TABLE OF CONTENTS

W9-BDT-428

TRADING CRYPTOCURRENCY

INVESTING IN BITCOIN AND CRYPTOCURRENCY

BITCOIN AND CRYPTOCURRENCY TRADING FOR BEGINNERS 2021

3 Books in 1

The Ultimate Guide to Start Investing in Crypto
and Make Massive Profit with Bitcoin, Altcoin,
Non-Fungible Tokens and Crypto Art

Nicholas Scott

NFT FOR BEGINNERS

TRADING
CRYPTOCURRENCY

A Comprehensive Guide to the Best Time-
Tested Cryptocurrency Trading Strategies.

Nicholas Scott

INTRODUCTION

If you decided to purchase this book, I assume you consider yourself a newbie. While this book will not make you a trading genius, it will help you to get across the newbie level.

Cryptocurrency is a disruptive concept, used in the current monetary system as an alternative to fiat currency. Entrepreneurs, startups, and large, small, and medium-sized enterprises take an interest in cryptocurrencies; hence they consider it a groundbreaking tool to combat transactional compliances.

As the cryptocurrency market is rapidly blooming, there is an increasing demand in the world for developers in blockchain technology. Companies are asking for people who can design software, contracts, applications, etc. in this very field. If you know the basic science of programming, cryptocurrency might be the start of a career for you.

Adhere to the values provided in this book; it can become your guide to success. Many people now are living an unimaginably good lifestyle due to the world of cryptocurrency. You could surely be one of them.

The cryptocurrency market is expected to be a highly lucrative market for those who understand how it works. With the right knowledge, as provided and revealed in this book, and continuous hard work, you can make your way to success and financial freedom.

Financial markets will never be an easy place to make money, and this will be even harder for newbies. It can be harsh and very confusing. In fact, one thing is for sure: it is not a get-rich-quick scheme. Such a mindset will do nothing but drown us in this market.

You may understand a few terms used in financial markets, but you may still be new to trading. If you are entering the financial markets with the mindset of a gambler, where you want to make tons of money in a few days, that is a faulty mindset that you should break, if you want to excel as a trader. If the first thing you do when you win a trade is to increase your trade amount the next time or double down when you lose money so that you get it all back, you have a gambler's mentality, which you should break. This book ensures you do not get burned too early in your trading journey. It seeks to ensure you no longer think like a newbie by the time you are done reading this book.

Plenty of people invest in building payment gateways and websites for their currencies. When a customer makes a purchase via cryptocurrency, the transaction often passes a fixed exchange rate through the payment gateway. It translates immediately to a commonly accepted fiat currency so that the merchant can escape the cryptocurrency market instability. Cryptocurrency payment has several advantages, such as improved transactional security, fraud protection, decentralized framework, low fees, customer chargeback protection, and rapid international transfers.

It is true that cryptocurrencies using blockchain technology ensure transactions are correctly recorded, which makes hacking very difficult. Blockchain software is a decentralized ledger that is not managed by any single person or institution; because all transactions are registered through multiple nodes, this provides transparency and makes it extremely difficult for any user to manipulate the system.

The fundamental problem with all cryptocurrencies is value fluctuation. While you are holding onto any specific digital currency, you may lose (or gain) money until you use it to buy something. Modern money (cryptocurrency supporters call it *fiat currency*) appears to be more robust, as it is backed by governments and a much more extensive global trading network.

CHAPTER 1

What is Cryptocurrency?

To understand what cryptocurrency is, you have to first decipher the meaning of the term.

Cryptography is the science of transmitting data in a way where only people authorized to see the data can see it and understand it. Thus, cryptocurrency is any digital currency that uses cryptography for protection. Because of this enhanced security feature, it is impossible to create a counterfeit. In addition, the originator of cryptocurrency can control its production. This means that all the time, demand will always outweigh the supply, thus making cryptocurrency very popular. It also means that cryptocurrency cannot be controlled or manipulated by governments. It is devoid of interference by nature. These benefits make cryptocurrency more attractive day by day.

In 2009, a pseudonymous entity known by the name Satoshi Nakamoto launched the first-ever cryptocurrency in the world of computers – Bitcoin. Barely six years later, there were about 14 million BTC coins in the world worth an estimated $3.4 billion. Quite huge! This great value contributed to the extreme growth of Bitcoin, much more than other digital currencies.

Since 2009, we can say that this secret money market has never looked back. It has continued to get better, with more people looking for digital currency.

It has increased more than a hundredfold in value. As more and more people come to trust and use cryptocurrencies, the value has only increased, making the holders of these currencies richer.

You could be one of them if you are brave enough to believe and trust the technology. With large financial institutions like JP Morgan Chase seeing the potential in Bitcoin and other cryptocurrencies, because of their cheap transaction costs, the currencies can only get better.

The cost for the transfer of funds and other payments is very cheap—way cheaper than what banks charge. Another quality is safety. Although there have been some thefts in the future with some Bitcoin lost, it is much safer than most other currencies we have in the world. Since it exists purely in digital form, it is much safer than other currencies, and transactions can be done super-fast. We will be looking at the safety of Bitcoin later, in more detail.

Should you get on the bandwagon today then? If you have not already, you should! The money train just went digital. While paper, coin, and plastic currency are not going anywhere soon, we can say the future is here with cryptocurrency.

Deciphering the Cryptocurrency Lingo

If you do not understand the language, then you cannot benefit from the information. In your search for cryptocurrencies, you will find that a lot of technical jargon is used. Some of IT can be outright dumbfounding. No need to worry though because that is not what we will talk about here.

We will be more concerned about the "Bull and Bear" of trading in cryptocurrency. After all, should we delve into all the lexicon used, we may never see the end of it as there are so many.

Just as an introduction, here are some of the more common cryptocurrency terms:

Altcoin: This refers to any cryptocurrency coin, other than Bitcoin

HODL: This means to "hold on" to the Bitcoin/coin even in times of plunge of the price. In other words, it means to hold the coin.

Choyna: It is another name for China. This is revered, as it is where most coin mining takes place.

Whale: It means the same as a Wall Street Bull but in the cryptocurrency world—a person who believes the Bitcoin price will rise.

ICO: This means Initial Coin Offering, where the coins bought at the first stage before they get to the exchange, where they can be sold for a much higher price. Price rises at the exchange mostly because of the hype that is created as the coin is about to be released.

Bear: This refers to a person who believes coin prices will fall

Bear Whale: A trader considered very dangerous because of his tendency to flood the market with coins, affecting the overall prices as he sells aggressively, believing prices will fall.

Bagholder: This refers to a coin investor who holds for longer than advisable.

FOMO: This stands for 'fear of missing out'. This is the fear that you experience when you see a rise in the coin price, and you do not have that coin.

FUD: This is short for 'fear, uncertainty and doubt'. Usually, people or institutions with malicious intentions against coins spread FUD.

Shill: It is the endorsement of a coin mostly by the trader, who wants to catalyze public interest in a coin they have bought.

Pump and Dump: It means to buy lowly priced altcoins in large numbers, in the hope of initiating fear of missing out in new investors, and then dump/sell the coins in large amounts.

Long: It means taking a long position (buy), in the assurance or hope that the price of the coin will rise in the near or distant future.

Short: It means to take a short position (sell) with the assurance that a coin's price will fall in the near future.

Borrowing rate: This is the rate you pay to borrow coins to leverage a position. The rates are usually predetermined.

Lending rates: The rate at which you lend coins to other traders who want to leverage a position. This is only possible if the coin exchange has lending accounts.

Moon: A lot of bullish behavior/upward movement of a coin.

Limit order: This is an order that is set to be executed only when a coin hits a certain price.

Market Cap: This shows how much dominance/share a certain coin has in the cryptocurrencies market.

DDOS: This means "Distributed Denial of Service;" traders take this to mean there is an attack in a volatile market, and therefore they cannot manually execute any order. Only limit orders or preset orders can go through.

Circulating supply: This means the number of coins in the market. This number is multiplied by the price to get the market cap.

There are almost as many jargon terms as there are coins, and therefore it is impossible to cover all of them here.

Be a smart trader and make every day at the exchange a learning experience.

The Most Common Types of Cryptocurrencies

Unlike what many beginners think, there are more cryptocurrencies than just Bitcoin, and more will come up in the future. However, you are smart if you only know of Bitcoin because it is way ahead of the pack. It is most popular; it started this wonderful technological revolution. So, Bitcoin it is! A name for the other cryptocurrencies has been coined and they are collectively referred to as altcoins or alternative coins.

Without any centralized authority over Bitcoin, we can say that it has practically set the trends for most other cryptocurrencies in the market. The other coins are the enhanced versions of Bitcoin; but the truth is that if Bitcoin was not here, they too would not be here.

Today, there are more than 1000 cryptocurrencies. In the future, this number can only go up. However, Bitcoin will remain way ahead of the pack, being the most preferred coin in the world since it is backed by perfect technology.

With so many cryptocurrencies in the market, what others are worth your attention? Well, take your pick from the few presented below:

Ethereum

The value of Ethereum as of June 2020 was $ 244.66.

In your search for information online, you will find Ethereum mentioned in many circles. This is another type of digital money, decentralized, and made to run without any form of interference, control, or fraud.

However, the most interesting part of it is the Ether, a cryptographic token that is used by developers to codify, secure, and run applications (other than money) on the Ethereum platform.

It occupies second place after Bitcoin in terms of value and distribution. Over time, Ethereum has become the technology of choice for many people, as it can be used to encrypt, codify, trade, and do much more in a very decentralized manner.

Only a few years of being in the market since it was released in 2015, Ethereum is worth looking into if you would like to diversify your cryptocurrency portfolio.

Litecoin

The value of Litecoin as of June 2020 was $ 46.58.

Called LTC, Litecoin has been present a good number of years in the market, and it is regarded second only to Bitcoin. It is perfect for you if you would like to diversify your coin portfolio.

It is built on the same concept as Bitcoin, i.e., decentralized, peer-to-peer computer networking, storage, and backup; most importantly, it uses a technology called *scrypt* for security. This technology can be decoded by consumer-grade CPUs, thus making it possible for everyone to invest in Litecoin.

There are caps designed to keep Litecoin safe from inflation. For example, it is said that the value of Litecoin in the market cannot exceed $84 million. This is designed to keep it scarce, attractive, and valuable for a good number of years.

Who uses Litecoin? Like Bitcoin, the list of international merchants who accept Litecoin continues to grow. Apart from that, developers and software vendors have no qualms at all about being paid in LTC.

BitcoinCash

The value of BitcoinCash as of June 2020 was $ 254.92.

While this is not exactly Bitcoin despite the relationship in names, it is a nice investment avenue that is up and coming very quickly. It is largely used by Bitcoin enthusiasts, but it is not expected to rise too high.

Dogecoin

The value as of June 2020 was $0.00258232.

Would you believe this coin was created just for fun, and when it was released, it was found it had staying power? It is not supposed to do as well as Litecoin, but it has many features similar to Litecoin. If you are a true Cryptocurrency enthusiast, maybe you can add several Dogecoins to your portfolio.

Namecoin

The value as of June 2020 was $0.486094.

This is regarded the same as Bitcoin because initially it was designed to be an upgrade of Bitcoin; later on, it seemed much better to release it as a standalone coin, fearing that it could cause problems if released as an upgrade. While it is a direct spinoff of Bitcoin, it is still very low in value.

Ripple

The value as of June 2020 was $0.203532.

Although it is one of the cheapest cryptocurrencies in the market, Ripple has been integrated into some banks, thanks to its design and purpose. It was created in 2012 as a remittance network, for currency exchange and gross settlement. With that kind of progress and purpose in the market, this coin will stick around even though it is one of the cheapest in the market today.

SexCoin

As of June 2020, the price for SexCoin was $0.00213763.

What a name for cryptocurrency and yes, this coin was created to help you stay anonymous if you are a consumer of adult content on the web. Thus, instead of using your credit card or bank wire for paying for such services, you can use SexCoin.

CHAPTER 2

Starting to Trade Cryptocurrency

C ryptocurrencies are traded differently since they use many different algorithms.

What you need to consider before buying or investing are:

- **Retailer Acceptance:** Owning a cryptocurrency is not any good if you cannot buy things with it. Before you decide to invest, you need to know who will and will not accept it. Some coins are built for certain purposes and were not designed to purchase goods. Some cryptocurrencies are accepted, while others can just be exchanged for other digital coins.

- **Verification Method:** The biggest difference between cryptocurrencies and other currencies is the way they verify transactions. The most common and oldest way is the proof-of-work method. A computer spends energy and time solving math problems to verify transactions. The problem with this is the computer uses massive amounts of energy just to operate. Systems that use proof-of-stake methods get rid of this problem, by allowing the users who have the biggest share to verify the transactions. This has a faster speed and uses less power to operate. Security concerns mean that fewer coins rely totally on proof-of-stake systems.

Create a Cryptocurrency Wallet

1. Create an account on the *Tradingview* platform and learn its tools.
2. Register an account on the exchange (it is better to get registered on several exchanges) and undergo verification.
3. Determine the ways of depositing and withdrawing funds from the exchange
4. Study the process of placing orders on the exchange
5. Create your own trading strategy
6. Start trading independently

Trading via Coinbase

Let us look at the process of starting to trade cryptocurrencies through *Coinbase*. It is a fairly simple process, but there are some crucial things you need to understand.

First, you will have to create an account with Coinbase.com, so that you can make a digital currency wallet where you are able to store your digital currency securely.

Connect your Coinbase account with your credit card, bank account, or debit card, so that you will be able to exchange digital currency with your local currency.

You will then trade US dollars for a cryptocurrency of your choice, which will likely be Litecoin or Ethereum, or both.

You should also use a bank account and avoid using a credit/debit card, as bank account fees are a lot lower than credit/debit card fees.

You will have to give them your bank account login when you sign up. It may seem shady, but it is safe and part of the process. You will also have to wait about three to five days to get your bank account approved. You will also have a limit on the amount that you can buy and sell in a single week. When you add a photo ID and other types of payment methods, it will help to increase your limits.

Developing a Trading Algorithm

For any work to be structured and, therefore, successful, we must develop a clear algorithm of actions. Trading is no exception. For example, we cannot start cryptocurrency trading without registering on the exchange or learning how to work with the Tradingview platform. Everything should be done in due order.

Of course, every trader has their own unique path and tailored algorithm of actions. However, as time passes and we gain experience, the sequence of your actions in trading can change. However, we should always have a certain algorithm. This will help save time and avoid financial losses.

Hence, if you need a basic and a short algorithm to start trading, you are welcome. Take a pen and write it down. This algorithm is shallow, but you still can use it and adjust it to your needs and preferences. And now, let us look at this algorithm with a fine-tooth comb and analyze the early stages of your trading in detail.

Reviewing the Cryptocurrency Market Dynamics

The first thing every self-respecting trader should do before they start to trade is analyze the current situation of the world financial markets. Try to identify the most prevalent activities.

After you find the answers to these questions, determine which coins, based on the information previously received, could be profitable now.

Choosing the Coins

The determining factors in the process of choosing a coin should be its volatility and liquidity.

Volatility is a statistical financial indicator that characterizes the change of a price. It is a crucial indicator in the management of financial risks.

Exploring the Chosen Tools for Trading – Technical and Fundamental Analyses

Technical and fundamental analyses are the main methods of evaluating the market as a whole, and types of cryptocurrency in particular.

Fundamental analysis helps us to determine the general trends and situations in the market, while technical analysis helps to choose the best moments for opening and closing a position.

When put differently, fundamental analysis is a telescope, which allows one to see the whole picture, while technical analysis is a microscope that helps to understand the smallest details.

Following the Latest News

First of all, pay attention to the latest information about the main macroeconomic indicators and news about particular coins. Macro statistics affect the volatility of financial instruments and the activity of traders around the world.

To stay informed, I strongly recommend that you remember, or even better, write down the exact time and day of the week when a news report on a particular coin is released. To simplify news monitoring, I recommend creating a separate tab (page) of a calendar of statistics on your computer, and to view it from time to time.

Drawing Up a Trading Plan

Although this section seems very simple, it is actually quite complicated, as it is the most important part of the activities of any trader.

If you think that you can open a position, after just scrolling through the newsfeed about a particular coin and making a technical analysis of its chart, you need to reconsider that.

Of course, you may be lucky once, but in the long term, this method will result in permanent losses. A trading plan is a prearranged, detailed scenario of a trader's actions in various market situations. That is, before you open a position, you determine the possible movements in a coin's price and the reaction of the bulk of traders. At the same time, we should not forget about the time when the news about a certain coin is released. Thus, having viewed the calendar of events and understood which time the statistics are released, you get the time of the highest volatility. This time is best suited to the most risk-loving and morally sound traders. Therefore, I do not recommend sluggish traders being active, fifteen minutes before or after the news about a coin release.

Understanding the Psychology of Trading Participants

Although many traders miss this step, I view it as one of the most important prerequisites for successful trading. After all, psychology, namely the sense of the market and a traded coin as well as an understanding of the desires of traders at a given time, is the lion's share of your profitable trades. In my opinion, about 70% of success comes from psychology; 20% from the systems of risk management and money management; and only 10% from your trading strategy. Therefore, once again, review your attitude towards the importance of understanding market participants' psychology.

Looking for Entry Points, Planning Stop Loss and Take Profit Placement

The fourth and fifth steps of our algorithm can brief you on an entry point. However, one should not treat the choice of such an important aspect too superficially. First, let us determine what the entry point is.

You should be very responsible when choosing the entry point, as the first step in trading has an impact on the final result and its size.

A stop-loss order is an order regarding the price level of an instrument on the chart, by which you close your position at a loss. In other words, you set the sum you are willing to risk in case of a price reversal.

CHAPTER 3

Trading Plan for Cryptocurrency

J ust like trading in securities and forex, trading in cryptocurrency requires you to have a trading plan.

A plan is important when it comes to trading and investment of any kind; cryptocurrencies are no exception. However, due to extreme volatility and high speculation associated with cryptocurrency markets, it is imperative to have a trading plan for them.

A trading plan is a framework that enables you to define your trading activity. It comprises criteria, rules, and guidelines that you need to follow in your trade undertakings.

While there is no perfect blueprint for a trading plan (as every trader is unique in terms of needs, attitude towards risk, and lifestyle), there are certain universally accepted principles to consider when developing your trading plan.

Every trader needs a trading plan. It is commonly claimed that the more experienced and knowledgeable you are in a certain trade, the less reliant you become on a trading plan. This is a fallacy. It could simply mean that you have internalized your basic trading plan, such that you do not need to keep on referring to it physically. However, this means that you have outgrown the basics, and thus you need to advance your trading plan to become a better trader at a higher level.

Trading Plan – Your Roadmap

A trading plan defines your trading objectives and how you are going to achieve them. A trading plan is your roadmap to follow, from where you are currently (just about to trade) to where you want to be (as a successful trader).

To be able to establish a clear vision in your trading plan, you need to ask yourself and provide answers to the following fundamental questions:

- What is your current status (SWOT)?
- What is your trading horizon?
- What is your level of knowledge and experience?
- What is your capital plan?
- What is your vision?
- What is your goal?
- What is your time-adjusted plan?
- What is the kind of success you wish to achieve?

A trading plan is a business plan tailored towards trading, in a certain specific product (funnel).

General Trading Plan Rules

Every plan is customized to your particular needs and predisposition. There is no universal plan or a blanket blueprint to implement. Nonetheless, the following are the important rules that you must consider in your plan:

- Write down your plan

21

- Record your progress
- Control your risk
- Question key trading plan

The best way to come up with an elaborate trading plan is to address key questions. Discussed below is the set of questions that you need to answer in your trading plan.

Creating a Trading Plan

Trading plans are customized by nature. You can personalize your trading plan to suit your style. However, there are certain basic components that you need to incorporate. The following are some of the considerations you need to make in order to have a good trading plan:

- Know your status as a trader. This means self-evaluate via a SWOT analysis.
- Clearly define your goals and mirror them to every step and decision you make.
- Decide whether you want to be a short trader or a long trader.
- Identify your key trading pairs and trading timeframes.
- Establish your personal trading system.
- Decide on how much risk you can afford.
- Determine the manner in which you will handle your open trades.
- Establish a proper record-keeping system.
- Back-test your trading system.

Personal Trading System

A trading system is part of a trading plan, which comprises a logical scheme of actions to take should certain events occur. This scheme is devised based on a set of rules that you have preset. A trading system automates your decision-making process so that you become less susceptible to psychological mistakes.

A simple trading system should have the following key basics:

- Set-ups: These are observable conditions, which you look for in the market, as indicators of a high probability of a successful trade. Set-up indicators include higher highs, lower lows, moving averages, etc. Set-ups you choose depend on whether you are a short trader or a long trader.

- Trigger points: These are exact moments when you have to take an action, based on your set-ups. Triggers can be manual or automated, depending on your expertise and the availability of required tools on your trading platform. While most forex markets have advanced setup and trigger tools, very few cryptocurrency platforms have them. Tools that are available are still rudimentary. Thus, you are more likely going to rely on manual set-ups and triggers.

Back-Testing of Your Trading System

Back-testing refers to passing your trading system through a testing mechanism, using hypothetical or historical, to determine its validity, reliability, and efficacy. This is extremely important as it can help you avoid the costly mistakes of relying on a defective trading system.

You can either do back-testing yourself, or you can outsource experienced and professional back-testers to carry it out on your behalf. While created through different systems and technologies, cryptocurrencies and fiat currencies both rely on the same principles of trading. Thus, a forex back-testing system can be used to back-test cryptocurrency trading systems with just minor customizations.

Risk Management

Risk management is an important and inevitable component of a good trading plan. Without risk management, you can hardly claim that you have a trading plan. Risk management depends on your risk appetite. It also depends on whether you are trading short or long.

Nonetheless, you need to have a basis for setting up your risk management strategy. The following are key questions you need to answer, in order to guide you in your risk management strategy:

- How much of my account (in terms of percentages) can I afford to risk on each trade?
- How many trading positions am I ready to run at any given time?
- What is the maximum level of my account exposure that I am ready to accept?

CHAPTER 4

The Best Trading Platforms

Trading in cryptocurrency has continued to become lucrative, due to the high levels of speculation and the increasing acceptance of cryptocurrency by the global online community.

Once you decide to trade in cryptocurrency, you need to have an appropriate platform, which will not only help you buy but also trade in cryptocurrencies.

Establishing the right criteria to guide you in your choice of trading platforms will help you avoid pitfalls that many beginners encounter, such as signing up for a trading platform in which preferred cryptocurrencies are untradeable or not purchasable using fiat currency. This will also help you avoid signing up for a platform that is not secure and prone to being hacked.

The following are criteria that will enable you to choose the best trading platform for your cryptocurrency:

- Safety – how safe is the server and its website?
- Liquidity – how fast is the cash flow?
- Fees and Spreads – how much fee is being charged per transaction?

- Transparency – how transparent is the exchange in terms of prices, volumes and coins transacted?
- Currency pairs – how many currency pairs are available? Does the platform trade in my preferred currency pairs? (e.g., cryptocurrency/cryptocurrency, fiat/cryptocurrency, cryptocurrency/fiat, etc.)?
- Means of payment – what means of payment are available for both buying and receiving sales proceeds?
- Customer support – is customer support good? Are customers happy? How fast and effective are customer issues being handled? What are the common customer complaints?
- Reputation – what is the current rating of the trading platform?
- Beginner-friendliness – is the platform friendly for beginners? Does it have sufficient resources to help beginners learn how to trade on its platform? Does it offer dummy accounts where beginners can practice before they are skilled enough to trade on the platform?

With the appropriate criteria in mind, you can now choose the best platform. The following are some of the best platforms you can consider:

Coinbase

Coinbase is the leading cryptocurrency trading platform. It is considered by most cryptocurrency users as the best exchange platform for cryptocurrencies. Most of the leading cryptocurrencies are traded on the platform.

Coinbase has recorded an increase in traffic by almost 70% from October to November 2017. By mid-2017, it had about 20 million cryptocurrency wallets and 75,000 merchants, who use the platform as a payment processor. It also had 15,000 app developers, who have created APIs based on its platform.

Bittrex

Bittrex is reputed for its comprehensive vetting process, especially of new coins and user security. It has a high-security module. It also supports a wide array of currencies. Currently, it supports trading in over 190 cryptocurrencies. It has a high level of stability accompanied by speedy transactions. Due to its high security level, it has one of the most secure wallets in the market.

Many cryptocurrency experts have placed a bet on it overtaking Coinbase in the near future. It is the most globalized exchange platform, as it is able to accept traders from over 180 countries around the world. This has been made possible by its online payment and verification partner, *Jumio*. This allows it to overshadow Coinbase, which struggles to serve clients from North America, Europe, Australia, and Singapore. Its junior competitor, Kraken, only serves the US, the EU, and Japan.

When it comes to traffic, Bittrex has already surpassed Coinbase, as it receives over 160 million visitors per month compared to Coinbase, which receives just about 125 million visitors per month (in the months leading up to the end of the year 2017). Kraken receives just 45 million visitors. It receives the highest volume of mobile traffic at 35%, which almost nears both Coinbase and Kraken combined.

Most users claim to have better engagement with Bittrex than with Coinbase. This could be attributed to its better utilization of social media networks, including Facebook and Twitter, in marketing and customer service.

Kraken

Kraken boasts of a high-security framework. It is preferred by intermediate and professional traders due to its fast funding, high liquidity, margin trading, low fees, and advanced orders such as stop-loss orders. The platform accepts both fiat and cryptocurrency transactions, which can be completed via wire transfer at that bank. However, the platform does not accept cash deposits or debit/credit cards.

Cex

Cex was launched in the UK, as a holding entity, for one of the world's largest Bitcoin mining companies, GHash. GHash controls about 42% of Bitcoin hashing power. Cex is based in the UK. CEX accepts deposits in US Dollars, Russian Rubles, and Euros through credit cards, SEPA, and wire transfers. It accepts transactions from users around the globe who want to trade in Bitcoins or GHash mining shares. Cex became one of the early platforms to accept Bitcoin Cash (BCH), a fork of Bitcoin.

Coinmama

Coinmama is a user-friendly platform that does not require one to have cryptocurrency to start trading. New users can start by using fiat currency to buy cryptocurrencies. This platform is available for users in almost all countries around the world.

Other Popular Trading Platforms

Bitstamp.net

LocalBitcoins

Gemini

Bitfinex

Bisq

Bitstamp

CEX.IO

eToro

Poloniex

HitBTC

BitMEX

GDAX.com

Etherdelta.com

Paxful.com

CoinATMradar.com

How to Join a Trading and Investment Platform

Sign up for your preferred trading platform.

Enable 2Factor authentication, where required.

Carry continuous benchmarking of altcoins against Bitcoin.

Focus on your margins of gain.

Keep an ear on industry influencers and opinion shapers.

Factor in your tax responsibility.

CHAPTER 5

How to Determine the Value of Cryptocurrencies?

You will find that when it comes to the value of digital currencies, the factors that determine it are different compared to what you will find with traditional currencies. For most users of these digital currencies, this can be a really good thing. It means that the government stays out of the mix and that the users get to determine the value through supply and demand. There are some people who worry a bit about the value of these currencies though; worrying that they may become overinflated and that the value will drop really quickly. However, right now, people seem to be following the market value.

When it comes to pricing traditional currencies, it is up to the government or financial institutions, which will decide how much the currency in that country is worth. They will release a certain amount of the currency and let it be circulated, to be used in trade. Over time, the government can decide to make more of the currency. They are not limited, by any factor, to make available a certain amount of currency.

In the past, our money was based on the gold standard. The government was able to make only enough money to match the amount of gold that it owned, to back it up. But today, money in our system is no longer based on the gold standard, meaning that the government can print off as much as they would want. Each time that the government prints out some more of the currency and places it into the market, it results in inflation.

Now, when a government or financial institution is responsible, it monitors the market and is careful about the amount of money that they release into the market at one time. A little bit of inflation can be good for the economy and can help it to grow, and this allows people to be better taken care of. However, there are plenty of examples where governments did not act responsibly; they saw that their economy was failing, so they kept printing and releasing more money into the system.

In this case, over-inflation can make the currency worthless. People can, at an extreme point, decide to go back to trading rather than use the money, because the currency may be worth something one day but be worthless by the next day. This may leave a country in turmoil, and so the country may have to restart a currency and build up trust again.

Things are a bit different when it comes to digital currencies. There is no central organization that is running the value of the currency, so the problems with releasing too much currency or relying on a government to make the right decisions, are not going to be an issue. After the worldwide economic collapse that happened in 2008 and after, many people were excited to find that there is a currency they can work with, which is not reliant on someone else to determine the value.

When it comes to digital currencies, there are a few things that will determine the value of the coins. For the most part, the demand for the coins, at a particular time, will determine how much the coins are worth. If a lot of people would like to have the coins at one time, the value is going to shoot through the roof. If there are not many people who want to have these coins, then the value is going to go down.

The number of coins that are in circulation will determine the price as well. Remember that most digital currencies have a limit on how many coins can be out on the market ever. For Bitcoin, there were only 21 million coins created, and no one can create more than that. Not all of them are in the market at one time though. The slow progress of miners protects the blockchain, and over time, the coins will be released.

If there are more people interested in purchasing the coins at one time, and the miners have not been able to release more coins by creating hashes, then the value of the coins will rise. If the interest has died down a little bit, and more coins are released by the miners, the value may go down a little bit.

This is a supply and demand issue, just like in a free-market model of the economy. So far, it seems to be working well to help keep the market going. No one has to worry about an individual or an organization determining how much their coins are worth, and they can rest assured that the value of the coins will be accepted in the future, no matter where they use them throughout the world.

Anyone can combine investment and trading, but the two should not be confused. The existing cryptocurrency markets are traders' markets, so those looking to invest will do well over time, to carefully construct positions to prevent price fluctuations.

All investing and trading require patience and control over one's emotions, and both can be challenging, but rewarding as well.

A cryptocurrency's value can change very quickly, but in time, one may see that the transaction volume has risen while the volatility has continued to drop. It remains to be seen whether this pattern will continue. It is essential to keep in mind the risk of a significant price correction. It is up to each trader and investor to weigh the considerable potential of cryptocurrencies on their own with the dangers that these currencies still face.

As with most goods and services, the economic value of cryptocurrencies is derived from supply and demand. Quantity refers to how much is available, i.e., the number of Bitcoins available to buy at any time. Demand refers to the desire of individuals to own it, i.e., how many people would like to buy Bitcoin and how much they want it. A cryptocurrency-monetary value will always be a combination of both variables.

There are other value types, as well. There is the interest you get from using cryptocurrency, for example. Most people love to spend or donate cryptocurrency because it gives them a sense of pride in helping an exciting new financial system. Likewise, some people enjoy shopping with Bitcoin because they like its low fees and want to inspire businesses to take it on.

In general, the value of a cryptocurrency is derived from its usefulness, frequency of use, and, eventually, demand, among other factors. Learning this will help you make good choices about which cryptocurrency coins you trade and invest in.

Today the value of cryptocurrency comes from two sources: People are expecting the cost to go up, and they buy it as an investment, so its value is rising. If expectations shift, the value may crash, then recover, and the pattern goes on.

Users need the cryptocurrency so that they can use it. The value goes up, and even if it falls, it remains significant. If the value goes down, it gets more from people who need that money, because they need that.

While thinking about the value of money, you may think about the native currency you use to buy groceries. Where do they come from? What determined the worth of these coins and bills?

The technology behind cryptocurrency plays a vital role. Decentralized currencies are resistant to censorship, but even more so, just shutting them down is almost impossible.

To determine whether a currency has a fair price or not, one may check for the node count and the cryptocurrency's total market capitalization, then compare those two metrics with other cryptocurrencies.

Supply and demand are significant factors deciding the value of anything that can be traded, including all of the market's digital currencies. For instance, if more people try to buy Bitcoins while others are willing to sell them, the price is going to go up and vice versa. Since many cryptocurrencies are restricted in availability, the increased popularity will drive up prices.

If a currency achieves mass adoption, this can fire its value through the roof. This is because the total number of most cryptocurrencies is small, and a demand rise leads to a direct price increase.

If a fiat currency's price falls, then Bitcoin's price will increase against that currency. This is because you'll be able to use your Bitcoins to get more of the money. This trend can be seen today, as more and more money is being printed by the FED, the ECB, and other central banks, which artificially keep interest rates low.

Although the energy used to create new Bitcoins may seem unnecessary, it is still the only way to provide users with protection. Mining is the reason why governments cannot quickly shut down the Bitcoin blockchain. Regardless, there is talk among programmers about how to make the process more efficient.

Critics say transactions will be reduced due to regulations imposed, as governments may see cryptocurrency as insecure. Some organizations could even prohibit them; such attempts have been demonstrated in Russia and China.

How Are Prices Calculated?

How do those digital currency forms compare to traditional currencies? Especially considering that there is no gold or anything else of worth behind them?

The most obvious difference to spot between the two currencies is that centralized governments back traditional currencies. Governments declare the legal tender for their currencies. The fiat currency value is derived from announcements by the central government. This means everyone who owns the money puts their trust in the government. That is the case today for most countries around the world. Central banks control the money supply, foreign reserves, and the inflation rate, indirectly.

On the other hand, cryptocurrencies do not come under a central authority or government umbrella. They are not recognized or approved through any legal tender. Also, cryptocurrencies typically have a fixed supply, ensuring that the inflation devaluation of digital currencies is virtually non-existent. Part of the reason is where the data comes from for the Bitcoin value. Bitcoin is never sold in a single location. Instead, it is exchanged on multiple different markets, all of which set their average prices, depending on the transactions that the exchange makes at any given time.

Indices collect and average prices from multiple exchanges, but not all indices use the same transactions for their results. You cannot trade Bitcoin anyway through these index sites— all they do is aggregate price details.

If you are keen to buy and sell Bitcoin, you have to choose a specific exchange that will list its average price. Bitcoin's price fluctuates at any given moment, depending on with whom you speak.

How Do the Prices of Cryptocurrencies Fluctuate So Much?

One of the main reasons why cryptocurrency prices are shifting so much is because of how new the market is. Beyond knowing the terms 'blockchain' and 'cryptocurrency', this area of finance is still unfamiliar to most people.

The emerging markets possess other qualities that make them competitive. Let us take a look at a few of them:

- Lack of liquidity: The cryptocurrency market does not deliver as much cash compared to a traditional, established market. The gap between fiat currency and cryptocurrency in the overall market cap is over $89 trillion. That is a 36,000 percent difference.
- Daily trading rates: The regular volumes of traded cryptocurrency hover about $14 billion. On the other hand, traditional markets are at about $5 trillion.
- Thin market: The market shifts rapidly, suggesting a probable rise in digital currency volatility.
- Early adopters: Numerous new users enter the cryptocurrency market every day. Recent reports indicate that more than 100,000 new adopters become a part of the digital currency economy, daily. Most new users have an interest in whether particular cryptocurrencies shift upwards or downwards. It contributes to the market's volatile nature, which leads to instability.

Alternative Ways to Acquire Cryptocurrency

There are two problems with most online cryptocurrency exchanges:

Not Everyone Can Get Approved

Many online cryptocurrency exchanges are highly regulated, and demand that all new users undergo a background check. The exchanges then have the power to deny an account, based on the information that applicants provide—exactly the sort of restriction that cryptocurrency was initially meant to do away with. Some people cannot prove identity, or are under-age, or are from a country that the exchanges do not support. For them, the doors to enter the online cryptocurrency exchanges remain bolted.

LocalBitcoins

The website *LocalBitcoins.com* helps strangers to transact in Bitcoin with one another directly, avoiding online cryptocurrency exchanges. Here is how it works: Users log in to the website and enter their location. Then, they can view the traders in their area offering to buy and sell Bitcoin. There are many payment options, including bank deposit, PayPal, and using cash in-person. In-person cash transactions afford the maximum universal access and anonymity.

The website also displays the following information for traders registered on their site:

- Reputation score
- Maximum and minimum they will trade
- The price they offer to buy and sell at
- Where to meet

An in-person cash transaction using *LocalBitcoins* will look something like this: The Bitcoin buyer shows up with cash and a destination wallet address, while the Bitcoin seller arrives with a device with access to their Bitcoin wallet. The buyer will hand over the cash, and the seller will make a transfer of Bitcoin to the buyer's address. No banks or online cryptocurrency exchanges are involved, and the only record is on the blockchain—nothing identifying the buyer, seller, or why the transaction occurred.

Here are a few things to watch out for, if readers decide to trade in cryptocurrency through this website:

- **Reputation**: A trader's reputation score is a measure of how many people have used them before, and also the collective feedback that others have given in past dealings. This score will be familiar to anyone who has used a service like Uber or Airbnb. If the cryptocurrency trader already has hundreds of positive reviews, then it is fair to expect a positive experience, as no one wants to ruin their hard-earned reputation.

- **Safety**: Once banks and online cryptocurrency exchanges have been left behind; the protections they provide are forfeited too. When dealing with substantial amounts of cash, it pays to be aware of personal security. Insist on meeting in a public place to minimize risks, even when dealing with traders with positive feedback scores.

- **Price**: One of the major disadvantages of in-person cash trades is that the prices offered are usually quite higher than the online cryptocurrency exchanges. There is less competition on *LocalBitcoins* than in centralized marketplaces. Because meeting in person involves time and travel, the traders expect to be compensated for the inconvenience. Before trading, compare the price of *LocalBitcoins* with the price offered at the major online cryptocurrency exchanges, to be aware of the premium being paid on the website.

Meetup

Cryptocurrency get-togethers are regularly organized through *Meetup.com* all over the world. After signing up on the website, users can enter their location and search for 'Bitcoin, 'cryptocurrency', and 'cryptocurrency'. So long as they are in a sizable town, the calendar will likely have events coming up for them, to meet other cryptocurrency enthusiasts.

Someone at the meeting will probably be willing to trade, especially for anyone buying for the first time. Most people in the cryptocurrency community want it to grow and will be all too happy to sell a cryptocurrency to help a newcomer get started.

If *Meetup.com* is not available nearby, try to find a friend who already owns cryptocurrency and is willing to sell some. Simply get the friend to send the cryptocurrency to the desired wallet address and pay them in cash.

Gift Card Purchases

Another way around the online cryptocurrency exchange compliance procedures is to avoid fiat money entirely and deal in other instruments which still act like cash.

Several websites enable users to buy and sell Amazon gift cards using Bitcoin. Amazon is 'the everything store', meaning Amazon gift cards can be used to purchase practically anything. There are less-developed marketplaces for other gift cards too, such as Apple iTunes cards.

The current list of gift-card purchase websites can be accessed at *citizen-softheworld.io/thecryptocurrency-intro.*

Credit Card Purchases

Services exist to enable the direct purchase of cryptocurrency using a credit card. They charge about 5% for this, on top of the value of cryptocurrency being bought. These websites often have a much simpler sign-up process than online cryptocurrency exchanges. All that is required is an existing wallet address to send the purchased cryptocurrency to.

The websites enabling credit card purchases are always changing.

An up-to-date list is available for download at **citizensofthe-world.io/thecryptocurrency-intro**.

Whether through an online cryptocurrency exchange, as described in the previous chapters, or through the alternative options outlined in this chapter, there is a way of acquiring cryptocurrency for everyone. If the first method tried does not work, try another. With persistence, it will be possible for the reader to get their first cryptocurrency.

CHAPTER 6

Automated Trading

utomated trade uses a programmed computing system that allows traders to establish certain trade rules for entry and exit into the market. Once these rules are met, the computing systems execute the set instructions. Traders can add specific entry and exit points into the system and let the system monitor the trades. Once the entries match the set criteria, trades are placed automatically. Traders can create the entry and exit points using any of the criteria discussed in the preceding sections.

There are different types of automated trading software on the web, and traders can choose one and customize it to meet their trading needs.

Trading Bots

A **trading bot** is a program created to do repetitive tasks. The program is set based on specific parameters or rules, making them a faster way to trade. The bots monitor price movements and analyze market trends in terms of trade volumes, trading orders, price, and time. It makes trading decisions based on the analyzed information and preprogrammed rules.

Due to the increased market volatility, trading bots have become more popular in the cryptocurrency market. Traders are using bots to control their cryptocurrency investment 24/7, even when they are away. Setting the bots correctly with clearly specified entry and exit points will enable trades to be automatically executed, and they are more effective compared to observing and setting trades manually.

Bitcoin traders trade passively and spend the majority of their time analyzing the market. Therefore, trading bots will help them be more effective, as traders do not have to constantly watch the market.

When using bots, you must be very careful to avoid phishing attacks. There are phishing bots designed to specifically steal personal data from the web, such as your account details. When looking for a trading bot, choose the one that is free from coding errors and has minimal downtime. Look at the user's feedback before investing in a particular bot.

Top Trading Bots

Cryptocurrencyhopper

This is a popular trading bot that has a paper-trading option. It simplifies trading processes and helps users increase profit margins. This type of trading bot runs on the cloud and offers 24/7 services to users.

The platform has an interactive user interface, which only requires the user to log in to its dashboard, before starting to trade. Once you buy the trading bot, it only requires five minutes to set up to be ready to start trading.

Cryptocurrencyhopper offers advanced trading tools which are easy for traders to use. Next to the dashboard is an embedded external signaler, which allows new subscribers to join other trading analysis lists online. It uses machine learning to determine market prices and trading volumes, then sends signals directly to users' bots. The bots make automatic buy and sell orders on behalf of the users after receiving the signals.

This type of bot allows users to take advantage of the bull market, and to set stop-loss limits when entering a trade. Users rely on the dashboard to monitor price trends and trades made. It also uses technical analysis tools like RSI, MACD, and Bollinger Bands.

3Commas

3Commas is another reputable trading bot in the market. It provides web-based services to users so they can trade 24/7.

When you buy this trading bot, you can monitor trading activities on your dashboard from any device. The bot allows you to set stop-loss limits, to maximize your profits and minimize your losses.

This web-based platform has a cryptocurrency portfolio feature, which enables you to not only create and analyze trades but also to back-test a cryptocurrency portfolio.

MetaTrader

MetaTrader is an automated trading platform that is popular among stock and forex traders. It is a little different than the other trading bots listed here because it requires a separate broker to do the trades.

Traders must choose a reputable broker to link to *MetaTrader*. Be very careful choosing a broker because there are many scam brokers.

Because of its stock market and forex history, *MetaTrader* has a rich library of functions, from analyzing charts to generating trading signals. The platform provides advanced technical analysis, expert advice, and an automated trading system.

You can install the application on your computer or your mobile device and enjoy its benefits.

MetaTrader4 and *MetaTrader5* are customizable based on user preferences. After downloading the free application (*MetaTrader* makes its money from the brokers it connects to), a user can define the market conditions based on predetermined factors and set stop-loss limits and profit targets. Once the conditions are met, the trading bot can place buy and sell orders. Investors with an Android device can additionally install the *MetaTrader* app and monitor their trade at any time.

Access Trading Bots Via Mobile Device

You can build and run a trading bot through your mobile device. You can also back-test or run automated trading strategies on the cloud, using mobile-based apps. The apps allow you to create your trading strategy based on predefined parameters. You can also monitor and control the trades using your mobile device. The apps are easy to use and community-driven, so traders can trade and interact with other like-minded individuals on the platform forums.

You do not have to be an expert in programming since no coding skills are needed for automated trading. You can test the automated trading strategies on the cloud through your mobile device.

You will have total control of your trading account. All you need is to build your strategy on your mobile app and test your strategy with real market conditions. Constantly monitor and control your trading strategies using your mobile device.

You can also turn the alert feature on. Set alerts to receive Bitcoin news via your mobile device. This can be through email or an SMS to your phone.

DIY Python Programming

The Python coding language has become a preferred choice for algorithmic trade developers since it has free library packages for commercial use. Automated trading developers rely on its open-source scientific library which includes packages like *Pandas*, *PyAlgoTrade*, *NumPy*, and *Pybacktest* to produce statistical data.

Python trading programs are popular, and many free examples are available to traders. Only experienced traders who know how to program should jump into using Python for trading. However, once familiar with the trading essentials, these programs allow the trader to customize their algorithms.

FreqTrade

FreqTrade is a cryptocurrency trading bot built using the Python language. This trading bot requires that you have basic knowledge of the Python programming language to run any trading patterns.

You also have to learn how trading works and expect the number of profits or losses you can incur if you use *FreqTrade* as your trading tool. You can read through various analyses before you commit money. You can use the dry run to practice paper trading with the bot, before investing real money.

With the *FreqTrade* platform, you can use features like back-testing, which provides you with a simulated environment to test, buy and sell signals based on historical data. The platform also provides edge position sizing where traders can calculate their win rate, determine risk/reward ratio, enter stop-loss points, and adjust the position size.

Advantages of Automated Trading

- **Speed of execution:** Since automated trading systems are designed beforehand, they can execute instructions automatically. They can scan and execute multiple market conditions at a fast rate compared to manual analysis.

- **Accuracy of information:** Automated trading is a computer-programmed platform that executes trades based on given parameters. The parameters or predefined conditions entered into the system are double-checked for any errors before execution. This ensures data accuracy and the use of trade signals to complete a transaction. Double-checking eliminates errors made by humans in manual entries to the system.

- **Removes human emotions:** Automated trading systems eliminate human emotion while trading because traders are constrained within particular predefined criteria. This avoids irrational decisions made by humans based on their emotions.

- **Back-testing:** Automated trading systems allow traders to analyze trading patterns, to know what works, and what does not work for them based on their past data. If past data worked for them, there is a possibility that the new data and algorithms will work for them as well. Looking at past data also allows traders to tune their algorithms, to eliminate any flaws that can affect their current trading activities.

- **Reduce transaction cost:** In automated trading, you do not have to spend a lot of time monitoring the trading market. Repetitive transactions are done without any constant supervision of the markets, which reduces the costs of monitoring the market and transaction costs.

Cryptocurrency Exchanges

Cryptocurrency exchanges are web-based platforms designed to allow traders to buy and sell cryptocurrencies using fiat money.

It is ironic that even though Bitcoin was designed as a decentralized currency; the crypto ecosystem has evolved into using centralized exchanges to exchange fiat money for cryptocurrencies.

Cryptocurrency Exchange Policies

Payment merchants and cryptocurrency exchange companies have to comply with established banking regulations, to operate as a financial company in the United States and Europe.

These exchange firms are required by the government agencies to monitor internal policies and procedures and control any illegal activity. Exchanges are required to pay close attention to AML and KYC procedures.

KYC (Know Your Customer)

KYC is a requirement for financial institutions to identify and verify customers. Exchanges monitor whether clients are using the exchanges for money laundering operations. Typically, this requires proving your identity by submitting an ID or passport, when opening an account on the exchange.

If you only buy and sell cryptocurrency without using an exchange, you may not run into KYC barriers. If you trade outside centralized exchanges, you do not have to declare your identity either.

Although KYC tools are mostly used by centralized organizations, cryptocurrency exchange firms apply KYC in their decentralized ecosystem. Many people assume that Bitcoin is anonymous, but as a result of KYC, it really is not. The transaction is recorded forever in the Bitcoin block-chain. Although the Bitcoin transaction does not require anyone to disclose their identity when performing a transaction, if the coin eventually is sent to a cryptocurrency exchange, the government will be able to subpoena the identity of the person who received the Bitcoin and then trace it backward. Think of unraveling the transaction history as pulling a thread on a sweater.

AML (AntiMoney Laundering)

Anti-money laundering laws and regulations were created to control the exchange of illegal money. AML laws are expansive and cover tax evasion, corruption, abuse of public money, and market manipulation via the use of wash-trading techniques, among others.

The exchange firms must comply with AML regulations. The firms should monitor all transactions and report any suspicious accounts to AML. Cryptocurrency exchange firms and other companies use KYC software tools to detect any fraudulent activity, and also to verify customer identity and viability.

AML and KYC are used interchangeably in the cryptocurrency market, and they are both associated with identifying and accepting clients, monitoring transactions, and handling risk management.

Automated Trading with Exchanges

There are ways to exchange one cryptocurrency coin for another, without going through an exchange and the associated KYC or AML, but that is outside the scope of this book.

Bitcoin traders use Bitcoin exchange platforms to exchange fiat currency and altcoins. Exchanges act as the intermediary between the buyers and the sellers.

The cryptocurrency exchange publishes an Application Program Interface (API) to allow bots to connect to them. The bot uses the API to connect to the cryptocurrency exchange, to buy and sell cryptocurrency.

Automated transactions through an exchange platform have to be registered with the exchange, to be verified and authenticated for access to the system. Once the verification is complete, your account is opened. After establishing an account, you can transfer funds to your account and begin buying and selling cryptocurrency coins.

Conversion Fees

Depositing or withdrawing money to your account typically results in a transaction fee, imposed by the exchange. The fee charged depends on the payment option used. Bank transfers are usually cheaper than credit card purchase fees.

Bitcoin exchanges also attract transaction fees which are applied when you make buy and sell orders on the exchange platform. The fee depends on the volume of your transactions.

Hacking of Bitcoin Exchanges

Although almost all Bitcoin exchange platforms have safeguards for cryptocurrency security, there is no guarantee against threats. In the past, hackers have been able to make their way into exchange platforms like *Mt. Gox* and *Binance,* where they stole customers' cryptocurrency.

The cryptocurrency itself is very secure, but exchange platforms concentrate a lot of cryptocurrencies in one place and thus, are a profitable target for hackers. When the exchange platform experiences a major hack, users are affected. Some exchanges have insurance for all or part of your account.

CHAPTER 7

Technical Analysis

Technical analysis (sometimes abbreviated as TA) forecasts future cryptocurrency prices and market trends based on historical data. It anticipates whether the price trends will be up (bull) or down (bear). This is done through the use of technical indicators, which calculate the historic and current market price of an asset and analyze price trends.

Analyzing historical price charts and collected volume data determines whether the coin is undervalued or overvalued.

Technical analysis is based on the following assumptions.

The price movement follows certain trends. Bitcoin prices do not change randomly but tend to follow particular trends that last for either short or long periods. It uses past performance to predict future prices.

Bitcoin prices are determined by multiple variables. The price movement of the coin is due to past and future demand of the coin, current market prices, and regulations governing the cryptocurrency market.

History tends to repeat itself. What happened in the past is used to predict what will happen in the future. Past changes can easily predict future market changes. Traders tend to behave the same way when presented with similar market conditions.

Types of Technical Analysis

There are three components used in technical analysis:

- Chart lines: Chart lines are used to indicate the points where price changes. Using historical price data, current prices, and volume data, analysts can draw charting lines to show the exact points where the prices tend to change.
- Patterns: Chart patterns predict price movement. They show the price direction and extrapolate to show where prices are headed to.
- Indicator oscillators: This analysis tool uses statistical methods to determine the buy and sell signals.

Analysts and cryptocurrency investors rely on the charts, to get visual data on price trends and market momentum.

Technical Indicators

Technical indicators are investment analysis tools used to calculate and interpret market trends. Traders rely on these tools to determine the right time to invest in cryptocurrencies. Investors can receive alerts on any new investment opportunities and price changes.

Traders can know the price movement of cryptocurrency assets whether they move up, down, or sideways. The price movement is calculated using historical price data, current prices, and trade volume data.

Technical indicators are very important in analyzing cryptocurrency investments. They help investors to:

- Predict price movement and future price direction.
- Confirm market trends in the price movement of cryptocurrencies, such as Bitcoin.
- Alert investors to whether prices are going up, down, or sideways to allow traders to plan ahead for trade.

Cryptocurrency investors rely on these indicators to determine the short-term price movement. They also evaluate the asset's long-term price changes to determine when to enter or exit the market.

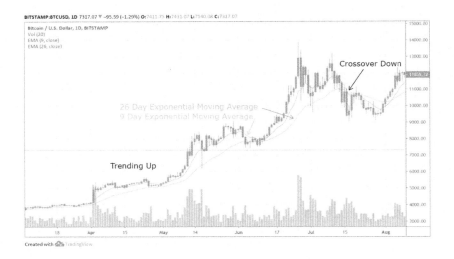

Some of the common technical indicators used include calculating Moving Averages (MA) and the Relative Strength Index (RSI). For example, you can plot a chart to show the Bitcoin price direction for 12 and 26 days, respectively.

There are several indicators to observe when analyzing a particular cryptocurrency asset. To choose the right indicator, you need to first understand how each indicator works and how each indicator will affect your investment strategy.

Because of the volatile nature of cryptocurrency assets, monitoring the price direction or a Bitcoin price chart will help the investor evaluate both high and low trading patterns. If the chart assumes an upward trend, this will indicate higher trendlines; a downward trend indicates a series of low trendlines.

Sometimes the cryptocurrency will move sideways. In such a case, it does not move in any particular vertical direction at all. Investors should be very careful when using only one indicator, such as trendlines, to predict future prices, since the trends can move in any direction. It is much better to use two or more indicators as confirmation of a move, up or down.

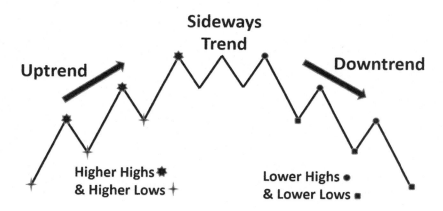

A technical analysis chart, drawn based on historical prices and trading volume data, represents the past decisions made by investors on the buying and selling of cryptocurrency assets. As investors, we use past data to predict future investments. For example, a typical investor who bought Bitcoin will monitor the price of Bitcoin. If the price falls in comparison to the initial buying price, the investor may wait until the price reaches the break-even point to sell the cryptocurrency. As savvy investors, we recognize this as Support/Resistance (explained later in this book) and can use this to our advantage.

Price movement is influenced by both internal and external constraints. Multiple forces including human emotions like fear, panic, greed, anxiety, hope, and hysteria affect the prices of cryptocurrency. These emotions lead to dramatic shifts in the prices of the cryptocurrency asset. Therefore, price movement is not only based on facts but also on expectations.

Trend Analysis

Trend analysis uses technical tools to determine price movements; it helps traders know when to buy, sell, or hold a cryptocurrency asset.

This technique analyzes past cryptocurrency prices to predict future price movements. It determines an upward trend when asset prices continue to rise and detects a downward trend when prices keep decreasing over several consecutive days.

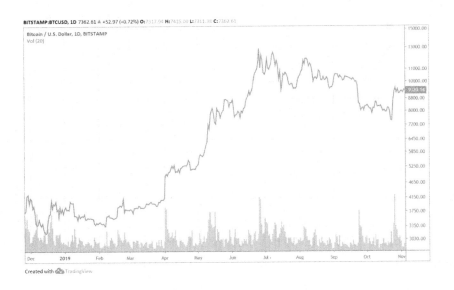

Trendlines, moving averages, and polarity analysis are the major tools used to determine price trends. In this chapter, we will focus on the use of trendlines.

Using trendlines is one of the most popular techniques used in technical analysis. They are used to show the consistent movement of prices either up, down, or sideways. Price movements vary, based on the timeframe and whether the investor is observing on a daily, weekly, monthly, or quarterly basis.

Drawing Trendlines

Trendlines indicate the general direction of the price. Straight lines are drawn above and below the price line. Trendlines also show support and resistance areas, which can determine when to enter or exit a trade. Trendlines can show increased supply or demand.

Downward trendlines are drawn above the price of the plotted chart, while upward trendlines are drawn below the price. The upward trendline is used to estimate support, while the downward trendline is used to estimate resistance.

Rules of Thumb for Trendlines

1. There must be at least two highs or lows to have a valid trendline (3 points are preferred). The trendline is further validated if it intersects the price line a 3rd time. Bitcoin is so volatile, that it may be hard to find the 3rd point validation.
2. Larger time frames result in better trendlines. Start with weekly or daily charts, and then check the smaller time frames to confirm.
3. Sometimes trendlines cut through the low or high portion of a candle. Try not to cut through the body of the candle. If the trendline does not fit without being forced, it probably is not a valid trend.

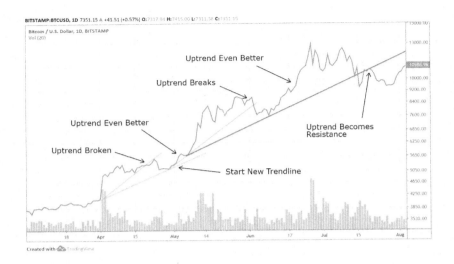

In the above chart, the prices touched the trendline at least two times in the given timeframe. The line represents the area of support, and it indicates when traders should be looking for buying opportunities. Sometimes the upward trendline can become a resistance line, as shown on the right side.

We will discuss support and resistance in more detail below.

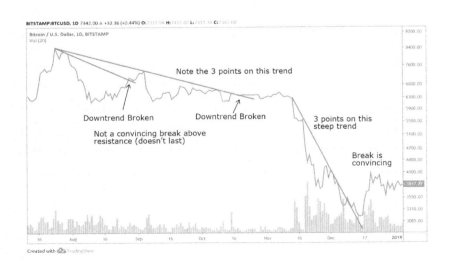

The downtrend touched the trendline three times in the given timeframe. The trendline in the graph represents resistance, and this indicates where the buyers are expected to slow down their buying. Traders use this to sell their cryptocurrency near the top.

How to Draw Trendlines

Open the *TradingView* website, and then choose BTC/USD charts. This displays the real-time trending price for Bitcoin in US Dollars.

You can customize the chart and draw trendlines on it. To do so, click on the **full-featured chart** icon, to open advanced chart tools to customize your chart.

You can change the chart trend to be daily, weekly, or monthly, and then draw trendlines from the available tools. Select the **Trendline** Tool on the left side of the chart.

Trading Channels

A channel consists of a pair of straight lines, with one line drawn at the top of the uptrend line, and the other line drawn in parallel at the bottom, linking the troughs of a price series chart.

Channels are used in visualizing data to determine when to buy and sell cryptocurrency assets. The top and bottom lines are drawn to show both the support and resistance levels on the trade chart.

Trading channels show where prices will likely reverse direction. If an asset trades between the boundaries of two trendlines for a certain period, then it is trading within the channel. If the trading price is on an uptrend, then it is an ascending channel. If the price moves downward between the trendlines, it is referred to as a descending channel. When the price moves in horizontally, then a horizontal channel is created.

The channel can be drawn by either using the trendlines to draw two lines or by using channel tools available in the software.

Let us walk through what happened above.

When Bitcoin was at $274 (the bottom left corner of the channel), many people bought it. As a result, the price increased to $400. Investors who bought at $274 wanted to sell their Bitcoin at the increased price and take their profits. This led to increased supply and less demand, which dropped the Bitcoin price to $320.

At that point, investors may have started buying Bitcoin, expecting that the price would increase back to $400. The rise was not as rapid this time, but it eventually hit $452, before the sellers took control and pushed the price back down to $360.

The buyers and sellers traded back and forth without much rise or fall in price, until late May 2016 when Bitcoin became more attractive and rose quite fast from $450 to $750 in mid-June.

Using Channels to Make Trading Decisions

Traders rely on the channel for trading, under the assumption that the price will typically remain enclosed within the channel.

If confirmed by other signals, a trader sells their Bitcoin when the price touches the upper boundary of the trendline or buys Bitcoin when the price touches the lower boundary.

Note how selling was not a good decision when the price touched the upper right channel, because Bitcoin continued to rise. This is an example of where a good trader would realize the mistake and buy back in.

Sometimes, you may have a false breakout, which occurs when the price breaks outside the channel. In such a case, some investors may immediately buy in thinking the cryptocurrency is rocketing upwards. It is best to wait until it closes outside the channel before you trade. Many times, the price will immediately return inside the channel, and the extra caution is worth the confirmation.

Volume Analysis and Price Action

Volume analysis is a very powerful tool in trading. Volume analysis determines the number of times a cryptocurrency asset has been traded for a certain period. It measures how many units are sold or bought, within a specific timeframe. Traders use this tool as the key metric in determining the asset liquidity level.

The tool also enables traders to know how easy it is to enter and exit the market. If well utilized, traders and investors can maximize profits as well as reduce the risks involved.

If the assets have a higher volume, then it will be easy to trade either a large number or a smaller quantity of assets, since there are several traders available.

False Volume on Exchanges

Unfortunately, the volume can be falsely indicated inside a cryptocurrency exchange. Since the exchange is its own ecosystem, some exchanges report more volume than actually trading. They do this for publicity since an exchange with a lot of volume would be better at matching buyers and sellers and, thus, would attract more traders.

You could look at the cryptocurrency blockchain to determine the number of actual transactions. This still does not capture the actual demand because people are buying and selling on the exchanges. The exchange only needs to settle the transactions with the blockchain if it needs more liquidity. It is helpful to look at the charts for several exchanges and compare the volume.

Buying and Selling Volume

Volume determines the strength of price trends and warns investors about the weakness of price movements. Buyers need increased asset volume to push the prices higher.

If there is an increase in the price but a reduced number of units, then there is a lack of market interest that is likely to lead to a price reversal.

On the other hand, if the price does not change, but large volumes that do not affect price have occurred, this is called **churn**. At some point, the buyers and sellers will be exhausted, and the price will likely remain steady.

Large volumes of assets traded may result in price declines or gains if the buyers and sellers are not evenly matched. This indicates a major fundamental change in the market.

Let us go back to the supply-demand graph. When prices rise, this is because buyers are controlling the price movement. More buyers in the market push the prices higher, resulting in increased buyer volume.

The volume of each cryptocurrency asset is shown at the bottom of the price chart. The real-time charts show the trading volume in the form of vertical bar graphs at the bottom, with each bar representing the number of units exchanged for a specific period.

BITSTAMP:BTCUSD, 1D 7169.67 ▼ −130.76 (−1.79%) O:7299.20 H:7299.20 L:7102.24 C:7169.67

Bitcoin / U.S. Dollar, 1D, BITSTAMP

Low Interest (not much volume)

Buyer Volume

Seller Volume

Created with TradingView

Volume bars are either red or green. A red bar indicates that the prices of the asset decreased for a specific time frame. It also indicates a selling volume in the market.

If the volume bars are green, it is an indication that prices increased during that time frame, resulting in increased buying volume.

CHAPTER 8

Fundamental Analysis

Fundamental analysis is also called the lifeblood of investment. The key to using it is to gather as much information and real facts as possible. It stands on the premise that the more you understand a particular cryptocurrency, the more likely that you will be able to predict its price movement in the market. Hence, when you use fundamental analysis, you should follow the latest news. The news has a powerful influence on the price of a cryptocurrency.

Just to give you an idea: when CNN featured just how high the price of Bitcoin was increasing at that time; it further pushed the price of Bitcoin upward. When China declared that it would close down all its cryptocurrency exchanges, the price of Bitcoin and other cryptocurrencies dropped. When Russia removed its ban on the use of Bitcoins and other cryptocurrencies, the price of Bitcoin experienced a significant increase in value. As you can see, by being aware of the latest news and analyzing its implications in the market, you can get a good idea of how the price of certain cryptocurrencies will most likely be affected.`

News is not the only source of information. You should also check the white paper released by the developer of a cryptocurrency. Although it may be hard to understand due to the technical terms, it will nonetheless provide you with useful information regarding cryptocurrency.

You should also join related online groups and forums. Many developers are active in these places, and this will allow you to not only get information from the developers, but you can also even contact them if you want. Needless to say, you can also learn from the other members of the cryptocurrency community. From time to time, you will surely come across interesting points of view, as well as useful strategies that you can use to make a profit in the cryptocurrency market.

This tool is important because it deals with the basics. If you do not understand the basics; how do you think you can make the right investment decision otherwise? Therefore, always do your research and analysis of the different cryptocurrencies in the market. Do not be lazy.

Fundamental analysis can be used with other tools. People usually use this tool together with technical analysis. If you consider yourself a true and professional cryptocurrency investor/trader, then it is a must that you use it, regardless of other tools that you may want to use. After all, if you do not know the fundamentals, it would be hard to think of yourself as a real investor/trader.

CHAPTER 9

Drawing Support and Resistance Levels

The basics of technical analysis deal with identifying and forecasting the trends on cryptocurrency charts. After determining the trend, we can proceed to graphical analysis (analysis of patterns), and computer analysis (analysis of indicators and oscillators data).

A trend is a direction in which the market moves. It is a series of zigzags that resemble a series of waves; a rise is followed by a fall.

Types of Trends:

To determine the current trend in the market, we need to look for the highest and the lowest prices of a coin on the chart.

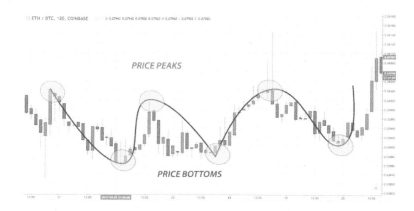

For example, if we connect a large number of highest and lowest points with a line, we will see that the market is flat.

Upward/Bullish Trend

We need a chart to grasp the essence of this and other trends.

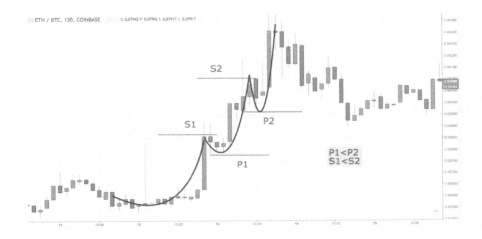

The chart above shows different points; some of them are marked with the letter S; others are marked with the letter P. What do they mean?

There is a simple formula for determining an upward trend. S1 and S2 are price peaks, while P1 and P2 are price bottoms. The essence of this formula is that P1 will always be less than P2, and S1 will always be less than S2. This means that at the upward trend each subsequent peak will be higher than the previous one, and each bottom will also be higher than the previous one.

Downward/Bearish Trend

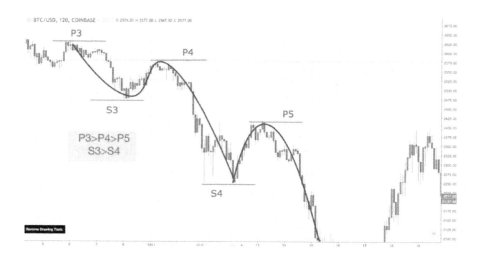

In case of a downward trend, P3 is more than P4 and P5. Each subsequent peak will be lower than the previous one, while each subsequent bottom will be lower than the previous one (S3 located higher than S4).

Flat Trend

Here, F1, F2, and F3 are peak price points, and F4 and F5 are bottom price points. Both peak and bottom points are on the same level. The price moves horizontally, along a corridor, not updating the highs and lows. This indicates a flat market trend.

Thus, it is obvious that to start to do technical analysis to determine the trend in the market, you only need to know the peak and bottom prices of a coin.

How do you trade amid different trends? Of course, it is safer to trade when there is a bullish (upward) trend in the market. Except, you can also trade amid a flat trend. A downward trend poses the biggest risk to trading. Put simply, if the peaks and bottoms continue to be updated on the chart, there is no reason to worry. If peaks and bottom points are not updated, it is a warning that a trend may reverse.

Support and Resistance Levels

We have already discussed what support and resistance levels are, so I suggest switching to practice immediately.

The lower line on the chart is the **support level**, and the upper line is the **resistance level**. These levels help us to determine that this chart shows an upward trend.

Thus, a support level is a level below the market, where the desire to buy is so strong that it can withstand the pressure of sellers. As a result, the fall is suspended, and prices start to move up again. Usually, a support level can be determined in advance, according to the level of the previous decline. A resistance level, on the other hand, is the direct opposite of a support level. It represents a level above the market, where the pressure of sellers exceeds the pressure of buyers.

The support and resistance levels can be different in magnitude of strength. We need to learn how to pick out strong levels.

- The First Rule: The longer the price hovers in the area of support or resistance, the more important this area is. For example, if the price was hovering near the support level for two weeks, and then went up, this area of support is more significant than if the same price fluctuations occurred for only two days.

- The Second Rule: if the support level formation is accompanied by a large trade volume, this level is very significant. Conversely, the smaller the trade volume is, the less significant the support level is.

- The Third Rule: It deals with the remoteness of a support or resistance level in a time away from the present moment. Since we deal with the reaction of traders to the market movements and positions (either already opened or not), it is clear that the closer the event is, the greater importance it has, because the market is activated to a greater extent.

How to Draw a Support Level and a Resistance Level in Tradingview?

We draw one level by linking the price peaks and bottoms. Afterward, to make the second level parallel to the first, we clone it and place prices on the other side of the price chart. To do this, click on the first drawn level and select **Clone** in the taskbar. Thus, we get a level that is parallel to the one we drew before. Now just move it to the area we need – to the area of the largest number of points above or below the price chart.

Apart from these levels, many traders also draw horizontal lines on the chart. The principle of drawing is almost identical: we link the biggest number of points on one horizontal level with a line.

Trendline

A trendline is one of the simplest and clearest elements of technical analysis.

A trendline may be ascending and descending. We draw these lines the same way we draw support and resistance levels. The ascending line is drawn by connecting ascending lows, while the descending line is drawn by connecting descending highs. In order to verify the presence of a particular trend in the market, we need at least three points to draw a trendline. Once you find the third point on the chart and confirm the nature of the trend, you can use the trendline to solve a number of tasks.

For example, one of the fundamental principles of technical analysis is: a trend on the move will seek to continue its movement. Therefore, as soon as a trend gains pace and a trendline positions itself at a certain angle, this angle will usually remain unchanged through the course of further development. In this case, a trendline will allow us to determine the extreme points of the correction phases, and also will indicate possible changes in the trend.

Suppose we have an upward trend on our chart. On any chart, corrective or intermediate price drops are inevitable. They, as a rule, will either approach an ascending trendline or touch it. When there is an upward trend, we expect to buy an asset at a low price. In this case, a trendline serves as a support level below the market. It is our buy zone and vice versa; if our chart shows a downward trend, then we use a trendline as a resistance level for sale.

And as long as there are no breaks in the chart, a trendline helps us determine the buy and sell zones. However, if a trendline breaks, it is the first sign of a change in the nature of the trend.

Technical Line Break

Did you notice something interesting in this chart?

I hope you have noticed the breakout through a resistance level. The price did not continue to move in the historical direction, thus updating the highs and lows; instead, it jumped one level and went up. This happens when the closing price of the candlestick is fixed above the level.

What does this situation mean in the market? If we see a candle formation (especially its closing) behind a support or resistance level, this indicates a price reversal is looming. But if a candlestick, at first glance, makes its way beyond the level yet closes below it, it is a false breakout.

Acceleration of a Trend

This chart shows an ascending trend, but a resistance level break also occurred. We see here not a breakdown—which would signify a price reversal and change in trend—but a breakout. That is, the price breaks through a resistance level of an ascending trend and continues to move upwards. Now our resistance level has turned into the support level. Thus, the trend is accelerating.

If a trend is accelerating, the higher the degree of ascension, the shorter in time this trend will last.

Drawing a Channel

A channel is drawn automatically on your chart when you draw support and resistance levels. The area between these levels is called a channel.

A channel contains a channel line and a trendline. A trendline is the main line to focus on. If this line breaks on the chart, it means that the trend in the market has changed.

The main ascending trendline can be used for opening new positions. A channel line can serve as a guide for making profits in short-term operations. Some traders use a channel line to open short positions, in the direction opposite to the main trend. However, it is very dangerous and, as a rule, it is unprofitable to trade against the market trend.

As in the case with the main trendline, the longer the channel lasts, the more important and reliable it becomes.

A main trendline break always indicates a change in trend. However, a break of a channel's ascending line has the opposite meaning; it indicates an acceleration of the existing trend. Many traders open additional positions after the breakout amid an upward trend.

In my opinion, building graphic patterns and channels is a very subjective concept. They are built with the help of inclined lines, and these lines can be drawn in different ways. For example, a trader may draw a line along either a body or a shadow of a candlestick, and the results can be different.

I will cite an example of an interesting situation concerning the building of a channel on the chart. We had drawn a channel, but the situation in the market changed after a while, and all our lines turned out to be below the price chart. What should we do?

The crossed area of the chart is the future we did not see when drawing a channel. In order to correct the situation and "return the chart into the channel" we have two options: change the angle of lines to capture the new highest point of the chart or expand the channel itself. We will get the following result.

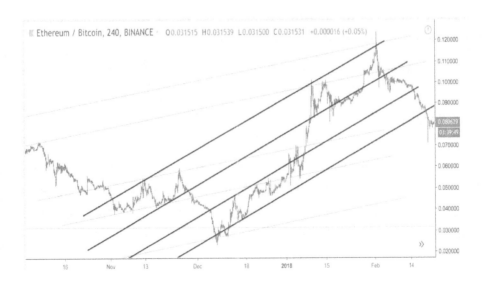

The first option is depicted with thick lines; the second one, with the thin ones.

Which of these two options is more correct? The answer is both.

The lines in both options help identify breakdown or breakout points, i.e., the zones where we receive a signal. So, it does not matter how you draw the lines, because if they show you the points of opening the position, your lines are drawn correctly.

To sum up, such an analysis of a chart shows us the zones we need to monitor, as we will open or close positions in these zones. However, this analysis does not show whether the price will break this zone or not.

Finally, write down and always remember the golden rule of technical analysis: Always conduct transactions following a dominant trend, i.e., if there is an upward trend in the market, you should buy; if there is a downward trend, you should sell.

CHAPTER 10

How to Hold Your Coins Safely and Securely

What Is a Cryptocurrency Wallet?

Your public address is like a vending machine; anyone can put money into a vending machine. Similarly, anyone with your wallet who has a public key can send you money. However, to get money from the vending machine, the owner needs an actual key to the machine. Without the key, no one can remove the money from the machine. This is represented by your private key. It is important to note that the cryptocurrency wallet does not actually store your coins; it only stores the keys that you need to send and receive the coins. When you send or receive coins, no coins are actually exchanged. Instead, the transaction is simply a record on the blockchain that changes the balance in your cryptocurrency wallet.

Choosing a Cryptocurrency Wallet

Today, there is a wide variety of cryptocurrency wallets to choose from, which makes choosing the right one a challenge, especially if you are just getting started with cryptocurrency. Making the right choice boils down to striking a balance between the security of your coins and convenience.

To make the choice easier, you need to consider the following two variables: transaction value and transaction volume. Transaction value is the number of coins you need to transact at a time, while the transaction volume refers to how frequently you will need to send or receive coins in a given period of time. There is no absolute figure for these two variables. They are relative and will vary for different people.

Let us take a look at the different types of wallets, and how the above variables influence which wallet you should use.

Online Wallets

Also known as cloud wallets, online wallets are the simplest to use and are also very convenient. Online wallets store keys online. If you intend to have low transaction volume and value, an online wallet is an excellent choice. This means that you should opt for an online wallet if you intend to store fairly small amounts of coins and make relatively few transactions. While the term 'low transaction value' is relative, you should only store your coins in an online wallet, if you would be comfortable walking around with a similar amount of money in your pocket on the street.

Mobile Wallets

Mobile wallets are also very user-friendly and are the most convenient to use. These are a good choice for someone who intends to frequently send or receive low amounts of cryptocurrency. For example, someone, who frequently makes cryptocurrency payments to gain access to online gaming platforms, should consider using a mobile wallet. The convenience of mobile wallets stems from the fact that most people always carry their smartphones with them. This allows them to make on-the-spot cryptocurrency payments. Mobile wallets offer better security in comparison to online wallets. To avoid losing access to your coins in case you lose your phone, you should note down your seed phrase on a piece of paper and keep it safe.

Paper Wallets

Paper wallets have a fairly good amount of security. However, they are the least convenient to use. As such, you should only consider a paper wallet if you intend to store huge amounts of cryptocurrency while making relatively few transactions. To ensure maximum security for your coins, you should set up your paper wallet yourself, instead of relying on an online service. One thing you should note about paper wallets is that you cannot spend your coins directly from the paper wallet.

Hardware Wallets

Hardware wallets offer the highest level of security. They are also quite convenient. This makes them a great choice if you intend to make high-value transactions every now and then. Most hardware wallets look like USB flash drives. However, unlike flash drives, they do not have any storage space for your media and other files. Instead, they are fitted with a specialized chip that stores your wallet's private key. This allows them to keep your coins safe, even in the event that a malicious person gains access to your computer. Hardware wallets require a password for access to the wallet private key, which keeps your coins secure, in the event that someone manages to steal your hardware wallet. As is the case with mobile wallets, you should jot down your seed phrase on a piece of paper and keep it safe. This allows you to retrieve your coins if your hardware wallet gets lost or damaged. Unlike the other kinds of wallets which are free, you have to pay for a hardware wallet.

Desired Traits of a Cryptocurrency Wallet

Apart from considering the transaction value and transaction volume when choosing the type of wallet you require, there are other factors that you should keep in mind when it comes to choosing the actual wallet. These are:

- **Cost**: Some wallets are free while you have to pay for others. Are you willing to spend money to keep your coins safe?
- **Security**: Does the company, providing the wallet, have a solid record of excellent security? Have there ever been any security breaches within the company?
- **Mobility**: Can you access your wallet any place, any time?
- **User-friendliness**: Does the wallet have an intuitive design? Does it support different kinds of cryptocurrency?
- **Convenience**: Can you easily make a fast transaction when you need to?
- **Style**: This is mostly for people who are looking for cool tech gadgets.

Other Important Things to Keep in Mind When Securing Your Coins

Never Leave Your Coins on Exchanges

This is one rule every cryptocurrency user should abide by. Once you buy your cryptocurrency coins, immediately transfer them to your wallet. By leaving them on the exchange, you put yourself at risk of losing your coins, in case the exchange shuts down or gets hacked (as it happened with *MtGox* and *Cryptsy*).

Keep Your Assets in a Wallet Where You Have Control Over the Keys

Whoever is in control of the keys to your wallet, has control over your funds. Therefore, you should only store your coins in a wallet, that gives you total control over your keys. When you leave your coins on the exchange or store them in online wallets that have access to your keys, you are basically handing over the responsibility of keeping your coins safe to these third parties. You should also consider using a unique passphrase to encrypt your wallet, for extra security.

Use Two-Factor Authentication on Exchanges

Always secure your exchange accounts with two-factor authentication. Sometimes, it is necessary to transfer your assets to exchanges when you need to trade. In such instances, a hacker, who has compromised your password, can easily steal your cryptocurrency coins. However, with two-factor authentication, they would also need your 2FA code before logging into your account. Since these codes are usually sent to your phone via text message, it would be impossible for an attacker to log into your account, unless they had access to your phone.

Take Care When Sending Coins to Others

When sending coins to another user, it is quite easy to erroneously send them to the wrong address. Since cryptocurrency transactions are irreversible, this means that your coins will be gone for good. To avoid such occurrences, you should first send a small amount of cryptocurrency to the address you intend to send it to. If that transaction goes correctly, you can then move large amounts of cryptocurrency with the assurance that you are sending them to the correct address.

Always Back Up Your Wallets

Always keep several online and offline backups of your cryptocurrency wallets. For instance, Exodus offers online backups that allow you to restore your wallet via email. You can also use a USB flash drive, or never write down your private keys on a piece of paper and keep them in a safe place.

CHAPTER 11

Things to Watch Out for When Trading Cryptocurrency

W hether you look at cryptocurrency as just an alternative transactional mode, or as the next big thing in investment, you ought to be aware of the potential dangers of this new currency on the block.

Absence of Government Regulation

In the case of cryptocurrency, there is not a single international government that has established a comprehensive framework for the regulation and monitoring of transactions denominated by cryptocurrency. Some governments have let organizations and individual users decide for themselves, while other governments have taken the extreme route of outright banning transactions in cryptocurrency. The perils of investing in any cryptocurrency in such a de-regulated climate cannot be ignored.

Remember to Wait Until the Transaction is Approved

Cryptocurrency relies on the approval of a transaction, to ensure that the money is really transferred. Therefore, if you are a seller, never act too hastily when a cryptocurrency transaction is complete. Always wait for approval no matter how much time it takes. The approval comes from the systems that are keeping track of all the transactions; therefore, it might take some time.

Decentralization

Remember that cryptocurrency is a much-decentralized type of currency. There are no banks that have a hold of it, and it does not emanate from a single location. The currency depends on the thousands of people, who keep their systems running all the time, by keeping a track of the transactions that are carried out.

If you fall into any sort of trouble, you might choose to go to a number of places for help; but none of them may be able to offer you a solution, since the currency is not centralized.

Security from Cyber Threats

Cryptocurrency is an entity that has taken shape solely in the digital landscape. Herein lies its most beneficial yet dangerous attribute: this form of currency is the least protected from cybercrimes and hackers. You are out there on your own, while you decide to invest and hold on to cryptocurrency. Risks of your account being hacked into are high, and to make matters worse, conventional channels of dispute resolution are of no use.

Market Value Fluctuations

As mentioned earlier, the value of cryptocurrency is not pegged directly to any specific market. That is not to say that it is free from value fluctuations. On the contrary, speculation-based trading is indeed very high, and the value is often based on the perceived levels of acceptance of this currency. What this means is that your investment could lose half its value overnight without any concrete reason to warrant that depreciation.

Taxation

In the United States, the IRS considers cryptocurrency like Bitcoin, etc. as property, for taxation purposes. Moreover, at present, this form of currency is not acceptable as a part of a tax-qualified IRA. Hence, there are no legal solutions to shield it from being fully taxed.

Keeping Your Digital Codes Safe

Keeping your digital codes safe is crucial if you are going to be involved in cryptocurrency in any way. Your digital codes, be it your passwords, keys, etc. are akin to the key to your bank locker. These can give someone access to all your fortune and hard work very easily. Therefore, it should be important that you take care of these digital codes carefully. It should not be written out so that the outside world can peek into it.

Furthermore, like your cryptocurrency wallet, your private key is your only hope of accessing and making use of your cryptocurrency. If you lose your private key, you cannot recover it, and your account as well as the money inside it may be lost. Therefore, make sure that you have your digital codes securely with you, and you do not lose them in any case.

Cryptocurrency and the Darknet

If you are not familiar with the darknet, it is the anonymous region of the Internet filled with all sorts of content and markets that cannot operate legally on the open regulated Internet we access.

This darknet is accessed through secure proxy-based browsers, like the Tor browser. You can find everything imaginable on the darknet, no matter how punishable it may be by law.

The darknet hosts a lot of markets that deal with drugs, arms trafficking, etc. Since these markets wish to stay anonymous and untraceable from the law, all the transactions that are made there are made through cryptocurrency.

Therefore, you need to ascertain that your cryptocurrency account is not used for any such transactions. Law enforcement works hard in trying to catch up to people who operate these markets, and to the customers who reach out to these markets. Therefore, make sure that your account and its cryptocurrency amount are only used for safe transactions.

CHAPTER 12

The Magic Formula to Make Money

The Mindset

Before you start taking money out of the bank, set your mindset on making money, not just on learning the technology or on experimenting with other folks. Always remember, you are investing your time and money to make money, not just some money but a lot more than average returns from other channels.

That would also require you to take some risks. Taking decisions without a lot of data is hard for many, including experienced traders, but sometimes following your gut pays off immensely.

Set goals with a timeframe to keep track of it. Make sure you create a goal, e.g., $100k in 1 year. Then create a portfolio to reach that goal.

Portfolios

For any investment, the general rule of thumb is to not put all your money in one basket, whether it is cryptocurrency or stocks.

Cryptocurrency investments fall into a high-risk category, so we suggest taking 1% to 5%, or whatever you feel comfortable playing around with.

The investment should not make you go broke if you lose it. Create a portfolio of cryptocurrencies with it and execute it as planned. Treat the investment as money expensed, to be recovered only later. If the coins do well in the future, you make a ton of money. If not, you would lose the investment.

High-Risk Tolerance – Short Term High Returns

For people with high-risk tolerance, the cryptocurrency space could be rewarding. The market fluctuates so much that you can enter and make quick money easily.

Pick any coin, and the price of that coin could fluctuate a lot within just a week. Wait for a week or two, to identify the pattern of the price movement. Based on that trend, invest in the dip, and exit when it rises. When using this method, do not plan to hold the coin for long. Focus on selling, even if the profit is low, and then buy it again when it dips. The goal is to execute as many profitable trades as possible.

Medium Risk Tolerance – Mix of Long Term and Short Term

If you want to have a balanced mix of risks and long-term growth, then you need to pick coins that are fundamentally sound. For example, Bitcoin and Ether are good coins with long-term sustainability. Pick a few coins that are moving constantly and trending in the cryptocurrency community.

Plan to keep changing these coins, based on the changes in trends. Book profit as often as you can on the trending coins and hold strong coins for a little longer. The goal is to extend the trading cycle by a little longer by optimizing your portfolio. Book profit in the short term and stay invested for long-term growth as well. Picking the right coins is critical and changing the coins as often as needed is important.

Low-Risk Tolerance – Long Term Investments

Holding the strong coins longer could be less risky. We know many businesses are starting to offer Bitcoin to accept payments. If this trend continues, then the value of the coin would multiply significantly.

Look for the best timing to invest in Bitcoin or Ether. Since the goal is long-term holding. Timing is crucial. You can even wait for weeks to find the best time to enter.

Timing of Your Investment

Just like any other investment to maximize the return, you need to find the right time to invest your money. The key to trading and making money is knowing when to enter and exit.

Remember the cryptocurrency market is a socially driven network. The coins perform based on future predictions on the uses for business.

There is no real value for the coins right now. Yet the coins are performing at an unbelievable pace; it is all because of speculation from the social networks.

The right time to invest in any coins can be found easily when you start spotting the trends in social media. Before you invest, join these groups (mentioned later in this book) and participate in the ongoing discussions.

Enter

The coin market fluctuates quite frequently. This gives you a pattern of minimum and maximum limits over a period of time. You must carefully watch the cryptocurrency rates for a couple of weeks, before you invest, to understand the fluctuations. Then, pick the limit that you are comfortable going in with, and invest before it gets traction.

Some of the coins in the market might be relatively new, but often have strong backing from a solid financial team. It is advisable to invest in it before it has a major upswing.

Exit

Profit does not always depend on when and how you enter the market; how and when you exit is also important to make a good profit. For every coin you have invested in, you should have a plan on when and by how much you are going to cash out.

Your portfolio should have a combination of both long-term and short-term stock of coins. Some cryptocurrencies have a long-term growth (1-3 years), and some have a comparatively shorter lifespan (1-3 months).

Stop Loss

Dramatic financial collapses are a part of many big investments. Fluctuations of market trends, positive or negative, are in no one's control. Hence, if you picked the wrong coin at a bad time, it may fall drastically. Therefore, it is very important to set up a stop-loss order and sell the currency before you lose it all. At the same time, you must also be aware to not sell prematurely.

CHAPTER 13

Buying and Selling at Cryptocurrency Exchanges

We all like the short and simple route. For a person who just wants to buy cryptocurrency, doing so at the exchange need not be hard; just buy anywhere! *Coinbase.com,* for example, is a great place to start trading.

You need to find a Bitcoin exchange, pay dollars/euro/any other currency to the equivalent Bitcoins. Then you can transfer the Bitcoin to your online wallet, and you are good. Or are you?

While the securities exchange is controlled and centralized, Bitcoin exchanges are not, as they are built on the same concept of decentralization as Bitcoin itself.

There are hundreds of huge exchanges, where you can trade your Bitcoin for cash or vice versa.

The problem therefore would be how to know you have the best exchange. Apart from the common benchmarks like safety, privacy, and reputation of the exchange, there are other important things that you should look for in an exchange.

Limits

This should not be a problem if you just want a few Bitcoins, as pretty much any exchange can allow that. However, when you have some money that you really need to put away in Bitcoin, you want an exchange that does not limit you. You want to be able to buy as much Bitcoin as your money will allow.

Speed and Ease of Access

This is about how fast you can use your Bitcoin for whatever you need it for. For example, maybe you want to buy software or transfer money to someone across the globe. How fast does the exchange allow you to access your coins after you have bought them?

I would say the faster, the better. It is your money after all, and the sooner you can have it, the more you will feel in control.

The Fee

Just as it happens in regular money and securities exchanges, there is a fee to be paid for the transactions. This fee varies from exchange to exchange, and as you trade more Bitcoins, some exchanges can waive the fee for you. However, do expect to pay a fee most of the time.

Withdrawal and deposit fees should not be too high; do your research before choosing an exchange.

The Bitcoin Average Rate of Exchange

While there is no standard rate for Bitcoin exchange in the market, the exchange rate is arrived at via an average of rates across all the exchanges.

Before buying your coins, find out the exchange rate from sites like *CoinDesk*. They daily update Bitcoin and altcoin exchange rates.

Buying from the Local Bitcoin ATM

In major cities around the world, it is possible to find one or two Bitcoin ATMs. If there is one in your city, you can buy Bitcoins from there. It is as simple as that!

What methods of payment are generally acceptable for Bitcoin trading? You can start with credit card payments. This is fast and very convenient, and there are no blockades regarding what you can or cannot buy. The exchange rates are high though.

You can also use bank transfers. The exchange rates for banks are low, but the transfer could take anywhere from three to five business days for the transaction to go through. It is just the way banks work. This method is best for buying many coins though.

The other method of paying for Bitcoin is to pay cash. You know someone who is selling his coins; you meet, you transfer the coins to your wallet, and you pay cash. This old-age method of trading is very convenient, but the exchange rate could be high too.

When looking for information about buying Bitcoin, you will find some sites telling you about PayPal. It is best to avoid PayPal as they prohibit it. If they find out you have traded in Bitcoin with your account, they could limit your account, and you do not want that.

Exchanges to Avoid

Avoid exchanges that have a hacking attack history. No one can overemphasize the importance of safety and security for your Bitcoin. At the high exchange rate, this is the hottest thing after the discovery of fire in the world. Many hackers attack exchanges all the time.

CHAPTER 14

Learning How to Avoid the Scammers

There is a lot of commotion in the world of digital currencies. Many people are excited about joining the community. They want to be able to trade with people all over the world, they want to be able to invest, and they like the security that comes with using these digital currencies.

The good news is that there are some different methods that you can use that will help you avoid scammers and keep your coins safe. When you are in the market to invest in digital currencies; you want to make money for yourself, not for scammers.

You Can Never Have Enough Security

The first step that you should take is to make sure that the passwords on your wallet are as safe as possible. You should have some form of backup in place, to help keep the coins safe, rather than just leaving them in your online wallet. Nevertheless, you should still protect the online wallet as well. Remember that while the wallet is a convenient place for you to leave your coins, you need to realize that depositing coins there will not be the same as when you deposit the money into a bank. There is no one watching over your money, or an FDIC that will be able to guarantee no theft/loss. You have to be the one, who takes the right steps, to keep others from accessing your coins.

Watch Out for the Exchange Service You Are Using

Remember that not all exchanges for digital currencies are going to be the same. There are some really great exchange platforms that you can choose to work with. These may charge a small fee to do the exchange, but it is not that much. You will not be cheated from the money that they take from you. However, there are some services that have just sprouted up, in the hopes of taking your coins and running away. These are sometimes easy to find but harder to figure out. If you pick out the wrong exchange service, you are going to feel like you were fooled, especially if this company just takes your money and runs off.

Knowing How the Technology Works

To do well with investing in digital currencies, you need to make sure that you understand the technology that helps run them. These digital currencies rely completely on technology. If this is something that scares you a little bit, then this may not be the best investment option for you. Just by learning a little bit about technology, you get to work with cryptocurrency without falling into any traps that possible scammers may set.

Purchasing Online

There are many times when you will want to make a purchase online using your digital currencies. This is one of the benefits of being able to use digital currencies in the first place. If you are going with one of the major retailers that have started accepting digital currencies, such as *Overstock*, you will not have anything to worry about. However, there are a lot of individual sellers that you can work with. While many of these will provide you with a good experience, there are also some that are just looking to trick you once the transaction is done.

Other Methods to Use to Avoid Scammers

There are a lot of other things that you can do to avoid the scammers getting ahold of your personal information and digital coins, some of which are mentioned below:

- Never let someone else remote access the computer you are using. This includes support staff for your exchange site or anyone else that you are working with.

- Never hand out your 2FA codes. No reliable exchange site is going to ask you to hand these over.

- Double-check that the channel you are using for support is considered a legitimate site before you try to send over funds.

- Before sending any money to another person, you need to search for some reviews on that person. There are often some good reviews online about the different businesses that you want to work with, so make sure they are reputable, before sending the money.

- If you get a link in your email, it is always best if you can copy and paste these links rather than clicking on them. This is true even if you recognize the website. There is the possibility that a scammer would have placed in a hidden link to redirect you, without you realizing it

- Any time you email or peruse through a website, look for grammatical errors. Many times, scammers are not going to take the time to proofread their scam websites, so their emails/sites will be full of mistakes.

- Beware of emails that say someone has sent you money. Often this is going to redirect you to some place where you will accidentally send money out of your account; then you cannot get the money back.

- No exchange site is going to ask you for your password, through email or call. If someone is asking you for this information, then you know that it is a scammer.

- Make sure that you are regularly scanning your computer with an antivirus. This will ensure that the scammer has not been able to put malware on your computer without you noticing.

- The operating system and other programs on your computer need to be kept up to date. This will ensure that all discovered malware and other issues will be prevented.

- If you ever notice anything unusual, it is important to scan your computer and talk to the exchange site that you are using. They will be able to help you figure out what is going on, and they may be able to prevent a scammer from causing more damage ahead of time.

Scammers are always interested in getting ahold of money that you have in your wallets. Without any type of security in place or a reliable agency to go through and protect your information, you could be out of luck and end up falling victim to one of these scammers. Make sure to follow some of the tips in this chapter; then you will be able to keep the scammers away.

CHAPTER 15

Cryptocurrency Trading Broker

Here are the standards to look for in prospective brokers:

Trading Platform

Your broker is an entity that will provide you with a platform that you can use to buy and sell, as well as open trading positions. Your broker should provide you with a professional-looking platform. Although the design of the platform may not be as important as its features, it is still beneficial to have a professionally designed platform to help set the right mood for trading/investing.

Customer Support

It is important that you work with a broker that has an active and professional customer support team. The customer support team will help you in case you have questions, and especially if you face technical issues. Your broker lets you know how you can get in touch with the customer support team. Normally, an email address will be provided, or a certain page on the platform may be used where you can directly send a message to the support team. A live, on-page chat service may also be provided by your broker. Sometimes a broker may even provide you with a number that you can call, to reach the customer support team.

Latest Reviews

Just like when looking for other services or products online, you should also read the latest reviews given to a trading broker. Be sure to read the reviews before you make any form of commitment. Also, do not rely on just one website for reviews. This is because many cryptocurrency trading brokers hire writers to come up with a positive write-up about their business. Hence, read as many reviews as you can. It is also good if you can read some negative reviews. This usually shows that the reviews are honest and true. To find the reviews on a particular broker, simply open your browser, type the name of the broker, and add the word 'reviews.' The SERP will then give you a list of related pages. Also, pay attention to the dates when the reviews were written.

Mobile Trading Platforms

The mobile version should be easy and convenient to use. Although it may not provide all the features that you can enjoy when you use a desktop computer, it should at least provide you with the important parts of the trading platform. You should be able to manage your account easily, as well as open and close trading positions. It should also allow you to make deposits and withdrawals easily. Last, but not least, it should be easy to use and navigate. Again, your broker should help you and make the experience of trading more convenient and interesting for you.

Deposit Requirements and Withdrawal Limits

Check the minimum and maximum deposit and withdrawal requirements for a broker. Also, keep in mind that making a deposit is usually easier than making a withdrawal. Normally, making a deposit can be done in-stantly, provided you transfer funds from your wallet into your trading account.

It is worth stressing that you should not rush the process of choosing a cryptocurrency trading broker.

It is very important that you work only with a trustworthy and reliable broker; so, take as much time as you need, to identify the right broker for you.

CHAPTER 16

Strategies for Making Money in Cryptocurrency

A good trading strategy should have a well-thought-out plan with specific trading objectives, a trading timeframe, and a risk tolerance plan.

The plan involves developing methods aimed at buying and selling cryptocurrency assets. It should also have a strategy that meets your investment goals. Trading strategies help identify the entry and exit points in the cryptocurrency market.

Buy & Hold

Buy-and-hold (sometimes referred to as HODL) is the basic trading strategy where you buy the cryptocurrency asset, hold it, and later sell it. To hold the asset requires a lot of confidence. You have to be optimistic about the rising prices, to hold the asset and sell at a higher price later. The investor holds the asset as long as the prices are rising. The bull market fuels the buy-and-hold strategy.

HODL means "Hold on for Dear Life," and has been used in the Bitcoin and cryptocurrency-sphere, to indicate the buy-and-hold strategy for cryptocurrency investments. Holding the coin for a certain period can result in long-term benefits to cryptocurrency traders.

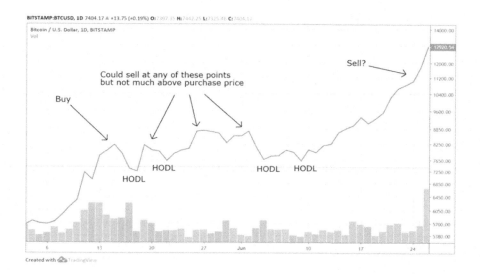

Many HODL investors have been able to achieve their long-term business goals. Investing in multiple cryptocurrencies such as Ethereum, EOS, Ripple, etc. is one way to diversify investment risks.

As cryptocurrencies increase in value, the gains are not as large as they are for lower-priced cryptocurrencies. Right now, an investor can buy almost 50 Ethereum for the same price as 1 Bitcoin. The spread varies; at the Bitcoin/Ethereum price peak, it was about 20 Ethereum to 1 Bitcoin. Diversifying the cryptocurrency portfolio can result in better returns and can also re-balance the portfolio.

Most buy-and-hold investors do not set a stop-loss. A stop-loss would set a sell order if the price dropped to an amount that is uncomfortable for the investor. However, setting a stop-loss removes the emotion from the trade. It locks in the loss but prevents an even larger loss incurred by a stubborn investor. Setting stops to limit the downside is recommended by most successful investors.

Bitcoin Mining Strategy

The process of creating new coins is called mining. Mining Bitcoin (or other cryptocurrency coins) is another way to obtain coins. Unfortunately, Bitcoin mining has progressed to the point where custom hardware "rigs" are needed.

However, you can mine less popular coins, using second-hand rigs, and exchange the coins for Bitcoin on the exchange website. You can also hold the coins for a while and sell them when the price increases.

Miners incur the expense of buying and operating the rigs. In some cases, there are significant costs of electricity and cooling since the rigs create heat while running.

Bounties

As you become more involved in cryptocurrency trading, you are going to see the word 'bounty,' eventually. If you have ever seen forums or ads about bounties, bounties probably seem like a treasure hunt, and that is kind of true. Bounties are projects, jobs, or tasks that have been typically made by a coin developer. If you are able to finish the job, then you will get a reward in the form of a coin. These simple jobs/tasks normally take place during the coin's Initial Coin Offering.

Types of Bounties

- **Signature Campaign:** These campaigns will typically consist of posting a signature that the company created. The signature will have to be posted on a *Bitcointalk.org* forum. Depending on your ranking, you may get a few or more stakes. You will have to be a junior member in order to participate.

- **Video/Blog Post Campaign:** This is a great option if you are a big media user. The stakes you receive not only depend on the quality of your work, but also on the number of views your content gets.

- **Translation Campaign:** This is a great option for native language speakers. These jobs will typically involve translating three subject types.

- **Facebook and Twitter Campaign:** If you have a decent number of followers on your social media pages, then this could be a lucrative choice of bounty for you.

Where to Find Bounties

Nowadays, you can find the most active bounty campaigns on *Bitcointalk*. If you know the right keywords and places, you should be able to find thousands of them. Another way to find them is to Google something similar; you may just get lucky and find something interesting.

Some other places you can find bounties are:

- Cryptocurrencycointalk.com
- Cryptocurrencymoms.com
- The Viral Exchange

Arbitraging Strategy

In an arbitrage strategy, you buy coins at a lower price and sell them at a higher price, in a different location. As an example, the price of Bitcoin is $8500 on *Coinbase* and $8600 on *Binance*. Buying a Bitcoin on Coinbase, and then selling the same Bitcoin on Binance, could return a profit of $100 minus the Binance and Coinbase fees.

This is less viable now because the technique is now widely known. Some companies and people are constantly scanning for price discrepancies and are more likely to act quickly. However, this may be a good technique with lesser-known coins.

Passive Income from Dividend Payouts Strategy

In some cases, lending cryptocurrency coins can earn dividends between 5% and 10% per year. These dividends are usually limited to a few coins like Bitcoin, NEO, and VeChain. If the coin price goes up for a certain period, you gain more profits.

Recently, coins that use proof-of-stake verification, instead of proof-of-work verification, can earn dividends on coins held in cryptocurrency exchanges such as Coinbase, Bittrex, or Kraken.

Long Trade

A long trade is a term used when purchasing cryptocurrency assets at a cheaper price, with the expectation of selling them at a high price in the future to gain profit.

Day-traders can also use a long trade strategy when they buy the asset with the expectation that the price will rise during the day. 'Buy' and 'long' are common terms in the trading sector. If an investor says, 'Going long,' it means he/she has an interest in buying a particular asset and holding onto it, with the expectation that it will increase in value.

Long trades have unlimited profit gains since the price of the coin can go up indefinitely.

Short Trade

In a short trade, the coin is sold because the trader expects the price to decrease. If the coin is not owned, traders can borrow the coin for a fee. This is called a "naked" short and is only recommended for experienced traders when the price could go up.

In a "naked" short trade, the trader sells the borrowed coin to repurchase it later at a lower price and return the coin to the person it was borrowed from. If the selling price is higher than the repurchase price, they keep the profit.

Short sales have high financial risks. Be very careful when using this strategy, because sometimes key market players can drive the price up, forcing short position speculators to buy back the asset before the price goes too high. This is referred to as a "short squeeze" and ironically, this can cause the price to zoom even higher since there are more buyers.

Day Trading

Cryptocurrency day-trading involves buying and selling cryptocurrency assets for a profit. The practice has become popular in recent years due to high volatility and trading volumes.

Daily cryptocurrency trading is characterized by high risk. Before you enter into any trade, you have to know when to take profits. You also need to know the price at which to stop the trade to avoid major losses. Smart investors control the size of their position in the market. They also do not risk a significant portion of their investment portfolio or use too much leverage in a single trade.

To succeed in day-trading, you have to be tuned in constantly. Receiving any big news or announcements just a few minutes later than everyone else can result in huge profits or losses.

Altcoin Spread Out

The proper way to use this strategy is to divide your capital. There is no hard-and-fast rule as to how many times you should divide your capital, but it is suggested that you divide it into at least five parts. Hence, if you have an invested capital worth $1,000, you should be able to invest in five positions, $200 per position.

Dollar-Cost-Averaging

Dollar-Cost-Averaging (DCA) is a simple investment technique that does not require much skill or knowledge to perform. The problem with trading is that we will never know exactly how the market will turn out. With the DCA technique, you will have more control over market fluctuations. The idea behind Dollar Cost Averaging is to cut down the risks, by breaking up the total investment into smaller parts and investing them over a period of time.

Stop Loss

This is an important technique that every trader needs to know how to use, as it will be like a protection for your investment. Basically, a stop-loss order is an order to sell your coin when it reaches a certain price.

Pump-And-Dump Advantage

As the name already suggests, it is where a certain cryptocurrency is pumped. This is where an individual or a group attempts to increase the price of a particular cryptocurrency through the use of promotions. The problem with this is that it is usually done through the use of false promotions, where you make a bad investment to appear as if it were profitable. This is why it is not a recommended method, as it is fraudulent in nature. Now, due to the promotional hype, it will draw the interest of some people, which would lead them to make an investment in the cryptocurrency, the subject of the said scheme.

Of course, this will further increase the price of the cryptocurrency being pumped, which will make it look even more convincing, especially if it gets featured in the news. Once people behind the scheme are happy with the increase in value, they then sell the cryptocurrency. This is when the people responsible for the scheme, now dump the cryptocurrency. The effect of this is that the people behind the pump-and-dump scheme will enjoy a nice profit, while all the other investors will realize that they have become victims, holding a losing asset, whose price simply keeps on decreasing.

The problem with this scheme is that there is no real value. This is why you should check if the price of a cryptocurrency really justifies its value.

CHAPTER 17

Tips for Cryptocurrency Trading

Have a Purpose for Each Trade

Before placing any trade, you need to have a reason as to why you want to trade cryptocurrency assets. In the cryptocurrency market, there is always a winner and a loser. It is a zero-sum game; for every win, there is a corresponding loss.

Whether you are a day-trader or long-term trader, you must be patient. Do not rush a trade and cause losses. Sometimes it is better to make a small gain than to rush into losses with a single trade.

Set Profit Targets and Stop-Loss Orders

You should always know when to enter and exit the market, and how much profit you want to make. If you plan to get out of the market when you make a certain profit, or if the price hits a set target, stick to that plan. Do not be greedy.

Place stop-loss orders to help you cut down on losses. When trading, put emotions aside and set a stop-loss point so that when the price drops to the stop-loss points, the asset is sold automatically.

Manage Risks

You need to learn how to manage risk in the business. It is better to accumulate a lower profit from small, regular trades than to risk everything by investing big. If the market is less liquid, invest small amounts and set both stop-loss and profit targets further away from the buying price.

Know Exactly When to Take Profit and When to Cut Losses

Before you enter a trade, please do technical analyses beforehand, so you will know exactly when to take profits and when to cut losses. Stick with this plan, and never be greedy or stubborn. Discipline is the only way to survive in this market.

Do Not Over Trade

Newbies usually fall into the mentality of overtrading, where they constantly put themselves in a position of buying or selling. Newbies enter these trades hoping that they will make some kind of profit, magically. They have the fear of missing out. However, most of the time, they will exit those same trades with a loss. In addition, the trading fees collected by the exchange can eat up their investment really quickly.

Cut Loss

As I mentioned previously, cutting losses is crucial when it comes to trading. No one wants to lose, but failure is a part of the game. When a trade does not go as planned, cut losses immediately and wait for a new opportunity. If you have not lost all of your investment, you still have another chance. Again, if things go wrong, cut losses, and move on.

Trade with the Trend

Trends come in waves. There will be long waves and there will be short waves. The waves can go up, or they can go down. Our main purpose in doing technical analysis is to identify the trend and go along with it. Many traders make the mistake of trying to buy at the bottom and sell at the top. They want to profit from the whole wave, from the start till the end. This is a risky strategy since no one will ever know where the bottom is or where the top is until they have happened. The best way to trade is to buy when the trend has already started and sell before it ends. We are not trying to win big; we are trying to win little by little, but consistently.

Never Stop Learning

In trading, it is important to never stop learning to enhance trading skills. Every time we win or lose a trade, write down the lessons that we can learn from that trade. Everyone has a different personality and mentality so the learning path for every individual can be very unique. In trading, the best way to learn is through self-experience; there will be no book or guru that could guide us well to success. We all have got to learn how to win, by making mistakes. Patience, persistence, and discipline are the keys.

Welcome FOMO

FOMO (fear of missing out) is a trading psychology experienced by traders, and one of the reasons why the majority of traders fail. There are times when almost everyone wants to trade, and you feel like jumping into the market by buying the coins. Bitcoin whales are watching every move that small traders make. This will lead to an oversupply of coins in the market, and the price will drop as demand vanishes.

If you can harness your emotions, you can exploit the FOMO and sell when you see that people are in FOMO mode.

Do Not Buy Because the Price Is Low

Buying coins because the price is low is a common mistake made by amateur traders. You need to look out for other factors before buying the coin. You should not base the decision to buy the coin only on its affordability. You should also look at the market cap of the coin. The higher the cap, the more suitable it is to invest in it.

Be Vigilant of ICOs

Some startups encourage the public to invest in their ICO (Initial Coin Offering) with a promise to get promoted coins at lower prices, for you to sell at a profit. ICOs' high returns attract a large number of investors. Recently a large number of firms using ICO strategies were found to be scams. Therefore, be careful when investing in an ICO. Scrutinize all information provided to attract investors. Do a background check on the people behind that firm and analyze them to see whether they can deliver as promised. Do not just buy because of the returns they are promising.

Diversify Your Investment

Although cryptocurrency investments can offer large returns, they are very unpredictable. A slight change in market conditions can make them fall within a day. You can also lose everything you hold, in just seconds, especially if the exchange platform is hacked. Diversification will allow you to cope with this uncertainty.

CHAPTER 18

Trading Psychology

One of the biggest hurdles new traders have to overcome is acquiring the mindset of a successful trader. This is even more prevalent in the cryptocurrency market because the sheer volatility allows the potential for large losses in addition to large gains. Having a successful mindset is the single most important skill a trader must possess. Given below is a list of important psychological factors that you must be aware of if you are going to become a successful trader.

Paralysis by Analysis

You have spent your time reading and studying charts; now it is time to go to *CEX.io* or your preferred trading website and deposit money into your account. You do so, and begin looking at charts, waiting…and waiting…but you just cannot seem to pull the trigger. This happens to a lot of new traders, especially those who are naturally risk-averse. You want everything to go perfectly, and you want to start out on a good note.

Knowing When Not to Trade

One of the more important qualities of a good trader is restraint. In other words, being able to understand that there are days where you do not need to make a trade. Maybe there are no obvious patterns appearing, maybe it is just a slow day in the market. Either way, you need to learn to take days off. This is good for preventing trade burnout, especially in the cryptocurrency market that operates round the clock.

Accepting That the Market Is Always Right

One of our great cognitive biases as human beings is believing we are better than we actually are at certain things. For example, are you an above-average driver? Bets are 90% of people will answer yes; statistically, only 50% of people can be above average at anything, that includes trading as well.

Accepting That You Are Wrong

Following on from the above point, the market is not wrong, you are. You need to be able to accept that you will be wrong in many trades, even in multiple trades in a row. Remember, judge yourself by your results, and not on any perceived clever moves you may have made. You will always have losers, but you need to be able to take a step back and accept this, in order to move forward.

Taking Intermediate Profits

If your profits are only on paper, you have not made much progress. You need to convert some of your gains back to fiat from time to time. Taking profits helps you mitigate your need to earn more money on paper, which leads to greed taking over, which inevitably leads to losing money in the long run.

Recency Bias

"You are only as good as your last trade" is a concept many traders adhere to, especially if they have a run of losses. This leads to negative mental energy and a loss of confidence in oneself. What you need to learn to do, is not focus on these losses, but look at the bigger picture. Instead of focusing on your next trade, focus on your next hundred trades. By focusing on the next hundred trades, you remain committed to your trading fundamentals, as opposed to just chasing short-term results and experiencing dopamine highs.

CHAPTER 19

Professional Trading Practices

Research and Analysis

It is also important that you do sufficient research. It is true that many investors and traders do their research before making an investment; however, a very common mistake is to do little research. Just because you have spent three hours on your computer, trying to understand the market does not mean that you are in the position to make the best and profitable investment. You should know that truly professional and successful traders spend hours every day studying and analyzing the market, and yet, they are still very careful each time they make a trade or investment. Never enter any trade position, or make any investment, without doing enough research and analysis.

Only Invest the Money That You Can Afford to Lose

This is common advice that is given to casino gamblers. The truth is that there is no amount of preparation and research that can guarantee that a particular investment will end up in your favor. The cryptocurrency market is highly volatile, and there are so many things that can happen in the course of an investment. Therefore, you should never use the money you otherwise need, say, to pay for your electric bill and other obligations.

This is also a good way not to be too pressured. When you use the money that you need for your obligations, you will not be able to think clearly. Therefore, only invest the money that you can afford to lose. This way you will not be pressured even if you stake a losing investment. This will allow you to think more clearly and effectively.

Self-Discipline

Self-discipline is extremely important to your success. Unfortunately, many investors and traders learn about it the hard way. Normally, they only realize the importance of self-discipline after losing an investment. This is another reason why experts advise that you should start out small when you are a beginner. This way you can learn about self-discipline and make mistakes, without risking too much.

Self-discipline is also the best way to combat greed. As you already know, greed is your serious enemy. It has caused many investors to lose their profits and investments.

Cryptocurrency Trading Journal

Although having a trading journal is not required, there are many experts who strongly recommend it. The reason is that a trading journal will allow you to see yourself from a new perspective, one that is free from any form of bias and/or prejudice. It will also allow you to learn things that you might not be able to learn without the use of a journal. Do not worry; keeping a journal is not easy. You do not have to be a good writer just to maintain a trading journal. However, there are two things that you need to do: You need to be completely honest, and you need to update your journal regularly.

Professional Approach

Although there is nothing wrong with participating in the market just for fun, you should not expect to make so much of a profit if you only consider it a mere hobby. Approaching it just as a hobby usually signifies a lack of dedication and commitment. You should understand that truly professional and successful cryptocurrency investors/traders take their work seriously. They spend hours researching, just to understand a single cryptocurrency better.

Practice

You cannot be a successful and experienced cryptocurrency investor, by simply reading books on how to invest in the cryptocurrency market. Being a successful investor or trader takes actual practice. You need to practice how to apply the strategies, effectively and properly. You should also develop your own strategy. You should understand that the strategies in this book only serve to give you an idea of how professional traders deal in the market; these strategies should not limit your creativity.

Take A Break

It is easy to get absorbed into the activities of being a cryptocurrency investor. It is not uncommon to find people who do not notice the time, as they analyze the market and the different cryptocurrencies that they can invest in. Although it is good to work hard, you should also understand that taking a break is also important. By allowing yourself to take a break, you will be able to clear your mind and relax your body. This will allow you to be able to think more clearly and effectively.

Patience

You need to learn to be patient and observe proper timing. A common mistake is to keep on investing and trading, even when the market is down. Of course, there is still an opportunity to make a profit, but the chances are low. Sometimes the best way to deal with the market is to be inactive. Simply be patient and observe the market. Soon enough, a better opportunity will arise, and be sure that you are ready to take advantage of it.

Enjoy

Although being a cryptocurrency investor can be sad, in the sense that you immerse yourself in a market that is ruthless, there are perks that you can enjoy. Enjoy the fact that you are your own boss, you have complete control over your schedule, and you can earn a very high amount of profit. You can also function more effectively if you enjoy what you do.

CHAPTER 20

The Future of Cryptocurrency

Many cryptocurrencies saw a lot of growth in recent years, with some like Bitcoin, Bitcoin Cash, Dash, and Ethereum seeing exponential growth. As we move forward, the cryptocurrency space will only keep growing. According to some industry experts, the coming year will see mass public awareness for cryptocurrencies. Here are some of the things expected to happen in the cryptocurrency world in the future:

Taxation Will Become a Huge Issue

While many people have amassed wealth in the cryptocurrency market, many have been keeping it away from the eyes of the government. In the coming years, you can expect that the IRS will be more focused on clamping down on cryptocurrency investors, to make sure they pay their taxes.

Bitcoin to Develop into a Payment Network

Though it was meant to be an electronic payments system, many people currently consider Bitcoin as a store of value and a speculative asset.

However, according to Trevor Konerko, CEO of a cryptocurrency technology company, Bitcoin's utility and price will increase dramatically, leading to its emergence as a fully-fledged payment network. This will be driven by the emergence of scaling solutions such as Lighting Network. However, for Bitcoin to become a fully-fledged payment network, its community needs to be willing to adopt these upgrades.

Cryptocurrencies Are Here to Stay

To some people, cryptocurrencies are a passing fad, something that will lose momentum as fast as it gained it. However, industry experts believe that cryptocurrencies and blockchain technology are here to stay. Some platforms like NEO and Ethereum will push for the widespread adoption of the technology since they help people create blockchain applications that have meaningful uses in the real world. The adoption of these real-world applications by the corporate world will increase the demand for cryptocurrencies and will therefore ensure their longevity.

Diversification of Assets by Investors

Currently, most investors hold their assets in Bitcoin and Ethereum. However, you can expect that more people will start diversifying their portfolios into other cryptocurrencies like Dash, Litecoin, IOTA, NEM, and many more. Many investors will diversify their cryptocurrency assets in the same way that they approach other traditional assets. Many more cryptocurrencies will also emerge in the coming years. Some will be introduced to tackle the challenges being experienced by existing cryptocurrencies, while others will introduce new niches altogether. There is a high likelihood that some of the new cryptocurrencies will become very profitable.

Increased Regulation

Currently, many countries do not have any policies for cryptocurrencies. However, several governments have been keenly watching their use and growth. As more people adopt cryptocurrencies, governments will start putting regulations in place surrounding their use.

Cryptocurrencies Will Force Conventional Financial Systems to Level Up

Currently, banks and traditional payment processors are enjoying extremely high transaction fees. They are also very slow, with most international transactions being processed in 1-3 days. Cryptocurrencies, on the other hand, are very fast and have extremely low processing fees. These advantages might push more businesses towards cryptocurrencies. If they are to remain relevant, banks and traditional payment processors will need to up their game.

Technological Future

Cryptocurrency, as a concept, has a bright technological future. Increasingly powerful computers accompanied by an algorithm that is becoming easier to mine means that cryptocurrency will be less cumbersome to mine.

Changing Dominance

Currently, Bitcoin is the leading cryptocurrency. However, as technology advances and as demand for tokens increases, there will be a shift towards other cryptocurrencies. Thus, Bitcoin is likely to cede ground in the future as the dominant cryptocurrency. Nonetheless, its position as the 'gold' standard of cryptocurrencies is going to remain unchallenged for a long time. Ripple, Litecoin, and Ethereum are going to take a greater role in the near future, as many financial institutions are actively exploring them. Ripple is being preferred to form an automated algorithmic clearinghouse. Ethereum is attractive due to its many customizable features such as smart contracts, among others.

Performance of Fiat Currency

One of the main factors that have driven many people towards cryptocurrency, is the instability of their own fiat currencies. For example, the Zimbabwean Dollar has become worthless. The Venezuelan Bolivar has depreciated at such a high rate that it is hard to keep it as a store of value. When a given fiat currency becomes unstable, users become more willing to take up cryptocurrency. In most jurisdictions where the economy is overheating, to such an extent that they are facing hyperinflation, countries restrict the flow of foreign currency so that people cannot buy them. Since governments have no control over cryptocurrencies, they can become the available options for citizens to safeguard their monetary investment.

CONCLUSION

This brings us to the end of our learning journey. All the information in this book is very crucial for beginners. Read it carefully, apply it to real-life trading, and learn from it. Start out with money you can afford to lose and enjoy the process of learning to trade. Remember, do not think you can get rich overnight by trading.

This book aimed to provide you with up-to-date information on cryptocurrencies and the know-how to trade them and maximize profit. I hope you have gained valuable information that has enabled you to start trading in cryptocurrencies. If this is the case, please help others achieve success in cryptocurrency trading, by encouraging them to acquire a copy of this book for knowledge and reference.

Due to the many advantages offered by cryptocurrency, many businesses and individuals are gradually starting to accept it. Many investors have also switched from traditional investment avenues to cryptocurrency assets.

Always remember that the safety of your cryptocurrency, your cryptocurrency wallet, and everything associated with it, is entirely up to you. This form of transacting enables a more secure way of transferring currency between two parties; therefore, always keep it so.

Always keep your passwords and keys securely with you. Do not share the private keys with anyone. The implications of this could be quite hazardous. All your money could be stolen, or even worse, used in an illegal manner.

With that said, using cryptocurrency is adjusting to the speed of the modern and the futuristic world. Cryptocurrencies are the way to transfer money in today's world. Not only is it secure, but the benefits are innumerable. Therefore, use it wisely and be a benefactor of it.

Cryptocurrency can be an intelligent investment that may generate a fortune. All you need are some smart skills.

Also, while diving into this cryptocurrency world, you should do in-depth research, so you are ready from the start. This book will serve as a good source of research for you. Additional research can be done through the internet as well.

You should make up your mind about which cryptocurrency you wish to invest in. Which wallet do you want to use? What would be the purpose of the cryptocurrency? These things should be clear in your mind, so you can take decisive steps.

Additionally, even if you do not really wish to invest in cryptocurrency, there are many other ways related to cryptocurrency, through which you can make good money, without actually investing in coins.

Cryptocurrency requires patience and good use of your mind. Therefore, put smart work into the field and have patience. You are gradually but eventually going to profit.

INVESTING IN BITCOIN AND CRYPTOCURRENCY

A Beginner's Guide to Obtain Passive Income by
Investing in Bitcoin and Other Cryptocurrencies.

Nicholas Scott

INTRODUCTION

A s the world becomes heavily digitized, digital currencies are here to stay. Cryptocurrencies created an entirely new, up-and-coming asset class that is attracting increasing interest from institutional investors. Cryptocurrency investment funds are provided by hedge funds, such as Fidelity Investments. Given the potential market capitalization of $265 billion today, there is clearly room for growth. It is hoped that this book can help you gain a better understanding of the technology behind cryptocurrency and its viability as an investment. *Blockchain* technology is, no doubt, one of the biggest breakthroughs of the 21st century, as big data continues to expand into one of the most lucrative fields today.

Understanding what blockchains and cryptocurrencies are gives you an edge in cryptocurrency investing, and you can better understand the industry. It is advisable to spend a significant portion of your time studying trading theory before you begin trading your hard-earned coins. Remember, at its very core, trading comes down to two factors, and two factors only.

Investing is the ultimate rush: it is a 'game' played against one another via a computer screen, your mind against another person, your money against theirs. Some days you come home a conquering hero, and other days you will be left beaten, demoralized, and broken. Hopefully, you will be experiencing more of the former than the latter, after studying this book, and you will become a consistently profitable trader going forward.

CHAPTER 1

Cryptocurrency Basics

What Is Cryptocurrency?

Essentially, you can think of a cryptocurrency transaction as you would a PayPal transaction between friends. The biggest difference is that instead of transferring a traditional (fiat) currency with a set price, you are trading a digital token, whose worth fluctuates based on what the market says it is worth. More precisely, the label 'cryptocurrency' can be applied to any digital token that utilizes programmed cryptographic processes to remain secure, without the need for any type of active oversight. Cryptocurrencies function thanks to what is known as *blockchain* technology, the basics of which will be discussed.

While interest has been building around all types of cryptocurrencies for several years, this interest is largely associated with speculative investment, as the opportunities to spend any acquired coins remains slim. Due to this imbalance, speculative investors typically exert a higher-than-average amount of influence on the prices of cryptocurrencies. For this reason, and many others, the cryptocurrency market remains highly volatile when compared to more traditional investment markets.

Because it served as a proof-of-concept for blockchain technology, *Bitcoin* quickly rose to the top of the cryptocurrency pile, where it remains to this day, occupying fifty percent of the total cryptocurrency market capitalization.

While the movement of fiat currencies is limited due to their direct ties to a specific economy, all cryptocurrencies routinely react to specific incidents that take place around the world. The only qualifier, as to whether a specific event will affect the price of a specific cryptocurrency, is if enough investors believe that it does; as a result, this causes even more price volatility.

It is mainly for this reason that cryptocurrencies range everywhere from $0.01 all the way up to $10,000 per unit.

Broadly speaking, there are two different types of cryptocurrencies: decentralized and centralized. A vast majority of the cryptocurrencies on the market today are decentralized. This means that they can operate effectively, despite a lack of human oversight or guiding authority. The opposite of this arrangement is a centralized cryptocurrency, which is controlled by a third party.

Many countries around the world, including China and Russia, have announced they are working on such cryptocurrencies. There are those out there who are fairly certain the US is also working on a version that is yet to be announced.

Before any cryptocurrency transaction can be completed, it has to be verified by a network of computers. These computers verify the transaction by solving complex mathematical equations in a process known as *mining*. By verifying transactions, this network of computers keeps the whole system running.

In return, the system creates and awards new coins to the computers in the network after a predetermined number of transactions. One thing that totally sets cryptocurrencies apart from ordinary currencies is that they are not backed or regulated by any bank, government, or central authority.

How Do Cryptocurrencies Work?

Cryptocurrencies work based on the same concept as debit cards. except bookkeeping is not done by banks, but by the public. Cryptocurrencies have no centralized clearing house. Bookkeeping for each cryptocurrency is carried out through a *blockchain,* which are publicly available ledgers, distributed across the Blockchain network.

Since every person has a copy of the ledger/register, there is transparency and accountability, which helps to build trust. By being distributed, it avoids intermediaries who would be responsible for the storage of the register. With no intermediaries, there are no agency costs.

Like fiat currencies, cryptocurrencies also have an exchange market. This is a market whereby one cryptocurrency is exchanged against another, or against a fiat currency. In the next section, we will explore the best trading platforms for these markets.

Understanding Blockchain Technology

Blockchain is a technology that is built on sharing transparency and ensuring the highest levels of incorruptibility. Data transmitted on a blockchain network can only be seen, but it cannot be altered in any way. To put this into perspective, there are millions of computers connected to a blockchain network and all of them operate a blockchain client (which is downloaded into your computer automatically when you join the network). You can imagine the magnitude of computing power that would be required to alter data across the whole network. It is impossible.

Consider blockchain a database that is open to anyone on the network. It keeps current records of who owns what coins. Thus, there is the need for anonymity when using the network. You do not want vandals to bludgeon into your house and force you to transfer your coins to them.

Once a transaction takes place, it is then kept in a 'block' of transactions that have taken place in the last ten minutes. Shortly afterward, this data is copied all across the network, to any computer in the network. Since all data is replicated across the network, this means that a hacker would have to replicate his hacking scheme millions of times over, which is impossible.

In all simplicity, we can say that blockchain is a transparent, incorruptible peer-to-peer technology that ensures data is not kept in one central database, thus eliminating the need for intermediaries when performing transactions. Blockchain technology is useful when it comes to financial transactions, as well as any other type of transaction that requires extremely close monitoring. Instead of requiring external verification, a blockchain can successfully sort and verify all of its own data whilst the nodes interact with one another, to ensure it is possible for countless users to interact with the blockchain at the same time.

Attributes of Cryptocurrency

Cryptocurrencies have certain attributes that set them apart from fiat currencies. These include:

- **Anonymity**: This attribute is one of the reasons behind the popularity of cryptocurrencies. Cryptocurrency wallet addresses are not linked to a person's name or physical address. This allows cryptocurrency users to make transactions without having to reveal their identity.

- **Transparency**: This means that anyone can see all the transactions and the number of coins owned by every cryptocurrency address. Despite this transparency, the addresses cannot be used to identify the owner of the coins.

- **Decentralization**: Instead, cryptocurrencies operate on a devolved system where the processing and validation of transactions are done by all the computers within the network. Due to their decentralized nature, no government or financial central authority can influence cryptocurrencies. The decentralized nature of the network also means that cryptocurrencies are always active. If some of the computers in the network go offline, others simply step in to fill the gap.

- **Speed**: Another attribute that has contributed to the massive uptake of cryptocurrencies is their transaction speed. It only takes a couple of minutes for the computers in the network to verify a cryptocurrency transaction, allowing you to instantly send money to any part of the world. Compare this to banks, which need several days to process and confirm transactions.

- **Ease of setting up**: Getting started with cryptocurrencies is a breeze. There are no checks. Simply set up a cryptocurrency wallet in a few minutes and you are good to go. Compare this to banks, which require you to go through a number of checks before you can create a bank account.

- **Irreversibility**: Unlike regular money transactions, cryptocurrencies do not have chargebacks. Once a transaction is completed, it cannot be reversed.

Advantages of Cryptocurrency

The massive popularity and uptake of cryptocurrencies in recent years has been driven by the distinct advantages offered by cryptocurrencies. Some of these advantages include the following:

Instant Funds Transfer

One of the inconveniences of banks and regular payment processing systems is that it usually takes several days to process and confirm payments. Cryptocurrencies get rid of this inconvenience by allowing you to transfer funds anywhere in the world within a matter of minutes.

Fraud Protection

Many credit card fraudsters buy items online and then, later on, claim chargebacks, which lead to losses for online businesses. With cryptocurrency payments, businesses are protected from such fraudsters since cryptocurrency transactions are irreversible. Cryptocurrency transactions have to be validated by the entire network before the transaction is completed, thereby eliminating the risk of counterfeit payments. By paying for goods using cryptocurrency, customers also keep their financial information safe from hackers who usually target small businesses.

Privacy

One of the attributes of a cryptocurrency is that it offers anonymity. By not linking personally identifiable information to your cryptocurrency wallet, you are able to exchange money with other people without revealing your identity. This is important when you want to keep your transactions away from prying eyes.

Total Control Over Your Funds

One of the disadvantages of a payment system is that it is controlled by a central authority. Unlike Blockchain and cryptocurrencies, you are never in full control of your account and funds. The bank or company has the final say over them.

Low Transaction Fees

Another disadvantage of banks and conventional payment processing companies is that every transaction is accompanied by processing fees. With cryptocurrency, there are no third parties, which means that you can make transactions for absolutely no fee. However, due to the technical complexity of cryptocurrency, many users rely on third parties to maintain their wallets. These third parties will definitely charge a fee for their services, though their fees are nowhere near as high as what banks will charge you.

Are Cryptocurrencies Real Money?

Ever since Bitcoin was first introduced to the world, there has been a raging debate as to whether cryptocurrencies can be qualified as money. The back-and-forth arguments have attracted support from big players in the cryptocurrency and financial industries. Just recently, the CEO and Chairman of JP Morgan Chase & Co. referred to Bitcoin as a fraud. But is this really true? Are cryptocurrencies really money? To answer this question, we need to understand what money is.

Money is defined by the following properties:

Uniformity: For something to be termed as money, each unit of measure should have similar purchasing power to another equal unit of measure. For example, one dollar has similar purchasing power to another dollar.

Portability: For something to be used as money, it should be easy to carry and transfer to others. For instance, you cannot use a sack of potatoes or a goat as money because you cannot easily carry them.

Fungibility: This means that a unit of money should be interchangeable with another similar unit without profit or loss. This means that one unit of money should not be superior to a similar unit. For instance, a ten-dollar bill can be exchanged with another ten-dollar bill without gain or loss.

Based on the above properties of money, we can now deduce whether cryptocurrencies meet the requirements of money. Cryptocurrencies are uniform since each unit of cryptocurrency has similar purchasing power to another equal unit of the same cryptocurrency. Since cryptocurrencies exist digitally, they are extremely portable. They have no weight and size restrictions. You can store them online, on your computer, or on your smartphone. Transferring them to others is easy and frictionless. Compare this to paper money, which is cumbersome and dangerous to carry around in large quantities.

Cryptocurrencies have high divisibility, with most being capable of division up to 8 decimal places. Despite not having the same level of acceptance as fiat money, it is steadily growing. Currently, there are over 35 million active cryptocurrency wallets. Hundreds of thousands of businesses also accept cryptocurrency payments. Considering that cryptocurrency is still in its infancy stage, its acceptance will only keep growing.

Cryptocurrencies are digital entries that do not exist physically. This means that they do not face the risk of physical degradation. Cryptocurrencies cannot be destroyed as it happens to paper money. So as long as you have your wallet password and you keep it safe, you cannot lose your cryptocurrencies. Finally, cryptocurrencies are highly fungible. You can interchange a unit of cryptocurrency for another similar unit without gain or loss. Based on the above properties, it becomes evident that cryptocurrencies can be used as real money.

Supply and Demand

There are far more people who hold cryptocurrencies than there are people who spend them. As such, this leads to a pricing bubble (prices rise above what the market alone would dictate) that all cryptocurrencies are influenced by to some degree or another. This problem is further magnified for smaller cryptocurrencies as there could only be a few thousand people holding units of it at a given time which means that even a moderate change by one individual could cause ripples across the limited market.

The basic principles of cryptocurrency investing are the same as any other type of trading: buyers look to buy low, and sellers look to sell high. The average smaller cryptocurrency can experience as much as a 15-percent movement in its price per day, which means there is significant potential for either profit or loss if the proper caution is not applied. In fact, because the market is highly speculative, it is practically impossible to find a cryptocurrency listed on a major exchange that is not experiencing some degree of price bubble or another.

This is not to say that price bubbles are completely without merit; as long as you are able to get out before things get too out of hand, you may make tons of money. When buying any cryptocurrency, this means you are going to want to do your research and determine where the price would likely be if the market was not being influenced by speculation. As long as you do not simply follow the crowd, in an effort to jump on the next big thing, there is no reason you cannot get in early on a cheap cryptocurrency and ride its wave of speculation, making a significant profit in the process.

Cryptocurrency Laws and Tax Structures Around the World

Cryptocurrencies are primarily coins or tokens released on a cryptographic network and tradable around the world. As cryptocurrencies are more or less the same across the world, countries with different laws and regulations may give different returns to investors, who may also belong to other countries.

Different laws for investors from different countries will render a tiring and tedious exercise in the estimation of returns. This would mean expending energy and money and also employing techniques that unnecessarily prolong procedures.

Cryptocurrencies were created with the fundamental idea of worldwide transfer of funds. We have a meaning which is more or less comparable across exchanges, except for negligible arbitration.

A worldwide regulator for cryptocurrencies is the need of the hour and could lay down global rules to govern new modes of financing. Every country is currently trying to regulate virtual currencies through legislative processes. If economic superpowers reached a consensus with other countries—to establish a regulatory body with legislation that knows no national frontiers—this would be one of the biggest catalysts for the creation of a crypto-friendly, most open fintech system ever.

Uniform control of sub-part trading, returns, taxes, fines, KYC procedure, trade laws, and punishments for unauthorized hacks will give us the following advantages:

- This can make it super easy for investors worldwide to measure income because net profit would not vary due to common tax structures.

- Countries worldwide would agree to share a certain portion of the profit as tax. The share of the countries in taxes collected would, therefore, be standardized throughout the world.

- It would be possible to save time by forming various commissions, writing bills, and debates in the legislative arena (like the Indian Parliament and the US Senate).

- You do not have to go through stringent tax laws in each region, especially with multinational people and organizations involved.

- Only companies that offer tokens or ICOs must adhere to international law. Calculating post-tax revenue would, therefore, be a piece of cake for companies.

- A globalized system would allow more firms to come up with better ideas and increase jobs worldwide.

Such laws may be sponsored by an international surveillance dog or global currency regulator, which may have the power to mark an ICO bid as not compliant with the requirements.

However, a law that would regulate cryptocurrencies worldwide is not just about benefits.

CHAPTER 2

Benefits of Investing in Cryptocurrencies

When it comes to finding a good investment opportunity, there are a few different options that you can choose from. Some people like to go into real estate because they like to invest in market trends while probably making a lot of money. Some people like to start their own business and work at a job that they love each day. And still, others will spend their time with the stock market because of all the different options that are available.

They Are Growing Quickly

It only takes a few days of watching the market to find out that digital currencies are growing exponentially. They are in high demand, and since they can be used by people throughout the world, they are a great option that will continue to grow in popularity in the near future. If you jump in at the right time, you can see a huge return on investment in no time.

No Government Controls

One of the things that a lot of people like about working with digital currencies is that they do not need to worry about government control. There is no one entity—company, government, or otherwise—who is in control of these digital currencies. This can pose a few problems, but overall, people like the ability to control their money without having to worry about how the government is going to react to it.

Ability to Be Anonymous

When you do any transaction on these networks, you will be able to keep your identity hidden, something that is almost impossible when it comes to traditional financial institutions. With all the recent news about how hackers have been able to get on traditional databases and steal your information, it is nice to know that there is now a system available that will keep your information safe.

Huge Growth Possibility

Right now, many cryptocurrencies are growing exponentially. People around the world are hearing about these digital currencies, and they like the benefits that cryptocurrencies present. They like that they can use these currencies, regardless of where they are located in the world, and this makes it easy for them to make a purchase. Moreover, with the security that comes from blockchains, they can do these transactions in no time.

There is something bigger than knowing and it is participation; with regards to cryptocurrency, you actively participate by investing. When you invest, you take your interest up a notch and grow your coins steadily. This chapter is split into two parts; the first part provides in-depth knowledge on the why and how of investing in cryptocurrencies and much more.

But first, why should you invest in cryptocurrencies? Why is it important to use your resources for something that is internet-based? The answers to the questions above can be found below, as we answer the question of "why?"

Blazing Growth

With increased awareness of the importance of the internet, many people have made a fortune just by utilizing its potential. The impact of crypto-currencies is growing at the same speed as the internet did. This means that you can bank on the profitability of cryptocurrency because it has the potential to grow beyond its current reach.

More People Are Involved

As the year goes by more people board the wagon of cryptocurrency. The figures increase with every year, and it has not shown signs of slow-ing down. A reasonable investor considers numbers when investing, and with Bitcoins, you have got this very assurance backing up your invest-ments.

It Is Secure

Everyone wants their investments secured and you can be sure that your cryptocurrency investment is safe. Regardless of the amount of money you invest, you can go to bed knowing that it will produce the right result for you because it is in a secure network.

Cryptocurrencies have become a part of our financial system. If you want to be a part of the revolution, be ready to take the plunge and invest significant time. The second part of this chapter focuses on the "how". How does one go about investing in cryptocurrencies? What are the five most straightforward steps to take?

Send Money Instantly

If you have ever sent money to others, for travel expenses, transactions, or otherwise, you know that this process can be really slow. This is because both banks—your bank and the bank of the recipient—have to reconcile their records to record this money and verify the transaction. This could end up taking up to five days or more, depending on the type and amount of the transaction.

Saves Money

The blockchain technology underlying many of these cryptocurrencies can actually help you to save money. You will have to exchange a small amount of traditional currency for digital currency and back again. However, it is a lot less expensive compared to working with most banks and financial institutions. Moreover, since you can trade without a broker if you want (something that is really hard to accomplish with other forms of investing), you can end up reducing expenses on your investment, putting more of that money back in your pocket.

Many Options for Investing

There are different options when it comes to investing in digital currencies. You are not stuck with one option that you do not like. And even if you try out an option and find it is not the best one for you, it is pretty easy for you to make some changes and try out one of the other options.

Do Not Require a Lot of Work

You will be surprised at how little work you will have to put in to start investing in these digital currencies. There are some strategies that you can use that will require a bit more work, such as *day trading*, where you need to watch all of the daily fluctuations of the market. For the most part, you can just place your money into the market and get results.

Easy to Access

The money that you can place into these digital currencies will be easy to access at any time. Even if you execute a *buy-and-hold* strategy—which requires you to invest your money into the market, leave it there while the market grows, hence making you money—you can take out the money at any time.

As you can see, there are many reasons why an investor, especially a beginner investor, will choose to go with digital currencies as their investment option of choice. It is hard to work in some of the other investment options, but digital currencies can actually be pretty easy. Take these reasons into consideration when you are ready to start out with a new investment.

CHAPTER 3

Different Types of Cryptocurrencies to Invest In

Bitcoin (BTC)

New Bitcoins are created as a reward for mining, which is what keeps the Bitcoin protocol running. The Bitcoin protocol is configured in a way that keeps the rate of production of new Bitcoins around a certain average. If more processing power is deployed to mine for new Bitcoins, mining becomes harder. If some processing power is taken from the network, the difficulty of mining new Bitcoins decreases. The protocol was created with a limit of 21 million Bitcoins, after which no more Bitcoins will be released.

Bitcoin can be divided into smaller units known as MilliBitcoins, Micro-Bitcoins, and Satoshis. The smallest unit of Bitcoin is the Satoshi (0.00000001), which was named after the mysterious inventor of Bitcoin. As the first-ever modern cryptocurrency, Bitcoin is the easiest to get and enjoys the widest acceptance.

Ethereum (ETH)

In the long run, Ethereum holds much more promise than Bitcoin. While the two competing cryptocurrencies both rely on blockchain technology, they have major differences in terms of objective and capability. Bitcoin is strictly a payment system, which is only one application of blockchain technology. Instead of focusing on one use like Bitcoin did, Ethereum allows developers to build all kinds of decentralized apps. This means that Ethereum has the capability of revolutionizing all services and sectors that are currently centralized. Today, there are two parallel Ethereum blockchains, Ethereum (ETH) and Ethereum Classic (ETC). Ethereum Classic was introduced after a split that came following the hacking of the Ethereum-based DAO project in September of 2016, where about $50 million Ether was stolen.

Litecoin (LTC)

One of the major changes that Lee made was the cryptographic 'hash' function used by Litecoin. Unlike Bitcoin which uses the SHA256 hash, Lee introduced 'scrypt' in Litecoin. Switching to scrypt allowed Litecoin to process and confirm transactions faster. Litecoin transactions are verified in about two minutes, while Bitcoin might take up to 10 minutes to verify transactions. Another advantage of using 'scrypt' is that it allowed users with consumer-grade CPUs to mine for coins, unlike Bitcoin which requires miners to have CPUs that are specialized for mining.

By doing so, Lee gave Litecoin more liquidity, since there are more coins available for purchase, preventing the hoarding that has become so common with Bitcoin buyers. Another major difference between Litecoin and Bitcoin is that Litecoin uses a slightly different mining protocol, which allows a fairer distribution of mined coins. Litecoin also allows for faster testing and implementation of new technology. For instance, Lite-coin pioneered and implemented *SegWit (Segregated Witness)* technology way before Bitcoin. All in all, Litecoin is a strong cryptocurrency with a good reputation and solid economic principles.

IOTA (IOT)

IOTA includes things like internet-enabled cars, computers, kitchen ap-pliances, microchips, home automation devices, hospital devices, and so on. By being the backbone of IOT, IOTA aims to achieve its call of being the 'Ledger of Everything'.

Apart from being the backbone of IOT, IOTA was also developed to solve some of the challenges faced by Bitcoin, including issues of scala-bility, speed, and transaction fees. IOTA has one key difference from other cryptocurrencies like Bitcoin. With blockchain-based cryptocurren-cies, the network of computers needs to verify a transaction before it is completed. With the *Tangle*, verification does not rely on the network. Instead, the Tangle relies on a system that requires the sender to perform some proof of work before they can make their transaction. By doing so, the sender approves two transactions, thereby combining the transaction and its verification. Since it is up to the sender to provide proof of work, there is no need for miners.

This has two benefits. First, by eliminating miners, the Tangle makes IOTA fully decentralized. Instead of having players who have an effect on the network without actually using it (miners simply enable the net-work, but they do not use it), the IOTA network is maintained solely by the 'users' who are actually making transactions. Second, by having the sender approve two transactions before they can make their transaction, this system makes the IOTA protocol faster. It also means that an in-crease in the number of users leads to a faster validation speed. This is unlike what normally happens with other cryptocurrencies like Bitcoin, where an increase in the number of users slows down the validation time. Since there are no miners, users do not have to pay any fees for maintaining the network either.

Ripple (XRP)

Unlike many cryptocurrencies out there, *Ripple* was not built as a variant of Bitcoin. Instead, its developers built it from scratch and incorporated some major changes in its architecture. Unlike most cryptocurrencies which use a proof-of-stake or proof-of-work system to verify transactions, Ripple uses a unique consensus system, where the computers in the network keep monitoring any changes. Once a majority of the computers in the network observe a transaction, it is added to the public ledger. The consensus system has a number of advantages over the proof-of-work or proof-of-stake systems. Transactions verified under the consensus system are validated faster and require less processing power. While it might seem possible for hackers to compromise the consensus system, it is designed in such a way that any unreliable results are rejected by the network.

Since the Ripple network is meant to facilitate cross-currency conversions, Ripples can be exchanged for a wide range of fiat currencies and altcoins. Some businesses also allow customers to exchange Ripples for air miles and reward points. Unlike altcoins, like Ether and Litecoin, which are sold on cryptocurrency exchanges, you have to go through Ripple Gateways to buy Ripples. The Gateways work in the same way PayPal works.

Dash (Dash)

Dash is a cryptocurrency that was developed by Evan Duffield and Kyle Hagan. Launched in 2014, it was originally known as *Darkcoin*. After a year in existence, it rebranded to *Dash*, which is the shortened version of 'digital cash'. By developing Dash, Kyle and Evan wanted to create a cryptocurrency that is totally secret and anonymous. Most cryptocurrencies are not thoroughly anonymous. Though addresses are not linked to personally identifiable information, the network knows the number of coins within each address, and anyone can keep track of coins as they move from one address to another. This makes it possible for someone to independently know the identity of those users who do not take measures to protect their identity. To keep users anonymous, Dash uses a decentralized mastercode network which makes Dash transactions practically impossible to trace.

The high level of anonymity offered by Dash is enabled by a system known as *Darksend*. With this system, specialized computers known as *mastercodes* collect several transactions and execute them simultaneously, thereby keeping the transaction untraceable. It becomes impossible to track the source and destination of the coins. To make your transactions even more anonymous, you can choose to have the mastercodes mix your transaction for multiple rounds before completing the transaction. To maintain this anonymity, the Dash ledger is not publicly accessible. The high level of anonymity has also prevented wide acceptance by businesses.

Another distinguishing feature of Dash is its hashing algorithm. Instead of using the SHA256 or scrypt hash, Dash uses a unique X11 hash which requires less processing power, allowing users with consumer-grade CPUs to mine for Dash coins. Other notable advantages of Dash include its speedy transaction verification (4 seconds) and low transaction fees.

However, the fees are likely to rise once more people join the network. Dash also has a voting system in place to allow the quick implementation of important changes.

Monero (XMR)

Monero is another cryptocurrency that, just like Dash, is focused on privacy and anonymity. Monero was launched in 2014 by a team of seven programmers, five of whom chose to remain anonymous. Due to its anonymity features, it quickly gained popularity with cryptocurrency enthusiasts. Like most other cryptocurrencies, Monero is completely open source. Development of the platform is driven by the community and donations. This technique is a digital version of group signatures. Each transaction on the Monero network is enshrouded by a group of cryptographic signatures. This way, it is impossible to pinpoint the actual sender or recipient in the transaction. Even with a person's wallet address, it is impossible to see the number of coins in the wallet or keep track of where they are spent. This means that it is impossible for Monero coins to become tainted, as a result of any previous dubious transactions.

Monero transactions are verified using the same proof-of-work system that Bitcoin uses. However, a major difference between Bitcoin and Monero is that while Bitcoin block sizes are limited at 2MB, there is no limitation on Monero block sizes. The lack of limited block sizes presents the risk of malicious miners using disproportionately huge blocks to clog up the system.

Neo (NEO)

NEO is a Chinese cryptocurrency that was founded by Erik Zhang and Da Hongfei. NEO is designed to be a smart economy platform, much like Ethereum. It has even been referred to as 'China's Ethereum'. NEO first launched under the name *Antshares*. In August 2017, it rebranded to *NEO Smart Contract Economy*. NEO's objective is very similar to that of Ethereum. NEO provides a platform where developers can develop decentralized applications and deploy smart contracts. Unlike Ethereum, which only supports its Solidity programming language, NEO can be used with common programming languages such as C#, Python, and Java.

Since consensus under the dBFT system only needs to be achieved by a subset of the network, this system requires less processing power and allows the network to handle a higher transaction volume. NEO claims that it is capable of handling over 1000 transactions per second, whereas Ethereum only handles 15 transactions per second. The dBFT system also eliminates the possibility of a hard fork, which makes NEO a great option for digitizing real-world financial assets.

OmiseGO (OMG)

OmiseGO is a cryptocurrency that has gained a lot of popularity from cryptocurrency enthusiasts lately. Launched in 2013, it is an interesting yet very ambitious project which aims to use Ethereum-based financial technology to un-bank the banked. OmiseGO is currently built on the Ethereum platform as an ERC20-token, though it will eventually launch its own blockchain. OmiseGO's vision is to become the leading P2P cryptocurrency exchange platform. Instead of being just an altcoin, OmiseGO is built to act as a financial platform with the aim of disrupting the financial sector as we currently know it.

OmiseGO intends to solve a challenge that most cryptocurrency exchanges have failed to address. To purchase a cryptocurrency in most cryptocurrency exchanges, you have to start with a fiat currency. To exchange one altcoin for another, you have to convert the altcoins to fiat currency or Bitcoin, and then convert the fiat currency/Bitcoin to your desired altcoins. Throughout this process, the exchange charges fees for each transaction. This means that you will pay fees to convert altcoins to fiat currency/Bitcoin, and then pay fees again to convert the fiat currency/Bitcoin to other altcoins.

OmiseGO plans to solve this problem by linking all existing cryptocurrency wallets to a central OmiseGO Blockchain. This way, users can easily exchange altcoins for other altcoins without having to convert them to fiat currency or Bitcoin. This means that instead of multiple fees, users will pay a one-time fee.

OmiseGO also aims to bring decentralization to cryptocurrency exchanges. Currently, most exchanges are centralized operations. The records of all transactions as well as data about different users are stored in databases that are stored on the company's servers. OmiseGO aims to decentralize the exchange functionality by having all the transaction info and user data stored on the blockchain. This way, the data is more secure, since a hacker would then need to perform a 51% attack (gaining control over 51% of the computers in the network) in order to breach the blockchain, which is virtually impossible.

NEM (XEM)

NEM is a revolutionary cryptocurrency that was launched in March 2015. Unlike many other cryptocurrencies which were created as variants of existing projects, NEM was built from the ground up, with its own unique source code. NEM derived its name from the *New Economic Movement*, the group which came up with the cryptocurrency. NEM is designed as a blockchain-based technology that can be customized to fit different business purposes. At the core of NEM's protocol is what is known as the *'Smart Asset System'*.

Since NEM can be customized to fit multiple use cases, it has unlimited potential uses. It can be used as a central ledger in the banking sector, a means of keeping secure records, a blockchain-based voting system, an escrow service, a means of rewarding points in loyalty programs, a crowd funding platform, as a means of stock ownership, and so on. This shows how much potential NEM holds.

Unlike most cryptocurrency platforms, NEM has a messaging platform. It also has a reward system and supports multi-signature transactions. One of the key differences between NEM and other cryptocurrencies is the verification method. Instead of proof-of-work or proof-of-stake systems, NEM relies on a unique proof-of-importance system, where block calculation chances are allocated based on the contribution of a user to the development/distribution of the platform. Users who make a lot of contributions get rewarded with more chances. This allows a fair distribution of mining chances among users.

The NEM network is fast, with a transaction verification wait time of about one minute. This means that you can rely on NEM to make instant global money transfers. With the proof-of-importance system, users do not need expensive hardware to mine NEM coins.

CHAPTER 4

What You Need to Know Before Investing in Cryptocurrency

Why Invest?

People make cryptocurrency investments for various reasons. However, there are three important reasons why you should invest in cryptocurrency. Firstly, investing in cryptocurrency is a way of hedging your assets against the impending fall of the dollar imperium. Cryptocurrency is a wave that is silently revolutionizing money. By investing in cryptocurrency, you are essentially betting on the success of this revolution. Secondly, you should only invest in cryptocurrency if you support the vision behind cryptocurrency – the vision of universal currency that is free from control by governments. Finally, you should invest in cryptocurrencies only if you understand the technology behind them.

Unfortunately, some people are investing in cryptocurrency because of the fear of missing out (FOMO), in the hopes of making a quick buck. They do not even understand the technology. This is a very bad investment strategy.

You should also note that cryptocurrencies are not like any ordinary investment. They are more volatile than any other investment class. They are unregulated assets. and are a very high-risk investment. There is always the risk that you could lose your key, an exchange, or your wallet might get hacked, or they might even get outlawed altogether.

Know Which Cryptocurrencies You Should Buy

For most people, the only cryptocurrency they have thought of investing in is Bitcoin. This is because up until recently, Bitcoin has been the only dominant cryptocurrency. Other altcoins have only been penny stocks with little chance of profitability. However, things have now changed. While Bitcoin remains dominant, its share in the cryptocurrency market has dropped to around 40%, down from 90%. This is mostly a result of the growth of Ethereum, as well as the scalability problems facing Bitcoin. This shows why it is important to always keep yourself abreast of any occurrences in the crypto-sphere.

While Bitcoin is still a standard asset to invest in, you should balance and diversify your portfolio. Some good options to consider include Ethereum, Ripple, Dash, Litecoin, Monero, and the other coins discussed in Chapter 3. However, before you invest in a certain cryptocurrency, take your time to do your research on the coin, and decide if you believe in their vision and objective. New coins are coming up each day, while others are dying each day, so do your research to avoid losing your money.

Some factors you should consider before deciding on whether you want to invest in a specific cryptocurrency include:

- The transaction processing speed
- The number of coins currently in circulation
- Is the supply of coins limited or unlimited? If limited, what is the limit?
- The real-world applications of the cryptocurrency

- Real-world adoption of the technology
- Background of the founders
- Does the project have any big investors?

Know How to Buy Your First Coins?

For beginners, the first time buying crypto-coins can be confusing and challenging. Before you can buy your first coins, you need to set up your digital wallet. The issue of how to choose the right cryptocurrency wallet for you has been covered in detail in Chapter 4. Once your digital wallet is set up, the next thing is to figure out how you are going to pay for your crypto-coins. Although they are also a form of money, you have to exchange them for fiat money, similar to how you would exchange your dollars for another currency when traveling abroad. The complexity of buying cryptocurrencies depends on your country's financial system, though it may not be a complicated process. Some of the methods you can use to pay for crypto-coins include:

- **Bank transfer**: This is a simple but slow way of paying for cryptocurrencies. Simply make a transfer to the seller's account, and they will send you your coins the moment they receive the money. Bank transfers take about 1-2 days for the money to reflect in the seller's account, therefore you will have to wait for 1-2 days before you receive your coins.
- **Credit card**: Despite being the most common online payment method for fiat money, it is widely unaccepted by cryptocurrency sellers. This is because with credit card payments, malicious buyers can claim chargebacks, therefore defrauding the seller. Since cryptocurrency transactions are irreversible, the seller would have no way of getting back their coins. Still, some exchanges accept

credit card payments, though they charge higher prices for cryptocurrencies.

- **PayPal**: Just like credit cards, PayPal payments are widely unaccepted by cryptocurrency sellers because of the issue of chargebacks. Some exchanges support PayPal payments, though they also charge significantly higher prices.

- **Other payment channels**: Different exchanges accept many different payment methods such as Skrill, Sofort, iDEAL, and many more.

- **Private payment channels**: It is possible to pay for crypto coins through other private channels such as Western Union, Paysafecard, or using good old cash. Some P2P online platforms like LocalBitcoins link buyers and sellers in the same region, allowing them to decide on their own payment methods.

Once you have figured out the best payment method for you, you can now go ahead and purchase your preferred cryptocurrency. Some common places where you can buy cryptocurrencies include exchange platforms, brokers and direct commercial exchanges, P2P markets like LocalBitcoins, cryptocurrency ATMs, and through gift cards and vouchers.

Know Cryptocurrency Exchanges

If your intention is to get into cryptocurrency trading, then you will definitely need to join a cryptocurrency exchange. These are platforms that allow users to exchange cryptocurrencies for fiat currencies as well as other cryptocurrencies. There are various kinds of exchanges, each meant to serve a specific kind of user. There are advanced exchanges with complex trading tools to serve professional traders, while others are there to serve people looking to make the occasional trade.

The three main types of exchanges are:

- **Trading platforms**: These connect traders and perform the role of an escrow. They handle the processing of orders and charge fees for each transaction.

- **Direct trading platforms**: Also referred to as P2P markets, these link buyers and sellers directly without playing the role of an intermediary. Instead of having fixed prices, they allow sellers to set their own rates.

- **Brokers and direct commercial exchanges**: These operate similar to forex brokers, exchanging cryptocurrencies for other cryptocurrencies/fiat money at fixed prices.

Factors to Consider When Choosing an Exchange

Type the words 'cryptocurrency exchange' into your browser and you will find several exchanges to choose from. With such a wide pool to choose from, you want to make sure you join a cryptocurrency exchange that best serves your needs. Some factors to keep in mind when choosing a cryptocurrency exchange include:

- **Reputation**: Before joining, find out what other users are saying about the exchange. Read online reviews and scour cryptocurrency communities and forums.

- **Fees**: Cryptocurrency exchanges make money by charging transaction, deposit, and withdrawal fees. Find out the fee structure of an exchange before joining to avoid unanticipated charges.

- **Payment methods**: Does the exchange support payment methods that are convenient for you? You should also keep in mind that charges will be higher for exchanges that accept PayPal and credit card payments, and that bank transfers are not convenient when you need to make fast transactions.

- **Verification requirements**: Are you looking for complete anonymity? Most exchanges will ask you for identity and proof-of-address documents before you can start trading. Are you willing to provide this information?

- **Geographical restrictions**: Does the exchange offer full support in your geographic region?

- **Exchange rates**: Cryptocurrency exchanges also make profits from their spreads. Check their rates and spreads to ensure you are getting the best deal.

- **Liquidity**: This is the value of the coins that the exchange has. If an exchange has low liquidity, you may be unable to withdraw your coins.

- **Volume of trades:** If the volume of trades is high, then the exchange has a lot of customers, which is an indication that they are in business for the long haul.

- **Spread:** This is quite hard for the average person to understand but generally, a high exchange spread indicates greater difficulty in making a profit for you. Good exchanges will help you and advise you about this.

- **Security:** This is another term that is hard for the average person to understand. Good exchanges will help you and advise you about this.

- **Comprehensibility (user-friendly?)** This obviously refers to the helpfulness and user-friendliness of exchanges. The online world can be very daunting if you do not really know what you are doing.

Evaluating an exchange based on the above considerations will ensure that you join a cryptocurrency exchange that is best suited to your needs.

Some popular cryptocurrency exchanges that you might consider include Coinbase, Kraken, Poloniex, Shapeshift, and LocalBitcoins.

Know When Should You Buy?

If you listen to cryptocurrency traders, you will hear them talking about good and bad times to buy. So, when is the best time to buy? There is no rule of the thumb for when you should buy cryptocurrencies. However, you should avoid buying at the peak of a bubble, also when prices are crashing. As the trader's saying goes, 'Never catch a falling knife'. The best times to buy are when prices are relatively low and stable.

To be a successful trader, you need to learn how to determine when a bubble is about to burst and prices nosedive. However, no one can predict this with complete certainty. For instance, when Bitcoin rose to $1000, many people were afraid of buying, thinking that this was the peak of the bubble. The price rose to $10000 and many more thought that this must certainly be the peak. However, Bitcoin defied their prediction and continued rising, nearly hitting the $20,000-mark. You should also avoid comparing cryptocurrency bubbles to financial bubbles since cryptocurrencies are highly volatile.

Know the Risks of Cryptocurrency Investing

Despite some people having become instant millionaires and billionaires through cryptocurrency investing and trading, this does not mean that there are no risks to it. Here are some risks you face when you decide to become a cryptocurrency investor:

- **Some technologies will fail**: You should keep in mind that cryptocurrencies are basically software or lines of code. Remember the dot.com bust? Some cryptocurrencies will fail in the same way that some software companies failed in the dot.com era.

- **It requires technical savvy**: Cryptocurrencies were developed by super-geeks, and to most people, cryptocurrencies are still geeky. To get into cryptocurrency, you need to be good with computers.

- **Broker and technology risk**: Cryptocurrencies are still in infancy, therefore there are still lots of unknowns. Many things could change. New security vulnerabilities might emerge. Remember how millions of traders lost their money after the hacking of *MtGox*? If anything, you should consider dealing with cryptocurrency brokers to be about twice as risky as dealing with forex brokers.

Know Factors That Affect the Price of a Cryptocurrency

Cryptocurrency prices are affected by several factors, sometimes leading to very abrupt changes. Some factors you need to keep in mind include:

- **Exchange listing**: This is a major mover of cryptocurrency prices. Whenever a large cryptocurrency exchange announces that it will start listing a certain cryptocurrency, you can expect the price to skyrocket in the near future.

- **Software upgrades**: Cryptocurrencies undergo software upgrades, to either solve existing challenges in the network or to improve functionality. For example, there was a hot debate about making a software upgrade to improve Bitcoin's transaction processing speed. This argument ended with the split of Bitcoin Cash from Bitcoin. Watch out for software upgrades since they are highly likely to affect the price of a cryptocurrency.

- **Public hype**: Just like company stocks, cryptocurrency prices can be affected by fake news.

- **Wallet improvements**: Some investors buy cryptocurrencies and hold them for a couple of years as they wait for prices to rise.

- **Platform applications**: Some cryptocurrency platforms are more than digital currencies. For instance, Ethereum is a platform that allows the building and deployment of other applications. If one of the applications built on a cryptocurrency platform does well, it can lead to an increase in the value of the underlying platform. Therefore, it is good to watch out for any promising apps that are hosted on the cryptocurrency platform you are trading in.

- **Government regulation**: Government policies also have an effect on cryptocurrencies. For instance, Bitcoin prices fell before rebounding in September 2017 after China announced that it had banned cryptocurrency trading in the country. You should keep abreast of any relevant government policies and avoid cryptocurrencies that are likely to be flagged by governments.

CHAPTER 5

Setting Up Your Own Cryptocurrency Account

Before you can decide what digital currencies are worthwhile for your investment, you need to be able to find a way to get ahold of those currencies. You cannot go to the bank and exchange money for those currencies, although this may be something that changes in the future. You will need to set up your own cryptocurrency account and have it available, so you can reach the coins whenever you would like. Some people choose to work on mining to get coins, but since this is a hard job that requires technical knowledge to be successful, it is not the right option for everyone. The good news is you can use an exchange site to get some of your own coins.

Most people choose to go onto an exchange site and exchange some of their current traditional currency for the digital currency of their choice. You will find, with a little bit of research, that there are a few exchange sites that will work for you. The one you will pick often depends on which currency you would like to invest in, and which one has the best offers at the time. To help you get your account set up and ready to handle any and all digital transactions/investments, let us take a look at how to find these exchange sites and how to get started.

What Are the Best Exchange Sites?

The first step that you need to work with is finding an exchange site in order to switch your traditional currencies to a digital currency. This is one of the easiest and fastest methods that you can use to get Bitcoin because you will be able to switch currencies in no time. You will find that most of these exchange sites are set up like the traditional ones; you will exchange your traditional currency for digital currency just like you would exchange it for a fiat currency from another country.

Some exchanges are pretty basic, and they are just available so you can take your traditional currencies and exchange them out for the digital currency of choice. Others will provide some more services to you, such as monitoring your transactions or providing you with a wallet to store your currency. Picking out the right exchange site can often depend on what you wish to do with your currency, and how much you want the exchange site to help.

One thing that some beginners do not realize is that they will need to show some proof of their identity before they can get started with these exchange services. Beginners think this information should not be necessary since they would remain anonymous at all times on these networks. However, many countries require that the exchange site collect this information, so you will need to provide it before you can proceed.

Using Your Exchange Site

Setting up an account can be pretty easy, but there are a few things to consider when moving your traditional money over to a digital currency. Each exchange site is going to be different, but we will take a look at how *Coinbase* works, since this is a popular option to use for options like Ethereum, Bitcoin, and Litecoin.

With Coinbase, you can choose between using a credit/debit card, your bank account, or a PayPal account. The bank account can be convenient because you will have higher transfer and exchange limits. If you want to be able to invest a large amount of money, then this is the option that you should go with. However, it is important to note that because you are working with your bank, the transfer is not going to be instant. It will often take, at least, three to five days for the transaction to be processed. This can slow you down your entry into the market, so you need to weigh whether that option is good for you.

Some people like to use their PayPal accounts or their credit/debit cards. These have the benefit of resulting in instant transactions. If you want to be able to enter the market right away, then you should consider using these to help you get started. You will have a limit on how much money you will be able to invest. If you are just interested in getting into the market and trying it out, and you do not want to wait around to see how long the bank will take, then using one of these options will help you get started.

Once you have exchanged your traditional currency with the digital currency of your choice, it is time to find a place to store it. Coinbase and some of the other exchange sites will provide you a wallet to use, and you can choose to store the coins in it if you like. If you plan on using the coins right away to make purchases or to send money, these wallets are fine. If you plan on storing the coins for some time as an investment option, it is probably best to find a different wallet.

These exchange sites are often under attack from scammers and hackers who want to get ahold of the coins for free. The longer you let your money sit in that wallet, without having some extra safeguards in place, the easier it will be for these hackers to take the information that they want. For long-term storage, it is much better to move the coins to another location to keep them safe and to ensure that no one else can get ahold of them.

Setting up an account for your digital currencies and making sure that you can get ahold of the currencies that you intend to use, can take some time and a little bit of planning. Make sure you look at the various sites that are available because this can help you out a lot. Some are going to have special features that you may want to utilize. With research, you will be able to figure out the one that is best for you.

CHAPTER 6

How Can You Earn Cryptocurrencies?

Like anything else in the market, there are free as well as paid-for ways to earn Bitcoin, the cryptocurrency that we will concentrate on here. By "earning" cryptocurrency, we mean other ways of getting cryptocurrency, apart from buying it at the cryptocurrency exchanges.

There are millions, possibly hundreds of millions or even billions of coins out there, some of little value, others like Bitcoin of great value, hence earning the moniker digital gold.

Work for Coins

Online, there are many sites willing to pay for your work in coins or units of coins. For example, with Bitcoin, now worth about $5000, you may freelance online, and they will pay you with Bitcoin. Know that one full coin has many units. For example, one Bitcoin can be divided into 100 units, each worth $50 or thereabouts.

With the office going virtual, if you have skills and a little time to spare every day, there are many online tasks to do. From surveys, web design, referral programs to regular freelancing tasks like content writing, video transcription, and others, there is something for everyone on the internet. When you get paid, you can store your coins safely in your digital wallet.

Steemit is one of the most trusted, blockchain-based blogging platforms that is dedicated to coin enthusiasts only. You can try it. Joining is free of charge and on the network, you can post your own content or upvote the content of other people. By doing so, you will earn tokens like STEEM which is a crypto-coin, or STEEM-backed dollar which is regarded as almost equal to the US dollar. After that, you can then send your STEEM and STEEM-backed dollars to an exchange where you can then trade them for Bitcoin.

Earn Bitcoin from Your Blog or Website

This is another way of earning Bitcoin. You can display a banner on your site, for which you will be paid in coins. Just join CoinURL, and get your own affiliate link, which you will encode on your site. At the same time, you can also promote shortened links from CoinURL and earn Bitcoin.

Mine Your Coins

This requires a powerful machine and decent mining software and hardware with some kickass features. For example, consider a computer with four graphic cards and advanced software.

Mining usually means committing your computer to the task and dedicating a lot of its processing power to solving complex ledger accounting sums across the entire BTC blockchain network, where every correctly verified or balanced ledger entry earns you Bitcoin. You will earn by maintaining public ledgers on the Bitcoin blockchain. Bitcoin miners from China have excelled in this science.

You will need a GPU, which can perform repetitive tasks faster and better than a CPU. Now, a GPU will cost you a good amount of money, especially one that is made for mining.

You Can Also Mine Altcoins

With the growth of the Bitcoin and altcoin networks, you can be sure that mining coins will become increasingly competitive, and you need a good computer. However, mining is still one of the "free" ways to earn coins. Is there a way to mine altcoins using your regular computer?

Of course, there is. Just get the right software. For example, when you are using *Minergate*, you can mine Ethereum, Bytecoin, Classic, Monero, and other coins with your computer. The software picks the altcoins that are doing very well in the market at that time and then it gets to work.

Do not expect much though when using your regular computer. Say, a day's mining effort can earn you 10 cents maybe. But hey, it is still some experience, isn't it?

CHAPTER 7

How to Get Started with Cryptocurrency Investing

Understanding Cryptocurrency

Asmart investor must understand the terrain he is about to go into, so before you invest in cryptocurrency understand the terminologies that are associated with the investment. You do not have to fret over this, because you already have an introductory guide at the beginning of this book. Get familiar with the terms by going over the first and second chapters of this book. Know your blockchains, Bitcoins, ledgers, etc.; these words serve as a guide. If you ever are lost or uncomprehending of the investing process, these terms will aid your understanding. Once you have nailed the terminologies; it is time to move to the next step: buying a coin.

Buying a Coin

There are several platforms through which you can purchase your currency, but for credibility, I will use Coinbase as an example, because it is currently the safest and most reliable platform where you can buy Bitcoins (this book is all about giving you the best).

First, you have to create an account with the platform using your email address. You will have to verify your email address, and within minutes the first stage of registration is done. Next, you have to go through the validation process which requires you to sign up as an individual or business. Connect your bank account or credit card right after the validation phase, and you are ready to start purchasing crypto-coins. You can start off with Bitcoins, Ethereum or Litecoin because more people trade with these than other cryptocurrencies. After your purchase, confirm that it was successful by checking your "accounts". If your coins appear, your transaction was successful, and you can start trading.

Investing Starts Now

After buying coins, they are stored in your wallet. If you do not want to commence trading right away, you can download software and save your coins on your computer's hard drive; this protects your coins till you are ready to use them. When you want to commence trading, ensure that your coins are on the exchange's wallet. Your wallet has an address, a unique hash key, and a QR code; whenever you receive or send coins. It is vital to be very careful because if you send coins to the wrong wallet address, you may lose all of your coins, and nobody wants that. There is a myriad of platforms you can use for exchange purposes. What you should look out for is a platform that has a good reputation and trades in lots of coins. We will stick with *Bittrex* because they fulfill these criteria.

Sign up to the Bittrex, set a password, and go to **Wallets**. Click on the positive sign on the type of coin you have (Bitcoin etc.), then click on **New Address.** Once the address is generated, double-check to be sure it is correct, then copy and paste it. Log on to your Coinbase account and go to **Send**. Click on **Send Funds**. Switch to your open Bittrex account, and you will see a pending deposit that indicates the funds you just sent.

Press **Confirm** so that the process is complete. You are now ready to trade.

Seek Out the Best Coins

You might become confused over the myriad of coins you can trade with because there are a lot of projects ranging from banking, gambling, etc. The solution lies with *Coinvision Research*, through which you will be able to get notifications on the best deals. Just go to the webpage of the coin you want to invest in and check if they have a stable system in place. Check out the price and get advice on the pros and cons of buying the coin. If you are still unsatisfied, carry out research, and when you become confident in your choice of coin, go ahead and purchase. It is imperative to note that results may vary according to the projects you invest in.

Monitor Your Investment

Make frequent checks on your investment, be sure that everything moves smoothly; being able to stay in full control of your investment makes it possible for you to monitor your progress.

This third chapter launched you into the world of taking risks with your coins and learning all the way. We have completed a run-through on the steps of how best to invest in crypto-coins. The next section is all about the dos and don'ts of investing in crypto coins. You will get the cliff notes to investing.

CHAPTER 8

Investing in Blockchains

According to many sources, a sure way to earn an income is through investing in blockchains. The demand for blockchain developers cannot be kept abreast with by the current job market, hence the business opportunities and possibilities for innovation just keep growing.

Blockchain technology intimidates many people because they cannot understand it, hence they end up not investing in cryptocurrency startups and blockchains. In order to invest, a basic knowledge of how blockchains function, as in this book, will suffice. Cryptocurrency is one of the easiest, most profitable investment avenues. The leading cryptocurrencies to invest in are:

- Bitcoin Cash: Bitcoin Cash is similar to Bitcoin, but the difference is the block size capacity, which is larger. At the time of this writing, its current value is over a thousand, and it has been multiplying since it was created.
- Ripple: Ripple has been a serious contender, with incredibly low transaction fees and with lightning-fast settlement speed. You might not be what you are comfortable with because it is utilized

and centralized and pre-minded by banks for example Bank of America.

- Ethereum: Ethereum is said to be the future for both blockchain technology and cryptocurrency. Prospects for Ethereum seemingly increase since, in the last year only, its price has risen by three thousand percent. Perhaps it is best to invest in both Ethereum and Bitcoin if it is affordable for you so that both of your bases are covered.

- Litecoin: This is another big competitor; its value has increased by two thousand percent, though not with magnanimous fanfare as with Ethereum. It is ideal for those starting to invest, with its much lower price. Like Bitcoin, it is a peer-to-peer digital currency and compliments Bitcoin. It is recommended to invest in both Bitcoin and Litecoin, just the same as Ethereum because they complement each other properly.

- Bitcoin: There is a reason why Bitcoin is still the biggest cryptocurrency name, even though it might be showing its age. People have calculated and established that the BTC market capitalization of 21 million will never be reached. Different from fiat money, you are not to be worried about your Bitcoin losing its value because someone is producing more for fun.

Blockchain Companies You Can Invest In

- First Bitcoin Capital: This company operates similar to Concilium Group, but it only focuses on startups, in which Bitcoin is utilized as their cryptocurrency.

- Concilium Group: This company was founded in London, assists other blockchain startups, and invests in them to get them off the ground.

- BTL Group: Blockchain solutions and alternatives are created by this company for various existing web spaces like online shopping, fantasy football, and banking.

- DigitalX: A mobile app was created by this company that helps people to make payments of cryptocurrency internationally. It has supported in creating payment transactions that are secure in over 30,000 locations.

- Global Area Holding: Patents acquired by this company are related to blockchain technology. It is also working on a bigger project, of how blockchain technology is implemented into ATMs, which has huge implications for the financial world. This is a solid company to invest in because shares will skyrocket if they succeed in this endeavor as yet there is no reason to suggest that it will not succeed.

- BTCS: To start investing, this is a good company. In the United States, it is the first public company that has a market capitalization of over seven million, and it is centered on blockchain technology.

Another Way to Invest in the Blockchain?

The companies that are supporting blockchain technology, like Microsoft and IBM, should be invested in. They will be encouraged to invest further, since they are helped by the Blockchain technology to go on putting money into it, and companies that appear the last are the ones that throw their weight behind the Blockchain, so do not worry about having invested in them.

Potchain is another good sector to invest in. In the United States, Potchain is the slang term used for buying and selling medical, legal marijuana.

States are scrambling to catch up with marijuana, since it is not well regulated, but is an accelerating economic sector. Many people sell marijuana on their own, as entrepreneurs. They are being helped by blockchain technology to fill the gaps, whether it is financially or legally, while they are coping with varying state laws. The reason being while having or smoking marijuana can be legal in different states now since it is prohibited for banks from performing marijuana-related businesses. This means that in order to make transactions and secure money, marijuana-related business owners and entrepreneurs will turn to the blockchain and cryptocurrency. Those dealing in the legal marijuana market, as agreed by all financial experts, are making money hand over fist, and banks are allowed to do business with them as well.

It may not take many of the companies to add a "pay by Bitcoin" button to their options of payment. For the investor, there can be solid rewards, so it is not a huge risk. Another way is investing in private blockchain networks like the ones that companies are developing. It is a good parallel for how blockchain technology should be implemented in your company if you are running your own company. Begin with baby steps; for instance, Bitcoin should be added as a payment method. Looking at what other governments and large companies do, will help you to implement blockchain technology. Blockchain can also be used internally, by making it a database where your physical and virtual assets can be stored. Henceforth, you can continue to create an organizational blockchain for your company.

CHAPTER 9

How to Invest in Cryptocurrencies

Investment is about safeguarding your earnings or wealth into programs that are not only secure but also grow in value.

For an investment to be deemed as a promising investment, it must have:

- A standard of measure
- A store of value
- Converted into a form that is universally recognized as an investment option

Cryptocurrencies, such as Bitcoin, differ from fiat currencies (government-issued currencies) due to their limited volume. This means that when someone hoards a unit, fewer units are available for circulation into the market. For example, Bitcoin has a maximum volume of 21 million tokens. Litecoin has a maximum volume of 84 million tokens. This is unlike fiat currency, where that unit could be replaced by the printing of more units.

Due to the limited supply of cryptocurrencies, hoarding and speculation have become the norm. Hoarding means of investing and holding cryptocurrencies. Speculation becomes the real driver that determines whether one should hoard or release his/her hoarded stock to the market.

Establish a Measure of Your Investment

Every investment has a yardstick for measuring its value. When it comes to fiat currencies, the US Dollar remains the international yardstick. When it comes to commodity currencies, gold remains the yardstick. Cryptocurrencies also have their yardstick - Bitcoin.

Bitcoin is the first cryptocurrency to use blockchain technology. Before Bitcoin, there had been many unsuccessful attempts. Bitcoin became the first successful attempt. Bitcoin has dominated the cryptocurrency market such that it has become the de facto cryptocurrency standard, just as gold remains the de facto standard for both commodity and fiat currency.

Its dominant position and recognition as a cryptocurrency standard have made other cryptocurrencies to be recognized as *altcoins*, which simply means alternative coins/cryptocurrencies.

Thus, to be able to establish the performance of your investment in the cryptocurrency market, you have to gauge it against Bitcoin.

What are the failures of fiat currency that cryptocurrency has come to remedy? While you desire to invest in cryptocurrency, you need to understand its rationale. Why does it exist? What problem(s) was it created to solve?

From an investment perspective, the following are some of the failures of fiat currency that cryptocurrency has come to remedy:

- Low returns
- Low levels of speculation
- Unlimited supply
- Government manipulation
- Legal limitations – sanctions, political upheavals, etc.

The Best Cryptocurrency to Invest In

Which is the best cryptocurrency for investors? Many would-be investors pondered this question before making an investment decision. However, unlike investment in securities and forex, cryptocurrency is a relatively new phenomenon. It is not easy to predict which cryptocurrencies will last and which ones will eventually collapse.

You can easily choose a currency to trade in, but investment, being long-term, is not such an easy choice. The best thing to do is to follow the old adage 'never put all your eggs in one basket'. Every investor knows the importance of diversification when it comes to dealing with highly risky and volatile markets. The cryptocurrency market is extremely risky and volatile. It is not a market for the risk averse. It is a market for risk-takers.

Why go for high-risk volatile markets such as cryptocurrency? The underlying principle of investment is 'high risk, high returns.' You get little return on a risk-free investment.

While Bitcoin has shown high potential, this does not guarantee that it will never fade into obscurity. New blockchain and non-blockchain technologies are emerging. Many cryptocurrencies have already submerged into obscurity while more are coming up. You cannot ignore Bitcoin, but you have to look beyond Bitcoin as you diversify your portfolio.

How to Buy Cryptocurrency

Acquiring a cryptocurrency is the first step to owning it. While miners can acquire cryptocurrencies without buying them, you as an investor will have to buy them. Once you decide on your portfolio, and the cryptocurrencies to buy based on your portfolio, you will have to look out for a trading platform where you can buy your cryptocurrencies. We shall look at these cryptocurrency trading platforms in our next section.

While there are many cryptocurrencies, not all of them are traded on every platform. The only cryptocurrencies that you can easily find on most platforms are:

- Bitcoin
- Ethereum
- Litecoin

For the other cryptocurrencies, you have to ascertain the platform it is traded on.

How to Store Cryptocurrency for a Long-Term Hold?

Cold storage is a term that refers to the storage of cryptocurrencies for the long term. Due to their digital or virtual nature, you need to store your coins on a medium that will not allow your digital codes/keys to be erased, due to blackout, viruses' attacks, or other threats. An online wallet or your exchange platform is a *warm storage* facility. They are temporary in nature. They are ideal for traders but not investors. You cannot store coins in them for a long time. Online wallets and exchange platforms can be hacked, and they can even fold up.

Cold storage facilities are offline facilities for storing cryptocurrency. The following are some of the common cold storage facilities:

PC Wallet

This is a wallet (folder) that you create on your own personal computer to store your cryptocurrency codes.

Hardware Wallet

A hardware wallet is a dongle specifically created to store encrypted data. Thus, you can block any other unintended use of your hardware wallet.

Ledger Wallets

These are special kinds of hardware wallets. Unlike dongles, they have their own tiny screens that enable one to monitor and manipulate the storage facility. However, ledger wallets are specifically designed to store certain kinds of cryptocurrencies. Thus, while buying one, you must confirm it can store your kind of cryptocurrency.

Paper Wallets

These are impressions specifically created by software and imprinted onto paper. To help minimize the risk of erasure, tear, and wear, you need to ensure that you have quality paper. The paper wallets have a QR Code printed on them, to help you easily capture the keys into the computer during the transaction.

Brain Wallets

These are biological wallets that you etch commit to memory, through the process of coding and consolidation, in such a manner that you can easily remember. Use of mnemonics is the most usual way of creating brain wallets.

Cryptocurrency Exchanges

Coinbase

Pros:

- It is one of the most popular trading websites.

- The fees for this website are pretty reasonable, in comparison to other websites.

- It has a user-friendly interface. Hence, as a beginner, you will not struggle to figure out your way around this website.

- The currency that you store here is automatically covered by the website's insurance.

Cons:

- The customer service offered by this website is not as good as the other sites.

- This website supports only limited countries.

- This website has limited payment options, which reduces your flexibility.

- The services rolled out by this website are not uniform across the globe. Hence, it might cause a bit of inconvenience if you wish to trade on-the-go.

CEX.IO

Pros:

- It is one of the most popular trading websites.

- It has a user-friendly interface. Hence, as a beginner, you will not struggle to figure out your way around this website.

- You can easily access and trade from this site using your mobile phone.

- It also supports the use of credit cards for making payments.

- The exchange rates offered by this website are reasonable when compared to the other sites.

- It provides worldwide support.

Cons:

- The customer service/support offered by this website is not as good as the other sites.

- This website has an elaborate and long verification process. The long process can dissuade you from joining this site.

- Depositing money to this website is expensive compared to other websites.

Kraken

Pros:

- It is one of the most popular trading websites.

- The exchange rates offered by this website are reasonable compared to other sites.

- The customer service/support provided by this website is excellent.

- This website has more features than most trading websites.

Cons:

- It does not have an interactive, intuitive user interface. Hence, as a beginner, you might find it difficult to navigate through this site.

- This website has limited payment options, which reduces your flexibility.

Shapeshift

Pros:

- It is one of the most popular trading websites.

- It has a user-friendly interface. Hence, as a beginner, you will not struggle to figure out your way around this website.

- The exchange rates offered by this website are reasonable when compared to the other sites.

Cons:

- This site does not support fiat currencies.

- This website has limited payment options, which reduces your flexibility.

Bitstamp

Pros:

- It is one of the most popular trading websites.

- The transaction costs associated with this website are also minimal when compared to the other websites.

- It provides worldwide support.

- It provides high security for your transactions and the currency is stored on the website.

- This website is well suited to voluminous trading.

Cons:

- It does not have an interactive and intuitive user interface. Hence, as a beginner, you might find it difficult to navigate through this site.

- This website has limited payment options, which reduces your flexibility.

- Depositing money to this website is expensive compared to other websites.

Poloniex

Pros:

- You will be able to create your account faster here, as compared to the other trading sites.

- This website is well-suited to carrying out transactions in large volumes.

- The transaction costs associated with this website are minimal as compared to the other websites.

- It has a user-friendly interface. Hence, as a beginner, you will not struggle to figure out your way around this website.

Cons:

- This site does not support fiat currencies.

- The customer service/support offered by this website is not as good as the other sites.

CoinMama

Pros:

- It is one of the most popular trading websites.

- It has a user-friendly interface. Hence, as a beginner, you will not struggle to figure out your way around this website.

- Transactions can be carried out quickly.

- It provides worldwide support.

- It provides multiple payment options.

Cons:

- The exchange rates offered by this website are higher when compared to other sites.

- There is no function to sell Bitcoin.

- There is a premium that is being levied for the usage of credit cards.

- The customer service/support offered by this website is not as good as that offered by other sites.

Bitsquare

Pros:

- It is one of the most popular trading websites.

- It provides a secure and private interface to transact.

- This website supports trading several types of cryptocurrencies.

- It provides worldwide support.

- The transaction costs associated with this website are also reasonable compared to the other websites.

Cons:

- The customer service/support offered by this website is not as satisfactory as other sites.

- This website is well suited to advanced traders.

- It does not have an interactive and intuitive user interface. Hence, as a beginner, you might find it difficult to navigate through this site.

- This website has limited payment options, which reduces your flexibility.

Gemini

Pros:

- It provides a highly secure interface for carrying out your transactions.

- This site provides you with analytics, which will help you with your trading decisions.

- This website also provides higher liquidity.

- It has a user-friendly interface. Hence, as a beginner, you will not struggle to figure out your way around this website.

Cons:

- This website has limited payment options, which reduces your flexibility.

- It supports the trading of limited cryptocurrencies.

- This website does not provide for margin trading.

- The customer service/support offered by this website is not as good as other sites.

This website is available in limited countries.

LocalBitcoin

Pros:

- It has a user-friendly interface. Hence, as a beginner, you will not struggle to figure out your way around this website.

- It provides worldwide support.

- Transactions can be carried out in a fast manner here.

- It provides the user with multiple payment options.

Cons:

- The exchange rates offered by this website are higher compared to other sites.

- It will not be possible for you to buy Bitcoin in large quantities.

If you are keen to learn more about trading, do not rush in. Take your time. It is optimal to take it very slowly. It is best if you can find an experienced individual to take you through your first trades. There are YouTube tutorials on all aspects of trading; however, be careful as it is very easy to make mistakes, and once you have lost cryptocurrency it is gone for good!

Choosing a Broker

These are websites, which you can visit to buy cryptocurrencies at a price determined by the broker. These brokers are similar to dealers in the foreign exchange market.

There are a few criteria that will help you choose the right exchange for trading purposes. Make sure that you pay attention to these before you start trading.

- **Reputation:** The internet has information about the different trading sites available. I have already listed the most popular trading websites above. You can choose from any of the sites above.
- **Fees:** The owners of cryptocurrency exchanges want to make a living and to do this they charge fees. These fees are usually a percentage of the trade, and they vary greatly with some being twice as much as others.
- **Payment Methods:** Each exchange has its own payment modalities. Check out the payment methods before you make up your mind. If an exchange has only limited payment options, you may

not choose it, because it might turn out to be inconvenient to use at a later point in time.

- **Geographical restrictions:** Certain exchanges permit only individuals from certain countries to access and trade. Hence, make sure that you choose an exchange which does not restrict access, and allows everyone across the globe to trade.

- **Verification requirements:** Most exchanges in the UK and US require you to verify your identity before you can engage in trading. On the other hand, there are certain exchanges that let you stay anonymous and trade. While you might prefer to stay anonymous, I strongly suggest that you get the verification done. This will ensure that you are not caught in any scams at a later point in time.

- **Exchange rates:** Each website has its own exchange rates. Before you decide on the exchange, make sure that you visit all these sites and look at their rates. Compare these rates, and choose the one that is the most advantageous, keeping in mind the features that come along with that price.

Long-Term Crypto Investment

Long-term investment in cryptocurrency is about having long-haul future projections and deciding to commit your resources to them for a longer period.

Long-term investment in cryptocurrency has two major advantages:

- Less risk: Short-term investment is prone to short-term swings. Without proper timing, you may lose your short-term investment simply because you waited longer than necessary to recoup your gains. The challenge is that this timing is undefined.

- Lower fees: Short-term investment means that you have to keep on withdrawing and reinvesting. Both withdrawals and reinvestments have their own transaction costs. The more frequently you do it, the higher the transaction cost. On the other hand, long-term investments are less frequent and thus have lower transaction costs.

Indicators of Long-term Value

One of the most important things to a long-term investor is the future value of a given investment. While you cannot establish, with certainty, the future value of a given cryptocurrency investment, the following are key indicators to watch out for:

- **Market share**: Market share refers to the percentage of market capitalization that a given currency has relative to the rest of the market. If this market share becomes persistent in its trend, then, that is a solid currency. You can make a long-term investment depending on whether you just want to secure your investments against volatility (in case of a horizontal trend), or you want a long-term return (in case of an upward trend). Currently, Bitcoins control above 50% of the market share.

- **Utility**: Utility is the ability of a currency to satisfy market wants. Currencies that satisfy the most investor requirements (e.g., exchange of value, or store of value) will receive more attention and demand, than other currencies in the market. A currency with a higher utility in the market will be the most sought-after.

- **Transaction volume**: Transaction volumes indicate the level of activity of a given currency. A currency that increases in its traded volume indicates how lucrative it is for the public. A currency with higher or steadily increasing trading volumes has a higher long-term value.

- **Technological development**: Cryptocurrencies have no other value except that derived from their unique technology. Technologically advanced cryptocurrency will be increasingly adopted in the future, and become the leader of other cryptocurrencies, possibly even the standard benchmark. Thus, a cryptocurrency that keeps on churning new technological breakthroughs (in terms of mining, transacting, and storage) has a higher long-term future value.

- **Market sentiments**: Market sentiments can shape the demand for a given currency, and thus affect its transaction volume and market share. This can be either positive or negative, depending on the market sentiments. Consistently positive market sentiments grant a given cryptocurrency long-term positive value. On the contrary, persistently negative sentiments in the market erode a cryptocurrency's future value.

Risk Appetite as An Influencing Factor of Your Investment Strategy

Risk is an important consideration of any investment one makes. Equity markets and money markets are, by their very volatile nature, more prone to risk than other investments. Whether you will invest long-term or short-term and whether you will choose a riskier, yet higher premium investment or a less risky with lower premium investment depends on your risk appetite.

CHAPTER 10

Making Money with Cryptocurrency

aking money requires work. Getting a job is a good way, winning the lottery is another. Making money is possible with cryptocurrency as well, either through buying, trading, and investing, or by diving into the process directly and mining cryptocurrency yourself.

Buying, Trading, and Investing

You can make money from the cryptocurrency market as you would in the stock market. That is to say, it is a full-time job and not so easy to do. Most returns are realized with buying and trading. With only a couple of dollars' worth of Bitcoin, for example, you can begin exchanging digital forms of money. There are no agent charges; there are no intermediaries to manage; there are no real boundaries to stop you. Therefore, there is no reason not to attempt it.

Initial Offerings

While the name comes from the more traditional *initial public offering* that occurs when a company issues stock for the first time, the two have relatively little in common. While IPOs provide investors to own part of the company in question, they only offer early adopters the opportunity to purchase a new type of cryptocurrency at a low rate in hopes that it will increase to the point where doing so was a good decision. A majority of all ICOs these days are built on the Ethereum blockchain.

While a majority of the funding for these ventures comes from China, by no means do they hold a monopoly on the practice. While investing in cryptocurrency, in general, is a high-risk proposition, investing in an ICO is even riskier, because it is functionally an unknown quantity. ICOs face several unique issues that make them a less than ideal investment choice. For starters, the companies that offer them are not regulated by the SEC, which means they are not held to any of the standards that an IPO must meet to move forward. Additionally, there are fears that any past ICO success has just been a part of the larger cryptocurrency bubble, and that such success is not feasible in the long term.

Mining

Cryptocurrencies and Blockchains are more popular than ever these days, thanks to the rise of some more popular cryptocurrencies like Ethereum (Ether). Now, because mining has become more competitive, people are either setting up a home-based system, or they are setting up multiple rooms filled with computer systems intended just for mining. That, then, creates a rise in the price of graphic cards, and the need for producing larger and more powerful ones. This business has the potential of bringing in huge wealth, with mining enabling one to earn as much cryptocurrency as possible.

Computers that are used to mine digital currency run huge electricity expenses and require the latest technology graphic cards, to be able to solve complex mathematical issues.

Mining is an essential aspect of how most cryptocurrencies work. In order for a user to send or receive crypto-coins, the user initiates a transaction which is then broadcast to the entire network. Before this transaction can be completed, it has to be validated and recorded on the public ledger. As a reward for mining, miners are issued these newly created coins. In other words, miners act as bookkeepers for the cryptocurrency network and earn via newly created coins as payment for work. Anyone can become a cryptocurrency miner as long as they have internet access and sufficient computer hardware.

The Different Ways to Mine Cryptocurrencies

Computer Mining

You can mine using your computer. For example, you can download *GUIMiner*, join a mining pool, and start mining Bitcoins using your computer. However, a computer alone does not have enough hash power to mine a decent amount of cryptocurrency. You will probably end up paying more for your electric expenses than the amount of cryptocurrency that you could mine.

Hardware Mining

Since a computer alone does not have enough mining power to earn you a decent amount of cryptocurrency, you may want to do hardware mining. When you use hardware mining, you will mine using both your computer and mining hardware. This way you will have more mining power, which will enable you to mine more cryptocurrencies.

Software mining

With this mining method, you will download software on your computer and use it to mine cryptocurrencies. Normally, you will have to purchase it from a company. The software provider may also allow you to upgrade your account, to mine for more cryptocurrencies. Of course, an additional fee is often charged for upgrading your account or software. Again, since you will still be using your computer, you will have to pay attention to any overheating problems, and you still need to mine cryptocurrencies yourself.

Cloud Mining

Cloud mining is the most popular type of method for mining nowadays. With cloud mining, you no longer have to use your computer nor worry about any overheating issues. Instead, you simply have to wait for a mining company to send you cryptocurrencies, which are normally on a weekly/monthly basis, or every time that you reach the minimum threshold amount.

The Block Reward

Cryptocurrency mining is based on the concept of block rewards. For cryptocurrency transactions to be verified, miners are required to solve complex, computationally demanding mathematical equations. The solutions to these mathematical puzzles are based on the results of the previous block solutions. Therefore, it is impossible for a miner to calculate the solution of a future block in advance without the solution to the previous block.

Setting Up Mining Software

There are several options when it comes to cryptocurrency mining. Some algorithms like *CryptoNight* can be run on CPUs. Others like *Ethereum*, *Vertcoin* and *Zcash* are best run on GPUs, while others like Bitcoin and Litecoin can only be run on ASICs (Application Specific Integrated Circuits). However, there is more to mining, besides having the mining hardware.

Mining Pools

Mining pools work by having every participant contribute their computational power to mining. Similarly, all rewards are distributed among all the pool members, based on the percentage of computational power they provide. Your hardware is assigned small tasks by the pool, which it submits as shares. By joining a pool, you increase your chances of earning a small percent of a reward. If you were to solo mine, you would get to keep the whole reward for yourself. However, your chances of finding a valid block solution would be next to zero.

The Actual Mining

With your hardware ready and joined to a mining pool, you are now ready to start mining. All you need to do now is to download the correct software and configure it to your hardware and mining pool. Most mining pools will help you with instructions on where to download the software and how to configure it. It is good to note that your mining speed will be affected by things like memory, clock speeds, drivers, and even firmware revisions. To get the most out of your mining software, you should check various forums for ideas on how to optimize your hardware.

Understand the Market

The surest way to enjoy the profitability that comes with cryptocurrency is by understanding the market. You can buy Bitcoins at a specific price and then sell them at higher prices; this is one of the most profitable aspects of Bitcoins because it is akin to getting a multiple of what you invested in the first place.

Holding Bitcoins

Another viable way through which you can make a lot of profits through Bitcoins is by purchasing a Bitcoin wallet that is used to receive, send, and store your Bitcoins. There are online platforms that render such services, including *Coinbase* and *Blockchain.info*. They are the most commonly used Bitcoin wallets that come with an online and mobile version for easy access. The safest way to store your Bitcoin is on an offline platform.

Engaging in Tasks for Bitcoin

Here is a fun way to earn Bitcoins by completing works on platforms that encourage the use of Bitcoins. *Coinbucks* is a smartphone app that makes it easy for you to earn Bitcoins by playing mobile games and downloading apps. *Bitcoin Rewards* also makes it easier for you to get Bitcoins by downloading and testing apps and fulfilling other minor tasks that make it possible for you to get Bitcoins upon completion. You can watch videos on the smartphone app known as *Bituro* and get paid in Bitcoins. Fill out surveys and test apps for platforms and grow your Bitcoin wallet to entry-level trading funds.

Purchasing Goods and Services in Exchange for Bitcoin

This is gradually becoming the most common means of generating profits through Bitcoins. Currently, there are a lot of sites that accept Bitcoins as a payment option, but more importantly, you can sell items and get Bitcoins as payment. Examples of sites that encourage the exchange of products for Bitcoin include *Bitify.com* and *Purse.io*. Bitify can be likened to a digital eBay, where Bitcoins are accepted as payment. A fascinating aspect of this site is the fact that customers can pay for goods after delivery; by securing their Bitcoins initially they get the assurance of products in excellent shape. Purse.io is mostly utilized by individuals with an Amazon account. Here, products are sold at a discounted rate, and Bitcoin becomes the currency of trade. So here we are, with a whole bunch of platforms that thrive using Bitcoin, the question is what are you going to do with what you have heard? These platforms can serve as an avenue for increased profitability.

For the Love of Gambling

The sources of profit with cryptocurrency just do not end. If you love to gamble and enjoy having a great time at the casino, then your Bitcoins may become very useful and can multiply your Bitcoins. Some online casinos also utilize Bitcoins; you can play roulette, lottery, or slots and if you hit it big, you can decide to get paid in Bitcoins. So, you get your money secured up in layers of cryptography, and this improves your chances of building true lasting wealth.

Interests Payments

If you have Bitcoins in your wallet, lend it out and receive more Bitcoins as interest. You can lend directly to close friends and can create an interest stream that ensures the inflow of more Bitcoins to your wallet. It is a safe and exciting way of earning Bitcoins.

Gifts

Who does not love presents? Did you know that you can receive crypto-currencies as gifts? If you are focused on adding Bitcoins to your wallet, then you can insist that your peers give you cryptocurrency gifts. The more Bitcoins you have in your purse, the easier it gets for you to invest and grow your Bitcoin wallet.

CHAPTER 11

How to Master the Art of Cryptocurrency Investing

To make sure you get the most out of your experience, and to help you truly master the art of trading in cryptocurrency, we are going to discuss some tips that you can use to master the art of investing and trading in cryptocurrency. Using these tips will ensure that you do not make any fatal beginner mistakes and that you protect your assets and maximize the returns you get from your investments from the get-go.

It is a good idea to review these tips before you begin investing to ensure that you know as much as you can before you get started. Although it is a fairly simple concept and you can get started relatively easily, it is important that you know as much as you can before you invest any of your cash into these currencies. If you do it right, you are likely to make a great return. Plus, it is always proper investment etiquette to make sure that you effectively research any investment before you actually invest in it. This way, you do not make any uneducated decisions that could result in you losing out on cash!

Buy with Funds You Do Not Need

Especially when you are getting started, you should only invest funds that you do not need. If you think you may be able to invest critical funds in a cryptocurrency and hit the jackpot, think again. Investments, especially in cryptocurrencies, are something that takes time to accumulate and build money. While you may get lucky and make some money in a relatively short period of time, you should not expect that this will happen. Generally, when you invest in cryptocurrencies, you should expect your investment to stay put for a fairly lengthy amount of time. The longer you leave your investment, the better your return on it will be. For that reason, you only want to use money that you do not need.

Research First, Buy and Trade Later

It is imperative that you research cryptocurrency before you buy it. You are off to a great start by reading this book. Now, you have a strong idea of what the most popular forms of cryptocurrency are, how you can acquire them, how you can store them, and how you can trade them. That is important. However, you should not let it stop here.

When you are investing in anything, including cryptocurrencies, it is important that you invest in them after you have researched them. You do not want to find yourself investing in something that you do not fully understand, only to lose your investment because you were not clear on what you were doing. It is important that you spend time researching the exchange network you are going to use, the cryptocurrency form that you want to invest in, and the recent and historical market figures for that particular coin.

A great way to research cryptocurrency comes from basic internet searches, but you should go deeper than that too if you want to make an informed decision. There are many cryptocurrency forums and groups online that you can get into that will connect you with people who have already been trading in cryptocurrencies for quite some time. Getting involved in these forums gives you the opportunity to communicate with other traders, and helps you find out what is the best move for you to make as a beginner. The market is constantly changing, and so are the available currencies. For this reason, anything we may be able to recommend to you right now in this book may quickly become invalid. That is why we have not recommended any one specific coin for you to get started with but rather educated you on the most popular coins at the time of writing this book.

In addition to researching before you trade the first time, make sure you continue to research before every major trade, and also throughout the duration of your investments. As we just discussed, the market is constantly changing, and so is the range of available cryptocurrencies. It could change at any given time with the introduction of a new technology or cryptocurrency, so you want to make sure that you stay on top of it and pay attention. The more you research first, the more likely you will make wise, educated investment decisions. This can protect you from making uneducated decisions that could cost you in the long run and can help you get more out of your investments.

Diversify Only If You Understand

To expand on the importance of researching first, make sure that you only diversify when you understand what you are diversifying into. Some people suggest that you buy a small amount of every cryptocurrency currently available. This is actually a really poor investment choice. Some, you can clearly tell, are not going to pay back very much, and if you were to do some research, you would know that. Some cryptocurrencies are experimental ventures intended for learning about new technology and to see what can be improved. Others are revealed as an opportunity for new developers to get in on the cryptocurrency buzz and are not actually developed that well at all, making them virtually useless to you. There is no sense in wasting your funds on these types of cryptocurrencies when you could simply research them and invest in ones that are more likely to succeed.

Unless Circumstances Change, Do Not Take Profits

Many people feel that you should take the profits of your funds out right away. Of course, this is entirely up to you. Most people will say that you should go ahead and quickly sell so that you can collect a massive profit. If that is what works for you and that is what you are looking for, then, by all means, do that. For example, if your income changes and you really need the funds, you can sell them and reap your profits. Otherwise, you may choose to remove your funds and invest elsewhere. You may also choose to remove your initial investment for peace of mind so that you know for sure that no matter what happens, you are not going to lose your original investment.

Of course, you may have other personal reasons for wanting to remove your profits that may be entirely up to you. However, it is worth noting that the longer they sit, the bigger they grow. Rather than dipping into them, unless absolutely necessary, it may be a better idea to leave them alone and let them continue to accumulate, so that one day when you do actually need them, they are available to you.

Cryptocurrency Is Not for Day Traders

Many modern traders tend to skim the market on a daily basis. They enter in the morning with low buy-ins and sell in the evening with high payouts. This strategy is completely fine in many marketplaces, but it is not a viable practice in cryptocurrency. When it comes to cryptocurrency, you want to hold it for as long as possible. Rapidly buying and selling your funds can result in you losing out on valuable growth.

If you want to invest in cryptocurrency, you should look to it as a long-term investment instead of something that you can get in and out of in a relatively short period of time. While some people choose to take the profits and make massive returns in a short period of time, the real prize is in letting it sit and grow in value. It is not unheard of for people to buy in with $1,000 and walk out with $80,000.

Buy Low, Sell High

When it comes to buying low and selling high, this is virtually always true no matter what market you are trading in. So, naturally, it counts for cryptocurrencies as well. However, because of how volatile the crypto-currency market can be, this may not always be practical. It is hard to predict when the peaks and dips will occur, as cryptocurrencies can often trend on the volatile side at any given time.

Instead of worrying about buying low and selling high, focus on buying low, holding onto the coins as long as you can, and then selling when they are high. You may not be able to predict the peaks due to the vola-tility of the market, so you may want to make sure that you are focused on the long-term gains, not the short-term ones. Trying to predict the market in a short period of time can become stressful, and this may result in you losing out on potentially major gains. Instead, look at the bigger picture and pay attention to it. Look beyond 24-hour timespans and into weeks, even months or years. This makes it much easier to determine where the general market is going and what trading moves you should make, as a result.

Buy Now

Many people are worried about when to buy into the market. They are unsure about when they should buy in, they do not know if it is the right time, and they want to make sure that they get the most back. This is completely normal and natural. Obviously, this is likely why you are investing in cryptocurrency: to make a return. However, there is no optimal buy-in time. The longer you wait, the higher the price goes, and the higher your buy-in price will be.

Do not wait for the right time, or try and predict when a valley will come so that you can buy in. Instead, buy in right now with only what you can afford. Thenceforth, focus on buying more once it hits a low point. That makes it much easier for you to actually get started, and to not feel quite so intimidated in the world of cryptocurrency. For the first week or two, make it about learning the market. Then, once you have done so, you can start paying attention to pulling the right moves and getting your low buy-ins and high payouts.

Buy the Rumor, Sell the News

Although this can sometimes result in you not always making the best trades or losing out, it also puts you in the running to stand for a lot of gains. Since the entire idea is to earn as many funds as you possibly can, the more knowledgeable you are, the better. Of course, you do not want to make an uneducated decision, so make sure that the rumors you are listening to are coming from reputable sources. Pay attention to other traders, to media surrounding trades and investments, and other similar sources. As long as the rumor comes from a credible source and there are many people talking about the rumor, there is a good chance that it may come true. If you are worried about it not coming true, however, you can always invest a smaller amount.

Practice and Get Comfortable

The ultimate goal when it comes to trading and investing in cryptocurrencies is that you take your time, practice, and get comfortable. If you practice with uncritical funds, unlikely to impact you heavily should you lose them, then any mistakes you make early will be easy to forgive.

Getting started in anything new, especially trades and investments, can be confusing. Early on, you are learning to navigate new software, store your coins, and understand the market. Give yourself some time and practice money to figure it all out, and then once it begins to make sense to you, you can start investing more into it. The more you learn to navigate the software, get used to transferring your funds and storing them, and knowing when to buy and when to sell your coins, the easier it becomes. Also, this will give you time to learn how to be patient and accumulate overall market gains, rather than getting antsy and trading too frequently. Once you get used to the entire process, it will be simple for you, and you will likely find that you can generate incredible returns with this form of investment and trading.

Your Risk Should Be Managed Wisely

Do not invest everything in one trade or coin. Look for a lot of small profits that will accumulate, but do not look for the peak coin movement.

Have Purpose for Each Trade That You Make

This might seem a bit thoughtless, and maybe a bit obvious, but is not the rush of financial gain or trading reason enough? Nevertheless, it is essential to identify why you are beginning the trade and to recall the idea afterward.

CHAPTER 12

Which Investment Strategy is Right for Me?

Here are a few general approaches to investing that may suit you.

Go All-In and HODL

Although this is not recommended, the simplest thing to do today is go all-in and then "just HODL." The problem with this strategy is that it is like walking up to the roulette table and putting everything on black. That is true, but there is no complexity in the plan. If you do not manage to time the absolute bottom of the market, you will end up watching your on-paper capital disappear, without many choices to do more than cut losses or wait.

Establish an Overall Average and Then HODL

This is a conservative and straightforward technique that helps alleviate worries about regular prices. Either you buy irrespective of the price at regular intervals, or you buy incrementally as if the price is down over time. This helps to avoid mistiming the market, by creating an extended duration over months or even years. This can be a robust high-risk strategy, for an unpredictable reward asset such as Bitcoin. You could end up paying long-term capital gains tax as a bonus rather than the short-term tax (it is about half as much). You, most probably, will avoid some of the headaches of disclosing complicated crypto-tax trades.

Trade, Targets at Buying Low and Selling High

To do this, you need not know more than just how to buy and sell. Purchase at rates you think are small, whatever the price is after a few days of falling prices, then try to sell when prices are higher. You can either set a 'stop-loss' if you get it wrong, or you can 'hold bags' (mainly reverting to a policy of 'build an average position and hold' if you get it wrong). If you like to do it like a pro, then Technical Analysis (TA) is required. TA allows you to base your buy and sell on support levels, moving averages, etc. If you get it right, TA will help you boost the profitability of your trades, but if you get it wrong, it could psych you out. Watch out for commissions and portfolio depletion while you trade.

Unbalanced Portfolio

This is a strategy where you allocate every investment depending on your projection of its performance. For example, if you think Bitcoin will perform the best over time, you would allocate a significant proportion of investment to it, and continue allocating to the next-best downwards, based on predetermined percentages:

- Bitcoin (50%)
- XRP (30%)
- Monero (15%)
- DASH (5%)

This strategy is ideal for those investors who are able to carry out extensive research so that they can make informed predictions.

Balanced Portfolio

A balanced portfolio is whereby you allocate all your shortlisted currencies an equal share of your portfolio. For example, if you have a total portfolio fund of $4,000, you will allocate to your chosen four currencies as follows:

- Bitcoin ($1,000)
- XRP ($1,000)
- Monero ($1,000)
- DASH ($1,000)

Any subsequent investment fund will be allocated equally to your preferred currencies. This strategy is ideal for those who are not active followers of the currency market, and they may be unable to make more accurate predictions of which preferred currencies will perform better.

Reinvesting Profit

Reinvesting profits is a strategy where you reinvest profits from a high-return portfolio into new currencies, to expand the portfolio. This way, profits cover the risk of a new adventure rather than a new source of capital from your pocket. However, you only need to reinvest a given percentage of your profits (e.g., between 10% and 50%).

Reinvesting is a good strategy for long-term investors who are risk-averse, yet they are not in a hurry to withdraw their profits.

Dollar Cost Averaging

Dollar Cost Averaging is a strategy that allows you to invest a fixed amount of dollars (or any other fiat currency) into cryptocurrency at predetermined intervals. It is more of a blind investment strategy whereby you continue investing to increase your stock level, regardless of price movements in the market (for as long as your allocation is enough to buy some currencies).

This strategy is ideal for passive investors who do not have time to follow up on market activities on a day-to-day basis. They only need to have a long-term projection of a given currency based on its fundamental analysis to make their investment decision.

Use A Trading Bot to Deal

Trading bots are apps designed to handle your trades. The real benefit is that while you are sleeping, it can do your bidding. If you are going to trade, the time, effort, and resources needed to get a bot up and running are likely worth it. You do not have to do something fancy with it, just let it put stop losses for you, or if you know any simple TA, try making it trade things like death crosses and golden crosses on 2-hour+ candles (this technique is popular enough that you need to watch out for any time frame; if everybody automates this without any additional parameters, then each crossover will be more unforgettable than it already is.

Do a Mix of the Above?

A mix of the above can be used to play safe when learning about and enjoying everything that cryptocurrency has to offer. In investment mode, you can have one instance of your bot, one in trade mode, you can trade a little by hand, and you can store the rest of your funds in a safe offline wallet. Perhaps your wallet exceeds all your other good intentions, and maybe your bots will save you from your emotional trade? Here's the thing, if one thing works very well for you and the others do not, now you know what kind of investor/trader you might want to concentrate on being.

CHAPTER 13

Tips for Success in Cryptocurrency Investing

Knowing the Market Cryptocurrencies May Imitate Traditional Financial Assets

Still, they are undeniably exceptional, acting both as a forward-looking representation of natural products and, at the same time, as an ultimate innovation.

Cryptocurrencies are infamously unpredictable and erratic. Sometimes inexplicable spikes in prices are typical for the crypto-investor. Such occurrences have resulted in add-ons to the crypto-sphere lexicon. *HODL*, a misrepresentation of 'hold' that has become a mantra for crypto investors, is intended to ease the fears of investors as uncertainty inevitably comes in.

Bitcoin Is Volatile

This is the first fact you should know when investing. Bitcoins are the most commonly used cryptocurrency and are volatile, hence while investing be mindful of this. The prices of Bitcoin fluctuate and plummet occasionally. There are reports of cyber hacks, and the exchange rates may not be the same through the year. Although the percentage fluctuation in Bitcoin price has reduced over the years, you have to be careful before making a move; study the history of the coin and know when to take a plunge or withdraw. Investing is good, but do you know what is better than investing? Smart investing. Rule number one: Be smart with your coins.

Hold on to Profits

When you start trading Bitcoins and receiving profits, it is important that you hold on to your profits for a while before selling or reinvesting. One reason why you should hold on for a while is it keeps you prepared for a viable investment that may come your way. Sometimes, people are in a hurry to sell off their coins; thus, they have an empty wallet. When a great opportunity presents itself, they are unable to buy in because they have an empty wallet. Rule number two: never have an empty wallet.

Transfers Are High-Speed

Unlike other financial institutions that take a lot of time, sometimes even days to complete a transaction, Bitcoin transactions do not take so long to go through. Besides the speed with which transfer can be done, there are no delays because of the absence of intermediaries, so it is just you and your network. More importantly, processing fees are not high as other financial institutions; you have got a good deal here so start investing.

Secure Your Wallet

Your cryptocurrency wallet must be secure for you to generate good returns. As you already know, there are hacking attempts and scamming reports of cryptocurrencies, but if you have a secure wallet/safe, then you do not have to fret over this. When you download a secure app that protects your coins, you can be sure that they will be safe from hackers. In the preceding chapter, we discussed some of the excellent apps you can rely on to secure your wallet, so benefit from them.

Buy Early Enough

If you want to get the best out of cryptocurrencies, then you must be an early bird; this rule reigns supreme. Buy when others have not, when prices are lowest. You will be amazed at the price at which you will sell. This is one of the quickest ways to invest and make a lot of profit. If you study the market long enough, you will be able to predict when digital coins are cheap, buy them, store them in your wallet, and get ready to sell for more returns.

Profits Should Be Higher Than Loses

Even if you lose money in the process of investing, your overall profit should be substantially more than your losses. It can be very frustrating when you lose too much money. Hence, always weigh your profit margin and ascertain if you have made progress or have regressed.

Do Not Invest What You Are Not Ready to Lose

This is a vital piece of information. As much as you know of the security and user-friendliness of cryptocurrencies, it is important that you invest money that you can afford to. So do not invest money that will put you in a very tight position if you end up losing them because of a bad deal. Remember that you may want to leave your coins for a while so invest money you wouldn't want to withdraw in a hurry.

Stay Up to Date

Information is key in the world of cryptocurrencies. People get into trouble when they use stale information in recent times. Cryptocurrencies are within the confines of the internet, and a lot of changes take place quickly here. You will be helping yourself considerably when you stay relevant and up to date. If you are not sure of something, ask questions and more importantly, read! Read material on cryptocurrencies. There is a lot of information as well as plenty of books and training available; do everything you can to be informed. Remember the saying: knowledge is power!

Diversify Your Portfolio

Do not put all of your eggs in one basket. Too many people get it wrong here; they place all their money in one investment, and when its returns dip, they are left with losses. There are a lot of cryptocurrencies you can invest in; you do not have to invest in just one currency. So, diversify your portfolio; spread your investment by diversifying your portfolio. When you diversify, you reduce your risk level, and you have numerous avenues through which you can make a profit. It also helps you get a feel of the various platforms, which informs your decision to pull out your investment from a source or increase it.

Be Rational

Investing in cryptocurrencies is an excellent move in this day and age, but you must be armed with information on what to look out for before leaping. I believe it is not about investing but investing properly, taking the right steps, and getting the best results. The rules shared here will help you make the right decisions. Remember this book is a definitive guide that contains all you need, so feel free to read it over again. The next chapter takes us into the future of cryptocurrencies; you will get a glimpse into what the future holds for digital currency, and how far it can go in a world where technology is an ever-spinning wheel.

Choose the Best Platforms

To produce a fantastic crypto portfolio, you need to choose the exchanges and wallet services that suit your needs.

Every product is full of its own set of complexities, but investors can, in general, value certain aspects more than others. Priority must be provided to inter-operability, as well as security and functionality. If you are struggling to choose a platform, consider some of the tools and feedback that can help you select the platform that is right for you.

Be Consistent

Make regular contributions to your assets that have been allocated. Cryptocurrencies can be the hottest investment class. Nevertheless, they are not a get-rich-quick scheme. Buying digital tokens like lottery tickets might help some people make sumptuous headlines. However, it will not let most investors develop a long-term investment strategy for cryptocurrencies.

Creating the ultimate portfolio on cryptocurrencies will not occur overnight. Nonetheless, when investors understand the market intricacies, diversify their assets, and use the best channels, they can continually grow these assets, which could produce the vigilant investor's high returns.

Ignore Sources That Are Biased

When you decide to trade in cryptocurrency, it is extremely important that you do not rely on biased sources for investing ideas. The minute you start browsing online for trading options, you will come across multiple sites promising good returns. As a beginner, it is extremely important that you stay away from phony sites, which offer surprisingly high returns. Seek advice only from reliable sources before you begin investing. Rely on your judgment and risk appetite and choose your portfolio accordingly. Do not get swayed by disingenuous success stories posted on certain websites and make a hasty decision.

Start Small

As a beginner, until you get a good grasp on how the market works, it is important that you do not exhaust your life savings at once. Start small. Keep aside a small portion of your income every month, for trading purposes. Invest small amounts at first and understand the nuances of the trading process. As you start making a profit, slowly increase your investments. Do not make the mistake of investing huge sums, as soon as you experience a profit for the first time. Take your time to decide the optimal portfolio for your risk appetite. Once that is figured out, you can gradually increase your investments.

Have Realistic Goals

Do not perceive cryptocurrency trading as an easy and quick way to become rich. As you already know, the cryptocurrency market is highly dynamic and volatile. It will take you some time to get a grasp of the trading process.

Do Not Try to Guess and Trade

Trading is not about making the right guesses. When it comes to an extremely volatile market, such as that of cryptocurrencies, it is not possible to sustain your returns, purely by making guesses. You might get lucky once or twice, but your guesses can only help you to a certain extent. You need to do your homework before you make an investing decision. Even if you are not a beginner, you cannot predict exactly how the market will react tomorrow. Make sure you keep an eye on the trends and ensure you watch out for market reports before you invest. Despite all the homework, there is still a possibility of you not making a profit. However, one failure should not deter you from doing your homework.

Be Patient and Do Not Panic

When it comes to trading with cryptocurrencies, it is extremely important that you learn to be patient. As a beginner, you might make some trading mistakes. Or it might take you more time to understand the nuances of the market. Do not immediately give up on trading with cryptocurrencies because of a few mistakes. In fact, you will learn more from the mistakes, which will help you make more informed decisions in the future. You must embrace the uncertainty element of the future and be prepared for the worst-case scenario too. This way, you will not panic if you make a mistake or incur a loss. You will be able to regard it as a short-term phenomenon and try to come up with a strategy to overcome this.

Learn from Your Mistakes

Given that the market for these cryptocurrencies is booming, it is only a matter of time and effort from your end before you make a tidy profit. Hence, it is absolutely important that you learn from your mistakes and correct your investing strategy accordingly. Your mistakes should be an opportunity for you to learn and better understand the market.

Plan Ahead

If you want to sustain your profits from trading, in the long run, you will have to come up with an investing plan. You cannot aspire to make huge profits by just focusing on trading for the day, without keeping the future implications in mind.

Do Not Trust Others Completely

When it comes to trading with cryptocurrencies, you are out on your own. You cannot rely on the success stories of others alone and make your investing decisions. While it is extremely important that you seek the inputs of others, who are regular traders, you cannot blindly rely on their trading advice. This is because a certain investing strategy or choice of investments might have worked for a certain individual at that point in time, due to various reasons. There is no reason for it to work that way for everyone another time. Hence, you should not be basing your investment decisions solely based on what worked for others.

Pick Currencies That Have Huge Communities

With over 800 cryptocurrencies to date, you can be confused about which cryptocurrency you should pick. If you want to invest in something new, do not go into a currency that no one has ever heard of.

Instead, choose a currency that has a good and established platform. The currency that you choose should have the support of a lot of community members. People should know about the currency. Having a community dedicated to a particular currency would mean that the currency is popular with the people, is stable, and going to last.

Do Not Forget to Have Fun!

Do not consider trading as a mundane job or activity. At the same time, do not spend too much time overanalyzing the market. This will just ruin your experience. You will forget to enjoy trading when you are overstimulated with market information. Learn to draw a line between being prudent and paranoid. When you are prudent, you will be willing to play around, have some fun and make money on the go. On the other hand, if you are paranoid, you will be overthinking before making any investment decision. Time is of the essence when it comes to trading. When the market is quickly changing, you cannot forever question your decisions and lose out on the opportunity to make money. Enjoy trading. That way, you will learn more than you expected! With time, you will be able to develop a passion for trading. When that passion sets in, it is going to be an interesting journey for you!

Now, if you are new to trading, it might be difficult for you to come up with an investing plan for the future on your own. This is where you need to take that extra step and learn from others. Seek the advice of other experienced traders, study the market, watch out for trends, and come up with your tentative plan. When you see that your plan is working, see how you can further improve it to optimize your returns. If your plan is not working, well, it is a lesson learned! Remember, you cannot just rely on others' counsel before investing. You need to do your bit of research as well, to validate their counsel.

CONCLUSION

Investing is a matter of knowledge, practice and information management, and preparation, regardless of the asset you are willing to work with.

Cryptocurrency has attracted millions of users and amateur investors around the world who are, in most cases, guided by the emotions on the market over an asset that's value is only based on supply and demand, generating huge gaps and instability of the price.

If you are planning to invest in cryptocurrency, make sure to get the right information, study as much as you can about how the currency behaves. Be aware of news and related material that can have an impact on its price. Getting started can be intimidating, especially if you have never been directly involved in investments or trades before. Unlike traditional currency, whereby you can hire an investment portfolio manager to do the work for you, you are responsible for investing in and trading your own cryptocurrencies. Fortunately, there are many exchange networks you can use that make this process easy, even for beginners who have very little background knowledge on the trading side of finances. However, before you fully commit to any particular cryptocurrency, it is important that you take additional time to research that specific cryptocurrency. There are constantly new forms of cryptocurrencies emerging, and each one has unique traits, properties, and benefits. They also change rapidly, and so can their popularity. If you want to make the best move, it is a good idea to investigate the specific coin you are most interested in before you commit to purchasing anything.

The main thing required of you is to believe in yourself and the cryptocurrency market. After all, it is those people who believed in Bitcoin a few years ago that now possess huge fortunes and are influential today. Therefore, believe in the dawn of the cryptocurrency economy.

NFT

FOR BEGINNERS

How to Make Massive 100x Gains from
Non-Fungible Tokens and Crypto Art

Nicholas Scott

INTRODUCTION

U nless you've been living under a rock (which I seriously doubt!) you must have heard about NFTs, especially with some of the jaw-dropping prices certain NFTs have been sold for in recent times. However, if you are like the average person, you might be scratching your head and wondering what the hype is all about.

If you have been wondering what NFTs are, how they work, where you can buy and sell them, and how you can create your very own NFT (trust me, they are not difficult to create), you do not need to wonder anymore!

After making a respectable ROI of 1,050% from my NFT transactions, I decided to explain what NFTs are, how they work, their use cases, and how you can make money from them in clear and simple terms. Additionally, I will be sharing the secrets behind generating a high ROI on any NFT you invest in.

In a few short words, I will be explaining everything you need to know to get started in the world of NFTs.

Let's get started!

CHAPTER 1

NFTs

B asically, NFTs are Non-Fungible Tokens. They are pieces of digital content that are linked to a blockchain. In case you didn't know, a blockchain is a digital database that underpins cryptocurrencies such as Bitcoin, Ethereum, Litecoin, and Ripple. It is this same blockchain that NFTs are linked to.

Before I further explain what NFTs are, you need to understand the concepts of fungibility and non-fungibility as well as the concept of a token. Understanding these three concepts will help you easily comprehend what NFTs are all about. First, I will explain the concepts of fungibility and non-fungibility before I proceed to explain the concept of a token.

Fungibility vs. Non-Fungibility

Essentially, fungibility refers to the ability of an asset or good to be interchanged with other individual assets or goods of the same type. Let me explain better with an example. Money is a prime example of fungibility. Let us assume for a minute that a friend of yours loans you a $100 bill. It does not matter if you repay the loan with two $50 bills or even ten $10 bills because the total value of those dollar bills equals the $100 bill you loaned from your friend. That is to say that fungible goods or assets can be easily exchanged with other similar goods or assets without any change to the value.

Conversely, non-fungibility refers to the inability of a good or asset to be interchanged with other individual assets or goods of the same type due to the uniqueness of the initial non-fungible good or asset. Let me also explain this better with an example. Let us assume that your friend lends you their car. Without being told, you know it will not be acceptable if you return a different car to your friend, even if it is the same model. Likewise, you know it will not be acceptable if you break up the car into different parts and return it to your friend. Unlike money, cars are not fungible with respect to ownership; however, the gas that powers the car is fungible because you can easily replace it with an equal amount of gas. Therefore, this is to say that non-fungible goods or assets cannot be exchanged with other similar goods or assets due to the unique properties of non-fungible goods or assets.

Put simply, while fungible goods or assets are interchangeable, non-fungible goods or assets are non-interchangeable. Also, while fungible goods or assets are uniform, non-fungible goods or assets are unique. Furthermore, while fungible goods or assets are common, non-fungible goods or assets are rare. Finally, while fungible goods or assets are divisible, non-fungible goods or assets are non-divisible.

Tokens

Now that you know the distinct difference between fungibility and non-fungibility, it is time to understand what is referred to as a token.

Basically, in the real world, tokens are anything that serves as a tangible representation of a quality, fact, or even feeling. For instance, real-life tokens can include a driving license – which represents the fact that you have successfully completed the training required for you to become a driver. Similarly, your student ID card is a real-life token that represents the fact that you are a student of a particular institution.

Comparably, in the crypto-universe – which is colloquially referred to as the cryptoverse – tokens are representations of "something" in their re-spective ecosystem. In the cryptoverse, a token can represent value, vot-ing right, ownership of something unique, or anything, depending on the token. However, I should also add that a token is not usually restricted to a single specific role; it can perform different roles in its native ecosys-tem. That is to say that a token can represent a store of value, provide ownership to something unique while allowing its owner to utilize it as an exchange of value.

What Are NFTs?

Now that you understand the distinctive difference between fungibility and non-fungibility as well as what token means, I believe you are starting to understand what an NFT is as well as what makes them valuable.

As I mentioned earlier in this chapter, NFT is simply an acronym for Non-Fungible Token. NFTs are digital assets who's non-fungibility makes them unique. Due to the fact that they are tokens, they are used to represent ownership of unique items such as collectibles, music, art, or even real estate in the digital world. Also, I mentioned earlier that NFTs are pieces of digital content that are linked to the blockchain. This essentially means that NFTs are units of data stored on the blockchain which serve as digital ledgers that ensure the authenticity of any NFT and provide buyers of such NFT with proof of ownership.

Therefore, in a few short words, an NFT is a piece of data that transmutes digital works of art as well as other collectibles into one-of-a-kind, verifiable assets that can be traded easily on the blockchain. Additionally, the piece of data in an NFT serves as a verification that you are the owner of a digital item which can include tweets, virtual real estate, virtual trading cards, GIFs, images of physical objects, and more. Furthermore, due to the non-fungibility of NFTs, they are not interchangeable. As a matter of fact, NFTs have been likened to digital passports due to the fact that each NFT contains a unique non-transferable identity that distinguishes it from other tokens — this, in essence, means that no two NFTs are the same as it is impossible for one non-fungible token to be equal to another.

While NFT is the latest cryptocurrency phenomenon to go mainstream, the attention of the general public was drawn to it due to the recent price records certain NFTs have generated this year. For instance, the first-ever NFT artwork — which is a collage of the first 5,000 images created by Beeple (who is a digital artist) — sold for an astounding $69.3 million! Similarly, Jack Dorsey, the CEO of Twitter, put up his first tweet for auction as an NFT which is now bidding for an equally astonishing $2.5 million. However, NFTs did not just spring up this year; they have been around since as early as 2012. In the subsequent subtopic, I will be discussing the historical background of NFTs and how they have evolved to the point of successfully penetrating the mainstream.

The History Behind NFTs

While you might just be getting acquainted with NFTs in 2021 due to the recent buzz generated by the pulse-quickening prices some NFTs have been sold for, NFTs have been around for almost a decade. Let us take a look at how NFTs originated and how they have evolved since then.

Colored Coins (2012-2013)

Colored Coins are arguably the earliest NFTs that existed. Colored Coins are made up of small denominations of bitcoin and can be as small as the smallest unit of bitcoin – which is referred to as a satoshi.

Colored Coins have multiple use cases which include access tokens, digital collectibles, issue shares of a company, coupons, property, and subscriptions, to mention a few. While Colored Coins demonstrated a huge leap in the capabilities of Bitcoin, their major downside was that they could only represent value if everyone agreed on their worth. For example, let us assume that a certain number of people reach an agreement that 200 Colored Coins represent 200 shares of a particular company. The moment one of the participants decides that the Colored Coins no longer equates to the company shares, the entire system fails.

Consequently, while Colored Coins were not without flaws, their creation highlighted the potential opportunity of creating digital tokens and laid down the groundwork for the subsequent creation of NFTs linked to the blockchain.

Counterparty (2014)

The creation of Colored Coins subsequently opened the eyes of a lot of people to the enormous potential benefits of issuing digital assets onto a Blockchain.

Hence, in 2014 Adam Krellenstein, Robert Dermody, and Evan Wagner founded Counterparty. Counterparty is a peer-to-peer financial platform and distributed, open-source Internet protocol which was built on top of the Bitcoin blockchain by the aforementioned individuals. The platform allowed asset creation on a decentralized exchange and even created a crypto token which was identified as XCP. In addition to that, the platform also created a lot of digital projects and assets which included meme trading and a trading card game.

Spells of Genesis on Counterparty (2015)

The success of Counterparty led some game creators to create Spells of Genesis and issue in-game assets onto a blockchain via the Counterparty platform. While this was a pioneering move from the creators of Spells of Genesis, they took it a step further by being among the first set of people to launch an Initial Coin Offering (ICO). They launched a token which they called BitCrystals. This token was then utilized as an in-game currency, which, in turn, was used to fund the development of the game.

Force of Will Trading Cards on Counterparty (2016)

Unsurprisingly, the success of Spells of Genesis in issuing in-game assets onto a blockchain generated some interest and in August 2016, Counterparty teamed up with Force of Will to launch their playing cards on the Counterparty platform. This was a huge leap for NFTs because, at that time, Force of Will ranked as the fourth card game by sales in North America behind Pokémon, Yu-Gi-Oh, and Magic: The Gathering. Hence, their entry into the ecosystem indicated the value of placing digital assets on a blockchain.

Rare Pepes on Counterparty (2016)

Seeing as in-game assets and trading cards were already being placed on the blockchain as digital assets, the demand for more unique digital items increased. Therefore, in October 2016, people started to issue Rare Pepes as digital assets on the Counterparty platform.

In case you didn't, Rare Pepes are rare types of memes featuring the frog character in the image below.

Before you roll your eyes at the eccentricity of issuing memes as digital assets, you should know that this particular meme has a very large and intense fanbase. As a matter of fact, as you can see in the image below, Rare Pepe Directory was created as a type of meme exchange that allows users to buy and sell Rare Pepe Memes.

Rare Pepes on Ethereum (2017)

Colored Coins as well as the Counterparty platform was built on Bitcoin's blockchain. However, in the early part of 2017, Ethereum started to gain a reputation as the second most prominent cryptocurrency; hence, it was not long before people started to issue memes as digital assets on Ethereum's blockchain as well.

In March 2017, Peperium was created as a decentralized meme marketplace and trading card game that allowed people to create memes on Ethereum's blockchain. Peperium was just like Counterparty and had its own crypto token which identified with the ticker symbol of RARE. This crypto token – RARE – is used to create the memes on Peperium and is also used to pay a listing fee for a created meme.

Cryptopunks (2017)

In June 2017, just as the trading of Rare Pepes gathered some momentum on Ethereum, Matt Hall and John Watkinson decided to create a special NFT project on Ethereum's blockchain. They discovered that they could create unique characters on the blockchain; these unique characters were limited to 10,000 and none of the characters were the same. They tagged this NFT project as Cryptopunks in reference to the Cypherpunks that experimented with precursors to Bitcoin in the 1990s.

Surprisingly, after creating the 10,000 unique characters, John and Matt allowed anyone with an Ethereum Wallet to claim a Cryptopunk for free. The Cryptopunks were promptly claimed by people and a secondary marketplace was subsequently created on the platform which allowed people to buy from existing owners and resell to anyone interested in purchasing a Cryptopunk.

Fascinatingly, Cryptopunks do not follow the ERC721 standard – as the standard had not been invented by the time they were created – but they were also not entirely ERC20 due to the limitations of the standard. Therefore, Cryptopunks can best be described as a hybrid of ERC721 and ERC20 (more information on these token standards and what they stand for will be divulged in a later chapter).

CryptoKitties (2017)

CryptoKitties is a virtual game based on a blockchain that allows players to adopt, raise, and trade virtual cats. This virtual game was instrumental in helping NFTs break into the mainstream due to the enormous attention generated by the game when it launched in October 2017.

Coincidentally, CryptoKitties went viral just as the 2017 bull market of cryptocurrencies was underway and this immensely contributed to the popularity of NFTs during this period. A lot of people started trading virtual cats as digital assets and this led people to realize the massive potential of NFTs. In fact, Axiom Zen – the company that developed the virtual game – ended up creating a new company which they called Dapper Labs. This new company ended up securing $15 million in funding from various investors, amongst which was Google Ventures.

The huge trading activity within the CryptoKitties community, as well as the massive investment capital investors funneled into Dapper Labs, began to make people realize the incredible power of Non-Fungible Tokens.

NFT Stabilization and Consolidation (2018-2019)

In many ways, 2018-2019 was the year of stabilization for the NFT ecosystem. During this period, following the boom CryptoKitties in 2017, the NFT entered what was referred to as a "phase of consolidation and stabilization".

However, despite the slowdown after the CryptoKitties excitement, several new developments began to occur in the NFT space as new projects were created. This period saw NFT marketplaces such as SuperRare and OpenSea thriving as the trade volume on these marketplaces began growing at a brisk pace.

Additionally, there are now several websites – such as NFTcryptonews.com and nonfungible.com – that are dedicated to the NFT space; just as there are numerous wallets such as Dapper Wallet and Metamask that have made the onboarding process into the NFT ecosystem as easy as possible.

The image below illustrates the current ecosystem of NFTs and as you can see from the graphic, the ecosystem is now very robust with its own dedicated marketplaces, substantial infrastructure, and lots of games and collectibles that contribute to the ecosystem.

During the 2018-2019 period, a lot of NFT projects generated record-breaking sales and this helped the NFT space garner a lot of attention from people. For instance, two of the most expensive NFTs (at that time) were sold in 2019 and this included a one-of-a-kind digital sports car tagged "F1 Delta Time Apex Race Car '1-1-1'" which was sold for 415.9 Ethereum and whose dollar equivalent is $113,124. The second most expensive NFT that was sold during this period was a plot of virtual land tagged "The Secret of Satoshi's Tea Garden" which existed in the virtual reality platform Decentraland; this virtual land sold for 1.3M MANA and its dollar equivalent was $80,663 at the time. These two sales generated a lot of interest to the point that even celebrities started utilizing NFTs as a source of income; for instance, Paris Hilton auctioned off a cryptograph drawing of her pet cat, and it was sold for 40 Ethereum whose dollar equivalent was $17,000 at that time.

Mainstream Adoption (2020–2021)

The enormous attention NFTs have been generating really began to pay off in 2020-2021 when a lot of major companies as well as big brands started to take interest and get involved in the NFT industry.

After realizing the opportunity NFTs provide, several big brands began to develop blockchain-based games, virtual worlds, and collectibles. The big brands I am referring to include National Football League (NFL), National Basketball Association (NBA), Ultimate Fighting Championship (UFC), Louis Vuitton, Nike, Formula 1, and Samsung to name just a few.

Besides these big brands and companies, several influential personalities such as Elon Musk and Jack Dorsey also got involved in the NFT industry. The involvement of these companies, brands, and influential personalities contributed to the mainstream adoption of NFTs as a lot of people became introduced to the concept of NFTs through the channels they were passionate about and already familiar with while the support of several influential personalities helped the mainstream adoption gain traction as well.

This mainstream adoption in 2020 led to a massive growth of the NFT space in 2021 with over $100 million transacted on NFT Marketplaces within the first two quarters. For instance, since its launch in October 2020, NBA Top Shot has successfully sold over $70 million worth of collectible NBA moments. Also, in just a single month – February – sales on OpenSea (which is the leading marketplace for NFT resales) increased from $8 million to $32 million! Similarly, the leading marketplace for crypto art, Nifty Gateway, saw a trading volume of $8.72 in January 2021 and over $6 million in February 2021. Likewise, SuperRare generated a total sales volume of over $10 million. As you can see from this gigantic boom in the NFT space, it is no surprise that NFTs crossed over into the mainstream with a lot of people looking to own their own piece or pieces of NFTs.

A lot of people are of the opinion that CryptoKitties led to the explosion of NFTs into the mainstream; however, while that is partly accurate, they could not have done this without the other aforementioned projects laying the groundwork of creating unique digital assets. Hence, it is important to acknowledge the roles of these previous projects in paving the way for the inevitable crossover of NFTs into the mainstream.

As you can see from this brief exposé into the history of NFTs, they have been around for quite some time. Starting from the first attempts to create NFTs in the Colored Coins era down to the CryptoKitties era, NFTs have evolved, and they keep evolving with the acceleration of the growth of the NFT ecosystem.

In just 2021 alone, the buzz around NFTs has been incredible, with several eye-popping NFT sales being made such as Beeple's First 5000 Days digital artwork which was sold for 38,474.82 ETH with a dollar equivalent of a whopping $69 million! Additionally, big names such as Elon Musk and Jack Dorsey contributed to this buzz when they both created their own NFTs and put them up for sale. This and other aforementioned factors led people to regard NFTs as a viable tool for investment in 2021, especially when you consider the fact that NFTs are still a relatively young investment vehicle with a rapidly increasing market cap.

What Are NFTs Used For?

You can use your NFTs in the following ways:

- By constructing and curating NFT collections.
- By displaying your public NFTs inventory through various means such as decentralized applications or even social media platforms.
- By utilizing them in several decentralized applications and games.
- By gifting to friends and family.
- By trading them on NFT marketplaces.

The Connection Between NFT and Cryptocurrency

By now, you must be wondering about the connection between NFTs and cryptocurrencies, especially when every NFT you hear about is bought and sold with a certain cryptocurrency. For example, Mike Winkelmann aka Beeple sold his digital piece of artwork for 38,474.82 ETH which is an equivalent of $69.3 million. So, why are NFTs ultimately intertwined with cryptocurrencies?

Well, the answer is not that difficult to understand. You see, every NFT is linked to a particular blockchain. For instance, as I mentioned earlier,

Colored Coins – which was the first attempt to create an NFT – was created on Bitcoin's blockchain. However, in recent times, following the successful creation of Rare Pepes as an NFT on Ethereum's blockchain in 2017, most NFTs have subsequently been created on platforms that are built on Ethereum's blockchain. For this reason, the transactions of NFTs are done using Ethereum as the purchasing currency.

Hence, purchasing an NFT will require the cryptocurrency of the blockchain that the platform is built on. That is to say, if you are purchasing or selling an NFT on a platform that is built on Bitcoin's blockchain, then Bitcoin will be the transactional currency. Similarly, if you are purchasing or selling an NFT on a platform that is built on Ethereum's blockchain, then Ethereum will be the transactional currency.

Benefits of Owning an NFT

You now know what an NFT is, as well as some of its use cases. However, you might be wondering what the advantages or benefits of owning an NFT of your own are. Well, you do not need to wonder anymore! Let us take a look at some of the top benefits of owning your own NFT.

- **They are easily transferable:** When you buy and own an NFT, you can easily transfer it to another individual either by selling it on dedicated NFT marketplaces or gifting it to them. However, you should keep in mind that the value of any NFT depends on the uniqueness of the NFT. That is to say, the more unique an NFT is, the higher the price you can sell it for.

- **They are authenticated:** Due to the fact that NFTs are powered by blockchain technology, their authenticity is guaranteed. It is impossible to create a counterfeit NFT due to the decentralized nature of blockchains. Hence, you do not need to worry about spending your hard-earned money purchasing fake NFTs as they are impossible to create.

- **Preservation of ownership rights:** Yet again, due to the fact that NFTs utilize decentralized platforms which are linked to a blockchain, any and all NFTs are embedded with data that can be used to determine the original creator of the NFT. Regardless of how many times the NFT is bought and sold, the data cannot be altered. Therefore, if you create an NFT, your ownership rights will be preserved regardless of how many times the NFT changes hands. Also, when you sell an NFT you create, if the person you sold it to sells it, you can potentially earn a certain percentage of the resale – which is referred to as royalty rights.

- **Value Growth:** NFTs tend to appreciate in value depending on how scarce they are, how unique they are, and due to the fact that some of them are used in games and other decentralized platforms. Therefore, the more popular the game or platform becomes, the more the value of the NFT increases. For instance, CryptoKitties is a blockchain-based game that allows players to create their own tokenized virtual cats. These NFT cats then began to increase in value as the game became more popular to the point that some of the NFT cats sold for as high as $600,000. Hence, you can purchase an NFT as an investment and sell it later for a handsome profit.

CHAPTER 2

How NFTs Work

I n the previous chapter, I laid down the foundation to help you understand what Non-Fungible Tokens are by discussing their fungibility, the history behind them, and their connectedness to cryptocurrencies. Basically, I dedicated chapter one to explaining what NFTs are. Now that you know what they are, it is time to take a look at how they work. Understanding how NFTs work will help you to further understand the concept behind them. Hence, in this chapter, I will be explaining how NFTs work by discussing their key characteristics.

Blockchain-Based

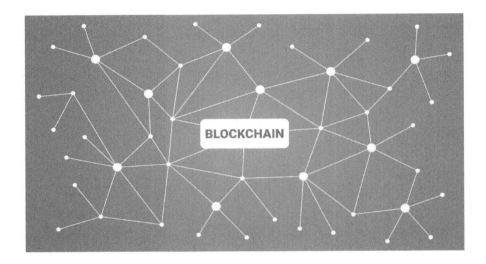

Prior to the emergence of NFTs and their subsequent adoption by the mainstream, non-fungible digital assets existed since the dawn of the internet. These non-fungible digital assets included in-game items such as in-game currencies, domain names, event tickets, and user handles on social media platforms like Twitter. However, these non-fungible digital assets varied in their standardization, liquidity, interoperability, and tradability. As a result, while we have a lot of non-fungible digital assets, we never really owned any of them in the real sense of ownership. For instance, when you purchase a skin on Fortnite, you own the in-game item in the game. You cannot decide to remove the skin from your Fortnite game and sell it on a secondary marketplace such as eBay. Similarly, you cannot use a skin you purchased in Fortnite in another game like PlayerUnknown's Battlegrounds (PUBG). Hence, the ownership of non-fungible digital assets is purely contextual. That is to say, you only own certain digital assets in the context of the platform providing them.

However, the emergence of NFTs solved this ownership problem as every NFT is based on a particular blockchain. Blockchains provide a synchronization layer for digital assets that provide users with ownership and management permission. That means that with blockchains, you can completely own a digital asset that is blockchain-based, and this gives you the freedom to indefinitely hold and transfer such an asset. Furthermore, several unique properties are encoded into blockchain-based digital assets and these unique properties transform a user's and developer's relationship with such assets.

There are certain features that are intrinsic to blockchain-based NFTs, and these features are what makes blockchain-based digital assets stand apart from traditional digital assets. These features include the following:

Standardization

As I mentioned earlier, traditional digital assets vary in their standardization based on the type of digital asset as well as the platform they are issued on. This is to say that none of the traditional digital assets have a unified representation in the digital world. For instance, the way an in-game item is represented in a game will differ from the way an event ticket is represented in an event ticketing system. However, by representing Non-Fungible Tokens on blockchains, creators are able to develop common, reusable, and inheritable standards that are relevant to all Non-Fungible Tokens. These standards include the rudimentary basics such as simple access control, ownership rights, and transfer rights for any NFT that is blockchain-based.

In the event that certain additional standards need to be added to certain NFTs such as specifications on how to display a particular NFT, such standards can easily be layered on top of the existing standards. Layering a new set of standards will then provide creators with a new set of what is known as stateful rudimentary basics.

Interoperability

Unlike traditional digital assets, Non-Fungible Tokens can easily be transferred across multiple ecosystems due to the standardized nature of blockchain-based NFTs. Therefore, as soon as a developer creates a new Non-Fungible Token project, the project is immediately displayable inside virtual worlds, viewable inside different wallet providers, and tradable on different marketplaces. This interoperability is made possible as blockchain standards provide a clear, consistent, reliable, and permissioned Application Programming Interface (API) that allows easy reading and writing of data.

Tradability

Essentially, the interoperability of blockchain-based NFTs makes it possible and easy to trade such NFTs across different marketplaces. Furthermore, the interoperability feature of blockchain-based NFTs allows free trading on open marketplaces. This means that, unlike traditional digital assets, users of blockchain-based digital assets are able to move items out of their original environments and into different marketplaces for sale. This allows users of blockchain-based digital assets to take advantage of advanced trading capabilities, such as eBay-style auctions, bundling, bidding, and the ability to sell in any currency like stablecoins and application-specific currencies.

Additionally, the tradability of blockchain-based digital assets represents a transition from a closed economy to an open, free-market economy specifically for game developers. This means that game developers do not have to constantly manage every single aspect of their economy; instead, they can just let the free market take care of the supply of resources, pricing, as well as capital controls of their respective game economy.

Liquidity

Naturally, higher liquidity is expected due to the instant tradability of NFTs. Therefore, as long as NFTs are based on blockchains, liquidity will not be a problem for developers of NFTs. Additionally, due to the increasing number of NFT marketplaces, NFTs are provided with greater exposure to a wide pool of potential buyers as well as sellers.

Immutability and Provable Scarcity

Since NFTs are blockchain-based, developers of NFTs can utilize smart contracts to cap the supply of NFTs while imposing unalterable properties on their NFTs after issuance. For instance, a developer can programmatically enforce the creation of a specific number of a rare digital asset just as such a developer can programmatically enforce the creation of an infinite supply of a common digital asset.

Additionally, a developer can programmatically enforce specific immutable properties on certain digital assets by encoding them on-chain. This is especially useful for digital art assets that heavily rely on the provable scarcity of an original piece of art.

Programmability

If there is anything that NFTs share with traditional digital assets, it is the fact they are both programmable. Certain functions can easily be programmed into NFTs before they are released. For instance, CryptoKitties programmed a breeding mechanic into their tokenized virtual cats. That means that two cats can be combined to breed an entirely new cat.

Nowadays, NFT developers tend to program complex mechanics into their NFTs such as random generation, forging, crafting, redeeming, etc. There are endless programming possibilities in the NFT universe.

Token Standards

As I mentioned earlier, most of the recent NFTs have been created on Ethereum's blockchain; however, the creation of these NFTs requires specific token standards that focus on how a token interfaces with the blockchain. These NFT standards ensure that the smart contract behind an NFT remains composable so that when a new project issues a token, such token remains compatible with the existing decentralized exchanges. In fact, these NFT standards are what is responsible for the standardization of an NFT.

There are various token standards on Ethereum; however, three of those popular token standards include the ERC-20 (fungible), ERC-722 (non-fungible), and ERC-1155 (non-fungible). In addition to these, there are also different token standards that are not based on Ethereum, and I will be explaining some of them as well.

Ethereum Token Standards

On Ethereum, tokens can be used to represent anything from lottery tickets to the skills of a character in a game to financial assets such as a company's share. Therefore, creating a healthy ecosystem on Ethereum – or any other blockchain – requires each token to be able to interact with each other. For instance, let us assume that two tokens were created with different structures of smart contracts. For both tokens to be able to interact with each other, their developers will need to carefully study each contract before mapping out how each token will work together – which will make scalability a bit difficult. Now, imagine that there are 1,000 different tokens with 1,000 different smart contracts. Narrowing down all the qualifications and specifications that are necessary to ensure that each of the 1,000 tokens are able to work together will require a colossal number of complex calculations – which is time-consuming and does not make for an ideal scenario. This is why token standards were created to standardize the rules that regulate a token's underlying architecture on Ethereum's blockchain. These sets of rules are called "ERC" which stands for "Ethereum Request for Comment". While the number attached to the end of the "ERC" – such as ERC-20 – represents specific token standards.

Let us take a look at the popular token standards available on Ethereum's blockchain.

ERC-20

The ERC-20 standard is a fungible token standard that helps standardize the functionality of any token that utilizes its smart contract structure. This, in essence, means that such a token is provided with properties that make it the same type and have the same value as any token that utilizes the same contract structure. This token standard is an interface for fungible tokens such as staking tokens or virtual currencies. This standard allows developers to build tokens that are able to interact with other products and services that recognize and/or utilize the same standard. In essence, this standard allows a token to be interoperable with other products and services.

This standard includes certain functionalities that are built into its foundations, and they include:

- name
- symbol
- decimal
- totalSupply
- balanceOf
- transfer
- transferFrom

- approve
- allowance

These functionalities allow the token standard to transfer tokens from one account to the other, get the total supply of available tokens on the network, as well as get the current token balance of an account. In addition to these, it also has other functionalities that allow the addition of a name, a symbol as well as certain decimals.

Now, due to the fact that ERC-20 is a fungible token standard, this means that one token can be used to replace another, and the tokens are divisible – i.e., smaller fractions can be used to pay back a larger amount. For instance, 1 ETH can be paid back with 0.50 ETH, 0.30 ETH, and 0.20 ETH.

Now, let us take a look at the two other token standards with non-fungibility that make it possible to create NFTs.

ERC-721

The ERC-721 standard is a free Non-Fungible Token standard that is unique in nature. Its uniqueness is due to the fact that any token that utilizes this standard can have a different value from another token that utilizes the same smart contract structure. This is important because, as I mentioned earlier, all NFTs are intrinsically different from each other – which is a major reason for their non-interchangeability.

Furthermore, all NFTs have a uint256 variable referred to as tokenId; hence, for any ERC-721 smart contract, its uint256 tokenId must be globally unique – as this is used to distinguish one NFT from another. Therefore, a dApp – decentralized app – can have what is referred to as a "converter" that utilizes an NFT's tokenId as an input before outputting a programmable image such as a weapon, zombies, or even animals such as cats. This "converter" is what CryptoKitties uses to project their NFTs as cats – in essence, those cats are simply smart contracts.

This standard includes certain functionalities that are built into its foundations, and they include:

- **balanceOf:** This functionality counts and displays every NFT assigned to a particular user.
- **ownerOf:** This indicates the current owner of an NFT.
- **transferFrom:** This functionality is responsible for the transfer of ownership of a particular NFT.
- **approval:** This occurs when an approved address for a certain NFT is changed or reaffirmed. It also occurs when a Transfer event is triggered.
- **approve:** This functionality sets or reaffirms the approved address for a particular NFT.

Essentially, the balanceOf function allows you to know your balance of tokens, the ownerOf function allows you to know the owner of a particular NFT, the transferFrom function allows you to be able to transfer ownership of a token, and the approve function allows you to approve transfer of ownership.

There are a couple of things you need to understand before I explain the key functions of an ERC-721 token. You see, when you purchase an ERC-20 token, your ownership right is usually written into the smart contracts. This smart contract also includes other data such as the number of tokens an address has after a deal and that is all. An ERC-20 smart contract does not have to concern itself with specific tokens because due to their fungibility, they are all the same. However, this is not the same for ERC-721 smart contracts. As I mentioned earlier, the value of one ERC-721 token differs from another ERC-721 token due to their non-fungible nature. Hence, simply adding an address and a balance of token will not be enough; the details of a token's unique ownership need to be added as well.

Now that you know that, an ERC-721 token deals with two major functions which are otherwise referred to as events. These events are "transfer" and "approval". Basically, the "transfer" event is activated every single time an ERC-721 token ownership moves from one person to another. The "transfer" event details three things: the account that sent the token, the account that received the token, and which token, in particular, was transferred. The second event – "approval" – is then activated whenever a user grants another user ownership of a particular token. The "approval" event details two things: the account that currently owns the token and the account that is being granted permission to own the token in the future. Additionally, the "approval" event also checks the token's identification tag so as to determine which particular token is being approved for ownership transfer.

The ERC-721 standard is supported by numerous projects including OpenSea, 0x Protocol, Trust Wallet, Decentraland, NonFungible.com, imToken, MyCollectibles.io, and Emoon to mention a few. To determine if an NFT fully follows the ERC-721 standard, simply copy the contact address of such an NFT and paste it on erc721validator.org. The website will let you know if the NFT is following the ERC-721 standard. This is useful as you do not want to be misled into purchasing an NFT that is not created according to the Ethereum standard.

ERC-1155

The ERC-1155 standard is also a unique type of tokenization standard. Its uniqueness arises from the fact that it introduces the idea of semi-fungibility to the NFT ecosystem. While identification tags in ERC-721 tokens represent single assets, ERC-1155's identification tag represents classes of assets. For instance, an identification tag might represent "cats", and a wallet can contain 10,000 cats. In this case, the balanceOf function would show the number of cats owned by the wallet, and the owner of the wallet can easily transfer any number of these cats by using the transferFrom function and inputting the ID of the cat.

With ERC-721, if a user wants to transfer 2,000 cats from their wallet, they will need to modify the state of the smart contract by utilizing the transferFrom function for 2,000 cats. However, with ERC-1155, the user only needs to use the transferFrom and input the number of cats they want to transfer – which is 2,000 – and perform such a transaction with a single transfer operation. Therefore, the ERC-1155 increases efficiency; however, it has one downside, which is the loss of traceability. That means that we would not be able to trace the history of the individual cats.

However, a lot of people have been utilizing ERC-1155 contracts because the efficiency of the smart contract trumps the loss of traceability.

Non-Ethereum Non-Fungible Token Standards

When it comes to the creation of Non-Fungible Tokens, Ethereum's network is currently the most developed as well as the most convenient platform available for that. However, there are other available networks that utilize non-Ethereum standards in creating an NFT. Let us take a look at some of those other networks.

dGoods

dGoods is an open-source and free standard that provides ownership and liquidity of digital goods and assets on blockchain. The platform provides cross-chain features that allow interoperability between two independent blockchains. This cross-chain feature enables different blockchains to communicate with each other since those blockchains are built in a standardized way. The platform currently facilitates this cross-chain feature between just two independent blockchains – Microsoft Azure and EOS – with plans to include other independent blockchains in the future. However, for now, NFTs created using the dGoods standard will be able to interact across EOS and Microsoft Azure's blockchains.

COSMOS

Cosmos is a decentralized network of independent parallel blockchains which is another way of saying that the platform is an ecosystem of multiple blockchains. The platform is an Internet of Blockchains, designed to communicate with each other in a decentralized way. Hence, just like dGoods, the blockchains under the Cosmos platform are able to interoperate with each other.

The platform is able to achieve this interoperability between platforms by utilizing a set of open-source tools such as Tendermint, The Cosmos SDK, and IBC. These open-source tools allow people to build custom, secure, scalable, and interoperable blockchain applications.

The platform's development team is currently developing an independent NFT module which is spliced into the Cosmos SDK. Therefore, NFTs created using the Cosmos Standard will be able to interoperate between multiple blockchains without restrictions.

FLOW

Flow is a relatively new blockchain that is built to power next-gen applications, games, and other digital assets. The team behind the creation of the CryptoKitties game created a new form of programming called Cadence on the Flow's blockchain. This programming converts NFTs to resources which users can store in their accounts. Cadence programming possesses important ownership rules that are strictly enforced by the platform. The rules behind the programming ensure that all NFTs created with the Cadence standard possess just one owner and cannot be accidentally or maliciously duplicated or lost. The essence of these rules is that they serve as protections that allow owners to be safe in the knowledge that their NFTs are safe and represented as a digital asset that possesses real value.

CHAPTER 3

Types of NFTs

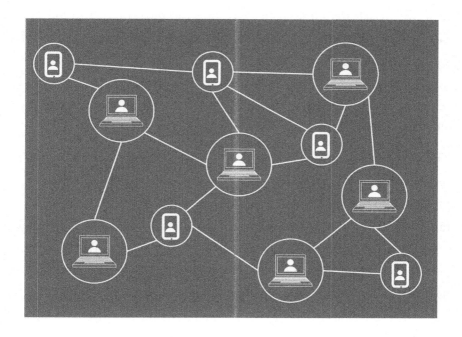

Now that you know what an NFT is, the history behind them, and the key characteristics that drive their functionality, it is time to take a look at how NFTs can be used.

The use cases of NFTs are currently focused on four major categories, namely art, gaming, collectibles, and virtual worlds. However, there are several other use cases of NFTs in several other categories such as fashion, sports, and real-world assets. These use cases determine the types of NFTs that you can create or purchase.

Let us briefly take a look at the current use cases of NFTs, and some other use cases that are steadily developing in the NFT space.

NFT Use Cases

Collectibles

In terms of sales volume, collectibles are the most popular applications of NFTs. Cryptopunks, which launched in June 2017, is one of the first collectible NFTs which sold for tens of thousands of dollars. Likewise, the launch of CryptoKitties in November 2017 is an example of the usage of NFTs as a collectible – with the sales of the virtual cats generating an all-time volume of over $38 million.

The collectible category of NFTs continues to develop and expand as the technology behind NFTs is being leveraged to create tokenized versions of celebrities and star athletes for fans to collect. For instance, Sorare – a fantasy soccer game – allows players to collect "limited-edition digital collectibles" of their favorite athletes from over 100 football clubs. Similarly, in collaboration with the NBA, Dapper Laps launched NBA Top-Shot which is a token-powered platform that allows fans to purchase and own tokenized pieces of action that happen on the basketball court. NFTs collectibles are not just restricted to sports as it includes other traditional collector items such as coins, trading cards, and stamps.

Collecting is the heart of the NFT industry; therefore, collecting NFTs collectibles allows a collector to either keep them for ownership or sell them as digital assets in secondary marketplaces for a profit.

Gaming

The gaming market is a perfect target for NFTs since gamers are already familiar with the concept of virtual worlds and in-game currencies. Hence, it is only logical that one of the most popular use cases for NFTs would be in the gaming industry. Within the gaming industry, NFTs allow the tokenization of in-game items such as skins, pets, and any other thing you purchase in the game. These tokenized in-game items can then be easily sold on secondary marketplaces or transferred/exchanged with peer-to-peer trading. If you are a gamer, you will know that this is quite unlike traditional games which do not allow the sale or transfer of in-game items such as rare weapons. While you can purchase in-game items for use in traditional games; the moment you are done playing the game, the item becomes useless to you. However, with NFTs, you can easily sell such game items on any NFT marketplace when you are done playing the game. This way, you can recoup your money and even make a decent profit if the item is in high demand.

The usage of NFTs in the gaming industry also makes the gaming experience more tangible and rewarding as it allows players to have true ownership over their digital assets. NFTs have also succeeded in creating a new economy for gamers which provides them the opportunity to earn money by building and developing their in-game assets. For instance, Gods Unchained is a digital collectible card game that issues cards as NFTs which players can own and trade with the same level of ownership as physical cards.

In order for games to be successful, they need to be fun and enjoyable; however, another crucial feature that plays a significant role in the mass adoption of NFT games is the Play2Earn feature of some of the games.

The fact that you can earn something while playing a game is a very attractive feature for many people, especially in developing countries, where playing the Axie Infinity game can earn you as much as a salary!

Simply put, NFTs provide you with ownership records for in-game items, power in-game economies, and provide a host of other benefits to players.

Art

The biggest challenge most digital artists face is how to protect their digital creations against copyright infringement. However, the advent of NFTs provided a solution to that problem as NFTs provide authenticity, proof of ownership while eliminating concerns of fraud and counterfeiting. NFTs provide digital artists with a way to tokenize their art and sell them on various NFT platforms and marketplaces such as Markerplace, Rarible, and SuperRare. These platforms and marketplaces also allow artists to streamline their revenue by directly connecting them to consumers through blockchain-based payment and exchange solutions.

Virtual Worlds

The final major use case for NFTs is virtual worlds. Virtual reality platforms such as The Sandbox, Cryptovoxels, and Decentraland enables users to create, own, and monetize virtual lands as well as other in-game NFT items. Additionally, owning a piece of virtual land allows you to build virtual conferences, create virtual art galleries, develop virtual games amongst a host of other things. Therefore, as an investor in NFTs, you can own a piece of virtual land in the virtual world, develop such land and sell the land later on for a profit. Or you can purchase a piece of virtual land and rent it out to influencers or anyone in need of a virtual land; this way, you retain ownership of the land while earning rent on it!

Other Use Cases for NFT

Real-World Assets and Documentation

Just as you can tokenize in-game items and digital artworks, you can also tokenize documentation such as licenses, birth and death certificates, and qualifications or real-world assets such as property and shares. It is important to note that converting real-world assets into NFTs is still a work in progress as NFT development in this category is still at an early stage.

However, as NFTs and the crypto world in general continues to develop and expand the possibilities of tokenizing real-world assets and documentation continue to develop and expand as well. Do not be surprised if in a not-so-distant future you can purchase a tokenized deed to a piece of land located in another continent!

Domain Names

NFTs can also be used to create unique domain names which automatically makes the domain name a digital asset that can be sold on secondary NFT marketplaces. The creation of tokenized domain names is easy to create via Ethereum Name Service. Ethereum addresses are usually long chains of numbers such as 3x435532859343383226; however, with Ethereum Name Service, you can create unique and easy-to-remember addresses like theboss.eth. This means you can easily ask someone to send you cryptocurrencies to theboss.eth instead of 3x435532859343383226 – which is cooler if you ask me.

Just like traditional domain names, ENS names are valuable; however, the value of the domain name depends on its uniqueness, relevance, and length. Unlike traditional domain names you do not need a domain registry to facilitate the sale of your ENS domain name; instead, you can easily trade it on any NFT marketplace.

Additionally, you can use your ENS name to receive cryptocurrencies as well as other NFTs just as you can use it to store arbitrary information such as email addresses or Twitter handles.

Proof of Attendance Protocol

Some platforms have taken the use of NFTs further by utilizing them as proof of attendance protocols for certain physical as well as virtual events. This means that you can get an NFT as an attendance badge whenever you attend events that utilize them. Who would not want to attend an event that gives out tokenized attendance badges which are digital assets that can be bought and sold on secondary marketplaces? Therefore, certain events give out NFTs as a way to encourage people to attend the events.

POAP is one of such platforms that allows you to hand out attendance badges as NFTs during events and Decentraland provides something similar for its virtual events.

Events Tickets/Access Tokens

NFTs have also been generated as event tickets or access tokens that allow people to gain verified access to certain physical and virtual events. For instance, such access tokens are used for special HQ access in Decentraland while Kakao uses them to verify investors.

Music

A lot of musical artists usually have issues with the digital ownership of their music; however, such artists can now utilize platforms such as Mintbase and DaoRecords to sell their music as NFTs. This helps musical artists to solve their digital ownership issues while streamlining the process of connecting artists directly to their fans.

Funding and Sponsorship

Certain platforms are now issuing NFTs as proof that an individual funded or sponsored a project. One of such platforms is Based. Money which issued NFTs to individuals who committed $50,000 to the development of version 1.69 of the platform.

The aforementioned use cases of NFTs are just a few of the numerous applications of NFTs. The NFT space is still developing. The more it develops, the more its case uses will expand and develop as well.

CHAPTER 4

High-Value NFTs

I t's no secret that the NFT space has been awash with news of high-value NFTs, a couple of which have been sold for millions of dollars, and a host of others that have been sold for hundreds of thousands of dollars and tens of thousands of dollars. In fact, according to CoinTelegraph, over $300 million was realized in NFT sales between January and February 2021. This raises the question: what makes NFTs highly valuable?

Well, like a lot of things in the world, NFTs are valued based on extrinsic factors rather than intrinsic factors. These include factors like authenticity, scarcity, transferability, immutability, and utility. I will briefly discuss these factors below before we take a look at some of the most expensive NFTs that have ever been sold.

Factors That Affect the Value of an NFT

- **Authenticity:** In the physical world, physical collectibles undergo several authentication procedures; however, none of these authentication methods are completely foolproof. For instance, despite the high level of scrutiny that acclaimed art appraisers submit pieces of art to, there have been several cases of them being duped by high-level forgeries. However, when it comes to NFTs, their originality is guaranteed due to the fact that they are based on blockchains. As a result of this, they cannot be fraudulently duplicated. This means that purchasing any NFT is a guarantee of purchasing something completely authentic. Therefore, this authenticity feature is responsible for the high value placed on NFTs. Essentially, owning an NFT is just like owning the original version of Mona Lisa.

- **Scarcity:** NFTs also have a scarcity feature attached to them as most of them are either one-of-a-kind creations or available in limited numbers. For example, CryptoPunks released just 10,000 copies of Cryptopunks. Out of these 10,000 copies, just 24 of them are "apes", and out of those 24 apes, only one of them wears a fedora. The scarcity of these Cryptopunks greatly contributed to the high value placed on them.

- **Transferability:** Besides the aforementioned factors, the fact that NFTs can be resold to nearly everyone, anywhere in the world, contributes to the value attached to them. This is because the ease of transferability means that there is a large pool of potential buyers vying to purchase a limited amount of NFTs. This is where the law of demand and supply, coupled with the aforementioned factors comes in. Assuming you created a one-of-a-kind NFT, and its uniqueness catches the fancy of the NFT market, making it scarce can easily skyrocket the price as demand exceeds the supply of the NFT.

- **Immutability:** The code and metadata used to create an NFT cannot be changed, and this contributes to the permanence of any NFT. Therefore, an NFT created today will still be around and available with the same initial properties as long as the internet continues to exist.

- **Utility:** The fact that certain NFTs can serve functional purposes, be exchanged for physical assets, or be used to generate revenue also contributes to the high value placed on certain NFTs. For instance, owning a virtual land can lead to a generation of steady income due to rent. Depending on how large or how developed the virtual land is, you can rent it for several virtual events while maintaining ownership of the land itself. You can also decide to lease it to a developer to develop and use the land for a certain number of months or years before returning the land back to you. Or you can simply decide to flip the land and sell it for a handsome profit. Basically, you can use the virtual land to do everything you can do with a physical land and more. Hence, it is no surprise that people are paying high prices for such lands.

- **Sentimental value:** Another reason why certain NFTs have sold for high prices is due to the sentimental value buyers attach to such NFT pieces. The more sentimental a person feels about a piece of NFT, the more they are usually willing to pay it.

- **Intense bidding:** Most NFT pieces are sold via bidding. Hence, the more people want the piece that is on sale, the higher the bidding price. By putting an NFT piece up for sale via bidding, an NFT seller can take advantage of market forces to increase the price of the NFT. The more interest an NFT piece generates, the more people bid for the piece, and the more people bid for the piece, the higher the price of the NFT keeps going.

A combination of the factors discussed above is responsible for the high prices you see some NFTs being sold for. Let us now take a look at some of the most expensive NFTs that have ever been sold.

List of the Most Expensive NFTs

Everydays: The First 5,000 Days

Price: $69.3 million

On the 25th of February 2021, a digital collage of 5,000 JPEG pictures belonging to Mike Winkelmann aka Beeple was put up for auction by Christie's — a major auction house — as an NFT. The digital collage consisted of 5,000 pictures which were created one at a time for 5,000 days by Beeple. This means that the collage was a product of over 13 years, and this is one of the things that made the digital art unique.

The collage was minted as an NFT on the 16th of February 2021, before it was placed on auction on the 25th of February. The opening bid price was $100; however, its value quickly jumped to millions. The auction was closed on the 11th of March 2021, and was sold for a whopping $69, 346,250 million!

CryptoPunk #7804

Price: $7.6 million

Cryptopunks were developed by Matt Hall and John Watkinson before they were launched in June 2017. The initial 10,000 pieces of Cryptopunks were given away for free; however, Dylan Field purchased his CryptoPunk – CryptoPunk #7804 – in 2018. The Cryptopunk was the most unique of the initial 10,000 Cryptopunks released and was sold on March 11 for an impressive $7.6 million.

Axie Infinity Virtual Game "Genesis" Estate

Price: $1.5 million

On the 9th of February 2021, nine plots of virtual land located on the Axie Infinity was sold for a record-making amount of $1.5 million. The sale of this virtual estate made it the highest NFT sale in a virtual game and it was bought by an anonymous entity named "Flying Falcon". According to online sources, the virtual estate was purchased for an upcoming game mode that will be created within Axie Infinity. This game mode will allow players to purchase, build, and decorate properties, gather resources, and fight digital monsters called "Axies".

Hashmasks

Price: $16 million

The Hashmasks project was launched in January 2021, and it was created by 70-plus artists globally. Each "hashmask" had distinct features and the project was heavily inspired by the graffiti-esque movement started by Jean-Michel Basquiat in the 1980s. The masks were sold on the open market and generated $16 million with the most expensive Hashmask selling for $650,000.

Rick and Morty Artwork

Price: $1 million

January 21ˢᵗ saw Justin Roiland selling a collection of his original artwork tagged "The Best I Could Do" as an NFT on Nifty Gateway for over $1 million. The sale of that collection was one of the biggest sales handled on the platform to date.

NBA "Top Shots"

Price: $230 million

NBA's Top Shots is a trading card system that is blockchain-based. It features digital artwork and iconic highlights from the National Basketball Association (NBA) games. The project was created when the NBA teamed up with Dapper Labs in 2019 and since then it has generated over $230 million in sales — with a highlight of LeBron James selling for $208,000, making it the highest valued NFT sold by NBA to date.

Grimes's Artwork and Music Videos

Price: $6 million

A partner to Elon Musk, Grimes — a Canadian music artist — made over $6 million selling her music videos and artwork as NFTs on the 28ᵗʰ of

February 2021 via Nifty Gateway. Her highest-selling piece was a music video titled "Death of the Old" and was sold for $389,000.

Hairy

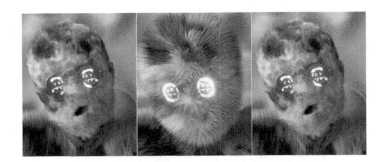

Price: $888,888

Hairy is an NFT project created by Steve Aoki in collaboration with Antoni Tudisco. The NFT depicts a purple and blue figure dancing to the tune of Aoki's music and was sold on Gateway for $888,888.88 in February 2021.

Nyan Cat

Price: $590,000

The Nyan Cat is a GIF that depicts a cat floating around space and after clocking 10 years on February 2021, its creator – Chris Torres – decided to auction it on a platform called Foundation. The cat meme ended up being sold for $590,000 and earned the record of being the most valuable crypto cat to date.

Crossroad

Price: $6.6 million

February 24th saw Beeple selling a digital art that features an anti-trump message as an NFT via Nifty Gateway for $6.66 million.

CryptoPunk #6965

Price: $1.54 million

This particular CryptoPunk is the third most expensive of all the Cryptopunks. It was sold on the 19th of February on Larva Labs.

The Complete MF Collection

Price: $777,777

This collection of Beeple's art is one of the most unusual NFT to be sold to date due to the fact that it contained a physical component as well as blockchain-based art. The collection, which was sold via Nifty Gateway, included several pieces of digital art alongside a physical artifact of the NFT which featured a numbers titanium backplate that was signed by Beeple himself.

Not Forgotten, But Gone

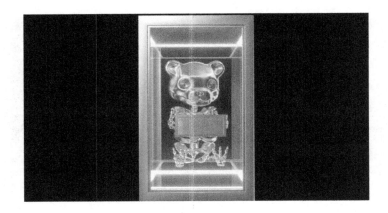

Price: $1 million

This NFT featured a 16-second clip of a spinning gold skeleton of a gummy bear and was sold on Nifty Gateway by Artist WhIsBe.

The EverLasting Beautiful

Price: $550,000

The EverLasting Beautiful was created by an 18-year-old artist from Las Vegas who goes by the name FEWOCiOUS. The artwork was originally created as physical artwork before it was minted as NFT and sold for a little over half a million dollars.

Forever Rose

Price: $1 million

The selling of this piece of NFT created by Kevin Abosch in February 2018, was a record-setting sale back when NFTs were still shrouded in mystery. It was dropped for sale on Valentine's Day in 2018 and was bought by a collective group of investors.

CHAPTER 5

NFT Market

Over the past three years, the NFT market has seen a rapid increase in value, with the market growing nearly tenfold between 2018 and 2020. The NFT market saw its market cap rise from $40.96 million to $141.56 in 2019 before skyrocketing to $338.04 in 2020. With its fast-rising market cap, the NFT market has begun to attract the attention of major investors, venture capitalists, celebrities, and several influential personalities as everyone is looking to get a piece of the NFT action.

Besides the fast-rising market cap of the NFT market, according to non-fungible.com – which tracks NFT data across 120-plus NFT market-places – all-time sales of NFTs now stands at 5.48 million with a generated revenue of $542,474,788! Dividing this total revenue by four years provides an average of $135,618,697 per year which means that the average yearly sales volume generated by the sales of NFT is around $135 million per year!

However, despite this impressive figure, I believe that the NFT market still has an enormous upside to capture, especially when you consider the fact the $135 million yearly sales volume is just a fraction of the $63.7 billion yearly volume generated by traditional art marketplaces. If I am to make a modest estimate of the yearly sales volume the NFT marketplace will generate within the next decade, it will be 10% of the traditional art marketplace's yearly volume. This means that within the next decade, NFT yearly sales can easily rise to $6.3 billion!

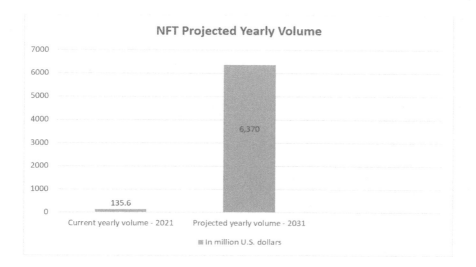

A yearly sales volume of $6.3 billion will mean that the current highest NFT sale – which is Beeple's 5000 Everydays – of $69 million does not amount to 0.01% of the projected yearly sales volume. Imagine what that means for future sales of NFTs. This means that NFT sales in the million zone will be a commonplace occurrence in the NFT space.

Buying and Selling of NFTs

The buying and selling occur on dedicated NFT marketplaces. Due to the various types of NFTs that are available such as art NFTs, trading card NFTs, and virtual land just to name a few, they are different dedicated platforms that primarily handle transactions for certain NFTs. Besides these primary NFT marketplaces, there are also several secondary markets on which you can resale any NFT you purchased from the primary market. Hence, you have to consider the type of NFT you want to transact before you choose a marketplace that suits your NFT transactions.

Let us take a look at a mix of both primary and secondary NFT marketplaces that are highly reputable.

OpenSea

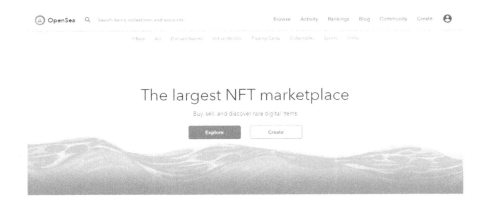

This platform was launched in 2018 – which makes it the first decentralized NFT marketplace in the NFT space. The platform refers to itself as the largest marketplace for digital goods and you can trade a host of unique digital items on the platform. These unique items can include anything from game items and domain names to collectibles and even digital representations of physical assets. Essentially, the platform is the NFT version of eBay as it hosts numerous assets systematically organized into hundreds of categories while allowing its users to visit other NFT marketplaces through its platform.

The platform has experienced an undeniable, significant growth level since its inception. It now has over 84,000 traders on its platform and has generated a trading volume of $261.89 million, which makes it the second marketplace with the highest number of users and trading volume.

When it comes to the decentralized NFT marketplace, there is no doubt that OpenSea is one of the biggest there is. With over 4 million assets, 135-plus dApps, and an estimated monthly trading volume of 4,000 ETH, the platform has been able to interest several big-name players such as

Gary Vaynerchuk, Chamath Palihapitiya, Logan Paul, and Mark Cuban to mention a few.

Rarible

This platform is Moscow-based and was created by Alex Salnikov and Alexei Falin before it was launched in early 2020. The platform is a dedicated marketplace for art assets; however, it allows users to trade various digital collectibles. Besides trading NFTs on the platform, users are also able to mint their own NFTs. In case you don't know, minting is the process of converting anything digital into an NFT. As a result of this, the platform has attracted tons of content creators who mint their music albums, movies, music, etc., into NFTs and sell them via the platform.

In addition to minting, content creators have the option to either release the full content of their NFT for the perusal of potential buyers or simply offer them a sneak peek of the content before releasing the full content when the NFT is purchased. However, after encountering a couple of scammers trying to sell fake projects, Rarible has created a verification process that helps it to minimize the risk of users dealing with fake projects.

Additionally, content creators on the platform can also set a certain percentage which they will receive anytime the NFT is resold – this allows them to receive royalties of their NFT creations for a lifetime. The platform also has its own dedicated token, which is named RARI and, in order to encourage activity on the platform, it distributes 75,000 RARI tokens weekly to traders on its platform. Furthermore, the platform keeps working toward developing itself into a completely autonomous platform driven by community governance. To achieve this, it is developing itself into a Decentralized Autonomous Organization (DAO) which will put its users in charge of all the decisions on the platform without external interference. This makes its RARI token crucial in achieving community governance.

So far, the platform has been able to attract over 37,000 traders and has successfully generated a trade volume of $79.84 million. The platform has also attracted a couple of big players, among which is Linsey Lohan who has a profile on the platform and, in one of the biggest sales on the platform, sold her NFT creation – Bitcoin Lightening – for just over $50,000.

Nifty Gateway

Nifty Gateway is a platform created by The Cock Foster Twins and launched in 2018 before it was acquired by the Winklevoss twins – Tyler and Cameron. The platform allows you to purchase digital items – which they refer to as Nifties – and it facilitates Nifty purchases for popular crypto-games and applications such as Gods Unchained and CryptoKitties.

The ease of purchasing NFTs on the platform is one of the things that makes it a favorite of the NFT space. Purchasing an NFT on the platform is as simple as visiting the marketplace via your browser, picking a nifty, entering your credit card information, and hitting purchase. You can then choose to either keep the NFT you purchased in your Nifty Gateway account, or you can decide to move it to a wallet.

While it is possible to create your own nifties for sale on the platform, you have to submit an application before you are allowed to do so. The platform also allows creators to set royalty rates on their creations; hence, whenever such a creation is resold, the creator receives the predetermined rate.

Currently, the platform has notable artists and brands such as Michael Kagan, Chris Cyborg, and Lyle Owerko and is backed by Gemini whose world-leading security technology is used to keep any Nifty you purchase and keep on the platform safe.

SuperRare

SuperRare

Editorial   Discover   Market   Activity   Sign In

Collect SuperRare
Digital Artworks

START COLLECTING   LEARN MORE

SuperRare is an NFT marketplace that was launched in 2017. The platform is dedicated to digital art, and it enables artists to convert their art into NFTs and sell it on the platform.

As a buyer, all you need to do is select any of the artwork that catches your fancy, then you can either purchase the artwork at the asking price or make an offer by placing a bid. Once you have successfully purchased the artwork, you can either decide to keep it in your collection or resell it on the secondary market to other collectors. You can display your art collection on the platform, or you can display them in any digital gallery, virtual reality gallery, or anywhere else you like.

As an artist trying to sell your digital art, you have to first authenticate your work, which involves you signing your work digitally and generating a tokenized certificate proving your ownership of the art. After your work has been authenticated, you can then set a fixed price for your art or allow collectors to place bids on your art. However, the platform is still in early access, therefore, they are only onboarding a small number of hand-picked artists. Regardless of this, you can still complete a form that might get you an invitation to display your art in the near future.

The platform has a dedicated user base with some collectors collecting as high as 510 artworks while some top artists on the platform have earned up to half a million dollars. Currently, the platform has 3,558 art owners, 20,644 art assets, and a total trade volume of $31.75 million.

Terra Virtua

Terra Virtua is an immersive collectible cross-platform that was launched in 2019. The platform provides a seamless cross-platform ecosystem that cuts across augmented reality and virtual reality which allows users to share, trade, and interact with digital collectibles in a social, engaging, immersive way.

You can collect unique art collectibles from various creators and display them in your personal art gallery. Likewise, you can use your digital collectibles as real game items on the platform by utilizing the immersive capabilities provided by the platform. Put simply, Terra Virtua allows you to view and interact with your digital assets online, via their mobile app, and in a 3D environment using Augmented Reality and Virtual Reality.

The platform's collaboration with several industry leaders such as Paramount Pictures, Legendary, Unity, Big Immersive, Varrow Interactive, and Unreal Engine allows it to provide unique social, gaming, and creative experiences. Essentially, Terra Virtua provides an Augmented Reality and Virtual Reality digital collectibles experience which can be enjoyed via PC or mobile. The platform also provides a personalized Fancave and Terra Dome that allows users to view and interact with their collectibles.

Ultimately, Terra Virtua is a platform that allows you to trade and share digital collectibles from top brands.

The platform also has its own dedicated token called Kolect which currently sells for $0.7607 and has a circulating supply of 219,201,959 Kolect tokens with a $167.14 million market cap.

NBA Top Shot

NBA Top Shot is a Non-Fungible marketplace with the backing of the National Basketball Association (NBA). This platform was launched in 2020 as a marketplace where anyone can purchase and sell pieces of NBA action. Basically, Top Shot converts action-filled highlights into digital collectibles called a moment. By converting an action-filled highlight into an NFT, the buyer or owner of the NFT is given ownership over that particular moment.

Since its launch, the platform has attracted over 271,000 traders and has generated an all-time trade volume of $449.37 million – effectively making it the number one marketplace with the highest number of users and trading volume. However, the platform is solely dedicated to the sales of

NBA moments which initial buyers can resell on any secondary market-place.

Ultimately, the NBA Top Shot platform is a highly competitive NFT marketplace where users can trade NBA moments and virtual cards with the aim of gaining exponential profits. One such case is the sale of the Cosmic edition Series 1 – which features LeBron James dunking – which sold for $208,000.

Axie Infinity

Axie Infinity is a blockchain-based game that is similar to the Cryp-toKitties breeding game. The game allows players to collect fantasy crea-tures known as Axies. These creatures are unique NFTs that have certain characteristics which make them valuable in the game. Just like Cryp-toKitties cat, Axies can be bred with other Axies to produce other unique Axies that possess unique and scarce characteristics. Since Axies are used in the game to participate in battle tournaments – which sees the winner of such tournaments earning crypto prizes – this makes them valuable as players are constantly seeking out Axies with scarce qualities that perform well in battle and win. Winning a battle tournament in the game requires players to strategically purchase the NFT game assets to augment their gaming experience and as a result of this, such NFTs are in high demand on the platform.

Besides battle tournaments, players can own lands and use such land to farm resources, go for dungeon raids, and gain AXS tokens which can be used for upgrades in the game. While Axie Infinity is a blockchain-based game, players can sell their cultivated lands and strengthened Axies in the Axie Infinity NFT marketplace whenever they like. The ability of players to sell their in-game items provides Axie Infinity users with the element of true digital item ownership which is not available in traditional games.

Since its launch in 2020, Axie Infinity has gone on to attract 27,169 users and has generated an all-time trade volume of $21.61 million in its in-house marketplace. Its users have also made massive profits from their transactions on the platform. For instance, an Axie was sold for $533,916 – which makes it the most expensive Axie ever sold on the platform to date. Besides that, 15 plots of Axie Land were sold for 888.25 ETH with its dollar equivalent being $1.5 million.

Foundation

Foundation is a community-led digital collectibles platform that has seen impressive growth since it launched in 2020. When the platform first launched it invited 50 artists who were then each given two invites to share with subsequent new members on the platform.

Providing a home for artists while pushing the platform forward is one of the core objectives of Foundation. Hence, when it first launched, it invited 50 artists who were then each given two invites to share with subsequent new members on the platform. The community team on the platform is responsible for selecting curating artworks that are featured on the platform's homepage, its newsletters as well as its social media channels. The platform keeps experimenting with new creative approaches while providing a platform that provides a spotlight to marginalized artists.

Since it launched in 2020, the platform has been able to attract 4,292 users and generate a total volume of $11.37 million in digital collectible sales. Several noteworthy individual artists and groups have gravitated to the platform to sell their art as digital collectibles. For instance, electronic music composer Richard James aka Aphex Twin minted an audiovisual NFT on the platform – which was quickly bought for $127,000. Similarly, another noteworthy sale was made on the platform when Pussy Riot – a Russian punk rock group – minted a video of theirs as an NFT which was sold for $175,000.

AtomicMarket

AtomicMarket is a unique marketplace for NFTs that is integrated into the AtomicAssets hub. This NFT market allows its users to list NFTs for sale or put them up for auction. However, the uniqueness of this NFT market lies in the fact that as a seller you get to keep ownership of the NFT until someone purchases it. Let me explain better.

When listing NFTs for sale on other NFT marketplaces, a seller has to put the NFT itself up for sale on those platforms. However, in the case of AtomicMarket, when you put up an NFT for sale, you do not have to immediately send it over to your account on the platform. Instead, a trade offer feature is used to list your NFT for sale on the platform and you only transfer the NFT to the platform when someone accepts your offer and purchases the asset. This means that you can list that particular NFT on other platforms or even continue to use it in dApps, pending for when someone accepts your trade offer on AtomicMarket.

However, this feature is only available for listings. For auctions, you need to transfer the NFT to your AtomicMarket account because once the auction starts you are not able to cancel it anymore.

In addition to this, the platform charges low base fees and allows customizable dApp fees. The base fee for any sale or auction is 2% and, as a seller, you can specify a certain percentage to be paid to you as a royalty whenever your NFT is resold.

Since the platform launched in the early part of 2021, it has attracted 35,953 traders to its marketplace and has generated $8.64 as total trade volume.

Sorare

Sorare is a platform where users create and trade football-related NFTs. The platform operates on Ethereum's blockchain – which it uses to secure ownership of the NFT player cards as well as their distribution.

Just as NBA Top Shot focuses on basketball-related NFTs, Sorare focuses on facilitating transactions of digital player cards – which are licensed as digital collectibles. On the 15th of March 2021, a one-of-a-kind Cristiano Ronaldo NFT player card sold for $290,000 on the platform thereby making it the world's most expensive soccer trading card.

Ultimately, Sorare is the platform to consider if you are interested in collecting player cards as more than 120 football clubs have launched their digital cards on the platform. Since launching in 2019, Sorare has attracted 14,536 and has generated a total trade volume of $46.79 million.

Other NFT Marketplaces

- SimpleMarket
- Enjin
- MarkerPlace
- Known Origin
- Cargo
- Mintbase
- Blockparty
- Collectible.io
- Waxplorer
- Myth.Market
- CryptoSlam
- Waxstash
- CryptoCats
- Aavegotchi

- The Sandbox
- BakerySwap
- Solible
- GhostMarket

The increase in demand for NFTs over the years has led to the launch of several NFT marketplaces. There are certainly a lot of promising NFT marketplaces you can buy and sell NFTs on; however, when looking to buy or sell NFTs, it is important to consider the trading volume as well as the number of a marketplace. The higher the trading volume and number of users, the more liquidity such a marketplace has to offer. The table below lists out some NFT marketplaces with their trading volume as well as number of users. You can use the list to determine the most liquid marketplace to conduct your NFT transactions.

Marketplace	Users	Trade Volume
NBA Top Shot	271,170	$449.37 million
OpenSea	84,645	$261.89 million
CryptoPunks	2,444	$179.84 million
Rarible	37,809	$79.84 million
Sorare	14,536	$46.79 million
Axie Infinity	27,169	$21.61 million
Aavegotchi	2,600	$13.49 million
Foundation	4,292	$11.37 million
AtomicMarket	39,953	$8.64 million
CryptoCats	127	$2.45 million
Myth.Market	9,163	$596.55 thousand
Waxplorer	7,947	$359.91 thousand
Collectibles.io	1,789	$63.35 thousand
CryptoSlam	341	$40.91 thousand
Waxstash	499	$9.02 thousand

CHAPTER 6

How to Easily Create and Sell an NFT

The creation of NFTs is a relatively straightforward process that you can execute without any prior knowledge about the crypto industry. Before you mint your NFT, you have to first consider which of the blockchains you want to issue it on. There are several blockchains you can issue your NFT on. They include:

- Tron
- Tezos
- WAX
- Polkadot
- EOS
- Flow
- Binance Smart Chain
- Cosmos
- And, of course, Ethereum

Before selecting which blockchain you want to issue your NFT on, you need to keep in mind that each blockchain has its own NFT token standard, compatible wallet services, and dedicated marketplaces. For example, if you issue your NFT on Flow, you will only be able to sell such an NFT on marketplaces that support Flow's digital assets. That is to say that you will not be able to sell it on OpenSea which is based on Ethereum's blockchain.

Therefore, before you select which blockchain to issue your NFT on, you need to consider the following factors:

- **Pool of users:** You need to consider which blockchain commands the greatest number of NFT buyers and sellers. You do not want to select a blockchain that is not popular with NFT buyers and sellers; you want to create your NFT on a blockchain that has a large pool of existing users.
- **Secondary markets:** Secondly, you want to use a blockchain that is connected to the largest amount of NFT marketplaces. This is because there is no point issuing your NFT on a blockchain that only supports a few marketplaces as this will hurt your chances

of easily selling your NFT. The more marketplaces that are connected to a blockchain, the higher chance of finding a buyer for
your NFT.

- **Additional apps and services:** You also need to use a blockchain that supports a large pool of additional services you will
  need to create your NFT. This includes wallets that you will use
  to receive payments as well as make payments and exchanges that
  you will use to fund your wallet.
- **Minting fees:** Finally, you need to take minting fees into consideration. While minting fees are mostly determined by the platform you utilize in minting your NFT, some blockchains charge
  lower fees than others.

As I mentioned earlier in the book, Ethereum possesses the largest NFT
ecosystem – it has the largest pool of users, it is connected to several
marketplaces (with some primary marketplaces even based on the platform), and there are a host of wallets and exchanges that support the
blockchain. Hence, for the purpose of this book, I will be explaining how
you can create your NFTs on platforms that are based on or supported
by Ethereum's blockchain. Now let us take a look at how you can create
your own NFT and sell it.

Creating Your NFT

Step 1: Get Your File Ready

The first step to creating your NFT is to prepare the media you want to
mint ready. You can mint any type of media file, including:

- Image files such as PNG, JPEG, GIF, BMP, TIFF, etc.
- Music files such as MP3, AAC, DTS, WMA, AIFF, FLAC, OGG,
  WAV, DOLBY DIGITAL, etc.

- 3D files such as GLB, STL, AMF, STEP, DAE, FBX, etc.
- Text files such as TXT, DOC and DOCX, RTF, PDF, etc.
- Video file formats such as MOV, AVI, AVCHD, MPEG-1, MPEG-2, MPEG-4, MKV, DivX, etc.

Regardless of whichever file you want mint, you need to get the traditional file ready by making all the edits you need to do. Once you start the minting process, you cannot change the content of the file. Once, you have the traditional file ready, you can proceed to the next step.

Step 2: Get Your Wallet Ready

After getting your traditional file ready, the next step is to get an Ethereum wallet that supports ERC-721 – which is the Ethereum-based NFT token standard I explained in chapter 2. An Ethereum wallet helps you to manage your ETH assets and also helps you interact with decentralized applications built on Ethereum via the wallet.

Ethereum wallets that support storage of ERC-721 tokens or NFTs include:

- Metamask
- Coinbase Wallet
- Trust Wallet
- Gemini
- imToken
- Blockchain Wallet
- Status

When you decide on which wallet you prefer to use, you then need to fund the wallet with about $50 to $100. Some of the wallets – such as Coinbase Wallet – allow you to purchase Ether (ETH) directly in the wallet with a debit/credit card, while some do not. For wallets that do not support direct purchase, you can use exchanges that support the purchasing of Ether – which is Ethereum's cryptocurrency and also what you will use for your NFT transactions.

Exchanges that support the purchase of Ether include:

- Coinbase
- Huobi
- Binance
- Kraken

After purchasing your ETH via an exchange, the next step is to move the ETH into your wallet. This is because you will be required to connect your wallet to the platform you want to use for the creation of your NFT – and the wallet has to contain a certain amount of ETH which you will use for certain expenses such as "gas fees". Additionally, your wallet will be used to securely store any NFT you create.

Once you have successfully created a wallet and funded it, you can proceed to the next step.

Step 3: Upload Your File

The next step involves selecting an NFT-centric platform that is based on Ethereum's blockchain and allows you to connect your wallet as well as upload your file for conversion into an NFT.

Platforms that allow you to do this include:

- Mintable
- OpenSea
- Rarible
- Makersplace

- infiNFT
- Mintbase
- Cargo
- Async Art
- SuperRare

Most of these platforms – such as OpenSea, Rarible, Mintable, Cargo, etc. – allow a permissionless minting of your NFTs regardless of the type of file. However, some platforms – especially those in the digital art arena – are exclusive membership-only NFT minting platforms that require you to apply and be accepted before you can mint via the platform. This type of platform includes Async Art, Makersplace, and SuperRare, to mention a few.

Let me walk you through the process of creating your NFT on one or two NFT minting platforms.

Minting Your NFT via OpenSea

- **Step 1:** Access the platform by typing "opensea.io" into your browser.
- **Step 2:** Find and select the "Create" button on the platform.
- **Step 3:** Link your wallet to the platform. Alternatively, you can choose to create an OpenSea wallet that is powered by Fortmatic. However, if you already have a wallet, simply link that wallet to OpenSea. OpenSea supports the following wallets:
  - WalletConnect
  - Trust Wallet
  - Opera Touch
  - Metamask
  - Coinbase Wallet

- Arkane
- Authereum
- Torus
- WalletLink
- Fortmatic

- **Step 4:** After linking a wallet to the platform, you will be prompted to "create your collection". This is essentially where the NFTs you will be creating subsequently will be displayed. You can include a logo for the collection; this is strictly required. Next, you need to name your collection; this is also strictly required. After this, you can add a description that describes what the collection is all about; this is not required.

- **Step 5:** After successfully creating your collection, find and select the "Add New Item" button. This will take you to the page where you will be able to upload the file you want to mint. OpenSea supports the minting of images, video, audio, or 3D models as NFTs. After uploading your file, you need to add a name that will be the NFT's name. Next, you can choose to add a description to the NFT and an external link that links to a webpage that has more details about the NFT, although neither is strictly required. Next, you can also choose to add certain properties, levels, and stats, as well as certain unlockable content for your NFT. Due to the fact that you do not need to pay any "gas fee" for the minting process, the number of copies you can mint is restricted to just one. Finally, when you are satisfied, you can click on the "Create" button.

Congratulations! You have successfully minted your first NFT. You can either view the NFT in your collection or decide to sell it.

Minting Your NFT via Rarible

- **Step 1:** Access the platform by typing "rarible.com" into your browser.

- **Step 2:** Find and select the "Create" button on the platform. You will be directed to a webpage where you get to select if you are creating single or multiple collectibles. Select "Single" if you want your collectible to be one of a kind. Select "Multiple" if you want to sell your collectible multiple times.

- **Step 3:** If you selected "Single" you will be directed to a webpage where you can upload the file you want to convert into an NFT. You can choose to instantly place your NFT on the market as soon as it is created or not. You can also choose to create a collection under which your NFT will be displayed, or you can choose to simply create the NFT without creating a collection. Next, add the name and description of the NFT you are creating; the description is optional. Next, input your royalty percentage; this stipulates the percentage you will receive every time your NFT is resold. Then you can add properties that make the NFT unique as well as certain content that will be unlocked after someone successfully purchases your NFT; the properties, as well as unlockable content, are optional. If you choose "multiple", the only difference is that you will be required to input the number of copies you want to mint.

- **Step 4:** Connect your wallet to the platform. Rarible supports the following wallets:

  - WalletConnect
  - Coinbase Wallet
  - Torus
  - Fortmatic

- **Step 5:** After linking a wallet to the platform, you will be able to create your NFT for a certain "gas fee". After paying the gas fee, you will then be able to create a contract for the sale of the NFT before signing the sell order using your wallet.

Congratulations! You have successfully minted your first NFT. You can either view the NFT in your collection or decide to sell it.

Selling Your NFTs

After creating your NFT, it will show up in your wallet. The next step is to then consider which NFT marketplace you want to sell your NFT on. The easiest platform to sell all kinds of NFTs on is OpenSea. Not only is it easy to list your NFT for sale on there, but the platform is also the largest secondary NFT marketplace with the largest pool of users. Hence, listing your NFT on this platform will put your NFT in front of hundreds of thousands of eyes.

To sell your NFT via OpenSea, all you have to do is connect the wallet that holds your NFT to the platform. This will enable your NFT to show up on your account with the platform on which you can list it for sale. Additionally, listing your NFT for sale on OpenSea provides you with the ability to program in a certain percentage as royalty to be received on resales of your NFT. This allows you to earn a commission every time the NFT is sold to other people – thereby providing you with lifelong passive income.

However, you should keep in mind that while you can freely mint your NFT on OpenSea without paying any gas fee; listing them requires you to pay a certain fee. Hence, you need to take this into consideration when listing your NFT for sale. You also need to make certain that you have enough Ether in your wallet to cover the listing fee.

CHAPTER 7

Picking Profitable NFTs to Invest In

Now, you are getting to the part where you learn how to make money via NFTs! The previous chapters were written with the intention to introduce you to the world of NFTs. Now that you know how NFTs work, the different types of NFTs, how to mint your very own NFT, and where you can buy from other creators and re-sell them, it is time to learn how you can successfully select NFTs that will generate a massive return on investment for you.

Although the NFT market is relatively young compared to other markets, there is a lot of profit to be made from it. For instance, an acquaintance of mine made an ROI of 7,400% on a single piece of NFT when he resold "Temporal Shark Dream" – an NFT art he acquired from a creator named Max Osiris. This same acquaintance has made an overall ROI of 2,005% across 19 resales of several NFT he bought on the cheap. His NFT sales exploits have made him one of the top three collectors on SuperRare in terms of resales.

While you might not make an ROI of 7,400% on your first NFT investment, I can teach you the secret principles that underlie the process of profitably selecting NFTs that can generate at least an ROI of 100%. You should keep in mind that these secrets I am about to share with you are not hard and fast rules that guarantee you a 100% ROI on your NFT investments; rather, they are like guidelines that can help you systematically invest in NFTs that have the potential to produce a 100% ROI on your investment. As a matter of fact, these principles are what helped me generate a respectable 1,050% ROI across my NFT investments within a space of two years. If I can generate such ROI with these principles, I am positive that you can utilize them profitably as well.

So, what are these secret principles that can help you profit on your NFT investments? Let us take a look at them.

Secret Principles Behind Selecting Profitable NFTs

Creator's Reputation

The first thing to consider before investing in any piece of NFT is the reputation of the collectible's creator. In the traditional world of art, before a piece of art is purchased, the reputation of the artist that created the art is usually considered. The more popular and enigmatic an artist is, the more valuable their art is considered to be. This phenomenon also occurs in the NFT space. In fact, this phenomenon was one of the contributing factors that made Beeple's NFT art sell for as high as $69 million.

Hence, when considering an NFT investment – especially in the NFT arts – you want to make sure that the NFT you are considering is one created by a creator with a considerable reputation. Investing in such an NFT will make it easier for you to resell it at a much higher price than you initially bought it for.

However, the NFT space is not just restricted to digital art. There are other niches of NFTs you can choose to invest in – such as the game items, players cards amongst others. In the event where you are considering purchasing such NFTs, the next set of principles will help you select profitable ones to invest in.

Scarcity

When it comes to investing in NFTs with the expectation of massive ROIs, scarcity is an important factor to consider. In the traditional world, scarcity tends to lead to an increase in demand for the scarce item. The same holds true in the NFT space as the scarcer an item is, the more value it is presumed to have. For instance, an NBA Top Shot moment of LeBron James making a dunk sold for over $200,000 because that was the only copy available. Its scarcity made other buyers on the platform bid its price higher until it was eventually sold for $208,000. Although the collector who bought the piece is yet to list it for sale, you can imagine how much it would be sold for when it eventually gets listed for sale in a secondary market. Similarly, a player card featuring Cristiano Ronaldo ended up selling for $290,000 due to its one-of-a-kind nature. Imagine how much the card will sell for in the next two to three years when the NFT market further develops.

Hence, when seeking out NFTs to invest in, it is usually more profitable to invest in NFTs that are one of a kind as opposed to NFTs that have several other copies. People will pay more for an item that is one of a kind; however, when an NFT has multiple copies, people tend to pay less because of a lack of uniqueness.

Volume of Transactional Activity

You need to pay attention to the amount of volume of transactional activity related to any NFT project you want to invest in. The higher the volume of transactional activity surrounding an NFT project, the higher the liquidity. High liquidity helps you to easily get a buyer for your NFT whenever you decide to sell it. You do not want to invest in an NFT project that has low volume as this will make it difficult for you to sell in the future.

Specialized Knowledge

There is a saying in the world of investment – especially on Wall Street – and it goes like this: "invest in what you know about". This saying cannot be truer when it comes to investing in NFTs. In chapter three, I mentioned different industries that NFTs are revolutionizing; industries such as gaming, art, virtual land, and music to name a few. When you are planning on investing in an NFT, it is wise to consider NFTs that deal with what you know about. For instance, if you are an avid gamer, your primary investment focus should be on NFTs that are game-related. Likewise, if you are an art connoisseur, your primary investment focus should be on art-related NFTs.

Focusing on and investing in what you are knowledgeable about will help you spot valuable opportunities that other people might not be able to identify until it is too late. For instance, if you are a keen follower of football games, you can easily identify players that have the potential to become great players in the future. By identifying such players, you can decide to buy their player card and hold till they start gaining recognition for their ability in football. Furthermore, due to the fact that you will be purchasing their player card when they are still relatively unknown, such cards will not cost you a lot as some player cards sell for as low as $20 dollars. Now, imagine you purchased Ronaldo's player card when he was first signed by Manchester United for $50. Imagine what such a card will be worth today after he has successfully won 5 Ballon d'Ors.

Utility

The utility an NFT provides can also help you determine if it is going to be a good investment that yields a high ROI or not. The utility of an NFT depends on how it can be used and one of the major categories of NFT that provides high-utility NFTs is the game category. Game-related NFTs have a high utility value, especially if such game assets can be used in a different application. For instance, in 2019, a rare and powerful Crypto Space Commander Battleship was sold for a little over $45,000. Now, imagine if this same game asset were usable in a different game or dApp, the value would have been even much higher.

Hence, the more utility an NFT is able to provide, the higher the value it would command in the marketplace. When looking to invest in NFTs, keep an eye out for those that provide more utility than others as such NFTs have the potential to generate an impressive amount of ROI.

Ownership History

An NFT's ownership history is also a good metric you can utilize in identifying NFTs that can generate a respectable ROI for you. Imagine purchasing an NFT that was previously owned by an influential individual. Reselling such NFT can generate a substantial ROI because people love to own things that were previously owned by influential people. The more influential or popular an NFT's previous owner is, the higher the price you can resell such NFT for – thereby generating a respectable ROI.

While the NFT space is highly speculative in nature, the aforementioned principles are the secrets behind selecting highly profitable NFTs for investment. As the NFT ecosystem becomes more mature, these principles might evolve into a more standardized and systematic approach to selecting profitable NFTs that can generate substantial ROIs for you. In addition to these secret principles, I will be sharing a couple of NFT projects I am looking forward to investing in before the end of 2021.

Top NFT Projects I Am Investing in for 2021

One of the most important rules in the world of investment is to always do your own research. Hence, the following list of projects is not a recommendation or investment advice. This list is just an indication of certain NFT projects I am looking forward to investing in before 2021 runs out.

Virtual Land: One of the most interesting projects I am looking to invest in is virtual land on dApps like Decentraland. Decentraland is a decentralized virtual universe that allows its users to engage in the governance process of the universe. Before you can purchase an asset on the platform, you need to first set up a unique avatar which is a representation of your identity in the universe.

Once you have gained entrance into the platform, you can then direct your avatar to purchase Lands, build virtual cities, and use those assets however you see fit. In case you have not realized the reason why I am considering this as a top investment, you only need to reread the fifth principle behind selecting profitable NFTs – which is utility. If there is a particular NFT asset that provides a high level of utility, it is virtual lands. This is because you can use virtual land the same way you can use land in the real world. You can develop it, lease it out, use it to host virtual events amongst a host of other functionalities.

Just imagine this: you buy a virtual land and you rent it out to a virtual developer who pays you a certain amount of crypto-tokens on a weekly, monthly, or quarterly basis. The end result is that you own an asset that is generating passive revenue for you while you still retain ownership. With this model, the virtual land could possibly generate an ROI of more than 1,000% within the space of a year!

In case you didn't know, there is a high demand for virtual land especially by influencers, brands, and even celebrities that are looking to hold virtual events due to the restrictions caused by the Coronavirus pandemic.

Domain names: In the real world, a lot of people have made impressive ROIs on their domain name investments; hence, there is no reason why the same cannot be done in the NFT space. By utilizing decentralized naming and certificate authorities such as Handshake Domains or even Ethereum Naming Service, you can create unique domain names which you can then resell with a wide margin or profits. The more unique the domain name is, the more value it holds.

Ultimately, domain names are easy NFT assets you can create to generate a substantial amount of ROI.

Player cards and NBA Top Shot Moments: I am an avid football and basketball lover, and I have a good sense of the game; hence, I am able to spot premium opportunities in the space. Therefore, I am looking to collect several sport-related collectibles that have the potential to provide a high ROI. However, this is a long-term play as it takes a while before sport-related collectibles become very valuable – especially when you are looking to purchase collectibles of players that are not in the limelight yet. Who knows I might be lucky to collect the cards of the next Kobe Bryant or Lebron James and the next Messi or Ronaldo – and so might you!

CONCLUSION

Congratulations on making it to the end of this book!

While it might seem a little bit technical in nature, I have tried to make the subject as simple as possible so that you can understand what NFTs are about as well as the opportunities they possess, even if you had no previous knowledge of the cryptoverse.

NFTs have greatly revolutionized as well as provided a new meaning to the ownership of digital properties, and this has greatly contributed to their increasing level of value. If there is one thing I hope you can take away from reading this book, it is the fact that there are countless and multifarious opportunities in the NFT space. With the recent attention the industry has been generating – especially with the record-breaking prices of some NFT sales – there is not one iota of doubt in my mind that the industry will keep expanding. Furthermore, as more applications and use cases are discovered, the NFT phenomenon will continue to permeate a lot of industry – and this, in turn, will contribute to an increase in the value of the industry.

Right now, the knowledge of the potential and intrinsic value that NFTs can provide continues to spread, and this is leading to an increasing number of investors, major brands, and venture capitalists taking notice of the industry and getting involved in it. A lot of celebrities and other influential personalities are also racing to release their own flagship NFTs and this, in turn, is helping the industry gain more traction and more acceptability within the general populace.

As I mentioned earlier in the book, the NFT industry has the potential to hit a $6.3 billion market cap within the next decade. Hence, you can expect increasing growth and trading volume within the NFT industry as more and more NFTs continue to hit mainstream media. Additionally, due to the nascent nature of the industry, the opportunities available are plentiful, and an increasing number of people are busy grabbing their share. I hope you are able to grab yours as well!

Made in the USA
Middletown, DE
26 August 2022

72315856R00176

An Interpretation of Religion

By the same author

PROBLEMS OF RELIGIOUS PLURALISM
FAITH AND KNOWLEDGE
EVIL AND THE GOD OF LOVE
ARGUMENTS FOR THE EXISTENCE OF GOD
GOD AND THE UNIVERSE OF FAITHS
DEATH AND ETERNAL LIFE
GOD HAS MANY NAMES
FAITH AND THE PHILOSOPHERS (*editor*)
THE MANY-FACED ARGUMENT (*editor with A. C. McGill*)
CHRISTIANITY AT THE CENTRE
PHILOSOPHY OF RELIGION
THE SECOND CHRISTIANITY
WHY BELIEVE IN GOD? (*with Michael Goulder*)
THE EXISTENCE OF GOD (*editor*)
CLASSICAL AND CONTEMPORARY READINGS IN THE PHILOSOPHY OF
   RELIGION (*editor*)
TRUTH AND DIALOGUE (*editor*)
THE MYTH OF GOD INCARNATE (*editor*)
CHRISTIANITY AND OTHER RELIGIONS (*editor with Brian Hebblethwaite*)
THREE FAITHS – ONE GOD (*editor with Edmund S. Meltzer*)
GANDHI'S ELUSIVE LEGACY (*editor with Lamont C. Hempel*)
THE EXPERIENCE OF RELIGIOUS DIVERSITY (*editor with Hasan Askari*)
THE MYTH OF CHRISTIAN UNIQUENESS (*editor with Paul F. Knitter*)
DISPUTED QUESTIONS IN THEOLOGY AND THE PHILOSOPHY OF RELIGION
THE FIFTH DIMENSION
DIALOGUES IN THE PHILOSOPHY OF RELIGION
JOHN HICK: AN AUTOBIOGRAPHY

An Interpretation of Religion

Human Responses to the Transcendent

Second Edition

John Hick

Yale University Press
New Haven and London

First published in the United Kingdom in 1989 by The Macmillan Press Ltd.
First published in the United States in 1989 by Yale University Press.

Second Edition published in the United Kingdom in 2004 by Palgrave
Macmillan.
Second Edition published in North America in 2004 by Yale University Press.

Published in North America under license from Palgrave Macmillan,
Houndmills, Basingstoke, Hants RG21 6XS, United Kingdom.

Library of Congress Control Number: 2004108302
ISBN 0–300–10668–8 (pbk. : alk. paper)

A catalogue record for this book is available from the British Library.

The paper in this book meets the guidelines for permanence and durability of
the Committee on Production Guidelines for Book Longevity of the Council on
Library Resources.

10   9   8   7   6   5   4   3   2   1

Dedicated to
Mike

Michael John Hick, 1961–1985

Praise for the first edition

'A major breakthrough in the understanding of the world's traditions and should be read by the adherents of all faiths.' – **Rabbi Prof. Dan Cohn-Sherbok**, *University of Wales*

'This book strengthens Hick's position as one of the most significant thinkers in the second half of the twentieth century . . . It has the patina of decades of careful scholarly reflection . . . It is Hick's most comprehensive, bold, and challenging work.' – **Chester Gillis**, *Journal of Religion*

'A leader in interfaith interpretation of religion, Hick has written what will probably become a classic in the philosophy of religion'. – *Library Journal*

'Hick has drawn together his many provocative insights into a masterful summary statement. – **Peter Hodgson**, *Religious Studies Review*

'An Interpretation of Religion is distinguished by its breadth and erudition and by its author's willingness to examine religion as a cross-cultural phenomenon.' – **Garrett Green**, *Theology Today*

'A masterful survey of world religions . . . Writing from a Christian point of view, Hick is sympathetic toward other world religions and clearly argues for the validity of a faith response. The book is highly recommended for college and seminary libraries as well as for public libraries seeking to expand resources for readers interested in religion on a world scale.' – *Choice*

'[This work] evinces Hick's many virtues: ingenuity; fairness toward all arguments; deference to the standards of analytic philosophy; familiarity with Eastern as well as Western religions; and, not least, a clean, clear prose.' – **R. A. Segal**, *Christian Century*

'Hick's Interpretation of Religion offers an appealingly simple and comprehensive argument for world ecumenism . . . The argument for the pluralistic hypothesis is lucidly presented, while it controls a broad range of materials and uses simple language that should appeal to non-philosophically trained readers.' – **Ellen T. Charry**, *Journal of Ecumenical Studies*

'Professor Hick is . . . to be warmly commended for his bold and comprehensive undertaking. His work is very clearly written and is well organized and structured. The main issues are argued forcefully yet with a rather quiet, assured open-mindedness. It is certainly a fine and important work 'of and for its time.' . . . *An Interpretation of Religion* is surely among the best of its kind. It is the work of a generous philosophical mind looking closely and broadly at what it is reasonable to hold with regard to religious beliefs, values, claims, and experience itself.' – **Eliot Deutsch**, *Philosophy East and West*

'The book is delightful to read.' – **Donald Wiebe**, *Toronto Journal of Theology*

'Those who work through this lengthy book will be richly rewarded. They will be drawn deeply into the politics, pain, frustration and even the courage, humor and hope present in this fascinating and tragic part of the contemporary world.' – **Charles A. Kimball**, *The Christian Century*

'A monumental achievement in the philosophy of religion which, I believe, will become a classic . . . Hick's lucid presentation has moved the discussion of the central issues in the philosophy of religion a large step forward, and for this we are all in his debt.' – **Owen C. Thomas**, *Anglican Theological Review*

'An extraordinarily ambitious piece of work . . . As a work of comparative religion, *An Interpretation of Religion* is an eloquently written, richly erudite piece. It also treats with fairness, and a striking degree of comprehension, many critical issues in the philosophy of religion.' – **Stephen Paul Foster**, *Modern Schoolman*

Contents

Contents

16 The *Impersonae* of the Real

PART FIVE   CRITERIOLOGICAL

17 Soteriology and Ethics

18 The Ethical Criterion

19 Myth, Mystery and the Unanswered Questions

20 The Problem of Conflicting Truth-Claims

Contents   xi

Preface to the First Edition

This book is an expanded version of my 1986–7 Gifford Lectures, delivered in the University of Edinburgh. I would like to record appreciation to the electors for the opportunity to present a systematic interpretation of religion under such famous auspices; and to Professor Ronald Hepburn of the Philosophy Department and Dean James Mackey of the Faculty of Divinity, and their colleagues, for their hospitality and encouragement while I was in Edinburgh.

The book is intended to contribute to a project which no one person can hope to complete, namely the development of a field theory of religion from a religious point of view. I propose here a philosophical ground-plan and suggest some of the more concrete interpretations to which it points. Behind this endeavour lies the belief that a philosopher of religion must today take account not only of the thought and experience of the tradition within which he or she happens to work, but in principle of the religious experience and thought of the whole human race. In order to contribute to this work philosophers must be prepared to learn from the historians and phenomenologists of religion. I have tried to do this. But the body of knowledge is immense, and growing all the time, so that my acquaintance with it is inevitably selective and second-hand, relying on first-hand experts in the different areas. There are indeed whole regions, such as the religious life of China, that I have had largely (though not entirely) to leave aside. Again, in concentrating on the 'great world religions' I have given primal religion less attention than it ought to have. However the aim has not been to produce something complete and definitive, but to make a preliminary exploration of a range of problems that are only now entering the purview of western philosophy of religion, and to suggest a possible approach to them. Those who find this approach inadequate or misleading will I hope feel under obligation to propose another, so that the various options can be progressively clarified and their merits considered.

The references within the book do not fully reveal the author's indebtedness to co-workers. For example, although I do not discuss his writings here in any detail I have been deeply influenced by the work of Wilfred Cantwell Smith; and I have learned more, in their respective fields, from the publications and conversation of Masao Abe, John Bowker, Ninian Smart and several others than the references to them here might suggest.

The writing of this book has occupied some five years, and I probably could not have written it without moving when I did to the academic environment of the Claremont Graduate School, with its tradition of discussion of the problems of religious pluralism and of East/West interaction. I am grateful not only to colleagues and students here, but also to the administration for a special research leave in the spring of 1986 to enable me to devote my time at a critical point entirely to this book. I am likewise indebted to the John Simon Guggenheim Foundation for making me a Guggenheim Fellow for the second time, in 1985–6; and to the Rockefeller Foundation for a delightful and productive period of residence at their Study Center at Bellagio on Lake Como in the spring of 1986.

I wish to thank a number of colleagues both in Claremont and elsewhere who have read one or more of these chapters in draft form and have given me their comments, criticisms and suggestions: Rex Ambler, Paul Badham, John Cobb, Stephen Davis, Gavin D'Costa, Chester Gillis, Ariel Glucklich, David Griffin, Peter Heath, James Kellenberger, Gerard Loughlin, Edmund and Tova Meltzer, Dewi Phillips, William Rowe, Joseph Runzo, Norman Solomon, Richard Swinburne, John Vickers. They have saved me from a number of errors and have pointed out difficulties to which I had not been sufficiently alert. I am likewise grateful to a number of graduate students at Claremont who, in seminar discussions of draft chapters and in research assistant and secretarial capacities, have contributed to the development of the book: Dale Breitkreutz, Shawn Burn, Dennis Dirks, Alvin Ethington, Ken and Elizabeth Frank, Cheryl Fields, Gregory Garland, Matthew Hawk, Harold Hewitt, Nancy Howell, Laurie Huff, John Ishihara, Chris Ives, Karl Kime, Kyoung Kae Kim, Joseph Lynch, Melissa Norton, Maura O'Neill, Leena Pullinen, Thandeka, Paul Waldau, James Wallis, Wang Jang. Henry Sun on the ancient near-eastern material and Linda Tessier from a feminist perspective have been particularly helpful; as also has Earlyne Biering in the Religion Department office, in organising and enabling the processing of the numerous successive draft versions, Bruce Hanson in making the Bibliography and Lynn Isaak in checking quotations. I should also like to thank Gary Chartier for help with proof-reading and Ellen Sun with the indices; Naomi Laredo for very helpful editing; and my wife, Hazel, for the background of happiness which is so conducive to productive work!

My hope is that this book will make it clear that a viable justification of religious belief, showing that it is rational to base our beliefs upon our experience, including religious experience, leads inevitably to the problems of religious pluralism; and that there are resources within the major world traditions themselves that can, when supported by important philosophical distinctions, point to a resolution of these problems. In so far as such a resolution proves acceptable within the different traditions it provides a basis for the mutual respect that is necessary for fruitful inter-faith dialogue and for practical collaboration in face of the common threats – of nuclear destruction, of North–South and East–West confrontations, of irreparable damage to the environment – that face the human family on this small and fragile planet.

John Hick
Department of Religion
Claremont Graduate School
Claremont, California 91711
June 1987

Introduction to the Second Edition

Since this book was first published fifteen years ago its proposals have given rise to a number of critical discussions in journals and books, focusing particularly on its 'pluralistic hypothesis'. (Because there are several versions of religious pluralism, I shall use the term 'pluralistic' here to refer to my own version, presented in this book).[1] This new edition provides an opportunity to consider to what extent these criticisms can be met and to what extent they require some revision of the theory. There are several quite important points at which critics have enabled me to develop or modify the hypothesis and thereby strengthen it, and I am extremely grateful to them. Because of the large number of journal articles (over a hundred and thirty) and of critical discussions in books (more than a hundred, ranging from a few pages to a chapter to whole books),[2] with many of the same or overlapping points being made by different writers, it is impossible even to mention here all the authors to whose arguments I am responding. But although I only quote from a very few, a number of others are being addressed at the same time. I am not however responding here to the numerous criticisms from Christian theologians which consist in a reassertion either of an exclusivist (Christianity alone is true/salvific) or inclusivist (Christianity alone is fully true/salvific, but non-Christians can be included within the sphere of Christian salvation) theology of religions, having replied to these, as well as to a number of earlier philosophical critics, in _The Rainbow of Faiths_ (1995). In _Dialogues in the Philosophy of Religion_ (2001) I have responded to some more recent philosophical contributions by philosophers, some of whom have written further new material for the book. However in this new Introduction I have collected criticisms thematically, rather than (usually) under individual writer's names. But it will be well first briefly to summarise the hypothesis.

The hypothesis. The starting point is the religious ambiguity of the universe, the fact that it can be understood and experienced both religiously and naturalistically. But given this ambiguity it is, I

Darwin

xvii

argue, entirely rational for those who experience religiously to trust their religious experience and to base their living and believing on it. The principle on which this argument rests has recently been aptly called 'the critical trust approach' (Kai-man Kwan 2003, 152f). The important qualification indicated by 'critical' is that it is rational to trust our experience *except* when we have some reason to doubt it. In the case of sense experience if we did not normally proceed on this basis we would be unable to act in relation to our environment and hence to survive within it. But this 'normally' allows for exceptions when we have reason to think or suspect that, for example, we are being subject to an optical illusion or are, or were, hallucinating or otherwise deluded. Given that qualification the principle of critical trust is an aspect of what we ordinarily count as sanity. The present question is whether it properly applies to religious experience also. Against this it is argued that sensory and religious experience are too different for the same principle to apply. For whereas the former is compulsory, the latter is not; whereas sense experience is reported by all human beings, religious experience is not; and whereas sense experience is largely uniform around the world, religious experience sometimes differs widely between, and indeed within, the religious traditions. However these differences correspond appropriately to differences between the respective putative objects of sensory and religious experience. The compulsion to be aware of the physical world sets the scene within which we exercise our moral freedom but does not undermine that freedom itself. But – putting it in monotheistic terms – if we could not avoid being conscious of being all the time in the direct presence of a God of limitless goodness and power, who knows us through and through, and always wishes us to act in a particular way, we would have a formal, but not a real, moral freedom in relation to the deity. However if God preserves an epistemic distance from us, so that we are free to be aware or unaware of the divine presence, then it can reasonably be expected that at any given time not everyone will have freely opened themselves to an awareness of that presence. And if, as the pluralistic hypothesis holds, religious experience is always culturally conditioned, it is not surprising that it takes different forms within the different traditions. In view of this I believe that it is reasonable to apply the critical trust principle (with its proviso) to religious experience.

In practice, and with or without any philosophical backing, this is accepted within each of the great post-axial traditions on behalf of its own adherents. But if the principle is sound it must apply to the other traditions as well, and it thereby validates a plurality of incompatible religious belief-systems. The pluralistic theory is a response to this apparently anomalous situation.[3]

The hypothesis is that there is an ultimate reality, which I refer to as the Real – though sometimes, because there is no ideal term, also speaking of Ultimate Reality, the Ultimate, the Transcendent – which is in itself transcategorial (ineffable), beyond the range of our human conceptual systems, but whose universal presence is humanly experienced in the various forms made possible by our conceptual-linguistic systems and spiritual practices. The basic epistemological principle invoked here was well stated by Thomas Aquinas in his dictum that 'The thing known is in the knower according to the mode of the knower',[4] although his own use of it did not extend to the problem of religious plurality and diversity. For all awareness of our environment is interpretative, a form of experiencing-as. And whereas in relation to sense perception the 'mode of the knower' is much the same throughout the world, in relation to the Ultimate, the Transcendent, the Real, the mode of the knower differs considerably as it has been variously formed by the different religious traditions.

I am thus suggesting that we use something analogous to Kant's distinction between noumenal reality and its phenomenal appearance(s) to human consciousness. Kant's 'Copernican revolution' gave a central place to the mind's contribution to perception. In this strand of his thought the noumenal world exists independently of our perception of it and the phenomenal world is that same world as it appears to human consciousness, given form by the categories which structure this. Kant did not apply this epistemology to religion, and might well not have approved of our doing so today. But this is nevertheless what I suggest that we do in the theory that the noumenal Real is thought and experienced by different human mentalities, forming and formed by different religious traditions, as the range of divine *personae* and metaphysical *impersonae* which the phenomenology of religion reports. This hypothesis has been subjected to serious and responsible criticism at a number of points.

(1) *The concept of the Real*. This is the concept of the transcategorial (or ineffable) Real, to which we cannot apply literally the attributes that we apply to its humanly thought and

experienced forms, such as being good, loving, powerful, just, etc. Several issues have been raised. The ineffability of the Real has been described as transcendental agnosticism.[5] But this is inaccurate. The reason why we cannot apply these terms to the Real is not that we do not profess to know whether or not they apply, which would be correctly characterised as agnosticism, but because all such terms are part of our human conceptual field, the range of ideas embodied in our languages, and according to the pluralistic hypothesis the Real is beyond, or outside, this conceptual field. Further, to speak of God as ineffable should not be confused with a negative (apophatic) in distinction from a positive (cataphatic) doctrine. Transcategoriality excludes the attribution of properties either positively or negatively. This is in fact taught by virtually all[6] the great thinkers of the different traditions (see Chapter 14), but monotheistic theologians then regularly undermine this basic insight by making a wealth of positive claims about the nature of the supposedly ineffable reality. Christian theologians, for example, having declared that 'God transcends even the mind' (Augustine)[7] or that 'by its immensity the divine substance surpasses every form that our intellect reaches' (Aquinas),[8] nevertheless profess to know that this ineffable reality is in its ultimate nature a Trinity of Father, Son and Holy Spirit, the second Person of whom became incarnate as Jesus Christ. But we ought to be consistent at this crucial point, despite the far-reaching implications of doing so. We cannot rationally hold both that the ineffable, or transcategorial, ultimate reality is indescribable in human terms and also that it is correctly describable in the terms provided by one's own religious tradition. We are, it seems to me, driven instead to distinguish between the ultimate reality in itself, beyond human description, and the describable mental images of it which we can comprehend and to which we can respond.

However, this notion has been challenged on the logical ground that anything, including the Real, must have one or other of any two mutually contradictory qualities, x and non-x, and therefore cannot be outside the domain of our human concepts. My response has been to appeal to the familiar idea of concepts which do not apply to something either positively or negatively. It does not make sense, for example, to ask whether a molecule is clever or stupid, or whether a stone is virtuous or wicked, because they are not the kinds of thing that can be either. And I have suggested that it does not make sense to ask of the transcategorial Real whether it is personal or non-personal, good or evil, just or unjust, because these concepts do not apply to it – either positively or negatively. My suggestion (in Chapter 14) is that we have to distinguish between what I call substantial properties (such as being personal, being good, etc.), which would tell us something significant about the Real, and purely formal attributes (such as being able to be referred to) which do not tell us anything significant about it. It is only the latter that can properly be applied to the Real.

However William Rowe is not satisfied. His 'chief difficulty with Hick's Real' is that 'I cannot see how the Real can avoid having one or the other of two contradictory properties . . . [E]ven though to ask whether the number two is green or non-green may be to presuppose that it's an entity of the kind that could be green or non-green, and would thus be an inappropriate or senseless question if asked by someone who knows that no number can be green, it hardly follows that the proposition that the number two is non-green is false or in some way meaningless. Indeed the proposition that the number two is non-green is necessarily true' (Rowe 1999, 146). Likewise Alvin Plantinga says:

> If Hick means that none of our terms applies literally to the Real, then it isn't possible to make sense of what he says. I take it the term 'tricycle' does not apply to the Real; the Real is not a tricycle. But if the Real is not a tricycle, then, 'is not a tricycle' applies literally to it; it is a nontricycle. It could hardly be neither a tricycle nor a nontricycle, nor do I think that Hick would want to suggest that it could.
>
> (Plantinga 2000, 45)[9]

In reply to both of them, I do indeed hold that the Real cannot properly be said to be either a tricycle or a non-tricycle, and either green or non-green, on the ground that the concepts of tricycality and greenness do not apply to it either positively or negatively. But I now want to add a distinction between properties such as being green or being a tricycle that are religiously irrelevant, in the sense that in religious discourse no one would think for a moment of attributing them to the ultimate divine reality, and those that are religiously relevant, such as being personal, good, loving, wise, etc. Although still in my view a mistake, it would do no harm religiously to say that God, or the Ultimate, or the Real is non-green, non-blue, a non-teapot, a non-tricycle, a non-heap of manure, a non-Mount Everest, etc., etc., because from a religious point of view these are trivial truths from which nothing significant follows. However it would importantly infringe the principle of divine transcategoriality to do the same with religiously significant concepts. For the opposite of personhood, goodness, justice, etc., are being non- or im-personal, being evil, being unjust, etc. It follows from Rowe's argument that if the Real cannot possibly be personal, because it is not the sort of thing that *could* be personal, then it must necessarily be non-personal – which rules out all forms of theism. Likewise, Plantinga's argument that the Real must be either a tricycle or a non-tricycle, if carried over from the trivial to the significant, produces the claim that the Real must be either a personal or a non-personal reality; and this would at a stroke falsify either all the theistic or all the non-theistic religions – for the argument can be deployed equally well either way according to preference! But either way it would be unacceptable from a global religious point of view.

(2) *Experiencing the Real?*   The question has often been raised, According to the hypothesis do we or do we not experience the Real? 'Clearly', says Alvin Plantinga (and there are others who think likewise), 'Hick is ambivalent about the answer to this question' (Plantinga 2000, 44). On the one hand, I say that we cannot experience the Real directly, as it is in itself, but on the other hand I say that we *can* experience the Real as its presence is mediated to us in the forms made possible by our limited human cognitive capacities. The epistemology in play here is the 'critical realism' which holds, in the case of sense perception, that there is a real external world that exists independently of all observers, but that we can only be aware of it in the distinctive forms that our own cognitive capacities permit. My proposal is that we apply this same principle to religious experience. There is a transcendent reality which is the ultimate focus of religious concern but it can only become an object of human awareness in the range of forms made possible by our conceptual repertoire. In the intriguing (and paradoxical) words of a Hindu religious text, 'Thou art formless. Thy only form is our knowledge of thee' (Parriskar 1978, I, 144).

(3) *The nature of the Real.*   If the Real is truly transcategorial (or ineffable) on what grounds can we say, as the pluralistic hypothesis does, that it is authentically manifested within the domain of human experience as a loving rather than a hating God, or as a benign rather than a hostile structure of reality, and that some

kinds of attitudes and behaviour, such as compassion and seeking human flourishing, are in alignment with the Real whereas others, such as hatred and aggression, are not? Must we not at least say that the Real is *such that* it is authentically manifested within human thought and experience in these ways and not in their opposites? The answer is both Yes and No. Yes, in that if the Real is appropriately humanly imaged (amongst other ways) as a loving God, then it is a tautology that it is such that it is appropriately imaged (among other ways) as a loving God. And 'being such that' equals 'having a nature such that'. But No, in that this does not entail that the Real in itself is a loving God, or indeed that it has any of the other qualities that we can attribute to a deity, such as personality, goodness, knowledge, justice, etc. But nevertheless it's unknown (to us) nature is such that, in relation to us, it is experienced, among other authentic ways, as a loving God.

Are there any analogies for a reality which in itself, *an sich*, has none of the humanly conceivable and experienceable qualities of the forms in which it is humanly conceived and experienced? There is a partial analogy in sense perception. We experience, for example, the table as a solid object with which we can interact, for example by putting plates and knives and forks, etc. on it. It has solidity, a certain varied expanse of colour, emits a sound when banged, and it has weight and odour and stable position. We do not experience what the physicists describe as millions of sub-atomic particles in continuous rapid motion in largely empty space, none of which particles has solidity, colour, odour, sound, or even fixed position. But to see it as a stationary solid object is appropriate for animals at our point in the macro- micro-scale, whilst to see it as a whirling cloud of particles would bewilder us and make us unable to act appropriately in relation to it. And so we experience it as it appears to animals with our kind of sense organs and organising concepts. We also see it in different shapes from different angles, and with different degrees of clarity or distortion according to the state of our eyes and optic nerves and the visual cortex at the back of the brain. If we did not exist as we are, what *we* call the table – i.e. the solid piece of furniture that we can use – would not exist, although the millions of particles would. Thus the table exists, with the particular qualities that we experience, only in relation to the perceiver. But we must now adapt the analogy by prescribing, contrary to fact, that unlike the physicists' table, which is describable – even if only in terms of sub-atomic physics – the table-in-itself has no humanly describable qualities. We would then have an ineffable reality which is humanly experienced in a variety of mostly slightly different ways as a table. (Why then believe that there *is* any unexperienceable table-in-itself, or Real-in-itself? See 10 below.) Analogously, the Real is in itself transcategorial, but is humanly experienced in a variety of forms which exist only in relation to those for whom they are the objects of their religious attitudes.[10] It is important to stress the place in this of the human activities of worship and meditation. To open oneself to the universal presence of the Ultimate in the I–Thou mode of prayer and worship is to experience it as a divine Thou, but quite differently in the mode of *zazen* or *satipatthana* or other non-discursive methods of meditation.

But nevertheless must not the Real be *such that* certain human values and actions are, and their opposites are not, in alignment with the Real?[11] The answer is again both Yes and No. Yes, the Real is such that, for example, love of one's fellow humans is, and hatred of them is not, an appropriate response to the Real; but No, it does not follow from this that the Real in itself loves or is loving. For love and hate, knowledge and ignorance, wisdom and folly, being just and being unjust, etc., are attributes of persons, and it is only by identifying the Real with a God made in our own image as a person, but magnified to infinity, that we can attribute such qualities to it. But whilst we cannot apply to the Real in itself such terms as loving and wise, which presuppose personality, we can use a more general concept and say that *in relation to us* the Real is serendipitous[12] or benign. The term 'serendipity' was invented by Horace Walpole to refer to the course of events when they turn out well for us. They are happiness-making and *as though* planned for us by a benevolent power. Accordingly, serendipity can be experienced either as the structure of the cosmos or as the work of a personal Being. Likewise 'benign' can be used in both personal and non-personal senses: we speak of a benign ruler and a benign climate. And so the benign or serendipitous character of the Real, in relation to us, can be expressed both theistically as the benevolence, goodness, love of a personal deity, and non-theistically as the process leading to *nirvana* or *moksha* or being at one with the *Tao*, the eternal order. . . . These are different human ways of conceiving and experiencing what I have called (Chapter 4) the cosmic optimism of the great world faiths.

Is this a doctrine of analogy, as when theologians say that God is good, just, etc., in a sense analogous to that in which humans may be good, just, etc., but without our knowing what the divine analogues of these qualities are? I think not. We cannot say that the Real has attributes analogous to such personal qualities as love, goodness, etc., in humans. For the Ultimate Reality, the Real, is beyond the personal/impersonal duality. But on the other hand, from our human point of view it is experienced as serendipitous, benign, rather than as hostile or indifferent. The point of view of the perceiver is crucial. A mountain is experienced visually as smaller the further we are from it and larger the nearer we are. But the mountain itself cannot be said to be either large or small – these are relational terms. It is what it is, and it is experienced differently from the point of view of different perceivers. And the Real is what it is, but is experienced from the distinctively human point of view as benign or serendipitous. There may conceivably be other kinds of being from whose point of view it is experienced as hostile. But friendly and hostile, benign and dangerous, are relational terms which do not apply to the Real *an sich*.

But how do we know, or why do we believe, that the Real in its relation to us is benign rather than malign? As Plantinga asks, '[The Real] is an unknown and unknowable X. But then why associate this unknowable X with religion, as opposed to warfare, violence, bigotry, and the horrifying things human beings often do to each other?' (Plantinga 2000, 56). Again, 'If the Real has no positive properties of which we have a grasp, how could we possibly know or have grounds for believing that some ways of behaving with respect to it are more appropriate than others?' (57). The answer comes from a point often ignored by critics, namely the origin and point of the hypothesis as arising within one of the great streams of religious life, in my case Christianity. It starts, in other words, within what Paul Tillich called 'the circle of faith'. I am seeking a *religious* interpretation of religion globally, an interpretation which starts from the conviction that there is transcendent reality of limitless importance to us. As Christians we believe that Christian religious experience is not purely human imaginative projection, although there is a large element of this within it, but that it is also and at the same time a cognitive response to sacred reality beyond us. Applying an epistemological analogue of the Golden Rule, I propose that we apply to religious experience within the other great world faiths the same principle that we apply to our own, namely critical trust: it is to be trusted except when we have reason to distrust it. And the test by which both Christians and people of the other major faiths judge the authenticity of religious experience is its moral and spiritual fruit in human life. The general form of this fruit is identified within each tradition as – in the formulation used in this book – a transformation of human existence from natural self-centredness to a new orientation centred in the Transcendent, the Ultimate, the Real.

(4) *The religious criterion.* I maintain that so far as we can tell this salvific transformation is taking place – and also failing to take place – to more or less the same extent within each of the great world faiths. There is no one religion whose adherents stand out as morally and spiritually superior to the rest of the human race. (If anyone claims such a superiority for their own religious community, the onus of proof, or of argument, is clearly upon them.) But this creates a problem: the different religions have different images of the Transcendent and different associated belief systems. How then can they be, as seems to be the case, equally effective – although in each case only limitedly effective – contexts of the salvific transformation? The pluralistic hypothesis, as an answer to this question, is thus not an *a priori* or free-standing theory, unrelated to living religion, but an attempt from within it to make intelligible sense of the actual religious situation world-wide. Unless this is taken into account, as it has not been by many critics, the debate becomes off-target.

The criterion of facilitating the transformation of human life from self-centredness to a new orientation centred in a manifestation of the Real, progressively freeing us *from* ego-concern and *for* love and compassion for others, functions as the criterion for assessing religious organisations and movements. The result is usually ambiguous. Religious institutions in general have probably done as much harm as good in the long course of history. But some, such for example as the Japanese sect which put sarin gas in the Tokyo underground, and such semi- or pseudo-religious movements as Nazism and Fascism, fail spectacularly under this criterion.

(5) *Why one Real rather than many?* Keith Ward says that '[Hick] argues that since one unknowable is indistinguishable from another, they are all the same' (Ward 1990, 313, also Ward 1994, 313). Or as Robert Cook says, 'Hick slips into the logical fallacy of the quantifier-shift when he adduces references to an ineffable reality in the sacred texts of the world's religions and deduces from this that they must all be referring to the same object, namely the

Real' (Cook 1993, 11). However that there is one ultimate reality rather than many is offered as a 'best explanation', not an iron dogma. Whether the idea of many *ultimate* realities is coherent is debatable. But even if it is, a single Real is the most natural, as well as the most economical, hypothesis to account for the identity of the salvific transformation from self-centredness to centring in the Transcendent produced within the different world faiths.

(6) *Polytheism?* A different question that has been raised is, does not the plurality of divine *personae* amount to polytheism? George Mavrodes says, 'Hick is (in my opinion, at least) probably the most important philosophical defender of polytheism in the history of Western philosophy'! (Senor 1995, 261–2). Debate about this has continued in my response (Hick 1997) to his original paper (Mavrodes 1995), and his response to that (Mavrodes 2001) and then my comment on that response (Hick 2001). But it would be misleading to describe as polytheism the concept of a single ultimate reality which is differently experienced, in many cases as a personal deity, through the prism of the varying conceptualities and spiritual practices of the different religions. There are both 'mono-' and 'poly-' sides to this conception, so that it is, to coin phrases which I hope never to have to use again, both mono-ultimate-reality-ism and poly-manifestations-to-humanity-of-the-ultimate-reality-ism. But the mono- aspect is not monotheism, because the ultimate reality, the Real, cannot be described as a personal God who is the creator of everything other than Him/Herself, and the poly- aspect is not polytheism both because it does not consist in a plurality of such Gods and also because its manifestations to humanity include its *impersonae* as well as its *personae*.

Another of Mavrodes' arguments which has been taken up by several writers imagines a prince who, wanting to find out for himself how his subjects are thinking, goes among them in several different disguises – in one place as an itinerant monk, in another as a journeyman stonemason, and so on (Mavrodes 1995, 273f). Mavrodes' question is whether this is a good analogy for the different *personae* of the Real as they figure in the pluralistic hypothesis. On this interpretation the Real reveals itself by taking on different appearances within different religions. Or, he asks, would a better analogy be several artists painting the same landscape? Because they are of the abstract and non-representational school their paintings do not look like the landscape in the way that a photograph would, nor do the different paintings look like one another – they constitute different individual artistic impressions of the landscape. 'So the landscape has contributed something to each painting. There is a real input there, and some sort of dependence. . . . [But] There is also the aesthetic creativity of the artist, his or her artistic interpretation. . . . The painting itself is a construct, the product of an artistic reaction to, and interaction with, a (largely) natural landscape' (274). Are the divine *personae* constructions in this sense? Is the 'disguise model' or the 'construct model' the correct analogy? And Mavrodes cites passages in *An Interpretation of Religion* which seem to support each of these interpretations.

They only *seem* to, however, because when I speak of experiencing the Real I do not mean, as Mavrodes seems to assume, experiencing the Real itself directly, as the prince is directly perceived even in his deliberate disguises, but experiencing its phenomenal appearances to consciousnesses as formed by the different religious traditions. Thus far this is more like Mavrodes' construct model. But that does not fit either. For the artists all see the landscape in the same way, in that they would all confirm that a photo of it is indeed an accurate representation of it. But in their paintings they are not trying to emulate photography, for Mavrodes has prescribed that they are not of the realist but of the abstract and non-representational school. So the fact that they see the landscape directly but deliberately paint it differently distinguishes it from the pluralist hypothesis that we do *not* experience the Real directly, as it is in itself. There is no kind of religious experience corresponding to perceiving directly the scene which the artists then present in their different ways on canvas. (But see 12 below.) Thus neither analogy applies properly to the pluralistic hypothesis.

(7) *Does the Real act causally upon us?*   This raises the often asked question of how the transcategorial Real *affects* or *impacts* us, so that we can be aware of it, not indeed as it is in itself, but in the humanly knowable forms of which we can be aware? This was a notorious problem for Kant in relation to sense perception. According to him causality is one of the categories imposed by the mind on the raw impacts of the world-in-itself in the process of its coming to consciousness within us. But in that case how can the noumenal world be said to *cause* our consciousness of the phenomenal world? However this problem does not arise in

the adapted use of Kant's distinction within the pluralistic hypothesis. For according to the great religions there is a 'spiritual' aspect of our nature – the *imago dei*, or our capacity to receive divine revelation, or the *atman*, or the Buddha nature – that resonates to the universal presence of the transcendent reality, in virtue of which quality we are religious animals. However 'resonates', 'impacts', 'produces', 'grounds', etc., are all metaphors in an area in which we have no entirely appropriate language.

(8) *The status of the* personae *and* impersonae *of the Real.* What, it is very properly asked, is the ontological status of the divine *personae* and metaphysical *impersonae*? Let us take the *personae*, the God figures, first. It is clear that, phenomenologically, Jahweh or the Adonai of rabbinic Judaism, and the Holy Trinity, and Allah, and Vishnu, Shiva, Devi, etc., are not identical. Each has his or her own unique personal profile and unique history of interactions with humanity. In Chapter 15 I offer two possible accounts of their status, both of which are compatible with the pluralistic hypothesis, so that it is not necessary to the hypothesis to chose between them. One is that they are joint constructs of the 'impact' of the universal presence of the Real and the human creative imagination. Each then exists as an experienced reality only in relation to his, or in the case of many Indian deities, her worshippers. For example, the Jahweh of the Hebrew scriptures exists as a vital factor in Jewish history, and his covenant relationship with the Hebrews is an integral part of Jahweh's own biography. The Gods are, on this option, beings who exist in relation to their worshipping community, but not independently of it. The other possibility is that they are objectively existing beings of great but not infinite benevolence, power and knowledge – the *devas*, 'demi-gods' of eastern, or the angels and archangels of western, traditions.

However I now think that it is possible to venture a step further by combining elements of these two options. In moments of individual prayer and communal worship there is often, or at least sometimes, an experience of being in the presence of God and of being in an I–Thou (or We–Thou) relationship with God. I do not think that this is illusory, but neither do I think that the Thous with whom people of different faiths are in contact have the infinite attributes – as the omnipotent and omniscient etc., creator of everything other than oneself – that the developed monotheistic theologies have come to ascribe to them. For it is not possible to experience that an encountered being has *infinite* dimensions –

infinite power, infinite knowledge, etc. The omni- qualities are the
result of philosophical thinking congealed into religious dogma.
And the possibility that I am proposing is that in each case the
experienced Thou is a being analogous to the *devas* (gods with small
g) of Indian religion or to the angels and archangels of traditional
Jewish, Christian and Muslim belief, or to the heavenly Buddhas –
Amida, Vairocana, etc. – of some understandings of the *trikaya*
doctrine of Mahayana Buddhism, each being the object of
veneration by their own devotees. These are intermediate beings
between ourselves and the transcategorial Real. But in our
awareness of these beings we tend, at least within the western
traditions, to invest them in our minds with the omni- attributes
created by the vast superstructures of theology that have been
developed over the centuries.

(9) *The religions contradicted?*   Several criticisms of the pluralistic
hypothesis depend (in my opinion) upon leaving aside the basic
distinction between the Real in itself and the range of humanly
described and experienced forms which are the direct objects of
worship or focus of meditation within the different religions. Thus
Plantinga says that, 'Hick's idea, I think, is that those who practice
the great religions refer to [the Real] when (as it seems to them)
they refer to God, Allah, Brahman, Shiva, Vishnu, the Dharmakaya,
or whatever. So Christians *think* they refer to a being who is
personal, loving, knowledgeable, and the like; the fact is, however,
that they do *not* refer to such a being, but to a being who doesn't
have any of these properties or, indeed, any other positive
properties of which we have a grasp' (Plantinga 2000, 49–50). In
distinction from this, however, my suggestion is that Christians,
when they refer to the object of their worship, are referring to the
distinctively Christian image of the ultimate reality as a Trinity of
Father, Son and Holy Spirit. The Christian faith begins in an
experience, coming originally by contagion from Jesus, of being in
the presence of the Heavenly Father of whom he spoke, this
experience being theologised in the course of time (or to some
extent by Jesus himself on the basis of his Jewish inheritance) into
the conception of the Creator of the universe, with the infinite
qualities of omnipotence, omniscience, omnibenevolence, omni-
presence, etc. Likewise when Muslims refer to Allah (Arabic for
'God') they are referring to the image – mental image not graven
image – of the ultimate reality given to them in the Qur'an. Their
faith begins with a response to the immense power of the Arabic

text accepted from their tradition as the verbal self-revelation of God. They are thus referring to a different mental image of the ultimate reality from the Christian one. And Christian theology spells out the Christian image, whilst Islamic theology spells out the Muslim image, of the Ultimate. But both (and the many other such) images are, according to the pluralistic hypothesis, human images arising at the interface between the Real and human minds, given form by the different conceptualities and associated spiritual practices of the different streams of religious life. But the Real in itself is not a direct object of worship. There is no cult of the Real.

It may help to make this both more intelligible and more acceptable if we remember, as an example, the way in which the Christian image of God has changed through the centuries. The mainline Christian concept of God today is that of a God of limitless love, with Jesus as love incarnate. But for several centuries in mediaeval Europe God was imaged and experienced in a quite different way, as a remote and terrifying power to be dreaded. To quote Dennis Nineham in his study of tenth century Christianity in France . . .

In an age which . . . had little understanding of secondary causes, the evils that befell society were assumed to be punishment from God; he must indeed be angry with his people, it was felt, if he visited so much suffering upon them. At the personal level also, the deaths and illnesses of individuals were interpreted as divine punishment for what they had done, even if in many cases no one could be sure what this had been. God was believed capable of bringing about the slaughter of countless enemy troops – mostly conscripts at that – to ensure the victory of an army which had won his favour; and it must be remembered that orthodox doctrine had no doubt or qualms about his intention to damn the great majority of the world's population, including all babies who died unbaptized. Small wonder if such a heavenly lord seemed quite as arbitrary and high-handed as any earthly lord.

(Nineham 1993, 48)

And Christ himself was not seen as the embodiment of divine love but as the strict judge whom they must face on the last day. They prayed for mercy to their local saint or to the Virgin Mary. It was only in the thirteenth century that the understanding of God as gracious and merciful began to return and eventually to supplant for many Christians the previous threatening conception. Again, the image of God in the Hebrew scriptures develops through the centuries from a warrior god leading his people in battle to the universal Lord, blessed be he, of the later scriptures and of rabbinic Judaism. Yet again, the Vedic gods of India had their individual biographies involving many changes and sometimes mergers in a complex mythic history.

And so the question arises whether it is God who has changed in these ways through the centuries, or our human images of God? Clearly, the latter. Does not this show that between ourselves and the ultimate reality there is a screen of varied and changing human images of that reality? At different points through the centuries and around the world humans have conceived, and have correspondingly experienced, the ultimate reality in this vast range of different forms. The direct object of the conscious activity of a worshipping community is always their own concrete image of the ultimate. Now Plantinga, and others, might say that this is precisely what they mean when they say that, according to the pluralistic hypothesis, the worshipper thinks she is worshipping a personal loving God when in fact she is worshipping an ineffable ultimate reality. But this would be to forget the epistemological distinction on which the hypothesis hinges. The principle that, in Aquinas' words, 'The thing known is in the knower according to the mode of the knower', applies to all our awareness of reality beyond us. All our intercourse with other people and with our material environment is with those people and that environment as they appear to us, given our specific cognitive equipment and conceptual and emotional resources. But this does not mean that we are being deceived all the time in either our sensory or our religious experience. It just means that this is the nature of all human cognition. Once this is accepted, naïve realism, in both sense perception and religious experience, has to be abandoned and we have to proceed on the basis of the critical realism which holds that there is a reality beyond us of which we are aware, but that our awareness is always and necessarily mediated through and limited by our cognitive faculties and conceptual systems. Plantinga is, it seems, a naïve realist about Christian experience (only), and this leads him to dismiss by implication the many forms of non-Christian religious experience as spurious. The predictable outcome is the Christian exclusivism which he advocates (Plantinga 1995).

(10) *Why affirm a transcategorial Real?*   A number of critics (e.g.

Plantinga 2000, 59f) ask, Why believe that there *is* a transcendent and transcategorial Real 'behind' the many God figures and non-personal absolutes which are said to constitute its humanly known *personae* and *impersonae*? One can equally well ask, Why believe that there is a personal God? Why believe in a transcendent reality of any kind? Here I am in agreement with Plantinga that we cannot go beyond what he calls 'warranted belief'. And, as he says, in the end 'theistic belief has warrant if and only if it is true; hence whether one thinks it has warrant will depend upon whether one thinks it is true' (Plantinga 1997, 389). But I hold that we do have to go beyond our conviction that Christian belief is warranted to an acceptance that Jewish belief and Islamic belief and Buddhist belief . . . are also and equally warranted. We therefore need a more comprehensive understanding of religion than one confined to the philosopher's own tradition. A key premise for me is the (so far as we can tell) salvific parity of the great world religions, referred to above. Since each is consciously related to a different image of the Real or the Ultimate, no one of these images alone can be exclusively identified with the Real in itself. It cannot be, identically, the Holy Trinity, or the strictly unitary Allah, or the strictly unitary Adonai of rabbinic Judaism, or Vishu, or Shiva, or the Dharmakaya, or the Tao, or Brahman . . . It cannot even be any two of these, let alone all of them at once. If, then, they are not all, or (according to religious exclusivists) all but one, figments of the human imagination, the simplest explanation of the situation is that they are different humanly formed images of the Real. The Real itself is thus that which there must be if our human religious experience, in its variety of forms, is not purely imaginative projection but is at the same time a mediated awareness of the ultimate transcendent reality. Putting it in Kantian-like terms, the Real is the necessary postulate, not of the moral life, as Kant held, but of the global religious life of humanity.

(11) *Literal and mythological truth.* Yet another set of questions concern the distinction between literal and mythological statements (e.g. Gillis 1989, chap. 5 and 1991, 37–40). According to the pluralistic hypothesis we can make true and false literal and analogical statements about our own image of the Ultimate, truth or falsity here being determined internally by the norms of our tradition. But statements about the Real in itself have mythological, not literal, value. A statement about X is mythologically true if it is not literally true but nevertheless tends to evoke an appropriate

dispositional attitude to X. Mythological truth is thus a kind of practical or pragmatic as distinguished from theoretical truth. Using the common criterion among the world religions of their fruits, in terms of treating others as one would wish to be treated oneself,[13] we can say that the beliefs that God is love;[14] that Allah is *rahman, rahim*, gracious and merciful; that within Judaism God's command is to 'do justice, to love kindness, and to walk humbly with your God';[15] that the requirement of the eternal Buddha nature is 'As a mother cares for her son . . . so towards all living beings a man's mind should be all-embracing';[16] that for those for whom the *Bhagavad Gita* is a sacred text God is 'as a father with his son, a friend with his friend, a lover with his beloved'[17] . . . are literally true of these divine *personae* and metaphysical *impersonae* of the Real, and mythologically true of the Real in itself.

This naturally provokes the question, Can mythological truths have any power to move us? Are they religiously relevant? Surely it is only if, for example, I 'accept the splendid and powerful doctrines of traditional Christianity' literally that they will affect my behaviour. '[H]ow can I possibly accept them, adopt *that* attitude toward them [i.e. being influenced to move from self-centredness towards God-centredness], if I think they are only mythologically true – that is, really false?' (Plantinga 2000, 81). To put this more concretely, how can anyone be significantly influenced by the Christian story of God the Son, second Person of the Trinity, being born at Christmas of a virgin mother, dying on the cross to atone for the sins of the world, being bodily resurrected from the dead at Easter, subsequently ascending bodily into the sky, and being present today in the Church through the Holy Spirit, if this is not all believed to be literally true? I accept of course that there are very many on the conservative-evangelical and fundamentalist wings of the churches who operate in terms of a naïve realism and who accordingly cannot see this story as other than either a literally true historical narrative or as a lie. For them there is nothing in between. Unhappily, their faith is today very vulnerable, for the modern historical study of the New Testament and of Christian origins has made nearly all the historical elements of the story a matter of serious debate and responsible doubt[18] – the one exception being that Jesus, who undoubtedly existed, was executed by crucifixion. But it is only by retaining a pre-critical use of the scriptures that what Plantinga calls 'traditional Christianity' (including for him the rejection of the scientific discovery that *homo sapiens* has developed out of earlier forms of life in the long process of biological evolution: Plantinga 1991) can be maintained. But among many other Christians today within the mainline Churches there is an appreciation of the poetic, or symbolic, or metaphorical, or mythological nature of much religious language. They accept and respond to the immense power of Jesus' teaching about how to live, calling us to love our neighbour and even our enemies, to reject the 'eye for an eye' ethic, to be generous and forgiving, and by extension into an age when political power and responsibility has been distributed far beyond emperors and kings, to work for justice and peace throughout the world. But none of this depends upon a literal belief in a miraculous conception of Jesus, or on his having two complete natures, one human and the other divine, or on his bodily resurrection and ascension, or indeed on sharing his conviction that the end of the Age was coming in the lifetime of those then living. Jesus' moral teaching shines in its own light as true and as claiming our response. Indeed if we, and the earliest disciples, did not bring an existing moral discernment to our encounter with Jesus we would never have recognised him in the first place as a 'window onto God'. If we had reason to believe that he was devious, selfish, dishonest we would never have come to take him as our lord. And so his moral teaching, which presupposes whilst it deepens and widens our existing moral discernment, does not depend upon questionable miracle stories for its validity and for its inherent claim upon us. But the Christmas story nevertheless remains beautiful and moving even when it seems likely that Jesus was not in fact born in Bethlehem – more likely at Nazareth, and several years BCE – and that the artificial genealogies and legendary birth and infancy stories in the Gospels of Matthew and Luke, which decorate our Christmas cards and are celebrated in our Christmas carols, are very probably not historical. Bethlehem seems to have entered the tradition to fulfil Old Testament prophecy, and the perennially inspiring stories of the guiding star and the kings or wise men from the east, and the shepherds in the field, were very probably added by pious imagination in an age when modern standards of historical writing did not exist. But even amidst its modern ruthless commercial exploitation, Christmas can still be used joyfully to celebrate the life and teaching of Jesus. During this season we suspend critical questions as irrelevant to its enjoyment and to participation in its uplifting transcendence of ordinary life. I think, then, that much of

Christianity will be able to survive because of its intrinsic moral power. And the same can apply within the other world faiths. It is already acceptable to many Hindus to recognise the mythic character of its rich tapestry of traditional stories of the loves and wars of the gods, or for many Buddhists to regard as non-historical the *Jakata* stories of the previous lives of Siddhartha.

(12) *Refuted by direct mystical experience?* The criticisms discussed so far come from western Christian sources, and indeed often from very theologically conservative Christians for whom the mystical strand of their own tradition is more of an embarrassment than an enrichment. But nevertheless mysticism may well create problems for the pluralistic hypothesis. Does not the claim that our awareness of the Real is always a mediated awareness conflict with the claim of many mystics, both eastern and western, to have attained a direct unmediated unitive experience of the Ultimate? Mysticism has often been defined as union with the divine. William James said that the 'overcoming of all the usual barriers between the individual and the Absolute is the great mystic achievement. In mystic states we both become one with the Absolute and we are aware of our oneness' (James 1960, 104). And R. C. Zaehner says that 'in Christian terminology mysticism means union with God' (Zaehner 1961, 32). This has been much discussed in contemporary philosophy – in, for example, Katz 1978 and 1983.

Taking Christian mysticism first, unitive language has indeed often been used, particularly during the period of the dominance of Neo-Platonism within Christian thought. For example, 'the most divine knowledge of God, that which comes through unknowing, is achieved in a union far beyond mind' (Pseudo-Dionysius 1987, 109), and 'when the divine light pours into the soul, the soul is united with God, as light blends with light' (Meister Eckhart 1941, 29). But the majority consensus among Christian mystics is that such language is not to be understood literally, but rather as ecstatic metaphor. Thus Ruusbroec, who uses unitive language freely, adds that 'Yet the creature does not become God, for the union takes place in God through grace and our homeward-turning love: and therefore the creature in its inward contemplation feels a distinction and an otherness between itself and God' (Ruusbroec 1985, 265). Again St John of the Cross insists that in the unitive experience the human soul remains 'as distinct from the Being of God as it was before' (St John of the Cross 1958, 182). And Bernard of Clairvaux held that 'The union between God and man is not unity. . . . For how can there be unity where there is a plurality of natures and difference of substances. The union of God and man is brought about not by confusion of natures, but by agreement of wills . . .' (Butler 1967, 114). I think it is safe to say that whilst many Christian mystics have freely used the language of divine-human union, in doing so they have been speaking poetically or metaphorically rather than literally.

It is likewise true, I believe, that the unitive language used so freely by some of the Sufis of Islam is to be understood as poetic metaphor, not as literal description. One of them, Al-Ghazali, analyses the situation very clearly when he says that the mystics 'after their ascent to the heavens of Reality, agree that they saw nothing in existence except God the One . . . Nothing was left to them but God . . . But the words of lovers when in a state of drunkenness must be hidden away and not broadcast. However, when their drunkenness abates and the sovereignty of their reason is restored – and reason is God's scale on earth – they know that this was not actual identity' (Zaehner 1961, 157–8). And I believe that the same is true of the Jewish mystics of the Kabbalah. I have argued this more fully elsewhere in relation to each of the great monotheisms (Hick 1999, ch. 16; 2004, ch. 17). I do not think that they affirm a literal numerical identity between the human creature and God, but rather the experience of a temporary complete openness of the human ego to the divine presence which fills their entire consciousness. For monotheistic metaphysics maintains a fundamental distinction between creature and Creator.

But on the other hand the metaphysics of advaitic Hinduism does allow for a literal identity. The *atman* which we all are in the depths of our being is ultimately one with Brahman. Shankara, in the *Crest Jewel of Discrimination* (which may not be by Shankara himself but a disciple expressing the master's thought), uses the analogy of clay jars each enclosing a particular volume of air. Break the jars and what remains? 'The air in the jar is one with the air everywhere. In like manner your Atman is one with Brahman' (Shankara 1978, 80). And in mystical experience we may transcend the ego to become conscious of our true identity as Brahman. He describes this experience. 'My mind fell like a hailstone into the vast expanse of Brahman's ocean. Touching one drop of it I melted away and became one with Brahman. And now, though I return to human consciousness, I abide in the joy of the Atman.' Again, 'I am Brahman, one without a second, bliss without end, the eternal, unchanging Truth' (Shankara 1978, 113, 115). This certainly sounds like a claim to attain in this life the union-without-distinction with Brahman that is, according to advaitic metaphysics, our ultimate destiny.

However there is a difficulty here. If the mystic, having returned from the unitive state, is able to remember and describe the experience, must there not have been a continuity of individual consciousness and memory formation during that experience? Must there not have been a continuous thread of individual memory-bearing consciousness throughout? To become totally dissolved in the infinite reality of Brahman, like a drop falling into the ocean – which is a familiar analogy in the advaitic literature – would be a state from which there could be no return to the same finite individuality. This may well be the final state far beyond this life. But I am in agreement with Louis Duprés when he says, as regards unitive mysticism in this life, that 'such a total elimination of personal consciousness remains an asymptotic ideal never to be reached but to be approached ever more closely' (Duprés 1987, 248).

I therefore do not think that the pluralist hypothesis is incompatible with the reports of unitive mysticism when we take into account their characteristically poetic language and the logical problem of claiming a personal memory of a state beyond individual personal existence.

(13) *Feminist criticism.*   A different kind of criticism, not so much logical as cultural, come from some feminist theologians. Thus June O'Connor (O'Connor 1991), commenting on pp. 52–4 of this book, suggests that the idea, which Valerie Saiving Goldstein promoted in her pioneering work, that whereas the characteristic sin of men is too strong an ego, leading to pride and self-assertion, women's characteristic sin is an underdevelopment or negation of the ego due to the long history of male domination and repression. Acknowledging Goldstein's thesis I suggested that in so far as anyone, women or men (for many men also have been damaged by oppression), lack a sense of their own worth, it may be necessary for the ego first to be built up as a prerequisite of the salvific transformation. O'Connor thinks however that women's experience is too varied and multi-layered to be categorised in this neat way. I think she is right, and I have not stressed this sufficiently in the text. I do not however accept her further and more radical suggestion that the salvific change – which she rightly emphasises

is a gradual process – occurs purely on the natural level, involving no transcendent reality, and is exclusively a turning from self to the human other. She is here supporting the humanist or naturalist position of Mesle (1991) and others. However this is not the place to return to the basic argument for religious experience as a ground for warranted belief in a transcendent reality.

(14) *A Post-Enlightenment western imposition?*   An objection to the pluralistic hypothesis from yet another quarter is summarised by one writer as that 'most adherents of most religions will see the pluralistic hypothesis [as] derogatory to the visions of religious truth to which they adhere, [and] also as another form of Western or Christian religious reinterpretation and reduction to foreign assumptions of what they hold as the deepest truths of life' (Rose 1996, 102).[19] There are two distinguishable points here. As to the first, it is true that most 'ordinary believers' within the different traditions assume that the religious beliefs in which they have been brought up are literally true, so that any that are incompatible with them are false; and they often regard any questioning of this as an attack upon their faith. But this is an historically short-sighted position. The traditions have in fact all developed and changed very considerably in the course of time. Christian theology, for example, was transformed by the discovery in the nineteenth century of the age of the earth and the process of biological evolution, requiring the abandonment of the centuries-long assumption that the Bible, literally understood, is verbally inspired by God. We know now that the account of creation and of the origin of man and then of woman in the first book of the Bible is not factually credible and must be understood as religious myth. This is now so generally taken for granted that many forget that in the second half of the nineteenth century the abandonment of these beliefs was profoundly traumatic. There were fierce debates, heresy trials, divisions even within families, and real pain and anguish were caused. But none of the leading theologians of the twentieth century or today subscribe to biblical literalism. They all accept that there is myth and legend as well as history (some of it being exaggerated history) in the scriptures, and they regard as mythic such stories as that the universe was created in six days, that the first woman was made out of the rib of the first man, that a serpent tempted the first pair to disobey God by eating some fruit from a particular tree, and most no longer infer from that story that all subsequent humans have inherited the original sinfulness of Adam

and Eve. New knowledge and new ideas do, unfortunately, often cause real mental and emotional distress; but this is not a valid reason for rejecting them. If it were we would all still believe today that the sun revolves round the earth. Today the challenge comes from the growing realisation that one's own religion is not the one and only true faith and path of salvation/liberation/enlightenment. However within the pluralist position there are many variations, and we are in a period of continuing discussion of different options, the one that I have propounded here being one of them.

As to the charge that religious pluralism is a 'Western or Christian' or a post-Enlightenment European invention, this is just historically false. So far from religious pluralism being a recent creation from within Christianity, Christianity is among the last traditions to begin to take it seriously! And so far from it being a modern western invention, it was a familiar and widespread outlook in the East centuries before the eighteenth century western Enlightenment. The thirteenth-century CE Muslim Sufi, Rumi, is famous for the pluralistic teaching embodied in such sayings as – referring to the religions of his time – 'The lamps are different, but the Light is the same: it comes from Beyond' (Rumi 1978, 166). Again, 'Hindus do Hindu things. The Dravidian Muslims in India do what they do. It's all praise, and it's all right' (Armstrong 1993, 278). In fifteenth-century CE India, Kabir, who was venerated by both Hindus and Muslims, taught that the 'formless God takes a thousand forms in the eyes of His creatures' (Kabir 1977, 75). In the same century Guru Nanak, founder of the Sikh faith, began his ministry in a period of Hindu–Muslim tension by declaring 'There is no Hindu and there is no Musalman' (Harbans Singh 1969, 97) and preached that 'The one God is the Father of all. We are all His children. . . . He is not far, He is not near, He is with us all' (Trilochan Singh 1969, 44). And so we have to look for the earliest expressions of the pluralist insight to fifteenth century India, or indeed to some extent at least to the Buddhist emperor Asoka in the second century BCE. So far from it being a modern western discovery which we have foisted on the rest of the world, it is an aspect of a widespread eastern outlook which we in the west are independently discovering many centuries later – although there are also earlier Christian intimations of it in the fifteenth century Nicholas of Cusa with his teaching that 'there is only one religion in the variety of rites' (Nicholas of Cusa 1990, 7) and the seventeenth- to eighteenth-century Quaker William Penn who wrote that 'The humble, meek, merciful, just, pious and devout souls are everywhere of one religion, and when death has taken off the mask they will know one another, though the divers liveries they wear here makes them strangers' (Penn 1926, 99–100). No doubt it was the European Enlightenment that has freed the west to take this insight on board; but it's origins lie much further back in human history.

(15) Finally, an important clarification. What about atheists, humanists, Marxists, and what about those who engage in spiritual practices in an eclectic or syncretistic way but who adhere to no religious tradition? Very often self-professed atheists in the west are upside down Christian fundamentalists, in that the concept of God which they reject is one that very many non-fundamentalist Christians also reject. But the important point to be made is that from the point of view of the pluralistic hypothesis people can, and increasingly do, respond in their lives to the universal presence of the Real, the ultimate reality, without using any religious concepts or indeed whilst explicitly rejecting them all. For they may feel, and act upon, an unconscious awareness of that presence as a responsibility to seek justice or to create peace or to serve their fellow humans in a great variety of ways. In post-Christian Europe this is a widespread phenomenon, worthy of the utmost respect and support.

Notes

1. There are many theological, but only a few other philosophical, versions of religious pluralism. These latter include Christian 1964, 1972 and 1987; Runzo 1986; Neville 1991; the contributors to Kellenberger, ed., 1993; Rose 1996; Kaplan 2002.
2. These books, philosophical and theological, are: Terry Mathis 1985, Gavin D'Costa 1987, Olof Franck 1988, Chester Gillis 1989, Gregory Carruthers SJ, 1990, Kenneth Rose 1996, Adnan Aslan 1998, Gerhard Gade 1998, Heather Meacock 2000, Christian Heller 2001, Christopher Sinkinson 2001, Paul Eddy 2002, David Cheetham 2003, with others in Japanese, Chinese, and Turkish; and on other aspects of my interpretation of religion: Carl Reinhold-Brakenhielm 1975, Douglas Geivett 1995, Robert Mesle 1991, Lindsey Hall 2003.
3. It is at this point that I part company with William Alston, with whom I share the argument for trusting religious experience. I maintain that in affirming the exclusive truth of doctrines based on Christian experience he has really propounded the principle that religious

experience generally produces false beliefs, with the sole – and arbitrary – exception of Christian religious experience. We have debated this is in *Dialogues in the Philosophy of Religion*, 2001.

4. Aquinas, *S.T.*, II/II, Q.1, art.2, trans. ed. Anton Pegis, *Basic Writings of Saint Thomas Aquinas* (New York: Random House, 1945), vol. 2, p. 1057.

5. D'Costa 1991, 7f.

6. I accept Alvin Plantinga's correction to my including Calvin at this point (Plantinga 2000, 46).

7. Augustine, *De Vera Religione*, 36, 67.

8. Thomas Aquinas, *Summa contra Gentiles*, I, 14, 3.

9. Plantinga is, incidentally, mistaken in thinking (Plantinga 2000, 47) that I allow the negative concepts of the *via negativa* as applying to the Real. I treat these as 'a way of saying that it lies beyond the range of our positive substantial characterisations' (p. 239).

10. This is not a new idea. We find it in some of the great mystics. Meister Eckhart says that 'before there were any creatures God was not "God", i.e. the humanly known and worshipped God (Eckhart 1981, 200). Again, the great Islamic mystic Al-'Arabi, distinguishing between the essence and the manifestations of God, says, 'The Essence . . . is not a divinity . . . it is we who make Him a divinity . . . Thus He is not known [as Allah] until we are known' (Al-'Arabi 1990, 92).

11. The question is eloquently raised by, e.g., Stafford Betty (Betty 1991, 100f).

12. The term 'serendipity' was introduced into theology in Gordon Kaufman 1993.

13. See Chapter 18 on 'The Ethical Criterion'.

14. I John 4: 8.

15. Micah 6: 8.

16. Sutta Nipata, 144.

17. *Bhagavad Gita*, 11: 44.

18. For more about this see Hick 1993, *The Metaphor of God Incarnate*.

19. Others who make this objection include Surin 1989 and 1990, Verkamp 1991, Loughlin 1990. I should make it clear that this is not the main burden of Rose's book, which also contains more important arguments which I have discussed under other headings above. He is also rare among critics in proposing what he regards (though I do not) as a way of improving the pluralistic hypothesis.

1

Introduction

Everything has been said before, but usually by people who did not know that they were saying it.

1 A RELIGIOUS INTERPRETATION OF RELIGION

There are many general interpretations of religion. These have usually been either naturalistic, treating religion as a purely human phenomenon or, if religious, have been developed within the confines of a particular confessional conviction which construes all other traditions in its own terms. The one type of theory that has seldom been attempted is a religious but not confessional interpretation of religion in its plurality of forms; and it is this that I shall be trying to offer here.[1]

In offering a religious interpretation of religion I do not claim that the naturalistic, or reductionist, accounts advocated by such thinkers as Feuerbach, Freud, Durkheim and their successors can be shown to be mistaken. It is evident that each of these is more convincing in some areas than in others; but although severally limited they are in principle capable of being combined into comprehensive theories of religion as a self-regulating response of the human animal to the pressures generated by its particular niche within the biological system. The impossibility of refuting such interpretations is an aspect of the pervasive ambiguity of the universe. So also is the equal impossibility of refuting the interpretation of religion as our varied human response to a transcendent reality or realities – the gods, or God, or Brahman, or the Dharmakaya, or the Tao, and so on.

However, although ancillary, the findings of the human sciences are far from irrelevant to a religious interpretation of religion. It has been customary to treat the view of religion from within, through the eyes of faith, and the view of it from without, through the eyes of anthropological, sociological and psychological theory, as mutually exclusive. It has accordingly been assumed that one can

1

understand religion either religiously or scientifically but not in both ways at once. However a contemporary religious interpretation of religion requires us to do precisely that. I shall therefore attempt to construct a comprehensive hypothesis which takes full account of the data and theories of the human sciences but which uses them to show how it is that the response to a transcendent reality has taken the bewildering plurality of forms that history records.

Such an endeavour is likely, as a matter of biographical fact, to be launched from within a particular religious tradition, which in this instance is Christianity. But it cannot restrict itself to that tradition.[2] For it is evident that in some ninety-nine per cent of cases the religion which an individual professes and to which he or she adheres depends upon the accidents of birth. Someone born to Buddhist parents in Thailand is very likely to be a Buddhist, someone born to Muslim parents in Saudi Arabia to be a Muslim, someone born to Christian parents in Mexico to be a Christian, and so on. There are of course conversions from one faith to another, but in the case of the great world religions these are peripheral to the massive transmission of each from one generation to the next within its own population. It is also true that we have to speak today of post-Buddhists, post-Muslims, post-Christians . . . However the post-religious are still deeply influenced by their religio-cultural past and it remains true that much of the life of humanity flows through the channels of thought and imagination formed by the ancient traditions that we know, in rough order of antiquity, as Hinduism, Judaism, Buddhism, Taoism, Confucianism, Christianity and Islam.

That there is not just one but a plurality of such historical channels is prominent among the facts for which an interpretation of religion must account. In doing so it will inevitably have to go beyond the dominant self-understanding of each tradition. For each has come over the centuries to regard itself as uniquely superior to the others, seeing them either as lying outside the sphere of salvation, or as earlier stages in an evolution of which it is the culmination, or as less full and authentic versions of itself. But this cannot be sustained on impartial grounds. A genuinely pluralistic hypothesis will thus inevitably call, at least by implication, for further development within each of the traditions. Change is in fact going on all the time by means of interpretation, exegesis, commentary, midrash, theological experiment; and insofar as each of the world religions comes, in today's global city, to see itself as one among many it will use these methods to de-emphasise its own absolute and exclusive claim, allowing this to fall into the background and eventually to become absorbed into its past history.

2 RELIGION AS A FAMILY-RESEMBLANCE CONCEPT

Scholars have proposed an immense range of definitions of 'religion', attempting to discriminate between that to which the word does and does not properly apply.[3] The major division, as we have already noted, is between religious and naturalistic definitions. According to the former, religion (or a particular religious tradition) centres upon an awareness of and response to a reality that transcends ourselves and our world, whether the 'direction' of transcendence be beyond or within or both. Such definitions presuppose the reality of the intentional object of religious thought and experience; and they are broader or narrower according as this object is characterised more generally, for example as a cosmic power,[4] or more specifically, for example as a personal God.[5] Naturalistic definitions on the other hand describe religion as a purely human activity or state of mind. Such definitions have been phenomenological,[6] psychological[7] and sociological.[8]

These varied formulae solve in different ways the problems of inclusion and exclusion: for example, should Theravada Buddhism, with its lack of belief in a supreme being, or classical Confucianism, which is often regarded as essentially a social ethic, or again Marxism, which is militantly atheistic, be regarded as religions? Or should we perhaps, in order to accommodate these problematic cases, distinguish between religions and 'quasi-religions' (cf. Tillich 1963, 5–12)? Or again, should we see religions and secular ideologies as different species of the wider genus of world-views (cf. Smart 1981)?

All these definitional strategies embody decisions and either reveal or conceal commitments. Each can be, and has been, attacked and defended; and indeed much time and energy has been devoted over the years to the debate between rival definitions of 'religion'. But Wittgenstein's discussion of family-resemblance (or, as they have also been called, cluster) concepts has opened up the possibility that 'religion' is of this rather different kind. He took the example of games. These have no common essence. Some are solitary, others competitive; some individual, others team activities; some depend on skill, others on chance; some are capable of being won or lost, others not; some are played for amusement, others for gain; some are played with balls, others with cards, sticks, etc. What makes us apply the name 'game' to this wide assortment of activities, ranging from football to chess, and from a solitary child playing with her doll to the Olympic Games, is that each is similar in important respects to some others in the family, though not in all respects to any or in any respect to all. Instead of a set of defining characteristics there is a network of similarities overlapping and criss-crossing like the resemblances and differences in build, features, eye colour, gait, temperament and so on among the members of a natural family (Wittgenstein 1963, para. 66; cf. McDermott 1970, 390–400, Smart 1986, 46–7). There are no characteristics that every member must have; but nevertheless there are characteristics distributed sporadically and in varying degrees which together distinguish this from a different family.

Using this analogy it is, I think, illuminating to see the different traditions, movements and ideologies whose religious character is either generally agreed or responsibly debated, not as exemplifying a common essence, but as forming a complex continuum of resemblances and differences analogous to those found within a family. But as in the case of 'game' we need a starting point from which to begin to chart this range of phenomena. No one would look, for example, to the act of childbirth or to the act of murder for an example of a game; and no one would look to a teapot or a post office for an example of a religion. We must and do have some general agreed notion of where to look. I suggest that Paul Tillich's concept of 'ultimate concern' (Tillich 1957, 1–4) can serve as a pointer in the right direction. For religious objects, practices and beliefs have a deep importance for those to whom they count as religious; and they are important not merely in the immediate sense in which it may seem important to finish correctly a sentence that one has begun or to answer the telephone when it is ringing, but important in a more permanent and ultimate sense. This quality of importance pervades the field of religious phenomena. Not everything that has more than transient importance to us is religious; but all authentic as opposed to merely nominal religiousness seems to involve a sense of profound importance.

However within the wide domain of this very general characteristic religion takes such widely different forms and is interpreted in such widely different ways that it cannot be adequately defined but only described. Thus we can say that the worship of a 'higher unseen power' is a widespread feature among this family of phenomena. It is however absent from Theravada Buddhism, which nevertheless shares many other prominent characteristics of the family, such as claiming to teach the true nature and meaning of life and to show the way to final liberation from suffering. Again, the bloodthirsty worship of Moloch in the ancient Near East had nothing directly in common with Theravada Buddhism; but on the other hand, although in most other ways in startling contrast to Christianity, the cult of Moloch overlaps with it in involving the worship of a personal deity; and Christianity in turn overlaps with the Theravada in the quite different respect that it offers a comprehensive interpretation of life. Thus all three are members, at considerable removes from one another, of the same large family of phenomena.

This understanding of the concept also enables us to locate the secular faith of Marxism as a fairly distant cousin of such movements as Christianity and Islam, sharing some of their characteristics (such as a comprehensive world-view, with scriptures, eschatology, saints and a total moral claim) whilst lacking others (such as belief in a transcendent divine reality). Accordingly when within what we may call the Oxford–Larousse–Brockhaus linguistic world[9] we are speaking of the more central members of the religious family we usually exclude Marxism, although when speaking more broadly we include it. But the question 'Is Marxism, or Buddhism, or Confucianism, or Christian Science, a religion?' ceases to have a straightforwardly correct answer. It becomes a matter instead of noting their positions within a complex, ramified network of related phenomena. Having done this we have resolved – or perhaps dissolved – the problem of the definition of 'religion'.

3 BELIEF IN THE TRANSCENDENT

Given this family-resemblance understanding of the concept, different scholars and communities of scholarship are free to focus their attention upon the features that specially interest them. Thus sociologists of religion legitimately focus upon one set of features, ethnologists upon another, psychologists upon another. The feature upon which I shall primarily focus in this book is belief in the transcendent. Although this is not of the essence of religion – for, as I have just suggested, there is no such essence – nevertheless most forms of religion have affirmed a salvific reality that transcends (whilst also usually being thought of as immanent within) human beings and the world, this reality being variously conceived as a personal God or non-personal Absolute, or as the cosmic structure or process or ground of the universe.[10] One might call the systematic discussion of this topic 'theology' except that the term restricts the concept of the transcendent by implication to the notion of *theos*. Wilfred Cantwell Smith has tentatively suggested the more comprehensive term 'transcenden-tology' (W. C. Smith 1981, 183). But however we name it the topic of the transcendent is to be a central concern of this book. One of the merits of the family-resemblance analogy, however, is that it does not push the controversy between believers and disbelievers in the transcendent out onto the borders as a battle between religion and its external enemy, irreligion, but gives it a place within the ongoing religious discussion. For in a growing contemporary debate it has become a vital *religious* question whether religion requires or can on the contrary dispense with belief in a transcendent reality. In focusing upon this issue we shall thus be addressing what is both the most momentous and the most contested issue in religious discourse today. It is so momentous because a whole understanding of life flows from one's response to it; and it is so intensely debated precisely because it is so momentous.

Until recently the debate has almost invariably been conducted in terms of one or other specific conception of the transcendent, embedded in a distinctive system of religious symbols and myths and authoritatively expressed in its related scriptures. Belief in the transcendent has thus generally been defended from the standpoint of a particular tradition and has accordingly been identified with belief in the reality of the Jahweh of the Torah, or the Vishnu of the Bhagavad Gita, or the heavenly Father of the New Testament, or the Brahman of the Upanishads, or the Dharmakaya of Mahayana Buddhism . . . However we have already noted the anachronistic character of single tradition treatments of basic religious issues in our consciously pluralistic twentieth and twenty-first centuries.

A further important reason for a global treatment is that it reveals with unmistakable clarity the human element in religion. For each tradition, whilst able to acknowledge peripheral cultural influences, has assumed that there has been no human and therefore fallible contribution to the formation of its own core conceptions. These are believed to be integral to the eternal Dharma or to have been divinely revealed in Torah, Bible or Qur'an. But it is abundantly evident today that each tradition has been deeply influenced by cultural forces which rest in turn upon a complex of geographical, climatic, economic and political factors. Xenophanes, centuries ago, noted that 'Ethiopians make their gods black with turned up noses, Thracians make them with red hair and blue eyes; mortals think that gods are born and have their own food, voice and shape; but if oxen or lions had hands and could draw or produce images like men, horses would draw the shapes of the gods like horses, oxen like oxen, and they would produce such bodies as the bodily frame they have themselves' (Preller and Ritter 1913, 100). And modern historians of religion have made such observations as that ancient nomadic pastoral communities tended to think of the divine in male terms, in contrast to settled agricultural peoples who tended to think of the divine in female terms (Ling 1968, 27). Thus the sociobiologist Edward O. Wilson says:

> The God of monotheistic religions is always male; this strong patriarchal tendency has several cultural sources. Pastoral societies are highly mobile, tightly organized, and often militant, all features that tip the balance toward male authority. It is also significant that herding, the main economic basis, is primarily the responsibility of men. Because the Hebrews were originally a herding people, the Bible describes God as a shepherd and the chosen people as his sheep. Islam, one of the strictest of all monotheistic faiths, grew to early power among the herding people of the Arabian peninsula . . .   (1978, 190)

Again, we cannot help noticing that in conflicts between 'God-fearing' nations each warring group has invariably believed that the deity was on its own side. There are thus unmistakable correlations between the ways in which particular communities have believed religiously and the nature of their environmental and historical circumstances.[11] We shall have occasion to note other such correlations later; but at this stage it is sufficient to make the point, which the history of religions abundantly illustrates, that human factors manifestly enter into the formation of religious concepts and into the ways in which the transcendent is believed to be encountered.

In saying this we are in effect acknowledging an important element of truth within the naturalistic theories of religion. These have claimed that God is a projection onto the universe of ideal human qualities, or of buried infancy memories of one's father, or of the social reality of the community with its absolute claims and supporting presence; and that the belief in a life to come has arisen to satisfy our insistent desire to continue in being. Such theories, when generalised into comprehensive interpretations of religion, turn out to have significant flaws and limitations (see Chapter 7.1). However the issue between the naturalistic and religious interpretations of religion must not be allowed to become one of total opposition. The alternatives are not that the intentional object of religious worship or contemplation is either entirely illusory or else exactly as described in this or that sacred text. It will be a major theme of this book that we always perceive the transcendent through the lens of a particular religious culture with its distinctive set of concepts, myths, historical exemplars and devotional or meditational techniques. And it is this inexpungible human contribution to religious awareness that accounts for the fascinating variations of religious thought, experience and practice around the globe and down the centuries, in all their rational and irrational, profound and shallow, impressive and absurd, morally admirable and morally reprehensible features.

This last polarity is worth stressing. For the ethically mixed character of human nature is reflected in the religions of humanity. We see individuals and societies being morally and spiritually elevated by the claim of the Real touching them through their religious traditions, but we also see those same traditions being used as instruments of human selfishness, greed, cruelty and prejudice, both individual and corporate. On the one hand religion has been responsible for the saintly lives of men and women who have risen above self-centredness to serve God or to live out the Dharma; it has also been a major influence in such developments as the abolition of slavery, the beginning of the liberation of women, the struggle against racial discrimination, the rise of political concern for the unjustly disadvantaged and the search for international disarmament and world peace. On the other hand religion has sanctioned human sacrifices and the torture and burning of 'witches' and 'heretics'; it has blessed almost every war that has ever been fought; and it has been used as an instrument for gaining power over and exploiting large groups of people, bestowing its validation upon massively inequitable social systems. Thus to defend the conviction of the reality of the transcendent is not to affirm the moral worth of religious phenomena simply as such. On the contrary, the recognition of the human element in all religion emphasises the need for rational and ethical criticism and discrimination.

A contemporary apologetic for belief in the transcendent, then, must start from the new situation revealed by our modern awareness of religious plurality and conceptual relativity.[12] It must see religious thought and experience as a global continuum containing an immense variety of forms in a history moving from archaic beginnings to the present still-evolving state of the great world traditions.[13] It must recognise to the full the presence of culture-relative projection and symbolisation within this long history. And it must show reason to believe that this vast and multifarious field of human faith is nevertheless not wholly projection and illusion – even though there is much projection and illusion within it – but constitutes our variously transparent and opaque interface with a mysterious transcendent reality.

4 PROBLEMS OF TERMINOLOGY

Any discussion of religion in its plurality of forms is inevitably beset by problems of terminology. Each tradition has its own vocabulary, expressing its own system of concepts; and whilst these overlap with those of other traditions, so that there are all manner of correspondences, parallels, analogies and structural similarities, yet each set of terms is only fully at home in its own particular linguistic environment. We have very little in the way of a tradition-neutral religious vocabulary. Accordingly we have to improvise, sometimes using words in stretched senses to cover two or more related ideas – and thereby risking the wrath of those who can see the semantic stretching but not the communicational need which it serves.

For example, in the next chapter I shall be referring to the soteriological character of the great world faiths. 'Soteriological' comes from the Greek *soter*, saviour, and 'salvation' from the Latin *salus*, and both have become linked historically with the specifically Christian notion of being saved by the atoning death of Christ from God's righteous judgment upon sinners. But it is not difficult to see that this is a specific form of the more general idea of being brought from an evil situation into a radically better one. It is in this sense that it is possible to speak, for example, of 'Buddhist salvation' (Abe 1985a, 212) and to refer to Zen enlightenment as salvation (Suzuki 1982, 99), in spite of the fact that the more usual Buddhist, and also Hindu, concept is that of liberation as awakening – from metaphysical ignorance and illusion. In the same general sense one could speak of 'Christian liberation' – from sin and guilt. These are both forms of what in these chapters I propose to refer to by the hybrid term 'salvation/liberation':[14] for they both speak of the transformation of our human situation from a state of alienation from the true structure of reality to a radically better state in harmony with reality.

An even larger problem concerns the term to be used for the putative transcendent reality which is affirmed when the different traditions speak of the God of Abraham, Isaac and Jacob, or of the Holy Trinity, or Allah, or Vishnu, or Brahman, or the Dharmakaya/Nirvana/Sunyata, and so on. It is possible to use the term God with the proviso that it remains an open question whether God is personal or non-personal, or both personal and non-personal in different aspects or as differently conceived and experienced. But nevertheless the theistic associations of the term are so strong that such a usage is always liable to misunderstanding and could well appear to Buddhists, advaitic Hindus, Taoists and Confucians as linguistically imperialistic; and this would only hinder the presentation of a general theory of religion which is intended to be acceptable to the more global-minded members of all traditions. We therefore have such options as the Transcendent, the Ultimate, Ultimate Reality, the Supreme Principle, the Divine, the One, the Eternal, the Eternal One, the Real. There is no clearly right choice among these and different people will legitimately prefer different terms. In previous writings, struggling to find the most appropriate word, I have used the Transcendent, the Divine, and the Eternal One. However 'the Divine' and 'the Eternal One' are perhaps too theistically coloured. 'The

Transcendent' is possible; but on balance I prefer to speak of 'the Real'.

This term has the advantage that without being the exclusive property of any one tradition it is nevertheless familiar within all of them. In Christian terms it gives rise to no difficulty to identify God, the sole self-existent reality, as the Real. Within Islam the Real, *al Haqq*, is one of the names of Allah. Within the Hindu family of faiths it is natural to think of the ultimate reality, Brahman, as *sat* or *satya*, the Real. Within Mahayana Buddhism the Dharmakaya or *śūnyatā* is also spoken of as *tattva*, the Real. In Chinese religious thought the ultimate is *zhen*, the Real. 'The Real' is then, I suggest, as good a generic name as we have for that which is affirmed in the varying forms of transcendent religious belief.[15] For it is used within the major theistic and non-theistic traditions and yet is neutral as between their very different ways of conceiving, experiencing and responding to that which they affirm in these diverse ways. I shall also however, for the sake of stylistic variety, sometimes use as synonyms 'the ultimately Real' and 'ultimate Reality' or even simply 'the Ultimate' or 'Reality'.

There are many other terminological problems on a lower level. In discussing Hinduism and Buddhism, Judaism and Islam, it will be necessary to use terms taken from their sacred scriptures and their theological or philosophical literature. I propose to treat some of these – such as Karma, Nirvana, Samsara, Dharma – as English words; for I believe that in the increasing inter-cultural study of religion these must be accepted into whatever language is being used. Others however – such as *śūnyatā* – I shall usually leave in their (transliterated) Sanscrit or other original form, because the standard English equivalents (in this case 'Emptiness', 'Void', 'Nothingness') can be seriously misleading. Such terms as *śūnyatā* cannot be satisfactorily translated by any one word but have to be understood from context and commentary.[16] On the other hand I shall sometimes use Sunyata (without the diacritical marks) as an adopted English word along with Dharmakaya, Dharma, Nirvana, Brahman, Tao, God, when referring to the different concepts of the ultimate. I hope that such liberties and superficial inconsistencies will be forgiven in a situation in which usage is fluid and somewhat arbitrary and in which we are all still groping for satisfactory ways to express ourselves inter-culturally.

5 OUTLINE OF THE ARGUMENT

It may be helpful to conclude this Introduction with a brief sketch of the argument in the book. Our field of interest is the great world faiths, each of which has its roots in the axial age of the mid-first millennium BCE. Whereas pre-axial religion was generally concerned to keep life on an even keel, post-axial religion has been concerned with salvation/liberation as the realisation of a limitlessly better possibility. These traditions affirm that this possibility is grounded in reality and is thus actually available to us (Chapters 2–4).

The universe is religiously ambiguous in that it is possible to interpret it, intellectually and experientially, both religiously and naturalistically. The theistic and anti-theistic arguments are all inconclusive, for the special evidences to which they appeal are also capable of being understood in terms of the contrary world-view. Further, the opposing sets of evidences cannot be given objectively quantifiable values (Chapters 5–7).

This religious ambiguity is a special case of the general fact that our environment is capable of being construed – in sense perception as well as ethically and religiously – in a range of ways. In a continuous activity of interpretation, usually operating in unconscious and habitual ways, we form hypotheses about its character or practical meaning for us which we then test in our behaviour. For the meaning of an object or a situation is its perceived (or misperceived) character such that to perceive it as having that character is to be in a distinctive dispositional state in relation to it. We are continuously experiencing aspects of our environment as having kinds of meaning in virtue of which it is appropriate for us to behave within it in this or that way or range of ways. Thus all conscious experiencing is experiencing-as.

Three levels of interpretation or meaning have long been recognised: physical, ethical and religious. In terms of its physical meaning we experience the world as an environment in which we learn to survive and flourish as animal organisms; and in doing so we exercise a minimum degree of cognitive freedom. Ethical meaning presupposes physical interpretation but involves a much greater degree of cognitive freedom. At this level we are aware of other human beings as persons whose co-presence with us creates mutual claims and obligations. The further religious mode of experiencing involves a yet greater exercise of cognitive freedom, in virtue of which it can take many different forms. As religious beings we continue to live in the world in terms of its physical and ethical meanings, but do so in new ways required by its religious meaning.

The religious awareness of the world and of our life within it ranges from, for example, the experiencing by the ancient Hebrew prophets of historical events as divine acts to the Mahayana Buddhist experiencing of Samsara, the fleeting round of birth, death and suffering, as Nirvana. Both the religious and the naturalistic ways of construing the world arise from a fundamental cognitive choice, which I call faith, which is continuous with the interpretive element within our experience of the physical and ethical character of our environment (Chapters 8–10).

The religious and naturalistic modes of experience both connect with conceptions of the structure of the universe and with expectations concerning the course of future experience within and (in the religious case) beyond our present life. Thus the issue between them is ultimately a factual one in which the rival world-views are subject to eventual experiential confirmation or disconfirmation (Chapter 11). This understanding of the situation is challenged by contemporary non-realist understandings of religion, which are however themselves ultimately naturalistic, presenting us again with the same fundamental options (Chapter 12).

Confronted with this choice it is rationally appropriate for those who experience their life in relation to the transcendent to trust their own experience, together with that of the stream of religious life in which they participate and of the great figures who are its primary experiential witnesses, and to proceed to believe and to live on that basis. It is likewise rationally proper for those who do not participate in any way in the wide field of religious experience to reject, *pro tem*, all belief in the transcendent. In view of the ultimately factual character of the issue both groups are running the unavoidable risk of being profoundly mistaken and both are entitled in this situation to make the choice to which their own experience leads them (Chapter 13).

The argument that (with various qualifications and caveats) it is rational to believe what our experience leads us to believe opens up the problem of religious plurality; for different forms of religious experience justify different and often incompatible sets of beliefs. The hypothesis proposed at this point hinges upon the distinction (first given philosophical prominence by Kant) between something as it is in itself and as it appears to a consciousness dependent upon a particular kind of perceptual machinery and endowed with a particular system of interpretive concepts congealed into a linguistic system. An analogous distinction is drawn within each of the great religious traditions between the Real in itself and the Real as humanly thought and experienced. This distinction, in conjunction with the principle that it is rational for people within each tradition to trust their own form of religious experience, suggests the hypothesis that the infinite Real, in itself beyond the scope of other than purely formal concepts, is differently conceived, experienced and responded to from within the different cultural ways of being human.

Experience of the transcendent is structured either by the concept of deity, which presides over the theistic traditions, or by the concept of the absolute, which presides over the non-theistic traditions. Each of these is schematised in actual human experience to produce the experienced divine *personae* (such as Jahweh, the heavenly Father, Allah, Vishnu, Shiva) and metaphysical *impersonae* (such as Brahman, the Tao, the Dharmakaya, Sunyata) to which human beings orient themselves in worship or meditation. The function of religion in each case is to provide contexts for salvation/liberation, which consists in various forms of the transformation of human existence from self-centredness to Reality-centredness (Chapters 14–16). Given this interpretive hypothesis, are there criteria by which to assess particular religious phenomena and the religious traditions as totalities? The basic criterion is soteriological; and the salvific transformation is most readily observed by its moral fruits, which can be identified by means of the ethical ideal, common to all the great traditions, of *agape/karuṇā* (love/compassion) (Chapters 17–18).

The contrasting and often conflicting beliefs of the different traditions are of several kinds. There are opposed historical beliefs, which are in principle resolvable by historical evidence, though in practice generally not; and these should simply be acknowledged and tolerated. There are conflicts of trans-historical belief, concerning origins (creation/emanation/beginningless flux) and destinies (resurrection/reincarnation/heaven and hell/trans-cendence of egoity). These concern either questions to which we do not and do not for the purposes of salvation/liberation need to know the answer, or questions which cannot be answered in terms of our present earthly systems of concepts. Our human response to the latter has been the creation of myths. But alternative myths, functioning in their separate mythic spaces, do not clash with one another. Finally there are the different ways of thinking-and-experiencing the Real. According to our hypothesis these represent different phenomenal awarenesses of the same noumenal reality and evoke parallel salvific transformations of human life. None of these differences, then, is incompatible with the overall hypothesis (Chapters 18–20).

Finally, in the Epilogue, there is some consideration of the implications of such an hypothesis for the ongoing religious traditions and for spirituality in a pluralistic age.

Notes

1. Although he was concerned with the phenomenology rather than with the philosophy of religion, the massive work of the late Mircea Eliade, one of the greatest twentieth-century scholars in the field of comparative religion, was based upon the premise that I am assuming here. He wrote that

   a religious phenomenon will only be recognized as such if it is grasped at its own level, that is to say, if it is studied *as* something religious. To try to grasp the essence of such a phenomenon by means of physiology, psychology, sociology, economics, linguistics, art or any other study is false; it misses the one unique and irreducible element in it – the element of the sacred. Obviously there are no *purely* religious phenomena . . . Because religion is human it must for that very reason be something social, something linguistic, something economic – you cannot think of man apart from language and society. But it would be hopeless to try and explain religion in terms of any one of those basic functions . . .

   (Eliade 1958, xi)

2. The appropriate programme has been well defined by Wilfred Cantwell Smith as

   to interpret intellectually all human faith, one's own and others'; comprehensively and justly. Seeing one's own group and its history thus far as making up one complex strand in the total history of religion until now, a total history that one is endeavouring to understand from within, one may essay a theory that aspires to be part of a movement towards the truth. Seeing one's own group as a component in the total community of humankind, a total community whose corporate critical self-consciousness in this matter has yet to be articulated, again one may endeavour to

contribute to its formulation. A Christian, no more but no less than
any other member of that human community, may and must think
in these realms.   (W. C. Smith 1981, 152)
3. It seems to have been mainly in the late nineteenth and early
   twentieth centuries that scholars discussing religion felt obliged to
   begin by offering a definition of the word. In 1912 James H. Leuba
   published a list of forty-eight such definitions, adding two more of;
   his own (1912, Appendix). More recently, however, there seems to
   have been a growing – though still by no means unanimous – feeling
   that the range of religious phenomena is so various and many-sided
   that no single definition can ever be adequate to it. On some of the
   difficulties of defining 'religion' see William Alston 1967.
4. For example, 'Religion is the consciousness of our practical relation to
   an invisible, spiritual order' (Josiah Royce, quoted by Leuba 1912,
   357).
5. For example, religion is 'the belief in an Ever-living God, that is, a
   Divine Mind and Will ruling the Universe and holding Moral relations
   with mankind' (Martineau 1889, I:1).
6. For example, 'One's religion . . . is one's way of valuing most
   intensively and comprehensively' (Ferré 1970, 11).
7. For example, religion is 'man's faith in a power beyond himself
   whereby he seeks to satisfy emotional needs and gain stability of life,
   and which he expresses in acts of worship and service' (Galloway
   1914, 184).
8. For example, 'A religion is a unified system of beliefs and practices
   relative to sacred things, that is to say, things set apart and
   forbidden – beliefs and practices which unite into one single moral
   community called a Church, all who adhere to them' (Durkheim
   [1912] 1963, 47).
9. 'Recognition on the part of man of some higher unseen power as
   having control of his destiny, and as being entitled to obedience,
   reverence, and worship' (*Oxford English Dictionary* 1971); 'Rapport
   que l'homme établit avec la divinité en lui rendant un culte; Ensemble
   spécifique des croyances, des règles morales et des pratiques cultuelles
   par lesquelles l'homme établit ses rapports avec la divinité' (*Grand
   Larousse de la langue française* 1971); 'Glaube an eine überirdische
   Macht sowie deren kultische Verehrung; Gottesglaube, gläubige
   Verehrung eines Gottes, einer göttlichen Macht' (*Brockhaus Deutsches
   Wörterbuch* 1960).
10. 'In brief: <u>what the great religions claim, against radically secular
    ideologies, is that there is a Beyond or an Unborn, and this is
    somehow accessible to the religious</u> experience of the human race,
    and is not just a <u>philosophical speculation or a theory about the
    world'</u> (Smart 1981, 178).
11. It was Max Weber, in the early years of this century, who first
    showed this systematically in tracing, for example, the sociological
    basis of the theistic and monistic religions respectively ([1922] 1963,
    55–9), the differences between ancient Greek and Roman religion
    (11), the different statuses of war gods (19), the sociological pre-

conditions for the emergence of the idea of universal love (212), etc., etc.

12. On conceptual relativism see Runzo 1986.
13. On the unity of human religious history, despite the often fragmented awareness fostered by the different traditions, see W. C. Smith 1981.
14. Another term, preferred by Martin Prozesky and having much to commend it, is 'ultimate well-being' (Prozesky 1984).
15. The same choice is made by Keith Ward in his recent comparative study of concepts of God in five religious traditions (Ward 1987).
16. I say this despite the weighty words of Kees Bolle in his essay on translating the *Bhagavadgita* (Bolle 1979).

Part One
Phenomenological

2

The Soteriological Character of Post-Axial Religion

Definition p. 12 (handwritten)

> The existence of an axial time, which is placed in the first millenium B.C.: it was then that our intellectual, moral and religious civilization was born and that the foundations were laid on which we continue to build, despite differences in the superstructures we have erected and go on erecting.
>
> (Weil 1975, 21)

1 THE UNIVERSALITY OF RELIGION

The phenomenology of religion is a vast jungle of proliferating diversity in which discordant facts have continually attacked and destroyed large-scale theories and in which few generalisations have been able to survive. Nevertheless, two broad interpretive concepts have emerged to very widespread acceptance, and both are important for the argument of this book.

The first concept is the virtual universality throughout human life of ideas and practices that are recognisably religious. Talcott Parsons says:

> This view that belief in the supernatural is universal has been completely confirmed by modern anthropology. Religion is as much a human universal as language or an incest taboo, which is to say a kinship system. Any conception of a 'natural man' who is not encumbered by such 'cultural baggage' belongs to a fictional picture of prehistory, for which there is no solid evidence for the human, socially organized stage. The view that such 'baggage' *ought* to be dispensed with and that rational man should 'face reality' without any 'superstition' is a product of sophisticated culture, in no way true of the original human condition.
>
> (1963, xxviii)

21

This statement reflects the general consensus among modern historians of religion that, as Mircea Eliade puts it, 'the "sacred" is an element in the structure of consciousness and not a stage in the history of consciousness' (1978, xiii).

This does not of course mean that every man and woman, particularly since the gradual emergence of autonomous individuality, has been actively religious. There are wide variations in degree of personal religiousness, doubtless descending to zero. It does however mean that all human societies have displayed some religious characteristics. This even applies to such officially secular societies as the contemporary Soviet Union. For the Communist ideology constitutes a mythic framework for life, providing both a motivation for idealism and a validation of the existing social order; and the Communist Party is, sociologically, a church with its own hierarchy, its sacred scriptures, its system of dogma, including doctrines of the fall (the development of capitalism) and eschatology (the eventual classless society), and having its exegetical disputes and heresies.[1] Thus the sociologist Robert Bellah speaks of the 'religio-political system of Marxism' (1970, xix). Accordingly if (as recommended in Chapter 1) we understand 'religion' as a family-resemblance concept, referring to a network of partly overlapping and partly distinct phenomena, Communism in its Marxist and Maoist forms belongs within this extended family. It does not constitute a counter-instance to the virtual universality of religion within human societies.

2 PRE-AXIAL RELIGION

The second widely accepted large-scale interpretive concept is the distinction between pre-axial religion, centrally (but not solely) concerned with the preservation of cosmic and social order, and post-axial religion, centrally (but not solely) concerned with the quest for salvation or liberation. Recognition of what is often referred to as the axial period or axial age is more widespread than the use of these particular terms. Thus Robert Bellah notes as one of 'the massive facts of religious history' that

in the first millenium B.C. all across the Old World, at least in centers of high culture, [there occurred] the phenomenon of religious rejection of the world characterized by an extremely negative evaluation of man and society and the exaltation of another realm of reality as alone true and infinitely valuable . . . [Now] the religious goal of salvation (or enlightenment, release, and so forth) is for the first time the central religious preoccupation. (Bellah 1970, 22, 32)

The terminology of current history of religions scholarship is not uniform, but selecting from the range of uses I propose (following Eliade and others) to refer to the pre-axial forms of religion as archaic – using this term in its original sense of 'characterising the earliest times'. This will cover both the 'primal', 'pre-literate', or 'primitive' religions of stone-age humanity and the now extinct priestly and often national religions of the ancient Near East and Egypt, Greece and Rome, India and China. For our present purpose I am grouping these together as pre-axial in contrast to the post-axial movements which have their roots in the 'axis time' and which we now know as the great world faiths. But the pre- and post-axial periods are nevertheless not stages such that the second definitively succeeds and replaces the first. Earlier forms of religion generally continue to some extent both alongside and also within the later ones.[2] Thus the chronological distinction refers primarily to origins.

Pre-axial religion has both psychological and sociological dimensions. Psychologically it is an attempt to make stable sense of life, and particularly of the basic realities of subsistence and propagation and the final boundaries of birth and death, within a meaning-bestowing framework of myth. This serves the social functions of preserving the unity of the tribe or people within a common world-view and at the same time of validating the community's claims upon the loyalty of its members. The underlying concern is conservative, a defence against chaos, meaninglessness and the breakdown of social cohesion. Religious activity is concerned to keep fragile human life on an even keel; but it is not concerned, as is post-axial religion, with its radical transformation.

Pre-literate forms of archaic religion have existed down to our own day in parts of Africa, the Americas, Indonesia, Australasia and the Pacific Islands; but in ever smaller pockets and in ever less pure forms as a result of the invasions during the last two centuries of western imperialists, missionaries and scientific anthropologists. Such religion takes a wide range of forms.

Whereas in the thinking of modern technological people 'the spiritual' is generally relegated to a margin of private fantasy or 'faith', it seems that for pre-literate people it has always been part of the everyday world. The forest, hills, streams, rocks, sky are full of unseen beings and forces which have to be taken into account. There are the local gods and spirits, sometimes ancestors, sometimes totem animals, who are to be variously worshipped, placated or subtly negotiated with. There are magical and ritual practices of many sorts. In all this there is no division between ordinary secular life and special religious moments but rather a single seamless fabric in which what the modern world sees as the 'natural' is everywhere suffused with 'supernatural' presence and meaning. The world of humans, animals and earth forms a unity and life is, in Stanner's phrases, 'a one-possibility thing', 'a kind of standstill' (1979, 515, 521). For example, for the Australian aborigines or 'blackfellows' there is, he says,

> no notion of grace or redemption; no whisper of inner peace and reconcilement; no problems of worldly life to be solved only by a consummation of history; no heaven of reward or hell of punishment . . . [S]ameness, absence of change, fixed routine, regularity, call it what you will, is a main dimension of their thought and life. Let us sum up this aspect as leading to a metaphysical emphasis on abidingness. They place a very special value on things remaining unchangingly themselves . . .
> (1979, 518, 521)

The same basic concern continued, though taking much more complex forms, in the national religions of the ancient world. The archaic structure was cyclical, its flow of meaning beginning afresh each new year and thus maintaining human existence in the same familiar place. This was achieved by a ritual return to the pristine state of the world as depicted in the creation myths. In the new year festival there was an 'annual expulsion of sins, disease, and demons' which was 'basically an attempt to restore – if only momentarily – mythical and primordial time, "pure" time, the time of the "instant" of creation. Every New Year is a resumption of time from the beginning, that is a repetition of the cosmogony' (Eliade [1949] 1971, 54). The function of this 'annulment of time' was to prevent a slippage away from the existing order and so to avoid chaos and disaster:

the cosmos and man are regenerated ceaselessly and by all kinds of means, the past is destroyed, evils and sins are eliminated. Differing in their formulas, all these instruments of regeneration tend toward the same end: to annul past time, to abolish history by a continuous return *in illo tempore*, by the repetition of the cosmogonic act. (1971, 81)

Thus for the ancient Egyptians life existed in a tension between finite ordered existence and a limitless surrounding chaotic non-existence which manifested itself in darkness, in the unbounded desert, in the annual flooding of the Nile, in states of sleep and in death (Hornung [1971] 1982, 179–80); 'But gods and people must together ensure that disorder does not come to overpower justice and order; this is the meaning of their common obligation toward *maat*' (1982, 213).

The cosmic events which revealed the nature of divine life were connected with Ma-a-t, the order which the sun-god, as creator, called into existence once and for all at the beginning of time. Ma-a-t held good unconditionally. The consequence of this truth was that the ancient Egyptians entertained a static image of the world. Unlike modern man, they did not feel themselves borne by a dynamic stream of involvements which carried them to an uncertain future. They had scarcely any eschatology. They firmly believed that, in spite of periods of social disruption and moral deterioration, Ma-a-t would prevail. They believed in a sacred order which was normative in all spheres of life.
(Bleeker and Widengren 1969, 41)

In this world-view the king was the vital link between earth and the gods. When Egypt became unified its divine pharaohs functioned as guarantors of the land's stability:

the monarch was believed to perform a cosmic role. The life of his people and the life of nature throughout his territory was thought to be closely bound up with his life, his vigour, his virility. Chaos might ensue at his death if his natural successor were not immediately enthroned in his stead; by this was understood not only political chaos, but something more akin to cosmic chaos. The king was deity incarnate, the guarantor of life and fertility, the upholder of the whole natural order.
(Ling 1968, 5)[3]

And so the mythic system centring upon the pharaoh was designed to preserve the existing orderly balance of life.

> This 'immobilism', which is characteristic of Egyptian civilization but which is also found in the myths and nostalgias of other traditional societies, is religious in origin. The stability of hieratic forms, the repetition of gestures and exploits performed at the dawn of time, are the logical consequences of a theology that considered the cosmic order to be supremely the divine work and saw in all change the danger of a regression to chaos and hence the triumph of demonic forces.   (Eliade 1978, 86)

Accordingly ancient Egyptian civilisation valued stability – in its hierarchical social order, in the pyramids and other vast public edifices, and in its cosmic mythology.[4] There was no thought of renouncing the established goods of this life to realise a limitlessly better possibility. 'The Egyptians never succumbed to the temptation to find in the transcendence of the existent release from all imperfection, dissolution of the self, or immersion in and union with the universe' (Hornung 1982, 182).

Further east an interaction of cultures produced the Mesopotamian civilisation, ruled by Babylon and presided over by the supreme deity Marduk. Although the king was not himself divine, he was God's representative on earth, and the whole life of the empire and of nature hinged upon him: 'he was responsible for the regularity of the rhythms of nature and for the good estate of the entire society' (Eliade 1971, 55). Hence the annual enthronement festival which seems in varying forms to have occurred throughout the ancient Near East (Ling 1968, 6–8). This was a systematic performance to ensure a continuation of the orderly existence of the land and the people. 'The ritual pattern represents the things which were done to and by the king in order to secure the prosperity of the community in every sense for the coming year' (Hooke 1933, 8). Once again continuity and conservation were the themes, rather than any hope of a radical transformation, personal or national. Indeed 'Eschatological conceptions appear to have been entirely absent or scarcely known in ancient Mesopotamia' (Romer 1969, I:120).[5]

Further east again, in the Indus valley, there was an urban civilisation contemporary and perhaps comparable with those of ancient Mesopotamia and Egypt. This too had its many deities –

primarily, it would seem, female deities representing the fecundity of mother earth. Little is yet known about this ancient culture before the Aryan invasions from the west which began toward the end of the second millennium BCE. Much more however is known from the Rig Veda and Brahmanas of the state of the sub-continent immediately prior to the axial period. This pre-axial Indian religious life involved, together with many gods, the idea of the cosmic law (*rta*), observed by the proper performance of liturgical acts. Vedic religion seems indeed to have been largely a matter of ritual sacrifice in which every detail was important and the slightest error or omission could cause the sacred spell to fail and chaos and calamity to ensue. Here was a system clearly formed for preserving and benefiting from the existing order (cf. Dasgupta 1981).[6]

We see the essentially conservative, rather than revolutionary, nature of the archaic religious outlook again in its attitude to death. Some form of survival of bodily death seems almost always to have been assumed. But in the ancient civilisations of Mesopotamia and Greece, and among the Hittites and Hebrews (as also among many pre-literate tribes down to quite recent times) the persisting aspect was generally thought of as a 'shade', an insubstantial shadowy counterpart body which descends into the darkness beneath the earth. In this underworld individual identity continued, but without any real life. The shade was to be pitied; in some cases feared lest it should envy the living; but its state was in no way one to be looked forward to with pleasurable anticipation. There was no heavenly recompense beyond the grave to which hope might cling amid perils and hardship. The only people whose fate was sometimes thought of as different from this – and the exception underlines the conservative character of the picture as a whole – were the kings and chiefs. For the differences of status prevailing in this life were generally thought of as being continued in the life beyond, so that a great king or warrior would have his treasures buried with him together sometimes with his slain wives and slaves (Eliade 1978, 322; 1982, 8). This represented essentially a preservation of the status quo, though sadly depleted for the great majority. And within the 'megalithic' cultures that produced Stonehenge, Carnac and the other great stone erections which are spread from Malta and the Aegean islands through Spain, Portugal, France, England, Ireland and Denmark to southern Sweden, the vision of the dead, whilst more optimistic, seems to have contributed no less surely to the validation and perpetuation of the existing framework of meaning. The ancestors continued to be real and influential and were joined with their living descendants in a single system of life which their presence enriched and strengthened. They were immortalised as part of the human village, extending beyond the grave, whose indestructibility was symbolised by the massive stones, living and dead being linked by the timeless solidity of the rocks – the central theme in all this being, once again, continuity, order, stable borders against chaos and darkness.[7]

What however we do not find in archaic religion is the hope, central to the post-axial movements, for a radically new, different and better existence, whether in this life or in a further life to come. The sacrifices to the gods, the placating of ill-disposed spirits, the rules for using without being injured by *mana*, the new year festivals, the observance of taboos, the methods of disposal of the dead – all were intended to keep the life of the community on an even keel and the fabric of society intact. Even the high God was creator and preserver but not saviour or liberator. The religious system functioned to renew or prolong the existing balance of good and evil and to ward off the possible disasters which always threatened. But it did not have in view any basic transformation of the human situation. There was no sense of a higher reality in relation to which a limitlessly better future is possible.

Before turning to the post-axial forms of religion, which are to be the main concern of this book, may I remind the reader that no religious stigma should be attached to the term 'archaic'. It is not implied that it is better, from a religious point of view, to be literate than pre-literate, or to live within a contemporary rather than a now extinct form of life. The profound changes initiated during the axial age brought loss as well as gain. In pre-literate tribes life's hardships are endured and its joys communally celebrated in ways which are largely unknown to us modern individualised men and women.[8] In the archaic religions of the ancient Near East and of India there were an affirmation of earthly life and a natural acceptance of death which have been largely lost since the discovery of sin and salvation, *avidyā* and illumination. Indeed the axial age could even be seen as the fall of humanity from a state of religious innocence. But we have to live and work in the period into which we have been born; and this is for us emphatically within the post-axial age as the twentieth moves towards the twenty-first century. There are however fundamentally important values that we can re-learn from the continuing precarious threads of primal religion in the modern world: a sense of continuity with other forms of life and of the living unity of nature, which might restrain our ecologically destructive uses of the environment; and a sense of the moral reality of community, which might moderate our now extreme western individualism.

3 THE AXIAL AGE

Through centuries and millennia the conditions of human life remained essentially the same, and generation after generation lived and died within the same familiar mental horizons. But in the imperceptibly slow evolution of human life through long periods of time the conditions gradually formed for the emergence of individuality. What these conditions were and how they developed are still, in detail, largely matters of speculation. But in what Karl Jaspers has identified as the *Achsenzeit*,[9] from very approximately 800 to very approximately 200 BCE, significant human individuals appeared through whose insights – though always within the existing setting of their own culture – human awareness was immensely enlarged and developed, and a movement began from archaic religion to the religions of salvation or liberation.[10]

It must be emphasised that such large-scale changes are visible only from a distance of centuries. Further, they are not firmly engraved patterns but rather movements within a fluid medium, like changes in the patterns of a river surface resulting from inflow from a new source. For we are dealing with a very large-scale transition, without precise boundaries and complicated by contrary eddies. The axial age was spread over centuries, and much more was going on during these centuries than is captured by the axial image. It was not a clean break with the past but had been prepared and anticipated by earlier movements and has since always been qualified by elements of pre-axial religion persisting within each of the great world traditions and within the secular societies of today. The inevitable danger in identifying and naming this immensely significant transition of some two and a half millennia ago is that it may thereby be made to appear more dramatic and sharply delineated than it must have been at the time. But with this caution in mind let us attempt a long-distance view, focusing on this religious transformation and allowing the rest of the scenery to recede into the background.

In China during this period Confucius and Lao Tzu (or the unknown writers of the Taoist scriptures) lived, and thus two great traditions, later to be labelled Confucianism and Taoism, began.[11] In India Gautama the Buddha and Mahavira the founder of Jainism both lived and taught, the Upanishads were produced and, probably, towards the end of this period the Bhagavad Gita. In Persia Zoroaster transformed the existing pre-revelational religion into what has been called Zoroastrianism, a movement which survives today as a living religion only among the relatively small Parsi community, but whose eschatological ideas nevertheless influenced developing Judaism, and through Judaism Christianity and probably also Islam. In Israel the great Hebrew prophets – Amos, Hosea, Jeremiah, the Isaiahs, Ezekiel – lived and the scriptures were largely written. In Greece this period produced Pythagoras, Socrates, Plato and Aristotle. Individuals were emerging into self-consciousness out of the closely-knit communal mentality of their society. They were now able to hear and respond to a message relating to their own options and potentialities. Religious value no longer resided in total identification with the group but began to take the form of a personal openness to transcendence. And since the new religious messages of the axial age were addressed to individuals as such, rather than as cells in a social organism, these messages were in principle universal in their scope. As Bellah says,

> From the point of view of [the post-axial, or in his terminology the historic, religions] a man is no longer defined chiefly in terms of what tribe or clan he comes from or what particular god he serves but rather as a being capable of salvation. That is to say that it is for the first time possible to conceive of man as such.   (1970, 33)

The period of tribal and national religions was waning and that of the world religions was beginning. Only in ancient Mesopotamia and Egypt, in northern Europe and in the Meso-American cultures does an axial discovery of the transcendent not seem to have taken place.

Thus the axial age was an uniquely significant band of time. With certain qualifications we can say that in this period all the major religious options, constituting the major possible ways of conceiving the ultimate, were identified and established and that nothing of comparably novel significance has happened in the religious life of humanity since. To say this is of course to see Jesus and the rise of Christianity, and again Muhammad and the rise of Islam, as major new developments within the prophetic stream of Semitic religious life; and the growth of Mahayana Buddhism as a development from early Buddhism. At the other end of the axial period there are also qualifications to be noted. Judaism may be said to have begun, not with the work of the great prophets, but with the exodus some four centuries before the beginning of the axial age; or indeed with the prehistoric figure of Abraham. Nevertheless, while Abraham is the semi-legendary patriarch of Judaism and the exodus its founding event, yet the distinctive Jewish understanding of God, and the ways in which this understanding became embodied in a tradition, were formed very largely by the great prophets and biblical redactors of the axial period. Again, in India the Vedas existed before the axial age; but while these are foundational scriptures, the transformation of early Vedic religion into the complex of Brahmanism, the Vedanta and Bhakti, constituting what has come to be called Hinduism, began during the axial period. Finally there was, prior to this period, a brief moment of pure monotheism in Egypt under the Pharaoh Amenhotep IV; but this was quickly extinguished and left no lasting influence.[12]

The concept of the axial age is thus not that of a block of time with a precise beginning and end; nor on the other hand is it so elastic as to be capable of being stretched out to include everything of significance in religious history.[13] It is the concept of a concentration of events which, although without exact boundaries, forms a large-scale event in its own right. Because of the magnitude and widespread incidence of these changes we must suppose that it was made possible by a new stage in human development, occurring at much the same time in these different ancient cultures, in which outstanding individuals emerged and were able to become centres of new religious awareness and understanding, so that from their work have developed what we know today as the great world faiths. But the whole subject of the axial age, its causes, nature and consequences, is ripe for further research and clarification.

4 THE AXIAL SHIFT TO SOTERIOLOGY

In terms of religious phenomenology the new movements arising in the axial period exhibit a soteriological structure which stands in marked contrast to the relatively simple world-acceptance of pre-axial religion. In the archaic world life was variously endured and enjoyed but not fundamentally criticised. Bellah's suggestion carries conviction that this world-acceptance 'is largely to be explained as the only possible response to reality that invades the self to such an extent that the symbolization of self and world are only very partially separate' (1970, 45) whereas, in contrast, in the axial age the human mind began to stand back from its encompassing environment to become conscious of itself as a distinct reality with its own possibilities. Accordingly, whilst archaic religion accepted life as it is and sought to continue it on a stable basis, there came through the outstanding figures of the axial period the disturbing and yet uplifting thought of a limitlessly better possibility. Among the new streams of religious experience by no means every wave and eddy is soteriologically oriented. Nevertheless a clear soteriological pattern is visible both in the Indian religions of Hinduism, Buddhism and Jainism, and in the Semitic religions of Judaism, Christianity and Islam, as well as in their modern secular offspring, Marxism.

They all recognise, first, that ordinary human existence is defective, unsatisfactory, lacking. For the Jew we suffer from an innate inclination to evil, the *yetzer ha-ra*, and we live in a world in which evil forces have long been harassing God's chosen people, so that life is often precarious and survival a constant preoccupation. For the Christian this is a 'fallen' existence ruined by the primordial sin of our first ancestors. Inheriting their fault, or its consequences, we live in alienation from God, from ourselves and from one another. For the Muslim we human beings are weak and fallible and our life is commonly lived in *ghafala*, forgetfulness of God. And for the Marxist capitalist life is a condition of alienation in which we are divided into classes with irreconcilably competing interests. For Hindus of all kinds, as also for the Jains and in modern times the Sikhs, the ordinary human condition is one of immersion in the relative illusoriness of *avidyā*, subject to the recurrent pains and sorrows of the wheel of birth and death round which we are propelled by our karmic past. And for the Buddhist the first Noble Truth is that all life involves *dukkha*, an 'unsatisfactoriness' which includes pain, sorrow and anxiety of every kind. 'Birth is *dukkha*, decay is *dukkha*, sickness is *dukkha*, death is *dukkha*: likewise sorrow and grief, woe, lamentation and despair. To be conjoined with things which we dislike; to be separated from things which we like, – that all is *dukkha*. Not to get what one wants, – that also is *dukkha*' (*Saṃyutta Nikāya*, 5.241; Woodward 1956, 357).

Whereas in the various forms of pre-axial religion there had always been a realistic awareness of suffering, insecurity and mortality, in the great post-axial traditions these are now thought of in terms implying a contrast with something fundamentally different – whether that different state lies in the future (as also perhaps in the remote past) or in the unrealised depths of the present moment. Thus Christianity speaks of redemption and eternal life; Judaism of the coming kingdom of God; Islam of judgment and paradise; Hinduism of *mokṣa*;[14] Buddhism of enlightenment and *nirvāṇa*. Behind and giving substance to these varied conceptions of a limitlessly better state is the awareness of an ultimate unity of reality and value. For Judaism this is 'the God of Abraham, of Isaac and of Jacob' and of their descendants through the ages; for Christianity, the triune Father, Son and Holy Spirit; for Islam, Allah, most merciful, most compassionate; for Hinduism, the infinite being, consciousness, bliss (*satchitānanda*) which is Brahman; for Theravada Buddhism, the ineffable imperishable reality of Nirvana; for the Mahayana, the Emptiness (*śūnyatā*) which is also Suchness, or fullness of 'wondrous being'.[15]

In all these forms the ultimate, the divine, the Real, is that which makes possible a transformation of our present existence, whether by being drawn into fellowship with the transcendent Thou, or by realising our deeper self as one with the Real, or by unlearning our habitual ego-centredness and becoming a conscious and accepting part of the endlessly interacting flow of life which is both *saṃsāra* and *nirvāṇa*. And for the secular faith of Marxism the saving reality, transcending the alienated individual, is the dialectical process of history, whilst the way of salvation is that of class struggle leading to a new age beyond the revolution. Thus all these post-axial faiths are soteriologically oriented. We must therefore next look more closely at the forms of salvation or liberation which they profess to offer.

Notes

1. Edward O. Wilson remarks that 'The May Day rallies of T'ien An Men Square would have been instantly understood by the Mayan multitudes, Lenin's tomb by the worshippers of Christ's bloodied shroud' (1978, 184).

2. The continuing presence of archaic elements within Buddhism, Christianity and Islam is traced by Denise Lardner Carmody (1981, ch. 3). See also Eliade (1982, paras 304–6).

3. For a more detailed and nuanced account of the sense in which the reigning king was the earthly 'image of God' see Erik Hornung (1982, 138–42).

4. There was also evident, however, by the latter part of the second millennium, a development looking beyond the maintenance of cosmic order. This is reflected in the Egyptian *Book of the Dead*, which affirmed a better or worse after-life, now extended down from the pharaohs to a much wider circle, the soul's destiny being determined by an ethical judgment in the court of Osiris. Heaven and hell were still pictured in essentially earthly terms; but nevertheless in so far as moral considerations are in principle universal the outlook expressed in the *Book of the Dead* can be seen as preparing the way, even if still at a distance, for the great insights of the axial age – that there is a limitlessly better reality in which we can come to participate, and that this participation involves our own moral and spiritual transformation.

5. Within the religious life of Mesopotamia there was nevertheless also a certain wistful feeling out towards a better possibility in the form of a desire for immortality. This is expressed in the *Epic of Gilgamesh*, known in a written version of about 650 BCE but going back perhaps as far as the third millennium BCE. Here the hero Gilgamesh seeks the secret of everlasting life, finds it, but loses it before he is able to take advantage of it. This ancient poem seems to express a poignant sense of our mortality and a longing for immortality, together with an acceptance of the sad fact that this is beyond our grasp.

6. However the whole subject of pre- and post-axial Vedic sacrifice is under renewed discussion today. See J. C. Heesterman (1985, particularly chapters 6 and 7). There were also, in the pre-axial life of India as elsewhere, secondary movements, marginal to the main stream, that were to provide the setting for the great religious breakthroughs of the axial age. The *Āranyakas*, or 'forest writings', express a dissatisfaction with the Vedic rituals practised merely as ends in themselves, and evince a desire to discern the deeper spiritual significance behind them; and they reflect also the practice of yoga in the form of individual asceticism and meditation. The ideas of Karma and reincarnation were developed within this less cultic and more mystical stream from which the Upanishadic philosophy was later to emerge. This was also the seedbed in which Vardhamana, Mahavira and Gautama grew.

7. Cf. Eliade 1978, 118–24.

8. Cf. van der Post 1958.

9. The concept of the axial age is discussed by Jaspers (1953); A. C. Bouquet (1941); G. F. Moore (1948, 279f); E. Voegelin (1954–74, vols 1–4); Lewis Mumford (1957, ch. 4); John B. Cobb (1968, ch. 5); Georg Fohrer (1972, 279–91); Benjamin I. Schwartz (1975b); Samuel N. Eisenstadt (1982).

10. Of course during the pre-axial period there were also local enlargements of religious awareness due to new insights. For example Robert Bellah cites Australian research (by Ronald Berndt 1951) showing that 'dreams may actually lead to a reinterpretation in myth that in turn causes a ritual innovation' (Bellah 1970, 27). Bellah adds more generally that 'we should not forget the innovative aspects of primitive religion, that particular myths and ceremonies are in a process of constant revision and alteration, and that in the face of severe historic crisis rather remarkable reformulations of primitive material can be made' (29). However in comparison with the new insights of the axial age, which have shaped so much of the religious life of humanity since, these seem like hillocks in comparison with great mountains.

11. See Schwartz 1975a.

12. For a recent interpretation of this episode see Hornung (1982, 244–50).

13. Nor, again, is the use of the term 'axial' intended to suggest that this is the only period of critical significance in human religious history. The profound and far-reaching changes brought about by the invention of agriculture at the end of the Ice Age also constituted a crucial transition (Eliade 1978, 29); and it is possible to describe both the birth of the modern world at the end of Europe's medieval phase and the western secularisation of the last two centuries in similar terms.

14. On the move from self-centredness to God-centredness according to Sikhism see Mohinder Singh 1995, 254.

15. 'True Emptiness (*śūnyatā*) is Wondrous Being (*Shinku nyou*)'; from the tenth-century Hua-yen text, *Mojingengenkan*.

3

Salvation/Liberation as Human Transformation

So long as man clamours for the *I* and the *Mine*, his works are as naught;
When all love of the *I* and the *Mine* is dead, then the work of the Lord is done.

(Kabir, *Poems*, I:83)[1]

Thinking on there being no self, he wins to the state wherein the conceit 'I am' has been uprooted, to nirvana, even in this life. (The Buddha, *Anguttara-Nikáya*, IV:353)[2]

1 ACCORDING TO THE HINDU TRADITION

The great post-axial traditions, as we have seen, exhibit in their different ways a soteriological structure which identifies the misery, unreality, triviality and perversity of ordinary human life, affirms an ultimate unity of reality and value in which or in relation to which a limitlessly better quality of existence is possible, and shows the way to realise that radically better possibility. This may be by self-committing faith in Christ as one's lord and saviour; or by the total submission to God which is *islam*; or by faithful obedience to the Torah; or by transcendence of the ego, with its self-centred desires and cravings, to attain *mokṣa* or Nirvana. As I shall now try to show, these are variations within different conceptual schemes on a single fundamental theme: the sudden or gradual change of the individual from an absorbing self-concern to a new centring in the supposed unity-of-reality-and-value that is thought of as God, Brahman, the Dharma, Sunyata or the Tao. Thus the generic concept of salvation/liberation, which takes a different specific form in each of the great traditions, is that of the transformation of human existence from self-centredness to Reality-centredness.[3]

36

Let us consider first the Hindu tradition. 'Hinduism', which is a term that originated in the West, is not the name of a single cohesive tradition but rather of the spreading family of Indian religions which have in common a respect for the Vedic scriptures. The variations within this family are almost endless, but the theme that I shall highlight runs through them all. This is that spiritual liberation requires a transcending of the ego either (in the dualist strands) in self-giving to the divine Lord, the Supreme Person, or (in the monist strand) in union with the ultimate trans-personal Absolute. According to this latter version, which is better known in the West, we are in our true nature one with the eternal reality of Brahman. But this ultimate identity is at present obscured by the empirical ego, the self-positing 'I' which encases and conceals the inner self. The 'I' is part of the samsaric illusion of *māyā*, the world of perpetual change and unfulfilment through which the *jīva* or soul passes in the course of many earthly lives until it attains to liberation. Thus *mokṣa* is the freeing of the eternal self – which is ultimately identical with the divine reality – from the confining and distorting influence of its succession of false egos. 'How to realize this eternal soul and how to disengage it from its real or imaginary connexion with the psycho-somatic complex that thinks, wills, and acts, is from the time of the Upanishads onwards the crucial problem facing the Hindu religious consciousness' (Zaehner 1966, 60). Radhakrishnan expresses the religious challenge of this vision as follows:

> The divine consciousness and will must become our conscious-ness and will. This means that our actual self must cease to be a private self; we must give up our particular will, die to our ego, by surrendering its whole nature, its consciousness and character to the Divine.   (Radhakrishnan 1969, 105)

When this happens, in the words of a contemporary interpreter of advaitic Hinduism, 'The small human individualistic self disappears and the universal *atman* now takes its place' (Panikkar 1977, 417).

Hindu tradition teaches three ways to final liberation. These are not mutually exclusive but rather represent different emphases which are appropriate for different types of personality or even for the same person at different times. The *jñāna-marga*, the path of knowledge or spiritual insight, is a direct translation into religious practice of the advaitic philosophy. For according to this teaching we are in our deepest nature already one with the universal Being or Self. Our existence as separate egos is illusion – though an illusion which is entirely real so long as it lasts. Accordingly on the *jñāna-marga* one strives to realise, not merely intellectually but with one's whole being, the great truth: *tat tvam asi* (*Chāndogya* Up., VI:4 – Radhakrishnan 1969, 460), 'That art thou', the identity of one's deepest inner self with the eternal and universal Self. This is a knowledge that can only come about through the hard-won negation or transcendence of the ordinary conscious ego. As Rudolph Otto explains in his comparative study of Shankara and Meister Eckhart:

> the self (*atman*) comes into sharp conflict with that which we are accustomed to set up as self, as ego – 'I' and 'mine' . . . or 'I-sayer' as Eckhart puts it. The Ahankara is the erroneous act by which consciousness relates things to an 'I', . . . falsely imputing a relationship between possessions, relatives, friends, body, senses, will and action and the self, and wrongly calling them 'my senses, my body, my possessions'. Yet it is that faculty by which I regard myself as individual, separate and different from others. All this does not belong to the true self but to that 'ego', which, in true self-knowledge, is brushed aside as alien and false.   ([1932] 1957, 80)

The aspirant to saving knowledge must be totally dedicated to the quest, renouncing all worldly desires and ambitions. From an already realised guru such a one learns to meditate and in many hours of practice descends through the different layers of the earthly mind to that fundamental being which is the radiant reality of Brahman. And eventually after long years, indeed many lives, of perseverance he or she may finally attain to *mokṣa* and become a *jīvan-mukta*, a soul liberated from the illusions of ego-centredness whilst still in this world.

A second path is the *karma-marga*, the way of action. Traditionally, within Indian society, this is the path available to the 'householder' engaged in the life of the world – married, earning a living, contributing to the upkeep of an extended family, performing the prescribed rituals and having social responsibilities within the elaborate caste system. However in order to reach liberation through the faithful fulfilment of one's role in society one must achieve inner detachment. There must be action without concern for the fruits of action. As we read in the Bhagavad Gita:

> Fools are wedded to cultic work.
> A wise man should act as they do,
> But unattached,
> envisaging the totality of the world.
> (3:25 – Bolle 1979, 45)

This is not only true for people born in Hindu India. It has a universal meaning which was expressed very differently in western philosophy by Immanuel Kant as the life of duty for duty's sake, doing without self-regarding concern that which impartial reason can discern to be the right course of action. According to Kant the good will, instead of making practical decisions from the standpoint of a particular individual whose interests will inevitably conflict with those of others, makes them from the universal standpoint of impartial rationality. Practical reason, undistorted by individual desires, aversions, hopes and fears, sees and does what ought to be done, acting upon principles which are universally valid (Kant [1785] 1947, ch. 1).[4] Such true moral goodness is one form of Reality-centredness in this world – the form that consists in becoming an unselfish moral agent, a force in the world seeking human welfare rather than personal advantage. The most outstanding Indian example of one who has followed this path in modern times is Mahatma Gandhi, who sought to 'reduce myself to zero' (1968, II:754) as an active instrument of God or Truth (*Sat*).

The third way is that of *bhakti* or self-giving devotion to the Real encountered as the divine Thou. This is the path from self-centredness to Reality-centredness that has been followed in the broad *bhakti* stream of Hindu religious life, both Vaishnavite and Shaivite, as also in Christianity, Judaism, Islam, Sikhism and the Jodo strand of Buddhism.

Bhakti takes the form in these different contexts of loving devotion to a divine Lord and Saviour. It involves a radical re-centring in the divine Other, expressed in intense personal love and gratitude, in devoted temple ministry, in personal testimony and dedicated missionary witness, in a life spent in the service of the Lord. In all these forms it involves a transposition of the individual's existence from a state of self-centredness to a new centredness in the Real experienced and responded to as the divine Thou. In the Bhagavad Gita the personal Lord, incarnate as Krishna, says:

> But those who are intent on me
>   and dedicate all their rituals and doings to me,
> Who meditate on me, who revere and see me,
>   disciplined toward none but me –
>
> Them I lift up from the ocean
>   of the round of deaths
> As soon as they direct
>   their thought to me.
>
>   (12:6–7 – Bolle 1979, 147–9)

The rich Indian *bhakti* literature is pervaded by an intense fervour and devotion such as Christians are familiar with in the hymns of Bernard of Clairvaux or the Wesleys. Thus one of the hymns of the twelfth-century CE Vaishnavite poet Tukaram begins:

> O save me, save me, Mightiest,
>   Save me and set me free.
> O let the love that fills my breast
>   Cling to thee lovingly.
>
> Grant me to taste how sweet thou art;
>   Grant me but this, I pray,
> And never shall my love depart
>   Or turn from thee away.
>
> Then I thy name shall magnify
>   And tell thy praise abroad,
> For very love and gladness I
>   Shall dance before my God.
>
>   (Bouquet 1954, 246)

The point to be stressed here is that as a way of conversion from self-centredness to God-centredness *bhakti* is a form of human transformation. Thus, discussing Campantar, the great Tamil *bhakta* of the seventh century CE, Dhavamony says that 'Bhakti, for Campantar, implies surrender of the whole person to God' (1971, 142) and at another point, referring to the hindrances to

devotion, he speaks of 'the arch-impurity of egoism' (1971, 357).
The thirteenth-century CE Shaivite *bhakti* poet Arulnanti wrote
that 'egoism or self-centredness consists in doing everything in
the spirit of "I" and "mine", not realising that I am the servant (of
God) and that he (God) is the Lord' (Dhavamony 1971, 250). And
Dhavamony comments,

> [The Shaivite bhakta] lovingly dedicates himself to Siva; he
> consecrates all his acts to him and considers his acts as God's.
> Out of the abundance of love for God he renders loving service
> to other bhaktas, for it is said that those who do not love God's
> devotees love neither God nor themselves. It involves a whole-
> hearted self-surrender to God, self-dedication, and humble
> service.   (1971, 376)

Bhakti-yoga is regarded by the Advaitists as a lower path
provided for those who need a personal presence to cling to. On
the other hand the Vishishtadvaitists, experiencing the Ultimate
as personal, and seeing human selves as threads of finite life
within the infinite divine life, regard the way of devotion as a
fully valid path to the liberation which consists in self-giving to
the Lord. However we are not at this point concerned so much
with this difference as with the fact that in both Vedantic
approaches liberation requires the transcendence or negation of
the ordinary human ego and its centring in or its realised identity
with the ultimately Real.

2 ACCORDING TO THE BUDDHIST TRADITION

The conception of liberation as the transformation from self-
centredness to Reality-centredness is likewise powerfully evident
in Buddhism. Indeed a leading contemporary exponent of this
tradition to the West says that 'Buddhist salvation is . . . nothing
other than an awakening to reality through the death of the ego'
(Abe 1982, 153). This turning from ego to reality is both illuminated
and enabled by the *anatta* ('no self') doctrine, which D. T. Suzuki
translates as 'non-ego', 'selflessness', and which he says 'is the
principal conception of Buddhism, both Hinayana and Mahayana'
(1972, 120).
  In Buddhism the salvific human transformation is understood

as liberation from the powerful illusion of 'me' or 'self'. 'Me' forms a distorting lens through which the world takes on a false character.[5] The universe is misperceived as structured around 'me' and the world process is accordingly experienced as a stream of objects of my desire and aversion, hope and fear, giving rise to a grasping (*taṇhā*) which expresses itself in selfishness, injustice and cruelty, and in a pervasive self-regarding anxiety and insecurity in face of life's unpredictabilities and the inevitability of final decay and death – all of which constitutes, comprehensively, *dukkha*. To be liberated from the illusorily enduring and falsely evaluating 'me' is to exchange this samsaric realm of ego-infected consciousness for the glorious freedom of Nirvana. The *anatta* or no-self doctrine is thus not offered merely as a theoretical truth but above all as a practical prescription for liberation. Referring to David Hume and other western philosophers who have also questioned the substantiality of the self, Edward Conze says:

> Those who look to Buddhism for startlingly new and unheard-of ideas on the problem of self, will find little. Those who look for advice on how to lead a self-less life, may learn a great deal. The great contribution of Buddhist 'philosophy' lies in the methods it worked out to impress the truth of not-self on our reluctant minds, it lies in the discipline which the Buddhists imposed upon themselves in order to make this truth into a part of their own being.   (1975, 20–1).

Steven Collins, in his study of the Theravadin goal of the selfless person, says:

> There is [a] psychological 'realisation' of *anatta*, which is the loss of pride or 'conceit': this constitutes the attainment of Arhatship. This fetter is explained as the conceit of 'I am', *asmimana*; 'conceit' here is a particularly appropriate translation, since it suggests both the sense of something 'constructed' or 'made up' by a conceptual act, and also the pride with which this artificial mental object (the supposedly permanent 'I') is regarded. What this 'conceit' refers to is the fact that for the unenlightened man, all experience and action must necessarily appear phenomenologically as happening to or originating from an 'I'. The more enlightened, the less is this phenomenological datum converted into a theoretical belief, in *sakkayaditthi*; and

the final attainment of enlightenment is the disappearance of this automatic but illusory 'I'. (1982, 94)

In the Mahayana tradition the same basic conception of liberation operates. Here however the aim is not to become an arhat but a bodhisattva, an 'enlightenment-being' whose openness to the Real is expressed in boundless compassion for all life. For whilst to live as an ego is to seek happiness for oneself, to transcend the ego, becoming a manifestation of the universal Buddha-nature, is to seek the happiness of all: 'The benefit of others is their own benefit, because they desire it' (*Abhidharmakosa* – Conze 1975, 126). Accordingly a bodhisattva, having attained to the verge of full liberation, deliberately remains in or returns to the world in order to assist others to that same end:

The bodhisattva is endowed with wisdom of a kind whereby he looks on all beings as though victims going to the slaughter. And immense compassion grips him. His divine eye sees . . . innumerable beings, and he is filled with great distress at what he sees, for many bear the burden of past deeds which will be punished in purgatory, others will have unfortunate rebirths which will divide them from the Buddha and his teachings, others must soon be slain, others are caught in the net of false doctrine, others cannot find the path (of salvation), while others have gained a favorable rebirth only to lose it again. So he pours out his love and compassion . . . and attends to them, thinking, 'I shall become the savior of all beings, and set them free from their sufferings.'
(*Aṣṭasāhasrikā Prajñāpāramitā* 22:402–3 – de Bary 1972, 81–2)

Clearly the way to bodhisattvahood is a way of self-transcendence; and in Buddhism as a whole liberation consists in a transformation from self-centredness to what is believed to be true Reality-centredness.

3 ACCORDING TO THE CHRISTIAN TRADITION

In the Hindu and Buddhist traditions, as we have seen, the salvific change that is experienced is explicitly thought of as a radical turning from ego to the ultimately Real. Within the

Christian tradition a like turning occurs, consisting in a self-giving in faith to God's limitless sovereignty and grace, which engenders a new spirit of trust and joy that in turn frees the believer from anxious self-concern and makes him or her a channel of divine love to the world. However the official Christian conceptualisation of this, in the doctrine of the atonement, presents the transformation as a result of salvation rather than as itself constituting salvation. A distinction is drawn in much developed Christian theology between justification and sanctification, the former being a change of juridical status before God and the latter the resulting transformation of our moral and spiritual condition. As sinners we exist under a just divine condemnation and a sentence of eternal punishment, but Christ's sacrifice on the cross on our behalf cancels our guilt so that we are now counted as innocent in God's sight. The divine justice has been satisfied by Christ's death and the faithful are now clothed in the righteousness of their saviour. As a consequence they are opened to the re-creative influence of the Holy Spirit and are gradually sanctified – the fruits of the Spirit being 'love, joy, peace, patience, kindness, goodness, faithfulness, gentleness, self-control' (Galatians 5:22).

According to this official doctrine the transformation of human existence embodied in these new qualities of love, joy and peace is secondary to the juridical transaction of Christ's atonement for human sin. However that doctrine is only one possible way – the way that was promoted by the powerful influence of St Paul – of understanding the joyful consciousness of being accepted by God's grace and empowered to live a new life of outgoing love towards one's neighbours. But whereas the various forms of atonement doctrine – centring in different stages and strands of Christian thought on the idea of defeating or cheating the devil, on the medieval conception of 'satisfaction', on a penal-substitutionary model and on an exemplary model – are theoretical constructs, the new reconciled relationship to God and the new quality of life arising within that relationship are facts of experience and observation. It is this reality of persons transformed, or in process of transformation, from self-centredness to God-centredness that constitutes the substance of Christian salvation.

It is, I think, clear that in the teaching of Jesus himself, in so far as it is reflected in the synoptic gospels, the juridical conception was entirely or almost entirely absent. Virtually the whole weight of Jesus' message came in the summons to his hearers to open their hearts now to God's kingdom, or rule, and to live consciously in God's presence as instruments of the divine purpose on earth. It is true that as Jesus anticipated his death at the hands of the Jerusalem authorities he related it to the traditional belief that the blood of the righteous martyr works for the good of the people (Mark 10:45).[6] But there is no suggestion in Jesus' recorded teaching that the heavenly Father's loving acceptance of those to whom he was speaking was conditional upon his own future death. In the parable of the prodigal son (Luke 15:11–32), for example, the father – who clearly represents the heavenly Father – is ready to forgive his erring son and to receive him back as a beloved child as soon as he is truly repentant. There is no addendum to the effect that the father, because he is just as well as loving, must first punish either the prodigal himself or his other son before he can forgive the penitent sinner. Again, the words of the 'Lord's Prayer' presuppose a direct relationship to the heavenly Father in which men and women can ask for and receive God's forgiveness for their sins and are expected in turn to forgive one another.

But Jesus' teaching was not simply a vivid picturing of the 'amazing grace' and re-creating love of God. It was at the same time a profoundly challenging call to a radical change (*metanoia*), breaking out of our ordinary self-enclosed existence to become part of God's present and future kingdom. The summons was away from a life centred in the self and its desire for possessions, wealth, status and power to a new life centred in God and lived out as an agent of the divine love. Such a challenge cut through the normal web of self-concern, requiring a choice between the true quality and style of life, found in a free and perhaps costly response to God, and spiritual death within a stifling shell of self-concern. 'For whoever would save his life will lose it; and whoever loses his life for my sake and the gospel's will save it' (Mark 8:35). With the progressive deification of Jesus within the developing faith of the church the earthly lord became exalted into the heavenly Christ, virtually occupying the place of God, so that St Paul, expressing his own form of God-centredness, could say 'It is not I who live, but Christ who lives in me' (Galatians 2:20).

Both in the teaching of Jesus, then, and in the practical consciousness of Christians the reality of salvation is the transition from ego-domination to a radically God-centred life. The function of the official theories of salvation, according to which Jesus' death constituted an atonement for human sin, has been to provide a theoretical framework within which to understand this profound shift in human consciousness. But the reality of Christian salvation is no juridical abstraction but an actual and concrete change from sinful self-centredness to self-giving love in response to the divine grace.

If within ecclesiastical Christianity this has been partially obscured by the atonement doctrine, in the mystical life of the church it has been open and explicit. The mystical journey moves from the *cor curvatus in se* through a painful process of re-orientation to a total self-giving to God, finally returning to the world in loving service. The character of this path, as the approach to a God-centredness so complete that it is sometimes described in the language of union, is evident throughout Christian mystical literature. We shall be looking more closely at aspects of mysticism in Chapters 10.5 and 16.5, but for our present purpose it will suffice to refer to the accounts in Evelyn Underhill's classic study. Describing the mystic path, she speaks of 'the definite emergence of the self from "the prison of I-hood"' ([1911] 1955, 195), the 'giving up of I-hood' (317) and 'that principle of self-surrender which is the mainspring of the mystic life' (223); and says that 'a lifting of consciousness from a self-centred to a God-centred world, is of the essence of illumination' (234). Describing that unavoidable stage of the path known as the Dark Night of the Soul, she says:

> The act of complete surrender then, which is the term of the Dark Night, has given the soul its footing in Eternity: its abandonment of the old centres of consciousness has permitted movement towards the new. In each such forward movement, the Transcendental Self, that spark of the soul which is united to the Absolute Life, has invaded more and more the seat of personality; stage by stage the remaking of the self in conformity with the Eternal World has gone on. In the misery and apparent stagnation of the Dark Night – that dimness of the spiritual consciousness, that dullness of its will and love – work has been done; and the last great phase of the inward transmutation accomplished. The self that comes forth from the night is no separated self . . . but the New Man, the transmuted humanity, whose life is *one* with the Absolute Life of God.   (1955, 402)

Within Christianity, then, the concrete reality of salvation is the transformation of human existence from a sinful and alienated self-centredness to a new centring in God, revealed in Christ as both limitless claim and limitless grace. The experience of salvation is the experience of being an object of God's gratuitous forgiveness and love, freeing the believer to love his and her neighbour.

4 ACCORDING TO THE JEWISH AND MUSLIM TRADITIONS

In Judaism the hope of redemption from present evil into a radically better state has always been corporate rather than purely individual, and always the hope for an event within, even if it be the final event within, earthly history. It has been the expectation of a social and ethical as well as spiritual transformation, affecting the future of Israel and of the world. This hope began with the great prophets of the axial age. A prophetic voice, whose words have become part of the book of Amos, foresaw God's new age of peace and justice on earth (Amos 9:11–15).[7] Hosea likewise looked beyond impending disaster to a time of divine forgiveness and renewal (Hosea 14:4–8). First Isaiah, another prophet of immediately impending doom – in the very concrete form of the Assyrian invasion of Judah –, also spoke of the future birth of an ideal king (Isaiah 9) in whom in the coming time the people who walked in darkness will see a great light. Again, Jeremiah, the most pessimistic of the prophets, spoke of a future new covenant when 'I will put my law within them, and I will write it upon their hearts; and I will be their God, and they shall be my people . . .' (Jeremiah 31:33). But it is Second Isaiah who gave the hope a cosmic dimension in the thought of a new age, which Eliade refers to as a 'universal transfiguration',[8] to be established by God's power (Isaiah 51). This thought developed in later Jewish apocalyptic writings into the image (familiar also in the New Testament) of the two aeons, the present evil age and God's new age to come.

Gershom Scholem has shown that the older idea that the Jewish apocalyptic ended with the coming of Christianity is mistaken (1971b, ch. 1). Rabbinic apocalypticism has continued, sometimes more and sometimes less prominently, down to today. That the reality of God implies an eventual messianic redemption has been affirmed by many leading Jewish thinkers (for example,

Hermann Cohen, Rosenzweig, Martin Buber, Abraham Heschel, Soloveitchick) although also questioned today by some – for example, David Hartman (1985, ch. 11). But the hope for a new age, the Kingdom of God on a transformed earth, which arose in the axial period, has ever since been a part of the Jewish religious outlook, sometimes vividly and centrally and sometimes lying in the background of consciousness.

Islam does not use the concept of 'salvation' and does not think of the human condition in terms of a 'fall' involving a guilt and alienation from God that can only be cancelled by a divine act of atonement. However, the Qur'an does distinguish radically between the state of *islām* – a self-surrender leading to peace with God – and the contrary state of those who have not yielded themselves to their Maker and who are therefore in the last resort enemies of God. The state of *islam*, then, is the Muslim analogue of Christian and Judaic salvation and of Hindu and Buddhist liberation. It is the Muslim form of the transformation of human existence from self-centredness to Reality-centredness. For the Qur'anic summons is to turn to God, giving oneself in total self-surrender to Allah, the merciful, the gracious. An influential contemporary orthodox Muslim writer, Badr al-Din Muhammad ibn 'Abdallah al-Zakashi, says that 'those who hear in [the Qur'an] the words of the Truth [God], they become annihilated before Him and their attributes effaced' (Ayoub 1984, 25). The believer is to say, with Abraham, 'I bow (my will) to the Lord and Cherisher of the Universe' (Qur'an 2, 131). In Zafrulla Kahn's translation of Surah 2, 132: 'live every moment in submission to Allah, so that death whenever it comes should find you in a state of submission to Him'.

From the point of view of the understanding of this state of *islam* the Muslim sees no distinction between the religious and the secular. The whole of life is to be lived in the presence of Allah and is the sphere of God's absolute claim and limitless compassion and mercy. And so *islam*, God-centredness, is not only an inner submission to the sole Lord of the universe but also a pattern of corporate life in accordance with God's will. It involves both *salat*, worship, and *falah*, the good embodied in behaviour. Through the five appointed moments of prayer each day is linked to God. Indeed almost any activity may be begun with *Bismillah* ('in the name of Allah'); and plans and hopes for the future are qualified by *Inshallah* ('if Allah wills'). Thus life is constantly punctuated by the remembrance of God. It is a symptom of this that almsgiving ranks with prayer, fasting, pilgrimage and confession of faith as one of the five 'pillars' of Islam. Within this holistic conception the 'secular' spheres of politics, government, law, commerce, science and the arts all come within the scope of religious obedience.

Thus the Islamic way of life includes, in principle, the entire culture and organisation of a society. There is no distinction between church and state: the nation is a theocracy in which God's will is to be done in every aspect of life. It is needless to say that actual Muslim societies, as human communities involved in all the ambiguities and conflicts of historical existence, have only very partially exemplified this ideal of life lived in total obedience to God. Nevertheless the insistent demand of the Qur'anic revelation is to turn from human self-centredness to an individual and communal life in obedience to God's commands, as revealed in the Qur'an and expounded in the Shariah. And the *islam*, or God-centred existence, embodied in this earthly pattern is a life at peace with God, trusting in his mercy and compassion and hoping beyond this world for the joys of paradise.

This transformation of human existence by the total surrender of the self to God, basic to orthodox Islam, is further highlighted in Islamic mysticism. Indeed, the two central Sufi concepts are *dhikr*, God-consciousness, and *fana*, which is a total re-centring in God leading to *baga*, human life merged into the divine life or (in R. A. Nicholson's phrase) 'everlasting life in God' ([1914] 1963, 19). Expounding the Sufi path, Seyyed Hosein Nasr says:

> Sufism uses the quintessential form of prayer, the *dhikr* or invocation, in which all otherness and separation from the Divine is removed . . . Though this process of transforming man's psyche appears gradual at first, the *dhikr* finishes by becoming man's real nature and the reality with which he identifies himself. With the help of the *dhikr* . . . man first gains an integrated soul, pure and whole like gold, and then in the *dhikr* he offers this soul to God in the supreme form of sacrifice. Finally in annihilation (*fana*) and subsistence (*baga*) he realizes that he never was separated from God even from the outset.   (1980, 37–8)

Fana is thus a radical transformation from self-centredness or self-rule to God-centredness or divine rule, involving a total self-naughting. The ninth- and tenth-century Sufi master Junayd of Baghdad described it by saying that 'the creature's individuality is completely obliterated' and he is 'naughted to self' (Zaehner 1961, 166). As one of the greatest of the Sufi mystics, the thirteenth-century Jalal al-Din Rumi, wrote, 'No one will find his way to the Court of Magnificence until he is annihilated' (*Mathnawi*, VI:232 – Chittick 1983, 179). For 'With God, two I's cannot find room. You say "I" and He says "I". Either you die before Him, or let Him die before you' (*Mathnawi* XXV:58 – Chittick 1983, 191). The human I must give itself totally to the divine I. But this 'annihilation' is not of course a ceasing to exist. Beyond the death of the self comes its resurrection in a transformed state. This is *baqa*, union with the divine life. 'The spirit became joyful through the I-less I' (*Mathnawi*, V:4127, 39 – Chittick 1983, 193). Thus the human being lives, and lives in fullness of energy and joy; but it is now the divine life that is being lived in and through the life of the fully surrendered servant of God.

Thus whilst the Hindu saint attains to unity with the eternal reality of Brahman, or to a complete self-giving to the divine Person, by a path of detachment from the false ego and its concerns; and whilst the Buddhist saint, by overcoming all thought of 'I' and 'mine', attains to the ego-less state of Nirvana or to oneness with the eternal Buddha nature; and whilst the Christian saint can say 'It is not I, but Christ who lives in me', the Sufi saint likewise gives himself to God so totally that al-Hallaj could even utter *ana 'l-haqq*, 'I am the Real' (Arberry 1979, 59–60; Nicholson [1914] 1963, 149–50). This was the all too easily misunderstood affirmation that he had given himself to God in perfect *islam* so that God had taken over his life. He was saying in effect 'It is not I, but Allah who lives in me'.

Islam, then, is human surrender to God expressed outwardly in the ways detailed in the Shariah and inwardly in an individual self-giving which reaches its ultimate point in *fana* and *baqa*, when the divine life is lived through a human life. Islam is thus very clearly a form of the transformation of human existence from self-centredness to Reality-centredness.

5 TWO POSSIBLE OBJECTIONS

In tracing the transformative character of salvation/liberation within the different world traditions I have given prominence to the mystical element in each case. Indeed Hinduism and Buddhism as totalities are sometimes characterised as inherently mystical in contrast to the prophetic religions; and it is apparently in the more mystical strands of Christianity and Islam, as also of Judaism, that spiritual transformation is most clearly focused. And so it might seem that the theme of salvation/liberation as the transformation of human existence from self-centredness to Reality-centredness is a conception of mystical rather than mainstream religion.

This would however, I think, be a misunderstanding. I shall recommend using the term 'mysticism' to refer to those forms of religious experience in which the transcendent 'information' that is transformed into outer visions and auditions or inner unitive experiences reaches the mystic's psyche directly rather than being mediated through the world (see Chapter 10.5). But it is within the experiential spectrum as a whole, both mystical and mediated, that the transforming power of religion is felt. Religious institutions and their cultic activities depend for their vitality upon the streams of religious consciousness and emotion that flow through them, although they can persist as external structures even when their inner spiritual life is at a low ebb. Thus the institutional history of a religious tradition is not synonymous with the story of its experiential heart. It is true that Christianity is strongly institutionalised, even to the extent of being identified as an historical reality with the church. And Islam is equally strongly self-identified with a visible form of communal life patterned after the Shariah. This is no doubt why in these cases the mystical element has developed as a relatively distinct strand, marginalised by the main institutional and communal body of the tradition.

Hindu religious experience, on the other hand, is characteristically mystical. It does of course have its elaborate institutional expressions within family life and the public ceremonies. But so much importance is given to the inner quest for liberation and to the guru (who is above all a spiritual practitioner) that in this tradition the mystical–experiential element has never become separated out as distinct or peculiar. And the same is true, perhaps even more strongly, of Buddhism. But despite this difference between the highly institutionalised and the less institutional traditions, religious experience is the vital life-blood flowing within each. And when we recognise the essential role of the experiential aspect of religion in all its forms we are no longer tempted to think that the human transformation which it can effect is in any way secondary or peripheral.

Another possible objection comes from contemporary feminist Christian theologians, who are today contributing major and sometimes startling insights which it would be a serious mistake for others to ignore. One such insight is relevant to the view of salvation/liberation as the transformation of human existence from self-centredness to Reality-centredness. The idea of a shift from worship of self to worship of God is reflected in the ancient Christian doctrine that the basic sin is pride, or self-assertion against our creator, and that salvation involves the overthrow of the proud 'I' in humility and self-abasement. According to St Augustine, 'We had fallen through pride . . . We cannot return except through humility' (*Faith and the Creeds*, iv:6 – Burleigh 1953, 76; compare *Of Free Will*, III:xxv – Burleigh 1953, 76), and the theme has continued through the ages, its most usual contemporary form being in the identification of sin with self-centredness or self-enclosedness – for Pannenberg, for example, *Ichbezogenheit* in contrast to *Weltoffenheit* ([1962] 1970, ch. 1; compare 1985).

The feminist critique of this strand of Christian thought is that self-assertion is not the basic *human* temptation but rather the characteristic *male* temptation; and that its female counterpart, within the existing patriarchal world culture, is different. In societies which have been basically patriarchal (even when sometimes legally matriarchal) women have been condemned to a secondary and dependent role as 'help-meets' whose approved virtues have been other-regarding love, sacrifice, and self-fulfilment in the service of the family. As Valerie Saiving Goldstein argued in an important pioneering article, the specifically feminine dilemma is the opposite of that of the male:

The temptations of women *as women* are not the same as the temptations of man *as man*, and the specifically feminine forms of sin – 'feminine' not because they are confined to women or because women are incapable of sinning in other ways but because they are outgrowths of the basic feminine character structure – have a quality which can never be encompassed by such terms as 'pride' and 'will-to-power'. They are better suggested by such items as triviality, distractibility, and diffuseness; lack of an organizing center or focus; dependence on others for one's own self-definition; tolerance at the expense of standards of excellence; inability to respect the boundaries of privacy; sentimentality, gossipy sociability, and mistrust of reason – in short, underdevelopment or negation of the self.

> (1960, reprinted in Doniger 1962, 165; see also Dunfee 1982)

From this point of view the characteristic female sin is not self-assertion but self-abnegation and failure to achieve authentic selfhood; and the function of divine grace is not so much to shatter the assertive ego as to support a weak ego towards true self-realisation. For half the human race salvation will not bring a change from, but on the contrary a change to, self-centredness!

In considering the implications of this feminist analysis I suggest that we have to distinguish between, on the one hand, the large-scale historical reality of the male domination of the species, resulting in the social and structural repression of women, and on the other hand the distorted individual psychic developments which this has produced. Because of the effects upon them of patriarchal cultures – according to this feminist analysis – many women have 'weak' egos, suffer from an ingrained inferiority complex and are tempted to diffusion and triviality. But it would clearly be an over-simplification to assume that ego-weakness is confined to women and is synonymous with having been patriarchalised. The general sapping of the female ego in male-dominated societies is closely paralleled by, for example, the general sapping of the black male ego in white-dominated societies – not only in the colonial past but in South Africa and, residually but still powerfully, in the United States and Europe today. Both forms of oppression are massive social phenomena that distort innumerable lives. And quite apart from the effect of these vast structural influences, at the level of individual psychology many males, white as well as black, have come as a result of external pressures or through their own inner psychic development to see themselves as inferior or unworthy. On the other hand there are many women, past and present, with 'strong' egos, capable of powerful self-assertion and with notable achievements to their name, by no means trapped in triviality and diffusion.

This distinction between ego-weakness as a phenomenon of

individual psychology and the pervasive cultural forces, both sexist and racist, which are among its large-scale causes, enables us to see more accurately the implications of this feminist insight. In so far as anyone, female or male, lacks the ego-development and fulfilment necessary for a voluntary self-transcendence, the prior achievement of self-fulfilled ego may well be necessary for a true relationship to the Real. For in order to move beyond the self one has first to *be* a self. This means that the contemporary women's liberation movement, as a part of the larger movement for human liberation, is in the front line of salvific change in our world today. For every kind of moral evil works against human liberation: this indeed is what constitutes it as evil. And feminist theologians are pointing out that patriarchalism is a major such evil that has hindered and retarded, and continues to hinder and retard, the soteriologial process. At this point we are close to the wider political and economic issues of salvation/liberation in the world today, to which we shall come in Chapter 17.3.

Notes

1. Kabir [1915] 1977, 49.
2. Hare 1965, 233.
3. Cf. Keith Ward: 'Religion is primarily concerned with the transformation of the self, by appropriate response to that which is most truly real' (1987, 153).
4. Raghavan Iyer points out the affinity between the Kantian moral philosophy and *karma-yoga* (1983, 71).
5. George Eliot, in her novel *Middlemarch*, expressed this fact in a memorable simile:
   > Your pier-glass or extensive surface of polished steel made to be rubbed by a housemaid will be minutely and multitudinously scratched in all directions; but place now against it a lighted candle as a centre of illumination, and lo, the scratches will seem to arrange themselves in a fine series of concentric circles round that little sun. It is demonstrable that the scratches are going everywhere impartially, and it is only your candle that produces the flattering illusion of a concentric arrangement, its light falling with an exclusive optical selection. These things are a parable. The scratches are events, and the candle is the egoism of any person . . .
   > (George Eliot [1871–2] 1964, 258)
6. Concerning this Jewish assumption of the time see John Downing (1963). For further examples see D. C. Matt (1983, 19).
7. Some scholars today regard this passage in Amos as an interpolation from the post-exilic period: e.g. Hans Walter Wolff (1977, 350–3).

Others however see it as authentic: e.g. Gerhard von Rad (1965, 138) and Klaus Koch (1982, II:69–70).

8. Eliade 1982, 250. However, some scholars today see Isaiah's vision of the future as purely nationalistic, rather than universal, and would accordingly regard Eliade's words as exaggerated.

4

The Cosmic Optimism of Post-Axial Religion

> All shall be well,
> and all shall be well,
> and all manner of thing shall be well.
> (Julian of Norwich)[1]

1 COSMIC OPTIMISM

Each of the great post-axial streams of religious experience and belief has been shown to exhibit a soteriological structure: a recognition of our human moral weakness and failure or of the pervasive insecurity and liability-to-suffering of all life; the proclamation of a limitlessly better possibility arising from another reality, transcendent to our present selves; and the teaching of a way, whether by 'own-power' spiritual discipline or the 'other-power' of divine grace, to its realisation. They are thus centrally concerned with salvation or liberation or, in Martin Prozesky's alternative term (1984), ultimate well-being, and they all affirm a transcendent Reality in virtue of which this is available to us. Thus each in its own way constitutes a gospel, offering good news to erring and suffering human beings.[2]

We can express this abstractly by saying that post-axial religion embodies a cosmic optimism. It affirms the ultimate goodness from our human point of view, or to-be-rejoiced-in character, of the universe. William James was therefore, I believe, right when he formulated the two basic elements of what he called the religious hypothesis. First, religion 'says that the best things are the more eternal things, the overlapping things, the things in the universe that throw the last stone, so to speak'; whilst religion's second affirmation is that 'we are better off now if we believe her first affirmation to be true' (1905, 25–6; compare [1902] 1960, 464).

James' temporal metaphor, 'throwing the last stone', is

56

appropriate. For post-axial religious optimism does not affirm the goodness of our earthly life in its present untransformed state. On the contrary, at this point the post-axial faiths have been typically negative and in that sense pessimistic. In a very general sense we can even say that archaic religion – even though with ample exceptions – was optimistic and world-affirming whilst the new insights of the axial age brought a wave of world-denial and a widespread sense of the hollowness, transitoriness and unsatisfactoriness of ordinary human existence. This immediate pessimism is however linked with an ultimate optimism. Life was recognised to be pervaded by suffering, its satisfactions fleeting and unreliable, the human will trapped in sin; but at the same time a limitlessly better possibility was affirmed, on the basis of the experiential insights of the great religious figures, and a path traced out to its realisation. A structure of reality was proclaimed in virtue of which the limitlessly better possibility is indeed available to us. It is really there, waiting to be grasped or received or attained. And so the cosmic optimism of the post-axial religions is a vision of the ultimately benign character of the universe as it affects us human beings, and an anticipation in faith that the limitlessly good possibilities of existence will finally be realised. There is thus an essential temporal, and hence teleological or eschatological, dimension to this optimism. It is the present 'blessed assurance' that, in the words of the Christian mystic Julian of Norwich, in the end 'all shall be well, and all shall be well, and all manner of thing shall be well' (1978, 124).[3] This dimension of religious thought seems to have emerged within the intensified temporalisation of human consciousness in the axial period.

2 THE TEMPORAL CHARACTER OF EXPERIENCE

The other animals appear to live almost entirely in the present moment. Thus Friedrich Kümmel says that 'the main difference between animal and human life is the complete lack of time consciousness in the former' (Kümmel 1966, 50). Of course the higher mammals learn from their past experiences; but they probably only have occasional flashes of conscious recall of particular incidents. Again, they can take account of the immediate future – for example, when the hunting animal anticipates the movement of its prey. But normally and for the most part, it would seem, they live either in the present moment of experience and action or in a state of somnolence. This is not the case, however, at the human level. We normally experience the present in relation to both past and future. Recollection and anticipation colour our present awareness. For although the future does not yet exist, psychologically it is as real and important as the past. 'A subjective future is supposed', writes a psychologist, 'in all our activities. Without a tacit belief in a tomorrow nearly everything we do today would be pointless. Expectation, intention, anticipation, premonition and presentiment – all these have a forward reference in time. Our entire psychic life is permeated with the hope of things to come. Implicit in all our actions are plans, however vague and inarticulate, for the future . . .' (Cohen 1966, 262; compare Maxwell 1972).

It is this temporal dimension that opens up the distinctively human level of meaning. For example, I am at the time of writing sitting comfortably on the sun-deck of my house in Southern California on a warm January morning. Although there are moments of pure enjoyment of the present moment, entirely without reference to past and future, yet more generally my situation, as I am conscious of it, has an essential temporal aspect. It cannot be adequately described in purely non-temporal terms as simply a static tableau. Not only is the remembered past implicit in the present, giving it basic intelligibility, but anticipations of the future also enter into it. For in writing these pages I am trying to get something clear in my own mind. But I am not doing so as though I were the only person in existence and as though there were to be no future in which to continue to interact with others. If I were the only person in the world I should probably have no philosophical motivation; for philosophy is essentially a dialectical and hence social activity. One philosophises within a community of people who are interested in trying to get things clear, with whom one can share one's own attempts and amongst whom there are many other such attempts going on, so that all these different endeavours can interact with and, one hopes, correct and assist one another. So my situation has as part of its description that I am formulating thoughts of which I hope to receive criticism, in the light of which I propose to work further, intending eventually to have something to share with a wider community of people who are engaged in the same general quest.

Thus I cannot describe my situation as I now experience it without referring at least implicitly to an anticipated future.

And indeed it is true in general that any situation in which we are conscious of being has a temporal as well as a spatial dimension. The temporal unit of consciousness, called by William James (borrowing from E. R. Clay) the 'specious present' (1891, I:609), is not a durationless point but a brief period whose lower limit seems to be about 0.01 of a second with an upper limit of about 12 seconds (Cohen 1966, 260). But the situations in which we are conscious of living normally far exceed the limits of this specious present. Their structure is analogous to that of our field of vision, with a sharp central focus and vaguer surroundings that fade towards a horizon. Thus what we may perhaps call my situational present is a duration bounded by breakfast and lunch; for this period is being lived through more or less as a unity. Thus we often experience a situational present which considerably exceeds our specious present.

This situational present can be conceived on almost any scale. Although the setting of boundaries is to a great extent arbitrary there are nevertheless various distinguishable histories which we commonly recognise, such as a cultural epoch, or a dynasty, or that which falls within the biblical narratives, or the span of one's own life. This latter unit has an uniquely central organising role in our consciousness. In addition to experiencing and living through a present situation as a relatively autonomous incident one can also be aware of it as a cross-section in a longer history which is one's life as a whole. For we do ordinarily think in all sorts of ways in terms of an entire human life and see a person as being at this or that point on its temporal curve. Thus on many occasions, including most news reports, we tend to place individuals in the context of their lifespan.

Now a situation, whether in the life of an individual or of a community, receives much of its experienced meaning from the history of which it is believed to be a part; whilst it receives what we may distinguish as its objective meaning from the history of which it actually turns out to be a part. A number of philosophers have remarked that the meaning of a present situation depends upon the character of the future to which it leads. Jean-Paul Sartre, for example, brings out vividly the fact that our life subsequent to some particular choice or incident can retrospectively alter the meaning of that earlier event:

Now the meaning of the past is strictly dependent on my present project . . . I alone in fact can decide at each moment the *bearing* of the past. I do not decide it by debating it, by deliberating over it, and in each instance evaluating the importance of this or that prior event; but by projecting myself toward my end, I preserve the past with me, and by action I *decide* its meaning. Who shall decide whether that mystic crisis in my fifteenth year 'was' a pure accident of puberty or, on the contrary, the first sign of a future conversion? I myself, according to whether I shall decide – at twenty years of age, at thirty years – to be converted. The project of conversion by a single stroke confers on an adolescent crisis the value of a premonition which I had not taken seriously. Who shall decide whether the period which I spent in prison after a theft was fruitful or deplorable? I – according to whether I give up stealing or become hardened. Who can decide the educational value of a trip, the sincerity of a profession of love, the purity of a past intention, *etc.*? It is I, always I, according to the ends by which I illuminate these past events.   (Sartre [1943] 1956, 498)

The way in which later phases of one's life can affect the meaning of earlier phases suggested to Sartre the theoretical idea of a completion of life which fixes its meaning as a whole. For our existence is essentially a movement through time in which our possibilities may be or fail to be gradually realised.

Thus it is necessary to consider our life as being made up not only of waitings but of waitings which themselves wait for waitings. There we have the very structure of selfness: to be oneself is to come to oneself. These waitings evidently all include a reference to a final term which would be *waited for* without waiting for anything more. A repose which would be *being* and no longer a waiting for being. The whole series is suspended from this final term which on principle is never *given* and which is the value of our being – that is, evidently, a plenitude of the type 'in-itself-for-itself'. By means of this final term the recovery of our past would be made once and for all. We should know for always whether a particular youthful experience had been fruitful or ill-starred, whether a particular crisis of puberty was a caprice or a real pre-formation of my later engagements; the curve of our life would be fixed forever. In short, the account would be closed.   ([1943] 1956, 538)

He then goes on to criticise the suggestion that death, as he takes it to be understood in Christianity, is this final term. He argues that, if God decides the moment of one's death, it comes as an external cut-off rather than as a completion of one's inner development, and thus cannot be the 'plenitude of the type "in-itself-for-itself"'' which he has postulated. However the particular strand of thought to which Sartre refers does not represent by any means the only Christian understanding of death. There is also the picture of further living beyond this life through which the human person may continue to develop and may eventually attain the complete fulfilment of his or her possibilities. This end state would then be precisely that 'plenitude' of which Sartre speaks. But whether conceived as a fulfilment or enlightenment attained through a long development, or as a sudden completion bestowed by divine grace or by final self-discovery, the religious traditions point to an ultimate state which is 'no longer a waiting for being' and which imparts to our present existence the positive character of movement towards a limitlessly good end. As religiously understood, our life is a journey towards a final fulfilment – whether in time or beyond time – which gives value and purpose to the hard pilgrimage of samsaric existence.

3 THE ESCHATOLOGICAL CHARACTER OF THE SEMITIC TRADITIONS

This conviction of the great traditions that the eternal and overarching reality is good, and that the outcome of the human story will therefore be good, is an assurance not merely of a private but of a universal fulfilment. However pervaded by suffering the lives of hundreds of millions have been and are, and however unrealised their human potential, those lives as seen by the post-axial faiths nevertheless all have their place in a soteriologically structured universe. Their gospels declare that the project of human existence is not meaningless and in vain.

At this point however we must distinguish between two forms of teleological or eschatological outlook. One is the communal-historical type in which history is expected to come to an end and human beings to be judged and either incorporated into a divine kingdom on earth or finally relegated to outer darkness; the other is the more individual and ahistorical type in which it is believed that the self, at the climax of its long spiritual evolution, will finally burst out of a false egoity into consciousness of its true nature, thereby escaping from the trammels of earthly existence. These different conceptions are bound up with different ways of understanding and experiencing time and history. The communal-historical outlook, dominating the religions of Semitic origin, sees the human story as proceeding from a beginning to an end through a linear sequence.[4] Time is assumed to be an irreversible unidirectional flow of which every moment is unique and unrepeatable. History is thus an unfolding drama, each stage having its own special character. Religiously, the world is an arena in which God is purposefully at work and in which human volitions are significant as serving or opposing the divine intention in each new day and year and century.

The individual-ahistorical outlook, on the other hand, as exemplified in the religions of Indian origin, sees time either as a vast cyclical movement which endlessly repeats itself or as a beginningless and endless flow of interdependent change (*pratītya samutpāda*). As each point on the rim of a wheel is equidistant from the centre, so each moment of revolving time is equidistant from the eternal reality of Brahman, or each moment of the world's incessant flux from the 'further shore' of Nirvana; so that the transforming moment of enlightenment can occur whenever the individual is inwardly ready for it.

These two different conceptions of time and history have frequently been contrasted. It has been said, for example, that for one of them history has meaning whilst for the other it is without meaning; or even that for the one history exists (that is, events are seen as meaningfully related to one another in a linear pattern) whilst for the other there is no history (that is, events are not seen in that way as forming a meaningful sequence). In this sense, in which 'history' signifies the character of events as forming a coherent story, we can speak of the monotheistic discovery of history. For history in this sense seems to have first emerged as the awareness that the human drama is a divine theophany, a scene of God's powerful presence and activity. This took place first among the ancient Hebrews during the axial period, as an achievement of the great prophets, whose insights sharpened and intensified the Israelites' consciousness of life as a continuous interaction with their God. The succession of events was given a coherent meaning as the working out of God's purpose. This meaning was initially most clearly experienced and expressed by Second Isaiah, with his vision of a new age soon to be inaugurated when the scattered children of Israel would be reunited and paradisal conditions established; for God would make Zion's 'wilderness like Eden, her desert like the garden of the Lord; joy and gladness will be found in her, thanksgiving and the voice of song' (Isaiah 51:3).[5] And so Eliade is able to say that 'for the first time, the prophets placed a value on history, succeeded in transcending the traditional vision of the cycle . . . and discovered a one-way time' (1971, 104).

As a result of the prophetic influence this soteriological-eschatological outlook became an aspect of Hebrew consciousness, dominating the emerging canon. The creation of the canon was of course a gradual process which 'absorbed primary traditions and records of more than a thousand years, and overlaid them with interpretations, with interpretations of interpretations, with redactions and interpolations, and subtle imposition of new meanings through integration in wider contexts' (Voegelin 1954–74, I:145). But in the finished literary product the meaning bestowed by the divine purpose radiated backward and outward to form what is in principle a world history beginning with the creation.

During the 'inter-testamentary' period Judaism absorbed influences from Persian Zoroastrianism as well as from the surrounding Hellenistic culture. The hope for an Israel triumphantly restored by the messiah mingled with other conceptions, including resurrection and an individual fulfilment beyond the grave. This medley of ideas continued within Judaism's larger offshoot, Christianity. Here the unfulfilled expectation of the end of the age, when Jesus was to have returned in glory to inaugurate God's kingdom on earth, receded and turned into the hope of a future resurrection, which in the medieval period largely merged into the thought of departed souls being judged individually at death and going either to purgatory, on their way to heaven, or to hell. Likewise in Islam there was from the beginning a proclamation of the resurrection of the dead, the day of judgment, the joys of paradise and the sorrows of hell.

Thus in these traditions of middle-eastern Semitic origin soteriology and eschatology are united – though there is also, as we shall note in section 5, the ever-present and religiously all-important possibility of anticipating the eschaton by living now within the pattern of the ultimate future.

4 THE ESCHATOLOGICAL CHARACTER OF THE INDIAN TRADITIONS

But what of the religions of Indian origin? Does not Hindu thought generally see *saṃsāra* as a beginningless and endless process, a perpetual revolution of the *kalpas* in which the universe is formed out of chaos, goes through its enormous cycle, is consumed by fire, and then moves again into another round of its eternal recurrence? The consequent lack of any final resolution, and hence of any overall purpose, is powerfully expressed in the image of the cosmic dance of Shiva as he continually creates, destroys and re-creates the universe. Again, Buddhists generally think of the universe as a beginningless and endless flux of interdependent insubstantiality (*pratītya samutpāda*) within which streams of conscious life, falsely positing their own autonomous existence, are subject to the self-centred craving in virtue of which life is to them suffering, anxiety, unsatisfactoriness. This craving binds them to the wheel of *saṃsāra* so that they are continually reborn as part of a whirling cosmic process which does not come from anywhere and is not going anywhere.

This is indeed the general Indian conception of the realm of finite existence; and it stands in contrast to the general Semitic conception of the beginning of that realm in an act of divine creation, the progressive fulfilment through its history of a divine intention, and its eventual supersession by an eternal heavenly state. But from our present human standpoint, as part of the ongoing movement of the universe and immersed in its temporal flow, the two conceptions are alike eschatological in that they point to the end of our present state of suffering and to a limitlessly better quality of existence which the structure of reality makes possible. The Hindu hopes to attain liberation from the samsaric illusion into the infinite being-consciousness-bliss of Brahman; and the Buddhist hopes to attain enlightenment and thus to realise Nirvana. These are variant concepts of an ineffable state beyond the sufferings generated by egoity. Thus the contemporary advaitic Hindu philosopher T. M. P. Mahadevan, speaking of the turning wheel of birth and death, says, 'The purpose of transmigration is to enable the soul to gain the transcendental experience. Life in the world is a schooling which disciplines the soul and makes it perfect. Viewed in this light, life is a blessing and not a curse' (1960, 256). And concerning the ancient message of Buddhism Wilfred Cantwell Smith writes:

> It has sometimes been said that early Buddhist preaching is pessimistic. This is simply wrong: it is a gospel, good news, a joyous proclamation of a discovery of a truth without which life is bleak, is suffering, but with which there is not merely serenity but triumph. It is indeed fortunate for man that he has been born into a universe where evanescence is not the last word. Because there is Dharma, he can be saved . . . That we live in the kind of universe where such a truth obtains, firm, reliable, and permanent, is the 'good news' that the Buddha preached, and that his movement carried half across the world.
>
> (1979, 28–9)

Moksha/Nirvana, then, is for the Indian religions the blessed eschaton for which believers hope and toward which they strive; and they hope and strive for this as ardently as within the Semitic traditions believers hope and strive for the promised eternal life of heaven, paradise, the Kingdom.

5 REALISED ESCHATOLOGY

Further, in the Semitic and Indian traditions alike the eschatological reality is not only a future state occurring beyond death but also – giving their gospels an immediate excitement and challenge – a limitlessly better existence which can and should be entered upon now, in the midst of this present life. In Christianity this is an eternal quality of life, which is 'to know thee the only true God, and Jesus Christ whom thou hast sent' (John 17:3). A characteristic of this is joy. In the Spirit-filled early church 'the disciples were filled with joy, and with the Holy Spirit' (Acts 13:52). For we 'joy in God through our Lord Jesus Christ, by whom we have now received the atonement' (Romans 5:11). And in its more authentic moments Christianity has always produced a profound sense of release and joy at being forgiven and accepted by God, and a love of neighbour empowered by the conviction of the divine love for all human beings.

For Judaism, despite the perils and threats of history, it is possible to experience now the joy of life lived in conformity with the Torah and to enjoy the blessings of God's favour.[6] Psalm 119 expresses this joy in the Lord from its first verse, 'Blessed are the undefiled in the way, who walk in the law of the Lord'. Again, in Psalm 16:11, 'Thou wilt show me the path of life; in thy presence is fullness of joy'. And in the Qur'an the revelation of Allah, the compassionate and merciful one, comes as good news for all who are open to it. It offers a new life at peace with God, secure in a knowledge of the divine commands and the divine mercy:

> Surely God's friends – no fear shall be on them
> neither shall they sorrow,
> Those who believe, and are godfearing –
> For them is good tidings in the present life and
> in the world to come.
>
> (Qur'an, 10:64–5)

In Hindu experience, to attain *mokṣa* or liberation in this life is to attain to a profound inner peace and happiness. It is indeed to participate in the indescribable *ānanda* (bliss) of Brahman. This supreme reality is 'the source of joy (*modanīyaṃ*)' (*Kaṭh. Up.*, I:2:13 – Radhakrishnan 1969, 614), the 'supreme bliss (*paramam sukham*)' (*Kaṭh. Up.*, II:2:14 – Radhakrishnan 1969, 641), and those who know this reality within them have 'eternal bliss (*sukham śāśvataṃ*)' (*Kaṭh. Up.*, II:2:12 – Radhakrishnan 1969, 640). For 'The wise, who perceive Him as abiding in their self, to them belongs eternal (or supreme) happiness (*sukham śāśvataṃ*)' (*Svet. Up.*, VI:12 – Radhakrishnan 1969, 746). This goal is to overcome one's illusory separateness from Brahman, and this end is 'sorrowless, blissful (*aśokam ānandam*)' (*Mait. Up.*, VI:23 – Radhakrishnan 1969, 834). For 'when the mind is dissolved and there is the bliss (*sukham*) of which the witness is the self, that is Brahman, the immortal and radiant (*cāmṛtaṃ śukram*), that is the way' (*Mait. Up.*, VI:24 – Radhakrishnan 1969, 835). Again, 'The happiness (*śukham*) of a mind whose stains are washed away by concentration (*samādhi*) and who has entered the self, it cannot be here described by words' (*Mait. Up.*, VI:34 – Radhakrishnan 1969, 845).

Again, in the teaching of the Buddha Nirvana is attainable now as the joy that lies beyond ego-centredness. 'Thinking of there being no self, he wins to the state wherein the conceit "I am" has been uprooted, to the cool [i.e., to Nirvana], even in this life' (*Anguttara-Nikāya*, IV:353 – Hare 1965, 233); 'He who doth crush the great "I am" conceit – this, even this, is happiness supreme' (*Udāna*, II:1 – Woodward 1948, 13); 'Above, beyond Nibbana's bliss, is naught' (*Therīgāthā*, 476 – Davids 1964, 169). In the *Dhammapada*, the ancient collection of the Buddha's sayings that is widely used as a Bible, the stress is strongly upon opening oneself to the Dhamma in this present life, and upon the blessedness which this brings: for example, 'happily do we live without hate among the hateful . . . happily do we live without yearning among those who yearn . . . happily do we live, we who have no impediments (*kiñcana*, such as lust and hatred) . . . happily the peaceful live, giving up victory and defeat . . . There is no bliss higher than Nibbana . . . Nibbana, bliss supreme . . . Nibbana is the highest bliss . . . the taste of the joy of the Dhamma . . .' (Narada 1972, ch. 15). Or again, Nirvana is the inner peace and joy of the awakened mind as the Zen practitioner experiences the world without the distorting and anxiety-creating influence of self-centredness. As D. T. Suzuki says:

> Zen . . . opens a man's mind to the greatest mystery as it is daily and hourly performed; . . . it makes us live in the world as if walking in the Garden of Eden . . . I do not know why – and there is no need of explaining, but when the sun rises the whole world dances with joy and everybody's heart is filled with bliss. (1969, 45, 75)

And whilst the Communist faith is strongly oriented to a distant ideal future when, in Marx's words, 'we shall have an association, in which the free development of each is the condition for the free development of all' (Marx [1848] 1963), yet dedication to this ideal can produce now in varying degrees what is, in religious language, a state of blessedness. Thus the Chinese Maoist revolutionary Liu Shao-ch'i said of the good Marxist, in words which Buddhists might use of a bodhisattva, 'He will also be capable of being the most sincere, most candid, and happiest of men. Since he has no selfish desires . . . he has no personal losses or gains or other things to worry about . . .' (de Bary 1960, 917–18).

6 DARKNESS AND LIGHT

But is there not also another and darker side to religion?

Undoubtedly there is. In the Semitic traditions, as well as gratitude for the gift of life there can be a sense of guilt, shame and self-loathing; as well as the awareness of God's love and blessing there can be the destructive sense of divine hatred and condemnation; as well as the hope of paradise there can be the fear of hell. For traditional theistic religion envisages not only a heavenly fulfilment but also the contrary end-state of everlasting damnation. In the faiths of Indian origin there are likewise many hells and their torments, though these have a different and less ultimate significance than in the Semitic faiths. For the many hells of the Buddhist and Hindu cosmologies are temporary conditions encountered between earthly incarnations; and they serve the soul's gradual progress towards final liberation and its union with the eternally Real. These religions do however have their own distinctive form of pessimism in the thought of the long, hard round of rebirths through which one's Karma must be worked out before liberation is achieved.

Thus both the Semitic and the Indian traditions have their pessimistic as well as their optimistic aspects. And whether the religious outlook of a particular individual at a particular time is predominantly hopeful or fearful will no doubt depend largely on personal temperament and circumstances. If one is going through a bad period one can confirm one's sorrows with the apparently endless vista of returns to this same pain-ridden world; or can despair in the thought of being cursed by God and excluded from the joys of the blessed. But nevertheless whilst there is an ample store of religious imagery to feed our darker moods and to confirm our tragic fears, this imagery does not represent the central message of any of the great traditions. The long vista of returns to a hard existence has at the end of it, for those who listen to the teachings of the Indian faiths, the ultimate hope of Nirvana or Moksha. And it is noteworthy that within the Semitic traditions the final disaster of hell is almost invariably seen as befalling others, not oneself! Hell is for the irredeemably wicked, or for the infidel, the heathen, the enemy; but have any theologians failed to assume that they and theirs are among the elect who are to be saved by God's grace? Thus despite the pain-ridden field of Samsara, and despite the menacing thought of eternal damnation, the central message of the post-axial faiths is the proclamation of good news. It is the affirmation that human life is in reality more than the harsh experience that has always been the lot of so many; and it offers a hope of salvation or liberation or fulfilment which can even now suffuse our life with a positive meaning and value.

Notes

1. *Showings*, longer text [14th century] ch. 27 – 1978, 124.
2. This analysis, first influentially made by William James ([1902] 1960, 484), represents today a widespread view of the basic structure of religious thought. For example, John E. Smith represents all religion as involving, first, an Ideal that is the ground and goal of existence; second, the conviction that life as we know it is separated from that Ideal; and third, powers or methods for overcoming the present flaw in existence (Bertocci 1982, 28; cf. J. E. Smith 1965). And Frederick Streng describes religion as a means to an ultimate transformation which 'is a fundamental change from being caught up in the troubles of common existence (sin, ignorance) to living in such a way that one can cope at the deepest levels with those troubles'. (Streng 1955, 2) See also Keith Ward 1987, 43–4 and 165–6.
3. As one of many reports of the cosmic optimism of religion, Mark O. Webb writes: 'nearly all religious experiences result in the belief that the universe is an essentially friendly place; that is, that we shouldn't worry about the future. People who have had experiences of this sort tend to live more calmly than others, having acquired a strong feeling that the world is essentially just, and they in particular are "cared for". This is true even of those experiences that include a conviction that the world is fallen and sinful, because they also include a conviction that God is sovereign and loves his creatures' (1985, 85).
4. Though there are also other elements in these traditions – above all in their mystical strands of thought and in their Wisdom literature.
5. On Judaism as a religion of redemption see Greenberg 1988, 18.
6. Cf. Schechter ([1990] 1961, ch. XI); see also, e.g., Benno Heinemann (1973, ch. 4).

Part Two
The Religious Ambiguity of the Universe

5

Ontological, Cosmological and Design Arguments

All proofs or disproofs that we tender
Of His existence are returned
Unopened to the sender.

W. H. Auden

1 THE ISSUE

By the religious ambiguity of the universe I do not mean that it has no definite character but that it is capable from our present human vantage point of being thought and experienced in both religious and naturalistic ways. This ambiguity has only become widely evident since the rise of modern science in the seventeenth, eighteenth and nineteenth centuries. From the beginnings of human life to the spiritual ferment of the axial period, and through the more settled 'ages of faith', the reality of the transcendent was accepted as manifest fact, unquestioned except by an occasional boldly sceptical philosopher. The immanence of the divine was daily experienced in the organic unity of life, the regular procession of the seasons, the rage of storm and earthquake, the still beauty of a lake, the terror of eerie places, and its power was felt as benign or threatening in prosperity and calamity, health and sickness, fertility and sterility, victory and defeat. Or again, the one God who had spoken through the Torah or through Christ or through the Qur'an was a given reality whose presence was daily confirmed in personal prayer and public liturgy, manifest both in the usages of language and in the structure of society, celebrated in painting, sculpture, architecture and music, and lived out in the great public festivals. Or, yet again, the ultimate Reality, beyond the limitations of personality, was transformingly known in the spiritual exercises of yoga and meditation. Thus a religious understanding of the world, and

73

religious modes of experiencing human life, flowed on through the generations almost without hindrance. In traditional societies the faith of each reinforced the faith of all and communal experience reciprocally shaped the experience of the individual.

But with the western Enlightenment of the eighteenth century, stimulated by the rapid development of the modern scientific method and outlook, a scepticism that had hitherto hovered in the background as a mere logical possibility now became psychologically present and plausible within the more educated circles of Europe and North America, and the old religious certainties began to crumble. Matthew Arnold was acutely conscious of this as he reflected on Dover beach:

> The sea of faith
> Was once, too, at the full, and round earth's shore
> Lay like the folds of a bright girdle furl'd.
> But now I only hear
> Its melancholy, long, withdrawing roar,
> Retreating, to the breath
> Of the night-wind, down the vast edges drear
> And naked shingles of the world.
>
> ('Dover Beach')

And in this post-Enlightenment age of doubt we have realised that the universe is religiously ambiguous. It evokes and sustains non-religious as well as religious responses. The culture within which modern science first arose was theistic; and accordingly the prevailing form of modern scepticism has been atheistic. The sceptics have mostly been secularised Christians and Jews or post-Christian and post-Jewish Marxists. Distinctively post-Hindu, post-Buddhist and post-Muslim forms of scepticism have yet to arise. I shall therefore in this and the following two chapters be discussing the religious ambiguity of the world primarily in terms of the western theist/atheist debate.

That the world is today experienced both theistically and naturalistically or atheistically is an evident fact, not likely to be disputed by anyone. Dispute does however arise when we ask whether these different modes of experience are alike rationally defensible. For there are those who maintain that the existence, or the non-existence, of God can be established either as certain or at least as demonstrably more probable than the contrary. Accordingly the religious ambiguity of the universe, as permitting both theistic and naturalistic responses, is by no means universally accepted and the case for it has to be made by showing the inconclusiveness of the various philosophical arguments on both sides.

2 THE ONTOLOGICAL ARGUMENT

The ontological argument, first clearly formulated by St Anselm in the eleventh century CE, begins with the concept of God as that than which no greater, or more perfect, can be conceived; and argues that there must be such a being since to think otherwise would amount to the contradiction of supposing the most perfect conceivable being to lack the perfection of existence.

This argument has fascinated generations of philosophers, and shelves of books have been devoted to its examination. I have myself, in collaboration with the late Arthur McGill (whose premature death deprived American theology of one of its most brilliant representatives in his generation), contributed a volume to the growing library on the ontological argument (Hick and McGill 1976). This vast output of books and articles has by now made the subject almost impenetrably complex in its proliferating detail and yet has also, I venture to think, made its central points manifest to the discerning.

Thus it is, I think, clear that the proof in this classic form was refuted by Kant's counter-argument, later reinforced by Russell and many others, that existence is not a predicate comparable with, say, 'red' or 'four-footed' as qualities that a given entity might have or lack. To affirm that x exists is not to say that x has, among its several properties, that of existence; it is to perform the quite different operation of asserting that the concept of x is instantiated. Thus to say that God exists is to affirm that a certain concept, such as that of 'the infinite personal creator of the universe', is instantiated: that there is in reality such a being. But this cannot be certified by the concept itself: a concept, as such, is simply a thought that may or may not have an instance. Even if, with Anselm and later Descartes, we insist that the idea of existence is integral to the concept, so that God is defined as 'the existing infinite personal creator of the universe', then whether *that* concept is instantiated still cannot be determined by the concept itself but only by the facts of the universe.

In the third quarter of the present century a second form of ontological argument has been propounded by Charles Hartshorne (1944, 1961, 1962, 1963a, 1963b, 1965a, 1965b, 1968, 1969, 1970, 1977) and Norman Malcolm (1960) and in a different form by Alvin Plantinga (1974, ch. 10; 1977, part II) and others. This argument – a version of which can be found in Anselm's *Proslogion, III,* and in his *Reply* to Gaunilo – hinges upon the distinction of logical modality between contingency and necessity. The concept of God, it is said, is not the concept of a being that contingently exists or fails to exist but of one that necessarily exists or necessarily does not exist. For only a being who has necessary existence and whose non-existence is therefore impossible measures up to the concept of that than which no more perfect can be conceived. Thus it follows from the concept of God that divine existence is either necessary or impossible. But it would only be impossible if the concept were self-contradictory. Since this has not been shown, we must conclude that God necessarily exists – and therefore exists.

In assessing this argument a distinction has to be drawn between logical and factual or ontological necessity. Logical necessity is the property that some propositions have of being true in virtue of the meanings of the terms composing them. But existential propositions, declaring that *x* exists, cannot have this kind of necessary or analytic truth because, as we noted above, existence does not name a defining property but is a term used to assert that a certain concept is instantiated. Thus whilst it may be necessarily true, not only that 'triangles have three sides', but also that 'God is good', it cannot be necessarily true that there exist any objects with the properties of a triangle or any entity with the characteristics that would constitute it God. For logical necessity has no purchase on matters of fact and existence. There cannot be a logically necessarily existent being. Nor indeed has classical theism generally supposed that there could. Although the distinction was not explicitly drawn until modern times, it was the concept of ontological or factual necessity that figured in the classical discussions. A being has ontological or factual necessity if it exists eternally and independently as an uncreated and indestructible unity. Thus Anselm explains what he means by 'a being which cannot be conceived not to exist':

For in fact all those things (and they alone) that have a

beginning or end or are made up of parts and, as I have already said, all those things that do not exist as a whole in a particular place or at a particular time can be thought as not existing. Only that being in which there is neither beginning nor end nor conjunction of parts, and that thought does not discern save as a whole in every place and at every time, cannot be thought as not existing. (Anselm [11th century] 1965, 177)

Thus God's necessary existence is, for Anselm, God's eternal *aseity* or self-existence. In terms of this Anselmic concept of ontological necessity the existence of God is either necessary or impossible. For if an eternal being exists, it cannot cease to exist, and its existence is accordingly ontologically necessary; whilst if not, no such being can come into existence and its existence is therefore ontologically impossible.

Hartshorne and Malcolm have, in my view, illicitly transmuted the valid insight that the concept of an ontologically necessary being must be instantiated either always or never into the quite different claim that God's existence is either logically necessary or logically impossible. They then conclude that since it has not been shown to be the latter, we must take it to be the former. But no such conclusion follows from the valid premise that the concept of God is such that God exists either eternally and independently or not at all. For it cannot be logically necessary that there is a reality corresponding to the concept of an ontologically necessary being – or indeed to any other concept. (The 'necessary existence' of, for example, the square root of minus one, and likewise the 'necessary non-existence' of, for example, square circles, are not relevant; for the aim of the ontological argument is not to prove that God exists in the sense in which mathematical and logical concepts exist, but exists as the ultimate creative power of the universe.)[1]

Plantinga's version, based on the use of possible worlds logic, is in my view equally fallacious. He defines the property of 'maximal greatness' as the property of having maximal excellence (defined as entailing omniscience, omnipotence and moral perfection) in every possible world. He then asserts that

(1) There is a possible world (*W*) in which maximal greatness is instantiated.
(2) Necessarily, a being is maximally great only if it has maximal excellence in every world.
(3) Necessarily, a being has maximal excellence in every world if

it has omniscience, omnipotence and moral perfection in every world.

'But', he says, 'if (1) is true, then there is a possible world *W* such that if it had been actual, then there would have existed a being that was omnipotent, omniscient, and morally perfect; this being, furthermore, would have had these qualities in every possible world. So it follows that if *W* had been actual, it would have been *impossible* that there be no such being. That is, if *W* had been actual,

(4) "There is no omnipotent, omniscient, and morally perfect being" would have been an impossible proposition. But if a proposition is impossible in at least one possible world, then it is impossible in every possible world; what is impossible does not vary from world to world.

Accordingly, (4) is impossible in the *actual* world, i.e., impossible *simpliciter*. But if it is impossible that there be no such being, then there actually exists a being that is omnipotent, omniscient, and morally perfect; this being, furthermore, has these qualities essentially and exists in every possible world' (Plantinga 1977, 111–12).

As in the case of other formulations of the ontological argument, the reasoning looks suspiciously like an attempt to prove divine existence (or, in this formulation, necessary divine existence) by definitional fiat. I believe that the suspicion is justified. This is perhaps fortunate; for Plantinga's argument for a maximally excellent being, if valid, would also work for a maximally evil being:

(1) There is a possible world *W* in which maximal evil is instantiated.

(2) Necessarily, a being is maximally evil if it has maximal malignness in every world.

(3) Necessarily, a being has maximal malignness only if it has omniscience, omnipotence and absolute moral depravity in every world.

(4) If *W* were actual, (5) 'There is no omniscient, omnipotent and absolutely depraved being', would be impossible.

(6) But since (5) is impossible in one possible world it is impossible in all possible worlds, including the actual world.

(7) Therefore there is an omniscient, omnipotent and absolutely depraved being.

This conclusion is not only disturbing in itself but is incompatible with the conclusion of Plantinga's own argument. For there cannot be two omnipotent beings of whom one is good and the other evil, since a power which is opposed by an omnipotent power is not itself omnipotent. And yet the same form of argument would, if valid, prove that both exist. Clearly, then, that form of argument is faulty. Its flaw reduplicates the flaw in other versions of the argument. Plantinga himself concedes that it does not prove God's existence because its central premise (proposition 1) might be rejected by some (Plantinga 1977, 110). But even if one accepts (1), thus granting that the existence of God is not impossible, all that we have is the fact that it is a possible (that is, not self-contradictory) proposition that 'the property of maximal excellence in any and every possible world – including this world – is instantiated'. But if it is possible that this property is in fact instantiated, it is also possible that it is in fact not instantiated.

Thus it appears to me that the ontological argument, fascinating though it continues to be as a perennial stimulus to philosophical ingenuity, does not provide a firm ground for belief in the reality of God.

3 COSMOLOGICAL ARGUMENTS

I shall treat together the cosmological family of arguments which move from the observed cosmos to an eternal and self-existent creator as providing its ultimate explanation. Within the variety of forms displayed by this line of thought there is a common theme. We live as part of a continuous flow of events no one of which nor the ensemble of which is self-explanatory. The occurrence of each one is explained by reference to other earlier or simultaneous events. Thus we may explain the present movement of the ball by my having previously kicked it, and the present movement of my pen by the concurrent movement of my hand. But these earlier or contemporary events themselves demand explanation, which consists in referring to other events, which in turn refer us to yet others, and so on in a regression which is either endless or must end in a reality that neither requires not is susceptible of further explanation. The first possibility – an unending explanatory regress – is ruled out on the ground that the universe would then lack any rational character; and since we are committed in science, philosophy and the conduct of life to the principle of rationality we must prefer a rational explanation if one is available. The only possible such explanation would be that the universe is the product of a creative will which is itself eternal, uncaused, not dependent upon any other reality and therefore not capable of being rendered intelligible by reference beyond itself. The universe is then explained as the creation of a being whose nature excludes the questions When did it begin? (for it is eternal), What caused or created it? (for it is uncaused) and On what further circumstances does it depend? (for it is independent). Such a being simply *is*, as the ultimate, unconditioned and eternal reality. It provides a final explanation of the existence of everything else, although there is and can be nothing that could explain its own existence.

Why, however, should we not take the physical universe itself to be the ultimate unexplained reality? For it may be a beginningless procession of events which is, as a totality, eternal, uncaused and not dependent upon anything beyond itself. The theistic answer can, I think, only be cast in terms of the greater *de facto* acceptability to us, as conscious wills, of the existence of an ultimate conscious will, than of the (to us) sheer unintelligible mystery presented by the uncaused and beginningless existence of a complex realm of matter. As consciousnesses we can rest in the idea of an ultimate consciousness as the source of the existence and character of the universe, whereas the thought that the physical universe itself is ultimate leaves us unsatisfied: we still cannot help wondering *why* it exists and *why* it exhibits the particular basic regularities in virtue of which it is ordered. Thus the idea of a creative divine mind possesses to our human minds greater intrinsic intelligibility than that of a realm of purely material forces and movements. We are accordingly faced – a theist might argue – with the choice of accepting God (though with the divine nature thus far unspecified except as the consciousness and will responsible for the existence of the universe) or accepting the existence of the physical universe itself as a given unintelligible and mysterious brute fact.

This argument says something that is true concerning our cognitive situation. But nevertheless it does not compel us to believe that there is a God. For one may opt instead to accept the universe as a sheer unexplained fact. One can say, with Bertrand Russell, 'The universe is just there, and that's all' (Russell 1957, 152). For it could be that the stronger plausibility of theism only holds relatively to our human minds, and indeed only to some human minds, and may be no more than an illusion to which they are subject. Thus it seems that the cosmological family of arguments, although richly suggestive, nevertheless does not constitute a compelling theistic proof.

4 CONTEMPORARY SCIENTIFIC THEISM

The design (or teleological) argument can best be regarded today as a comprehensive and internally complex probability argument. It is not simply, as in the eighteenth-century version criticised by Hume, a matter of the unity and coherence of nature, with the solar system working like a vast machine and each plant and animal marvellously adapted to its function within the total economy of nature. F. R. Tennant (1930) broadened the argument to include: (1) the coincidental obtaining of a variety of cosmic circumstances as pre-conditions of an orderly universe producing animal and personal life; (2) the fact of moral ideals and conscience; (3) the aesthetic values of nature; and (4) the fact that the universe is knowable by and to some extent intelligible to the human mind. One further consideration, which Tennant omitted because he considered that it had been over-stressed in the nineteenth century but which has since Tennant's time again become prominent, is (5) distinctively religious experience.

Let us look briefly at each of these five factors – (1) in the present section, (2) in Chapter 6.1, (3) and (4) in section 5 of the present chapter and (5) in Chapter 6.2 – considered as potential evidences for the existence of God.

The eighteenth- and nineteenth-century design argument as elaborated by many writers, including William Derham and the other Boyle lecturers, Archdeacon William Paley and the authors of the Bridgewater Treatises, and as classically criticised by David Hume, dealt with the orderly functioning of the solar system, whose regular movements seemed analogous to those of a clock, and also with the innumerable evidences of design in the way in which living creatures are adapted to their environment. Eyes are as evidently for seeing and legs for walking as clothes are for wearing and pens for writing. However these older versions of the argument were severely damaged by two successive blows. Hume's philosophical critique suggested that the universe, as a

[handwritten margin notes: "Lucretius", "On the Nature of Things"]

realm of self-sustaining order, might have come about through the random movements of atoms (or whatever the ultimate constituents of matter may be) passing in unlimited time through every possible permutation; and further that even if one does see signs of a mind behind nature, that mind need not be the deity of traditional Christian belief – for we cannot, from a finite and apparently imperfect world, validly infer an infinite and perfect source. Then nearly a century later came Darwin's demonstration that organic adaptation to environment results from a continuous process of natural selection whereby characteristics – resulting from chance genetic mutations – that have survival value tend to be propagated, thus producing a slow cumulative development in the stream of life.

This immensely complex process is still by no means fully understood and the details of the evolutionary picture have from time to time to be revised in the light of new information. Recent discoveries suggest, for example, that the process may not be as smoothly uniform as had hitherto been supposed but may involve phases of relatively rapid change followed by long periods of stability. There are thus mysteries and missing links within the evolutionary theory. But nevertheless it is abundantly evident, and agreed by virtually everyone who has confronted the evidence, that life has indeed gradually developed on earth from the simplest unicellular organisms to the most complex mammals. This process has constituted a continuous organic evolution which leaves no gaps requiring to be filled by supernatural interventions. It is open to the religious mind to believe that this entire history fulfils a divine purpose, or constitutes as a totality a divine manifestation or a gradually unfolding divine self-awareness. But it is not plausible to suggest that at certain points a divine power must have worked upon the process from outside to cause events to occur that were not linked by natural law to the previous states of the universe.

However during the last twenty or thirty years the probability type of theistic argument has enlarged its purview from the solar system and the surface of the earth to the history of the universe as a whole. Cosmologists, physicists and astronomers have identified a number of special conditions which had to be fulfilled in the structure and evolution of the universe if human life was one day to exist within it. In continuity with the older design argument the fulfilment of these conditions is then viewed teleologically as the work of an intelligent designer who has programmed the universe to produce beings capable of worshipping their Maker. Such a theological interpretation has recently been propounded by Hugh Montefiore in *The Probability of God*, and I shall quote his summary of the main cosmological 'coincidences' that were necessary to produce a planet on which life, and then intelligent life, could come about:

The distribution of gas in the universe from the big bang onwards had to be delicately balanced if it was to produce galaxies, with perturbations neither so big that the galaxies imploded into themselves, nor so small that galaxies would not form at all. Without this fine balance, there would have been no galaxies, no stars, no planets, no life.

The distribution of gases needed to be uniform. The dispersal of even minute unevennesses (one part in 10^{40}) would have caused an alteration of temperature inhospitable to the formation of galaxies. Without this uniform distribution there would have been no galaxies, no stars, no planets, no life.

The initial heat of the big bang was so finely adjusted that it has enabled the formation of galaxies and stars. If the heat had been slightly different, we could not have now a life system based on oxygen. If things had been a little colder, there would have been insufficient turbulence for galaxies to form; and so no galaxies, no stars, no planets, no life.

The weight of neutrinos (unless they are weightless) is so finely tuned that it permits the orderly expansion of the universe and the rotation of galaxies and clusters. A very small increase in weight would mean that the universe would contract instead of expand. This contraction would mean that conditions would not be suitable for the emergence of life.

The total mass of the universe is such that it is stable, with an orderly rate of expansion and no tendency to implosion. A little more mass, and the force of gravity would have caused an implosion; a little less and the rate of expansion would not be orderly but runaway. Without this fine balance, conditions would have been too unstable to permit the evolution of life.

The whole universe as we know it depends on the existence of atoms. A minute reduction in neutron mass would probably result in no atoms at all. Without atoms no stars, no planets, no life.

A very small shift in the value of certain constants (such as the strength of the 'weak interaction' in relation to the strength of gravity, or the relation of electron mass to the mass difference between protons and neutrons) would have resulted in a different ratio of free protons to free neutrons. This would have resulted in a different proportion of helium to hydrogen in the universe. This in turn would have affected the possibility of stable stars existing. Without sufficient hydrogen, life could not have emerged on Earth.

If the force of gravity were slightly weaker, or the force of electro-magnetism slightly stronger, there would probably be no planets in the universe. If these differences were reversed, the universe would be very different from what it is. The existence of life on Earth depends on these constants.

The 'strong nuclear force' is so finely tuned that it makes possible the existence of life on Earth. Had it been a little weaker there would have been no deuterium, which is needed to enable nuclear process in the stars: had it been a little weaker, there would be little hydrogen in the universe. In either case the emergence of life on Earth would not have been possible.

A slight change in the 'weak interaction' would mean that supernovae could not have exploded, and therefore would not have produced those elements which are essential for living systems on Earth.

The interior of hot stars provides just the right temperature for the manufacture of large supplies of carbon, which is vital for living systems as we know them. Without this carbon, there would have been no life on Earth.[2]

These special conditions necessary for the emergence of the human species have continued, as Montefiore reminds us, on the surface of the earth in, for example, a sufficient constancy of the climate, the salinity of the oceans, and the depth and consistency of the ionosphere – all of which seem to have been necessary if the earth was to constitute a favourable environment for the process of biological evolution as we know it.

From these cosmic 'coincidences' and 'fine tunings', as Montefiore calls them, the new scientific theists infer that a divine power must have been at work controlling the universe. For it seems to them overwhelmingly improbable that the complex nexus of circumstances required for the emergence of intelligent life should have come about by chance. Perhaps we could allow that one, or even two, of such a series of conditions might have been fulfilled by chance, but to suppose this of a dozen or more distinct co-operating factors seems beyond reason. They therefore believe that we are authorised to infer a divine power which values human persons and which has wielded the immensities of space, time and energy for the purpose of creating us.

We should perhaps first note, in responding to this catalogue of providential arrangements, that they are not in fact a series of separate and unrelated conditions but that they all flow at various removes from the state of the primal fireball in the first few moments of its 'explosion'. The constitution and temperature of the condensed universe in the first seconds of its history were apparently such that the expansion would ultimately result in the formation of galaxies of suns, many with planets. Some physicists have tentatively extrapolated back within the earliest milliseconds of the universe's history and have concluded that 'the laws of physics deduced here on Earth apply back to 10^{-38} seconds after the beginning' (Rees 1981, 272). Thus rather than using the image of tunings and adjustments occurring during the history of the universe we should think of the original fireball as so constituted that it was going to expand into the universe that exists today.

I shall argue presently that, if the question is whether from all this we can validly infer God, the answer has to be No. But if the question is whether, from a religious standpoint, the universe can properly be seen as a creation or emanation or expression of the divine, the answer has to be Yes. There are two broad alternative views of the relation between the material universe and the supposed transcendent Reality of which religion speaks. One is the naturalistic conception that the physical universe is prior and that 'God', the 'Real' and so on are ideas formed in the consciousness of human animals after some fifteen billion years during which no such thought existed, and are likely to persist for only a few more pulses of cosmic time; the other is the religious conception of the divine as ontologically prior and the physical universe as secondary and derivative. This religious option entails that the material universe, with its actual structure and history, stands in some kind of instrumental or expressive relationship to the divine: the fact that the universe exists and has the character that it has, including its liability to produce human life, is ultimately to be attributed to the divine Reality. Thus the religious conviction implies that, at least in its general features, the universe was from its inception such as to go through the successive phases that have in fact transpired, including the phase in which we now find ourselves.

But a religious vision which thus embraces the current scientific account of the universe has neither arisen out of that account nor is dependent upon it. If the scientific picture should change in the future (as it almost certainly will) each new version will be equally amenable to a religious interpretation. There is indeed no way in which a description of the physical development of any universe bearing a family resemblance to our own can be strictly incompatible either with theism or with atheism. Certainly the presently observed and deduced facts concerning the universe's expansion are religiously ambivalent.

At this point the 'scientific theist' will want to remonstrate that, although the history of the universe *can* be construed naturalistically, yet such a construal has to face a formidable concatenation of improbabilities. Is it not antecedently immensely unlikely that the initial degree of cosmic perturbation, and the initial heat of the primal fireball, and so on, should have fallen within the comparatively narrow range that would lead to the eventual formation of galaxies of suns, many with planets?

This must not be accepted as a merely rhetorical question. We must ask precisely what is meant by 'improbable' in this case. One interpretation would be statistical. We have seen that all these factors were apparently implicit in the initial state of the universe. If we assume an enormous, or even an infinite, number of possible initial states of equal antecedent likelihood, then the actualisation of any one of them is indeed enormously – or perhaps even infinitely – improbable. But of course on that basis the actualisation of *any* of the possible initial states is *equally* improbable. It is only the fact that we are ourselves part of one of the possible options that singles it out for us as uniquely improbable and therefore miraculous.

Can we however perhaps say that a simpler universe, devoid of galaxies, would have been *a priori* more likely than one containing galaxies; so that the existence of the actual universe has an initial improbability that increases with every additional complexity? In that case we could judge our universe to be prodigiously improbable and might then invoke an anti-improbability factor (which we could call God) to account for it. But by what authority do we legislate for the universe in this way, declaring it to be inherently probable or improbable? Why should the fact that our human brains find simple things easier to process, and therefore more 'probable', than complex ones require that the universe should be simple rather than complex? There is only one universe. It is what it is, and we have to take it as we find it. We find it to be infinitely complex and to our minds infinitely wonderful. We are almost stupefied by its immensity, awed by the picture of the primal fireball exploding and the galaxies and worlds gradually forming; and chilled again by the thought of the fleeting character of life on a planet that must either burn up or become a frozen ball. But we have no reason to think of all this as being *a priori* either probable or improbable except in relation to our own preferences and prejudices. To say that its existence has an antecedent probability of less than one half is simply to clothe our natural wonder in a deceptive garb of scientific precision.

I have been speaking of the universe as singular. And if by the universe we mean the totality of all that is, then it is a tautology that there is only one universe. However the term is sometimes used in contemporary cosmology to refer to a space-time system; and there may in principle be any number of such systems. There would then be an ensemble of universes only one of which is cognisable by a given observer – as in the highly paradoxical parallel universes interpretation of quantum theory propounded by the physicists Hugh Everett and Bryce DeWitt.[3] Or again there might perhaps be many universes constituting different enclosed 'bubbles' within the same 'super-space'. Thus what we usually regard as 'the universe' might in fact be only a disconnected fragment of space-time. There could then be many other universes, each physically inaccessible to the others (Davies 1983, 42). If there is indeed an enormous (or even infinite) number of universes, having different characteristics, then the larger the number the more likely it is that there should among them be one with the features that ours has – in which case this would, naturally enough, be the one in which we find ourselves. But if such a multiple-universe picture is indeed correct it too preserves the characteristic of religious ambiguity. For although God could no doubt have created in this way, it remains no less conceivable that the super-universe, with ours as one component, is itself the ultimate uncreated reality.

Whether or not the universe is one of many, it is in either case equally wonderful that we should find it existing with ourselves as part of it. For on either supposition the odds against one's own present existence are truly prodigious. To take just one link fairly close to hand in the vast chain of improbabilities: in order for me now to exist my parents had to meet and conceive me. That these two particular individuals, out of all their contemporaries in the same social milieu, should have married is statistically highly improbable. But when they conceived me that improbability was thereby multiplied many million-fold. For the male contribution to conception consists of some three to six hundred million sperm – say, on average, four hundred million – each of which is unique in the genetic code that it carries. To quote from an account I have given elsewhere:

> In each case of the millions of formations of sperm cells, through the complex process of meiotic division, a partial reshuffling of the parental genes takes place, producing unpredictable results. For a slightly different course is taken each time in the selection and arrangement of the twenty-three out of the father's forty-six chromosomes that are to constitute his sperm's contribution to the full genetic complement of a member of the next generation. The ordering of the chromosomes in the sperm cell is partly a matter of chance, depending upon which out of each pair of chromosomes happens to be on one side and which on the other when the two sets separate to form new cells. But the degree of randomness thus introduced (calculated as at least eight million potentially different arrangements) is multiplied by scattered breaks and re-formations in many of the chromosomes in the 'crossing over' stage of meiosis. So it is that each of the four hundred million or so sperm cells carries, in its details, a different genetic code. But only one out of these four hundred million can win the race to the ovum. Approximately half of the four hundred million or so sperm carry the Y sex chromosome which will result in a male embryo whilst the other half carry the X chromosome which will produce a female. And each of these two hundred or so million possible or notional males, and likewise each of the two hundred or so million possible females, is unique, differing from its potential brothers and sisters in a number of ways, mostly very slight but some, arising from major mutations, far

from slight. But this family of some four hundred million potential children, only one of whom will actually be conceived and born, is really only a family of four hundred million half-children. For the sperm carries only half the total complement of human chromosomes. Meanwhile the mother has been producing egg cells, though not nearly as many as the father produces sperm cells and usually only one at a time. Each of these eggs contains its own unique arrangement of chromosomes, and the vast range of possibilities which lies behind the formation of a particular sperm cell likewise lies behind the formation of a particular egg cell. Thus there is a further enormous multiplication in the possibilities out of which a particular genetic code is selected when it is actualised by the union of a particular sperm with a particular egg. And it is out of this astronomical number of different potential individuals, exhibiting the kinds of difference that can occur between children of the same parents, that a single individual comes into being.

(Hick 1985b, 36–7)

The antecedent improbability of an individual being conceived who is precisely *me* is thus already quite staggering. But a comparable calculation applies to each of my parents, and then to each of their parents and grandparents and great grandparents, and so on back through all the generations of human life, with the odds against my own present existence multiplying at each stage. The resulting improbability of my now existing, on the basis of this one factor of genetic inheritance alone, is accordingly truly astronomical. But it still has to be multiplied by the improbability of all the innumerable other conditions required at each successive moment for distinctively human history to have occurred, and before that for the wider evolution of life on this earth, and before that for the formation of galaxies and our solar system, and before that for the whole cosmic evolution of the universe back to the big bang. As a result the antecedent improbability that the unique individual who is *me* should now exist is inconceivably great. To say that I am lucky to be alive is a monumental understatement! And the same kind of calculation applies to everyone and everything else in the universe. When we look past *any* event into its antecedent conditions, their improbability multiplying backwards exponentially towards infinity, the event appears as endlessly improbable. However, it is important to realise that this improbability is purely notional. The virtual infinity of unrealised world-states and unconceived people which seems to surround us as a cloud of rejected possibilities does not in fact exist. The only reality is the actual course of the universe, with ourselves as part of it. And there is no objective sense in which this is either more or less probable than any other possible universe.

The consciousness of our chancy and insecure place in the scheme of things can nevertheless induce a swirling intellectual vertigo. It can also elicit a sense of gratitude and responsibility in face of the extraordinary fact of our existence. From a religious point of view this response is appropriate. For according to the theistic faiths we have been created by God:

> I will praise thee; for I am fearfully and wonderfully made:
> Marvellous are thy works;
> And that my soul knoweth right well.
> My substance was not hid from thee,
> When I was made in secret,
> And curiously wrought in the lowest parts of the earth.
> Thine eyes did see my substance, yet being unperfect;
> And in thy book all my members were written,
> Which in continuance were fashioned,
> When as yet there was none of them.
>
> (Psalm 139:14–16)

And according to the Indian religions too it is a rare privilege to have been born into this world rather than into one of the innumerable other realms of existence, because it is only as an embodied being on earth that one can make progress towards liberation or enlightenment (see Shankara [7th–8th century] 1978, 32–3). The measure of this good fortune was expressed by the Buddha when he said that the number who are born as humans in this world, rather than in some other form or in some other sphere, is like a speck of dust in comparison with the whole earth (*Saṃyutta Nikāya*, V:474–5 – Woodward 1956, V:396–99). But that our existence has this religious significance cannot be proved, or even shown to be probable, from the facts of cosmology and evolution. One can be conscious of the prodigious notional improbability of one's existence, and can feel privileged to be alive, without interpreting this good fortune religiously.

Nevertheless the mystery of the universe's existence and character can only evoke in any reflective mind a sense of wonder, and even awe, which if not taken up into a religious faith will most naturally find expression in mystical poetry. Thus the Soviet scientist I. D. Novikov of the Space Research Institute in Moscow sets at the beginning of his standard text, *Evolution of the Universe*, this poem by B. Komberg (translated by M. M. Basko):

> The Universe once was also young
> And Her heart was in the flame of creation
> Like a woman having lost control of herself
> She gave in to the violent burst of expansion
>
> In a fiery dance of Space and Time
> With blind obedience to the laws of the Unknown
> She gave birth in labour and pain
> To the host of worlds, and the Sun with the
>   Earth – our home
>
> When the heat from a breath of the Greatest of
>   Mysteries
> Will whiff in your face with the flows of quanta,
> You will probably catch – through the darkness
>   of skies –
> The miraculous smile of the vast and impassionate
>   stranger – the Cosmos
>
> And once you have noticed the gleam of that
>   smile
> And started, and stood for a moment all struck
>   with amazement,
> You will never forget and will spend all your life
> In an anxious search for yet another glimpse of
>   that vision.
>
> (Novikov 1984, vii)

5 THE ANTHROPIC PRINCIPLE

Einstein is said to have remarked that the most incomprehensible thing about the universe is that it is comprehensible. And it has seemed to some that the fact that the universe is at least to some extent knowable by and intelligible to us supports the theistic hypothesis. F. R. Tennant distinguished two aspects of the contribution which this 'mutual adaptation of thought and things' makes to teleological reasoning (1930, 81). One

> consists in the fact that the world is more or less intelligible, in that it happens to be more or less a cosmos, when conceivably it might have been a self-subsistent and determinate 'chaos' in which similar events never occurred, none recurred, universals had no place, relations no fixity, things no nexus of determination and 'real' categories no foothold.   (1930, 82)

Certainly the fact that the universe is a cosmos rather than a chaos is fully compatible with theism; and indeed we might go further and argue that a chaotic universe would not be compatible with the existence of a rational and moral creator. Thus far, then, the orderly and hence (given the presence of minds) knowable character of the universe tells for rather than against theism. But it does not tell at all strongly. For the facts are also fully compatible with atheism. From a naturalistic point of view the universe is simply, as a sheer given fact, basically orderly. The theist might retort that if the universe had instead been a chaos this would have rendered naturalism more probable than theism; and therefore that this is not so stands in favour of theism. But it is also the case that theism and atheism alike, as humanly entertained hypotheses, presuppose an orderly universe that has produced life and intelligence. For otherwise no human minds would exist to consider the question. And when they do consider it they are able to come to each of the two contrary conclusions.

However the existence of human consciousness has been seen by some as a vital clue to the nature of the universe, and the term 'the anthropic principle' has been coined in recent decades to indicate this.[4] In its general or 'weaker' form this is the principle that 'what we can expect to observe must be restricted by the conditions necessary for our presence as observers' (Carter 1974, 291), so that 'our location in the universe is *necessarily* privileged to the extent of being compatible with our existence as observers' (293). This is unexceptionable. However some have gone on to propose the 'strong' anthropic principle that 'the universe possesses many of its extraordinary properties because they are necessary for the existence of life and observers' (Barrow and Silk

1984, 233). Thus 'the Universe (and hence the fundamental parameters on which it depends) must be such as to admit the creation of observers within it at some stage. To paraphrase Descartes, "cogito ergo mundus talis est"' (Carter 1974, 294). In other words, because we are here the universe *had* to be such as to produce us. This proposition, I suggest, is either an empty truth or a substantial falsehood. The empty truth derives from the tautology that what is, is. Since the universe is such as to have produced us, then it is such as to have produced us. The substantial falsehood is the inference that the universe *had* to be such as to produce us, so that there could not have been a different universe which did not include ourselves. But from the fact that a cosmos without observers would not have been observed we cannot legitimately infer that there could not have been a different universe, devoid of observers.

Tennant's other and to him more important consideration is that 'Nature evokes thought of a richer kind than is involved in scientific knowledge, and responds to thinking such as is neither logically necessary nor biologically needful, thus suggesting a Beyond' (1930, 83). It does indeed seem that human thought has developed far beyond biological necessity. An intelligent animal will, in order to survive and flourish, seek to understand the workings of its environment and may therefore be expected to develop some degree of science and technology. But why, simply as intelligent organism, should it also produce philosophy, art, imaginative literature, religious speculation and belief? Do not these suggest that the human being is not simply an intelligent animal but one through which some further purpose is being fulfilled?

Certainly this 'thought of a richer kind than is involved in scientific knowledge' is fully compatible with theism, whilst its absence would have been less readily so. But it is also possible to suggest a naturalistic interpretation of this cultural surplus. It could be that the degree of brain complexity, and consequent level of mental life, needed for the understanding and manipulation of our environment will, once in operation, inevitably range more widely, weaving philosophical and religious speculations. Perhaps *homo sapiens* cannot be single-mindedly pragmatic all the time, and philosophy, religion and poetry are products of an excess intellectual energy that is not harnessed to the struggle to survive. Or perhaps, as Wittgenstein suggested, language itself, originally developed for dealing with the world, generates when 'idling' the philosophical concepts and problems which have kept thinkers busy for two and a half thousand years. Or, alternatively, perhaps imaginative literature and consolatory religion are biologically useful fantasies which give relief from the anxieties to which our intelligence makes us vulnerable. Or yet again, as a more sombre possibility, perhaps this cultural surplus is not after all biologically useful but on the contrary biologically dangerous and will in the long run lead to the extinction of the human species through its creation of divisive ideologies and nuclear weapons in virtue of which it destroys itself.

There can thus be a naturalistic as well as a theistic understanding of our cognitive powers and mental activities, so that the pervasive religious ambiguity remains unimpaired. And much the same considerations can be extended to another area treated by Tennant, namely nature's aesthetic values. Nature is everywhere producing beauty – in the glory of sunrise and sunset, the colours and scents of flowers and trees and bushes, the grandeur of mountain ranges, the moving kaleidoscope of the clouds, the stillness of the desert, reflections on a lake, the strength and economy of movement of animals and the charms of their young. 'Nature's beauty', says Tennant, 'is of a piece with the world's intelligibility and with its being a theatre for moral life; and thus far the case for theism is strengthened by aesthetic considerations' (Tennant 1930, 93).

The fact that much of nature is aesthetically interesting and pleasing to the human eye and mind is certainly fully compatible with theism. But once again it is possible to find an alternative naturalistic interpretation. For it may well be that 'beauty is in the eye of the beholder', being not a quality of physical objects as such but of the perceiver's reaction to them. It may be that certain combinations of colour, shape, proportion, perspective and movement tend to stimulate us in the ways for which we have developed our aesthetic language. This stimulation may be partly physiological (perhaps continuous with the effects of colours in the mating behaviour of some animals and birds) and partly a matter of higher-level mental associations setting up wide-ranging emotional reverberations. Or there may be yet other kinds of natural explanation. The postulation of a divine source of natural beauty is thus optional; and once again the religious ambiguity of the world remains intact.

Notes

1. I have traced in more detail what I take to be the fallacy in Hartshorne's and Malcolm's versions of the argument elsewhere (Hick and McGill 1976, ch. 19).
2. Montefiore 1985, 169–71. (Quoted with permission.) For a more detailed and technical account see Barrow and Tipler 1986.
3. The theory is described by DeWitt 1970, 30–5. For technical discussions see Bryce S. DeWitt and Neill Graham 1973.
4. For a full bibliography of the anthropic principle see Barrow and Tipler 1986, 25.

6

Morality, Religious Experience and Overall Probability

To say [God] hath spoken to [someone] in a dream, is no more than to say he dreamed that God spake to him!

(Thomas Hobbes)[1]

1 MORAL ARGUMENTS

The ethical circumstances which have been seen as pointing to the existence of God include both the general fact that we are conscious of moral ideals as exercising a claim upon us, and the particular sense of a demand to perform or refrain from performing this or that act or type of act as morally obligatory or forbidden. We can treat these two ethical realities – general ideals and specific obligations – together and ask whether they require us to postulate a deity as their source or ground. It is the felt absoluteness of the claim upon us that has suggested this inference. When I am conscious that I ought to do something, particularly if it is something that I do not *want* to do, I feel what can only be described as a pressure upon me as a moral being, a pressure which is real and of which I cannot but take account. It imposes a magisterial demand, confronting me as, in Kant's terminology, a categorical imperative, an absolute claim that can be defied but cannot be wished away. The question then naturally arises, in what is this moral obligation grounded?

Some theists have argued that morality must derive its authority from a source outside the human beings who are subject to it; that this source must itself be ethical in character; and that such a transcendent ethical ground of human moral values and obligations is part of what we mean by God. However in response to this argument we have to raise a further question. Supposing that

96

God is related to moral obligation as its ultimate ground, how more precisely are we to understand that relationship? There would seem to be two possibilities: first, that it is a matter of external divine commands, or second, that it is a matter of God having created us as moral beings capable of feeling for ourselves the intrinsic authority of moral values and of responding to them.

The first option is well rooted in traditional theistic language, which has often depicted morality as obedience – and sin, correlatively, as disobedience – to God. But there is a difficulty in this position which was first pointed out in principle by Plato in the *Euthyphro*. Are actions right because God commands them, or does God command them because they are right? If the former, it would seem that they are not intrinsically right but only contingently so as a result of God choosing to command in this rather than in another way. However the insistent witness of our moral consciousness is that loving kindness, for example, is intrinsically good and cruelty intrinsically evil; with the implication that their rightness and wrongness do not depend upon the decision even of a supreme being. But if on the other hand God enjoins loving kindness because it is good, and prohibits cruelty because it is evil, it seems that the basic moral values are not created by divine commands; and even that the divine goodness itself can be measured by moral standards that hold in their own right, applying to God as well as to ourselves. But clearly if that is the case we can no longer say that morality is grounded in God.

The more attractive possibility, in my view, is to see morality as a function of our human nature.[2] We are gregarious creatures and it is our inherently social nature that has given rise both to law and to morality. In order for human beings to live in community they have had to develop rules regulating their interactions. Murder and theft, for example, must be forbidden, and strongly discouraged by the punishments attached to them. Such rules are necessary to the survival and flourishing of any society and enjoy an authority arising from pragmatic necessity. This network of law merges upwards into morality. For we are not only gregarious animals but persons, and personality occurs within the interplay of a plurality of persons. It is this inter-personal nature of personality that gives rise to the sense of mutual moral – as distinguished from purely legal – obligation. Because we are, without our own choice, 'members one of another' we are conscious of actions that harm our neighbours as wrong and forbidden, and actions that protect them from harm or promote their well-being as good and sometimes as a matter of positive obligation. Ethics, I suggest, is grounded in this *de facto* character of human nature as essentially inter-personal, in virtue of which we have a deep need for one another and feel (in many different degrees) a natural tendency to mutual sympathy. Morality is accordingly a dimension of this realm of personal interactions.[3]

If morality is thus based in the structure of our human nature it may well be that Kant succeeded, at least to a considerable extent, in uncovering its inner logic. The essence of morality, according to him, consists in commitment to act for the general welfare as discerned by impartial reason. One should do that which pure reason – which judges on objective and universal principles – can see ought to be done. Kant expressed this insight in his doctrine of the categorical imperative, requiring the universalisability of our policies for action. For practical reason functions in the same way in everyone, and to act rightly is to act rationally, on unrestrictedly valid principles, rather than on the basis of one's own personal desires and preferences.

From this point of view ethics derives from God, not in the sense that it is divinely commanded but in the sense that the personal realm, of which it is a function, is God's creation.[4] Ethics is autonomous and would hold if there were no God; but in fact, according to theistic faith, the whole realm of human existence, including our inter-personal nature, is an aspect of the divine creation. In this way faith in the reality of God is combined with an acceptance of the autonomy of the moral life. This seems to me to be the correct solution to the problem of the religious status of ethics. But of course the cost of this solution is that we can no longer argue from morality to God. For the view of ethics as grounded in the structure of human nature is capable of being incorporated into either a religious or a naturalistic world-view. From a religious standpoint morality has a function commensurate with the momentous character that we experience it to have; for it is the path along which we may move through time to eternal life, or to the Kingdom of Heaven, or to Nirvana, or to unity with the Absolute. From a naturalistic standpoint, on the other hand, morality is simply a remarkable human feature, continuous with though going far beyond analogous features of some of the other forms of animal life. On either view it is the aspect of our nature which generates the invisible dimension of moral value. This dimension is hospitable to a religious interpretation; but it is nevertheless not incompatible with a non-religious interpretation.

2 RELIGIOUS EXPERIENCE

The last of the 'theistic evidences' that we have to consider is distinctively religious experience. At the moment we are concerned with this as something from which it may or may not be possible to infer the existence of God – or, more broadly, the superior plausibility of a religious over a naturalistic interpretation of the universe. We are not at this point concerned with religious experience in the light of the very different part that it plays in the kind of natural theology to be developed in Chapter 13. It will be useful to distinguish between on the one hand the religious experiencing, shared by a number of people, of public events, and on the other hand private experiences of inner religious encounter and illumination.

The public events which have seemed to have religious significance are of a wide variety of kinds. Usually the initial experience was undergone by a comparatively small number of people and is accessible today only through a heightened and hallowed story that has been treasured within a religious community and that has indeed often, as the tradition has solidified, become an essential element within it. Consider as examples two such stories from the Judeo-Christian tradition: the exodus of the children of Israel from Egypt and the resurrection of Jesus.

In the case of the exodus the historian cannot at this temporal distance tell precisely what empirical events, capable in principle of having been recorded by camera and microphone, lie behind the religiously interpreted and elaborated story in the Hebrew Bible. The exodus appears in the narrative as a manifestly divinely enabled event. Its meaning was declared at the time by God through Moses and was understood both by the Israelites and by Pharoah and the Egyptians – and this in spite of God having repeatedly 'hardened Pharoah's heart' to justify the infliction of ever greater disasters, culminating in the death in a single night of the first-born child of every Egyptian family.

But what historically-minded person today can regard this story, as told in Exodus 3–15, as an accurate account of actual historical events? (And if we could so regard it, what should we then think of the moral character of the deity?) If all these things had happened as described they would surely have left some mark in the records of Egyptian history. All that we can safely say is that a group of Hebrew serfs successfully emigrated from Egypt and that they or their descendants ended up in Canaan, contributing to Jewish folk memory the story of how their God had delivered them from captivity. There may or may not have been natural disasters in Egypt at that time, and if so they may or may not have facilitated the Israelites' departure. The emigrants may have constituted the whole Hebrew people or only a comparatively small part of it. In either case their particular story became, through a process of natural selection, central to Jewish self-understanding. But when Jews today dwell upon, 'remember', 'experience', 'participate in' the exodus as a great act of divine deliverance they are not experiencing the actual historical events of some thirty centuries ago. They are participating in something contemporary – a living religious tradition, one strand of which is the foundational myth of a deliverance that revealed God's providential care for their race. That the myth is a true myth (see Chapter 19.2–3), evoking an appropriate response of trust in God, does not entail that the traditional story is literally true – though on the other hand it could hardly have come about without some historical basis.

It follows from this distinction between a now inaccessible fragment of history and the religious myth that has been built around it that someone who does not share the response embodied in the myth, acknowledging instead only the minimal core of historical fact, is not obliged to see the hand of God at work there. To appropriate the story religiously may – from a sceptical point of view – be due to the psychological conditioning of a Jewish upbringing whereby the exodus has become part of the story that gives meaning to one's life. On this interpretation the event itself recedes into the twilight between history and pre-history. It cannot be offered as an unquestionable public divine manifestation. For it may only have acquired that character retrospectively through a process in which a natural event later took its place in Hebrew folklore as God's dramatic deliverance of the chosen people.

As a miraculous divine act which is looked back to as the origin of a new historical movement the resurrection of Jesus has a place within Christianity comparable with that of the exodus in Judaism. In Christian tradition the resurrection was a public event in the sense that some of the encounters with the risen lord were group experiences – not only of the apostles but of more than five hundred of Jesus' followers on one occasion, according to St Paul's list (I Cor. 15:16). That Jesus was not seen by anyone outside the small Christian fellowship must have some significance, but it does not transfer the resurrection, as described in the scriptures, into the realm of purely private religious experiences. It figures in the Christian tradition as an event within publicly observable history and with the indelibly miraculous character of God's raising of his son from the dead. And yet modern histories of the Roman Empire, written in accordance with the accepted canons of historical research, include no such manifest miracle. Instead historians record that the early Christian community believed, or that within it reports circulated, that Jesus had risen from his grave. The detailed evidence in the Christian writings themselves – and there are no other first-century references – is too conflicting, and shows too many signs of a miraculous heightening in successive strata of the tradition, for the historian to be able to affirm with the scriptures that Jesus, having died on the cross, was raised again to bodily life on the third day, lived on earth during the next forty days and then ascended into the sky in the presence of his disciples, finally disappearing from their view upwards into a cloud.[5] For critical study of the documents has opened up other possibilities.

If we start with the earliest (though still not first-hand) account that we have of an encounter with the risen lord, namely that of St Paul on the road to Damascus, we notice that this did not involve the physical body of Jesus but rather a blindingly bright light and a voice (Acts 9:1–9; 22:6–11). Perhaps the experience of Peter, or of Peter and some of the other disciples, was of essentially the same kind as Paul's, and the stories of the empty tomb, with its shining angels and miraculous earthquake, and of Jesus eating and drinking with his disciples developed later as the original story was adapted and developed for the benefit of Jewish audiences to whom the idea of a future bodily resurrection was familiar and accepted. Or again it may be that Peter and the others were conscious of the unseen presence of their lord or saw visions of the glorified Jesus in shining light – as in the transfiguration story, which some have interpreted as a displaced fragment of the resurrection tradition. Or yet again it has been proposed that the resurrection consisted in the rising of new faith in the hearts of the disciples after the shock of the crucifixion (Bultmann [1941] 1984, 39–40). The psychological phenomenon of the intensification of conviction in response to cognitive dissonance has also been suggested to account for the state of mind of the disciples shortly after Jesus' crucifixion, including their projection of fleeting visions of him (Goulder 1977, 59). But clearly these possibilities are all capable of naturalistic interpretation; for the seeing of visions, the hearing of voices and the feeling of an unseen presence could all be hallucinatory in character.

Once again, then, we do not have an instance, acceptable by normal historical canons, of a publicly observed divine action. The original resurrection event is inaccessible to us, and the Christian response to it through the centuries has been to a gripping pictorial image and a powerful theological idea, a response that terminates for some in the private experience, whether enjoyed in solitude or amidst a worshipping congregation, of 'the risen Christ' or of 'the unseen presence of Jesus'.

It is obviously impossible to look here at more than a minute sample of the reports in the world's religious literature of public divine acts. I have referred briefly to two prominent such reports and have concluded that they do not qualify as examples of the public observation of a manifest miracle. In each case the original event is now irretrievable and we have only the continuing tradition-borne story to which it has given rise. But a naturalistic construal remains possible both of the conjectured event itself and of the use made of it by the religious imagination. And I think it is a safe working assumption that the examination of any other example would lead to a similar conclusion. In other words, reports of this first type of religious experience, namely 'the religious experiencing of public events, observed by a number of people', remain evidentially ambiguous: the naturalistic option cannot be excluded.

We have seen however that this first kind of religious experience tends to collapse into the second kind. The exodus has become a contemporary reality in the thoughts and emotions of Jews culminating in the experience of the annual Passover celebrations. As an imaginative picture informing cultic practice it mediates God to Jewish worshippers with an efficacy that is only partly dependent on the original grain of history round which this pearl of devotion has grown. Again, the resurrection of Jesus has become a contemporary reality in Christian imagination and theological thought. To 'live in the risen Christ' is to see possibilities of renewal and new beginning in every situation and to connect the hopeful and positive aspects of life with the thought of the resurrection triumph whereby Jesus has 'abolished death and brought life and immortality to light' (II Timothy, 1:10).[6]

But this contemporary resurrection experience does not depend upon the literal historicity of any particular element of the biblical narratives. Such contemporary modes of experience are continuous in kind with a wide range of other religious experiences that are private to the individuals who undergo them. These include not only meditation but also visions, photisms, voices, dreams, the sense of a transcendently good or of an overpoweringly evil personal presence. The prophet 'hears the voice of the Lord' or sees 'the Lord sitting upon a throne, high and lifted up' (Isaiah 6:1); mystics and others have visions of Krishna, or Kali, or Christ, or the Virgin Mary; people receive divine messages in dreams; or they experience a blinding light or a surrounding radiance and are conscious of an invisible presence; or before being resuscitated from a state of apparent death they encounter a 'being of light' from whom emanates a profound love and acceptance. In Chapter 13 I shall return to these and other forms of religious experience from a quite different point of view. But at the moment we are looking at them from the outside, as reported private experiences, and are asking to what extent they constitute objective evidence for the existence of God or for the truth of a religious interpretation of the universe. Clearly they are fully consistent with the religious option; and indeed, in some significant sense, more readily so than with its opposite. For *prima facie* the most natural way of understanding them is as manifestations of the divine. But on the other hand if we ask, Can they count as unambiguous evidence for the reality of God? the answer is No. The reason was succinctly put by Thomas Hobbes when he remarked that when a man tells him that God has spoken to him in a dream this 'is no more than to say he dreamed that God spake to him' ([1651]: see note 1). For there could be other causes of such experiences than the activity of a transcendent divine power. We know that there can be hallucinatory visions, voices and senses of presence, experienced both in insanity and in deep emotional states of grief, longing and so on; that new insights developed in the unconscious can suddenly present themselves to consciousness in the form of voices, visions and dreams; that meditation can release tensions and promote mental integration, bringing with it a heightened sense of contact with reality. Clearly, then, a naturalism that is large enough to recognise these deeper psychic aspects of our nature will not be defeated by the fact that religious experiences occur.[7]

To this general possibility of a naturalistic explanation of such experiences we have to add, as a difficulty attaching to their religious construal, the fact that they differ markedly from one religious tradition to another. On the basis of their own form of religious experience the Hebrew prophets thought of God as standing in a special covenant relationship with the people of Israel; whilst Muhammad, on the basis of his own experience, thought of God as the Qur'anic Revealer whose definitive revelation was addressed to the people of seventh-century Arabia; and Christian mystics have, on the basis of their distinctive forms of religious experience, thought of God as mysteriously Three in One and One in Three; whilst at the same time Hindu mystics, on the basis of their own different modes of experience, have thought of the divine Reality as the ultimately trans-personal Brahman, and Buddhists as the infinite Dharmakaya, or the ineffable *śūnyatā* which is the reality and meaning of the ordinary world experienced as 'wondrous being'. If religious experience constitutes an authentic window onto the Real, why does that reality look so different when seen through different windows?

The hypothesis to be developed in this book will offer an answer to that question. But at this stage we can only acknowledge that the reports of religious experience which abound within all the great traditions are capable in principle of naturalistic as well as religious interpretations, so that the universe, even in this aspect, remains stubbornly ambiguous.

3 SWINBURNE'S PROBABILITY ARGUMENT

The five features of the universe that were singled out by Tennant are included in Richard Swinburne's recent probability argument for the existence of God. In *The Existence of God* (1979) Swinburne seeks to show by the application of Bayes's Theorem that the probability of traditional theism in relation to the evidences of the world is greater than one half. Where P = probability, h = the theistic hypothesis offered as an explanation of the world, e = the items of evidence to be mentioned presently and k = background knowledge, which at the crucial point of the argument is described by Swinburne as tautological (perhaps more precisely irrelevant) knowledge, Bayes's Theorem holds that

$$P(h/e.k) = \frac{P(e/h.k) \times P(h/k)}{P(e/k)}$$

That is to say, the probability of theism is its explanatory or predictive power, multiplied by its prior or intrinsic probability and divided by the prior or intrinsic probability of the evidence occurring by itself.

The evidences which Swinburne considers are, on the positive side, the existence of the universe; its temporal orderliness (the fact that there is an infinite number of particles which have identical powers and liabilities); the existence of humans and animals; the fact of consciousness and the correlation between consciousness and brain function; the circumstance that humans have opportunities to co-operate in acquiring knowledge and in changing their environment; apparently providential aspects of history and such evidence as there is for the occurrence of miracles; religious experience; and the fact of morality (which last Swinburne regards as lacking any evidential significance). On the negative side he refers to the existence of evil in the forms of human wickedness and human and animal pain and suffering – which however he also regards as having no evidential weight. He then asks, 'Where all the relevant factual evidence is included in e, and k is mere tautological evidence, what is the value of P($h/e.k$)? We may not be able to give it an exact numerical value, but the important issue is whether P($h/e.k$) > P($-h/e.k$) and so > $^1/_2$. Do we have a good P-inductive argument to the existence of God?' (278).

He answers in the affirmative. Leaving religious experience aside for the moment, Swinburne argues that the probability of each of these phenomena occurring if there is a God is greater than if there is no God: P($e/h.k$) > P(e/k). From this it follows that, for each e, P($h/e.k$) > P(h/k). In other words each of these phenomena renders theism more probable than it would be without it and thus makes possible a valid C-inductive (confirmatory) argument for divine existence. The question is whether these valid C-inductive arguments can be built together into a valid P-inductive argument showing that the final probability is greater than $^1/_2$.

The three factors to be considered are the prior (or intrinsic) probability of the theistic hypothesis; its explanatory or predictive power; and the prior probability of the evidence on the supposition that there is no God. As regards the prior probability of the theistic hypothesis, $P(h/k)$, Swinburne argues that this is low because 'It remains . . . a source of extreme puzzlement that there should exist anything at all' (283). Further, the predictive power of theism, $P(e/h.k)$, although low, is 'not too low' (285). That is to say, whilst it could not have been predicted that God would make a world at all, yet if we suppose that he has the power to make a world and has done so we can see that he might have reason to make it broadly like the world that exists – an orderly universe in which human beings can learn and mature morally and in which the evils of life, although great, are not (he considers) excessive (ch. 9–12). In short, 'The world is such that, given God's character, he might well bring it about' (285).

Given that something does exist, the theistic explanation of the existence of this rather than something else is (according to Swinburne) much higher than the alternative hypothesis that the universe, in all its complexity, is simply an inexplicable brute fact. This is because of the much greater simplicity of the God-hypothesis. For (a) theism reduces all explanation ultimately to one kind, namely explanation in terms of personal intention, and (b) the intention is that of a reality which, being eternal, and unlimited in knowledge, power and goodness, is maximally simple in nature since it is not subject to any limitations requiring further explanation (ch. 5).

What, finally, is the intrinsic probability of the evidence by itself, the facts of the universe considered without God, $P(e.-h/k)$? Swinburne argues that this is extremely low, and in particular that it is much lower than the intrinsic probability of theism. That the universe should just exist for no reason, as an immensely complex interdependent system obeying the basic laws that it does rather than others, has (he claims) minimal prior probability. 'For all of these reasons,' says Swinburne, 'I conclude that $P(e.-h/k)$, the intrinsic probability of there being a universe such as ours and no

God is very much lower than P(*h*/*k*), the intrinsic probability of there being a God. It remains perhaps passing strange that there exists anything at all. But if there is to exist anything, it is far more likely to be something with the simplicity of God than something like the universe with all its characteristics crying out for explanation without there being God to explain it' (288–9).

Using Bayes's formula, in an elaborated form,

$$P(h/e.k) = \frac{P(e/h.k) \times P(h/k)}{[P(e/h.k) \times P(h/k)] + P(e.-h/k)}$$

Endeavouring to show that this equation (still omitting religious experience from *e*) may well equal $^1/_2$, Swinburne says, 'We have concluded that P(*h*/*k*) may be low, but P(*e*.−*h*/*k*) is very, very much lower, and that P(*e*/*h*.*k*) is low, but not too low. If P(*e*/*h*.*k*) is not too low, P(*e*/*h*.*k*) × P(*h*/*k*) will equal P(*e*.−*h*/*k*) and the probability of theism on the evidence so far considered (P(*h*/*e*.*k*)) will be $^1/_2$. If it is lower, then P(*h*/*e*.*k*) will be less than $^1/_2$' (289). Now if the probability of theism, in the light of all the evidence other than religious experience, is $^1/_2$, then clearly when we add this further positive factor theism's overall probability will rise above $^1/_2$. Accordingly, 'On our total evidence theism is more probable than not. An argument from all the evidence considered in this book to the existence of God is a good P-inductive argument' (291).

It should be stressed that this is only a bare summary of a complex argument which is developed with impressive rigour and thoroughness in Swinburne's book. For a fully adequate view of it one must study Swinburne's chapters at first hand. They not only constitute a continuous and tightly constructed chain of reasoning but one which also includes a number of interesting subsidiary contentions which are worth attention independently of their place in the main argument of the book. A full critique would therefore have to take up a variety of topics. I shall however restrict this discussion to what I regard as the central weakness of Swinburne's argument.

I shall approach this via his treatment of the problem of evil. His conclusion concerning this is that 'the existence of the evil which we find does not count against the existence of God. There is no good C-inductive argument from the existence of evil to the non-existence of God' (220). This surprising conclusion is carried forward in that unqualified form into Swinburne's final calculation of the overall probability of theism. But it has been arrived at as no more than a personal assessment of the outcome of conflicting considerations. For Swinburne has earlier discussed the objection that the evil in the world is too great in extent and intensity to be compatible with the existence of God, and has acknowledged that 'The objection seems to count against the claim that there is a God' (219): this is indeed, he grants, 'the crux of the problem of evil' (219). However after introducing various counter-considerations he eventually feels able to say that 'my own tentative conclusion, in the light of the considerations adduced, is that God does not have overriding reason for not making a world with this evil' (220). But should not this tentativeness, occurring at so vital a point, be reflected in the final calculation? We have a probability that the fact of evil does not reduce the probability of theism, together with the rider that if it *does* reduce that probability it will do so by a substantial amount. The difficulty is of course that neither of these values – the probability that evil does not reduce the probability of theism and the extent to which it reduces if it does in fact reduce it – can be given any precise value.

This impossibility of precise quantification leads directly to my main criticism, which is that a theorem which requires numerical proportions for its operation is here being used without any exact values. In order that

$$P(h/e.k) = \frac{P(e/h.k) \times P(h/k)}{[P(e/h.k) \times P(h/k)] + (P(e.-h/k)} = \frac{1}{2}$$

the values must have the following numerical relationships: if $P(e/h.k) = 1/3$, then $P(h/k) = 1/3$, and $P(e.-h.k) = 1/9$. (The fractions could of course be different provided the essential relationship remains the same.) Then

$$P(h/e.k) = \frac{1/3 \times 1/3}{(1/3 \times 1/3) + 1/9} = \frac{1/9}{2/9} = \frac{1}{2}$$

In other words the predictive power of theism must have a value which, when multiplied by the prior probability of theism, is equal to that of the probability of the world's existence without God. But Swinburne has, rightly, not even attempted to establish such precise relative values. He is fully aware of the impossibility of doing any such thing. He describes the key probabilities in such terms as 'low', 'very low', 'very low indeed', 'not too low', 'not too close to 0' and 'none too high' (289).[8] He acknowledges that 'All this so far is very imprecise, but, as we have seen we just do not have the criteria for very precise estimation of probabilities in science or history or most other fields' (289).

At this point Swinburne introduces the term 'qualitative'. The quotation continues, 'However I now suggest that it is reasonable to come to the following qualitative judgement about the force of the evidence . . .' (289), namely that 'although the predictive power ($P(e/h.k)$) of theism is quite low, and so too is its prior probability $P(h/k)$, nevertheless, its over-all probability $P(h/e.k)$ is well away from 1 or 0, because the prior probability of the evidence $P(e/k)$ is very low indeed (due to $P(e.-h/k)$ being very low)' (289). Accordingly 'the probability of theism is none too close to 1 or 0 on the evidence so far considered' – that is, without taking account of religious experience. However when we inject this factor the balance is then tipped in favour of theism and the conclusion can be reached that 'the evidence of religious experience is . . . sufficient to make theism over-all probable' (291).

We have, then, both a quantitative argument using Bayes's Theorem, hinging on the claim that the probability of theism, without taking account of religious experience, is at least $^1/_2$; and a qualitative argument, which emerges in the last pages of the book, hinging on the probability of theism (again without taking religious experience into account) being not very close to either 0 or 1 and thus somewhere towards the middle. In each case religious experience is then added in as the decisive factor. However I suggest that the quantitative argument, using Bayes's Theorem, has no force because we lack the quantitative data needed to put the formula to work.[9] And I suggest that the qualitative argument fails because its qualitative judgments are merely vague quantitative judgments and are much too vague for us to be able to determine whether the probability of theism has or has not risen above $^1/_2$. I conclude, then, that the argument, fascinating though it is, does not succeed. The universe does not permit probability logic to dispel its religious ambiguity.

Notes

1. Hobbes [1651] pt III, ch. 32 – 1966, 360.
2. For a different view see 'A modified divine command theory of ethical wrongness' in Adams 1987.
3. Cf. John Macmurray 1957–61.
4. This basic position could of course also be stated in non-theistic religious terms.
5. On the many contradictions between the biblical stories see, e.g., Marxsen 1970.
6. Cf. Williams 1972.
7. Cf. Goulder and Hick 1983.
8. All these phrases occur in Swinburne's concluding discussion on p. 289.
9. This is also a conclusion arrived at by a different route by R. Provost 1985 and M. Martin 1986.

7

The Naturalistic Option

I had no need of that hypothesis.   (Laplace)

The only excuse for God is that he does not exist.   (Stendhal)

1 THE NEEDLESSNESS OF THE THEISTIC HYPOTHESIS

There are two kinds of anti-theistic or, more broadly, naturalistic argument. The negative kind seeks to show that a religious interpretation of the universe is otiose because all the phenomena known to us, including religion itself, can be adequately described and explained without it. The positive kind goes beyond this, seeking to show that there is an aspect of the universe that is actually incompatible with a theistic, or a religious, world-view.

The negative arguments, then, consist in the fact that it is possible to understand all the known phenomena in naturalistic terms. We have already seen that this is true of the evolution of the universe as a whole and of our ethical, cognitive, aesthetic and religious modes of experience. We are not obliged to postulate a transcendent divine Reality to account for any of these aspects of our nature or our environment. It is true that no naturalistic theory can account for the *existence* of the universe, or for its having the basic character that it has; this simply has to be accepted as the ultimate inexplicable fact. But religion also has its own ultimate inexplicable fact in the form of God or a non-personal Absolute. And the sceptical mind prefers to rest in the mystery of the visible world without going beyond it to a further invisible mystery.

However a complete naturalistic world-view must include an interpretation not only of particular moments of religious experience but of the phenomenon of religion in its totality. The basic such interpretation, of which there are many variations, is that the gods and absolutes are creations of the human mind, projected to reflect back a comforting warmth amidst the harsh

111

pressures and perils of life. Such theories have mainly been developed in relation to Judeo-Christian monotheism. According to Ludwig Feuerbach, God is the projected personification of our highest human ideals.[1] Freud propounded two theories, one concerned with the origin of religion in the individual and the other with its origin in history. The first appears in *The Future of an Illusion*, where he depicted religious beliefs as 'illusions, fulfillments of the oldest, strongest and most urgent wishes of mankind' ([1927] 1961, XXI:30). He saw religion as a defence against the threatening aspects of nature – disease and earthquake, storm and flood, and death itself: 'With these forces nature rises up against us, majestic, cruel and inexorable' (1961, XXI:16). But such potencies are to some extent tamed by being personalised.

> Impersonal forces and destinies cannot be approached; they remain eternally remote. But if the elements have passions that rage as they do in our own souls, if death itself is not something spontaneous but the violent act of an evil Will, if everywhere in nature there are Beings around us of a kind that we know in our society, then we can breathe freely, can feel at home in the uncanny and can deal by psychical means with our senseless anxiety. We are still defenceless, perhaps, but we are no longer helplessly paralyzed; we can at least react. Perhaps, indeed, we are not even defenceless. We can apply the same methods against these violent supermen outside that we employ in our own society; we can try to adjure them, to appease them, to bribe them, and by so influencing them, we may rob them of a part of their power.   (1961, XXI:16–17)

In Christianity, more specifically, God the Father is a projection onto the heavens of the buried infancy memory of our earthly father as the ultimate benign power and authority in our lives: so that 'at bottom God is nothing other than an exalted father' ([1913] 1955, XIII:147).

Freud's historical theory, expounded in *Totem and Taboo* ([1913] 1955, vol. XIII) and *Moses and Monotheism* (1939, vol. XXIII), was based upon a supposed stage of human pre-history in which the social unit was the 'primal horde' consisting of a male with a number of females and their offspring. The dominant male retained exclusive rights over the females. His sons therefore banded together to kill (and also eat) him. This was the primal parricide out of which have developed both morality and religion. For having killed their father the brothers were struck with remorse and, since they could not all succeed to the leadership, with a need for restraint. And so the dead father's prohibition took on the inner authority of a taboo. The combined enmity and guilt of the Oedipus complex has ever since made us revere and feel guilty before our heavenly Father.

This primal parricide theory has not commended itself to anthropologists, and it would indeed be hazardous to regard it as other than a Freudian myth.[2] The Oedipus complex theory of religion as arising out of the male child's relationship to his father can, in so far as it is valid, only illuminate a limited part of the total religious spectrum. It says nothing about non-theistic religion; and even in relation to the theistic traditions it is a theory specifically about the origin of religion in males.[3] It thus cannot be regarded as a theory of religion as such. On the other hand it is today obvious – and it was Freud who made it obvious by supporting this basic insight with a wealth of detailed evidence and argument – that our mental representations of deity are formed out of childhood images of parents and, in the case of the Semitic religions, particularly of the father.[4] Further, the general 'Freudian' view of religion as a psychological crutch obviously has considerable truth. Religious faith does often provide support in times of stress, solace in times of grief, hope in times of danger, and it does constitute a defence against the threat of meaninglessness and despair. In these respects it can be described as a 'crutch' on which we lean or a 'lifeline' to which we cling. But it would be an elementary mistake to infer from this that the claims of religion concerning the nature of the universe are necessarily false. Truths as well as illusions may be such as to uplift and support us. The mere fact that a religious message comes as good news does not entail that it is not true: this must be established on other grounds. Nor of course is it the case that religion always offers consolation. It also offers challenge. God is not only our 'strength in time of trouble' (Psalm 37:39) but is also 'like a refiner's fire' (Malachai 3:2), and 'the word of God is quick, and powerful, and sharper than any two-edged sword, piercing even to the dividing asunder of soul and spirit, and of the joints and marrow, and is a discerner of the thoughts and intents of the heart' (Hebrews 4:12).[5]

One particular aspect of religion, however, in relation to which a wish-fulfilment theory might seem particularly plausible is the belief in an after-life. Is it not obvious that the human mind has created heaven as a fantasy world beyond the grave in which wrongs will be righted and present sufferings compensated? This may indeed seem likely as a matter of *a priori* psychology; but nevertheless it correlates poorly with such knowledge as we have of the earliest forms of after-life belief, as we had occasion to note in another context in Chapter 2.2. For whilst a relatively few pre-literate peoples have believed in a 'happy hunting ground' beyond the grave, the much more general expectation has been of a dismal, depleted, ghostly half-life in the darkness beneath the earth. This was not a future to be looked forward to. On the contrary, precautions sometimes had to be taken against the envy of the dead dwelling in their grey and shadowy *hades* or *sheol*. Thus whilst wish-fulfilment has no doubt played its part in the later developments of after-life belief it does not seem to have been responsible for its beginning. Nor, again, does the early history support a sociological theory of the origin of such beliefs as instruments of social control, reconciling the toiling masses to their present lot by the thought of a reversal of fortunes hereafter. For when there was thought to be a social distinction beyond the grave this merely reproduced the earthly distinctions. Kings and heroes who had enjoyed the privileges of this world would continue to enjoy them hereafter, whilst their servants and slaves would remain servants and slaves. The idea of a *moral* judgment, and of the distribution of souls according to their desert to eternal happiness or torment, arose later, perhaps first in the highly sophisticated civilisation of ancient Egypt.[6]

It seems then that the existing reductionist psychological theories of religion are by no means compelling in their own right. Their plausibility depends upon a prior naturalistic conviction; and to anyone with an opposite conviction they will seem implausible. Thus the universe does not at this point shed its seamless cloak of religious ambiguity.

However the basic fact, long evident to common sense but now scientifically elaborated in the modern psychology of religion, that there are innumerable correlations between the forms taken by human religiousness and the other aspects of our experience and our mental structure is beyond dispute. The idea of God the Father, for example, obviously reflects the human experience of fatherhood. Again, some people may need and find a deity who will comfort them in their afflictions, whilst others may need and find one who makes stringent demands upon them and holds them steady in face of temptation. And so on. But there is no incompatibility in all this with the basic truth of religion as humanity's varied response to the ultimately Real. For if there is a God, the parent–child relationship may well be one of the ways in which we come to form some analogous concept of the divine nature; and likewise it is possible that an unconscious memory of the womb may have helped to form the idea of unity with an encompassing Absolute. Thus, whether religion be wholly or only partly projection, psychological analysis can suggest legitimate and sometimes illuminating speculations about the ways in which it has taken its particular concrete forms. There is no reason, from the point of view of the hypothesis being presented in this book, to reject or resist such speculations.

The classic sociological theory is that of Emile Durkheim in *The Elementary Forms of the Religious Life* ([1912] 1963). Durkheim's central concern was with totemism as it still existed in Australian aboriginal societies at the end of the nineteenth century. But he believed that in the course of his work he had discovered the basic nature of all religion, namely as the way in which society renders itself sacred to its members. He noted that a clan's totem, usually an animal or plant, functioned as the symbol not only of the 'totemic principle or god' but also of the clan itself. 'So if it is at once the symbol of the god and of the society, is that not because the god and the society are only one? . . . The god of the clan, the totemic principle, can therefore be nothing else than the clan itself, personified and represented to the imagination under the visible form of the animal or vegetable which serves as totem'(206). Accordingly,

the believer is not deceived when he believes in the existence of a moral power upon which he depends and from which he receives all that is best in himself: this power exists, it is society. When the Australian is carried outside himself and feels a new life flowing within him whose intensity surprises him, he is not the dupe of an illusion; this exaltation is real and is really the effect of forces outside of and superior to the individual. It is true that he is wrong in thinking that this increase of vitality is the work of a power in the form of some animal or plant. But this error is merely in regard to the letter of the symbol by which this being is represented to the mind and the external appearance which the imagination has given it, and not in regard to the fact of its existence. Behind these figures and metaphors, be they gross or refined, there is a concrete and living reality . . . Before all, [religion] is a system of ideas with which the individuals represent to themselves the society of which they are members, and the obscure but intimate relations which they have with it.   (225)

But Durkheim was not content to see religion functioning in this way in the life of the Australian aborigines. He generalised his thesis, claiming that 'it is applicable to every sort of society indifferently, and consequently to every sort of religion'(214).

In a general way it is unquestionable that a society has all that is necessary to arouse the sensation of the divine in minds, merely by the power that it has over them; for to its members it is what a god is to his worshippers. In fact, a god is, first of all, a being whom men think of as superior to themselves, and upon whom they feel that they depend. Whether it be a conscious personality, such as Zeus or Jahveh, or merely abstract forces such as those in play in totemism, the worshipper, in the one case as in the other, believes himself held to certain manners of acting which are imposed upon him by the nature of the sacred principle with which he feels that he is in communion. Now society also gives us the sensation of a perpetual dependence. Since it has a nature which is peculiar to itself and different from our individual nature, it pursues ends which are likewise special to it; but, as it cannot attain them except through our intermediacy, it imperiously demands our aid. It requires that, forgetful of our own interests, we make ourselves its servitors, and it submits us to every sort of inconvenience, privation and sacrifice, without which social life would be impossible. It is because of this that at every instant we are obliged to submit ourselves to rules of conduct and of thought which we have neither made nor desired, and which are sometimes even contrary to our most fundamental inclinations and instincts.

                                                                    (206–7)

And so holding on the one hand the naturalistic conviction that religion cannot be, as religious persons suppose, their response to a transcendent divine reality, but recognising on the other hand its social power, Durkheim proposed that the divine is a mythic symbolisation of the undoubted reality of the society of which the believer is a member: 'the god is only a figurative expression of the society'(226).

That religion has an essential communal aspect is evident; for we humans are through and through social beings. As the common world-view and way of life of a community religion has functioned as a powerful force for social cohesion. It is also likely that in aboriginal societies, in which men and women were conscious of their existence as parts of a larger human organism rather than as separate self-directing individuals, the claim of the Real should have been felt as the claims of society. Thus Durkheim's researches throw valuable light on an early stage of the history of religions. But as a general naturalistic theory, applying to all ages and places, his suggestion lacks plausibility. It presumes a religiously homogeneous and unified state of society, such as he found in the tribes that he studied. But hardly any modern society exhibits this simple pattern. Indeed his theory presupposes the human condition before the emergence of the autonomous individual exercising a moral and intellectual judgment which may diverge from that of society as a whole. It refers, in other words, to the kind of pre-axial religion that has continued among the Australian aborigines and various other pre-literate societies into the present century. But it does not seem able to account for some of the most striking features of post-axial religion. Can it explain the thought of the universal scope of God's concern, conceived as Maker and Father or as merciful and compassionate Lord of the entire human race? Or the moral independence and creativity of some of the great religious figures who, so far from echoing the voice of their society, uttered a divine judgment upon it? If Durkheim's theory were correct, an Amos denouncing the Hebrew society of his time or a Trevor Huddleston rejecting the hegemony of his own race in South Africa, and deeply alienated from their surrounding society, would *eo ipso* feel alienated from God. But in fact the contrary seems to have been the case; such people have felt that they were God's agents against the prevailing norms of their community.[7] Again, Durkheim's theory has nothing to say about the phenomenon of mysticism, which is often highly individualistic, or about those streams of Hindu and Buddhist religious life which have led to detachment from society.[8]

But to find Durkheim's theory unproven, and indeed as losing plausibility when applied beyond the totemic religion in relation to which it was developed, is not to reject the considerable light that sociology has thrown and will continue to throw upon the history of religions. On the contrary I shall be drawing heavily upon sociological findings when we come to consider why the human awareness of the Real has taken such numerous and diverse forms.

2 THE CHALLENGE OF EVIL TO THEISM

The aspects of the universe that we have considered so far have each proved to be ambiguous in the sense that they permit both a religious and a naturalistic interpretation. The reality and extent of evil, on the other hand, seem to many positively to demand an atheistic conclusion. This is indeed the most serious challenge that there is to theistic faith. When we remember the afflictions that invade millions of human beings every day – bodily sufferings due to physical pain, disease, hunger and thirst, blindness, deafness, dumbness, senility, brain damage and other kinds of disablement; together with the distinctively human agonies of fear and anxiety, both for oneself and for others; and bereavement, loneliness, envy, remorse, jealousy, resentment, hatred, humiliation, contempt, unrequited love; as well as the pain occurring at every moment in the animal kingdom – we do indeed have to ask ourselves whether it is possible to think of this world as the work of an omnipotent creator who is motivated by limitless love.

Having written about this challenge at length (Hick [1977] 1985a) I shall not discuss again the different kinds of theodicy that have been proposed. The only line of response that seems to me at all adequate to the full depth of the challenge sees our human existence on this planet as part of a much longer process through which personal spiritual life is being gradually brought in its own freedom to a perfection that will justify retrospectively the evils that have been part of its slow creation. This kind of theodicy goes back within Christian thought to the second-century Greek-speaking apologists, particularly Irenaeus. He offered the story or picture of God creating humankind in two stages with significantly different characters. To describe these in more modern terms,

God first brings human beings into existence through the long evolutionary process as intelligent animals who are social and therefore ethical and who are also capable of response to the transcendent. They are not initially formed – as in Christianity's alternative Augustinian type of theodicy – as perfect creatures living in an ideal relationship to God in the Garden of Eden, but as imperfect creatures brought into being at an epistemic distance from their maker; and they were so formed as a way of endowing them with a genuine freedom in relation to that maker. At this stage human beings are, in Irenaeus' terminology, made in the 'image' of God. But as thus formed they are still only the raw material for the further phase of the creative process in which they are being drawn through their own freedom towards an individual and corporate perfection, which Irenaeus called (using the terminology of Genesis 1:26) the 'likeness' of God.

We find ourselves in this second stage of creation, which is co-terminous with human history, as morally and spiritually immature and developing creatures. As such we are genetically programmed for self-preservation as animal organisms and are thus basically self-regarding, seeing and valuing our environment from our own point of view as its perceiving centre. This fundamental self-centredness, operating in varying degrees throughout life, is the root of sin or moral evil. But we are also endowed with a capacity for self-transcendence in virtue of which we can respond to the divine grace and can come to realise ever more fully our higher human potential. And the world, as an environment in which such imperfect creatures have the opportunity to grow towards their perfection, is a rough and challenging place, a scene of problems to be solved and challenges to be met, with possibilities of failure as well as success, disaster as well as triumph, tragedy as well as fulfilment. For a paradise, in the sense of a world from which all pain and suffering have been eliminated and in which there are accordingly no problems or challenges, would not be a person-making environment. Although it might from a hedonistic point of view be the best of all possible worlds, from the point of view of allowing growth in freedom towards full human maturity it might well be the worst of all possible worlds. For in it there could be no morally wrong actions – since wrong action entails hurt to someone – nor therefore any morally right actions; and accordingly no ethical choices and no possibility of moral growth. Further, there could be no occasions for ethical restraint or self-sacrifice, or for mutual love and protection in face of danger. For, paradoxically, it is the pain and suffering built into the structure of nature and evoking mutual love and protection, together with the boundaries of birth and death, giving to life its distinctive shape and making time precious and action urgent, that provide much of the person-making potential of life as we know it. Personal growth is realised as a by-product, not directly sought, of a positive response to life's hardships and problems – a courageous response to our own and a compassionate and self-sacrificing response to those of others.

A theodicy is an abstract scheme of thought, and as such it can never match the felt intensity of the problem. We have to judge it as an interpretive hypothesis, allowing for the inevitable psychic distance between such theoretical constructions and life's pains and travails as they are actually experienced. But given this unavoidable abstractness and distance, it is, I think, a sound general proposition that it is the hardships and problems of life, both physical and emotional, challenging us to courage and self-command, together with the social nature that opens us to the claims of other-humanity upon our own humanity, that make it possible for men and women to reach whatever depth and nobility of character they may attain. The insight that suffering constitutes the intrinsic cost of person-making is supported by the fact that in our apparently haphazardly painful world there are heights of love, compassion, self-giving for others which could not occur, because they would not be called for, in a world that was free of 'the heart-ache and the thousand natural shocks that flesh is heir to'. This is not to say of course that a person-making sphere must contain the particular dangers and challenges, pains and disasters, that have in fact occurred. The person-making character of the world consists rather in its being a realm that functions in accordance with its own general 'laws' and whose contingent states can be unpredictably benign or dangerous to human life.

But it is also true that in such a world, taken by itself, human suffering is often excessive in relation to any conceivable person-making purpose, breaking people both mentally and morally and turning them into human wrecks or into cruel and depraved monsters. Thus the gradual creating of persons through challenge and free response within a law-governed universe demands a larger sphere than this world and a longer time-frame than this life.[9] The Irenaean theodicy accordingly declares, as an essential further dimension of the traditional theistic picture, that this earthly life is only a small part of an immensely longer creative process which continues to an ultimate end-state in which that purpose will have been fulfilled. And the theodicy consists in the claim that the long and agonising cost of creation will be rendered worthwhile by the limitless future good to which it is leading. Thus from the point of view of a teleological theodicy the tragedies of human breakdown and descent into moral evil, which are part of the price of creation through finite freedom within a challenging environment, are not finally incompatible with the eventual success of that process. Indeed a faith which rests in the reality and ultimate sovereignty of God must affirm the ultimate completion of the divine creative activity. Thus, given an already established belief in God and the picture of the universe which flows from that belief, a viable theodicy is possible. Theism can by no means be inferred from the grim facts of suffering and wickedness, but it can, I think, be shown not to be necessarily incompatible with them.[10]

There is one other aspect of the universe as known to us which seems on the face of it strongly to support a naturalistic conclusion. This is its sheer size and humanity's correlatively minute place within its spatial and temporal immensity. Modern conceptions of the extent of the universe stagger the imagination. Our star is one of about 10^{11} stars in a galaxy which is itself one of about 10^{12} galaxies in the visible universe, which extends over some fifteen billion light-years (Barrow and Tipler 1986, 2 and 613). Further, for approximately fifteen billion years the universe existed, so far as we know, without any human or human-like minds to observe and ponder it. The collective span of mental life may prove to be a mere flash of time within the total history of the universe. For if humanoid life manages not to destroy itself in a nuclear holocaust it nevertheless seems doomed to eventual extinction as this earth and comparable planets in other solar systems become uninhabitable by reason of either heat or cold. Must it not then be a pathetic fallacy on our part to suppose that the entire history of the universe, in its unimaginable vastness and complexity, exists for the purpose of producing us human beings? Does it not seem more likely that in some tiny insignificant corner of the universe the incessant movement of matter has formed for a brief moment a consciousness-sustaining web of neuronal connections, only to disperse it again a moment later, leaving no trace behind?

Certainly on the face of it we must count our minuscule place in the scheme of things as supporting a naturalistic world-view.

But nevertheless it is not finally incompatible with a religious interpretation. Consciousness, although fleeting and frail, is qualitatively unique. As Pascal said,

> Man is but a reed, the most feeble thing in nature; but he is a thinking reed. The entire universe need not arm itself to crush him. A vapour, a drop of water suffices to kill him. But, if the universe were to crush him, man would still be more noble than that which killed him, because he knows that he dies and the advantage which the universe has over him; the universe knows nothing of this.   (Pascal [1670] 1932, 97)

And this uniqueness lends some degree of renewed plausibility to the idea that the universe exists to produce consciousness. Further, it is possible that human-like consciousness exists not only on our earth but also at different stages of development, perhaps some far in advance of our own, on the planets of stars in other galaxies. If so, the picture of the universe as a consciousness-producing system seems after all by no means impossible. Once again then the universe retains its baffling ambiguity.

3 CONCLUSION

We have, then, a variety of considerations, some supporting, but not decisively so, a theistic conclusion and others, but again not decisively, an atheistic conclusion. Each aspect of the universe that we have considered has turned out to be capable of both a theistic and a naturalistic interpretation. And yet I selected these particular aspects precisely because they constitute *prima facie* evidence for, or against, theism. That is to say that, taken in isolation, the fact (for example) of theistic experience points to there being a God whilst, again taken in isolation, the fact of suffering and wickedness points away from there being a God. Likewise the inference to an uncreated creator as rendering the existence of the universe intelligible, and again its apparently designed character, together with the facts of our moral, aesthetic and cognitive experience, can reasonably be said to point towards rather than away from a theistic world-view; whilst on the other hand the reality of evil, the utterly insignificant place of human life within the universe and the lack of any need for the theistic hypothesis to explain the workings of nature can reasonably be said to point away from such a conclusion. For no one would be likely to appeal to the fact of distinctively religious experience as positive evidence for atheism, or to the fact of human and animal suffering as positive evidence for theism. As we have seen, the theistic evidences *can* be interpreted naturalistically, and the naturalistic evidences *can* be interpreted theistically. But in each case such a counter-interpretation works against the *prima facie* significance of the evidence. Thus despite their ultimate ambivalence these items nevertheless fall more naturally on one or the other side of the balance sheet.

The question is whether having thus set them out in two opposed columns we can conclude that one list outweighs the other. It appears to me that no such outcome is realistically possible. For it would require us to quantify the values of the different items of evidence, assigning so many points to the mystery of existence, so many to alleged divine self-revelations, so many to the epistemic 'fit' between the universe and the human mind, so many to our moral and religious experience, so many to the beauties of nature . . . and on the other side, so many to the facts of human and animal suffering, so many to the universe's explicability without reference to God, so many to the 'psychological crutch' function of religion, so many to the insignificance of human life within the vastness of space and time. . . But any such relative quantifications could only be arbitrary and subjective. It is questionable whether we can even, with any hope of consensus, arrange the items within the same list in an order of relative importance. Which is the single most weighty piece of theistic, or of atheistic, evidence? On the theistic side some will see a particular supposed divine revelation as decisive whilst others will be more impressed by the orderliness and beauty of the world, or by the moral nature of the human species, or by some other factor. On the atheistic side some will see the problem of suffering as decisive whilst others will be more impressed by the reductionist force of a sociological or a psychological analysis of faith, or by the evils caused by religion in human history. And so on.

If it is difficult to the point of impossibility to assign comparative values on any objective basis to different items on the same side of the ledger, it is even harder to evaluate comparatively items drawn from opposite sides. By what criterion can we assert that the orderliness of nature tells more strongly, or less strongly, in favour of theism than human and animal suffering tells against it? Or that the explanatory superfluousness of the theistic hypothesis tells more strongly, or less strongly, in favour of atheism than reported divine revelations tell against it? And yet the differences between the theist and the atheist are precisely differences about such comparative weightings.

It seems, then, that the universe maintains its inscrutable ambiguity. In some aspects it invites whilst in others it repels a religious response. It permits both a religious and a naturalistic faith, but haunted in each case by a contrary possibility that can never be exorcised. Any realistic analysis of religious belief and experience, and any realistic defence of the rationality of religious conviction, must therefore start from this situation of systematic ambiguity.

Notes

1. Feuerbach is discussed more fully in Chapter 12.1.
2. A. L. Kroeber describes Freud's picture as 'intuitive, dogmatic, and wholly unhistorical' (1948, 616). Bronislaw Malinowski said that 'It is easy to perceive that the primeval horde has been equipped with all the bias, maladjustments and ill-tempers of a middle-class European family, and then let loose in a prehistoric jungle to run riot in a most attractive but fantastic hypothesis' ([1927] 1953, 165).
3. Freud 'never mentions the influence of the father representation, or any other, on the girl's conception of her God. Freud does not concern himself with religion or God in women' (Rizzuto 1979, 15). He seems to have assumed that religion is a male creation culturally imposed upon women.
4. For a modified Freudian theory, offering evidence of correlations between representations of God and a number of factors, including relationship to parents, see Rizzuto (1979).
5. A perceptive philosophical criticism of Freud's theories of religion can be found in William Alston 1964.
6. See further my *Death and Eternal Life* ([1976] 1985b, ch. 3).
7. Cf. H. H. Farmer 1942, ch. 9.
8. A more recent Durkheimian type of theory is presented by G. E. Swanson (1960) and is powerfully criticised by John Bowker (1973, ch. 2).
9. I have discussed in *Death and Eternal Life* ([1976] 1985b) some of the

different forms that such a continuation might take and shall not repeat that discussion here.

10. The theodicy problem has been considered in this chapter as a challenge to traditional theism. However after a more complex conception has been presented, according to which the gods are *personae* of the Real, the problem of evil will (in Chapter 19, Appendix) have to be faced again.

Part Three
Epistemological

8

Natural Meaning and Experience

Knowing is not knowledge as an effect of an unknown external cause, but is knowledge as we so interpret that our meaning is the actual meaning of our environment.

(John Oman 1931, 175)

1 MEANING

We have seen that the universe, as presently accessible to us, is religiously ambiguous in that it is capable of being interpreted intellectually and experientially in both religious and naturalistic ways. Even when it has come to be understood, experienced and inhabited in a particular way, whether religious or non-religious, it still retains its ambiguity for the intellect. And so, ideally, the religious person should, even whilst experiencing and living in the world religiously, be able to acknowledge its theoretically equivocal character; and the same holds *vice versa* for the non-religious person. However we are now leaving that philosophical ambiguity behind and turning to the ways in which the world is actually experienced and responded to. For whilst the objective ambiguity of our environment consists in the fact that it is *capable* of being interpreted in a variety of ways, its consciously experienced and actively lived-in character consists in its *actually being* interpreted as meaningful in a particular way which, whilst it operates, excludes other possible ways.

The notion of meaning can enable us to understand the nature both of experience in general and of distinctively religious experiencing in particular. As is well known, the word 'meaning' has many meanings. These divide into two distinct groups. On the one hand there is semantic meaning, concerned with the significance of words and sentences; and there is a very large modern philosophical literature concerned with the ways in which

129

words can variously refer, express and perform. And on the other hand we can speak of the meaning of an event or of a situation or indeed of life as a whole. There has in recent years been some philosophical discussion of this non-linguistic sense of 'meaning'.[1] It is in this second sense that we are using the word when we speak of the religious meaning of situations or of historical events or of human existence.

The idea of meaning in this second sense provides a path along which, initially at least, religious believer and humanist or secularist can set out together. They can both examine the kinds of meaning which they profess to identify. Because they are able to go thus far together, they can also identify the point at which they part company. For even in advance of a precise definition of 'meaning' we can say that the religious believer and non-believer see the meaning or character of human life very differently. For the believer it is part of a vast cosmic process which leads, or can lead, to the limitless good of Heaven or Nirvana or oneness with eternal reality; whilst for the atheist or humanist there is no such cosmic process but only the life-experience of the wonderfully complex human animal, terminating individually at death and constituting a story which is contingently pleasant and unpleasant, welcome and unwelcome in various ways and degrees. These clearly constitute radically different conceptions of the 'meaning', or practical and emotional response-evoking character, of the universe.

The difference will have to be spelled out more fully.[2] But first let me define the concept of meaning which I am using. Its application is not restricted to this notion of the meaning of life. On the contrary, meaning is the most general characteristic of conscious experience as such. For to be conscious is, normally, to be discriminatingly aware of various features of our surroundings in such a way that we can act appropriately (or at any rate in ways that we assume to be appropriate) in relation to them. We do not find ourselves in a homogeneous continuum within which no distinctions can be made, or within a mere chaos or stream of kaleidoscopic change which would offer no purchase for purposefully appropriate action, but rather in a structured environment within which we can react differentially to different items and within diverse situations. It is a space-time field within which a vast multitude of objects are distinguishable – humans, trees, mountains, seas, birds, cows and so on – and are such that we learn, with greater or less success, to behave appropriately in relation to them. In other words, we experience things and situations as having this or that recognisable character such that it is appropriate for us to behave in relation to them in this rather than in that way. For our consciousness is the consciousness of physical agents. We are not bodiless observers viewing a scene with which we have no contact, but integral parts of the world that we are cognising, and we exist in continuous interaction with those parts of it that are adjacent to us. To be sane, or basically rational, is to live in terms of the perceived character of our environment. ('Perceived' here of course includes 'misperceived': there is no assumption that we always cognise correctly.) And for that environment to have meaning for us is for it to be such that we can conduct ourselves within it in ways which we take to be appropriate to its character.

Meaning, thus understood, is both a relational and a practical concept. Meaning is always *for*, or in relation to, a consciousness or a community of consciousnesses; and the meaning of which a consciousness is aware is the character of its environment perceived as rendering appropriate one rather than another type of behaviour or (more generally) of behavioural disposition. We can accordingly define meaning as the perceived (or misperceived) character of an object or situation such that to perceive it as having that character is to be in a distinctive dispositional state in relation to it. To find the world, or some aspect of it, meaningful is thus to find it intelligible – not in the intellectual sense of understanding it but in the practical sense that one is able to behave appropriately (or in a way that one takes to be appropriate) in relation to it.

So defined, meaning is a pervasive characteristic of our environment as we perceive and inhabit it. If there are states of mind – perhaps in very early infancy and in some forms of mental disassociation or insanity – in which a conscious being apprehends no kind or degree of meaning in its environment, that being will be incapable of purposive action since there will be nothing to trigger tendencies to act in one way rather than another. All consciousness, or at any rate all our normal consciousness, is consciousness of an environment which we perceive as having many kinds and levels of meaning, an environment such that we can act and react in response to its character as this varies through space and changes through time.

There are of course very many, indeed innumerable, different forms of non-linguistic meaning corresponding to the different characters that we find objects to have; and there are also, I shall suggest, various orders or 'levels' of meaning, namely the physical or natural, the socio-ethical and the religious. In terms of natural meaning we inhabit the physical world, moving about in it as animal organisms. In terms of ethical meaning we inhabit this same world as an environment mediating personal relationships and moral claims. And in terms of religious meaning we inhabit this same world again, with both its physical and its ethical significance, as an environment either mediating or manifesting the ultimately Real. Thus meaning, as the perceived character of an aspect of our environment which renders a particular type of response appropriate, occurs at various levels: all cognition is a tentative grasping of meaning on the basis of which we act, thereby confirming, developing or refuting our cognitive hypotheses. And at each level of awareness – natural, ethical and religious – we exercise a cognitive freedom which is at its minimum in relation to the immediate physical environment and at its maximum in relation to that ultimate environment of which the religions speak.

Perhaps at this stage it would be wise to pause to anchor the discussion in ordinary everyday experience – for example, my own situation as I was writing this chapter a few months ago. I was sitting in a deck-chair on the lawn in a morning in early summer, writing in a large exercise book, and at the same time being conscious of hearing bird songs, and in the background the sound of traffic, and of seeing green grass and trees and bushes with their leaves waving gently in the breeze. I take it, however, that in the production of this pleasant state my mind/brain (and we do not need to raise here the question of mind–brain identity versus mind–brain dualism) was actively at work, below the threshold of conscious awareness, continuously interpreting sensory clues and enriching them from the resources of memory, thus recognising the character both of individual objects and of the environing situation as a whole.[3]

The practical aspect of this continuous activity of recognition is the difference which it makes to one's total dispositional state. For example, I perceived the lawn before me as a solid surface on which I could tread; and my corresponding dispositional state was such that I might walk on it but would not try, for example, to dive into it or to eat it or use it for fuel. I perceived the daisies as flowers and not as (say) white insects. I perceived the table as a table – that is, as a hard surface on which I could put my papers. I perceived the bird songs as bird songs, with all sorts of charming and poetic associations. I perceived the noise of traffic as the noise of traffic and not – as a stone-age person miraculously transported there might have perceived it – as the sound of dangerous animals charging by on the other side of the fence. In all this I was operating with the 'schemas' with which my mind is furnished.[4] And my total response to the meaning of this complex situation, as I thus experienced it, was to go on sitting in the deck-chair in the sun and writing these pages.

It is clear that in the production of our ordinary conscious experience of the world there are involved both a host of particular concepts corresponding to our ordinary sortal words, such as 'grass', 'chair', 'table', 'traffic', etc., and also certain more general organising concepts, which Kant called the categories. For 'Seeing is something we do with ideas as well as senses. We cannot see what we cannot conceive' (Strick and Posner 1985, 215; compare Runzo 1982). Indeed Kant's project of identifying the general categories of experience – the necessary features of any unitary consciousness of a world – could also be described as the project of identifying the basic structures of natural or physical meaning.

We can also notice in this example at least a background awareness of another level of meaning, namely the personal, which is (as I shall argue presently) the ethical level. For as I sat in the garden, my wife brought me an encouraging cup of coffee, and this served as a reminder that I am not an isolated individual but part of a network of personal relationships. And if some family crisis had occurred my consciousness would at once have moved from my philosophical reflections and refocused at the personal level of meaning, another range of practical dispositions being thereby activated. We may also note that the wider life of the world is continuous with the personal and ethical; for one cannot extract oneself from a complex social, political and economic system which in turn ramifies out into the vast throbbing organism of the life of humanity as a whole. Further, sitting in the garden and reflecting upon the idea of meaning, with a view to understanding better the religious meaning of life, I was also fleetingly conscious of existing in the universal presence of the ultimate Reality that I know as God. This is the level of awareness, or order of meaning, towards which our discussion is moving.

2 NATURAL MEANING

However, before coming to this, let us look more closely at natural meaning. Here the idea of cognition as a search for meaning, or for intelligibilities in relation to which we can guide our activity, is well supported by current conclusions in the physiology and psychology of perception. It has been known in general terms at least from the time of Descartes, and known in much more intricate detail during the last century or so, that the three-dimensional world of objects reflects light which affects the retina of the eye, stimulating its light-sensitive cells in patterns which correspond in some way to that which is affecting them. Thus the three dimensions of the physical world are projected onto the two dimensions of the more or less plane surface of the retina. Here changes in the rods and cones are converted into electrical impulses which travel along the million or so fibres of the optic nerve to the *area striata* at the back of the brain. The three-dimensional object, having been converted into a two-dimensional image, has now become encoded as a series of electrical impulses. At the same time other streams of information from the same physical world – sounds, smells, tastes, and sensations of heat, cold, touch and pain – have also been encoded as electrical impulses and are being correlated in the brain along with the information received from the eyes. Thus what we perceive as the world of solid and moving objects, with its vivid colours, smells and tastes; the world of mountains, seas, forests and rivers, inhabited by innumerable animals, birds and fishes; the human society around us; the sun, moon and stars; indeed the whole infinitely varied universe as it impinges upon our senses is translated into electrical events in the brain and then mysteriously converted into the contents of consciousness.

But is the external world in fact reconstituted faithfully as the world of which we are aware, or is this latter a new and private creation, occurring only within our own field of consciousness? Since we can never experience the unexperienced we can never compare the world as it appears in consciousness with the postulated world as it exists independently of its impacts upon our human sensory and nervous systems. But we know that we are able to survive, and indeed to flourish, as physical entities moving about in a physical world with which our bodies intermesh in a single causal system. That aspect of the world which is our consciousness of other parts of the world seems to be connected in regular ways with those other parts. For on the basis of the private inner 'picture' of itself which our environment creates in us we are able, by and large, to live successfully within it. As the history of modern western epistemology has established, there is no theoretical proof that we perceive a real world, or even that there is a real environing world to be perceived. But nevertheless it would be irrational, because self-destructive, to proceed on any other assumption.

However it is clear that the world as we perceive and inhabit it is not the world in its virtually infinite richness and complexity, but only a humanly selected aspect of it. For we are parts of the world, occupying a portion of its space and perceiving the rest of it in an inevitably idiosyncratic perspective in which we are at the centre of our own field of vision. Further, being not only observers but also agents, our perceptual machinery, determined by biological need, is attuned only to a minute proportion of the total range of information flowing through and around us. For example, out of the electromagnetic spectrum extending from cosmic rays as short as four ten-thousand-millionths of an inch to radio waves as long as eighteen miles, our bodily receptors only respond to those between sixteen and thirty-two millionths of an inch; and we are likewise deaf to most acoustic stimuli and insensitive to the great majority of chemical differences.

Again, we perceive matter organised into entities only within a certain band of the macro-micro scale. And it is necessary to our survival and well-being as vulnerable fleshly organisms that this should be so (see Norman Kemp Smith 1924, 10–12). If, for example, instead of seeing water as the continuous shiny substance that we can drink we perceived it as a cloud of electrons in rapid swirling motion, and the glass that holds it as a mass of brilliantly coloured crystals, themselves composed of particles in violent activity, then drinking a glass of water, instead of being routine, would be a startling adventure. But most of daily life has to be routine if it is not to bewilder and exhaust us. Accordingly, 'Sources of variation that have no survival value in themselves and that do not even covary highly with those that do are, in the interests of simplification and generality, best not detected' (Anderson 1975, 28–9). And so both senses and mind/brain first select and then relate and organise within the framework of well-tried schematic patterns. The result is a constructed version of the world that is enormously simplified and yet such that we can live in it successfully.[5]

After the sense-receptors, with their massive incapacities, have screened out some 90 per cent of the environment, the mind/brain proceeds to interpret the information that has been received. For our ordinary conscious 'picture' of the world is formed out of remarkably slight and fragmentary clues. Shapes of various colours and hues are projected onto the retina; but what we consciously see is, for example, a solid three-dimensional book which we believe to contain printed pages and to have been produced by author, publisher, printer and binder in a co-operative effort that presupposes a whole complex commercial society and a wealth of cultural tradition. The visual clues have been interpreted with the aid of memory and given meaning in terms of the concept 'book'. Recognition has taken place by matching within the memory bank, and this has activated schemas which enable us to act appropriately in relation to the object before us as a book – being prepared, for example, to read it rather than to eat it!

In this way the meanings in terms of which we inhabit the world far transcend the perceptual clues which it offers us. For meaning is concerned with patterns that are not given in their totality within sense perception, but in relation to which we can nevertheless act and react appropriately. Thus the environment in which we are conscious of living always transcends the physical impacts of the world upon our sense organs. Accordingly we cannot avoid the idea of the transcendent: for meaning is always couched at least partly in terms that exceed the immediately given. And within this dimension of transcendence there are, as we shall see, various levels: not only the physical or natural, but also the socio-ethical and the religious.

This transformation of electrical impulses into our awareness of an environment in which we can act and react goes on all the time. The mind/brain, below the level of consciousness, is continually forming hypotheses which are being tested as we act upon them. If our perceptual machinery were to go wrong we would quickly be set at odds with the surrounding world, misperceiving it and attempting to live on the basis of false assumptions concerning its character. In what would soon become a fatal encounter the larger system would inevitably prevail and we should be eliminated. Thus at this level our cognitive freedom is minimal; the physical world compels us to interpret its signals correctly and to live in it in terms of its real meaning for beings such as ourselves. And therefore at this level the interpretive machinery of the mind functions in basically the same way in all of us. Indeed much of this basic interpretive activity is probably genetically controlled, being the evolutionary deposit of millions of confirmations of the brain's hypotheses. As Karl Popper, to whom we owe this insight, has put it, 'The tentative solutions which animals and plants incorporate into their anatomy and their behaviour are biological analogues of theories' (Popper 1975, 145).

But within the constraints of biological necessity there is nevertheless some scope for variation, revealed in the ways in which our powers of perception have become adapted to different circumstances or sharpened by special effort. It is well known, for example, that training can greatly enhance one's capacity for visual discrimination. I once, during the second world war, took a course in malaria diagnosis in which I was taught to notice and identify under a microscope the different kinds of malarial plasmodia made visible by a stain applied to a drop of the patient's blood on a slide. It was possible within two or three weeks (spent in my case in the fascinating city of Damascus) to raise one's diagnostic score from zero to almost 100 per cent by training the eye and mind/brain to notice appropriately. Such adaptations of the perceptual machinery to varying circumstances are familiar phenomena. For example, we unconsciously calculate the relative distances of objects from a variety of clues – including the angle of convergence of the two eyes; the disparity between the images which they receive, which is converted by the brain into an awareness of depth; and at greater distances by the location of images within the visual field – the higher up the further away. It seems that the art of judging distances is learned by practice, the necessary control being provided by touch and/or movement in space. Accordingly peoples living in dense forest and never experiencing objects at a distance have been found when brought onto an open plain to perceive distant things as small instead of as distant. For they have not had the experience of walking towards remote objects, correlating their position towards the top of the visual field with the time and effort required to move through the intervening space (R. L. Gregory [1966] 1978, 162). Such cases – and the literature of the psychology of perception contains a large range of relevant cases[6] – show that our psycho-physical perceptual apparatus is to a certain extent plastic and capable of being adjusted by our own volitions.

Nevertheless the basic fact remains that at the level of sense perception our environment insists upon our living in terms of its own inherent structure or meaning. To be conscious of a rock differs from being conscious of a tiger in that these two objects have different meanings for us – that is to say, it is appropriate to behave differently in relation to them! And to a very great extent our physiological pain mechanism, backed by the ultimate sanction of the death penalty, has trained us to cognise our physical environment correctly and to live within it in terms of its actual meaning for the particular kind of vulnerable fleshly organisms that we are.

The subjective correlate of meaning can be called interpretation: to perceive an object or situation as having a particular kind of meaning is to interpret it as having that distinctive character, awareness of which consists in part in an adjustment to our system of practical dispositions. Whereas the word 'interpretation' more usually refers to a conscious intellectual activity – as when a scientist interprets her observations or a detective his clues, or when a metaphysician offers an interpretation of the universe – in relation to sense perception it refers to the unconscious activity whereby the mind/brain correlates information and identifies individual objects and complex situations, activating or pre-activating an appropriate dispositional response. But the two procedures are similar in kind. The formation of expectations at an unconscious and non-linguistic level is analogous to the formation of hypotheses at the conscious and linguistic level. Here, to form hypotheses is to experiment in the medium of language, trying out different symbolisations which can, if they are useful, be corrected or refuted in the light of experience. In the unconscious genesis of our perceptual experience, to form hypotheses is to experiment not with symbols but with the perceiver's own body. The animal which interprets a moving object as dangerous and runs in the opposite direction may well be staking its life on its hypothesis.

Whereas the growth of our conscious interpretation of the

world, which is science, proceeds through our own deliberate killing off of inadequate hypotheses, the development of our perceptual interpretation of the physical environment has proceeded by the killing off of the creature which was acting upon an inadequate hypothesis. As Karl Popper says, 'Thus, while animal knowledge and pre-scientific knowledge grew mainly through the elimination of those holding the unfit hypotheses, scientific criticism often makes our theories perish in our stead, eliminating our mistaken beliefs before such beliefs lead to our own elimination' (Popper 1975, 261).

Human beings, however, are not as immediately vulnerable as the lower animals. We are committed to only a few genetically encoded hypotheses (such as the new-born baby's hypothesis that it is useful to suck) and are able to revise most of our working assumptions in the light of experience. When what we took to be an apple turns out to be made of wax our discovery of this consists in discarding the original hypothesis and forming, and confirming by acting upon, an new one. But since our perceptual hypotheses work in some 99 per cent of instances we do not normally notice their hypothetical character. Nevertheless it seems entirely appropriate to give the name of hypotheses to the stream of judgments underlying our ordinary conscious experience, for they can be confirmed or refuted by environmental feedback, and if refuted superseded by an attempt to interpret the data more successfully.

The continual formation and testing throughout animal life of what are by analogy hypotheses presupposes what can, again by analogy, be called the basic 'aim' of surviving and flourishing as a living organism. For any structure of practical dispositions involves an implicit aim or purpose in terms of which responses are rendered appropriate or inappropriate.[7] Given that the organism 'wants' to survive, it will seek to avoid mortal danger; but in the absence of that basic programme there would, for that organism, be no such thing as danger and hence no policy of avoiding it. This notion of the basic aim implicit within the dispositional aspect of our awareness of meaning will come to the fore again when we turn to the moral and then to the religious levels of meaning.

3 EXPERIENCING-AS

Returning for the moment to normal perception, we have seen that in relation to our physical environment the mind/brain is actively interpreting, though at this level its operation is largely controlled by the environment itself. The outcome in consciousness can be called 'experiencing-as' – developed from Wittgenstein's concept of 'seeing-as'.[8] Wittgenstein was particularly concerned with puzzle pictures: we may see an ambiguous figure as, for example, the picture of a duck facing left or of a rabbit facing right. But in fact all our seeing is seeing-as and, more broadly, all conscious experiencing is experiencing-as. For in the recognition of objects and situations as having a particular character, setting up a particular range of practical dispositions, the mind/brain is interpreting sensory information by means of concepts and patterns drawn from its memory. When we recognise what is before us on the table as a fork, or what is lying on the desk as a pen, or the object over there as a building and more specifically as a house, or the figure moving towards us as a human being and more specifically as the postman, we are experiencing an object *as* having this or that character or meaning: that is, as a reality in relation to which we are prepared to behave in a certain range of ways appropriate to its being the kind of thing that we perceive it to be.

At this point I have parted company with Wittgenstein in his discussion of 'seeing-as'. He believed that the notion only applies to those exceptional moments when we are confronted by ambiguous pictures and objects, like the famous duck–rabbit picture or like seeing a protuberance on the branch of a tree as a squirrel. But I want to argue that *all* seeing is seeing-as; or rather that all conscious experiencing, including seeing, is experiencing-as: not only, for example, seeing the protuberance – erroneously – as a squirrel, but also seeing it correctly as a knobble on the branch. On the face of it this sounds paradoxical – and Wittgenstein was very sensitive to such hard lumps in the flow of language. One might put the difficulty in this way: we may if we like speak of seeing the knob in the branch *as* a knob in the branch because it is evidently possible to misperceive it as a sitting squirrel. But what about something utterly familiar and unmistakable? What about the fork on the table? Would it not be absurd to say that you are seeing it *as* a fork? It seemed so to

Wittgenstein; and it must be granted that this particular locution would be distinctly odd in most circumstances. However we have more usual names for ordinary seeing-as in real life: we call it 'recognising' or 'identifying'.

Of course we are so familiar with forks that normally we recognise one without encountering even enough difficulty to cause us to notice that we are in fact performing an act of recognition. But if the fork were sufficiently exotic in design I might have occasion to say that I can recognise this exhibit in the museum of domestic artifacts as a fork – that is, as a purpose-made instrument for conveying food into the mouth. Stone age persons, however, would not be able to recognise it as a fork at all. They might identify it instead as a marvellously shining object which must be full of *mana* and must not be touched; or as a small but deadly weapon; or as a tool for digging; or just as something utterly baffling and unidentifiable. But they would not have the concept of a fork with which to identify it as a fork. Indeed to say that they do not have this concept and that they cannot perform this act of recognition are two ways of saying the same thing. That there is no ambiguity or mystery about forks for you and me is simply due to the contingent circumstance that forks are familiar parts of the equipment of our culture. For the nature or meaning of an artifact is determined by the purpose for which it has been made and this purpose always arises within a given cultural context. But simply as a physical object of a certain size and shape an artifact does not bear its meaning stamped upon it. To recognise or identify is to be experiencing-as in terms of a concept; and our concepts are social products having their life within a particular linguistic environment.

Further, this is as true of natural objects as of artifacts. Here too, to recognise is to apply a concept; and this is always to cognise the thing as being much more than is currently perceptible. For example, to identify a moving object in the sky as a bird is not only to make implicit claims about its present shape, size and structure beyond what we immediately observe, but also about its past (such as that it came out of an egg), about its future (such as that it will one day die) and about its behaviour in various hypothetical circumstances (such as that it will tend to be frightened by sudden loud noises). When we thus equate experiencing-as with recognising it is, I suggest, no longer a paradoxical doctrine that all conscious experiencing is experiencing-as.[9]

We must distinguish between recognitional capacities operating in the lower animals at the pre-linguistic level and operating in the human animal largely at the linguistic level. Let us define 'concepts' as recognitional capacities which have been focused, abstracted and fixed by language. Given this definition, we shall not speak of the lower animals as using concepts but rather as having pre-linguistic recognitional capacities. For they are undoubtedly differentially conscious of those features of their environment that are significant to them as organisms programmed for survival; and they react in the ways which instinct, as their encoded survival strategy, has selected for them. But they only possess that restricted range of recognitional capacities engendered in them (or in the species) by the pressures of their physical environment. Human animals, on the other hand, in virtue of their enormously more complex brains, have produced language, and with its magic power have created a wealth of conceptual superstructures, the worlds of meaning which are developed, explored and enjoyed both in our everyday existence and in the arts and sciences, philosophies and religions.

These conceptual creations are the inner skeletons structuring the various forms of life, or ways of being human, that constitute the different cultures of the earth. And it is at this level, at which experience is pervaded, moulded and coloured by human meanings, that I wish to maintain that all experience embodies concept-laden forms of interpretation. At the sub-human levels of life experience is shaped by recognitional capacities which are the analogues of concepts. And between the high ground of human culture and the lower ground of animal existence there is a somewhat indeterminate region. The human baby moves through this region towards human personhood; adults may regress into it in some forms of mental breakdown and brain decay or under the influence of certain drugs; and possibly some domestic pets, living within a human sphere of influence, may rise tentatively into it. However it is not necessary for our present purpose to explore this indeterminate area; for our concern is to be with the distinctively human levels of experience.

Notes

1. E.g. Kurt Baier 1957; Anthony Flew 1963; Kai Nielsen 1964; Ilham Dilman 1965; John Wisdom 1965, ch. 4; Marvin Kohl 1981; John Riser 1981; Albert Shalom 1982; James O. Bennett 1984; Joseph Wayne Smith 1984.
2. See Chapters 11 and 12.
3. Cf. Barry F. Anderson 1975, chs 2–3.
4. Cf. Anderson 1975, ch. 4.
5. On the constructed nature of our perceived environment, and a tentative extension of the discussion to religion, see Arbib and Hesse 1986.
6. See, e.g., William N. Dember 1960.
7. Cf. Anderson 1975, ch. 8.
8. Wittgenstein [1953] 1963, II:xi. On the importance of this concept in Wittgenstein's later thought see Hollinger 1974.
9. Hughes (1968), Keeling and Morelli (1977) and Malone (1978) have claimed that it is not permissible to expand Wittgenstein's notion into a much wider concept which is co-terminous with conscious perceiving, in which the distinction between seeing and seeing-as accordingly disappears. Certainly Wittgenstein himself held that we just *see* knives and forks but see the duck–rabbit picture *as* the picture of a duck. But respect for Wittgenstein's authority should not prevent us from recognising that ordinary perception is also, in N. R. Hanson's phrase (1958, 19), 'theory laden' and is in this sense a matter of 'experiencing-as'.

Others have asked whether in addition to conscious visual perceiving, which necessarily uses concepts, there must not also be a non-conceptual seeing or experiencing (e.g. Nielsen 1971, 86). In order to recognise what is there as a chair must I not first (logically rather than temporally first) be seeing – non-conceptually seeing – what is there? Fred Dretske calls this 'simple seeing' or 'non-epistemic seeing' (Dretske 1979). Joseph Runzo prefers to call it 'looking at' (Runzo 1982). But whatever we choose to call it, I suggest that it is not this presupposed fact of the world being present to our senses, but the further fact of our modes of recognition and response, that is important for the understanding of our human cognitive situation.

I should however add that, if ordinary seeing is seeing-as, certain cases (including puzzle pictures) require a distinction between primary and secondary seeing-as. For example, if I 'see a cloud as a unicorn' I am primarily seeing what it there in the sky as a cloud, and secondarily seeing the cloud as being like a unicorn. The primary seeing-as involves my believing that what is there is a cloud, whilst the secondary seeing-as does not involve my believing that it is a unicorn, but only that it is shaped like one (cf. R. W. Perrett 1984, 59).

9

Ethical and Aesthetic Meaning and Experience

Any animal whatever, endowed with well-marked social instincts, would inevitably acquire a moral sense or conscience, as soon as its intellectual powers had become as well, or nearly as well, developed as in man.　　　　(Charles Darwin 1875, 98)

1　SOCIO-ETHICAL MEANING

We have thus far been speaking of our environment in terms of individual objects, such as trees and rocks, books and tigers. But in fact our practical consciousness, or consciousness as agents, does not normally focus upon objects in isolation but rather upon groups of objects complexly related to form what we can call situations. By a situation I mean that particular selection from our total environment to which at a given time we consciously relate ourselves as actual or potential agents. This is made up of entities each of which has its own distinctive character or meaning; but the situation itself also has a meaning which exceeds that of the sum of its constituent parts. And our consciousness normally functions on this situational level as an awareness of a continuum of objects within which we act or react.

The various kinds of meaning of which we are conscious are the correlates of our modes of experiencing-as. We experience what is before us, or the situation around us, as having this or that kind of meaning and thus as such that it is appropriate for us to behave in relation to it in this or that way or range of ways. This also applies to our consciousness of personal meaning, or the experiencing of persons *as* persons. For in many situations we are responding not only to physical objects and a physical environment but at the same time to other persons and a social environment. In our awareness of other persons the interpretandum is a human body behaving in a certain way, a central aspect of which is the

144

use of language. The body in question may, for example, be eating supper and chatting about the news; or negotiating for the sale of a car; or discussing the weather; or quarrelling; or making love; or playing tennis . . . What all these and innumerable other instances have in common is a mutual responsiveness or inter-adaptation. Each participant takes account, in what he or she does or says, of what the other does or says, behaving differently from the way he or she would have behaved but for the other's presence and activity.

What, then, is going on when I am conscious of the presence of another person? The job which the word 'presence' performs here is to emphasise that which distinguishes a thou from an it. We are indebted to the personalist thinkers of two generations ago for drawing attention to this distinctive character of the personal. This is something of which people had of course always been aware in practice. But Martin Buber, above all, brought it to explicit and reflective consciousness in his *I and Thou* ([1923] 1937). The leading modern personalist figures among Christian thinkers have been John Oman, whose classic *Grace and Personality* was published as long ago as the first world war ([1917] 1961), Emil Brunner (1936), H. H. Farmer (1936) on the more theological side, and John Macmurray (1957–61) and the Boston personalists on the more philosophical side. These and many others have taught us that to be confronted by another human person is to be aware of another consciousness existing independently of and over against myself; another centre of judgment appealing to canons of rationality to which we both subscribe; another system of valuation; another set of purposes; another will. In the presence of another person two evaluators meet, so that in judging I am at the same time being judged. Not only am I conscious of the other but I am conscious that the other is conscious of me. Further, he or she will have aims and interests which may support or oppose my own.

Thus whilst I can be aware of the bare neutral *existence* of a stone or a tree, I can only be aware of the bare neutral existence of a fellow human being if I have degraded that being in my own eyes from a thou to an it. As a thou he or she evokes in me an awareness, not merely of the existence of a thing, but of the *presence* of a person. And the dispositional aspect of our awareness of persons is different in kind from the dispositional aspect of our awareness of things. The latter in its public, generalised and systematic form is technology, the organised ability to manipulate matter for our own ends; whilst the dispositional aspect of the former is morality, the capacity to act responsibly as a person in relation to other persons. The two sets of dispositions are correlated with two levels or orders of meaning, and a human being lives on both levels at once, interacting with other persons within a shared material environment.

For to be a person is to be in interaction with other persons. A permanently solitary person is a logical impossibility: one is personal in virtue of one's participation in an interacting community of persons. A human baby is not born a person but becomes one by being drawn into the human community. (Having once become firmly established as a person, one may of course retain the capacity for personal response through long periods of solitude; but nevertheless one's existence as a person remains a gift of human society.) Thus a person is not adequately characterised, in Boethius' classic definition, as an 'individual substance (or entity) of a rational nature' ([5th–6th century] 1962, 85). On this account there would be no necessity for more than one person to exist; whereas modern psychology and sociology have shown us that, as John Macmurray used to say, 'for there to be one person there must be at least two'. A person, then, is better described as an individual who is capable of inter-personal relationships and who is (or has been) a functioning part of a system of such relationships.

Thus a person is not a psychic substance or monad whose essential nature is unaffected by the existence of other persons, but is one of a plurality of centres within a vibrating field of force in which each continuously balances, sustains and influences the others. The special character of personal existence is mutuality. We are personal in so far as we live in mutual responsiveness to other centres of consciousness, rationality, valuation, purpose and will.

We may presume that in the genesis of personal awareness the baby's consciousness develops and becomes focused largely as a result of interaction and response. She feels discomfort and cries, and her needs are attended to. This interaction gradually takes on the character of mutual awareness and thus of personal relationship with another person. And having been thus drawn into a living field of mutual responsiveness, one eventually becomes aware of oneself and the other as distinct individuals. One thereafter exercises the concept of a person, in the sense of the capacity to recognise and respond appropriately to a thou as distinct from an it. One habitually experiences persons *as* persons. For we do not see or otherwise observe another consciousness; nor do we infer it, except perhaps when we are challenged to produce a philosophical justification for our belief in the reality of other minds. Rather, we experience the behaviour of a particular kind of physical organism which is akin to ourself *as* the presence of another embodied consciousness. Although colloquially we may say that we saw her embarrassment, or observed his anger, nevertheless we do not see emotions. We see the behaviour of a physical organism *as* the behaviour of an embarrassed or an angry person. Again, although we may say that we could see what she intended to do, we nevertheless do not see intentions but rather experience certain movements and patterns of movement *as* intentional activities. And so on. In short we have no direct cognition of another centre of consciousness, but we experience-as in the way which has given rise to and is reciprocally supported and maintained by the language of the personal (see Charles Dunlop 1984, 359–64).

It is also worth noting that when A experiences, say, the movement of B's arm *as* an angry gesture or B's flushed face *as* the face of an embarrassed person, A's experiencing in this way is integral to a way of experiencing the wider environing situation in which A and B are mutually involved. The movement of an arm or the reddening of a face, without any context, lacks a specific meaning. The arm movement could, in different circumstances, be experienced as expressing anger, fear, horror, delight, astonishment, aggression, fantasy, or as the swatting of a fly; and the flushing of the face could, in different situations, be experienced as expressing embarrassment, anger, fear, or as a sign of fever. Our awareness of personal meaning, that is, of bodies as thous, is accordingly a function of our awareness of the wider context as having a particular kind of social meaning.

Thus our consciousness of the presence of other people is a distinctively human form of experiencing-as. It is so basic that someone who did not perceive in this way would probably have to be controlled in a mental hospital; for this way of experiencing-as is the basis of the moral and therefore of social life. In so experiencing we are finding a particular kind of meaning in the organic life of our species. And it is natural that we should. As

Charles Darwin wrote, 'any animal whatever, endowed with well-marked social instincts, . . . would inevitably acquire a moral sense or conscience, as soon as its intellectual powers had become as well, or nearly as well, developed as in man' (1875, 98).

However my concern here is not to try to develop a view of the basis and nature of ethics, but rather to note the structural similarity between our awareness at the natural and at the socio-ethical levels. We have seen that the awareness of meaning, or the experiencing of a situation as having a particular character, has an essential dispositional aspect: it involves being in a state to behave within that situation in a range of ways appropriate to its being that kind of situation. The dispositional aspect of natural meaning presupposes the basic aim of self-preservation. Given this basic aim, our perception of the character of an environing situation generates its appropriate dispositional response. The next level of aim or desire, presupposing self-preservation, is indicated by the general term 'flourishing' or the more traditional term 'happiness'. Given that we continue to exist, we want to flourish or to attain happiness. And because our nature as persons is inter-personal, this desire gives rise (amongst other things) to that dimension of our lives which is expressed in the languages of law and ethics.

At a basic level, bordering on but going beyond that of physical self-preservation, any society needs a framework of mutually accepted rules of behaviour. This is morality as law – about which I shall say no more. But the higher levels of morality, transcending this basic framework, are expressions of inter-personality. Here our basic need is for that mutuality which is of the essence of personal well-being. As our physical nature is programmed to seek self-preservation and our social nature requires law, so our personal nature seeks mutual acceptance and reciprocity, indeed mutual valuing and love. The 'milk of human kindness' is the nuturing power of human-kind-ship or kinship (see Cupitt 1986, 19). Our basic need as persons is community. And given this openness of the personal to the personal, our awareness of the character of a situation involving other persons generates its own appropriate dispositional response, the dimension within which this occurs being morality in distinction from legality.

But these higher levels of morality, going beyond the requirements of law, depend upon an inner attitude and mode of experiencing-as. When, for example, someone has been knocked down by a car and is lying in the road injured and calling for help, a perception of the situation at the purely physical level will simply note the position of the body, the broken shape of a limb, blood on the ground and screams. But to function as a moral being is to allow oneself to be conscious at the same time of another level of meaning in the same situation, a level at which we are aware of a moral claim upon us. The dispositional aspect of this awareness will (if no contrary force inhibits it) lead to one's rendering aid as best one can. It is however possible to conceive of individuals perceiving at the physical but not at the moral level, and consequently not being conscious of any inner need to turn aside to help. And whilst it would no doubt be possible to train such beings by rewards and punishments to conform to a set of social rules, it would be impossible to induce them to experience at the ethical-personal level.

Since morality is thus generated by the inter-personal nature of personality, its basic principle is mutuality, or acceptance of the other as another person, someone else of the same nature as oneself. The fundamental moral claim is accordingly to treat others as having the same value as myself. This is in effect a transcription of the Golden Rule found in the Hindu, Buddhist, Confucian, Taoist, Zoroastrian, Jain and Christian scriptures and in the Jewish *Talmud* and the Muslim *Hadith* (see Chapter 17.5), and is likewise a translation of Kant's concepts of a rational person as an end and of right action as action which our rationality, acknowledging a universal impartiality transcending individual desires and aversions, can see to be required.

There is one further important aspect of our moral awareness which must be noted before we turn to religious awareness. We saw that in relation to the natural meaning of our environment the world teaches us by powerful sanctions to develop responses that are appropriate, given the basic aim of survival. At this level we have a very limited freedom of perception and of corresponding response. But at the moral or personal level we have a much greater degree of cognitive freedom. Indeed it is only too easy to limit our recognition of others as fellow persons, admitting some and excluding the rest. The growth of moral awareness has come about as much by the enlarging of its range as by the sharpening of its focus. Pre-literate tribal societies have commonly seen kinsmen of the same tribe as persons bound together in community with themselves but have generally not seen those outside the tribe as part of the field of potential moral obligation. Slave-owning societies have accorded their slave populations a lower status, lacking the moral rights of their masters. It has been, and still alas is, all too common for white people to think of black people in essentially this way. In industrialised societies it is easy for managers to think of their workers as 'hands' rather than as persons; and indeed for almost everyone to see others, beyond a relatively small circle, in functional rather than personal terms.

The perception of the human person as an end in him- or herself, as a neighbour to be valued as we value ourselves, is an ideal seldom achieved. This ideal does not of course exclude seeing others in their functional roles as well, as the driver of the bus in which we are travelling, or as the shop assistant from whom we are buying something, or as the lawyer from whom we are seeking advice, and so on; but it does involve the possibility that an awareness of the other as a fellow person and an end in her or himself may at any time supervene upon our awareness of that person as a means to our own ends. As Kant put it, the categorical imperative in one of its forms is: 'Act in such a way that you always treat humanity, whether in your own person or in the person of any other, never simply as a means, but always at the same time as an end' ([1786] 1947, 96). The difference made for us by the existence of other persons would be a matter of spontaneous awareness on the part of beings living completely at the personal level, but is felt by such imperfectly personal creatures as ourselves as a matter of moral claim and obligation. To quote Kant again, 'for the *divine* will, and in general for a *holy* will, there are no imperatives . . . Imperatives are . . . only formulae for expressing the relation of objective laws of willing to the subjective imperfection of the will of this or that rational being – for example, of the human will' ([1786] 1947, 81).

However even within a basic recognition of those with whom we are dealing as fellow persons, on the same level of value as ourselves, we are still able to summon up endless strategies to evade an unwelcome moral claim from dawning upon us. Joseph Butler said that 'It is as easy to close the eyes of the mind as those of the body' ([1726] 1888, xxx). We can re-focus the situation until it becomes clear that the responsibility to act belongs to someone else, or that the impending disaster is the victim's own fault, or that the wrong action in which we are engaged is really a lesser evil . . . and so obscure or diminish the claim upon us. This human capacity for moral self-deception has been a rich theme for psychologically perceptive novelists. Jane Austen, for example, in *Sense and Sensibility* (chapter 2) enables us to listen to a conversation between Mr and Mrs John Dashwood shortly after his father has died leaving a widow with three daughters who are John Dashwood's half-sisters. His initial impulse, in view of his affluence and their poverty, is to give each of his half-sisters a thousand pounds out of the sum he has inherited. However his wife supplies a series of reasons for doing less and less, until at the end of the conversation he is convinced that he will be doing all that could reasonably be expected if he helps them with their removal expenses and then from time to time sends them presents of fish and game when in season. The human capacity for self-deception so accurately portrayed here ensures for us a much greater freedom in relation to the ethical than to the natural meaning of the situations in which from moment to moment we find ourselves. For whilst a physical state of affairs imposes its character upon us, a moral state of affairs has to await our free recognition.

The epistemological pattern that we have been noting is also to be found, I shall be suggesting, in religious awareness. For there is an aspect of our nature which responds to the transcendent as there is an aspect which responds to the personal and an aspect which responds to our physical environment. And the freedom of response which we saw to be at its minimum in relation to our physical environment, but which plays a much greater part within the world of persons, is even more crucial in our awareness of the Real.

2 AESTHETIC MEANING

Having thus stressed the practical dispositional aspect of our awareness of meaning it must be added that there are also purely contemplative moments of consciousness, known in aesthetic experience and also under the influence of certain drugs, in which practical consciousness is suspended and one simply enjoys colours, shapes, tastes, sensations, movements, spatial and temporal relationships for their own sake. It has been suggested by a number of writers on the philosophy of art that aesthetic appreciation is essentially of this kind: in the aesthetic mode of consciousness one can gaze at an object (which may range in extent from a flower to the natural world as a whole) without connecting it with any practical response. Aesthetic experience in its purest form is on this view the enjoyment of something as though it constituted a universe to which the experiencer is not causally linked. One ceases to be conscious of the object as something affecting one's own practical dispositional state. As Eliot Deutsch says, 'Withdrawing interest from those functional or practical aspects of things and concentrating attention entirely on what is presented, aesthetic consciousness notices especially those qualities which reveal the singularity and power of things' (Deutsch 1984, 138). That which is contemplated in this way therefore has no meaning, in the sense defined above; it stands outside our life as agents and may accordingly be experienced as having an eternal or timeless quality.

I am not in fact confident that this view does justice to all the many kinds of aesthetic experience, and I would not want to affirm its adequacy. It may well be that art operates on both sides of the border between that which has meaning, in the sense of making possible an appropriate practical response, and that which does not and is enjoyed in a purely contemplative mode. However it is not vital to my project to be able definitively to locate art on the map of meanings, and I am content to leave the topic, for our present purpose, in this indeterminate state.

10

Religious Meaning and Experience

The thing known is in the knower according to the mode of the knower.
(St Thomas Aquinas)[1]

1 RELIGIOUS EXPERIENCE

By an experience I mean a modification of the content of consciousness. Such modifications are 'intentional' or 'non-intentional' according as they do or do not constitute apparent awareness of something external to one's own consciousness. For example, the experience of 'seeing a tree in front of me' is (even if it should turn out to be hallucinatory) intentional, whilst the experiences of feeling unaccountably cheerful or feeling a generalised anxiety are non-intentional.

I have argued that all intentional experience is experiencing-as. It arises from the interpreting and misinterpreting of 'information' (in the cybernetic sense of that term) impacting us from an external source. Further, such interpreting always employs concepts.[2] We describe as religious experiences those in the formation of which distinctively religious concepts are employed. The denotation of the term is however less easily settled. For the notion of a religious concept reduplicates the family-resemblance character of the notion of religion itself. Thus the range of religious concepts, and hence of the experiences that they inform, is not fixed and there can sometimes be no definitive answer to the question whether this or that experience should be classed as religious rather than non-religious.

However, despite this absence of hard boundaries, there have been and there are innumerable uncontroversial instances of religious experience. From the point of view of the interpretation being developed in this book, this is a transformation of the 'information' generated at the interface between the Real and the

153

human psyche. I now want to suggest a distinction between two kinds of such experiences. In the one kind the 'information' is mediated through our material environment: things, events and processes in the world are experienced as having a religious character or meaning in virtue of which they manifest to us the presence of the transcendent. For example, a healing is experienced as a divine miracle.[3] In the other kind, to be discussed in section 5 and often distinguished as mystical, the information is received by a direct influence, analogous to telepathy between two human minds, and then transformed into visual or auditory terms. (The further very important type of mystical experience which consists in an awareness of union with God, or with the universe, or with the absolute, will be discussed separately in Chapter 16.5.)

The kind of religious experience that consists in experiencing the world and our life in it religiously can be individual or communal, can occur on many different levels of intensity and may take endlessly different forms. These include the sacramental experience of a symbol or idol, or even a bead in a rosary,[4] as mediating the transcendent; participation in a ritual or festival as an enactment of sacred meaning; the experience of particular events as divine acts, or as the outworking of karmic law; the reading of scriptures as the Word of God or as the *sanātana dharma*; the sense, whether sharply focused or as a general background awareness, of one's life as being lived in the presence of God; the consciousness of ordinary life as *avidyā* (illusion) and of all things as *śūnya* (empty) . . . These are for the most part particular episodes of religious experiencing-as. But more broadly and comprehensively religious experience is 'the whole experience of religious persons' (Temple 1934, 334) – or, more precisely, the whole experience of persons in so far as they are religious. And in the great post-axial traditions the way to salvation/liberation involves a gradual or sudden conversion to this new way of experiencing, an enlightenment in which both the experiencer and her world are transformed. This occurs in many different degrees. In the lives of ordinary believers the new mode of experiencing usually occurs only occasionally and is of only moderate intensity. In the saints and prophets, mahatmas and gurus, arahats and bodhisattvas, on the other hand, it can be so powerful and persistent as decisively to change their awareness both of themselves and of their world. Let us briefly remind ourselves of some familiar examples, drawing from the traditions of both Semitic and Indian origin.

The Hebrew scriptures are written predominantly from the point of view of the prophetic awareness of God as an active agent on the field of earthly history. Yahweh, the Lord, enters into a covenant with the patriarchs of Israel, later rescues the nation from slavery in Egypt, leads them through the great desert to a promised land, sends them kings and judges, rewards them with long life and many progeny when they seek faithfully to serve him, threatens them when they forget him and punishes them with defeat, humiliation and dispersal when they disobey him; and, beyond all this, promises them an eventual fulfilment of his love towards them in the future Day of the Lord. Throughout this long history, spanning a millennium, Yahweh is depicted as dealing actively with his people, whether directly or through agents – some of the latter being foreign rulers who are unaware that they are God's agents.

But this prophetic interpretation of history was not a theoretical construction of the scribes as they wrote and re-wrote the biblical canon. It must have originated in the experience of the prophets themselves as they participated in the events of their own time. As one example among many, Jeremiah was conscious of the downfall of the kingdom in the seventh century BCE as God's just disciplining of the erring Israelites. It seems clear that this diagnosis reflected the way in which he actually experienced the national situation as it was developing around him. A well-known commentary says of the time when the Chaldean army was investing Jerusalem, 'Behind the serried ranks of the Chaldean army [Jeremiah] beheld the form of Jahwe fighting for them and through them against His own people' (Skinner 1922, 261). And indeed the whole panorama of Hebrew history during the biblical period is recorded in terms of a powerful divine presence, purpose and activity. The scriptural pages resound and vibrate with the sense of God's presence, as a building might resound and vibrate from the tread of some mighty being walking through it. And the standpoint from which the writers were able thus to construe their history, as the dramatic story of God's interactions with his people, must have arisen out of the way in which the religiously inspired minds of the great prophets actually experienced and participated in the events that were unfolding around them.

But these vast historical dramas which the prophets experienced and the scribes recorded in distinctively religious terms are also capable of being externally understood and described as purely secular events. At each point the history lying behind the biblical narrative can be reconstructed with Yahweh figuring as no more than an obsessive idea in some human minds. From this point of view it was the expansions and contractions of great middle-eastern empires in response to a variety of economic and political pressures that had the incidental effect of pushing little Israel and Judah to the wall or leaving them to flourish in peace. There is no necessity to postulate supernatural agencies and forces; so that whilst this Hebraic strand of ancient history invites a religious interpretation, it nevertheless does not require it.

The same epistemological pattern continues in the early Christian experience reflected in the New Testament. When they left their ordinary lives as fishermen or whatever to follow an itinerant charismatic healer and teacher, Jesus' disciples were clearly experiencing him as a prophet, indeed as the last prophet, mediating God's challenging call to repentance and new life in preparation for the imminent coming of the Kingdom. In the accepted shorthand description of his impact, they experienced Jesus as the Christ. For although it is not clear whether the historical Jesus himself accepted the role of messiah, we know that by the time the Gospels were written this had become an established Christian category which was already beginning to expand from its original Hebraic meaning to the point, finally reached in the fourth century, at which 'Christ' had come to mean God the Son, the Second Person of a divine Trinity. This development has coloured subsequent Christian consciousness, Jesus now being worshipped as the cosmic Christ.

But at the moment we are more concerned with the New Testament story of his life, death, resurrection and ascension, reflecting as this does a distinctively religious mode of experiencing and participating in the events of his public ministry. That this constituted a particular response to an objectively ambiguous phenomenon is shown by the fact that there were others who, so far from experiencing Jesus as the Christ, perceived him as a powerful wonder-worker or a highly unorthodox rabbi or a potentially dangerous political leader. Thus the religious meaning of Jesus' life did not lie on the surface for all to see. Pascal has eloquently expressed, from a religious point of view, the hiddenness of God's manifestation in the founder of the Christian tradition:

It was not then right that He should appear in a manner

manifestly divine, and completely capable of convincing all men; but it was also not right that He should come in so hidden a manner that He could not be known by those who should sincerely seek Him. He has willed to make Himself quite recognisable by those; and thus, willing to appear openly to those who seek Him with all their heart . . . He so regulates the knowledge of Himself that He has given signs of Himself, visible to those who seek Him, and not to those who seek Him not. There is enough light for those who only desire to see, and enough obscurity for those who have a contrary disposition.

([1670] 1932, 118)

Thus the Christian response to Jesus was and is an uncompelled interpretation, experiencing an ambiguous figure in a distinctive way as mediating the transforming presence of God.

Let us now make a wide-angled turn from the Judeo-Christian to the Buddhist religious world. In the Mahayana development, particularly as represented by Zen, we have a very clear example of religious consciousness as a distinctive mode of experiencing-as. For the startling central insight of the Mahayana is that Nirvana and Samsara are identical. In the classic words of Nagarjuna, 'There is nothing whatever which differentiates *samsara* from *nirvana* . . . There is not the slightest bit of difference between these two' (Streng 1967, 216–17).[5] Experienced in one way the world-process is Samsara, the stream of life, death and rebirth, ever vulnerable to suffering; but experienced in a radically different way it is Nirvana! 'The essence of Zen Buddhism consists in acquiring a new viewpoint on life and things generally' says Suzuki (1956, 83).

The hinge by which we may turn from the world experienced as Samsara to the same world experienced as Nirvana is *satori* or enlightenment. D. T. Suzuki says,

Satori may be defined as an intuitive looking into the nature of things in contradistinction to the analytical or logical understanding of it. Practically, it means the unfolding of a new world hitherto unperceived in the confusion of a dualistically-trained mind. Or we may say that with satori our entire surroundings are viewed from quite an unexpected angle of perception. Whatever this is, the world for those who have gained a satori is no more the old world as it used to be; even with all its flowing streams and burning fires, it is never the same one again. Logically stated, all its opposites and contradictions are united and harmonized into a consistent organic whole. This is a mystery and a miracle, but according to the Zen masters such is being performed every day. Satori can thus be had only through our once personally experiencing it.   (1956, 84)

Elsewhere he says 'Religiously, it is a new birth; intellectually it is the acquiring of a new viewpoint' (Suzuki [1949] 1969, 95). For *satori* is a sudden conversion from one mode of experiencing to another, from the samsaric to the nirvanic mode; and this latter is, according to the Buddhist claim, Reality itself manifested within a purified human consciousness. Thus the epistemological pattern recurs of an ambiguous realm which, when experienced religiously, reveals new meaning as mediating or (in Zen) as directly manifesting the Real.

2 FAITH AS THE INTERPRETIVE ELEMENT IN RELIGIOUS EXPERIENCE

The term 'faith' has had its primary home within the Semitic traditions and particularly within Christianity. Here it has generally meant propositional belief that is unwarranted, or only partially warranted, by evidence. Such belief, which can be distinguished as propositional faith, was classically analysed by St Thomas Aquinas. According to Aquinas the propositions that are accepted by faith speak of divine mysteries beyond the scope of human knowledge. He distinguished faith (*fides*) from both opinion (*opinio*) and knowledge (*scientia*). Faith differs from opinion in that whilst the latter involves choice, the chosen belief is held only tentatively, 'accompanied by doubt and fear of the opposite side' (*S. T.*, II/II, Q. 1, art. 4), whereas faith is not, for Aquinas, a tentative opinion but an absolutely firm conviction. On the other hand faith is not theoretical knowledge (*scientia*). We have this when the intellect is compelled by its object to assent to the reality of that object. In contrast, the object of faith leaves us cognitively free in relation to it: 'the intellect assents to something, not through being sufficiently moved to this assent by its proper object, but through an act of choice, whereby it turns voluntarily to one side rather than to the other' (*S. T.*, II/II, Q. 1, art. 4).

Because faith thus involves choice and commitment it is meritorious and is accordingly classified as one of the virtues. The virtue of faith is not however the merely legal merit of assenting to the propositions that God has commanded us to believe. It is ultimately the inner virtue of the heart that opens itself to God. For whilst the immediate object of faith is a body of credal propositions, its ultimate object is God himself as the First Truth (*veritas prima*).[6] Finally Aquinas says that whilst some of the divinely revealed propositions are also accessible to human reason, those not thus accessible, but believable only by faith, refer to mysteries beyond the scope of human knowledge.[7]

For Aquinas, then, faith expresses the individual's innermost choice of openness to the divine presence; and he located this decision on the level of intellectual belief. I have suggested instead that this fundamental option occurs at the deeper level of the cognitive choice whereby we come to experience in either a religious or a non-religious way. For the world as humanly inhabited is perceived in distinctive ways by the religiously illumined mind. This can happen because our individual and communal modes of experience include a variable element, an uncompelled interpretive activity, which I am identifying as faith.[8] Each aspect of the Thomist description of faith (other than its propositional character itself) does however have an analogue in this analysis of faith as the interpretive element within religious experiencing-as. Where propositional faith is related to the divine mysteries, faith as an act of interpretation is a response to a mysterious ambiguity; and where propositional faith is voluntary, in so far as it falls short of *scientia* or objectively indubitable knowledge, faith as interpretation is likewise a cognitive decision in face of an intrinsically ambiguous universe. And again, the observation that propositional faith is subjectively firm belief corresponds to the powerfully convincing character of much religious experience, leaving no room for doubt.[9] However it appears to me that, whilst the Thomist analysis is structurally correct, propositional faith rests upon something else, namely a distinctively religious mode of experiencing the world and one's life within it. And I suggest that the interpretive activity on which this depends should be equated with faith in its most fundamental sense.

However, having appealed to the distinction between religious experience on the one hand and the believing of religious propositions on the other, I must repeat that there is a conceptual and thus implicitly or incipiently propositional element within experience itself. The idea of God, for example, does not enter into theistic experience as a purely neutral concept, but in the positive judgment – which comes to consciousness as a mode of experience – that in this situation or event or place or person God is present.

Faith as the interpretive response through which we are conscious of the Real comes fairly close to Wilfred Cantwell Smith's well-known account of faith. He uses the term to refer to the basic religious disposition. It is 'that human quality that has been expressed in, has been elicited, nurtured, and shaped by, the religious traditions of the world' (W. C. Smith 1979, 6). Faith is, he says,

> an orientation of the personality, to oneself, to one's neighbour, to the universe; a total response; a way of seeing whatever one sees and of handling whatever one handles; a capacity to live at a more than mundane level; to see, to feel, to act in terms of, a transcendent dimension.   (1979, 12)

If one were to understand religious experience somewhat narrowly, as consisting in special numinous moments, then faith as the free interpretive element within this would be only one aspect of what Wilfred Cantwell Smith calls faith. But if on the other hand one understands religious experience very broadly, as the whole experience of persons in as far as they are religious, then the element of free responsive choice within this would seem to lie at the heart of faith in his sense.

3 FAITH AS THE EXERCISE OF COGNITIVE FREEDOM

Religious faith then, as I propose to use the term, is that uncompelled subjective contribution to conscious experience which is responsible for its distinctively religious character. This is continuous with the subjective contribution to our ordinary awareness of our environment as having this or that kind of physical meaning, and of inter-personal situations as having this or that kind of ethical meaning. But we have the special word 'faith' for the operation of cognitive freedom at the religious level because its exercise is so much more evident here. We have seen (Chapter 8.2) that at the physical level the members of each species are compelled, on pain ultimately of death, to experience the world in the way that is standard for their niche in the biological system. If we did not, for example, perceive solid objects as solid and have a reasonably accurate awareness of relative heights and distances, we could not survive. Nature eliminates any who do not perceive in the way prescribed for them. At the physical level our cognitive freedom is accordingly at a minimum.

At the ethical level it is however considerably greater – particularly since the emergence of the autonomous individual, apparently beginning in the distant axial period. This greater cognitive freedom is correlated with the fact that ethical meaning presupposes and is thus of a (logically) higher order than natural meaning. The dispositional aspect of the former is superimposed upon the dispositional aspect of the latter so that when we function morally we are acting, but acting differently, as physical agents in the material world. In tacit acceptance of the element of freedom within ethical awareness moral philosophy has adopted cognitive terms – 'intuition', 'insight', 'judgment' – which border upon 'faith' in their acknowledgment of an uncompelled recognition. But whereas we can de-emphasise, re-conceive, minimise a moment of moral awareness, thereby deflecting a particular claim upon us whilst continuing in general to be ethically responsible human beings,[10] at the religious level we have a much more comprehensive capacity to shut out of our consciousness that which we are not ready to face. We are in fact able to exclude the entire religious dimension, experiencing only such forms of meaning as can enter through the filter of a naturalistic world-view.

This greater cognitive freedom at the religious level is correlated with the greater claim upon us of the aspect of reality in question. For the Real is the ultimate ground not only of the human life that has generated our moral categories but also of the religious invitation or claim or challenge to a radical self-transcendence. Whether this takes the form of a self-giving to God, or a renunciation of 'I', 'me' and 'mine', or an acceptance of the insubstantiality and emptiness of the ego, it is always profoundly threatening to our ordinary consciousness.[11] To give up one's personal projects, desires, hopes and ambitions, as also one's fears and aversions, in absolute surrender (*islam*) to God, or in a fading away of the ego point of view, or in acceptance of one's existence as but a fleeting moment within the interdependent flux of life, inevitably seems to most of us like plunging into darkness – even though there is the promise beyond it of peace with God 'whose service is perfect freedom', or of union with Brahman as the universal Consciousness dawns within us, or of the indescribable joy of the ego-free state of Nirvana.

4 RELIGION AS COGNITIVE FILTER

In the face of this threatening and promising, promising and threatening message of the religions we have a dual capacity to allow the Real to become present to us as the all-transforming reality or to shut it out of our consciousness. On the one hand, in so far as we are in our deepest dispositional nature open and responsive to the Real, we can receive an authentic awareness of it in one (or more) of its manifestations. I shall discuss later (Chapter 14.4) the relationship between the Real in itself and the divine *personae* and metaphysical *impersonae* in terms of which it is humanly known; but the point at the moment is that it is the interpretive element within religious experience that enables us to enter into an uncompelled, though always necessarily limited and mediated, awareness of the Real.

On the other hand this cognitive freedom in relation to the Real also has a negative function, namely to protect our finite freedom and autonomy. For to be a particular kind of creature is to be structured to cognise and participate in reality in a particular way; and for a creature to have imposed upon it a more extensive or intensive awareness than it is able to assimilate, compulsorily revealing to it a more complex or more value-laden environment than it can respond to, would be destructive. In T. S. Eliot's words, 'Humankind cannot bear very much reality' ('Burnt Norton'). This need to shut out much in order to live as the finite creatures that we are, not only limited but limited in the specifically human way, is evident above all in our consciousness of the Real. In archaic life – both before the axial age and down to our own time in cultures largely unaffected by it – few individuals have had the intellectual independence necessary to criticise, still fewer to reject, the world-view into which they were born. The group mind of the tribe seems to have so dominated its members as to leave them virtually no personal intellectual autonomy. In those traditional societies ideas and customs passed down from generation to generation in only very slowly changing forms and the tendency to interpret life religiously operated almost without hindrance. Myths emerged in the communal imagination, forming secure and unquestioned frameworks of meaning within which life was lived.

The kind of rational criticism that notices inconsistencies and contradictions, vaguenesses, failures to explain, seems to have begun in the axial period, particularly in ancient Greece, India and China, and has become greatly intensified and more widespread in the West with the rise of modern science and the enthronement of its canons of explanation and evidence and its ethos of uninhibited criticism. In this new cultural situation our human freedom in relation to the Real has come to be typically maintained in a new way, namely by a radical scepticism which rejects transcendence as such. This is expressed in the characteristic atheism, humanism, secularism and theoretical materialism of the modern period.

But in the archaic world the human mind was protected from an overwhelmingly direct presence of the Real by religion itself, functioning as a system for filtering out the infinite divine reality and reducing it to forms that could be coped with. Religion has thus constituted our resistance (in a sense analogous to the use of the word in electronics) to the Real. The effect of the different 'sacred canopies' has been to enable us to be touched by the Real, and yet only partially and selectively, in step with our own spiritual development, both communal and individual. Or, putting it the other way round, in terms of divine revelation, 'Brahma suits His language to the understanding of His hearer' (Kabir [15th century] 1977, 92).

Religious traditions, considered as 'filters' or 'resistances', function as totalities which include not only concepts and images of God or of the Absolute, with the modes of experience which they inform, but also systems of doctrine, ritual and myth, art forms, moral codes, lifestyles and patterns of social organisation. For religions have been basically communal responses to the Real, rooted in the life of societies and forming an essential element of human culture.

In the circular movement of the argument, in which each phase presupposes and is presupposed by each other, we have yet to come (in Part 5) to the question of the criteria by which to judge religious traditions. In a word, the central criterion will be soteriological, the bringing about of a transformation of human existence from self-centredness to Reality-centredness – a transformation which shows itself, within the conditions of this world, in compassion (*karuṇā*) or love (*agape*). Linking this criterion, yet to be established, to our pluralistic hypothesis we can say that human openness to the Real accounts for the immense ranges of good, and closedness to the Real for the perhaps equally great ranges of evil, within the history of religions.

It is tempting, looking back from what we regard as our privileged twentieth-century vantage point, to see this history in evolutionary terms as the progressive development of an authentic relationship to the Real, with a consequent increase of its good and decrease of its evil fruits in human life. Must not the axial age, for example, have constituted a 'great leap forward' in human religious awareness? Do not the world faiths provide a more favourable context for human transformation than the primal and archaic religions? The answer is not self-evident. Our pluralistic hypothesis is compatible with different interpretations of this long history. Rather than try to settle the matter here I shall therefore be content to note some of the complicating circumstances which make the question so difficult.

The axial age saw the emergence in each of the great centres of ancient civilisation of the autonomous human person. Men and women became for the first time and to varying degrees conscious of being unique individuals each with his or her own sins, hope of salvation, and final destiny. In this new situation a more individual relationship to the Real began to supersede the older communal awareness; and the post-axial traditions, which filled the psychic space opened by the new consciousness, are naturally better adapted than was pre-axial religion to foster and guide this individual quest. But it would be hazardous to assume that human life is more truly centred in the Real in the new individualistic phase than in its earlier communal phase. It could be that on the one hand the spontaneous self-transcendence of pre-literate and archaic people, seeing themselves as cells in a living social organism and subordinating their own interests to those of the community, and on the other hand a deliberate turning from self to the Real on the part of autonomous egos within the post-axial traditions, are not related as lower and higher but simply as the forms of ego-transcendence that are appropriate to different stages of human history. In each period, of course, some people have lived in more and others in less propitious religious circumstances; and indeed this fact stands as one of the great question marks over most of our theologies and religious philosophies. But the mystery is not alleviated by the assumption that those living in an earlier age were, in general, religiously underprivileged in comparison with ourselves today. At any rate the pluralistic hypothesis being developed in this book, whilst it does not rule out that possibility, by no means requires it. At this point we can be content to await more light – which the historians and phenomenologists of religions may or may not one day be able to provide.

5 MYSTICAL EXPERIENCE

The term 'mystical' is one of the most elastic in the language. However it is convenient for our present purpose to use it in a restricted sense to refer to those forms of religious experience that express the presence of the Real, not as manifested in our material environment, but as directly affecting the human psyche. These are experiences in which the 'information' being presented to consciousness has been received by some kind of extra-sensory awareness of our ultimate environment.[12] Such mystical experiences are themselves of two main kinds, which have been distinguished as unitive and communitive.[13] The former are experiences of oneness with God or with the absolute reality of Brahman or the eternal Buddha-nature; and because of their wider implications these will be discussed separately in Chapter 16.5. The latter are moments in which a divine being seems to encounter the mystic through visions, auditions and/or photisms; and it is with these that we are presently concerned. I shall try to show that they share a common epistemological character with the rest of the spectrum of religious experience, being joint products of the impact of a transcendent reality and of the mystic's own mind-set; but that they differ from the kind of religious experience discussed in the previous section in that this 'impact', instead of being mediated through the outer world of nature and history, is directly prehended at some deep level of the mystic's psyche and then expressed in forms supplied by his or her mind.

It is clear that phenomenologically – that is, as directly describable – different visions and auditions have different contents. As modifications of consciousness Isaiah's vision of Yahweh in the temple (Isaiah 6) was different from Lady Julian's seeing a crucifix flowing with blood (Julian 1978, 181) and from Sri Ramakrisha's vision of Kali (Isherwood 1965, ch. 6); and Samuel's experience of hearing the voice of Yahweh (I Samuel 3:11–14) was different from Muhammad's hearing Gabriel recite passages of what was to be the Qur'an (Qur'an 2:97). There are indeed certain features of visionary experiences that occur cross-culturally: the direct awareness of light and the relational awareness of height, depth and magnitude. These seem to have universal symbolic significance.[14] However even the experience, for example, of seeing a bright light can take on a tradition-specific character. Thus in many of the reports of persons resuscitated after having almost died the 'being of light' is experienced by Christians, but not by people of other traditions, as the dazzling presence of Christ.[15] This suggests that the same experience is being differently interpreted and described. But this only applies to these rather few common features. Much the greater part of the phenomenology of visions and auditions comes unmistakably from the experiencer's own scriptures and tradition. The different persons encountered, symbols deployed, words heard, are clearly related to characteristic features of the tradition within which the mystic functions. As has often been pointed out, it is invariably a Catholic Christian who sees a vision of the Blessed Virgin Mary and a Vaishnavite Hindu who sees a vision of Krishna, but not *vice versa*.[16] This fact strongly suggests that the distinctive ideas and images, the historical and mythological themes, and the range of expectation made available by the mystic's tradition have provided the material out of which the experience is constructed.[17]

Religious and naturalistic interpretations of such experiences are both feasible. As possible indicators of the nature of reality they can either be dismissed as the remarkable hallucinatory projections of religious eccentrics or accepted as manifestations of the Real within the peak experiences of exceptionally sensitive individuals. In accordance with the programme of this book I am concerned to explore the latter possibility in the case of some at least of these experiences. The pluralistic hypothesis to be presented in Chapter 14 suggests that humanity has always been conscious of the universal presence of the Real in terms of a range of concepts and modes of experience which vary from one tradition to another. This model can also illuminate mystical experience within the different traditions. It assumes the impact of the presence of the Real upon the mystic, this impact or presence generating information that is transformed into a conscious mode which the mystic and the mystic's community can assimilate. In the transformation of information into meaningful human experience the mystic's mind employs the same constructive capacities that operate in the creation of dreams. But whereas dreams are (normally) means whereby the complex and many-levelled psyche communicates internally with itself, mystical experiences – on a religious interpretation of them – embody information deriving from the transcendent source which I am referring to as the Real.

There is, I suggest, an analogy between mystical visions and the 'crisis apparitions' that were recorded so abundantly in the early period of psychical research before radio had been invented and when news could still take days or weeks to be transmitted. A typical case would be one in which, say, a man travelling in India is suddenly killed in an accident, and that night his wife in England sees an apparition of him that includes some element suggesting death: perhaps he looks still and death-like, or there is a coffin in the background, or he speaks of his own death. Then, several weeks later, a letter arrives informing the family of his death. What would seem to have happened in such a case is that the man's sudden crisis experience makes a telepathic impact upon the wife's unconscious mind, and the information thus received is then presented to her consciousness (often at night, when the mind is relatively disengaged from the world) in the form of an apparition. The apparition – whose content is derived from the percipient's memory and imagination – is hallucinatory in that there is no physical body present where she sees one; but the hallucination is nevertheless veridical, embodying true information.[18]

This complex cognitive transaction in which illusion is the vehicle of truth may well take place in mystical visions and auditions also. The specific material out of which the vision is composed – the figure of an angel, or Christ, or Krishna, or Kali, or of a throne, a heart, a cloud – is supplied by the imagination and memory of the mystic. But, according to our hypothesis, the information dramatised in this way originates at the interface between the Real and the human psyche, being generated by the impact of the one upon the other. Such information is accordingly relational, expressing the relevance or meaning of the transcendent reality to human life.

If however we were to identify mystics initially by the power and vividness of their special experiences we should find that they are a motley crew, including unbalanced and morally depraved as well as eminently sane and morally admirable men and women. Some of the inhabitants of psychiatric hospitals undergo powerful hallucinatory experiences, often of a terrifying nature. And various hallucinatory drugs can induce visions, intense experiences of unity with the environment or of mental illumination, or a sense of profound but ineffable meaning, as well as appalling nightmares of horror and of indescribable bleakness and despair. It is thus impossible to suppose that overwhelmingly vivid visual and auditory experiences, simply as such, necessarily embody information arising at the interface between the Real and the human psyche. They may instead embody information rising from the individual unconscious and expressing itself in terrifying or destructive ways.

Nor have any of the great religions failed to be acutely aware of this ambiguity. On the contrary they have emphasised the ever-present possibility of delusion.[19] Thus, for example, the Catholic tradition has developed its own criteria by which to distinguish visions sent by God from those sent by the devil. The more universal criterion is the moral and spiritual value of the fruit of the experience in the individual's life; and a subsidiary tradition-specific criterion has been faithfulness to the accepted teachings of the church.[19] Those mystics, in all traditions, who have become accepted and revered have been immensely impressive human beings whose words have illuminated, challenged and encouraged others and whose lives have revealed the Real by embodying an appropriate human response to one of the *personae* or *impersonae* in which it has been manifested within human experience. For true mystics are those who are startlingly more open to the Real than the generality of us.

When we study the reports of these outstanding sensitives we find that their experiences exhibit a common pattern, not in their visual and auditory contents but in the 'information' which they express. For mystical experiences occurring within the great theistic traditions have embodied one or another, or more than one, of a range of aspects of the relevance of the Real, theistically conceived, to human existence: the goodness, love and mercy of God; the absolute claim of God upon our lives; the availability of salvation and eternal life, and the cosmic optimism which flows from this.

We shall look later (in Chapter 16.5) at the mystical experience of unity with the absolute or with the universal totality. But as regards the forms of mysticism that we have looked at briefly in the present chapter the hypothesis that I am proposing is that the universal presence of the Real, in which 'we live and move and have our being', generates within certain exceptionally open and sensitive individuals an unconscious awareness of an aspect or aspects of its meaning for our human existence. In cybernetic terms this is 'information' about the significance of the Real for our lives. In order to be consciously received and responded to this information is transformed into inner or outer visions or voices, the psychological machinery which transforms the transcendent information into such experiences consisting of the mystic's own mind-set and creative imagination.

Notes

1. St Thomas Aquinas 1945, 1057 (*Summa Theologica*, II/II, Q. 1, art. 2).
2. I am thus in disagreement with those who distinguish, both for experience in general and for religious experience in particular, between 'propositional' or 'interpretive' and 'non-propositional' or 'non-interpretive' experiences (see, e.g., Carl-Reinhold Brakenhielm 1985, 18–21). I hold that all conscious experience is interpretive in the sense that it has specific meaning for us in virtue of the concepts which function in the process by which it is brought to consciousness. I am thus in agreement at this point with Steven Katz in his influential paper 'Language, Epistemology, and Mysticism' (Katz 1978).
3. This is, in my view, not an intensified metaphor (cf. William Reese 1978) but an actual mode of experience.
4. Wilfred Cantwell Smith speaks of 'a moment on one particular

afternoon when a given Muslim . . . is telling his beads and touches, let us say, the twenty-seventh bead and names to himself that particular divine attribute and his soul is suddenly or deeply, or just a whit more deeply than before, suffused with a realisation that mercy, or patience, or whatever it be, is indeed of cosmic import, or that man is in the hands of a just or awesome or powerful or eternal God' (W. C. Smith 1981, 167).

5. For a different interpretation from the commonly accepted one see David Kalupahana 1986, 366–70.

6. In II/II, Q. 1, art. 1, it is established that the object of faith is the *prima veritas*; and earlier, I, Q. 16, art. 5, it has been established that God is the *prima veritas*.

7. 'To faith these things belong essentially, the sight of which we shall enjoy in eternal life', *Summa Theologica*, II/II, Q. 1, art. 8. I have discussed the Thomist account of faith more fully in Hick [1967] 1987a, ch. 1.

8. I do not argue for 'the coextensiveness of faith and perception', as supposed by James Heaney (1980), but for a continuity between faith as the interpretive element within religious experience and the interpretive element within other forms of experience.

9. How can religious experience be both powerfully convincing, leaving no room for doubt, and also an exercise of cognitive freedom in response to ambiguity? The answer is that these phrases refer to different stages. Behind all conscious experience there lies a phase of unconscious interpretive activity and it is here that, in the case of religious experience, the free response to ambiguity occurs. In the conscious experience the ambiguity has been resolved in a distinctively religious (or in the contrary case, in a distinctively naturalistic) way, and the resulting experience itself may have any degree of intensity and of compelling quality.

10. See Chapter 9.1.

11. On the possibility of unconscious resistance to becoming aware of the Real see Reinhold Niebuhr 1941, chs 7–9, and Donald Evans 1963, 197–204, and 1980, ch. 6.

12. Denis Edwardes (1984, ch. 9) treats Christian mystical experience in essentially this way, though instead of ESP he speaks of 'pre-conceptual experience'.

13. The term 'unitive' is also used loosely in the literature to refer to an intimate communion with God which does not involve an ontological unity.

14. Cf. Edwyn Bevan 1938.

15. Cf. Raymond Moody 1975, 46.

16. On this phenomenon see Runzo 1977.

17. There has been considerable discussion in recent writings on philosophy of religion about whether, as W. T. Stace, Ninian Smart and others have argued, 'phenomenologically, mysticism is everywhere the same' (Smart 1965, 87) but is differently interpreted within the different religions, or whether, as Steven Katz and others have argued, 'the experience itself as well as the form in which it is

reported is shaped by concepts which the mystic brings to, and which shape, his experience' (Katz 1978, 26). In this debate I side with Katz, though the phenomenological differences mentioned above are not directed against the Stace/Smart thesis, in as much as these two writers have been referring to the unitive mystical experience rather than to visions, etc. I shall come to the phenomenological differences within unitive mysticism in Chapter 16.5.

18. See Edmund Gurney 1886; F. W. H. Myers [1903] 1943; G. N. M. Tyrell 1953. On the relevance more generally of parapsychology to the study of mysticism see Emilio Servadio 1986.

19. See St Teresa of Avila [1565] 1960, ch. 25; Walter Hilton [1494] 1948, bk I, ch. 11; St John of the Cross [16th century] 1958, bk II, chs 27–9 – for example, 'And I am appalled at what happens in these days – namely, when some soul with the very smallest experience of meditation, if it be conscious of certain locutions of this kind in some state of recollection, at once christens them all as coming from God, and assumes that this is the case, saying: "God said to me . . ."; "God answered me . . ."; whereas it is not so at all, but, as we have said, it is for the most part they who are saying these things to themselves' (330–1). See further in Chapter 13.5.

11

Religion and Reality

Religion constitutes our varied human reponse to transcendent Reality.

1 RELIGIOUS REALISM AND NON-REALISM

Religious experience, then, is structured by religious beliefs, and religious beliefs are implicit within religious experience. We next have to ask whether this complex of experience and belief, taking as it does different shapes within the different traditions, is to be regarded simply as a human creation or as our response to a transcendent reality – though a response whose particular forms always involve the creative activity of the human imagination.

There is here – as at so many points in the present enquiry – a problem of terminology. None of the available descriptive labels for these two possibilities is entirely adequate without explanatory gloss. I propose to use, as the least unsatisfactory pair of terms, 'realist' and 'non-realist' and their cognates. (I shall also use 'anti-realist' when referring to the polemic against realism.) I intend 'realism' in a sense derived from its use in modern philosophy – in distinction from its use in the medieval debates, in which realism was opposed to nominalism. In modern epistemology realism is the view that material objects exist outside us and independently of what we take to be our perceptions of them. And by analogy religious realism is the view that the objects of religious belief exist independently of what we take to be our human experience of them. For each religious tradition refers to something (using that word in its most general sense) that stands transcendingly above or undergirdingly beneath and giving meaning or value to our existence. This is referred to in a wide range of ways as God, or the divine, or the absolute, or the Tao, or the *dharmakāya*, or the Spirit . . . These and other comparable concepts have in common that they point to something alleged to be more or other than our ordinary human existence, something

172

that is thus, in relation to us, transcendent. And what I am calling the realist option understands such language in a basically realist way as referring to an object of discourse that is 'there' to be referred to.

Thus in the case of Judeo-Christian-Islamic talk about God the realist assumption is that God exists as an unlimited personal being, so that in addition to all the millions of embodied human consciousnesses there is at least one further consciousness which is not embodied and which is the divine consciousness. Or in the case of Hindu language about the trans-personal Brahman the assumption is that in addition to (though ultimately as the true nature of) the millions of individual human consciousnesses there is the infinite and eternal consciousness of Brahman. In this latter case the otherness of the transcendent reality is only a provisional otherness: for when the streams of consciousness which each of us calls 'I' attain to enlightenment they will thereby become aware of their true identity as the universal *ātman* which is ultimately one with Brahman. This advaitic conception reminds us that religious realism does not necessarily involve the kind of divine-human duality that we find in the theistic schemes. Within both the theistic and the non-theistic traditions it is equally possible to construe the language in either a realist or a non-realist way.

Religious realism is not of course to be equated with a straightforwardly literal understanding of religious discourse. This point has to be made because some contemporary anti-realist argumentation[1] suggests that we have to choose between, on the one hand, a simplistically literal use of the language and, on the other, its complete subjectivisation and evacuation of all factual content. From the point of view being developed in this book such a dilemma is misleading. For we have already recognised the unavoidable element of interpretation within all conscious experience. Our awareness of the world is necessarily an awareness of it as it impinges upon us and becomes meaningfully organised in our consciousness. All awareness, whether of our more immediate or of our more ultimate environment, is accordingly formed in terms of conceptual systems embodied in the language of particular societies and traditions. We can therefore only experience the Real as its presence affects our distinctively human modes of consciousness, varying as these do in their apperceptive resources and habits from culture to culture and from individual to individual. And so I shall not be advocating anything analogous to 'naive realism' in relation to sense perception, according to which the world as it is in itself is just as we perceive it to be. This will of course involve a departure from the ordinary and natural presumption of 'simple believers' within each tradition, who have generally thought in a way analogous to naive realism, construing their scriptures and traditional teachings literally in terms of a God who is 'up there' or 'out there' in space, angels with wings and devils with malevolent faces, a heaven 'above the bright blue sky' and a hell beneath of fires and torment; or of a Pure Land in the west, rebirth of the present self in human or animal form . . .

In contrast to this the kind of religious realism that I shall advocate takes full account of the subjective contribution to all awareness. It is thus analogous to the epistemological 'critical realism' which emerged in the first half of the present century, and particularly to the type developed by R. W. Sellars, Arthur Lovejoy, A. K. Rogers and J. B. Pratt (as distinguished from the somewhat different type developed by George Santayana, Durant Drake and C. A. Strong).[2] Critical differed from naive realism mainly in taking account of the conceptual and interpretive element within sense perception. It accordingly acknowledged that the sensory data of which we are directly aware (or which we 'intuit') are private to the perceiving consciousness, but added that it is by means of these private contents of consciousness that we are able to live in relation to a physical world transcending our own minds. Thus sense perception is a complexly mediated awareness of the physical world. Some quotations from Sellars will serve to bring out this aspect of his position:

> Perceiving involves more than sensing. . . . There is belief, construction and interpretation, all this leading to what is taken to be the awareness of things . . . [We need] to distinguish between the intuition of the sensory appearance, which alone is given, and the denotative selection of a thing-object which is believed in and characterized . . . Naive realism is right in its contention that, from the first in sense-perception, we regard ourselves as perceiving public objects. It is wrong in that it does not fully recognize that such perception is guided and mediated by sensory data which are private and given . . . The critical realist thinks himself truer to sense-perception to assert that sensory-data are the direct objects of intuition and that thing-

objects are the intentional objects of cognition . . . In short, all sorts of facts about the thing perceived . . . influence our perceptual experience . . . Attitudes, expectations, memories, accepted facts, all operate interpretatively to make us regard ourselves as somehow aware of public, independent things . . . There is, if you will, stimulus and complex interpretative response . . .   (1938–9, 474–7)

In the form of critical realism that I am advocating in the epistemology of religion the element of interpretation plays an even larger part than it does in sense perception – thereby preserving our cognitive freedom in relation to the much greater and more demanding value of the reality in question. But whilst fully recognising this human contribution, critical realism holds that the realm of religious experience and belief is not *in toto* human projection and illusion but constitutes a range of cognitive responses, varying from culture to culture, to the presence of a transcendent reality or realities. It would be possible to call this position 'transcendentalism' or 'super- or supra-naturalism'. But its character is, I think, better brought out by the established epistemological term 'realism', which I accordingly propose to use.

I want to contrast with this a range of non-realist and anti-realist theories which deny that religious language should be interpreted realistically and which offer their own alternative ways of construing it.[3] One could also categorise these by such terms as 'naturalism' and 'humanism'. But these have different emotional colourings for different people and it seems better to focus on the central philosophical issue by referring to them as non-realist positions. Needless to say 'non-realist' here does not mean unrealistic in the sense of failing to recognise the realities of the situation. The question at issue is precisely which option is realistic and which unrealistic in that sense.

2 THE REALIST INTENTION OF TRADITIONAL RELIGION

In comparing the realist and non-realist construals of religious language it is desirable to distinguish several issues. The first is the historical question as to which interpretation corresponds to the intention of religious language-users within the great traditions.

The full range of religious utterance has always included a variety of non-cognitive uses of language: exclamations, commands and exhortations, performatives and so on. But it seems almost beyond dispute that such core religious statements as that 'God loves human beings', 'The Qur'an is the Word of God', 'Atman is Brahman', 'Samsara and Nirvana are one' have normally been intended cognitively. To say that such statements have been so intended is not of course to say that all their terms function as in their use in ordinary secular discourse: the love of God may well be analogous rather than identical in nature to human love; the Word of God is not literally a word; and so on. However, the realist–non-realist issue is distinct from the question of literal or metaphorical, univocal or analogical usage. For language can be employed in all these different modes to say something (whether true or false) about 'what there is' and 'how things are' in the universe beyond our own minds. Myths also (at any rate as I shall be using the term in this book) are capable of being in varying degrees true or false according as they serve to relate us appropriately or inappropriately to the Real (see Chapter 19.2–4)

Now although we cannot look into the minds of the seminal religious figures of the past, or of the body of believers from century to century within the great traditions, it nevertheless seems to me transparently evident that they have normally understood their own and one another's core language in a realist way. I shall restrict the discussion for the moment to theistic religion, in relation to which the modern debate has taken place, and then move later to the non-theistic traditions. That God-talk has normally been construed cognitively is clear from the ways in which it has connected with the speakers' emotions and modes of behaviour. If people begin to think and act differently when told, for example, 'There is a rabid dog in the room', we properly infer that they understand the statement in a realist manner. And when in response to the language of their scriptures, liturgies and creeds theistic believers address God in prayer; look about to see if their prayers are being answered; receive calamities as God's punishment and well-being as an expression of divine favour; are in fear of hell and in hope of heaven; feel guilty, forgiven, thankful in relation to God; or even, as in ancient days, sacrifice human lives to their gods, we properly attribute to them a realist interpretation of the realm of language in which they are participating.

A non-realist interpretation is, in contrast, radically revisionary. Some contemporary religious anti-realists are inclined to deny this, seeking to present their own analysis as an account of the normative use of religious language and to marginalise its realist use as a superstitious aberration. Others however are more historically self-aware. Cupitt, for example, is conscious that he is recommending a radically different use of Christian language for the new age in which the traditional realist or objectivist use has (as he thinks) been rendered implausible by our modern science-oriented culture.[4] But despite the failure of some to acknowledge this it seems to me abundantly clear that the core of religious language has normally been understood and is today normally understood by believers and disbelievers alike as basically cognitive.

3 LINGUISTIC ANALYSIS AND RELIGIOUS REALISM

The second question is whether this may not nevertheless always have been a logical mistake. Are religious statements perhaps so formed as to be incapable of being either true or false? This is the challenging question that was posed to western theology in the period after the second world war. In the 1920s and 1930s the logical positivists had tried and failed to formulate a rigorous verification criterion of meaning.[5] But nevertheless the basic insight which inspired them continues to be valid and to be relevant to the philosophy of religion.[6] This insight acknowledges the empiricist principle that to exist is to make a difference. For X to exist is for the universe to be in an X-inclusive rather than an X-exclusive state. And verifiability, around which the logical positivists' quest revolved, consists in the experiential accessibility of the difference made by X's existence. To observe the feature of the universe affirmed by 'X exists' is to verify that X exists, and to observe a feature of the universe which is incompatible with X's existence is to falsify 'X exists'.

This concept of direct all-or-nothing verification is however a limiting case, realised only under certain special conditions. It applies to propositions about finite entities with a particular spatial location (such as 'There is a clock on the mantlepiece in that room'). In such cases verification can consist in a single simple observation or close cluster of observations. But many propositions are, if true, capable only of some degree of indirect verification, thus generating the notion of confirmation in distinction from that of simple and direct verification. For example, statements about a person's moral character, such as that X is an honest person, and large-scale scientific theories, such as the theory of evolution or of the expanding universe, are not open to direct verification by a single observation but are nevertheless capable of progressive confirmation by an accumulation of evidential data. However the two concepts of direct and indirect verification, specifying respectively verification by unique observation and by cumulative confirmation, both point to the same ideal of the exclusion of rational doubt. Of course, given any non-tautological statement, however fully verified or confirmed, it remains logically possible that it be false and psychologically possible for it to be doubted. But when all grounds for rational doubt have been excluded, whether by direct observation or by cumulative confirmation, verification – in the sense in which this is possible for human beings – has been achieved.

It seems reasonable to apply this principle to God-talk by asking what observable difference it makes whether God exists. What actual or possible state(s) of affairs would on the one hand verify or confirm, or on the other, falsify or disconfirm the assertion that God is real? The answer must be in terms of indirect verification, or confirmation, rather than direct all-or-nothing verification – and likewise of indirect rather than direct falsification. For God is conceived in Judeo-Christian-Islamic monotheism as infinite, and an infinite reality cannot be observed or experienced in its infinite nature by a finite observer. It is possible to experience finite power, goodness, love, wisdom; but impossible in principle to experience infinite qualities as such.[7]

The experiential confirmation of God's existence will not, then, consist in a direct observation of God but in experiencing features of the universe, as it changes through time, which trace the difference that the existence of God makes. These constitute the fulfilment of the divine purpose for the creation. For according to the monotheistic traditions time is linear, leading from a divinely initiated beginning to a divinely intended end. The human pilgrimage will lead eventually to – and at this point there is a range of overlapping conceptions – the Kingdom of God, heaven and hell, eternal life, the world to come, paradise, a new heaven and a new earth. Generally a double destiny, of contrasting happiness and misery, has been assumed. However since the two possible end-states could each in their different ways confirm the theistic character of the universe I shall, for the sake of simplicity, restrict the discussion to the more positive possibility.[8]

Broadly understood, the idea of heaven is the idea of perfected human beings endlessly experiencing beyond this life the infinite depths of God's creative love. Their condition may well from our present point of view consist in such a completely altered state of consciousness as to be beyond the scope of our present imagining. But whatever its form it will – according to the theistic traditions – be a situation in which the ambiguities of our present existence have been left behind and in which the divinely ruled character of our environment is manifest to all. The awareness of existing in God's unseen presence, currently inhibited both by the ambiguity of our environment and by our own blinding self-concern, will be full and continuous, limited only by our own finitude. Whereas in this life the sense of God's presence occurs in tension with experiences of pain and suffering, of injustice and the triumph of evil, which continually challenge its authenticity, in the eschatological state there will be no such tension. Our God-consciousness will be unimpeded and free from any seeds of doubt.

In such a situation it must still of course remain a logical possibility that one's continuous sense of the divine presence, and of joyful interaction with God, is delusory. For in *any* situation, earthly or heavenly, however unambiguous its character, it remains theoretically possible that we are being deluded. However if we are considering the case of one who has accepted (or indeed of one who has rejected) the theistic picture of the universe as a creative process leading to a limitlessly good end-state in conscious communion with God, I suggest that to participate knowingly in that fulfilment would confirm the reality of God beyond the possibility of rational doubt. It is true that the infinite divine attributes, exceeding the personal grace and creative power encountered within our finite experience, could still only be humanly knowable, in a heavenly state as now, either by divine revelation or by philosophical reasoning. But that the theistic as opposed to the atheistic understanding of the universe has turned out to be true would be overwhelmingly evident, and as much so to the erstwhile atheist as to the theist. The prediction that the universe is leading to a limitlessly good end-state in communion with God would have been fulfilled.

It is worth emphasising at this point that such an end-state might take almost any number of different forms, so that its actual character could well be unexpected and could indeed prove to be entirely beyond the range of our present earthly imaginations. A very literal-minded Christian, following the lead of popular hymns, might perhaps expect to find a choir of saints in shining robes singing and casting down their golden crowns before the throne of God. However if what occurs is quite other than this but nevertheless in some unforeseen way fulfils the basic expectation of participation in the completion of a loving divine purpose of universal scope, that initial prediction, even though falsified in all of its details, will nevertheless have been confirmed in its main substance. And any acceptable theory of the eschatological verification of theism must make this distinction between the basic notion of an 'unlimitedly good end-state in communion with God' and the various concrete pictures of such a state produced by our human traditions.

4 REALISM AND HINDU LANGUAGE

Let us now direct the verification question to the non-theistic traditions. Here the shape of the problem changes. For theism generally assumes continued personal identity linking our present existence with the future heavenly state; so that some or all human beings may one day discover that the universe is basically as theism has depicted it. But according to advaita Vedanta – and according also in a different way, as we shall see, to Buddhism – the 'limitlessly better possibility' is attained precisely by transcending individual ego existence. Thus the self which now contemplates the advaitic conception of the universe will not, if that picture is correct, be present as a continuing separate consciousness in the final state to confirm its accuracy. For what is asserted, and is accordingly a candidate for experiential confirmation, is the reality of Brahman and the ultimate identity of each individual consciousness with the universal *ātman* which is ultimately Brahman. This teaching presents a cosmic picture that includes both our present existence and a final future state which supersedes it. However the nature of that postulated future state, and of our participation in it, are very different from that anticipated by theists.

According to advaita Vedanta our present existence as separate selves is a systematic delusion in which the temporary self-concerned ego obscures our deeper and eternal nature as the universal Atman/Brahman. When the separating ego-boundaries are transcended in *mokṣa*, liberation, we shall know ourselves as the universal Consciousness. Freedom from the powerful illusion of egohood can indeed occur in the present life if this is the culminating member of an immense series through which it has been gradually approached. There then occurs the *jīvanmukta* state, embodied release or living liberation. 'In this jivanmukta stage, being freed from all impure afflictions and karmas, the consciousness shines in its infinity' (Dasgupta [1924] 1973, 118). How does the jivanmukti know that he or she has attained to this ultimate state? Shankara asks:

> How are you to know for certain that you are liberated from the bondage of ignorance and have realized the Atman, which is absolute existence, pure consciousness and abiding bliss? The words of the scriptures, your own power of reasoning, and the teaching of your master should all help to convince you – but the only absolute proof is direct and immediate experience, within your own soul.   (Shankara [7th–8th century] 1978, 112)

Thus far, then, the advaitist can justifiably point to the fulfilment of the prediction that if one perseveres long and single-mindedly enough on one of the paths of liberation – the ways of knowledge, of devotion, or of works – one will eventually attain to the illumined state of consciousness. That the conditions which have to be met in order to experience this end-state are extremely arduous does not affect the logical relationship of prediction and fulfilment.

But advaita Vedanta asserts more than that a rare state of consciousness is attainable in this life by a fortunate few. It also claims that the structure of the universe in virtue of which this is possible is such as to make *mokṣa* eventually available to us all. For it teaches that we are all finite centres of consciousness whose present separate existence consists in our temporary unawareness of our true nature. It affirms that beyond each completed series of embodiments individual consciousness will be subsumed into the universal Consciousness which, in potentiality, it has always been. If this occurs it will constitute that teaching's being true, in the sense of corresponding with what actually happens. However the standard western concept of verification cannot accommodate this case without a certain amount of gentle stretching – which can happen in two stages.

The first stage occurs when we note that the model according to which someone propounds a theory, including within it a predictive element, and then observes the fulfilment of the prediction, is an ideally simple case. Scientific research readily accepts that it may be someone other than the original theorist who observes the fulfilment of the prediction. The second stage is prompted by the realisation, expressed in a number of recent western philosophical discussions of personal identity, that we need not restrict the range of possibilities to the simple continuation of psychic or psycho-physical entities. The deconstruction of this model of personal identity began with questions about the conceptuality that would be required if human beings were, like the amoeba, to divide.[9] Suppose, as a further possibility, that they were capable of fusion, two people becoming one. Derek Parfit sketches some aspects of this possibility:

> Any two people who fuse together would have different characteristics, different desires, and different intentions. How could these be combined?
>
> The answers might be these. Some of these features will be compatible. These would coexist in the one resulting person. Some will be incompatible. These, if of equal strength, would cancel out, and, if of different strengths, the stronger would become weaker. These effects might be as predictable as the laws governing dominant and recessive genes.
>
> (Parfit 1984, 298)

Let us develop this picture further in the direction suggested by advaita Vedanta. Let us suppose that when individuals reach a certain level of spiritual development (*mokṣa*) they fuse mentally with all others who have attained that same level; and that eventually *all* fuse in this way. There then exists a universal consciousness which is the successor of each of the individual streams of consciousness. Advaita Vedanta adds that the separate consciousnesses were merely fleeting swirls of cloudy delusion obscuring the perfect clarity of the universal consciousness, Brahman. If, then, in the eschaton all consciousnesses have united into a single consciousness, and if this was predicted in a theory propounded by some of the individual consciousnesses before they united, it would seem that the unitary consciousness may be said to have verified that theory in its own experience. The eternal Self will know (and indeed knows now) that It is the one ultimate Reality underlying the illusorily finite egos. And if the advaitic doctrine is true this would seem to be the kind of experiential verification that is appropriate to its being true.

5 REALISM AND BUDDHIST LANGUAGE

For Buddhism the question of verifiability is even more elusive. Whereas according to advaita Vedanta our present consciousness is the eternal consciousness of Atman/Brahman in concealed form, according to the Buddhist *anattā* (Sanscrit *anātman*) doctrine it is merely a momentary phase in an ever-moving wave which will in due course exhaust its karmic energy, leaving only the deep untroubled ocean of Nirvana. Since the self is nothing but this temporary wave of consciousness, existing one moment and gone the next, how could it be said ever to participate in the confirmation of this Buddhist conception? If our consciousness is simply a fleeting moment within the universal process of *pratītya samutpāda*, the beginningless and endless movement of interdependent co-origination, how can it know that this is what it is?

We need at this point to distinguish between questions concerning the present 'false' self, seeking *nirvāṇa*, and questions concerning that, if anything, which lies beyond the moment of liberation or enlightenment and, yet again, beyond the earthly embodiment of the enlightened one. So far as the status of the present empirical self is concerned the *anattā* doctrine is in essential agreement with the advaitic conception. The present 'I' or ego, which habitually perceives the world as centred on itself, whether supportively or threateningly, is illusory; and the world as so perceived is itself ultimately illusory. Both are of course real in that this self-centred consciousness of the world actually occurs; and yet both are illusions in comparison with the reality experienced in the non-ego-centred state of *nirvāṇa*. It is only from that new standpoint, transcending ordinary awareness, that the delusory nature of ordinary consciousness is revealed.

In the Pali scriptures the state of enlightenment, in which self-concern – the root of all sorrow, anxiety and suffering – has been transcended, is one of tranquil joy (*Dīgha Nikāya*, I:196 – Davids and Davids 1923, 261). And in the Mahayana development, culminating in Zen, with its central insight of the identity of Nirvana and Samsara, enlightenment is essentially a rejoicing in the world as it is, undistorted by the false perspective of the perceiver's ego. This experience of the world, rediscovered in its pure 'suchness', is authoritative for the one who has it. Thus Suzuki says:

> By this I mean that the knowledge realized in satori is final, that no amount of logical argument can refute it. Being direct and personal it is sufficient unto itself. All that logic can do here is to explain it, to interpret it in connection with other kinds of knowledge with which our minds are filled. Satori is thus a form of perception, an inner perception, which takes place in the most interior part of consciousness. Hence the sense of authoritativeness, which means finality.   (1956, 104)

Does Buddhist teaching, however, say more than that a very special and wonderful state of consciousness is possible to those few who seek it with sufficient persistence, this nirvanic state ending in each case at their death? Given that few seem to have the necessary spiritual and intellectual endowments and the practical possibility of devoting themselves wholeheartedly to the quest, and that the requisite spiritual guidance of an *arhat* or bodhisattva or Zen master can be available to fewer still, such a form of Buddhism could be relevant only to a very small proportion of human beings. And indeed the full *satori* experience is in fact probably attained by no more than a few thousand in each generation, and the arhatship of the Theravada tradition probably by even fewer. (There are at any one time only at most a few hundred authentic Zen masters; and in Theravadin Sri Lanka it is believed that at any given time there is at least one living *arhat* concealed somewhere within the community.)

Buddhism, interpreted in this way, would thus be good news for an elite few but, by contrast, bad news for the generality of the human race. There are some – particularly within the varied western appropriation of Zen – who by implication, though often without full consciousness of the implication, understand

Buddhism in this way. But clearly this cannot be the original or the historically normative understanding which has made Buddhism one of the great world religions. In the course of twenty-five centuries Buddhism has imparted a positive meaning and purpose in life to hundreds of millions of people. They have been grasped by a picture of reality in which there is hope not only for a fortunate few but ultimately for all, including themselves. This picture involves the characteristically eastern conception of the universe as enormously greater and more complex than western religious thought, until corrected by modern science, has usually imagined; and a time-scale of the salvific process which is enormously greater than a single human lifespan.

The fact that this vast picture has today lost its hold on the imagination of a number of westernised Buddhists and some modern Zen practitioners should not blind us to its dominant place within the long Buddhist tradition as a whole. According to this picture, which is common also to Hinduism, one's present life is only a moment in an immensely long series of such lives, leading finally to the presently unimaginable good of Nirvana or Moksha. One may still be a very long way from the goal, with many more lives to be lived before it is attained. But nevertheless one is participating in a universal process whose structure offers a limitlessly good fulfilment, beyond anything that the unilluminated mind can envisage.

That Buddhism rests upon a vision of reality which constitutes good news for suffering human beings as such, and not only for an elite few, is classically evident in the story of the Buddha's enlightenment. We have of course to remember that our knowledge of the historical Buddha's life and teachings comes to us through a very long developing and proliferating tradition, each stage and branch of which was inclined to attribute its own special insights to the founder. It may be that the person and teachings of the exalted Buddha of the later tradition stand in much the same ambiguous relationship to the historical Gautama as does the glorified Christ to the person and teachings of the historical Jesus. This is a question which I neither need nor am competent to settle. But in the Pali scriptures, which are the earliest extant Buddhist writings, we read that the Buddha, in the night of his enlightenment under the Bodhi tree, saw into the entire workings of the universe as a limitless karmic system and experienced a liberation from it in which he attained to the 'further shore' of Nirvana (*Dīgha Nikāya*, II:36 – Davids and Davids 1938, 29–30).[10] (In later Buddhist teaching this tradition developed into the doctrine of the Buddha's omniscience.[11]) He saw that human existence is in a worse predicament than most people realise, since even its best moments are still part of the universal interdependent system of life which is pervaded by *dukkha*; but also that the human predicament is limitlessly better than most people realise, since liberation is possible into the serene joy of Buddhahood. Perceiving that this total picture, the *dharma*, constitutes good news for all humankind the Buddha felt an obligation to make it known. He surveyed the world with a Buddha's eye, and after internal debate and in compassion for struggling humanity he set forth on the teaching journeys – occupying most of the remaining forty-five or so years of his life – without which there would have been no Buddhist movement.

The Buddha's self-giving to his fellow human beings was later reflected in the Mahayana ideal of the bodhisattva, the enlightened being who renounces final Nirvana until all human life has been brought to the same point. This bodhisattva concept clearly presupposes that the *dharma* is good news for all. For it discloses a reality, beyond *saṃsāra*, which offers us a limitlessly better possibility and which is such as to express itself in those who have become fully attuned to it as a limitless compassion for others. The picture of these shining beings, the bodhisattvas, invisibly surrounding us and ever seeking our welfare symbolises for Buddhists the ultimate goodness of the mysterious universe in which we find ourselves. This sense of the goodness, indeed grace, of reality pervades the Mahayana. Here the cosmic optimism of the religious outlook comes to rest in what J. B. Noss describes as 'a sort of Love-behind-things that produces Buddhas – a Buddha-essence at the heart of the universe' (Noss 1956, 206).

This is perhaps most explicitly expressed in Buddhism's Pure Land or Jodo development. Amitabha (known in Chinese as Omito and in Japanese and Korean as Amida) is one of the heavenly Buddhas who devote themselves in their infinite compassion to the saving of humankind. Amida Buddha has created a 'field' of spiritual force within which men and women can quickly come to enlightenment and so to the bliss of Nirvana. And such is the compassionate grace of Amida that simply by calling upon his name in faith we may receive his gift of rebirth within this spiritual force-field, Sukhavati, the Western Paradise or Pure Land.

Thus the Buddhist spectrum covers both sides of the boundary between realist and non-realist religious self-understandings. In its realist development, comprising the major streams of both the Mahayana and the Theravada, it arises from an insight into the nature of reality, discerning at its heart the eternal Dharmakaya, or Buddha nature, which can be unitively known by a transformed consciousness. That eternal reality cannot however be described, but only experienced, and this only at the end of a long and arduous process of de-egoisation. It is spoken of as *nirvāṇa*, and also as *śūnyatā*, Emptiness – not in the sense of being nothing at all but in the sense that no human conceptuality can grasp it. The religious significance of the Nirvana/Sunyata/Dharmakaya cluster of concepts is soteriological; and the liberation which it makes possible presupposes a structure of reality, knowledge of which constitutes good news for all human beings. I shall be looking more closely at the Buddhist conception of reality later (in Chapter 16.3–4). At this point it is sufficient to note that in its major forms Buddhism uses language in a realist way (though always with a lively sense of the inadequacy of all language) to refer to the ultimate source and ground of enlightenment.

On the other side of the realist–non-realist boundary there are those who see Buddhism simply as a way of meditation which can produce inner peace, stability and detachment. It need have no metaphysical implications or presuppositions and can (like many other forms of meditation) be practised independently of any religious commitment. The trappings of Japanese *zazen* – the meditation hall, the Zen roshi, the discipline, the gongs and drums and chants – can help us to meditate successfully but need not entail acceptance of the traditional Buddhist world-view. Further, in addition to the attraction of meditation, the Buddhist ideal of un-self-centred consciousness, living in compassion towards all life, has for many an intrinsic value that claims their allegiance. And like Buddhist meditation this ideal of the selfless person can be acknowledged and responded to within any or no religious tradition. Indeed, as we shall see in the next chapter, for some contemporary post-Christian thinkers this ideal is valid and salvific even within a basically naturalistic conception of the universe.

Granting then that there are non-realist as well as realist forms of religious commitment, I have sought to establish the basically cognitive and fact-asserting status of standard religious discourse, both western and eastern, by stressing its eschatological component. Because the religions of Semitic and Indian origin offer coherent world-views entailing verifiable expectations they constitute factually true or false systems of belief. But it is clear that these expectations are very different. Hindu and Buddhist expectations differ, and both differ even more markedly from Jewish, Christian and Islamic expectations, which also differ among themselves. Each separately constitutes a genuinely factual system of beliefs. But – looking forward now to the next stages of our enquiry, in Parts 3 and 4 – have we not, in showing the fact-asserting character of the plurality of religious options thereby established their radical incompatibility? This is ultimately the question of the conflicting truth-claims of the different religious traditions that will be discussed in Chapter 20.

Notes

1. E.g. Don Cupitt 1985, 119.
2. Both types are represented in Sellars 1938–9.
3. For an analysis of the different issues involved and of the ways in which contemporary philosophers of religion have dealt with them, see James Kellenberger 1985.
4. See further on Cupitt in Chapter 12.3.
5. This chapter in the history of philosophy has been chronicled in many places, e.g. J. O. Urmson 1956; John Passmore 1957; P. Achinstein and S. F. Barker 1969.
6. There is a considerable literature of religious response to the challenge of logical positivism. See, e.g., Kenneth H. Klein 1974; Malcolm M. Diamond and Thomas V. Litzenburg 1975.
7. Thus the conception of the *visio dei* has to be used with care, as indeed it would seem to have been in much medieval theology, in which according to Philip Wicksteed there was an 'identification of seeing God with seeing as God sees'. 'This conception', he says, 'is perhaps as fundamental as any to the developed religion of the Middle Ages' (Wicksteed 1899, 97). Accordingly, 'The medieval saint believed that to see God is to see as God sees, and that just in so far as we rise into true communion with Him and do in truth see God, so far shall we see things not in their fragmentary imperfection, but in their combined perfection' (25).
8. The negative possibility has already been noted more fully in Chapter 4.6.
9. Cf. David Wiggins 1967, 50.

10. There is another, largely parallel, account in the later *Mahavastu*, II: 314–24.
11. Cf. Conze 1967, 169, 226, 268.

12

Contemporary Non-Realist Religion

> Religion is a dream, in which our own conceptions and emotions
> appear to us as separate existences, beings out of ourselves.
>
> (Feuerbach [1841] 1957, 204)

1 FEUERBACH

The non-realist end of the Buddhist spectrum connects with the nineteenth- and twentieth-century non-realist western construal of religious language. This is not to be confused with traditional atheism (exemplified today by such philosophers as A. J. Ayer, Paul Edwards, Anthony Flew and Kai Nielsen). In contrast to this, non-realist interpretations of religious language are part of the wide overlapping family covered by the umbrella term 'religion'. Their 'atheism' must be described as a religious atheism and their 'humanism' as a religious humanism which find deep significance and important guidance for life in the religious symbols, myths, stories and rituals cherished by the great traditions.

The modern western non-realist interpretation of religious language begins with Ludwig Feuerbach. In *Das Wesen des Christentums* Feuerbach offered what he described as 'a faithful, correct translation of the Christian religion out of the Oriental language of imagery into plain speech' ([1841] 1957, xxxiii). In this translation what is on its surface language about God is identified as being, beneath the surface, language about our own moral ideals. God is the image of the ideal person, the human spirit projected in imagination onto the vastness of the heavens to exert a sacred claim upon us and to sustain us as a gracious divine presence.

Feuerbach's historic achievement is to have planted firmly in western thought the broad conception that the objects of religious

190

faith are human projections: mankind 'unconsciously and involuntarily creates God in his own image' ([1841] 1957, 118). In doing so he also formulated a series of supporting philosophical arguments. Whereas his presentation of the broad hypothesis is vivid and memorable, and has become part of the common discourse of the western study of religion, his specific arguments are generally lacking in rigour, their logical gaps being filled by positions in nineteenth-century idealist thought which may well have seemed self-evident to Feuerbach and to many of his contemporaries but which have since lost much of their plausibility.[1] They read today like the kind of metaphysics which F. H. Bradley described in one of his *obiter dicta* as 'the finding of bad reasons for what we believe upon instinct' (Bradley 1906, xiv). I therefore propose to leave Feuerbach's nineteenth-century argumentation aside and to confront instead his broad projection theory, which has now established itself as a serious and indeed unavoidable possibility for the understanding of religion.

The moral attributes of God – love, justice, mercy and so on – are qualities whose intrinsic value we intuitively recognise and whose claim upon us we immediately acknowledge. As religious beings – according to Feuerbach – we worship these qualities, thinking of them as actualised in a divine super-person. Thus God is the idealised reflection of our own nature: 'Not the attribute of the divinity, but the divineness or deity of the attribute, is the first true Divine Being' (Feuerbach [1841] 1957, 21). Again, 'God, as an extramundane being, is nothing else than the nature of man withdrawn from the world and concentrated in itself, freed from all worldly ties and entanglements, transporting itself above the world, and positing itself in this condition as a real objective being' (66). In a phrase, 'God is the self-consciousness of man freed from all discordant elements' (98). For

> Such as are a man's thought and dispositions, such is his God; so much worth as a man has, so much and no more has his God. Consciousness of God is self-consciousness, knowledge of God is self-knowledge. By his God thou knowest the man, and by the man his God; the two are identical. Whatever is God to a man, that is his heart and soul; and conversely, God is the manifested inward nature, the expressed self of a man. (12–13)

But of course the worshippers do not know that they are worshipping their own ideals. For

Religion, at least the Christian, is the relation of man to himself, or more correctly to his own nature (i.e., his subjective nature); but a relation to it, viewed as a nature apart from his own. The divine being is nothing else than the human being, or, rather, the human nature purified, freed from the limits of the individual man, made objective – i.e., contemplated and revered as another, a distinctive being. All the attributes of the divine nature are, therefore, attributes of the human nature.   (14)

This account of religion as projection could have been purely negative and destructive, as in its further development in the hands of Karl Marx and Sigmund Freud and their followers. But Feuerbach laid the foundations not only for the non-religious atheist's realist interpretation of religious language as making false statements about alleged transcendent realities, but also for the religious atheist's non-realist interpretation of it as making true though disguised statements about the human spirit and our human possibilities. His own attitude was both negative and positive. He was strongly critical of Christianity and the other religions as they have developed in history. For in these traditions love, the supreme value, is checked by faith – by which Feuerbach means (in contrast to the meaning adopted here in Chapter 10.2) theological belief. Whereas love is universal, making no distinction between person and person, faith as the belief-system of a particular group is divisive, creating hostility between believers and unbelievers. It is thus 'essentially illiberal . . . Dogmatic, exclusive, scrupulous particularity, lies in the nature of faith' (Feuerbach [1841] 1957, 251). Faith then, he says, 'is the opposite of love' (257). Whereas true religion symbolises the unity of the human race by the image of the universal love of God, faith sets up particular human theories which in practice restrict love within a circle of fellow believers. And so Feuerbach concludes, 'In the contradiction between Faith and Love which has just been exhibited, we see the practical, palpable ground of necessity that we should raise ourselves above Christianity, above the peculiar stand-point of all religion' (270).

Thus Feuerbach's reason for recommending the abandonment of organised religion was not only that its talk about a transcendent divine reality is false but also that such talk leads away from that celebration of human life and that mutual love of all human beings which are alone 'true religion'. For historically religion is not conscious that its elements are human; on the contrary, it places itself in opposition to the human . . . The necessary turning-point of history is therefore the open confession, that the consciousness of God is nothing else than the consciousness of the species; that man can and should raise himself only above the limits of his individuality, and not above the laws, the positive essential conditions of his species; that there is no other essence which man can think, dream of, imagine, feel, believe in, wish for, love and adore as the *absolute*, than the essence of human nature itself.

(Feuerbach ([1841] 1957, 270)

This means that true religion can only be lived out in the relations between the different members of the human species as, in religious terms, different aspects or elements of God:

If human nature is the highest nature to man, then practically also the highest and first law must be the love of man to man. *Homo homini Deus est* [Man is God to man]; – this is the great practical principle: – this is the axis on which revolves the history of the world. The relations of child and parent, of husband and wife, of brother and friend – in general, of man to man – in short, all the moral relations are *per se* religious. Life as a whole is, in its essential, substantial relations, throughout of a divine nature. (271)

Feuerbach's was thus a noble vision, eloquently expressed, and one which has now been no less eloquently revived in our own day by Don Cupitt, to whose work we shall come presently.

2 BRAITHWAITE AND RANDALL

The negative aspect of Feuerbach's thought was developed sociologically by Karl Marx and psychologically by Sigmund Freud, both of which developments are discussed elsewhere in this book (see Chapter 7.1). But it is the more positive developments that concern us at this point. We find them in the United States in the work of George Santayana (particularly 1900 and 1905), John Dewey (particularly 1934), Frederick J. E. Woodbridge (particularly [1940] 1961 and 1926), John Herman

Randall Jr (particularly 1958 and 1968), Paul F. Schmidt (1961), Paul van Buren ([1963] 1966), J. Wesley Robbins (1982), and in Britain in the work of Julian Huxley (1957), R. B. Braithwaite (1955), Peter Muntz (1959), T. R. Miles (1959), R. M. Hare (1973), D. Z. Phillips (1966, 1970, 1971, 1977, 1986), Don Cupitt (1980, 1982, 1984, 1985) and others. I shall not make any attempt to describe all these variations here. It will be sufficient for our purpose to select four contributions which between them cover the main aspects of the non-realist interpretation of religion: those of Braithwaite, Randall, Phillips and Cupitt.

R. B. Braithwaite, is his famous 1955 Eddington Lecture 'An Empiricist's View of the Nature of Religious Belief', accepted the logical positivist argument that religious utterances (particularly sentences about God) fall outside the three classes of statement whose truth-value can, at least in principle, be tested and which can therefore be accepted as being true or false: the three classes being statements about particular matters of empirical fact, which are in principle verifiable, if true, by observation; scientific hypotheses and other general empirical statements, which, although not usually conclusively verifiable if true, are nevertheless in principle falsifiable if false; and the necessary statements of logic and mathematics, which are hypothetical in character, making no categorical assertions that this or that exists. However Braithwaite argued that, although religious statements are not of any of these kinds and therefore lack cognitive meaning, they nevertheless have an established *use* and hence a meaning within human communication; and he suggested that this use is closely related to that of moral discourse. For this, too, lacks cognitive meaning and yet plays a major role in human life, namely as guiding conduct.

According to Braithwaite moral statements do not make factual assertions about goodness or duty or the right. Rather they express 'the intention of the asserter to act in a particular sort of way specified in the assertion . . . when a man asserts that he ought to do so-and-so, he is using the assertion to declare that he resolves, to the best of his ability, to do so-and-so' (1955, 12–14). He is also by implication recommending this policy to others. And Braithwaite proposes that religious statements are moral statements dressed in the symbols, metaphors and myths of religion. They function as 'declarations of adherence to a policy of action, declarations of commitment to a way of life' (1955, 15). He points out that the fruits of faith in a believer's life have always been regarded as the acid test of sincerity. But 'The view which I put forward for your consideration is that the intention of a Christian to follow a Christian way of life is not only the criterion for the sincerity of his belief in the assertions of Christianity; it is the criterion for the meaningfulness of his assertions' (15). Braithwaite is not suggesting that each article of the creed is a disguised commitment to a different specific form of action, but that each distinguishable component of a religious belief-system is representative of that system as a whole, which is as a totality the expression of a way of life. According to Braithwaite the central theme to which all other aspects of the Christian world-view are subsidiary is that God is love (*agape*); and the meaning of this belief lies accordingly in its use to express commitment to 'an agapeistic way of life' (18), not only in outward deeds but also in the inner dispositions of the heart.

Braithwaite observes that the basic ethical policies of most of the great religious traditions are very similar. (The Golden Rule of seeking the good of others equally with our own occurs in the Hindu, Confucian, Taoist, Zoroastrian, Jain, Buddhist, Hebrew, Christian and Muslim scriptures – see Chapter 17.5.) But what in that case constitutes them *different* religions? Setting aside ritual observances as secondary, Braithwaite points to the 'stories' associated within the different traditions with the ideal way of life. Thus 'On the assumption that the ways of life advocated by Christianity and by Buddhism are essentially the same, it will be the fact that the intention to follow this way of life is associated in the mind of a Christian with thinking of one set of stories (the Christian stories) while it is associated in the mind of a Buddhist with thinking of another set of stories (the Buddhist stories) which enables a Christian assertion to be distinguished from a Buddhist one' (23–4). Such stories may be believed to be literally true or they may be treated as myths, sagas, allegories, midrash, parables. But whether they are understood historically or mythologically it is the embeddedness of the life of love or compassion in *this* set of stories that is characteristic of one religious tradition and its embeddedness in *that* set of stories that characterises another tradition. In short, then, for Braithwaite 'a religious belief is an intention to behave in a certain way (a moral belief) together with the entertainment of certain stories associated with the intention in the mind of the believer' (32–3).

A neighbouring but somewhat different type of non-realist analysis sees religious language as using non-cognitive symbols to express some of our deepest feelings, appreciations, yearnings and commitments. The notion of religious language and ritual behaviour as the symbolic construction of contexts of meaning for human life naturally appeals to many who deal in the scientific study of religion. For whilst that about which religion ostensibly speaks – God, Brahman, the Trinity, the Trimurti, the Trikaya, heaven, hell, *nirvāṇa*, *fana* and so on – are not available for scientific study, the human use of symbols is. And so it is congenial to anthropologists and to the sociologists and psychologists of religion to see religion in the kind of way exemplified by Clifford Geertz's influential definition: 'a system of symbols which acts to establish powerful, pervasive and long-lasting moods and motivations in men by formulating conceptions of a general order of existence and clothing these conceptions with such an aura of factuality that the moods and motivations seem uniquely realistic'.[2]

The view of religion as expressing natural realities in supernatural symbols was beautifully expressed by George Santayana. It was also more cloudily and sometimes ambivalently expressed by Paul Tillich. Indeed John Herman Randall, whom I shall take as a philosophical representative of this approach, remarked concerning his own theory that 'The position I am here trying to state I have been led to work out in connection with various courses on myths and symbols I have given jointly with Paul Tillich . . . After long discussions, Mr Tillich and I have found we are very close to agreement.'[3] According to Randall, 'all religious beliefs without exceptions are "mythology". That is, they are religious "symbols"' (1958, 104). Religion 'offers men no independent "knowledge" at all, though it can give religious expression and consecration to the many kinds of knowledge and the many truths men can find in their experience of the world' (9).

Religion in its many forms, then, bears witness to an aspect of our human experience that evokes this symbolism for its expression. Randall calls this 'the Divine' (112). The Divine, as he uses the term, is a dimension of the natural. Although language about it appears on the surface to be about a transcendent reality, Randall is emphatic that 'the Divine' is a symbol and that religious symbols 'are both nonrepresentative and noncognitive' (114). Their function in human life is, he says, four-fold. They evoke an emotional response, which in turn affects our behaviour. They unite societies and stimulate communal action. They are vehicles of a shared experience, such as may occur in corporate worship. And they 'disclose' or 'reveal' aspects of the world – they 'make us "see" something about our experience and our experienced world' (116). Developing the analogy with art, Randall says:

The work of the painter, the musician, the poet, teaches us how to use our eyes, our ears, our minds, and our feelings with greater power and skill. It teaches us how to become more aware both of what is and of what might be, in the world that offers itself to our sensitive receptivity. It shows us how to discern unsuspected qualities in the world encountered, latent powers and possibilities there resident. Still more, it makes us see the new qualities with which that world, in cooperation with the spirit of man, can clothe itself. For art is an enterprise in which the world and man are most genuinely cooperative, and in which the working together of natural materials and powers and of human techniques and vision is most clearly creative of new qualities and powers.

Is it otherwise with the prophet and the saint? They can do something to us, they too can effect changes in us and in our world. They too can teach us something, about our world and about ourselves. They teach us how to see what man's life in the world is, and what it might be. They teach us how to discern what human nature can make out of its natural conditions and materials. They reveal latent powers and possibilities not previously noticed. They make us receptive to qualities of the world encountered; and they open our hearts to the new qualities with which that world, in cooperation with the spirit of man, can clothe itself. They enable us to see and feel the religious dimension of our world better, the 'order of splendor,' and of man's experience in and with it. They teach us how to find the Divine; they show us visions of God.

(Randall 1958, 128–9)

Thus Randall's main contribution to a non-realist religious hermeneutic is his emphasis on the capacity of religious symbols to enable us to experience further dimensions of meaning and value in the world around us. He does not spell this out with specific examples. But I presume that he might say that to think of the world as the creation of a good God may lead us to focus our attention upon, and to savour, its beauties and intricacies and the ways in which it constitutes a favourable environment for human habitation; or that to think of God as benevolent, and as forgiving men and women, may help us to see in our neighbours something lovable and forgivable. Randall's primary focus is on the awareness of the world and other people, and his sense of the use of religious symbols to express our own inner moral and spiritual states is less prominent, although not absent. In some other non-realist religious thinkers, however, this inward reference is more central. I shall take here as leading examples D. Z. Phillips and Don Cupitt.

3 PHILLIPS AND CUPITT

D. Z. Phillips' main philosophical inspiration comes from the later writings of Wittgenstein. Whether Wittgenstein's own intention, in his occasional non-systematic references to religion, was non-realist can be and has been argued both ways;[4] and since this is an historical question which does not affect the issue before us I shall not attempt to settle it. Regardless, then, of whether one thinks that Wittgenstein would have endorsed his proposals[5] Phillips has provided a clear and eloquent version of a non-realist interpretation of religious discourse.[6] I shall use as a representative sample his analysis of language about death and immortality. '[It] would be foolishness', he says, 'to speak of eternal life as some kind of appendage to human existence, something that happens *after* human life on earth is over.' For 'Eternal life is the reality of goodness, that in terms of which human life is to be assessed' (Phillips 1970, 48). Again, 'Eternity is not *more* life, but this life seen under certain moral and religious modes of thought' (49). Thus 'Questions about the immortality of the soul are seen not to be questions concerning the extent of a man's life . . . but questions concerning the kind of life a man is living' (49).[7]

Phillips amplifies this theme in ways which we need not pursue here, even finding a use for the notions of prayers for the dead (57) and – a *tour de force* indeed – of prayers by the dead for the living (58). We are concerned here with his central view that language which appears to be about unending life is really a coded language about our present spiritual states. Here two questions have to be distinguished. One is the factual question whether human personality does or does not survive bodily death; and the other concerns the meaning of such religious terms as 'eternal life'.

Given this distinction, one possible 'scenario' is that there is in fact continued consciousness after death, but that 'eternal life' does not refer to this but rather to a limitlessly better quality of existence which may begin now and may have unlimited scope after death. From this point of view the issue is not an eternal quality of life *versus* survival of bodily death. On the contrary it might be that the latter opens up the possibility of eternal life to that majority of human beings who do not seem to have attained it in the present life. However this is not Phillips' own position. He has previously argued (1970, ch. 1) that all conceptions of a continued post-mortem existence are either meaningless or patently false. Accordingly eternal life has to be defined in exclusively this-worldly terms, namely as 'living and dying in a way which could not be rendered pointless by death' (50). Phillips extends his non-realist interpretation to every aspect of religious language, including talk about God. Thus, concerning the love of God and receiving everything as a gift of God, Phillips says, 'In learning by contemplation, attention, renunciation, what forgiving, thanking, loving, etc. mean in these contexts, the believer is participating in the reality of God: *this is what we mean by God's reality*' (Phillips 1970, 55; his italics).

We have here, then, a philosophy of religion which respects and supports the use of traditional religious language, with all its emotional depths and reverberations, but which understands it throughout as referring, not to realities alleged to exist independently of ourselves, but to our own moral and spiritual states. Thus to say that God exists is not to affirm the reality of, in Richard Swinburne's definition, 'a person without a body (i.e. a spirit) who is eternal, is perfectly free, omnipotent, omniscient, perfectly good, and the creator of all things' (Swinburne 1979, 8). That 'God exists' means that there are human beings who use the concept of God and for whom it is the presiding idea in their form of life.

Phillips does not argue that the classical users of God-talk – for example, the biblical figures, or indeed ordinary believers through the centuries – consciously accepted or were even aware of this kind of non-realist interpretation. They doubtless normally believed in a real and powerful divine Person and in a literal conscious existence after death in heaven or hell. Phillips' contention is rather that in the light of twentieth-century philosophy, and particularly the revolutionary work of Wittgenstein, we are now in a position to analyse this language correctly and to distinguish between its merely literal and its authentically religious meaning.

But the positive claim that all that is important in religious forms of life and belief can continue, and indeed be enhanced, when the language is deliberately construed in a non-realist way, is perhaps most impressively made today by Don Cupitt. Like Braithwaite and Phillips, Cupitt holds that religious beliefs, understood as involving 'various supernatural beings, powers and events' (Cupitt 1980, 1), are manifestly false. It is impossible any longer, in the modern world, to believe in an 'objective' God who is 'there' independently of human believing. 'If . . . belief in God has to take that very objectified form then the religious consciousness must be obsolete' (xii). However religious belief expresses something of immense importance and can retain, or regain, a central place in human life by becoming autonomous. 'The main requirements . . . are a break with our habitual theological realism, a full internalization of all religious doctrines and themes, and a recognition that it is possible autonomously to adopt religious principles and practices as intrinsically valuable' (xii).

Cupitt argues that in the modern period human consciousness has finally become individualised and autonomous. Accordingly we now see morality as 'standing on its own feet': the rightness of right action and the wrongness of wrong action do not depend upon an external authority. Justice and love, for example, are intrinsically good and injustice and cruelty intrinsically evil and are recognised as such by our own rational nature. This has been widely accepted since it was asserted by Kant at the end of the eighteenth century. Cupitt argues that we must now recognise the autonomy of religion also. Like ethics, religion must be allowed to come of age, as the practice of a spirituality which is not dependent for its validity upon any outside authority and whose claim upon us is grounded in our own nature. The 'religious requirement' to rise to unselfish compassion and detached serenity expresses a possibility within us whose fulfilment is its own reward. From this 'objectively atheous'

(Cupitt 1980, 13) point of view the term 'God' does not refer to an 'immense cosmic or supracosmic Creator–Mind' (8). Rather, 'God is a personal religious ideal, internal to the spiritual self' (Cupitt 1985, 136). Again, 'God *is* the religious requirement personified, and his attributes are a kind of projection of its main features as we experience them' (Cupitt 1980, 85); 'God is, quite simply, what the religious requirement comes to mean to us as we respond to it' (88). And so 'the doctrine of God is an encoded set of spiritual directives' (107).

Given this non-realist hermeneutic, Cupitt's religious vocabulary is virtually indistinguishable from that of a religious realist. He frequently says such things as that 'God indwells the believer, enlightening his understanding, kindling his affections and enabling his will' (5), or that authentic love is pure and disinterested and 'When one loves in that way then one is in the love of God' (68). He is thus able to use all the familiar biblical and liturgical language. It is only the invisible brackets that turn the worship of God into 'an expression of allegiance to a particular set of values' (69). For

> The journey has taken us from an old world in which faith was experienced as a supernaturally prescribed and guided response to objective supernatural realities, to a new world in which faith is instead seen as a creative and freely-undertaken commitment to a life-path guided by rituals, myths, symbols and ideals; rituals, myths and so forth which, moreover, are fully and consciously acknowledged as such without even the most secret and residual attempt at self-deception. (Cupitt 1982, 1)

4 PENULTIMATE ISSUES

This growing movement of the non-realist construal of religious language raises both an ultimate issue and a series of penultimate issues. I want to argue that on many of the penultimate issues its advocates are right, and stand on common ground with many religious realists; but that on the ultimate issue there is a decisive difference.[8] Let us begin with matters penultimate.

First, it is surely right to emphasise strongly the fruits of faith in human life – both in the moral life and in what Cupitt (following a long tradition) calls the spiritual life. Religious realist and non-realist alike can agree that growth in love or compassion, the transcending of the self-centred point of view, purity of heart, are intrinsically good. They commend themselves to the deepest aspect of our nature. From a realist as well as from a non-realist point of view we can say that they are good whether or not there is a divine reality to which they may be a response. However, according to the realist, there is such a reality and these self-transcending qualities constitute the difference made within us by our conscious or unconscious awareness of it. The non-realist, of course, does not see self-transcendence in this way, as a response to a greater reality which draws us out of our enclosed egos, but simply as an achievement of human nature itself. But as to the central importance of self-transcendence, and the value of its moral and spiritual fruits, the religious realist and non-realist can be at one.

Second, realist and non-realist can today agree that the forms of religious belief, experience and practice have always been culturally conditioned. For example, the maleness of God as thought and experienced within the Semitic traditions reflects and validates the patriarchal human societies whose traditions they are; the hierarchical character of medieval Christendom was reflected in and validated by a hierarchical–monarchial theology; and so on. The relativity of religion to human cultures is today common knowledge – though like many other aspects of modern knowledge it has had to push its way to general consciousness against the weight of pre-modern dogmas. The epistemology of religion advocated in this book arises within this contemporary awareness. It understands that the postulated Real is thought and experienced by us in the ways made possible by the structures of our own minds, which in turn reflect cultural variations within the basic human form. Thus to affirm a reality to which our religious concepts ultimately refer is not to claim that that reality is accurately defined by those concepts, or that the Real in its unlimited ultimacy is identical with the personae and impersonae which its presence generates within our human consciousness. The cultural relativity of religious thought and experience can thus be fully acknowledged by both religious realist and non-realist.

Third, Randall's analogy between religious and aesthetic perception parallels a good deal of traditional realist discourse concerning the new appreciation of the natural and human world which faith can evoke. This kind of transformation of consciousness is exemplified in a number of the classic reports of conversions. George Fox, for example, the founder of the Quaker movement, recorded in his Journal that 'All things were new; and all the creation gave another smell unto me than before, beyond what words can utter . . .' (Fox [1694] 1924, 17). Jonathan Edwards (quoted by William James) tells how 'The appearance of everything was altered; there seemed to be, as it were, a calm, sweet cast, or appearance of divine glory, in almost everything. God's excellency, his wisdom, his purity and love, seemed to appear in everything; in the sun, moon and stars; in the clouds and blue sky; in the grass, flowers, and trees; in the water and all nature; which used greatly to fix my mind . . .' (James [1902] 1960, 248). James also quotes a simple convert: 'I remember this, that everything looked new to me, the people, the fields, the cattle, the trees. I was like a new man in a new world . . .' (James [1902] 1960, 248). Such a transformation of consciousness is also characteristic of many of the mystics.[9] It is also startlingly exemplified by the Mahayana Buddhist experience of enlightenment in which Samsara, the ever-changing flow of ordinary life, is discovered to be Nirvana, glowing with the 'wondrous being' of all things. And without elaborating further it is, I think, evident that the religiously transformed mind is frequently able to discern new dimensions of meaning and value in the natural world and in human life; and that this is something which can be fully acknowledged and appreciated by religious realist and non-realist alike.

Fourth, Phillips (1970, ch. 2) and Cupitt (1980, ch. 6) as well as others emphasise strongly the autonomy of the moral life. The rightness of loving actions which benefit or avert harm from others, and the wrongness of acts of cruelty, malice and injustice, do not depend upon external divine commandments or prohibitions. On the contrary, a divine command to be selfish, cruel and unjust would itself be a morally wrong command and a divine prohibition against love, compassion, honesty and justice would be a morally wrong prohibition. Further, good deeds done to win a heavenly reward or to avoid punishment in hell are, by that very fact, not done from a moral motive. This is not however a new or a distinctively non-realist insight. It was the Muslim mystic Rabia who prayed, 'O God! if I worship Thee for fear of Hell, burn me in Hell; and if I worship Thee in hope of Paradise, exclude me from Paradise; but if I worship Thee for Thine own sake, withhold not Thine everlasting beauty!'[10] And it was Immanuel Kant who classically asserted that ethics is autonomous because it is based upon the universal or rational aspect of our nature.[11]

To see morality as based in the structure of human nature (as I have presented it in Chapter 9.1) is as possible to a religious realist as to a non-realist – although there are of course also religious realists, of the literalist kind, who reject this.[12] From a modern realist point of view our ethical nature, which makes possible moral judgment and moral obligation, is an aspect of our existence 'in the image of God', or as servants of God, or as temporarily separate egos seeking to realise our true nature as the universal *ātman* or the eternal Buddha-nature. Thus from a religious point of view morality is independent of external support or sanctions because it already rests on the foundation of a religiously constituted human existence. Accordingly the autonomy of ethics is not an issue between advocates of a non-realist use of religious language and of the realist use that I am recommending.

5 THE ULTIMATE ISSUE

What then is the real issue? It concerns the nature of the universe – using this term in its most comprehensive sense – and our place within it. On a non-realist interpretation of religious language the situation within which we find ourselves is essentially as follows:

(a) The physical universe (including the consciousness generated by physical brains) is itself the only reality: it is not a creation or emanation of any more ultimate divine power, or a teleological process embodying a creative purpose or leading to some kind of nirvanic fulfilment, or reabsorption of the illusorily separate many in the ultimate One.

(b) The human species is a form of animal existence, part of the evolution of life on this earth. As such, humans are destined individually to perish like all other animals and plants; and the species itself is also likely to perish as the earth gradually ceases to sustain life – if not earlier, as a result of some sudden catastrophe. However whilst we humans exist we are the most cerebrally complex form of life on earth, capable not only of intelligent reflection and action but also of conceiving and being grasped and shaped by moral, aesthetic and religious ideals. We are animals to whom certain emotions and certain modes of behaviour are intrinsically valuable in ways which have led to the development of ethical language; and to whom certain characteristics of the surrounding world and of our own artistic creations are intrinsically valuable in ways that have led to the development of aesthetic language. In addition to this we possess a capacity for imaginative self-transcendence in virtue of which we have projected our values – particularly our moral values – onto the cosmos as personal gods and non-personal absolutes and in ideas of eternal life and of an ultimate existence beyond egoity.

(c) The supernatural beings and states of which the religious traditions speak exist only as ideas in our minds. Having realised this, however, we can move to a new point of view – the non-realist religious standpoint – from which we accept that the values which were formerly expressed in objective religious terms retain their intrinsic validity after this apparent foundation has dissolved. Indeed religious language, and the institutions whose discourse it is, can take on new life in a post-realist religious age as guides to spirituality, pointing us to ever greater possibilities of self-transcendence,

Non-realist religion can thus have a strong appeal, particularly in an age in which our natural human religiousness is increasingly unsatisfied by traditional forms.[13] It seems to offer everything that is of indubitable value in religion – the quest for inner peace and purity of heart, the development of love and compassion, the outgrowing of the natural ego with its obsessive cupidity and corrosive anxieties – without the encumbrance of a system of supernatural beliefs which has lost its plausibility for many modern minds.[14]

There is, however, a fundamental anomaly in this non-realist position: namely that whereas the central core of religious discourse interpreted in a realist way constitutes, if true, good news to all humankind, on a non-realist interpretation it constitutes bad news for all except a fortunate minority. This is a major and disturbing anomaly, for the non-realist interpretation professes to express the permanently valuable meaning of our traditional religious language. That language presents a picture which, whilst often grimly pessimistic in the short run – acknowledging fully the structural inevitability of suffering and the universality of moral wickedness – is nevertheless on the long view profoundly

optimistic. For it looks beyond death to resurrection, beyond sin
and suffering to an eternal heavenly life, beyond the pain-ridden
wheel of Samsara through the gateway of enlightenment to
Moksha or to the 'further shore' of Nirvana.

It is true that in the Semitic faiths there are also threats of
eternal torment, and that there have even been theologians who
could think of God as creating some human beings in order that
they be damned. But discounting this latter aberration, the
doctrine of hell leaves us with the choice between a life leading to
fulfilment and a life leading to disaster, and permits the hope that
the latter possibility will never in fact be realised.[15] Thus the idea
of hell need not negate our interpretation of post-axial religion as
an ultimate optimism concerning the character of the universe in
which we find ourselves (see Chapter 4.6). However austere
their sense of human sinfulness and however vivid their awareness
of human pain and suffering, the religions proclaim the good
news that, in the haunting words once again of Julian of Norwich,
in the end 'all shall be well, and all shall be well, and all manner
of thing shall be well'. Indeed they proclaim that the final
fulfilment is already present to those whose minds and hearts are
open to it: Nirvana and Samsara are one; eternal life can be
experienced now, in each moment of time.

But in order for the religious message, that the universe is from
our human point of view ultimately such as to be rejoiced in, to
be good news for all and not only for those few who can realise
Moksha, Nirvana, an eternal quality of existence in this life, the
structure of the universe must be such as to make this possible.
There are conceivable cosmic structures within which an eventual
universal human fulfilment would be possible and others within
which it would not. And the universe as described by the non-
realist users of religious language is clearly of the latter kind. For
if God/Brahman/the Dharmakaya are human ideas, existing only
in mente, and if life terminates definitively at bodily death, then
the universe is good only for a small minority of men and women.
It does *not* sustain a religious message that is good news for all.

It is good news *in principle* for all, in that no one is theoretically
debarred from attaining to Moksha, Nirvana, the eternal quality
of life at each present moment. But this permissiveness is
analogous to the fact that in a desperately poor country with great
social and economic inequalities no one is in principle debarred
from becoming a millionaire! Likewise it is logically possible for

anyone and everyone to become in this life jivanmukti, a bodhisattva, a saint. But this logical possibility falls far short of being good news for all. For the actuality of human existence in history, as also – so far as we know – throughout pre-history, has been that the relentless struggle to survive, the continual battle against natural dangers and human and animal predators, the restrictions and pressures and often pathetic brevity of life, have prevented the great majority of human beings from making more than a small beginning towards the fulfilment of which the religions speak. If that potential is ever to be realised – and that it is to be realised is the meaning for human life of the ultimate goodness of the universe – then reality must be structured accordingly. But to believe that it is indeed so structured is to construe religious language in a basically realist way.

The kind of non-realist religiousness advocated by such contemporaries as D. Z. Phillips and Don Cupitt offers, then, welcome news for the few which is at the same time grim news for the many. It is for this reason that it has to face the charge of an unintended elitism. This charge is not avoided by saying that the non-realist religious person, having found his or her own salvation, is called actively to spread the message, and also to work politically to change the social structures which make it virtually impossible for so many to respond. For, first, even if the human situation should presently change markedly for the better, so that a much greater proportion of people are able to find inner peace and fulfilment, it would still be true that thousands of millions have already lived and died, their highest potentialities unfulfilled – and, if the non-realists are right, permanently and irrevocably unfulfilled. This would negate any notion of the ultimate goodness of the universe. And second, non-realist missionary activity could only mitigate the bad news in so far as the mission succeeds. But the hope that the world is about to be dramatically transformed for the better, although entertained periodically throughout history, has so far always proved delusory. There would be little plausibility, in the circumstances of the world today, in a religious message whose validity depends upon that hitherto deceptive utopian vision.

There are analogies in past religious thinking to this elitism. They are not however flattering. In western thought the one which comes most readily to mind is the strand of Augustinian and Calvinist theology which consigned the large majority of human beings to a predestined eternal damnation whilst a minority were recipients of an arbitrary and unmerited divine grace. In this doctrine the distinction between the fortunate few and the unfortunate many was drawn by divine decree, whereas for contemporary non-realist religion it is drawn by the accidents of nature and history, and does not extend into eternity. But in each case the structure of the universe is such that this division occurs, and is such that most human beings have been its unhappy victims whilst a small minority have been its fortunate beneficiaries. Another difference is that whereas the Augustinian–Calvinist doctrine was developed explicitly, and its horrifying implications frankly accepted, the advocates of non-realist spirituality seem not yet to have noticed the harsh implication of their own teaching.

Needless to say, the fact that a religious doctrine constitutes bad news for ordinary struggling humanity – though at the same time good news for a fortunate few – does not show that it is false. It is possible that the fundamentally unwelcome situation which it depicts actually obtains. My argument, then, is not that a basically pessimistic creed is necessarily false. It is rather that it cannot credibly claim to represent the message of the great spiritual traditions. For it proposes such a reversal of their faith, from a cosmic optimism to a cosmic pessimism, as to offer a radically different vision. The positive argument for going beyond a non-realist understanding of religion will accordingly be an argument for accepting an account of the universe based upon the witness of the religious traditions interpreted in a basically realist manner; and this will be the task of the next chapter.

Notes

1. For example, Feuerbach maintained that human consciousness, in contrast to that of the other animals, involves an awareness of infinity. (He may perhaps have meant that in being aware of ourselves as individually finite we are implicitly using by contrast the concept of infinity.) He then, ignoring a logical gap, identified this awareness of infinity with awareness of the infinity of our own generic human nature. For 'The consciousness of the infinite is nothing else than the consciousness of the infinity of the consciousness; or, in the consciousness of the infinite, the conscious subject has for his object the infinity of his own nature' ([1841] 1957, 2–3). This is a variation of Hegel's elision of finite and infinite

consciousness, the human mind and Absolute Spirit. But in Feuerbach it is not so much an argument as an assertion. However it enables him to identify God with our own infinite nature, which we then in imagination project upon the heavens as the unlimited person. (Feuerbach's doctoral dissertation at Erlangen had been on the infinity, unity and community of reason, and expressed a conception of the infinite character of human nature that had its roots in a good deal of nineteenth-century thought which has since perished except as a chapter of intellectual history.)

2. Geertz 1979, 79–80. Cf. Don Cupitt's definition, 'Religion . . . consists in a set of symbolic forms and actions by which human beings relate themselves to the fundamental conditions of their existence' (Cupitt 1985, 153).

3. Randall 1954, 159. The article by Tillich that develops his doctrine of symbols most clearly in the direction taken by Randall is Tillich 1955.

4. See Joseph M. Incandela 1985.

5. For the negative view see Faghoury and Armour 1984.

6. Another contemporary neo-Wittgensteinian philosopher who has expressed similar views, and to whom Phillips often refers, is Peter Winch. See, e.g., Winch 1977.

7. Cf. Cupitt 1985, 54.

8. Cf. John Bowker 1987.

9. See Evelyn Underhill [1911] 1955, ch. 4, section 2, 'The illuminated Vision of the World'.

10. R. A. Nicholson 1963, 115. The same prayer is sometimes attributed to St Francis Xavier. Cf. also Gregory of Nyssa, *The Life of Moses*, II:320 (1978, 137). Long before, Plotinus had said, 'If a man desires the good life except for itself, it is not the good life that he desires'.

11. Immanuel Kant [1785] 1947, ch. 2.

12. Thus Archdeacon William Paley declared that virtue is 'the doing good to mankind, in obedience to the will of God, and for the sake of everlasting happiness' (Paley [1786] 1817, 36).

13. Although it is not completely clear whether they intend a full naturalistic reduction of the concept of God, a number of contemporary Christian thinkers write as though they do. For example Gordon Kaufman says, 'Though we understand ourselves to have been brought into being by a complex configuration of factors, powers and processes (physical, vital and historico-cultural), it is appropriate to symbolize and hold all this together in the single symbol or concept, God' (Kaufman 1985, 42). See also Kaufman 1981. Again, Charles Birch and John Cobb equate God with Life in Birch and Cobb 1981, ch. 6.

14. For a sympathetic Jewish response see Dan Cohn-Sherbok 1985. See also Harold Schulweis 1983.

15. I have developed this thought more fully in Hick 1985b, ch. 13.

13

The Rationality of Religious Belief

It is as reasonable for those who experience their lives as being lived in the presence of God, to believe in the reality of God, as for all of us to form beliefs about our environment on the basis of our experience of it.

1 IDENTIFYING THE QUESTION

I have argued thus far that religious belief does not properly depend upon inference from evidences discovered in the structure of the universe or in the course of human experience – for such evidences are always theoretically ambiguous – but upon unconsciously interpreting the impacts of the environment in such a way that it is consciously experienced as having the kind of meaning articulated in religious language. In interpreting in this way the believer is making a basic cognitive choice and thereby running a risk: the risk of being very importantly mistaken. For in proceeding in this way one is living 'by faith' and not 'by sight'. Under the influence of one of the great religious figures and/or traditions one is interpreting and experiencing one's situation in a way which will ultimately prove to be either appropriate or inappropriate. If inappropriate, we are being profoundly deluded. If appropriate, we shall have so interpreted our situation that the picture of it in terms of which we live is in basic conformity with its actual character. In either case we have made a cognitive choice which has some of the characteristics of a wager.

To treat religious belief in this way, as expressing a cognitive choice, has been a relatively modern development. Alasdair MacIntyre points out that Pascal was the first western theist to see the universe as religiously ambiguous and atheism as accordingly a serious option; and likewise the first to formulate a religious response to this situation (MacIntyre and Ricoeur 1969, 12–13).

210

This response was the calculation that (given Pascal's concept of God) the risk run by not believing is considerably greater than that run by believing; and therefore that it is prudent, and in that sense reasonable, to believe (Pascal [1670] 1932, No. 233). I want to replace the rationality of this kind of calculation of risks with the rationality, on the part of those who experience 'the presence of God', of accepting that experience as basically veridical. Pascal was however, in my view, importantly right in seeing that the justification of theistic belief does not consist in an argument moving directly to the conclusion that God exists but rather in an argument for the rationality of so believing despite the fact that this cannot be proved or shown to be in any objective sense more probable than not. The appropriate form of reasoning seeks to establish the reasonableness of religious persons trusting and proceeding to live on the basis of their own religious experience and, through it, of the wider stream of such experience in which they participate.

The relationship between experience and belief has been much debated in recent work in the philosophy of religion. This discussion has focused upon specifically theistic belief and I shall be discussing it here in these terms. However, as I shall indicate at the end of the chapter, essentially the same considerations apply to the non-theistic forms of religious experience and belief.

I am going to argue, then, that it is rational to believe in the reality of God. More precisely, by taking account of differences between different people, and also between the cognitive situations of the same person at different times, the thesis elaborates itself as follows: it has been rational for some people in the past, it is rational for some people now, and it will presumably in the future be rational for yet other people to believe in the reality of God. For what it is reasonable for a given person at a given time to believe depends in large part upon what we may call, in the cybernetic sense, his or her information or cognitive input. And the input that is most centrally relevant in this case is religious experience. Here I have in mind particularly the fact that people report their being conscious of existing in God's presence and of living in a personal relationship of mutual awareness with God; and being conscious of their life as part of a vast teleological process whose character as a whole gives meaning to what is presently taking place.

That modifications of human consciousness described in these terms have occurred and do occur can I think safely be affirmed as non-controversial. But from the point of view of epistemology the modifications of consciousness constituting our apparently perceptual experience are of importantly different kinds. In addition to true perceptions there are misperceptions (as for example when I mistake a leaf on a bough for a bird sitting on the bough), illusions (for example, the illusion that the straight stick in water is bent) and hallucinations (if for example I 'see' a person before me when there is no person physically present). If I am misled by any of these forms of perceptual error I am then deluded. In each case the delusion consists in a mistaken implicit belief about the cause of the experience: believing that it was caused by a bird on the bough, by an actually bent stick, by a physical body near me. Applying this concept of delusion to the realm of religious experience we have to ask whether those who assume that their 'experience of living in God's presence' is caused (in however complexly mediated a way) by their being in God's presence are believing truly or are on the contrary under a delusion. We can express the two opposed possibilities slightly loosely by saying that, according to one, the 'experience of being in God's presence' is a genuine whilst, according to the other, it is a delusory experience.

We shall not however be asking directly whether A's 'experience of existing in the presence of God' *is* genuine (for that would require us to know first, independently of this and all other such experiences, and as a matter of established public knowledge, whether God does indeed exist and was present to A), but rather whether it is rational for A to trust his or her experience as veridical and to behave on the basis of it; and also, as an important secondary question, whether it is rational for others to believe in the reality of God on the basis of A's report. It is thus evident that as we proceed to speak in this chapter of the rationality of belief in God, the reference is to the rationality of the believing, not of what is believed. A proposition believed can be true or false: it is the believing of it that is rational or irrational. (The content of the belief is however relevant to the rationality or otherwise of someone's believing it: see below, pp. 219–20.)

2 THEISTIC BELIEF AS A FOUNDATIONAL NATURAL BELIEF

Our ordinary daily activity presupposes a general trust in the veridical character of perceptual experience. For whilst we are aware that we are sometimes subject to illusions, hallucinations and misperceptions of various kinds, this awareness presupposes a general trust in the main bulk and normal run of our apparently cognitive experience. It is only on the basis of this trust that we can have reason to distrust particular moments of it which fail to cohere with the rest. We are here up against something that is for us foundational. We have to rely on our experience in general; for in order to go on living we must continually act, and we can have no reason to do so in one way rather than another except on the assumption that we inhabit the world that is apparently disclosed to us by our senses.

And yet, as has often been pointed out,[1] western philosophy from Descartes to Hume has shown by default that we cannot prove the existence of an external world. None of the philosophical arguments that have been advanced has proved generally convincing; and all the empirical evidences that might be taken as confirming our ordinary belief in the reality of the perceived world – such as the fact that the belief works successfully both in daily life and in the sciences – are circular, presupposing the reality of that world. We thus come to rest in something like the 'natural belief' that Hume – according to Norman Kemp Smith's interpretation (N. K. Smith 1941), in contrast to the older reading of Hume as a systematic sceptic – adumbrated. Kai Nielsen, referring to these basic givens, speaks of 'framework beliefs' (Nielsen 1986, 23f). That is to say, we are so constituted that we cannot help believing and living in terms of the objective reality of the perceived world. We may be able to suspend our conviction during brief moments of philosophical enthusiasm; but natural belief in 'the existence of body' (Hume [1739] 1968, 187) will soon reassert itself. As that eminently sensible philosopher Thomas Reid wrote, 'a man may as soon, by reasoning, pull the moon out of her orbit, as destroy the belief in the objects of sense' (1785, 274). This seems to be a given circumstance that we can only accept.

Now although Hume himself resisted such a move it would clearly be possible to offer a parallel account of religious belief. Penelhum calls this the Parity Argument (1983, chs 6–7). It grants that it is no more possible to prove the existence of God than the existence of a material world but claims that theistic belief arises, like perceptual belief, from a natural response of the human mind to its experiences. All that we can say of a form of natural belief, whether perceptual, moral or religious, is that it occurs and seems to be firmly embedded in our human nature.

> We cannot explain how we are conscious of sensory phenomena as constituting an objective physical environment; we just find ourselves interpreting the data of our experience in this way. We are aware that we live in a real world, though we cannot prove by any logical formula that it *is* a real world. Likewise we cannot explain how we know ourselves to be responsible beings subject to moral obligations; we just find ourselves interpreting our social experience in this way. In each case we discover and live in terms of a particular aspect of our environment through an appropriate act of interpretation; and having come to live in terms of it we neither require nor can conceive of any further validation of its reality. The same is true of the apprehension of God. The theistic believer cannot explain *how* she knows the divine presence to be mediated through her human experience. She just finds herself interpreting her experience in this way. She lives in the presence of God, though she is unable to prove by any dialectical process that God exists.[2]

This seems to me to be correct. But nevertheless it is by no means the end of the story. A full account of our cognitive situation must be considerably more complex. For within the basic epistemological similarity between perceptual and religious experience-and-belief there are important dissimilarities, which we must now note and ponder.

3 TRUSTING OUR EXPERIENCE

We have seen that we normally live on the basis of trust in the veridical character of our experience. We thus operate in ordinary life upon what Richard Swinburne calls the principle of credulity. That is, 'what one seems to perceive is probably so. How things seem to be is good grounds for a belief about how things are' (Swinburne 1979, 254 and 1986, 11–13). This does not however apply indiscriminately to any and every 'seeming'. That things seem to be thus and thus is not an indefeasible reason for believing that they are indeed so. It is a good reason only if there are no countervailing considerations, or only to the degree that remains after such considerations have been fully and fairly taken into account. The general principle on which we operate is that it is rational to regard our apparently perceptual experiences as veridical except when we have reason to doubt their veridicality. Such reasons may be of one or other of two kinds. First, we may be aware of positive circumstances which could well cause us to be deluded in this case; and second, without our knowing of any specific deluding causes, nevertheless the experience may be so fleeting and discontinuous with the rest of our experience, and/or its implications so dissonant with our existing body of belief, that it is reasonable for us to regard it as delusory, or at least to withhold positive acceptance of it as a genuine 'experience of x'.

As an example of the first kind of circumstance, if after I have consumed a considerable amount of alcohol the floor seems to me to be heaving up and down and the walls to be wobbling back and forth, my knowledge of the effects of alcohol on the nervous system would properly make me doubt (whether at the time or later) the physical reality of the heaving and wobbling. As an example of the second kind, if when apparently awake, alert and in good health I have the experience for a split second of 'seeing' a flying saucer, which the very next moment is not to be seen, I probably ought to dismiss the experience as due to some kind of malfunctioning of my perceptual machinery.

Returning now to the safer territory of normal experience, we can adopt the general principle that in the absence of adequate grounds for doubt it is rational to trust our putative experience of an external world that is apparently impinging upon us. This reflects our basic operative conception of what it is to be in cognitive touch with our environment. And to believe, without any positive reason, that that which persistently appears within our experience has no objective existence, or to fail to adjust our beliefs about our environment in accordance with our seeming experience of it, would border upon insanity. Let us then look at the operation of this principle in the case with which we are concerned here, namely the claim to have experienced the presence of God.

I want to focus attention initially on the great souls or *mahatmas* whose experience lies at the origin of the theistic traditions. Among these I shall refer particularly to Jesus, as the one through whom my own consciousness of God has been largely formed. The New Testament records show, I believe, that Jesus was vividly aware of 'living in the unseen presence of God' as *abba*, father. God, as personal loving will, was as real to him as his neighbours or as the hills and rivers and lake of Galilee. The heavenly father was not for him a mere concept or a hypothetical entity, but an experienced living reality; and the supposition that there is no heavenly father would doubtless have seemed as absurd to him, as incapable of being taken seriously, as the supposition that a human being with whom he was talking did not exist. And so let us ask: is it rational for *such* persons, experiencing on this level of intensity, to believe and indeed to claim to know, on the basis of their own experience, that God is real?

The question at the moment is not what *we* should make of Jesus' sense of the present reality of God, but what Jesus himself, as a rational human being, could properly believe on the basis of his own powerful religious experience. And I suggest that we can only say that for such a person, 'experiencing the presence of God' in this way, it was entirely rational to believe that God is real; and indeed that it would have been irrational on his part not to. For unless we trust our own experience we can have no reason to believe anything about the nature, or indeed the existence, of the universe in which we find ourselves. We are so made that we live, and can only live, on the basis of our experience and on the assumption that it is generally cognitive (though perhaps in complexly mediated ways) of reality transcending our own consciousness. Indeed what we designate as sanity consists in acting on the basis of our putatively cognitive experience as a whole. We cannot go beyond that; for there is no 'beyond' to go to, since any further datum of which we may become aware will then form part of our total experience. And if some aspect of it is sufficiently intrusive or persistent, and generally coherent with the rest, to reject it would in effect be to doubt our own sanity and would amount to a kind of cognitive suicide. One who has a powerful and continuous sense of existing in the presence of God *ought* therefore to be convinced that God exists. Accordingly the religious person, experiencing life in terms of the divine presence, is rationally entitled to believe what he or she experiences to be the case – namely that God is real, or exists.[3]

But having said this one must immediately add certain essential qualifications. The first is that however psychologically coercive an 'experience of existing in God's presence' might be, it would be entirely put out of court by our arrival, along some other route, at the knowledge or the well-grounded belief that there is no God. This would be the case if we could see that the concept of deity is self-contradictory and thus incapable of being instantiated. Some have argued that this is the case; but the concept has, to my mind, been sufficiently defended in the course of the modern debate for it to be reasonable to proceed on the assumption that it is logically viable;[4] and I shall accordingly do so. It has also been argued that there are strong negative evidences which effectively rule out the possibility of divine existence; but I have argued in Chapter 7 that these are not decisive and that, on the contrary, the universe is religiously ambiguous.

Nevertheless we still cannot be happy to say that *all* religious and quasi-religious experiences without exception provide a good grounding for beliefs. There are errors and delusions in other spheres and we must expect there to be such in religion also. Indeed almost everyone will agree that this is in fact the case. The sceptic dismisses the entire realm of religious experience as delusory; but even believers regard some forms, other than their own, as delusory. Most of us, for example, are confident that Jim Jones, who induced some nine hundred of his followers to commit suicide with him at Jonestown, Guyana, in 1978, was religiously deluded. Or suppose that someone experiences life in terms of influences from extra-galactic intelligences who control our minds by invisible thought rays; or experiences life in some other way that most of us regard as perverse or crazy? What are we to say about such aberrations? And indeed what are we to say about the rationality of beliefs held on the basis of modes of experience in very different cultures from our own, and particularly in earlier epochs in which different ways of understanding and perceiving the world gave rise to different beliefs – such as belief in good and evil spirits, in witchcraft, astrology and alchemy?

We meet a problem of this kind when pointing, as I have done, to paradigm cases of religious experience occurring within pre-scientific cultures. Jesus himself, for example, not only experienced his life as being lived in the presence of God but also experienced certain diseases (such as, possibly, epilepsy) as cases of demon possession (Mark 1:23–6). He may in addition have experienced temptation as the work of Satan, and the success of his disciples in their healing and preaching mission as the defeat of Satan – though it is also possible that the biblical accounts of Jesus' temptation in the wilderness (Mark 1:12) and of his seeing 'Satan fall like lightning from heaven' (Luke 10:18) are intended as midrash and metaphor rather than as literal reports. But we should in any case distinguish between the New Testament notion of Satan as the supremely evil spirit, opposing God's purposes, and demons as relatively low-level spirits which may invade human beings, causing physical illness or mental insanity. The first idea, although certainly out of tune with modern western culture, is not ruled out by any positive scientific knowledge. The possibility of disembodied minds continues to be a matter of perennial debate; and if there are such minds it is possible that there are evil (as also good) non-human spirits and among them a supremely evil one. Disease-causing demons, on the other hand, do conflict with modern medical accounts of the aetiology of disease. It is therefore belief in demons rather than in the devil that raises the problem we are considering. Such a belief, held by Jesus in first-century Palestine, is for us part of the general question of the rationality of the beliefs of pre-scientific cultures; but it also creates a special problem for the argument that Jesus' belief in the reality of God was well-founded because based on his own experience: for must we not then say the same of his belief in demon possession?

Let us separate out the two questions, (a) whether it may have been rational for the participants of pre-scientific cultures to have held beliefs which we today have reason to think false; and (b), if we answer that question affirmatively, whether it may be rational for us to hold those same beliefs on the ground that it was rational for the participants of another culture to hold them? As to the first question, the whole course of this discussion points to the conclusion that it *is* rational for people to believe what their experience leads them to believe. Therefore it was rational for people in the ancient world to believe that the earth is flat; it may well have been rational for some peoples in the ancient world to believe that disease and death are the result of hostile witchcraft; and it may well have been rational for Palestinian Jews of the first century CE, including Jesus, to have accepted a demonic diagnosis for certain diseases. It was, in general, as rational for them to have believed what they believed about these matters as for ourselves today to believe what we believe about them.

But the more important and difficult question is whether it is rational for *us* to adopt beliefs on the ground that someone else, in another culture, reasonably held them. Whether we judge it proper to adopt another person's beliefs, held on the basis of their own experience – be that person a great religious leader or an ordinary participant in another culture – will properly depend upon further questions concerning the content of those beliefs. Generally it can only be rational for us to hold a belief on the basis of someone else's experience if the belief is compatible with our other beliefs, supported as they are by the general body of our own experience. Everything that we know or think that we know, and every critical resource that we have, is potentially relevant in screening candidates for belief as coherent or incoherent and plausible or implausible. And it may very well be that the acceptance of witchcraft, astrology or alchemy, or the existence of extra-galactic intelligences controlling our minds by thought rays, or the demonic causation of disease, fails to cohere with what we believe on the basis of our experience as a whole and, in particular, with our contemporary scientific beliefs. In that case, although we may recognise that people of other cultures have reasonably held these beliefs, nevertheless we shall not feel obliged to hold them ourselves; indeed we may on the contrary feel obliged to reject them.

How does all this apply to the religious case? It means that a rational person will only be open to accepting others' religious experience reports as veridical, and indeed will only trust his or her own religious experience, if the beliefs to which they point are such as one judges *may* be true.[5] Thus the existence of God must be held to be possible – and not merely a bare logical possibility, but an *important* possibility – if the 'experience of living in God's presence' is to be taken seriously. This is where natural theology comes into its own. Its office is not to prove the existence of God, or even to show it to be probable, but to establish both the possibility of divine existence and the importance (that is, the explanatory power) of this possibility. I believe that reason *can* ascertain both that there *may* be a God and that this is a genuinely important possibility. In that case theistic religious experience has to be taken seriously. But whether reports of experiences of astrological influences and so on are to be taken seriously depends upon a corresponding rational scrutiny of the content of the knowledge-claims to which they give rise.

But is there not an inconsistency in accepting as veridical Jesus' 'experience of God's presence' whilst rejecting as delusory his 'experience of disease-causing demons' – or indeed his 'experience of the sun moving round the earth'? There seems to me to be no difficulty in principle in the thought that a person may be correctly experiencing some aspects of reality whilst falsely experiencing others. Indeed this is so common a situation that we have to accept it as endemic to our human condition. And if we regard the great religious figures as human, and therefore as historically and culturally conditioned, we may expect them to be part of this cognitively chequered history. Why then should we not accept Jesus' 'experience of the presence of God' as genuine, because it evokes a confirming echo within our own experience, and yet regard his way of experiencing disease, and the relation between the earth and the sun, as erroneous because they clash with our modern medical and astronomical knowledge?

4 COMPLICATIONS

It will be evident that this is not an argument for, still less a proof of, the existence of God. It must not be mistaken for an argument from religious experience to God as its cause, such as I criticised in Chapter 6.2. If we simply take a description of some moment of religious experience and ask, Who or what but God could have caused such an experience? there may be many answers. Conceivably it was caused by the experiencer's super-ego, or by a need for cosmic reassurance in face of danger or of the death of a loved one, or by the pressure of one's group, or even by a drug. But I have been suggesting that we should turn from experiences, considered as events whose cause we can seek, to consider the situation of the experiencer, and ask what such a person should rationally think and believe on the basis of his or her own experience. Thus, as I indicated at the beginning, what we are concerned with here is not directly an argument for divine existence but rather for the rationality of believing in the existence of God on the basis of theistic religious experience.[6] In William Alston's terminology, we are concerned with the justification of a doxastic practice, namely the practice of forming beliefs on the basis of religious experience; or, as he also puts it, of using a particular conceptual scheme, namely a theological one, to specify what we are encountering in religious experience.[7] Having posed the question in this way we are, I have suggested, led to conclude that in the absence of any positive reason to distrust one's experience – and the mere fact that in this religiously ambiguous universe a different, naturalistic, epistemic practice is also possible does not constitute such a reason – it is rational, sane, reasonable for those whose religious experience strongly leads them to do so to believe wholeheartedly in the reality of God.

This then, I suggest, is the way in which belief in the existence of God is to be justified. It is justified in basically the same way as our beliefs about 'what there is and how things are' in our total environment: namely, by the impact of that environment upon us, our consciousness of which is our experience of it. In order for it to be rational for us to believe in the reality of entities which are ostensibly given in our experience, whether directly (as when we experience what is before us as a chair) or indirectly (as when we experience our lives as being lived in the unseen presence of God), two conditions have to be fulfilled. One is that we have responsibly judged (or reasonably assumed) it to be possible for such an entity to exist. The other is that it seems to be given in our experience in a powerful, persistent and intrusive way which demands belief in its reality. When someone believes in the existence of God on the basis of compelling religious experience, his or her belief is accordingly a case of rational or reasonable or well-founded belief.

On this basis we must acknowledge that such persons as Moses, Jesus, St Paul, St Francis, Martin Luther, Catherine of Genoa, Julian of Norwich, Muhammad, al-Hallaj, Ramanuja, Guru Nanak and Ramakrishna have been entitled as rational persons to believe that God exists. But what about more ordinary believers who do not enjoy the same overwhelmingly powerful forms of religious experience? Does this line of thought point to any justification for belief in the reality of God on their part?

Persons, if such there be, who never experience religiously in any degree whatever cannot have the same justification for belief as those who do. They might possibly, however, be so impressed by the moral and spiritual fruits of faith in the lives of the saints as to be drawn to share, at least tentatively, the latter's beliefs – in which case it would, I think, be proper to count their being impressed in this way as itself a secondary kind of religious experience. Or again, very commonly, people may hold religious beliefs, in spite of participating only minimally in any form of religious experience, because they have accepted without question what they were brought up to believe. If what they have thus accepted at second hand is in fact true (or is a viable symbolic representation of the truth) they are thus far in a fortunate position. But still their hold upon this truth is very different from that of the first-hand believer, because it is always vulnerable to the kind of sceptical challenge from which any inhabitant of the modern world is increasingly unlikely to be isolated.

However the more common case is probably that of the ordinary believer who does have at least some remote echo or analogue within his or her own experience of the much more momentous experience of the great religious figures. This echo may not be at all dramatic or memorable. It may merely be a moment of greatly intensified meaning in the midst of a church, synagogue or mosque service, or in private prayer, or when reading the scriptures or saying a rosary. Or, on a higher level of significance, it may be the sense of a transcendent reality and goodness being disclosed to us at one of the deep points of human experience, love or birth or death; or through the insistent pressure of an ideal, leading to practical commitment against some social evil or for the realisation of some communal good; or in an awareness, when gazing up into the starry night, of the mysterious immensity of space around us; or again, in the presence of mountain or lake, forest or ocean, of

> A presence that disturbs me with the joy
> Of elevated thoughts; a sense sublime,
> Of something far more deeply interfused,
> Whose dwelling is the light of setting suns,
> And the round ocean and the living air,
> And the blue sky, and in the mind of man;
> A motion and a spirit, that impels
> All thinking things, all objects of all thought,
> And rolls through all things
> (Wordsworth, 'Lines composed a few miles
> above Tintern Abbey')

Such 'peak experiences' can include very small and barely perceptible molehills within the humdrum spiritual life of most of us as well as the mountain-top experiences that startle and tend to be recorded. But if, within this continuum, one experiences one's own life religiously, even only occasionally and to some slight extent, this makes it both possible and reasonable to be so impressed by the reports of the *mahatmas* that one's own experience is supported by their much more massive awareness of the transcendent. One's belief is not *as* deeply or solidly grounded as theirs. But I would suggest that it is well enough grounded for it to be reasonable for us to proceed in faith in the footsteps of a great religious leader, anticipating the full confirmation which our faith will ultimately receive if it does indeed correspond with reality.

5 THE PROBLEM OF CRITERIA

At this point, however, another complication occurs. William Rowe has argued that a valid principle of credulity must not only require that A has an experience which seems to be of *x*, and that A has no positive reason to think that this experience is delusory, but also that A's belief that there is no such reason is itself an *informed* belief. In other words, A must know what sorts of circumstances would render the putative 'experience of *x*' suspect and must also know that these circumstances do not in fact obtain. If one lacks this further knowledge, one's belief that *x* exists will not, according to him, be properly rational. For rational belief requires a critical attitude in which we do not simply believe whatever *seems* to be so, but test and probe and insist upon seeking and taking account of all relevant considerations (Rowe 1982, 90–1).[8]

In general Rowe's additional criterion would seem to be an appropriate one. He now proceeds to apply it to theistic belief, claiming that in this case we do not know what all the possible causes of delusion are. We do not know, for example, what purely natural circumstances might have caused Jesus to have his intense, continuous and coherent 'experience of the presence of God'. And since Jesus cannot have known this either, it was not rational for him to believe in God on the basis of his own experience. Nor, on the same principle, can it ever be rational for anyone else to hold beliefs on the basis of their own or anyone else's religious experience.

In order to isolate the basic issue raised by this challenge we must distinguish between what we may call the general and the specific religious convictions concerning religious experience. The general religious conviction is that such experience is not as such and as a whole delusory, not *in toto* a high-level hallucination of religious individuals and communities. But this does not entail that religious awareness always constitutes, simply and without qualification, cognition of the divine. On the contrary, it is compatible with the view that this range of experience, whilst constituting our human consciousness of a transcendent divine reality, takes a great variety of concrete forms developed within the different historical traditions. It is in that case neither a pure undistorted consciousness of the divine, nor merely a human projection, but rather the range of differing ways in which the infinite divine reality has in fact been apprehended by finite and imperfect human beings.

Under the umbrella of this basic religious conviction there are more specific convictions formed within the particular historic traditions and tested by criteria established within them. Thus a sense of the presence of Christ would, on the face of it, be good currency within Christianity, as a sense of the presence of Krishna would be within the Vaishnavite tradition of India, but not *vice versa*. Again, among the sub-divisions of Christianity, a vision of the Blessed Virgin Mary could count as a notable divine revelation within the Roman Catholic Church but might well be puzzling and even disturbing if it occurred within, say, the Southern Baptist, the Presbyterian or the Quaker bodies. Again, each of the great traditions fully recognises the possibility of error. In medieval Christendom it was accepted that the devil can sometimes cause people to have delusory religious experiences, so that it was important to be able to distinguish between true and false visions, auditions, senses of the divine presence and so on.[9] St Teresa of Avila, for example, was much concerned about the authenticity of her own mystical experiences. One of the main criteria that she and the church used was conformity with the scriptures. She says that,

as far as I can see and learn by experience, the soul must be convinced that a thing comes from God only if it is in conformity with Holy Scripture; if it were to diverge from that in the very least, I think I should be incomparably more firmly convinced that it came from the devil than I previously was that it came

from God, however sure I might have felt of this.
(St Teresa of Avila [1565] 1960, 239)

And at an earlier stage, before the scriptural canon was formed, St Paul had written that 'no one can be speaking under the influence of the Holy Spirit and say "Curse Jesus", and on the other hand, no one can say "Jesus is Lord" unless he is under the influence of the Holy Spirit' (I Cor. 12:3).

Another, less tradition-specific, test has been provided by the spiritual and moral consequences in the experiencer's life. Thus, referring to the effects upon her of her visions of Jesus, St Teresa says,

> all who knew me were well aware how my soul had changed: my confessor himself testified to this, for the difference was very great in every respect, and no fancy, but such as all could clearly see. As I had previously been so wicked, I concluded, I could not believe that, if the devil were doing this to delude me and drag me down to hell, he would make use of means which so completely defeated their own ends by taking away my vices and making me virtuous and strong; for it was quite clear to me that these experiences had immediately made me a different person.   ([1565] 1960, 265)

Another example in Christian mystical literature of the use of this criterion comes in St John of the Cross' *Ascent of Mount Carmel* (book II, ch. 24) where he describes the effect of divinely caused visions as 'quiet, illumination, joy like that of glory, sweetness, purity and love, humility and inclination or elevation of the spirit in God' (1958, 308). This criterion connects with one taught by Jesus himself concerning false prophets who were to come in the future. He is reported as saying, 'You will be able to tell them by their fruits. Can people pick grapes from thorns, or figs from thistles?' (Matt. 7:16) Again, St Paul listed as authenticating fruits of the Spirit 'love, joy, peace, patience, kindness, goodness, trustfulness, gentleness and self-control' (Gal. 5:22). This kind of moral criterion, applied to the outward effects in peoples' lives of their inner religious experiences and beliefs, is probably used more or less universally, at least within the large sphere of the great world faiths.[10]

But, it may well be said, these are only human criteria for what people within this or that tradition have decided to *count* as an experience of the divine. We do not know that they indicate that a religious experience actually *is* an experience of the divine. For the general possibility remains that apparently cognitive religious experience, as such and *in toto*, is delusory. Indeed, it will be said, this is more than a mere logical possibility. For various naturalistic theories have been offered to explain why and how people seem to 'experience God' even though no God exists to be experienced. There are well-known psychological theories depicting theistic ideas and experiences as projections of the human mind, powered by our desire for assurance and comfort in a threatening world. Again, there are well-known sociological theories which claim that a religious sense has been instilled into us in the process of socialisation as a means whereby the individual is led to serve the interests either of the group as a whole or of the governing class. And there are various other kinds and combinations of naturalistic analyses of religion.

These are all, necessarily, speculative analyses and have all been subjected to powerful criticisms. I have myself criticised some of the main such theories in Chapter 7. They have proved convincing to some and unconvincing to others – though even when finally unconvincing they can nevertheless be seen as correctly indicating the presence of elements of human projection and cultural conditioning within the various forms of religious experience. But when we take the naturalistic theories as total explanations, excluding any divine impact triggering a culturally conditioned religious apperception, it is, I think, clear that both their acceptance and their rejection arise out of a prior commitment. For we have seen (in Part 2) that, from our present standpoint, the universe is religiously ambiguous. Alternative total views confront one another, one interpreting religious data naturalistically and the other religiously. Each may in principle be complete, leaving no data unaccounted for; and the acceptance of either arises from a basic cognitive choice or act of faith. Once the choice has been made, and whilst it is operative, the alternative global view is reduced to a bare logical possibility. This is the status both of the various naturalistic theories of religion from the point of view of one who trusts one's own religious experience, and likewise of theistic theories from the point of view of one who is committed to a naturalistic interpretation.

6 THE RIGHT TO BELIEVE

The question then is whether the possibility, in a religiously ambiguous universe, that religious experience as a whole is illusory renders it irrational for those who participate in a form of such experience to believe in the reality of the divine. I think not; and my reason for so thinking is analogous to that classically expressed by William James in his famous essay, 'The Will to Believe' ([1897] 1905). As James later recognised this ought to have been called 'The Right to Believe' (James 1920, II: 207). For its thesis, when we omit various subsidiary excursions, concerns our right to choose how to proceed within an ambiguous situation in which the choice is unavoidable and yet of momentous importance to ourselves. The universe as it confronts us is ambivalent, in that we can construe it either religiously or naturalistically; but when one option has been adopted it constitutes one's life a religious, or a naturalistic, response to reality. Such a response is ultimately true or false according as it conforms or fails to conform to the actual nature of things. However there can at this stage be no confirmation of the final appropriateness of either response. Further, if the religious response is correct, it may be that it is only by living it out that one can progressively relate oneself to and thus be changed by the divine reality. On the other hand, if the naturalistic interpretation is correct, the religious option can only lead us further into error and delusion. Thus we run an unavoidable risk.

What is at stake is our relationship to reality. The possible gain is that of living in terms of reality and the possible loss is that of living in delusion. James argues that in such a situation it is entirely rational to follow the prompting of what he called our 'passional' or 'willing' nature. The weakness of his position, as he himself presents it, is that it would authorise us to believe anything that we may have a strong enough propensity to believe, providing the evidence concerning it is inconclusive. If we would *like* some unprovable proposition to be true, then, given that the option is for us a live, momentous and forced one, James' argument would justify us in believing it. But this virtually amounts to a licence for wishful thinking.[11] I suggest, however, that we can retain James' central insight, whilst avoiding this unacceptable consequence, if we substitute compelling religious experience for the mere desire to believe an unproved and undisproved proposition. James' basic argument then becomes an argument for our right to trust our own religious experience and to be prompted by it to trust that of the great religious figures. Thus if in the existing situation of theoretic ambiguity a person experiences life religiously, or participates in a community whose life is based upon this mode of experience, he or she is rationally entitled to trust that experience and to proceed to believe and to live on the basis of it.

There is, then, on the one hand an 'experience of existing in the presence of God', which may be approved as authentic by the criteria of the individual's tradition. Such experience constitutes a good *prima facie* ground for religious belief. But on the other hand there is the possibility that this entire realm of experience may be *in toto* illusory. I suggest that in these circumstances it is wholly reasonable for the religious person to trust his or her own experience and the larger stream of religious experience of which it is a part. Such a person will, if a philosopher, be conscious of the ever-present theoretical possibility that it is delusory; but will, I suggest, rightly feel that it would be irrational to base life upon this theoretic possibility. Why should one forego entry into a larger universe of meaning, which claims and seems to represent the actual structure of reality, simply because there is always the general possibility of delusion?

I have been presenting an argument for the rationality of belief in God on the part of one who experiences his or her life as being lived in the unseen divine presence. But it is evident that essentially the same argument could be formulated for non-theistic experience and belief. Thus those who report the advaitic experience of oneness with Brahman, or who experience in the ego-less state of Nirvana the reality of the eternal Buddha-nature, or who are conscious of the 'emptiness' of all things as their fullness of 'wondrous being', are entitled to base their belief-systems on those forms of experience.

This realisation opens up yet another vast range of issues. For if the different kinds of religious experience justify people in holding the incompatible sets of beliefs developed within the different traditions, has not our justification for religious belief thereby undermined itself? Does it not offer an equal justification for acceptance of a number of mutually contradictory propositions? Has not our line of reasoning led to the dilemma that Hume, in the *Enquiries*, formulated in relation to miracles:

Let us consider, that, in matters of religion, whatever is different is contrary; and that it is impossible the religions of ancient Rome, of Turkey, of Siam, and of China should, all of them, be established on any sound foundation. Every miracle, therefore, pretended to have been wrought in any of these religions (and all of them abound in miracles), as its direct scope is to establish the particular system to which it is attributed; so has it the same force, though more indirectly, to overthrow every other system . . .   (Hume [1748] sect. x, part 2 – 1902, 121–2)

Instead of miracles one could equally well speak of the forms of experience occurring within the different 'particular systems', and conclude with Bertrand Russell that 'It is evident as a matter of logic that, since [the great religions of the world] disagree, not more than one of them can be true' (Russell 1957, xi). In Part 4 we shall therefore be confronting the range of problems presented by the fact that there is a plurality of religious traditions, constituting different streams of experience and belief flowing along different channels of history and sometimes, it even seems, flowing in opposite directions.

Notes

1. E.g. William Temple 1934, ch. 3; and, more recently, Alston 1983; Penelhum 1983; Plantinga 1983.
2. Hick [1957] 1987a, 132. (The argument is discussed critically by J. W. Robbins 1974.) This notion of the fundamental character of beliefs based upon our experience, including religious experience, is related to although not identical with Alvin Plantinga's much discussed concept of 'proper basicality' (Plantinga 1983 and 1986). This is the view that belief in God is a belief that can be held, not on the basis of evidence, but as basic in its own right, a belief in holding which the believer is not violating any valid epistemological rules. At times Plantinga speaks of properly basic beliefs as ones which the believer has a 'natural tendency' to believe (1983, 78). This would surely be much too broad and permissive. However Plantinga also says that properly basic beliefs, although not derived from evidence, do have grounds: for example, the experience of 'seeing a tree' is generally a good justifying ground for the basic belief that I am seeing a tree. If religious experience is recognised as the parallel justifying ground of religious beliefs, then Plantinga's argument and the argument of this chapter virtually coincide.
3. Others who have argued along analogous lines include C. D. Broad 1939a and 1939b; Alvin Plantinga 1967; Richard Swinburne 1979, ch.

13; William Alston 1983; J. A. Taber 1986. I have myself previously argued in this way in Hick [1957] 1987a and 1970.

4. See e.g. on the negative side Anthony Kenny 1979, and on the positive side Richard Swinburne 1977; Keith Ward 1974; Stephen Davis 1983.

5. Sometimes however there appear to have occurred powerfully invasive experiences setting up new beliefs that were not compatible with much of the individual's previous belief-system and indeed that required its wholesale reconstruction. These are dramatic conversion experiences such as that of Muhammad when he first began to receive the Qur'anic revelation, or that of St Paul on the road to Damascus. However, in accordance with the principle of a cognitive freedom which is proportioned to the value of the aspect of reality being cognised (see Chapter 10.4), and in accordance also with plausible psychological analyses of conversion, it seems likely that even these apparently sudden and unexpected experiences were 'threshold' phenomena in which a new awareness that had gradually been growing in the unconscious suddenly spills over into consciousness. (See, e.g., William James [1902] 1960, 236.)

6. It should be noted that much of the contemporary philosophical discussion of religious experience deals with the different question whether it provides the basis for a valid inference to divine existence: e.g. C. B. Martin 1959; Wallace Matson 1965, pt I; T. R. Miles 1972; Goulder and Hick 1983; R. W. Clark 1984; J. W. Forgie 1985b.

7. Alston 1983, 108–9. Alston is discussing beliefs about manifestations of God ('M-beliefs') rather than the more basic belief that there is a God to be manifested; but these M-beliefs entail that God exists, and the same argument is also relevant to that more basic belief.

8. For different responses to Rowe from the one developed here see J. L. Kvanvig 1984 and P. Losin 1987.

9. See, e.g., St John of the Cross [16th century] 1958, 324–6; Walter Hilton [1494] 1948, bk I, ch. 11.

10. See further in Chapter 18.

11. I have developed this criticism more fully in Hick [1957] 1987a, ch. 2. For a more sympathetic response to James' argument see Stephen Davis 1978.

Part Four
Religious Pluralism

14

The Pluralistic Hypothesis

The lamps are different, but the Light is the same.
(Jalalu'l-Din Rumi [13th century])[1]

1 THE NEED FOR SUCH AN HYPOTHESIS

I have argued that it is rational on the part of those who experience religiously to believe and to live on this basis. And I have further argued that, in so believing, they are making an affirmation about the nature of reality which will, if it is substantially true, be developed, corrected and enlarged in the course of future experience. They are thus making genuine assertions and are making them on appropriate and acceptable grounds. If there were only one religious tradition, so that all religious experience and belief had the same intentional object, an epistemology of religion could come to rest at this point. But in fact there are a number of different such traditions and families of traditions witnessing to many different personal deities and non-personal ultimates.

To recall the theistic range first, the history of religions sets before us innumerable gods, differently named and often with different characteristics. A collection of names of Mesopotamian gods made by A. Deinel in 1914 contains 3300 entries (Romer 1969, 117–18). In Hesiod's time there were said to be 30 000 deities (Hume [1757] 1956, 28, n. 1). And if one could list all the past and present gods and goddesses of India, such as Agni, Vayu, Surya, Aryaman, Aditi, Mitra, Indra, Varuna, Brahma, Vishnu, Lakshmi, Shiva, Kali, Ganesh . . . and of the Near East, such as Osiris, Isis, Horus, Re, Yahweh, Baal, Moloch, An, Enlil, Ea, Tiamat, Enki, Marduk . . . and of southern Europe such as Zeus, Kronos, Hera, Apollo, Dionysus, Hephaestus, Poseidon, Aphrodite, Hermes, Mars, Athena, Pan . . . and of northern Europe, such as Odin, Thor, Balder, Vali, Freyr, Frigg, Woden, Rheda, Erce, Donar, Fosite . . . and of Africa, such as Nabongo, Luhanga, Ngai,

233

Nyama, Amaomee, Lesa, Ruhanga, Kolo, Naymbe, Imana, Kimbumba, Molimo, Ohe . . . and also of the Americas, Australasia, northern Asia and the rest of the world they would probably form a list as bulky as the telephone directory of a large city. What are we to say, from a religious point of view, about all these gods? Do we say that they exist? And what would it be for a named god, say Balder, with his distinctive characteristics, to exist? In any straightforward sense it would at least seem to involve there being a consciousness, answering to this name, in addition to all the millions of human consciousnesses. Are we then to say that for each name in our directory of gods there is an additional consciousness, with the further attributes specified in the description of that particular deity? In most cases this would be theoretically possible since in most cases the gods are explicitly or implicitly finite beings whose powers and spheres of operation are at least approximately known; and many of them could co-exist without contradiction. On the other hand the gods of the monotheistic faiths are thought of in each case as the one and only God, so that it is impossible for there to be more than one instantiation of this concept. It is thus not feasible to say that all the named gods, and particularly not all the most important ones, exist – at any rate not in any simple and straightforward sense.

Further, in addition to the witness of theistic religion to this multiplicity of personal deities there are yet other major forms of thought and experience which point to non-personal ultimates: Brahman, the Dharmakaya, Nirvana, Sunyata, the Tao . . . But if the ultimate Reality is the blissful, universal consciousness of Brahman, which at the core of our own being we all are, how can it also be the emptiness, non-being, void of Sunyata? And again, how could it also be the Tao, as the principle of cosmic order, and again, the Dharmakaya or the eternal Buddha-nature? And if it is any of these, how can it be a personal deity? Surely these reported ultimates, personal and non-personal, are mutually exclusive. Must not any final reality either be personal, with the non-personal aspect of divinity being secondary, or be impersonal, with the worship of personal deities representing a lower level of religious consciousness, destined to be left behind in the state of final enlightenment?

The naturalistic response is to see all these systems of belief as factually false although perhaps as expressing the archetypal day-dreams of the human mind whereby it has distracted itself from the harsh problems of life. From this point of view the luxuriant variety and the mutual incompatibility of these conceptions of the ultimate, and of the modes of experience which they inform, demonstrates that they are 'such stuff as dreams are made on'. However I have already argued (in Chapter 13) that it is entirely reasonable for the religious person, experiencing life in relation to the transcendent – whether encountered beyond oneself or in the depths of one's own being –, to believe in the reality of that which is thus apparently experienced. Having reached that conclusion one cannot dismiss the realm of religious experience and belief as illusory, even though its internal plurality and diversity must preclude any simple and straightforward account of it.

Nor can we reasonably claim that our own form of religious experience, together with that of the tradition of which we are a part, is veridical whilst the others are not. We can of course claim this; and indeed virtually every religious tradition has done so, regarding alternative forms of religion either as false or as confused and inferior versions of itself. But the kind of rational justification set forth in Chapter 13 for treating one's own form of religious experience as a cognitive response – though always a complexly conditioned one – to a divine reality must (as we have already noted) apply equally to the religious experience of others. In acknowledging this we are obeying the intellectual Golden Rule of granting to others a premise on which we rely ourselves. Persons living within other traditions, then, are equally justified in trusting their own distinctive religious experience and in forming their beliefs on the basis of it. For the only reason for treating one's tradition differently from others is the very human, but not very cogent, reason that it is one's own! Later (in Part 5) we shall be considering criteria by which one might judge and even seek to grade the religious traditions. The conclusions to be drawn there do not support the picture of a single 'true' religion in the midst of a number of 'false' ones. But in the meantime let us avoid the implausibly arbitrary dogma that religious experience is all delusory with the single exception of the particular form enjoyed by the one who is speaking.

Having, then, rejected (in Chapter 7) the sceptical view that religious experience is *in toto* delusory, and the dogmatic view that it is all delusory except that of one's own tradition, I propose to explore the third possibility that the great post-axial faiths constitute different ways of experiencing, conceiving and living in relation to an ultimate divine Reality which transcends all our varied visions of it.

2 THE REAL IN ITSELF AND AS HUMANLY EXPERIENCED

In discussing (in Chapter 1) problems of terminology I opted – partly as a matter of personal linguistic taste – for 'the Real' (in preference to 'the Ultimate', 'Ultimate Reality', 'the One' or whatever) as a term by which to refer to the postulated ground of the different forms of religious experience. We now have to distinguish between the Real *an sich* and the Real as variously experienced-and-thought by different human communities. In each of the great traditions a distinction has been drawn, though with varying degrees of emphasis, between the Real (thought of as God, Brahman, the Dharmakaya . . .) in itself and the Real as manifested within the intellectual and experiential purview of that tradition. Thus Hindu thought distinguishes between *nirguṇa* Brahman, Brahman without attributes, exceeding the grasp of human language, and *saguṇa* Brahman, Brahman with attributes, known within human religious experience as Ishvara, the personal creator and governor of the universe. In Mahayana Buddhism there is the distinction between, on the one hand, the ultimate Dharmakaya and, on the other hand, this diversified into the heavenly Buddhas constituting the Sambhogakaya and, again, these incarnate in the Nirmanakaya. There is also the related distinction, first enunciated by T'an-luan and taken up by Shinran into the Pure Land tradition, between the *dharmata dharmakāya*, the Dharmakaya *an sich*, and the *upaya dhamakāya*, or Dharma characterised, known as the personal Amida, the Buddha of infinite compassion. In a pasage quoted by Shinran, T'an-luan said:

> Among Buddhas and bodhisattvas there are two aspects of dharmakaya: dharmakaya-as-suchness and dharmakaya-as-compassion. Dharmakaya-as-compassion arises out of dharma-kaya-as-suchness, and dharmakaya-as-suchness emerges into [human consciousness through] dharmakaya-as-compassion. These two aspects of dharmakaya differ but are not separate; they are one but not identical.   (Shinran [1250] 1979, 5)

As a commentator says, 'the ultimate formless and nameless dharmakaya-as-suchness (nirvana) manifests itself in the world as Amida Buddha, dharmakaya-as-compassion, emerging in this samsaric ocean to make itself comprehensible to men' (Shinran [1250] 1979, 6).

Again, the Taoist scripture, the *Tao Te Ching*, begins by affirming that 'The Tao that can be expressed is not the eternal Tao'.[2] In the West the Jewish thinker Maimonides distinguished between the essence and the manifestations of God (*Guide to the Perplexed*, bk I, ch. 54); and the Kabbalist mystics distinguished between En Soph, the absolute divine reality beyond human description, and the God of the Bible. In Islam it is proclaimed that Allah transcends human experience and yet is manifested to human awareness: in a haunting Qur'anic phrase, 'The eyes attain Him not, but He attains the eyes' (6:103). And among the Sufis, Al Haq, the Real, is the abyss of Godhead underlying the self-revealed Allah. The Christian mystic Meister Eckhart distinguished between the Godhead (*Gottheit/deitas*) and God (*Gott/deus*). Again, Paul Tillich has spoken of 'the God above the God of theism' (1952, 189). And Gordon Kaufman has recently distinguished between the 'real God' and the 'available God', the former being an 'utterly unknowable X' and the latter 'essentially a mental or imaginative construction' (Kaufmann 1972, 85–6; compare 1981). Again, Ninian Smart speaks of 'the noumenal Focus of religion which so to say lies beyond the phenomenal Foci of religious experience and practice' (Smart 1984, 24; compare 1981, ch. 6). A more traditional Christian form of the distinction is that between God *a se* in God's infinite self-existent being, beyond the grasp of the human mind, and God *pro nobis*, revealed in relation to humankind as creator and redeemer.[3] The infinite divine reality must pass out into sheer mystery beyond the reach of our knowledge and comprehension and is in this limitless transcendence *nirguna*, the ultimate Godhead, the God above the God of theism, the Real *an sich*.

In one form or another such a distinction is required by the thought that God, Brahman, the Dharmakaya, is unlimited and therefore may not be equated without remainder with anything that can be humanly experienced and defined. Unlimitedness, or infinity, is a negative concept, the denial of limitation. That this denial must be made of the Ultimate is a basic assumption of all the great traditions. It is a natural and reasonable assumption: for an ultimate that is limited in some mode would be limited by something other than itself; and this would entail its non-ultimacy. And with the assumption of the unlimitedness of God, Brahman, the Dharmakaya, goes the equally natural and reasonable assumption that the Ultimate, in its unlimitedness, exceeds all positive characterisations in human thought and language. Thus Gregory of Nyssa:

> The simplicity of the True Faith assumes God to be that which He is, namely, incapable of being grasped by any term, or any idea, or any other device of our apprehension, remaining beyond the reach not only of the human but of the angelic and all supramundane intelligence, unthinkable, unutterable, above all expression in words, having but one name that can represent His proper nature, the single name being 'Above Every Name'
> (*Against Eunomius*, I:42 – Schaff and Wace [1892] 1956, V:99)

Augustine, continuing this tradition, declared that 'God transcends even the mind' (*De Vera Religione*, 36:67 – Burleigh 1953, 259). St Thomas Aquinas reiterated that 'by its immensity, the divine substance surpasses every form that our intellect reaches' (*S. c. G.*, I:14:3 – Pegis 1955, 96–7);[4] and 'The first cause surpasses human understanding and speech. He knows God best who acknowledges that whatever he thinks and says falls short of what God really is' (*In librum De Causis*, 6 – Copleston 1955, 131–2). Eckhart said that 'God is without name, for no one can comprehend anything about him' (Eliade 1985, 200). St John of the Cross said that God 'is incomprehensible and transcends all things' ([16th century] 1958, 310). The theme, indeed, runs through the history of Christian thought.[5]

In Islam the notion of *subhānahu* likewise means that God is above all that we say of him. God is 'beyond what they describe' (Qur'an 23:91; 37:180; 6:101). Within the Hindu tradition the Upanishads say of Brahman, 'There the eye goes not, speech goes not, nor the mind' (*Kena* Up., 1:3 – Radhakrishnan 1969, 582) and speak of 'unthinkable form' (*Muṇḍaka* Up., III:1:7 – Radhakrishnan 1968, 688); and affirm that Brahman is that 'before which words recoil, and to which no understanding has ever attained' (*Taittiriya* UP., II.4.1 and II.9.1 – Radhakrishnan, 1968, 545 and 552). And with this sense of the divine infinity there often comes the awareness that 'To say that God is Infinite is to say that He may be apprehended and described in an infinity of ways' (Underhill 1955, 238).

The traditional doctrine of divine ineffability, which I want to apply to the Real *an sich*, has however been challenged.[6] In considering the challenge we need to distinguish two issues: (1) Does it make sense to say of X that our concepts do not apply to it? and (2) If this does (though in a qualified formulation) make sense, what reason could we have to affirm it? A response to the second question will be postponed until we come to consider the relationship between the postulated Real *an sich* and its experienced *personae* and *impersonae*. But in response to the first issue: it would indeed not make sense to say of X that *none* of our concepts apply to it. (Keith Yandell (1975, 172) calls this no-concepts interpretation 'strong ineffability'.) For it is obviously impossible to refer to something that does not even have the property of 'being able to be referred to'.[7] Further, the property of 'being such that our concepts do not apply to it' cannot, without self-contradiction, include itself.[8] But these are logical pedantries which need not have worried those classical thinkers who have affirmed the ultimate ineffability of the divine nature.

Such points might however usefully have prompted them to distinguish between what we might call substantial properties, such as 'being good', 'being powerful', 'having knowledge', and purely formal and logically generated properties such as 'being a referent of a term' and 'being such that our substantial concepts do not apply'. What they wanted to affirm was that the substantial characterisations do not apply to God in God's self-existent being, beyond the range of human experience. They often expressed this by saying that we can only make negative statements about the Ultimate. It is *neti, neti*, not this, not this (*Bṛhadāraṇyaka Up.*, IV:5:15 – Radhakrishnan 1969, 286). 'We are unable to apprehend [the divine substance] by knowing what it is. Yet we are able to have some knowledge of it by knowing what it is not' (Aquinas, *S. c. G.*, I:14:2 – Pegis 1955, 96).[9] This *via negativa* (or *via remotionis*) consists in applying negative concepts to the Ultimate – the concept of not being finite, and so on – as a way of saying that it lies beyond the range of all our positive substantial characterisations. It is in this qualified sense that it makes perfectly good sense to say that our substantial concepts do not apply to the Ultimate. The further question, why we should affirm that there is an Ultimate to which our substantial concepts do not apply, will be taken up in section 4.

Using this distinction between the Real *an sich* and the Real as humanly thought-and-experienced, I want to explore the pluralistic hypothesis that the great world faiths embody different perceptions and conceptions of, and correspondingly different responses to, the Real from within the major variant ways of being human; and that within each of them the transformation of human existence from self-centredness to Reality-centredness is taking place. These traditions are accordingly to be regarded as alternative soteriological 'spaces' within which, or 'ways' along which, men and women can find salvation/liberation/ultimate fulfilment.

3 KANT'S EPISTEMOLOGICAL MODEL

In developing this thesis our chief philosophical resource will be one of Kant's most basic epistemological insights, namely that the mind actively interprets sensory information in terms of concepts, so that the environment as we consciously perceive and inhabit it is our familiar three-dimensional world of objects interacting in space. This is a highly generalised version of Kant's complex theory of the forms and categories of perception which he found to be inherent in the structure of any unitary finite consciousness. There is continuing debate about the precise character and implications of Kant's arguments in the *Critique of Pure Reason* as well as of the relation between this and his earlier and later works. For the first *Critique* contains several different strands of thought whose mutual consistency can be questioned and whose relative importance has been variously estimated. I do not however propose to enter into questions of Kantian exegesis: for to do so could only divert attention from the application of the basic Kantian insight to an area to which he himself did not apply it, namely the epistemology of religion.[10] For Kant's broad theme, recognising the mind's own positive contribution to the character of its perceived environment, has been massively confirmed as an empirical thesis by modern work in cognitive and social psychology[11] and in the sociology of knowledge.[12] In applying it to the epistemology of religion we are therefore employing a well consolidated development of contemporary understanding.

The basic principle that I am adapting from Kant's philosophy had in fact already been succinctly stated long before by St Thomas Aquinas, although without any thought of the kind of application being proposed here, when he wrote that 'Things

known are in the knower according to the mode of the knower'
(*S.T.*, II/II, Q. 1, art. 2). He applied this basic epistemological
principle to faith considered as propositional belief, concluding
that although God *a se* is simple and undifferentiated, God can
only be known by human beings through complex propositions. I
want to apply the same principle to faith understood (as in
Chapter 10.2) in a very different way, as the interpretive element
within all awareness of our environment; and to argue that in
relation to the divine the 'mode of the knower' differs within
different religio-cultural systems so that the Real is thought-and-
experienced in a wide variety of ways. A near contemporary of St
Thomas, the Muslim thinker al Junaid, drew precisely this
conclusion in a metaphor which he applied to the plurality of
forms of awareness of God: 'The colour of the water is the same
as that of its container' (Nicholson [1914] 1963, 88).

But whilst the Thomist maxim, that things known are in the
knower according to the mode of the knower, says in principle all
that is needed as the starting point for a pluralistic epistemology
of religion, Kant's later much more detailed development of the
theme is particularly helpful because he went on to distinguish
explicitly between an entity as it is in itself and as it appears in
perception. For the realisation that the world, as we consciously
perceive it, is partly our own construction leads directly to a
differentiation between the world *an sich*, unperceived by anyone,
and the world as it appears to, that is as it is perceived by, us.[13]
The distinction plays a major part in Kant's thought. He points
out that since the properties of something as experienced 'depend
upon the mode of intuition of the subject, this object as appearance
is to be distinguished from itself as object in itself' (*Crit. Pure
Reason*, B69 – 1958, 88). And so Kant distinguished between
noumenon and phenomenon, or between a *Ding an sich* and that
thing as it appears to human consciousness. As he explains, he is
not here using the term 'noumenon' in the positive sense of that
which is knowable by some faculty of non-sensible intuition (for
we have no such faculty), but in the negative sense of 'a thing in
so far as it is not an object of our sensible intuition' (B307 – 1958,
268). In this strand of Kant's thought – not the only strand, but
the one which I am seeking to press into service in the
epistemology of religion – the noumenal world exists independently
of our perception of it and the phenomenal world is that same
world as it appears to our human consciousness. The world as it

appears is thus entirely real: in being a 'transcendental idealist' Kant is, as he says, 'an empirical realist' (A370 – 1958, 346). Analogously, I want to say that the noumenal Real is experienced and thought by different human mentalities, forming and formed by different religious traditions, as the range of gods and absolutes which the phenomenology of religion reports. And these divine *personae* and metaphysical *impersonae*, as I shall call them, are not illusory but are empirically, that is experientially, real as authentic manifestations of the Real.

Kant's own reason for distinguishing between noumenon and phenomenon was peculiar to his complex philosophical architectonic. He came to it through a critical discussion of space and time which, he argued, cannot be objective realities but must instead be forms which the mind imposes on the sensory manifold. From this it follows that the world *an sich* differs from the world of human experience in not being temporally and spatially ordered. But we do not need to follow Kant at this point in order to arrive at the distinction between things as they are in themselves and those same things as humanly perceived. For it arises out of elementary reflection upon our experience. We quickly realise that the same thing appears in either slightly or considerably different ways to different people owing both to their varying spatial locations in relation to it and to differences in their sensory and mental equipment and interpretive habits. Again, physics tells us that the surface of the table, which looks and feels to us as a continuous smooth, hard, brown expanse is a whirling universe of minute discharging quanta of energy in largely empty space, and that these quanta are neither continuous nor smooth nor hard nor brown. And so we differentiate between the physicist's inferred table-as-it-is-in-itself and that same entity as it is perceived, identified, labelled, understood and used by us in ordinary life. The basic distinction seems unavoidable and indisputable, though Kant is the philosopher who has grappled most radically and most thought-provokingly with it.

However Kant himself (in his three *Critiques*) would not have sanctioned the idea that we in any way experience God, even as divine phenomenon in distinction from divine noumenon. God was not for him a reality encountered in religious experience but an object postulated by reason on the basis of its own practical functioning in moral agency. According to him the categorical character of moral obligation presupposes the reality of God as making possible the *summum bonum* in which perfect goodness and perfect happiness will coincide. God must accordingly be postulated as 'a cause of the whole of nature, itself distinct from nature, which contains the ground of the exact coincidence of happiness with morality' (*Crit. Pract. Reason*, II:2:5 – 1956, 129). The idea of God, thus indirectly established, then functions as a regulative idea whereby we 'regard all order in the world as if it had originated in the purpose of supreme reason' (*Crit. Pure Reason*, B714 – 1958, 559–60).

But for Kant God is postulated, not experienced. In partial agreement but also partial disagreement with him, I want to say that the Real *an sich* is postulated by us as a pre-supposition, not of the moral life, but of religious experience and the religious life, whilst the gods, as also the mystically known Brahman, Sunyata and so on, are phenomenal manifestations of the Real occurring within the realm of religious experience. Conflating these two theses one can say that the Real is experienced by human beings, but experienced in a manner analogous to that in which, according to Kant, we experience the world: namely by informational input from external reality being interpreted by the mind in terms of its own categorial scheme and thus coming to consciousness as meaningful phenomenal experience. All that we are entitled to say about the noumenal source of this information is that it is the reality whose influence produces, in collaboration with the human mind, the phenomenal world of our experience. This takes place through the medium of certain concepts which Kant calls the categories of the understanding. In Kant's system of thought these are *a priori* and hence universal and invariable modes of human perception. The pure categories or pure concepts of the understanding (for example, substance) are schematised in terms of temporality to produce the more concrete categories which are exhibited in our actual experience of the world. (Thus, for example, the pure concept of substance is schematised as the more concrete idea of an object enduring through time.) The impact of our environment upon our sensory equipment then comes to consciousness in forms prescribed by these schematised categories.

The situation is basically the same, I suggest, in the case of our awareness of the Real – though within the similarity there are also major differences. Some of these have been discussed by William Forgie, who characterises the kind of view I am presenting as

'Hyper-Kantianism' (Forgie 1985a). The main difference is that the categories (Forgie prefers to call them 'category-analogues') of religious experience are not universal and invariable but are on the contrary culture-relative. It is possible to live without employing them; and when they are employed they tend to change and develop through time as different historical influences affect the development of human consciousness. Forgie is however mistaken, in my opinion, in regarding such a theory of religious categories as a 'rival view' (208) to Kant's. For Kant was solely concerned, in his discussion of the categories, with the construction of the physical world in sense perception. One who is concerned with the construction of the divine within religious experience has the option of accepting or rejecting Kant's view of sense perception. One theory neither requires nor is incompatible with the other. We have already noted that Kant's own epistemology of religion was quite unrelated to his understanding of sense perception. But this fact does not bar others, inspired by his basic insights, from seeing religious and sense experience as continuous in kind, thereby extending Kant's analysis of the one, in an appropriately adapted form, to the other.

In the religious case there are two fundamental circumstances: first, the postulated presence of the Real to the human life of which it is the ground; and second, the cognitive structure of our consciousness, with its capacity to respond to the meaning or character of our environment, including its religious meaning or character. In terms of information theory, we are speaking of the transmission of information from a transcendent source to the human mind/brain and its transformation by the mind/brain into conscious experience.[14] The transference of information from a source to a receiver, and its transformability from one mode to another, are among the ultimately mysterious facts of which we have to take account. Information is conveyed not only by such physical means as electro-magnetic radiations but also by forms of mind-to-mind and matter-to-mind causation such as are observed in ESP phenomena.[15] These do not depend upon physical contiguity but perhaps upon a universal cognitivity of mental life which is restricted in individual organisms by the limited and selective processing capacity of the brain.[16] The 'presence' of the Real consists in the availability, from a transcendent source, of information that the human mind/brain is capable of transforming into what we call religious experience. And, as in the case of our awareness of the physical world, the environing divine reality is brought to consciousness in terms of certain basic concepts or categories. These are, first, the concept of God, or of the Real as personal, which presides over the various theistic forms of religious experience; and second, the concept of the Absolute, or of the Real as non-personal, which presides over its various non-theistic forms.[17]

The relation between these two very different ways of conceiving and experiencing the Real, as personal and as non-personal, is perhaps a complementarity analogous (as has been suggested by Ian Barbour[18]) to that between the two ways of conceiving and registering light, namely as waves and as particles. That is to say, the purely physical structure of light is not directly observable; but under different sets of experimental conditions it is found to have wave-like and particle-like properties respectively. If we act upon it in one way it appears to behave like a shower of particles, and if in another way, like a succession of waves. The reality itself is such that it is able to be validly conceived and observed in both of these ways. Analogously the divine Reality is not directly known *an sich*. But when human beings relate themselves to it in the mode of I–Thou encounter they experience it as personal. Indeed in the context of that relationship it *is* personal, not It but He or She. When human beings relate themselves to the Real in the mode of non-personal awareness they experience it as non-personal, and in the context of this relationship it *is* non-personal.

Each of these two basic categories, God and the Absolute, is schematised or made concrete within actual religious experience as a range of particular gods or absolutes. These are, respectively, the *personae* and the *impersonae* in terms of which the Real is humanly known. And the particularising factor (corresponding, in its function, to time in the schematisation of the Kantian categories) is the range of human cultures, actualising different though overlapping aspects of our immensely complex human potentiality for awareness of the transcendent. It is in relation to different ways of being human, developed within the civilisations and cultures of the earth, that the Real, apprehended through the concept of God, is experienced specifically as the God of Israel, or as the Holy Trinity, or as Shiva, or as Allah, or as Vishnu . . . And it is in relation to yet other forms of life that the Real, apprehended through the concept of the Absolute, is experienced as Brahman, or as Nirvana, or as Being, or as Sunyata . . .

On this view our various religious languages – Buddhist, Christian, Muslim, Hindu . . . – each refer to a divine phenomenon or configuration of divine phenomena. When we speak of a personal God, with moral attributes and purposes, or when we speak of the non-personal Absolute, Brahman, or of the Dharmakaya, we are speaking of the Real as humanly experienced: that is, as phenomenon.

4 THE RELATION BETWEEN THE REAL *AN SICH* AND ITS *PERSONAE* AND *IMPERSONAE*

It follows from this distinction between the Real as it is in itself and as it is thought and experienced through our religious concepts that we cannot apply to the Real *an sich* the characteristics encountered in its *personae* and *impersonae*. Thus it cannot be said to be one or many, person or thing, substance or process, good or evil, purposive or non-purposive. None of the concrete descriptions that apply within the realm of human experience can apply literally to the unexperiencable ground of that realm. For whereas the phenomenal world is structured by our own conceptual frameworks, its noumenal ground is not. We cannot even speak of this as a thing or an entity. (We shall see later – in Chapter 16.4 – that the Buddhist concept of śūnyatā in one of its developments, namely as an anti-concept excluding all concepts, provides a good symbol for the Real *an sich*.) However we can make certain purely formal statements about the postulated Real in itself. The most famous instance in western religious discourse of such a formal statement is Anselm's definition of God as that than which no greater can be conceived. This formula refers to the ultimate divine reality without attributing to it any concrete characteristics. And in this purely formal mode we can say of the postulated Real *an sich* that it is the noumenal ground of the encountered gods and experienced absolutes witnessed to by the religious traditions.

There are at least two thought-models in terms of which we can conceive of the relationship between the Real *an sich* and its *personae* and *impersonae*. One is that of noumenon and phenomena, which enables us to say that the noumenal Real is such as to be authentically experienced as a range of both theistic and non-theistic phenomena. On this basis we cannot, as we have seen, say that the Real *an sich* has the characteristics displayed by its manifestations, such as (in the case of the heavenly Father) love and justice or (in the case of Brahman) consciousness and bliss. But it is nevertheless the noumenal ground of these characteristics. In so far as the heavenly Father and Brahman are two authentic manifestations of the Real, the love and justice of the one and the consciousness and bliss of the other are aspects of the Real as manifested within human experience. As the noumenal ground of these and other modes of experience, and yet transcending all of them, the Real is so rich in content that it can only be finitely experienced in the various partial and inadequate ways which the history of religions describes.

The other model is the more familiar one in western thought of analogical predication, classically expounded by Aquinas. According to him we can say that God is, for example, good – not in the sense in which we say of a human being that he or she is good, nor on the other hand in a totally unrelated sense, but in the sense that there is in the divine nature a quality that is limitlessly superior and yet at the same time analogous to human goodness. But Aquinas was emphatic that we cannot know what the divine super-analogue of goodness is like: 'we cannot grasp what God is, but only what He is not and how other things are related to Him' (*S. c. G.*, I:30:4 – Pegis 1955, 141). Further, the divine attributes which are distinguished in human thought and given such names as love, justice, knowledge, power, are identical in God. For 'God . . . as considered in Himself, is altogether one and simple, yet our intellect knows Him according to diverse conceptions because it cannot see Him as He is in Himself.'[19] When we take these two doctrines together and apply them to the Real we see that, whilst there is a noumenal ground for the phenomenal divine attributes, this does not enable us to trace each attribute separately upwards into the Godhead or the Real. They represent the Real as both reflected and refracted within human thought and experience. But nevertheless the Real is the ultimate ground or source of those qualities which characterise each divine *persona* and *impersona* insofar as these are authentic phenomenal manifestations of the Real.

This relationship between the ultimate noumenon and its multiple phenomenal appearances, or between the limitless transcendent reality and our many partial human images of it, makes possible mythological speech about the Real. I define a myth as a story or statement which is not literally true but which tends to evoke an appropriate dispositional attitude to its subject-matter. Thus the truth of a myth is a practical truthfulness: a true myth is one which rightly relates us to a reality about which we cannot speak in non-mythological terms.[20] For we exist inescapably in relation to the Real, and in all that we do and undergo we are inevitably having to do with it in and through our neighbours and our world. Our attitudes and actions are accordingly appropriate or inappropriate not only in relation to our physical and social environments but also in relation to our ultimate environment. And true religious myths are accordingly those that evoke in us attitudes and modes of behaviour which are appropriate to our situation in relation to the Real.

But what is it for human attitudes, behaviours, patterns of life to be appropriate or inappropriate within this ultimate situation? It is for the *persona* or *impersona* in relation to which we live to be an authentic manifestation of the Real and for our practical response to be appropriate to that manifestation. To the extent that a *persona* or *impersona* is in soteriological alignment with the Real, an appropriate response to that deity or absolute is an appropriate response to the Real. It need not however be the only such response: for other phenomenal manifestations of the Real within other human traditions evoke other responses which may be equally appropriate.

Why however use the term 'Real' in the singular? Why should there not be a number of ultimate realities? There is of course no reason, *a priori*, why the closest approximation that there is to a truly ultimate reality may not consist in either an orderly federation or a feuding multitude or an unrelated plurality. But if from a religious point of view we are trying to think, not merely of what is logically possible (namely, anything that is conceivable), but of the simplest hypothesis to account for the plurality of forms of religious experience and thought, we are, I believe, led to postulate 'the Real'. For each of the great traditions is oriented to what it regards as the Ultimate as the sole creator or source of the universe, or as that than which no greater can be conceived, or as the final ground or nature of everything. Further, the 'truthfulness' of each tradition is shown by its soteriological effectiveness. But what the traditions severally regard as ultimates are different and therefore cannot all be truly ultimate. They can however be different manifestations of the truly Ultimate within different streams of human thought-and-experience – hence the postulation of the Real *an sich* as the simplest way of accounting for the data. But we then find that if we are going to speak of the Real at all, the exigencies of our language compel us to refer to it in either the singular or the plural. Since there cannot be a plurality of ultimates, we affirm the true ultimacy of the Real by referring to it in the singular. Indian thought meets this problem with the phrase 'The One without a second'.[21] The Real, then, is the ultimate Reality, not one among others; and yet it cannot literally be numbered: it is the unique One without a second.

But if the Real in itself is not and cannot be humanly experienced, why postulate such an unknown and unknowable *Ding an sich*? The answer is that the divine noumenon is a necessary postulate of the pluralistic religious life of humanity. For within each tradition we regard as real the object of our worship or contemplation. If, as I have already argued, it is also proper to regard as real the objects of worship or contemplation within the other traditions, we are led to postulate the Real *an sich* as the presupposition of the veridical character of this range of forms of religious experience.[22] Without this postulate we should be left with a plurality of *personae* and *impersonae* each of which is claimed to be the Ultimate, but no one of which alone can be. We should have either to regard all the reported experiences as illusory or else return to the confessional position in which we affirm the authenticity of our own stream of religious experience whilst dismissing as illusory those occurring within other traditions. But for those to whom neither of these options seems realistic the pluralistic affirmation becomes inevitable, and with it the postulation of the Real *an sich*, which is variously experienced and thought as the range of divine phenomena described by the history of religion. This is accordingly the hypothesis that is now to be developed.

Notes

1. R. A. Nicholson [1950] 1978, 166.
2. *Tao Te Ching* 1982, 17. There has been considerable discussion of the enigmatic first chapter of the *Tao Te Ching* and its different interpretations (see e.g. David Loy 1985); but the translation which I

have quoted seems to reflect the nearest there is to a current consensus.

3. Thus Calvin taught that we do not know God's essence but only God as revealed to us ([1559] 1962, I:xiii:21).

4. Cf. *Summa Theologica*, part I, Q. 12, art. 7. On this aspect of Aquinas' thought see further Wilfred Cantwell Smith 1979, ch. 5.

5. For example, Lactantius, *On the Wrath of God* (quoted by Otto [1917] 1936, 99); Dionysius the Areopagite, *On the Divine Names*, ch. 1; Augustine, *On Christian Doctrine*, I:6; John Scotus Erigena, *On the Division of Nature*, bk I; *Theologia Germanica*, ch. 1.

6. See e.g. William Alston 1956; Keith E. Yandell 1975 and 1979; Peter C. Appleby 1980; Alvin Plantinga 1980.

7. Thus Augustine goes too far when he says that 'God is not even to be called ineffable because to say that is to make an assertion about him' (*On Christian Doctrine*, I:6).

8. Cf. Plantinga 1980, 23 and 25.

9. Cf. bk I, ch. 30, para. 4, and *Summa Theologica*, part I, Q. 12, art. 7. See also W. A. Wolfson 1957.

10. The best-known use of the Kantian epistemology in the philosophy of religion is Rudolf Otto's view of the concept of the holy or the numinous as an *a priori* category of the human mind. He held that this religious *a priori* is non-rational but is schematised by the operations of rationality. Thus 'The *tremendum*, the daunting and repelling moment of the numinous, is schematized by means of the rational ideas of justice, moral will, and the exclusion of what is opposed to morality; and schematized thus, it becomes the holy "Wrath of God" . . . The *fascinans*, the attracting and alluring moment of the numinous, is schematized by means of the ideas of goodness, mercy, love, and, so schematized, becomes all that we mean by Grace . . .' (Otto [1917] 1936, 144–5). For a more recent use, with much more in common with the thesis being developed here, see Robert Oakes 1973.

11. See e.g. Barry F. Anderson 1975; William N. Dember 1960; S. T. Fiske 1984; Harvey, Hunt and Schroder 1961.

12. See e.g. Berger and Luckmann 1967; Burkart Holzner 1968; Arbib and Hesse, 1986.

13. And also as it may appear to creatures with different cognitive equipment from our own. Kant was conscious that he was investigating the specifically *human* forms and categories of perception (*Crit. Pure Reason*, B59).

14. For an important discussion of information theory in relation to the epistemology of religion see John Bowker 1978.

15. For indications that information is conveyed extra-sensorily in a non-linguistic mode, see Ian Gratton-Guinness 1985.

16. Cf. Naranjo and Ornstein 1971, 170–2.

17. The term 'Absolute' seems to be the best that we have, even though it is not ideal for the purpose, being more naturally applied to some non-personal manifestations of the Real than to others. It is more naturally applicable, e.g., to Brahman than to Nirvana – although

Edward Conze found it proper to say that 'The ultimate reality, also called Dharma by the Buddhists, or Nirvana, is . . . very much akin to the philosophical notion of the "Absolute" . . .' (Edward Conze 1975; Masao Abe also identifies *Mu*, Nothingness, with the absolute – Abe 1985a, 20).

18. Ian Barbour 1974, ch. 5. Cf. Conrad Hyers 1983.
19. *Summa Theologica*, part I, Q. 13, art. 12 – Regis 1945, I:133. Or, more succinctly, 'All divine perfections are in reality identical', *Compendium theologiae*, 22, cited by F. C. Copleston 1955, 135.
20. This concept of myth is developed more fully in Chapter 19.2–4.
21. *Chāndogya Up.*, VI:2:4 (Radhakrishnan 1969, 449). Cf. Shankara [7th–8th century] 1978, 54. Maimonides grappled with the same problem: 'It would be extremely difficult for us to find, in any language whatsoever, words adequate to this subject, and we can only employ inadequate language. In our endeavour to show that God does not include a plurality, we can only say "He is one", although "one" and "many" are both terms which serve to distinguish quantity. We therefore make the subject clearer, and show to the understanding the way of truth by saying He is one but does not possess the attribute of unity' ([12th century] 1904, 81).
22. 'If we do not postulate the ultimate Focus, the subject, the inaccessible X lying beyond the contents of belief and experience, we might consider the real Focus as it enters into lives itself to be a projection' (Ninian Smart 1981, 187).

15

The *Personae* of the Real

The Real is one – sages name it variously.[1]

1 THE NEED TO THINK-AND-EXPERIENCE THE REAL AS PERSONAL

If the Real is present to all forms of existence as the ground of their ever-changing being, and if 'things known are in the knower according to the mode of the knower', finite persons will naturally tend to be conscious of the Real as a divine Thou. And so we find that from the earliest forms of archaic religion through the still-developing post-axial traditions the forms of experience in which, according to our hypothesis, the Real is present to human consciousness have usually (though not always) been hypostatised divine persons.

This does not need to be spelled out at length. Archaic religion is populated by countless gods and goddesses. Some are nature deities, personifications of the fertile energy by which plants and animals live; others are deified ancestors; others good or evil spirits in animal shape or formlessly haunting numinous places. These are powers who are able to work us well or ill and whom humans can worship and try to beseech, flatter, bribe or cope with by the magic of sacrifice. The world is full of such spirit-life, whether floating benignly above us in the sky or actively present on earth in the shape of unseen neighbours who can be either powerful allies or dangerous foes.[2]

That the Real is experienced as the divine Thou in the post-axial traditions of Semitic origin – Judaism, Christianity and Islam – needs no arguing; and I shall be saying more about these major divine *personae* presently. But the personification of the Real is scarcely less characteristic of the oriental traditions. Until comparatively recently the West tended to think of the richly pluralistic religious life of India in terms of one only of its many schools of thought, namely advaita Vedanta. This simplification was aided by the reifying effect of the western term 'Hinduism'.[3] But neither in the past nor today has most of the wide and multifarious stream of life that we call Hinduism been other than theistic. The cities of the original Dravidian inhabitants that have been excavated in the present century contain images of deities; and the ancient Aryan hymns refer to many gods, prominent among them being Indra, Varuna, Agni and Soma. However in the *Rig-Veda* there is also the idea, which was to become a fairly universal Indian assumption, that the many gods are all aspects of the one ultimate divine reality:

> They call it Indra, Mitra, Varuna and Agni
> And also heavenly, beautiful Garutman:
> The Real is one, though sages name it variously.
> (*Rig-Veda*, I:164:46)

The continued mingling of Aryan, Dravidian and other religious influences in India in the millennium from about 600 BCE to about 600 CE created what the modern West thinks of as 'Hinduism'. Within this complex and many-levelled history we must distinguish between the reflections of the philosophers and the concrete religious life of the ordinary people as it was carried on in homes and village temples, at the annual festivals and throughout the fabric of a pervasively religious culture. This village religion has always been predominantly theistic, or indeed polytheistic. The same has not been true, on the other hand, of Indian philosophy. Most of its once flourishing but now defunct schools were non-theistic, some even sceptical or materialistic. The one now living classical school, the Vedanta, has itself taken both non-theistic and theistic forms. Advita or 'non-dualist' Vedanta, with Shankara as its greatest exponent, teaches that Brahman, the non-personal Absolute, is all; and that the atman, the eternal self within each of us, is ultimately identical with Brahman. Shankara did not despise the religion of ordinary people and he was himself a worshipper of Shiva; but he regarded devotional worship as the lower and popular side of the religious life, a help at a certain stage on the way rather than the goal itself. On the other hand the vishishtadvaitist ('modified non-dualist') Vedanta of Ramanuja and the dvaitist or 'dualist' philosophy of Madhva are monotheistic. The Ultimate is God, the eternal Person; and these philosophies have accordingly provided a framework for the Bhakti movement

whose principal scripture, the Bhagavad Gita, has long been in
effect the bible of most Indians. Bhakti, or devotion to the divine
Thou, spread rapidly from the ninth century CE, transforming the
Indian religious scene. Indeed 'From the tenth century on all that
is most vital in Hinduism manifests itself in the form of *bhakti*'
(Zaehner 1966, 134).

Thus whilst the philosophers were evolving and debating their
rival systems the ordinary people in the thousands of villages
were worshipping a god or gods. Two great alternative divine
figures came to dominate the scene: Shiva, with his female consort
Kali or Durga, and Vishnu, with his consort Lakshmi. The
Vaishnavites (worshippers of Vishnu) have always affirmed a
number of divine incarnations, including Krishna and Rama, each
of whom has been the focus of intense personal devotion. The
Shaivites (worshippers of Shiva) also have a tremendous devotional
tradition going back to the Shaiva-Siddhanta of the fifth century
CE, within which some of the world's most moving theistic
literature has been produced. But, whilst most Hindus are either
Vaishnavites or Shaivites, the more reflective among them do not
hold that Vishnu or Shiva, as the case may be, is the 'true' and
the other a 'false' god. Rather these are seen as alternative
manifestations of the ultimate personal divine reality, who can be
approached along a plurality of paths. As is said by the Lord
Krishna in the Bhagavad Gita, 'In whatsoever way men approach
me, in that same way I receive them (or return their love)!'[4]

Is not Buddhism, however, non-theistic or even atheistic; or
indeed perhaps not a religion at all but rather a philosophy? The
name covers a wide range of developments of the original
teachings of Gautama. John Bowker, with his eye primarily on the
Pali scriptures of the Theravada, concludes that there is a sense in
which 'Buddhism is irredeemably theistic' (Bowker 1978, 296). On
the other hand Masao Abe, from the Zen point of view, says that
'Buddhism is nontheistic in its basic nature' (Abe 1985a, 157). And
it is certainly true that the tradition does not affirm an ultimate
personal Being who is the creator *ex nihilo* of all else that exists. In
this precise sense Buddhism is presumptively atheistic or, more
precisely, agnostic. For Gautama himself the question whether or
not the universe had a beginning was unresolved (see Chapter
9.1); and the unexcluded possibility of a cosmic beginning carries
with it the further possibility of a creator. However the Buddha's
concern was soteriological rather than metaphysical, and the
theistic possibility was not within the horizon of his interest.[5]

But on a lower level it seems clear that Gautama and his followers accepted the current Indian cosmology with its vast hierarchy of heavens and hells presided over by innumerable gods and devils. Such a belief is reflected at many places in the Pali scriptures. For example in the account of Gautama's death it is said that 'the gods (devas) of the ten world systems assembled together to behold the Tathagata (i.e. the Buddha)' (*Dīgha Nikāya*, II:139 – Davids and Davids 1938, 151). The Maha–Samaya Suttanta is entirely concerned with the gods as they gather to do homage to the Buddha: 'gods from the ten thousand world systems oft-times assembled there that they might visit the Exalted One and the band of brethren' (*Dīgha Nikāya*, II:253 – Davids and Davids 1938, 284). Further, the supreme god Brahma plays a vital part in the inauguration of the Buddhist movement. For we read that when Gautama attained to enlightenment he thought that the truth was too high and difficult for humankind to receive. However Maha Brahma, Great Brahma, supreme God, intervened:

And the Great Brahma, brethren, draping his outer robe over one shoulder and stooping his right knee to the ground raised his joined hands towards Vipassi the Exalted One, the Arahant, the Buddha Supreme and said: 'Lord! may the Exalted One preach the Truth! May the Welcome One preach the truth! There are beings whose eyes are hardly dimmed by dust, they are perishing from not hearing the Truth; they will come to be knowers of the Truth.'[6]

And in due course the Buddha took pity on humankind and the Wheel of Dharma was set turning for the salvation of many.

There can, then, be no doubt as to the reality and activity of the gods in the thought-world of the Pali canon. They are however finite and temporal beings still within the process of imperfect existence which a Buddha has transcended. Accordingly we find the gods revering and being taught by Gautama. They are penultimate rather than ultimate realities, divine phenomena rather than the divine noumenon itself.[7]

The need for a personal god has played an even greater part in the development of the Mahayana, which emerged at about the same time as Christianity and has grown to be numerically the major form of Buddhism. Here the figure of the Buddha has been elevated, not merely by popular imagination but by religious reflection, from the greatest of human teachers to a being of universal power and significance. Indeed the cosmic Buddha is referred to in the Lotus Sutra (VII:31 – Müller [1884] 1908b, vol. 21) as Devatideva, supreme god of gods. In the *trikāya* doctrine the earthly Buddhas, such as Gautama, constitute the Nirmanakaya or 'body of manifestation'; these are incarnations of heavenly Buddhas who constitute the Sambhogakaya or 'body of bliss'; and these heavenly Buddha-figures are themselves all one in the Dharmakaya, or 'truth body', which is the ultimate Reality or (since it transcends human thought) the Void or the Formless which is also Nirvana.

In another important development the Mahayana produced the ideal of the bodhisattvas or Buddhas-to-be who (like Gautama himself) instead of entering Nirvana elect to remain as individuals in the human world to lead others from misery to enlightenment. They reveal the compassionate aspect of Buddhahood, expressing the kind of self-giving love for humanity that is, in another faith-world, expressed in Jesus' sacrificial death. As personal manifestations of ultimate compassion the bodhisattvas became objects of worship, and sects developed in which devotion is directed to a particular bodhisattva, such as Amitabha (or Amida) who in virtue of the immense holiness generated by innumerable lives of self-sacrifice is able to draw those who call upon him in faith into his own paradise, from which they can readily make their final transition to Nirvana.

The same kind of development has occurred, though perhaps less markedly, within the religious life of China. Confucianism is often listed among the world religions. And yet K'ung-fu-tzu himself, the sixth-century BCE sage, was much less a prophet than a moralist and social thinker, concerned to create harmony in society on the basis of mutual respect or reciprocity. It is true that K'ung referred to the Way which he taught as the Way of Heaven; and he apparently thought of Heaven as an overarching divine personal or quasi-personal reality. But he seems to have kept relatively aloof from the popular religious practices of his day, and his influence was exerted among the highly educated governing class rather than among the masses. But from long before to long after K'ung's time the ordinary people of China were regularly offering sacrifices to local gods and spirits of the earth and air, and venerating their ancestors. Rulers offered sacrifices to their regional deities and it was the duty of the emperor to offer sacrifices to Heaven on behalf of the whole realm. K'ung himself was elevated, by the first century CE, to a level at which sacrifices were offered to him; and in modern times (in 1906) he was formally declared by imperial decree to be 'Co-Assessor with the deities of Heaven and Earth' (Ballou 1948, 462). Thus popular Chinese religion through the ages illustrates again the tendency of the human mind to think of the transcendent in personal terms, as a being or beings with whom people can have dealings through the medium of their religious cult.

The other major Chinese religious influence stems from the *Tao Te Ching*. The central concept is the Tao, the eternal principle of the universe, in some ways analogous to the Stoic and to some Christian notions of the Logos. Thus Taoism was a quasi-theistic movement, though a highly philosophical one. But once again we must remember that the great majority of ordinary Chinese villagers, although affected by the pervasive influences of both Confucius and Taoism, have always gone their own traditional ways, appeasing local spirits and deities, observing the seasonal festivals, venerating their ancestors and believing in magic. Early in the Christian era Mahayana Buddhism spread northwards, adding a third major influence to the complex field of spiritual forces constituting Chinese religion. But down at least to the time of the Maoist revolution of the 1930s the ordinary people of China, like the ordinary people of the rest of the world, seem to have needed to think of the transcendent as a personal reality or realities, able to be approached by means of ritual, prayer and sacrifice. And even during the more recent period there was for a while a tendency virtually to deify Chairman Mao himself.

Given that there is this almost universal propensity of the human mind to think-and-experience the presence of the Real in personal terms, what is the status and nature, from the point of view of our pluralistic hypothesis, of the numerous gods, goddesses and mono-deities? As an approach to this question we shall do well first to take note of their phenomenological character.

2 THE PHENOMENOLOGICAL FINITUDE OF THE GODS

According to the pluralistic hypothesis, when we speak of God as known within a particular religious tradition – Jahweh or Adonai, the heavenly Father or the Holy Trinity, Allah, Shiva, Vishnu and so on – we are speaking of a humanly experienced *persona* of the Real. And in describing these *personae* we have to make the distinction that was before Pascal's mind when he wrote his famous memorandum, during or after a mystical experience on the evening of 23 November 1654, between the God 'of the philosophers and scholars' and the 'God of Abraham, God of Isaac, God of Jacob'. In developed western systematic theology God is normally defined as infinite in all deity-constituting respects: existence or being, love or compassion, power, knowledge, goodness, wisdom . . . But this expansion to infinity is not given in the original moment or stream of religious experience out of which each tradition came. Here the conceptual element is limited to that which can shape concrete experience; and infinity is an experience-transcending concept.

The gods known in the archaic forms of religion are for the most part explicitly finite, their worshippers knowing what each one can do and where the limits of their respective jurisdictions lie. And even the divine *personae* of the developed monotheisms, as they enter into the experience of worship and into the religious life considered as an extension of worship, are not explicitly infinite but rather indefinitely great, exceeding our human horizon. God is encountered as one who is great beyond our ken, absolute lord of our lives and all-sufficient in relation to our needs; but the philosophical question of infinity nevertheless does not arise within religious experience itself. It is present of course in much of the liturgical language which the traditions have developed; but it is, I think, clear that it has entered this from the adjacent realm of theological reflection.

Let us illustrate this from the Judaic-Christian tradition. God is defined in classical Christian theism largely in terms of omni-attributes. These include infinite goodness and love, infinite wisdom and justice, omnipotence, omniscience and eternity. It seems best to regard infinity, not as a separate characteristic, but as a second-order qualifier of the first-order characteristics. Thus God is experienced as being good, loving, wise, just, righteous, powerful and aware – and, as a further meta-statement, God has all of these qualities to an infinite extent. Aseity, or self-existence, can also be regarded as a kind of infinity, namely infinite uncaused existence. But are these various limitless attributes affirmed on the basis of religious experience or of philosophical reasoning? Clearly they cannot be direct reports of religious experience. For as finite observers we could never directly experience, observe, verify, the infinite dimensions of an infinite reality. Thus whilst it can be given in religious experience that God is good, loving and powerful, it cannot also be given in human experience that God has these attributes to an infinite extent.

God's goodness, for example, is affirmed by believers on the basis of their experience of divine grace. The way to verify this goodness is given in one of the Psalms: 'O taste and see that the Lord is good! Happy is the man who takes refuge in him!' (Psalm 34:8). But we cannot 'taste and see' that the Lord is infinitely good. We may believe that the divine goodness is unlimited, and this belief will of course colour our awareness of God, so that we can say that we are conscious of living in the presence of the infinitely good God. But it remains true that what is actually experienced is a goodness to which we do not find any bounds. The further conviction that this goodness extends to infinity is a conclusion of theological reasoning.[8] There is an analogy here with our visual observation of the physical universe around us. As we look into the night sky, gazing up at its millions of stars and reflecting on the immense galaxies and the vast inter-stellar spaces, we may well be inclined to say that we are gazing out into infinity. But nevertheless we are not actually observing the infinite dimension of space. The belief or assumption that what we are looking at is infinite derives – like our belief in the divine infinity – from theoretical considerations. We cannot make sense of the idea that space ends at a certain point, and so we assume its infinity. And theologically the thought of God's ultimacy naturally unfolds into the concept of divine infinity.

I suggest, then, that in the actual first-order business of the religious life (as distinguished from the second-order activities of theologians and philosophers) God is not apprehended as infinite, or as limitlessly this or that, but is apprehended under concrete images which vary in magnitude from the definitely limited to the indefinitely great. This is very evidently true of the experience of God recorded in the Hebrew scriptures. For the ancient Hebrews Jahweh had a proper name and a distinctive role as the unseen warrior-king of his people: 'The Lord is a man of war' (Ex. 15:3). He is described as speaking (Gen. 1:3), as hearing (Ex 16:12), as laughing (Ps. 2:4), and as having eyes (Amos 9:4), hands (Ps. 139:5), arms (Is. 51:9; Jer. 27:5), ears (Is. 22:14) and feet (Nahum

1:3), which he rests on a footstool (Is. 66:1). He comes down from heaven (Gen. 11:17), walks in Eden in the cool of the evening (Gen. 3:8), shuts the door of the ark (Ex. 33:22; Gen. 7:16). He expresses regret (Gen. 6:6; I Sam. 15:5), jealousy (Ex. 22:5; Deut. 5:9), disgust (Lev. 20:23) and hatred (Deut. 16:22; Ps. 11:5, 31:6, 45:7; Prov. 6:16; Is. 1:14, 61:8, 44:4); and he undergoes changes of mind (Ex. 32:14; II Sam. 24:16; Amos 7:3).

On rare occasions God is even seen by human beings. We read that 'When Abram was ninety-nine years old the Lord appeared to him, and said to him, "I am God Almighty; walk before me, and be blameless"' (Gen. 17:1); and again that 'the Lord appeared to [Abraham] by the oaks of Mamre, as he sat at the door of his tent in the heat of the day' (Gen. 18:1);[9] and subsequently that 'God appeared to Jacob . . . when he came from Paddan-aram' (Gen. 35:9). Later Moses is allowed to glimpse God (Ex. 33:22). Thus in this ancient thought-world it would seem that Jahweh was believed in as an immensely powerful local presence, capable of destructive violence, enjoying the smell of burnt offerings, dwelling in one region rather than another, the god of one people rather than of all peoples.

However, in a gradual development that was stimulated and guided by the great prophets of the axial age, there was a movement from the experience and thought of God in the early days, when he was (in Freud's phrase) a 'violent super-man of the beyond', to the God of the post-exilic period, who is too holy to be named, who is mysteriously transcendent and who has created the whole world by the power of the divine word.[10] And yet even in the later strata of the writings God is still spoken about in terms of indefinite greatness rather than in a strictly infinite mode. For the question of limitlessness is neither asked nor answered. It is true that when the Hebrew scriptures are seen through the spectacles either of later rabbinic thought or of post-biblical Christian theology there are passages which then seem to speak of divine infinity. For example, 'For as the heavens are high above the earth, so great is his steadfast love towards those who fear him' (Ps. 103:11). But when we remember that in the ancient world the 'heavens' were not thought to be endlessly distant from the earth, we see that the psalmist's expression speaks of the incomparable quality rather than of a quantitative infinity of divine love. Again, there is the wonderful poetry of Isaiah 40 extolling God's transcendent greatness. But here again the use of earthly comparisons – marking the heavens with a span, taking up the isles like fine dust, and the earth's inhabitants being like grasshoppers before the Lord – keeps the greater as well as the lesser term of the comparison within the realm of the truly immense rather than the strictly infinite.

Is not God described, however, as 'everlasting' or 'eternal' (Gen. 21:33)? Moses says 'The eternal God is your dwelling place, and underneath are the everlasting arms' (Deut. 33:27). Again, the psalmists say, 'Blessed be the Lord, the God of Israel, from everlasting to everlasting' (Ps. 41:13); 'Before the mountains were brought forth, or ever thou hadst formed the earth and the world, from everlasting to everlasting thou art God' (Ps. 90:2); 'the steadfast love of the Lord is from everlasting to everlasting' (Ps. 103:17); and Isaiah says, 'The Lord is the everlasting God' (Is. 40:28). However the word *olam* used in these passages is probably derived from a root meaning 'hide', so that it signifies that which is hidden, hence 'the time which was removed beyond human sight and which therefore could no longer be perceived by man' (Barr 1969, 93), and it is to be noted that the word is applied in this sense not only to God but also to the covenant with Israel. The idea seems to be that of something stretching away into the past or future, or both, beyond our horizon. God is thought of as in this respect great beyond our ken; but the question of eternity, in the sense either of unlimited duration or of infinite non-temporal being, has been neither asked nor answered. The question does not, I am suggesting, arise within first-hand religious discourse about 'the God of Abraham, of Isaac, and of Jacob', but rather in the reasonings and speculations of the philosophers.

But again, is not the deity of the Hebrew scriptures often described as infinitely powerful? God says to Abraham, and again to Jacob, 'I am God Almighty' (Gen. 17:1, 35:11). God is *el shaddai*, usually englished as 'the almighty'. But *shaddai* means 'mighty' or 'sufficient', so that in its translation as 'almighty', with the connotation of infinite power, a later and more theologically developed conception would seem to be at work. As an experiential expression it means, perhaps, 'the All-Sufficient one'.[11] And this, surely, is the way in which God is known in first-hand religious experience. In relation to humanity, and indeed in relation to all of reality in so far as this impinges upon human beings, God is known as the supreme power and determiner of destiny, the One upon whom we depend utterly and by whose grace alone we live. But questions that go beyond the scope of human experience belong to the province of the intellect engaging in metaphysical speculation; and this is to be distinguished from religious experience itself.

Essentially the same continues to be true within rabbinic Judaism. The rabbis have frequently affirmed that we know God as a transcendent moral reality impinging upon our practical living; and they have seen God's nature, revealed in scripture and history, as one of justice and mercy.[12] A wealth of rabbinic stories treat the Holy One, blessed be he, as just and wise, merciful and gracious in ways which do not indeed involve limits but which on the other hand do not and were not intended to raise the philosophical question of infinity.

In the New Testament the prophetic experience of God as the personal Lord making insistent ethical demands upon Israel is expressed again in the teachings of Jesus, together with a tremendous sense of the gracious personal character of God as our heavenly Father. But is this heavenly Father, this divine Thou to whom and about whom Jesus spoke, thought of as infinite? The Father exists 'in heaven' (e.g. Matt. 6:9); he has made humanity from the beginning as male and female (Matt. 19:4); he 'clothes the grass of the fields' (Matt. 6:30) and is able to care for all our needs (Matt. 6:25–33); his spirit enables Jesus to perform miracles (e.g. Matt. 12:28); and he could if he wished send 'more than twelve legions of angels' to save his son from death (Matt. 26:53). He is, then, as in the older Hebrew scriptures, the All-Sufficient One in whom Jesus can have total confidence and to the doing of whose will he can unreservedly dedicate himself. But the question of the Father's infinity is neither asked nor answered in the directly practical and existential teachings of Jesus. As one who lived by religious experience rather than by theological speculation, Jesus knew God as concretely related to himself and to his fellow children of Israel. He was aware of God's power not as an abstract infinity but in concrete and therefore finite manifestations, particularly in the healing of the sick. He was aware of God's knowledge, but again not as a conceptualised infinity but always in relation to particular concrete circumstances. God knows human creatures through and through, so that even the hairs of our heads are numbered (Matt. 10:30); knows the natural world, so that not a sparrow falls without his awareness of it (Matt. 10:29); and knows when the world's last day is to be (Matt. 24:36). But all this, whilst it indicates a vast and altogether super-human awareness, far beyond our own, still does not touch the philosophical question of omniscience.

Again, Jesus speaks of God's love or forgiveness as truly stupendous, so that we are to imitate the heavenly Father with a love that is all-embracing and a forgiveness that goes on and on towards the distant horizon of the 'seventy times seven' (Matt. 18:22). But he also speaks of a sin which God never forgives (Matt. 12:31), and perhaps (though this can be disputed) of the consigning of many to eternal torment (Matt. 25:41).[13] In St John's Gospel God does not appear to be the heavenly Father of all humanity, for there are both children of God and children of the devil (John 8:41–7) – though of course we must not assume that the speeches attributed to the Christ of the fourth Gospel were in fact spoken by the historical Jesus. The heavenly Father seems, often at least, to be the God of the Jews, comparatively little concerned with the rest of humanity. 'I was sent', says Jesus, 'only to the lost sheep of the house of Israel' (Matt. 15:21). He did indeed extend his vision of God's love in his parable of the good Samaritan (Luke 10:29–37) and in his healing of the Canaanite woman's daughter (Matt. 15:21–8). But in general he seems to have been aware of the divine love and claim and of his own mission in the circumscribed context of the life of Israel (Matt. 10:5–6, 15:24).

These streams of primary theistic experience in which the Real has classically been reflected have each subsequently been channelled into an interpretive framework of thought. In the case of Judaism this has always been somewhat unsystematic and flexible, whilst in the case of Christianity it has until recently generally been highly systematised and rigid. Within these frameworks the divine Thou, originally experienced as a present all-sufficient power of commanding authority and trustworthy goodness, has been defined by the speculative intellect as infinite. Philosophical issues which do not arise within experience itself, but which are unavoidable by philosophical thought, have been posed and settled; metaphysical questions have been asked and answered which go beyond the concerns of the practical religious life. But the point that I want to stress is that the experienced divine *personae* are not phenomenologically infinite, although – according to our hypothesis – they are manifestations within finite human experience of the Real which, being truly ultimate, has no limits.

3 THE GODS AS *PERSONAE* OF THE REAL

In developing this hypothesis further we must ask what it is to be personal. We have a family of words, 'person', 'personality', 'personhood', 'personal'; and they all arise ultimately from observation of the same basic fact. This is that as a human baby grows and interacts with other human beings, undergoing her own unique stream of experience and reacting in her own way – partly on the basis of a genetic ground-plan and partly in the spontaneous creativity of life through time – she develops an inner psychic structure, which is her individual character, with a public 'face' which is her personality. Each such living psychic structure can be called a self: roughly, the character is the unconscious self whilst the personality is the conscious self or ego. For the character is the underlying and only slowly changing ground-plan which the personality expresses, whilst the personality is the conscious surface which lives in interaction with other selves. Thus the psychic 'face' is in fact an interface and personality is essentially inter-personal: to be a person is to be so in interaction with other persons.

It follows from this that the Real *an sich* cannot be said to be personal. For this would presuppose that the Real is eternally in relation to other persons. Whilst this is of course conceivable, it constitutes a pure *ad hoc* speculation rather than the most economical interpretation of the available data. For these include the facts (a) that the only persons of whom we know, namely humans, have existed (in their present form, *homo sapiens sapiens*) for about fifty thousand years, and therefore cannot provide an eternal dialogue-partner for the Real, and (b) that among humans the Real is experienced in non-personal as well as in personal ways. We may reasonably conclude, then, that the Real is personal not *an sich* but in interaction with human (and/or other finite) persons.

Personality, then, is not a substance but a network of relationships consisting in the ways in which one is seen by, acts upon and is responded to by others. This relational character of personality is well expressed by the psychological concept of the *persona* as a role that one builds within a certain group. One's personality exists in and is constituted by the range of these overlapping *personae*. The word *persona* comes originally from the Roman theatre, where it referred to the mask worn by an actor to indicate his part in the play.[14] This mask-connotation is stressed by C. G. Jung in his use of the term.[15] However I want to put a somewhat different stress upon it. One's *persona* in relation to a particular group or individual is not an extrinsic mask that one puts on: it *is* oneself within that system of relationships. It constitutes one's self living and responding within that particular context. Thus my neighbours' image of me, which is my *persona* in relation to them, is *me* in so far as I am part of the community which I conjointly form with them. A *persona* is accordingly a social reality living in the consciousness, memories and ongoing interactions of a community.

Further, within the different overlapping groups of which one is a member, with their various and shifting centres of interest, one may present partially different *personae*. One may be, to varying extents, 'a different person' in one's family, with colleagues at work, drinking with a group at a bar after work, with other members of a squash-playing or mountain-climbing or stamp-collecting or other leisure group, with fellow activists in a political party and so on. One can thus live out several overlapping roles within different contexts of activity and sets of inter-relationship. And each such *persona* is built up through the sequence of events constituting the life of that group. Thus personality is not only essentially inter-personal but as a corollary essentially *historical*, having its concrete character within and as part of a particular unique stream of events in the creation of which contingency and freedom have been important factors. The intertwining threads of history of which one is a part can diverge or overlap to almost any extent, and one's *personae* may exhibit many different degrees of fixity and plasticity and may accordingly change more slowly or more rapidly. There is indeed immense variety in the subtle interactions and systems of inter-relationship and mutual perceptions of different human beings through time.[16]

Pressing further the idea of a range of *personae* of the same individual, we can imagine someone entering into several quite separate communities with no overlap or communication between them – like Gulliver finding himself first as a giant among the midgets of Lilliput and then as a relative savage among the superior equine Houyhnhnms. In each of these different and unconnected worlds he was a different *persona* – although of course in a later *persona*, writing *Gulliver's Travels,* he was able to recount the experiences of both.

The varying *personae* of an individual within different social contexts provides a partial analogy for the plurality of divine *personae* which have developed in relation to different human faith-communities.[17] According to our hypothesis the Real is always present to human life, with our capacity for religious awareness; and in its theistic forms that presence consists in the various divine *personae* who are known in different steams of religious history. Each of these has an experienced social reality and power within the life of the worshipping community in relation to which it has been formed, and it constitutes the Real as perceived and responded to by that community.

The analogy is however only partial in that, when we speak of different *personae* of the same human self, that self is a particular finite system of character dispositions, whereas when we speak of the *personae* of the Real, the Real *an sich* is not a greater self or a divine dispositional system, but the ultimate ground, transcending human conceptuality, of the range of *personae* and *impersonae* through which humans are related to it. However, despite this limitation of the analogy, the notion of a divine *persona* expresses well the way in which the gods are formed in interaction with their worshippers. For they are at the same time both idealised projections of the character of those worshippers *and* manifestations of the Real. A divine *persona* arises at the interface between the Real and the human spirit, and is thus a joint product of transcendent presence and earthly imagination, of divine revelation and human seeking.

Such an image or *persona* is not permanent and unchanging. On the contrary, it may well undergo development in the course of a faith-community's religious history, mediating a more or, as the case may be, less authentic awareness of the Real. Over long periods, far exceeding the scope of any individual's observation, the gods have changed. The historian of religion can sometimes write their biographies. We have already noted the development of the Jahweh *persona* in ancient Israel. There were even more complex developments of deity in ancient India. Thus Trevor Ling is able to speak of the 'career patterns of the Vedic gods' (1968, 32) whose interweaving trajectories, individual rise and fall, alliances, unions and bifurcations, constitute a rich mythic history.[18]

4 TWO DIVINE *PERSONAE*: THE HINDU KRISHNA AND THE JAHWEH OF ISRAEL

To show the theory of divine *personae* at work in the interpretation of religious history let us look briefly at two independent facets of the human experience of the Real as personal: Krishna and Jahweh. The character of the Lord Krishna, as worshipped in the Vaishnavite tradition of India, is revealed in the mythic story, elaborated in the Mahabharata and interpreted theologically in the Bhagavad Gita, of the incarnation of the supreme God Vishnu. Vishnu and Krishna cannot however, as hidden and manifest forms of the ultimate Reality, be separated within Vaishnavite devotion; and in the Gita the human Arguna is given for a moment a 'celestial eye' to see Krishna as Vishnu: 'Then did the son of Pandu see the whole wide universe in One converged, there in the body of the God of gods, yet divided out in multiplicity' (xi:13 – Zaehner 1969, 83). The Krishna myth is expressed in the individual's daily *puga*, in the communal worship, with its priesthood and its music and incense, in annual and regional festivals, and in innumerable pictorial representations and statues of Krishna and his consort Radha. All this constitutes a rich, complex and satisfying 'form of life' or 'lived myth', which is characteristically Indian and which has its own massive solidity accumulated in the believing participation of successive generations from time immemorial. This is the mythic world or 'space' which Krishna inhabits. It would be impossible to indicate who he is except in terms of this particular mythology set in the context of this particular strand of Indian religious history.

Israel's Jahweh is a quite different divine *persona*, instantiating the concept of God within a very different context. He is characterised, in narrative terms, as the God of Abraham, Isaac and Jacob, who brought the children of Israel out of bondage in Egypt and established them in the promised land, who made his covenant with them, raised up alien powers to punish them when they turned away from him and at the same time sent his prophets to recall them so that they might become a light to enlighten the peoples of the earth. This lived myth is made real to each new generation by the re-telling of the stories in the synagogue and in the family worship and rituals, and particularly at the great annual festivals – Passover, Yom Kippur, Rosh Hashanah. This tremendous mythic history in which Jews participate constitutes another powerful and spiritually nourishing form of life which has held the children of Israel together through so many centuries and through so much adversity. And once again it would be impossible to detach Jahweh or Adonai from his role in this particular stream of religious experience. His nature is revealed in the stories of his actions on the stage of Israelite history, and these stories construct a particular mythic world or 'space' within which Jahweh has his existence.

Thus Krishna and Jahweh, reflected respectively in Hindu and Jewish faith, are two quite distinct divine *personae* who appear within quite different cycles of stories. The two cycles are as independent of one another as two traditional fairy tales, each taking place in its own magic space and time. They differ however from fairy tales in that the latter are fantasies, akin to dreams, whereas the myths of a religious tradition are stories by which the story-telling community lives and in terms of which it understands its existence in the world. They thus shape its waking consciousness and affect in varying degrees its entire life.

Krishna and Jahweh, then, are real divine figures, central to different streams of human existence. Each is historical in the sense that he is part of the experience of a people as they have lived through the centuries. Their relationship to the publicly remembered sequence of past events is however different, reflecting respectively the keen Semitic interest and the vague Indian lack of interest in historiography. Jahweh's personal life – that is, his interactions with a group of finite persons – began indeed in the mists of pre-history with his self-revelation to Abraham, but then continued through relatively firm tracts of near-eastern history, religiously interpreted and remembered. As such he has a concrete personality, developed in interaction with his chosen people: he is a part of their history and they are a part of his. Krishna, on the other hand, is much more tenuously related to chronological history. His life on earth can only be very tentatively located by historical research within secular time.[19] The stories in which he appears have a legendary character. And yet he is a thoroughly historical figure in the sense that he has entered as a concrete personal reality into the life of generation after generation of people within the Vaishnavite religious world. Indeed so real is he as a person that a Roman Catholic living in Vrindaban, the legendary scene of Krishna's youth, where he had played with the gopi girls, can report that 'even today the great bhaktas of Vrindaban relate how it is possible to discover Krishna peeping archly from behind a tree, dancing his rose dance with gopis during especially blessed times, or to meet Radha on a lonely path, enquiring after her lover Krishna' (Klostermaier 1969, 15).

There are, needless to say, many other divine *personae*, each likewise describable only within the context of a particular strand of religious history: the heavenly Father of Christian faith, known through the distinctively Christian response to Jesus of Nazareth; the Allah of Islamic faith, known as self-revealed in the Qur'an through the prophet Muhammad; Shiva, known and intensely experienced within the Shaivite cults of India . . .

5 THE ONTOLOGICAL STATUS OF THE DIVINE *PERSONAE*

If we ask within the context of any one theistic tradition: What is the nature of the divine person to whom prayer is addressed? a minimal answer might be that, in addition to the many finite centres of consciousness, reason, emotion and will constituting the millions of human selves, there is another limitlessly greater such centre of consciousness which is the divine self. However this answer embodies the assumption (commonly made within each tradition) that there is only one divine person to be considered. But as soon as we recognise other objects of religious worship – Adonai, Allah, the heavenly Father, Shiva, Vishnu and many others – a more complex conception becomes necessary.

Can we achieve the needed additional complexity simply by supposing a plurality of divine selves? This is the polytheistic option. A cost-benefit analysis shows as its main advantage that it does justice to the fact that Christians worship the heavenly Father as a real divine person, whilst Muslims worship Allah as a real divine person, and Jews Adonai, and so on; so that thus far there appear to be a number of gods. On the other hand the main disadvantage of this model is that it conflicts with the affirmation of each tradition that its deity is the sole creator or source of all finite existence. Since there can only be one sole creator or source, polytheism reduces each of the gods from ultimacy to penultimacy. If, then, we want an hypothesis which retains the ultimacy as well as the experienced plurality of the divine this will require a more complex structure than a one-dimensional polytheism.

The next hypothesis that suggests itself is that of one God who is known within different faith communities by different names. Within this model 'Adonai', 'the heavenly Father', 'Allah', 'Shiva', 'Vishnu' and the others are different names for the same divine person. However if we start out on this road we shall soon find that we have to go a great deal further. For these different names express different understandings of deity which are integral to different traditions and are embedded in different histories. 'Adonai' as used by Jews signifies specifically the God whose covenant relationship with the children of Israel is documented in the Torah. The title 'God' as used by Christians refers to the heavenly Father of Jesus Christ, whose incarnation was the uniquely full and final divine self-revelation. The equivalent title 'Allah', as used by Muslims, refers to the Qur'anic Revealer whose message, delivered through the prophet Muhammad, completes and fulfils the earlier revelations contained in the Torah and the New Testament. And so on. Thus, if Jahweh and Shiva, Allah and Vishnu and the heavenly Father are all the same divine person, the different names by which that being is known must go with different 'faces' showing distinctive characteristics, each being central to a different historical drama of divine–human interaction. And so the question now arises of the relationship between these different 'faces' or (as I have been calling them) *personae*; and then of the relation between these collectively and the Real whose 'faces' they are.

Religious thought offers two important models of diversity in unity to which we can turn for illumination: the Christian concept of the trinity and the Buddhist concept of the *trikāya*. The doctrine of the trinity depicts God as three persons who are one-in-three and three-in-one. The meaning of 'person' is however understood in different ways in different versions of the doctrine. When 'person' is construed in something like the modern sense of an individual centre of consciousness and will we have 'social' conceptions of the trinity as three personal centres so intimately united as to form a complex unity of three-in-one. On the other hand when 'person' is construed in the sense of the Latin *persona*, as a mask or face, the *tres personae* are three different manifestations of the same divine reality: the one God, functioning as creator and ruler, is known as Father; functioning as redeemer, as Son; and functioning as inspirer, as Holy Spirit.

We are not concerned here with the respective merits of these different interpretations for the internal purposes of Christian theology but only with their value as possible models for the relationship between the different divine persons worshipped within the several monotheistic traditions, and between them and the Real. Using the 'social' conception of the trinity as a model we could suppose that the Godhead consists of Jahweh and the heavenly Father and Allah and Vishnu and Shiva . . . as a complex one-in-many which is also many-in-one. This model has a certain attractiveness; but it also involves an apparently prohibitive difficulty. For whereas the members of the Christian trinity were, so to speak, designed to fit together, the many Gods of the wider religious universe were not. How, then, can they form a harmonious many-in-one? It seems that the 'social' trinitarian model, enlarged from three to as many as may be required, cannot realistically include so wide and varied a range of independent divine beings. For the three persons of the Christian trinity have different but complementary functions, covering between them the total work of the Godhead. But the Gods of Jewish, Vaishnavite, Shaivite, Christian and Muslim faith do not divide the divine functions between them in any comparable way. Each of them is at once creator, redeemer and inspirer. The basic role of creator is particularly resistant to division. The Father-and-Son (John 1:1–3) and Allah (Qur'an 36:81) and Vishnu (Bhagavad Gita 9:4) are each, according to the traditions from which we learn about them, the sole creator or source of the universe. But clearly this is not possible. Nor would it make sense from the point of view of any of the traditions to say that Allah is the creator of Muslims, Vishnu of Vaishnavite Hindus, the heavenly Father of Christians and so on, or that each created and rules a different segment of 'the heavens and the earth'.

What however of a 'modal' construal of the trinity? Here the one God, known in the different relationships of creator, redeemer and sanctifier, is imaged as Father, Son and Spirit, these being three modes of activity of the one divine reality. Can we say, analogously, that the one God acting in relation to the children of Israel is imaged as Jahweh; acting in relation to the disciples of Jesus is imaged as the heavenly Father; acting in relation to Muslims is imaged as Allah; acting in relation to Indians within the Vaishnavite tradition is imaged as Vishnu . . . ? This comes close to our pluralistic hypothesis. For it depends upon a distinction between the one God and the different human images of that God formed within the different traditions. It thus points towards a noumenon–phenomena model such as is made more explicit (though not in that terminology) in the Buddhist *trikāya* doctrine, to which we may now turn.

This speaks of three modes of the infinite Buddha-nature. There is, first, the ultimate Dharmakaya, the eternal truth or reality of the Buddha nature, which is – I am following here the exposition of Hans Wolfgang Schumann – 'the indestructible, timeless Absolute, the one essence in and behind all that was, is, and will be . . . the absolute reality, besides which there is no other reality' (Schumann 1973, 102–3). Second there is the Sambhogakaya, the 'Body of Bliss', consisting of a plurality of transcendent Buddhas. 'Transcendent', says Schumann, 'means that they cannot be perceived by the senses, but only experienced spiritually' (Schumann 1973, 104). Many of these heavenly Buddhas are known by name, two on whom long-lived religious traditions have focused being Amitabha (or Amida), worshipped within the Pure Land tradition, and Vairocana, worshipped within Tibetan Buddhism. And third there is the Nirmanakaya, consisting of earthly human beings each of whom has attained to final enlightenment and become the perfect vehicle of a transcendent Buddha. In some schools of thought (particularly the Mahasanghikas) the earthly Buddhas have been thought of docetically, as appearances projected into this world from the Sambhogakaya, whilst in other schools they are regarded as beings of historical flesh and blood, human witnesses to the Dharma.

Our concern, however, is with the functional analogy between the heavenly beings constituting the Sambhogakaya and the objects of Jewish, Christian, Muslim and other worship. Considered as many-in-one, with emphasis on their unity, the transcendent Buddhas are all manifestations of the one ultimate Dharmakaya – as, according to our pluralistic hypothesis, the gods of the great monotheistic faiths are all manifestations of the Real.[20] However there are two different understandings of the ontological status of the Sambhogakaya (or the Dhyani or heavenly) Buddhas, and these suggest two alternative models for the status of the divine *personae*.

According to one conception (developed in the Trantrayana) the transcendent Buddhas are to be understood 'as mental creations, as ideations of the Bodhisattvas: to the Bodhisattva his ideal becomes so vivid and alive that it takes shape as a subjective reality' (Schumann 1973, 104–5). They are thus projections of the religious imagination. They are not however random projections, but appropriate expressions of the Dharmakaya. For this is humanly known as a boundless Compassion which we may think-and-experience in the form of a compassionate being or beings. But the existence of such beings is, on this view, purely relational; they are modes in which the limitless Dharmakaya affects our human consciousness. Applied to the divine *personae* this would mean that Jahweh, the heavenly Father, Allah, Shiva, Vishnu and so on are not objectively existent personal individuals with their own distinctive powers and characteristics. But neither on the other hand would they be mere hallucinations, devoid of any objective ground. They would be analogous to what have been called in the literature of parapsychology 'veridical hallucinations'. The term occurs particularly in connection with crisis apparitions: person A becomes telepathically aware at an unconscious level of a crisis, usually sudden death, occurring to B, who is at a distance; and the telepathically received information is presented to A's consciousness in the form of a vision of B, who may indeed not only appear visually but also be heard to speak. The experience is technically hallucinatory in that there is no physical body in the region of space which the apparition seems to occupy, and no physical sound waves corresponding to the words heard. But it is a *veridical* hallucination in that through it authentic information about B is being transmitted to A.

In the case of the religious experience of being in God's presence there is usually no visual or auditory component but rather a powerful and deeply resonant sense of personal presence. On the option that we are now considering, this experience is not caused by a particular invisible person – Jahweh or Vishnu, for example. It does however constitute a transformation of authentic information of which the Real is the ultimate source. The presence of the Real affects us in the appropriate, and in this sense veridical, form of a personal divine presence. In worshipping this divine Thou we are accordingly relating ourselves to the Real – whether or not we are aware of the complex way in which the relationship is being mediated.[21]

This kind of theory would seem to be in line with the thought of the Vedantic *Yogava'sistha*'s 'Thou art formless. Thy only form is our knowledge of Thee' (Parrisikar 1978, I:144) and also with the suggestion of Ibn al 'Arabi that God is known to human beings through our human ideas of God. He says:

> God is absolute or restricted as He pleases; and the God of religious beliefs is subject to limitations, for He is the God contained in the heart of His servant. But the absolute God is not contained in anything.

'Arabi seems to hold that the divine Reality as humanly known, namely as the Qur'anic Revealer, exists in that human knowing:

> The Essence, as being beyond all these relationships, is not a divinity . . . it is we who make Him a divinity by being that through which He knows Himself as Divine. Thus, He is not known [as 'Allah'] until we are known.[22]

Ibn al 'Arabi was, incidentally, fully aware of the pluralist implications of this insight:

> In general, most men have, perforce, an individual concept of their Lord, which they ascribe to Him and in which they seek Him. So long as the Reality is presented to them according to it they recognize Him and affirm Him, whereas if presented in any other form, they deny Him, flee from Him and treat Him improperly, while at the same time imagining that they are acting toward Him fittingly. One who believes [in the ordinary way] believes only in the deity he has created in himself, since a deity in 'beliefs' is a [mental] construction.   (1980, 137)

The other kind of view found in the history of the *trikāya* doctrine, offering a different model for the divine *personae*, is that the transcendent Buddhas of the Sambhogakaya are 'objectively existing, supramundane and subtle beings' (Schumann 1973, 105). On this view Amida, Vairocana, Ratnasambhava and the others are real persons, of immense but not limitless proportions. Applying this conception to Jahweh, Vishnu, Allah, Shiva, the heavenly Father and so on it would follow that they are real personal beings, independent centres of consciousness, will, thought and emotion.[23] We have already seen, however, and must not at this point forget, that it is entailed by the plurality of the gods that each of them is finite; for each exists alongside and is limited by the others with their own particular natures and capacities. Although the power of any one of this plurality cannot therefore be infinite it may nevertheless be so great as to be virtually infinite from our human point of view, as the gods exercise their powers in response to prayer and in the providential ordering of nature and history. Clearly this model will involve extremely awkward issues concerning the relations between the deities and their respective spheres of operation. However we need not explore those problems here. What distinguishes this model from straight polytheism is, for Buddhism, the assumption that the transcendent Buddhas are all manifestations of the ultimate Dharmakaya or, in terms of our hypothesis in this book, that the gods are different authentic *personae* of the Real.

As I have already indicated, the pluralistic hypothesis being propounded here could accommodate either of these models and does not require a decision between them. It therefore seems wise not to insist upon settling a difficult issue which, in logic, the hypothesis itself leaves open.

Notes

1. *Ekam sat viprā bahudhā vadanti* (*Rig-Veda*, I:164:46).
2. In addition to the accessible gods with whom people have regular dealings there has often also been talk of a high god dwelling in the sky who created the world and who was thought of in exalted terms comparable with those of developed monotheism. The high god was however generally too remote to be concerned with the problems of daily life and was accordingly not effectively in touch with the tribe's practical problems. It is the lower and implicitly finite deities who receive offerings, hear prayers and send weal or woe. Perhaps – though this is pure speculation – the high gods of tribal religion may represent some dim sense of the Real beyond the more familiar figures of the gods. Or perhaps – as an alternative speculation – the high gods are a product of rational reflection, an answer to the cosmological question, How did the world come to be?
3. The reification of the different complexes of religious life by post-Enlightenment western thought has been classically studied by Wilfred Cantwell Smith ([1962] 1978).
4. IV:11. On the interpretation of this passage see R. C. Zaehner 1969, 185–6.
5. Edward Conze summarises by saying that 'If Atheism is the denial of the existence of a God, it would be quite misleading to describe

Buddhism as atheistic . . . Buddhist tradition does not exactly deny the existence of a creator, but it is not really interested to know who created the Universe' (Conze 1975, 42, 39).

6. *Dīgha Nikāya*, II:37 – Davids and Davids 1938, 31. Cf. *Majjhima Nikāya*, I:168–9 – Horner 1954.

7. The gods continue to play their part in the religious life of the ordinary village Buddhist in the Theravada-dominated island of Sri Lanka. Shrines of the gods – principally the bodhisattva Nata; Vishnu (or Upulvan), the guardian god of the island; Kataragama, to whose festival thousands of pilgrims flock each year; and the goddess Pattini – often stand on the courtyards of the buldings that house images of the Buddha. Further, the Buddha himself is often worshipped through these images of him. Again, in recent times pictures of the Buddha have been replacing pictures of Sivali, one of his disciples who had become a symbol of providence; and the devotional songs formerly used in the worship of the devas, or gods, are now being used in adoration of the Buddha himself (de Silva 1974, 55). Thus the practical religious life of the ordinary village Buddhist in Sri Lanka seems to be clearly theistic, though pervaded also by the ideal of the selfless person taught by the Buddha.

8. Cf. L. Becker 1971.

9. On the other hand some Jewish commentators think that it may have been an angel who appeared to Abraham on behalf of God.

10. For an excellent brief summary of this development see Gordon D. Kaufman 1981, 25–6.

11. The same would seem to be true of the Qur'anic 'name of God', Al-Muqtadir. Al-Ghazali expounded the related terms *al-Qādir* and *al-Muqtadir* as signifying 'He who acts, or does not act, as he pleases' (Stade 1970, 106). According to Hans Weir *muqtadir* means 'possessing power or strength, powerful, potent; having mastery, being equal to; able to do' (1976, 747). The word occurs four times in the Qur'an (18:45, 43:42, 54:42 and 54:55) and in each passage the context refers specifically to God in relation to human beings.

12. Cf. Ronald M. Green 1978, 127–8.

13. On the dispute provoked by such passages see e.g. Hick [1976] 1985b, ch. 13.

14. Cf. C. C. J. Webb 1918, ch. 2.

15. C. G. Jung [1945] 1953 vol. 7, 155f. Cf. vol. 6, 465.

16. Cf. William James 1891, I:293–8.

17. For a different but related treatment of the idea of divine roles see Ruth Page 1985, 151–62.

18. For example, 'Visnu . . . was the name of a minor god of the Rig-Veda, who had the characteristics of a solar deity. Now centuries later, . . . his prestige had grown considerably and by means of brahman influence he was absorbing other, non-Aryan, regional deities. His cult was destined to go on increasing in importance . . .' (Ling 1968, 146).

19. However for countless Vaishnavite believers 'Krishna is at once an authentic historical personality and a god, the time and place of

whose earthly activities can be precisely indicated . . . According to Indian tradition, Krishna died shortly before the coronation of the King Parikshit in the year 3102 B.C., with which the last of the four ages of the present world cycle began' (von Stietencron [1985] 1986, 186).

20. Cf. Masao Abe 1985b. See also comments on Abe's paper in the same volume, 17–20.

21. Within this theory, divine providence and answers to prayer can probably best be understood in terms of psychic laws (ultimately grounded in the Real) which are brought into operation by the activity of prayer and by mental attitudes and expectations.

22. Ibn al 'Arabi [13th century] 1980, 92. 'Arabi writes elusively, but I believe that Frederick Copleston expresses his thought faithfully when he says:

In a poem Ibn 'Arabi speaks of man as giving God being by knowing him. This does not however refer to God as he is in himself. It means that God is given being in man's mind through man's idea of him, this idea being at the same time God's manifestation of himself. God reveals himself in a variety of ways, and the conceptions of God in human minds are so many divine epiphanies.   (Copleston 1982, 106)

23. For yet another possible view see Runzo 1986, ch. 8.

16

The *Impersonae* of the Real

Thou art formless: thy only form is our knowledge of thee.
(*Yogava'sistha*, 1:28 – Parrisikar 1978, I:144)

1 EXTENDING THE HYPOTHESIS

I have suggested that the Gods of the monotheistic traditions are
personae formed jointly by the presence of the Real to human
consciousness and by that consciousness itself as it has been
variously shaped by the different theistic cultures of the earth.
Thus Vishnu and Shiva, Adonai, the heavenly Father and Allah
are each the Real as thought-and-experienced from within a
particular stream of religious life. Does this extended Kantian
model of a noumenal reality that is phenomenally perceived in
different ways by different mentalities also apply to the non-
personal ultimates upon which some of the eastern traditions are
focused: the Brahman of advaita Vedanta, the Nirvana,
Dharmakaya, Sunyata, Tathata of the Buddhist traditions, the Tao
of Chinese religion?

The main motivation for seeking a comprehensive interpretation
embracing both of these very different types of religious thought-
and-experience comes from the perception that the personal
deities and non-personal absolutes have a common effect (as
described in Chapter 3) in the transformation of human existence
from self-centredness to a new centredness in the God who is
worshipped or in the Absolute that is known in *samadhi* or *satori*.
This transformed state is one of freedom from the anxious, sinful,
self-concerned ego, a consequent realisation of inner peace and
joy, and an awareness in love or compassion of the oneness of
humankind, or of all life. The devout Jewish or Christian or
Muslim or theistic Hindu or Pure Land Buddhist worshipper,
throwing him or herself in faith into the hands of the Lord, the
Bhagavan, the highest Person, the all-compassionate Buddha,
undergoes in varying degrees this salvific re-creation. And the

278

single-minded advaitic Hindu or Theravada or Zen Buddhist, persevering on a path of meditation that leads to the dissolution of the ego-boundaries, also undergoes in varying degrees this same liberating transformation. The spiritual disciplines and the inner resolves and actions through which theists and non-theists change, and the interpretive frameworks in terms of which they understand their own transformation, are very different. And yet the transformation undergone within these diverse forms of life and systems of self-understanding is recognisably the same. It is this common soteriological process that suggests that the gods and the absolutes that produce it are different modes of presence of the same ultimate transcendent Reality.

We saw that in the case of the theistic traditions appearances are initially against this hypothesis; and the same is true for the non-theistic traditions. As each of the monotheistic gods is believed to be the sole creator and lord of the universe, so likewise each of the non-personal absolutes is believed to be the sole ultimate and absolute reality. In other words, each of what I am calling the *impersonae* of the Real, no less than each of its *personae*, is regarded within its own faith-world as being the Real *an sich*. However we have seen (in Chapter 15) the kind of dialectic that can lead to the conclusion that the different gods can more intelligibly be regarded as different manifestations of the same transcendent Reality. Let us now see whether analogous considerations suggest a like conclusion concerning the non-personal absolutes.

2 BRAHMAN

According to advaita Vedanta the Real is one – the 'One without a second' (*Chāndogya* Up., VI:2:4 – Radhakrishnan 1969, 449) – and our ordinary experience of a multiplicity of things, persons and events is, from the ultimate perspective, delusory, constituting a cosmic mirage created by nescience, *avidyā*. Indeed we are ourselves, as separate egos, part of this mirage. For it is only the illusion of individual identity that separates us from the universal consciousness, the *ātman*, which is our true nature and which is one with the eternal Brahman. In a simile used repeatedly by Shankara, space enclosed in a jar appears to have a separate shape and identity; but break the jar and what remains is what was there all the time: limitless space.[1] So the enclosing wall of *avidyā* creates the illusion of separate finite selves; but when that wall is thinned and finally dissolved in enlightenment the self knows itself as the one Reality, Brahman, which it has always been. Enlightenment, or *mokṣa*, is thus liberation from the presently encompassing illusion in which the self-positing ego, with its unfulfilled cravings, propels itself through life after life, generating ever new waves of illusion in the effort to satisfy itself. Release from this is like waking up from a dream and realising that it was only a dream. For whilst the world of ordinary life – including the body and its needs, family, politics, religious obligations – is real whilst one is under its spell, it fades into unreality in the radiance of that final illumination.

Liberation as awakening from dream to reality is an expository simile but it is one that is close to the heart of advaitic thought. A more detailed analogy is set forth in the short but important *Māṇḍūkya* Upanishad. The highest reality, containing no element of illusion, is *nirguṇa* Brahman, Brahman without attributes, beyond the scope of human thought and imagination. Less high, because involving some element of illusion, is *saguṇa* Brahman, Brahman with attributes, known as Ishwara, the personal creator and lord of the universe. And then, much lower because largely illusory, is the inner world of human thought and imagination; and finally the wholly illusory outer world of the senses and of bodily life – illusory not in the sense that the physical has no existence but in the sense that it is dependent, ever changing, not an aspect of that which is alone truly real, namely the eternal consciousness of Brahman.

Related to these levels of the cosmos are corresponding levels of human cognition. The lowest is that of ordinary waking consciousness or the perceptual self (*vaiśvānara*), wholly immersed in *māyā*. Higher than this is the dreaming state or imaginative self (*taijasa*), capable of some degree of freedom from the fleeting unreality of *māyā*. The third level upwards is deep dreamless sleep or the conceptual self (*prājña*), 'verily, a mass of cognition, who is full of bliss and who enjoys bliss, whose face is thought' (*Māṇḍūkya* Up., 5 – Radhakrishnan 1969, 696). *Prājña* corresponds at the cosmic level to *saguṇa* Brahman, as the absolute manifested outside itself: 'This is the lord of all, this is the knower of all, this is the inner controller; this is the source of all; this is the beginning and end of things' (*Māṇḍūkya* Up., 6 – Radhakrishnan 1969, 697).

Beyond this is the fourth and final level, *turīya*, related to *nirguṇa* Brahman, the absolute Reality itself. Shankara says in his commentary on Gaudapa's *Kārikā*, 'that which is designated as *prājña* (when it is viewed as the cause of the world) will be described as *turīya* separately when it is not viewed as the cause, and when it is freed from all phenomenal relationships, i.e. in its absolute real aspect' (Radhakrishnan 1969, 697). *Turīya* then, as a human state, is the self-realisation in which the finite self is one with the universal Self; and as a cosmic state it is the ultimate *nirguṇa* Brahman, 'unseen, incapable of being spoken of, ungraspable, without any distinctive marks, unthinkable, unnameable, the essence of all knowledge of the one self, that into which the world is resolved, the peaceful, the benign, the non-dual' (*Māṇḍūkya* Up., 7 – Radhakrishnan 1969, 698). In this fourth state the human and the divine are one and the truth is realised of the central Upanishadic saying, 'That art thou (*tat tvam asi*)' (*Chāndogya* Up., VI:9:4 – Radhakrishnan 1969, 460).

The Upanishads are holy scripture rather than a single systematic work. They reflect the rich variety of Indian religious experience and thought without regard to dogmatic unity or even visible consistency. They have been capable of being interpreted both non-theistically, as by Shankara and his school, and theistically, as by Madhva and Ramanuja and their schools. But even within the advaitic interpretation there are what appear to be divergent strands of thought. On the one hand in *turīya* the mind, freed in deep meditation from its ego boundaries, becomes one with *nirguṇa* Brahman, which is beyond all concepts and distinctions and accordingly has no qualities or attributes. But on the other hand Brahman is repeatedly referred to as *satchitānanda*: being, consciousness, bliss. That is to say it has the attribute of consciousness and the further quality of bliss. And when we turn to Shankara's own account of the unitive experience of a jivanmukta we find that it is an experience of oneness with Brahman as *satchitānanda* rather than with an ineffable, distinctionless reality devoid of all qualities:

I am the supreme Brahman which is pure consciousness, always clearly manifest, unborn, one only, imperishable, unattached and all-pervading like the ether and non-dual. I am, therefore, ever-free . . .
I am unborn, deathless, devoid of old age, immortal, self-

effulgent, all-pervading and non-dual. Perfectly pure, having neither cause nor effect and contented with the one Bliss, I am free . . .

As I am changeless, the series producing pain, viz., the body, the intellect and the senses are not Myself nor Mine. Moreover they are unreal like dream-objects . . .

As I do not possess a body I have neither sin nor virtue, neither bondage nor liberation, neither a caste nor an order of life . . .

False conceptions of people, such as 'mine', 'this', 'thus', 'this is so', 'I am so', 'another is not so', etc. are all due to delusion. They are never in Brahman which is auspicious, the same in all and without a second.

All grief and delusion are removed from those great souls when there arises the very pure knowledge of the non-dual Self. It is the conclusion of those who know the meaning of the Vedas that there cannot be any action or birth in the absence of grief and delusion.

(*Upadeshasāhasrī*, X:1, 3, 5, 6, 11, 12 – Jagadananda 1970, 104–8)

I suggest that, on our interpretive map, we may locate that which is thus unitively experienced as (in Hindu terms) the *ātman* understood as the unity of mind when this is freed from all the limitations and imperfections of individuality. As Shankara says, 'The Atman . . . can be directly realized as pure consciousness and infinite bliss' (Shankara [7th–8th century] 1978, 64). For in transcending the ego the jivanmukta's consciousness becomes one with the universal consciousness; and the liberated one is able to report that this universal awareness has the quality of *ānanda*, bliss or happiness: 'This is the Atman, the Supreme being, the ancient. It never ceases to experience infinite joy. It is always the same. It is consciousness itself' (Shankara 1978, 52–3).

In advaitic Hinduism, then, the Real is experienced through inner union with the spiritual reality of the *ātman* which we become conscious of being as we transcend our separating ego. And in this mystical experience we, now merged into the unitary *ātman*, discover our true nature as *satchitānanda*. In offering this proposal from the standpoint of the pluralistic hypothesis I am treating the trans-personal reality of *satchitānanda*, experienced in *mokṣa*, and the personal reality of Ishwara, experienced in *bhakti*, as alternative manifestations of the Real to our human consciousness. Thus in this formulation the Real *an sich* is equated with *nirguṇa* Brahman, whilst both *satchitānanda* and Ishwara are identified as forms of *saguṇa* Brahman.

3 NIRVANA

It is impossible to locate Buddhism at any one point within the network of family resemblances to which the term 'religion' refers; for in its many forms it spreads across almost the entire range of features. During two and a half millennia it has included, and includes today, an individualistic meditational discipline leading to radical self-transformation, but practised without any accompanying metaphysical beliefs; the same meditative discipline, leading to the same transformation, but understood as the realisation within human experience of an eternal transcendent reality; philosophies in which the Dharmakaya, identified with Nirvana and with Sunyata, is thought of as the Absolute, comparable with the Brahman of advaitic Hindu thought; the limitless other-regarding compassion and self-giving of the bodhisattva ideal; a religion of fervent personal faith and salvation by the grace of Amida Buddha; and the timeless moment of Zen enlightenment in which the world is experienced in its pure 'suchness' and one begins to live simultaneously in Samsara and Nirvana. Thus instead of a single unitary Buddhism there are a variety of Buddhisms, each major development having produced scriptures in which its own interpretation is traced to the founder himself. It would however be a mistake to try to identify within this wealth of differences a single 'authentic Buddhism' – rather this vast multi-faceted tradition as a whole constitutes authentic Buddhism.

At one end of the spectrum are Buddhists who simply regard themselves as engaging in an ancient and well-tried system of mental discipline which they find to be profoundly beneficial. For them Buddhism takes a purely naturalistic or humanist form, making no claim concerning the nature of the universe beyond the psychological fact that meditation can cleanse our minds of their corrosive anxieties and free us for a more serene, centred and unselfish life. For such practitioners the traditional Buddhist beliefs in Karma and rebirth, the bodhisattvas, the *trikāya*, the *asura* and *deva* worlds, are colourful imaginative decorations. This demythologised Buddhism appeals to many in the West who have reacted against both the positive dogmas of Christianity and the negative dogmas of science-oriented secularism. (We saw in Chapter 12.3 the attractive use made of Buddhist themes in the contemporary religious humanism of Don Cupitt.) However, whilst this is today part of the wide and spreading influence of the Dharma, it represents only a selection from the teachings of the Buddha as they are recorded in the Pali canon and developed in the later layers of scripture.

In considering how our pluralistic hypothesis relates to the more central forms of the Buddhist tradition I shall concentrate on the key concepts of Nirvana and Sunyata. The one is basic to the Theravada but continues and develops in the Mahayana. The other is basic to the Mahayana but is also present in germ in the Theravada. Ultimately of course *nirvāṇa* and *śūnyatā* are identical, these being terms by which to refer to the one ultimate reality, which is also called the *dharmakāya* and the eternal Buddha nature. My contention will be that the modes of experience which both the Theravada and the Mahayana make possible are ways in which the Real becomes manifest to a human consciousness sensitised by the meditational practices and shaped by the conceptual frameworks of these ancient and profound traditions.

Buddhism starts from where we are, immersed in a world characterised by *dukkha*: suffering or unsatisfactoriness. That 'all life is *dukkha*' does not however mean that every moment of human experience is one of pain and anguish. It means that the human phenomenon as a whole is inescapably subject to *dukkha*; for though I may not myself be in a state of suffering at this moment, yet I know that many others are. The hardships of disease, old age and decay, and the personal sufferings of pain, frustrated desire and involvement in the sorrows of others, come in some form to us all, with death as the universal closure. Buddhism sees this experienced world, pervaded as it is by *dukkha*, as a ceaseless kaleidoscope of ever changing insubstantialities. Instead of enduring substances which vary their attributes through time there is a stream of ephemeral phenomena in an ever changing network of interdependent causality (*pratītya samutpāda*). This constitutes *saṃsāra*, the beginningless and endless round of birth, suffering and death, to which we are firmly bound so long as we experience it from the illusory standpoint of an enduring 'I' which views the world in relation to itself, as threatening or helpful, to be grasped or avoided. Thus *dukkha* is

created by the ego-centred point of view and mode of apperceiving.
And the liberation which the Buddha proclaimed is from this to
nirvāṇa. In a common Buddhist image the transition is from this
shore to the farther shore. This is a release from the entire process
by which our self-centred consciousness lives from day to day,
creating around itself the samsaric world of insecurity and
unsatisfied desire. When this liberation occurs a human being has
become an arhat or a bodhisattva, living no longer in *saṃsāra* but
now in a state that cannot be described but only experienced and
which the Buddha called *nirvāṇa*.

The Pali *nibbāna* signifies 'blowing out', as in the blowing out of
a flame. Thus etymologically Nirvana suggests a simple cessation;
and a number of the things that are said about it are compatible
with such an interpretation. This was very often the early
European understanding of the Buddhist Nirvana: one escapes
from the sufferings of life by ceasing to exist.[2] However few
Buddhists would regard this as other than a caricature. In the Pali
canon the Buddha himself expressly repudiated this nihilistic
interpretation:

There are some recluses and brahmans who misrepresent me
untruly, vainly, falsely, not in accordance with fact, saying:
'The recluse Gotama is a nihilist, he lays down the cutting off,
the destruction, the disappearance of the existent entity.' But as
this, monks, is just what I am not, as this is just what I do not
say, therefore these worthy recluses and brahmans misrepresent
me untruly, vainly, falsely.

(*Majjhima Nikāya*, I:140 – Horner 1954, 180)

But Nirvana does undoubtedly mean the cessation, indeed the
destruction, of something: 'The destruction of lust, the destruction
of hatred, the destruction of illusion, friend, is called Nibbana'
(*Saṃyutta Nikāya*, IV:250 – Woodward 1956, 170). More
fundamentally Nirvana is the cessation of the ego-centredness
which generates self-regarding emotion and awareness, thereby
turning the world into a threatening environment in which we
live in continuous conscious or unconscious anxiety. In radical
contrast to this, 'Thinking on there being no self, he wins to the
state wherein the conceit "I am" has been uprooted, to the cool
[i.e., nirvana], even in this life' (*Aṅguttara Nikāya*, IV:353 – Hare
1965, 233). Here Nirvana is clearly not thought of as annihilation.

but rather as liberation from bondage to the ego and as entry into self-less life.

Thus Gautama himself, after his enlightenment, continued to live in this world until his *parinirvāna*, or final nirvanisation, at physical death.[3] During these years he was not emotionally anaesthetised but would seem to have lived in a state of positive tranquillity and joy: 'When such conditions are fulfilled, then there will be joy, and happiness, and peace, and in continual mindfulness and self-mastery, one will dwell at ease' (*Dīgha Nikāya*, I: 196 – Davids and Davids [1899] 1923, 261); 'He who doth crush the great "I am" conceit – this, even this, is happiness supreme' (*Udāna*, II: 1 – Woodward 1948, 13). Nor did he retire from the human scene, but lived in active compassion, leading as many as possible to their own liberation: 'Observing all sentient beings with the eyes of a Buddha, he felt deep compassion for them; he wished to purify those whose minds had been lost in false views arising from hatred, greed, and folly' (*Buddhacarita* – de Bary 1972, 70).

However Nirvana is not regarded in the main Buddhist tradition as simply the psychological state of unselfcentredness, but rather as the fundamental and eternal reality that can only be realised through this state of unselfcentredness. Nirvana as a psychological state constitutes the immanence of the Ultimate within human life. This positive understanding of Nirvana rests upon a number of passages in the Pali scriptures, one of the most famous being *Udāna* 80 (iii):

> Monks, there is a not-born, a not-become, a not-made, a not-compounded. Monks, if that unborn, not-become, not-made, not-compounded were not, there would be apparent no escape from this here that is born, become, made, compounded.
>
> (Woodward 1948, 97–8)

Nirvana is also spoken of as 'the unborn . . . unageing . . . undecaying . . . undying . . . unsorrowing . . . stainless' (*Majjhima Nikāya*, I: 163 – Horner 1954, 206–7); it is 'deathless' (ibid., I: 172). Again, there is 'no bliss higher than Nibbana' (*Dhammapada*, 202 – Narada Mahathera 1972, 176), and 'Above, beyond Nibbana's bliss, is naught' (*Therīgāthā*, 476 – Davids 1964, I: 169). And in one passage a series of forty-three terms is applied to Nibbana, including 'the further shore', 'the unfading', 'the stable', 'the peace', 'the un-decaying', 'the invisible', 'the security', 'the wonderful', 'the marvellous', 'the free from ill', 'the island', 'the cave of shelter', 'the stronghold', 'the refuge', and 'the goal' (*Saṃyutta Nikāya*, IV:369–71 – Woodward 1956, 261–3). In accordance with this tradition the contemporary Theravadin, Narada Mahathera, describes Nirvana as 'the permanent, immortal, supramundane state which cannot be expressed by mundane terms' (1972, 24–5). And Takeuchi Yoshinori, a leading contemporary figure in the Kyoto school of Buddhist philosophy, quotes with approval Friedrich Heiler's words, 'Nirvana is the equivalent of what Western mysticism understands as the "Being of beings", the supreme and one reality, the absolute, the divine . . . Nirvana is the infinite, the eternal, the uncreated, the quality-free, the ineffable, the one and only, the highest, the supreme good, the best, the good pure and simple' (Takeuchi 1983, 8–9).

This conception of Nirvana – or (in the Mahayana development) the Dharmakaya – as *paramārtha-satya*, ultimate reality (Murti 1955, 244, 245–6), runs through most of the Buddhist tradition. From the point of view of our pluralistic hypothesis Nirvana is the Real experienced in an ineffable ego-lessness, unlimited and eternal, which can be entered by the moral and spiritual path taught by the Buddha. From a religious point of view the authenticity of this Buddhist experience is shown by the life-transforming response to the Real which it makes possible. The great liberation is not however to be quickly or easily attained. It demands an immensely long and arduous process of self-discipline in following the Eightfold Path, a development that requires many lives for its completion. In the time of the Buddha himself thousands of men and women apparently became ripe, under his influence, for the attainment of Nirvana, though this abundant flow of changed lives declined in later ages. There are however many degrees of approach to the final experience of liberation, with the possibility of advancing from a more restricted to a more complete transformation. For the great majority of ordinary people in the Buddhist world (as in all the other religious worlds) this recentring is very partial; and yet the possibility of the great liberation is always there as an inspiring challenge and promise.

4 SUNYATA

When Buddhism spread north from India into China, Tibet, Korea and Japan it moved from a largely world-denying into largely world-affirming cultures; and in this new environment fresh aspects of the Dharma came to the surface. The great discovery of northern or Mahayana Buddhism was (as we have already noted in Chapter 10.1) that Samsara and Nirvana are one. Experienced from the self-enclosed ego's point of view human existence is Samsara, an endless round of anxiety-ridden living and dying. But experienced by the ego-less consciousness of the liberated mind the same ordinary human existence is Nirvana! In enlightenment, *satori*, self and world are transformed together. The following report of this experience from within, by a contemporary Japanese Zen monk, perhaps succeeds in communicating it to the western mind:

> Enlightenment is an overwhelming inner realization which comes suddenly. Man feels himself at once free and strong, exalted and great, in the universe. The breath of the universe vibrates through him. No longer is he merely a small, selfish ego, but rather he is open and transparent, united to all, in unity. Enlightenment is achieved in *zazen*, but it remains effective in all situations of life. Thus everything in life is meaningful, worthy of thanks, and good – even suffering, sickness, and death.   (Dumoulin [1959] 1963, 275)

This Mahayana development is indeed carried to its limit in Zen. Zen is not a philosophy but an experience;[4] and it is hardly for those who have not undergone the distinctive Zen enlightenment to presume to describe it. But Zen is also highly paradoxical, and one paradox is that this experience, which eschews all philosophy, is in fact presented to the world wrapped in a philosophy. Zen teaches that the human mind, in its ordinary functioning, obscures reality. It does this by continually distinguishing, comparing and evaluating, and thus seeing the world through a distorting screen of its own ideas. Further, the mind not only distinguishes, compares and evaluates, but does so from the individual's own particular perspective. Each of us is thus at the centre of our own world, being aware of things, people and events in relation to ourself and responding to them accordingly as good or bad, welcome or unwelcome, interesting or uninteresting, propitious or dangerous and so on. The result of this continuous misperception is an enclosed realm of illusion. We accordingly live in an environment created by the self-centred ego, which is itself not the substantial and enduring entity that it seems to itself to be, but a mere fleeting ripple of ever changing consciousness. However by ending or suspending this self-centred discriminative activity we can at last experience the world as it is. By renouncing the ego point of view we can become part of the dynamic movement which is reality itself in its pure 'suchness', with its own ineffable fullness and richness.

The key term of many of the Mahayana schools is *śūnyatā* (Emptiness, Nothingness, Void, the Formless). But the statement that reality is Emptiness can be a more startling than illuminating use of the English language. For this particular Emptiness is also Fullness. When one is empty of the discriminative self-concerned ego, then the world is empty of all that human thought had projected upon it; and it is now just what it is, full of its own being, pure suchness (*tathatā*). That reality is Emptiness means, then, that the world in itself is devoid of all human distinctions, of all individual perspectives, of all self-centred valuations. As the Vietnamese Zen monk Thich Nhat Hanh says, 'true emptiness is identical to the *tathatā*, which is non-discriminated and non-conceptual reality' (Hanh 1974, 106), or as the Buddha himself said, 'Because it is empty of self or of what belongs to the self, it is therefore said: "The world is empty"' (*Saṃyutta Nikāya*, IV:54; cf. Woodward 1956, 29). When we cease to distort our environment by discriminating, comparing, contrasting and evaluating from our own perspective, we become clear mirrors reflecting the world as it is. Thus the mirror which perfectly reflects what is before it is an ancient Zen symbol of enlightenment. Again, Suzuki says:

> A field without an inch of grass in it, symbolizes *sunyata*, the ultimate reality of Buddhist philosophy. *Sunyata* is literally 'emptiness'. To say that reality is 'empty' means that it goes beyond definability, and cannot be qualified as this or that. It is above the categories of universal and particular. But it must not therefore be regarded as free of all content, as a void in the relative sense would be. On the contrary, it is the fullness of things, containing all possibilities. (Suzuki 1982, 103)

Masao Abe, explaining that the English term 'Emptiness' is liable to mislead as a translation of *śūnyatā*, says:

> So I think that 'everything is empty' may be more adequately

rendered in this way: 'Everything is just as it is.' A pine tree is a pine tree; a bamboo is a bamboo; a dog is a dog; a cat is a cat; you are you; I am I; she is she. Everything is different from everything else. And yet, while everything and everyone retain their uniqueness and particularity, they are free from conflict because they have no self-nature. This is the meaning of saying that everything is empty. (Abe 1985a, 223; compare 198)

From the point of view of our pluralistic hypothesis we can say that for Zen the Real is immanent in the world process and can be experienced in each present moment of existence by a mind purified of the ego point of view. Zen involves a complete acceptance of the world as a beginningless and endless flow and of ourselves as a part of that flow; and those who have achieved this acceptance report that the world so experienced takes on a new dimension as 'wondrous being'[5] and that life so lived is pure joy. To experience the world in this way, as a moving ocean of reciprocally conditioned change (*pratītya samutpāda*), is to see that nothing exists in and of itself but only in dependence upon everything else. This 'not existing in and of itself' is *śūnyatā* or emptiness: that is, emptiness of any aseity or autonomous substantiality. Thus the notions of *pratītya samutpāda* and *śūnyatā* point to the same reality, in which they also coincide with the further Buddhist notions of Nirvana, Prajna and the Dharmakaya. However this reality is not *a* reality; this indeed is essentially what is meant by saying that it is *śūnya*, empty. It is not *a* thing or object or entity or substance but rather reality itself, formless or 'empty' from our point of view because not objectifiable by human thought. It is reality manifested in the ordinary world of time and change when this is experienced without the falsifying power of the ego.

D. T. Suzuki says, '*Dharmakaya* or *prajna*, being "emptiness" itself and having no tangible bodily existence, has to embody itself in a form and be *manifested* as a stalk of bamboo, as a mass of foliage, as a fish, as a man, as a Bodhisattva, as a mind, etc. But these manifestations themselves *are* not the *Dharmakaya* or *prajna* which is more than forms or ideas or modes of existence' (Suzuki 1982, 97). Again, he says of *satori* that it is 'not the perception, indeed, of a single individual object but the perception of Reality itself, so to speak' (Suzuki [1927] 1949, 93). This 'Reality itself' is thought of by some Zen philosophers, for example within the

Kyoto school, as having a role analogous to that of God in monotheistic religion or that of Brahman in advaitic Hinduism: 'in Mahayana Buddhism,' says Abe, 'Emptiness replaces God' (Abe 1985a, 167). And Suzuki says that 'Reality is known by many names. To Christians, it is God; to Hindus, Brahma, or *ātman*; to the Chinese, *jen*, tao, or t'ien (Heaven); to Buddhists, Bodhi, *Dharma*, Buddha, *prājña*, tathata, etc.' (Suzuki 1982, 91). But in an important constructive article Masao Abe (1985b, 182–90) goes beyond this, suggesting that Sunyata, as the formless self-emptying ground or source of everything, is in effect the Real *an sich*, and that all particular things – including the experienced personal deities and presumably also[6] the experienced non-personal absolutes – are manifestations of it.

When Sunyata is understood in this sense, as referring to the ultimate reality beyond the scope of all concepts, knowable only in its manifestations, then it is indeed equivalent to what in our pluralistic hypothesis we are calling the Real. And the Madhyamika (or Sunyavada), which T. R. V. Murti has described as the central philosophy of Buddhism and which he says is 'the systematized form of the suggestions made by Buddha himself' (Murti 1955, 9), uses the notion of Sunyata in a way which also applies – up to a point to be noted presently – to our concept of the Real. Thus Sunyata is manifested in all things but is itself beyond the net of concepts and distinctions. The negative force of *śūnya* excludes all positive determinations – like the Upanishadic 'neti, neti', not this, not this. As Abe puts it, 'Nothingness must be emphasized to indicate the necessity of going beyond any conceptualization or objectification' (Abe 1985a, 198). Seiichi Yagi accordingly translates *śūnyatā* as 'the Formless'. Sunyata is 'devoid of thought determination' (Abe 1985a, 122), ineffable, beyond the scope of human concepts – except, as we must add (see Chapter 14.2), certain purely formal ones. 'The Absolute', says Murti, expounding the Madhyamika, 'is very aptly termed Sunya, as it is devoid of all predicates. Even existence, unity, selfhood and goodness cannot be affirmed of it' (Murti 1955, 229). 'The Absolute . . . is transcendent to thought (sunya)' (276). He presents the Madhyamika view of the relation between Sunyata and the experienced realm of Samsara in basically Kantian terms. 'The Absolute looked at through thought-forms is phenomenon (samsara). The latter, freed of the superimposed thought-forms, is the Absolute' (141).

Thus far our pluralistic hypothesis runs parallel to this central strand of Mahayana Buddhism. But there is also an all-important difference. For the Mahayana teaches that although the Real is inaccessible to the discursive and discriminative intellect it can nevertheless be directly intuited in the mystical insight (*prājña*) achieved in *satori*. This remains a characteristic Zen claim. Thus Suzuki says that in *satori* one

> apprehends reality as it really is, or as it actually asserts itself
> . . . it is reality itself which now comes in full view, shifting the
> stage, making the intellect see itself reflected in reality. Or put
> the other way around, the intellect seeing itself is nothing other
> than reality becoming conscious of itself.
>
> (Suzuki 1982, 97, 100)

Since the Buddhist claim to a direct intuition of the ultimate is one of a number of similar claims within the different traditions, it will be well now to turn to this subject of unitive or unmediated mystical experience.

5 UNMEDIATED MYSTICAL EXPERIENCE OF THE REAL?

The Madhyamika philosophy claims, as we have just seen, that in the experience of *satori* the human mind finally transcends egoity and with it the entire apparatus of concepts developed in the ego's dealings with its environment. It is then able to enjoy a unitive intuition of ultimate reality: 'the Intellect becomes so pure and transparent that no distinction can possibly exist between the Real and the Intellect apprehending it' (Murti 1955, 212); 'In intuition, Knowledge and the Real coincide' (214); 'The mind . . . in that state is non-distinct from the real . . . the unutterable ultimate experience wherein the real and the intellect cognizing it are non-different' (245–6); 'Intuition is the Absolute' (220). For our ordinary experience is a function of the dualistic consciousness in which the ego affirms itself over against a world of objects. But this dualistic structure is transcended in the moment of enlightenment in which the Real (*śūnyatā*) and our unitive awareness of it (*prājña*) become one. For the Real is beyond all human conceptions and distinctions; and the mind in the state of *prājña* has emptied itself of those same concepts and distinctions.

There is now simply the eternal Buddha-nature being conscious of itself in a timeless moment of a human *satori*.

This unitive knowledge is unique and final, radically different from all other knowledge. As Suzuki expresses it, 'Prajna is seeing into the essence of things as they are'; it is 'to see reality . . . just as it is' (Suzuki 1953, 250, 284). Like the theistic claim to an absolute revelation, *prājña* sets itself beyond questioning or criticism. And yet – and here is the complication which alerts us to the need for a more comprehensive theory – essentially the same claim is made, though with radically different content, by advaita Vedanta. This tells us that in our true being, presently obscured by the illusions generated by our ego-centred experience, we are identical with the universal atman which is itself one with Brahman. By the overcoming of egoity in a long spiritual growth through many lives one may achieve Moksha, liberation, and enter into a unitive awareness of the eternal reality of Brahman. Brahman is then known with the same direct apprehension with which one knows oneself. And what is thus unitively known is the eternal transcendent Reality: *satyasya satyam*, 'the real of the real' (*Bṛ*. Up., II:iii:6; cf. Radhakrishnan 1969, 194), in comparison with which earthly life is a dreamlike illusion.

Thus whereas the Real directly apprehended as Sunyata is totally immanent in the ever changing forms of concrete existence, directly apprehended as Brahman it is a totally other reality in relation to which the 'ever changing forms of concrete existence' are mere illusions. And whereas for the Mahayana Nirvana and Samsara are one, for advaita Vedanta they are distinguished as respectively reality and illusion. And so we have here two very different reports which, taken as accounts of direct, unmediated awareness of the Real as it is in itself, offer incompatible alternatives. Is the Real *an sich* the 'wondrous being' of the world process itself, undistorted by the web of concepts structuring the self–other dichotomy; or is the Real the eternal, transcendent being-consciousness-bliss with which we are ultimately identical and which the advaitic tradition speaks of as Brahman? Or again, is the Real *an sich* the personal loving Lord of the theistic traditions, said to be directly experienced in Jewish, Christian, Muslim and Hindu Bhakti mysticism, even sometimes to the point of union – as indicated by Meister Eckhart when he wrote, 'If I am to know God directly, I must become completely He and I: so that this He and this I become one I' (Underhill [1911] 1955,

420), or by Al-Hallaj when he uttered the words which cost him his life, *Ana 'l-Haqq*, 'I am God' (Nicholson [1914] 1963, 149–50).

These claims of Zen and of advaitic and theistic unitive mysticism are at variance with the epistemological theory that all cognitive awareness is a mode of experiencing-as in terms of concepts and patterns of meaning, and that at the level of religious awareness these concepts and patterns vary as between different cultures and historical periods. Unitive mysticism seems to stand outside this epistemological paradigm as a direct intuitive consciousness of the Ultimate in itself, rather than as thought-and-experienced through the lens of a particular human mind-set. And if the history of religions had included only one tradition of unitive mysticism, offering a single and consistent report of that of which the mystics have an apparently unmediated awareness, it would have been necessary to amend our hypothesis at this point. The theory would then have offered an experiencing-as account of most of the wide field of religious experience, including the kinds of mysticism discussed in Chapter 10.5, but would see its comparatively rare unitive form as something entirely different which bypasses the normal structure of human consciousness.

However does not the fact that there are a number of different traditions of unitive mysticism, offering their characteristically different reports of the nature of the Real, make it seem more likely that the otherwise universal structure of human consciousness holds here also, and that that which is being directly experienced is not the Real *an sich* but the Real manifested respectively as Sunyata, as Brahman, as God? For there is considerable evidence that if one performs *zazen*, or sitting meditation, for a number of years under the guidance of a Zen *roshi*, feeding on Zen literature and steeping oneself in the Zen ethos, one may finally attain *satori* and become vividly aware of ultimate Reality as immediately present in the flow of ordinary life; but such a one will not in the moment of illumination experience God or the transcendent reality of Brahman. On the other hand if one performs yoga for many years under the tutelage of an advaitic guru, meditating on the Upanishads and studying the classics of Hindu thought, one may in due course attain the awareness of oneness with Brahman and become jivanmukti; but such a one will not achieve either the Buddhist *satori* or the theistic *visio dei*. And again, if a mystic prays and meditates for many years under the guidance of a Christian confessor–director, feeding in spirit on the eucharist, reading the Bible and the classics of Christian spirituality, he or she may attain to the unitive vision of God, but will not attain to oneness with Brahman or to the Zen *satori*.

These observable facts suggest that mystics within the different traditions do not float free from their cultural conditioning. They are still embodied minds, rooted in their time and place.[7] They bring their Hindu, Buddhist, Jewish, Christian, Muslim or Sikh sets of ideas and expectations with them on the mystical path and are guided by them towards the kind of experience that their tradition recognises and leads them to expect.[8] This lends considerable support to the hypothesis that even in the profoundest unitive mysticism the mind operates with culturally specific concepts and that what is experienced is accordingly a manifestation of the Real rather than the postulated Real *an sich*. And so it seems reasonable to suppose that basically the same kind of interpretation that I proposed in the previous chapter, in relation to the divine *personae*, applies also to the *impersonae* experienced in the non-theistic traditions.

Notes

1. Shankara [7th–8th century] 1978, 53, 80, 97, 117, 126. The simile probably originated in the *Kaṭha* Upanishad, II:2:10.
2. See G. R. Welbon 1968.
3. What Nirvana is beyond physical embodiment, in the state of the Tathagata or perfected one beyond death, is a mystery beyond the grasp of the unilluminated mind – the truth is 'deep, difficult to see, difficult to understand, peaceful, excellent, beyond dialectics, subtle, intelligible to the wise' (*Majjhima Nikāya*, II:427). For further discussion see Chapter 19.1.
4. D. T. Suzuki, its greatest exponent to the West, said that 'Under no circumstances ought Zen to be confounded with philosophy' (Suzuki [1949] 1969, 106–7).
5. 'True Emptiness is Wondrous Being' (from the 10th-century CE Hua-yen text, *Mojingengenkam*). Nishitani says that this phrase is 'usually acknowledged as expressing the core of Mahayana Buddhism' (Nishitani 1982, 183).
6. Though his exposition remains lop-sided in that he does not explicitly say this.
7. Thus Robert Gimello, discussing Buddhist meditation, says that 'rather than speak of Buddhist doctrines as interpretations of Buddhist mystical experiences, one might better speak of Buddhist mystical

experiences as deliberately contrived exemplifications of Buddhist doctrine' (1978, 193).

8. Cf. Steven Katz's convincing argument that 'The Buddhist experience of *nirvana*, the Jewish of *devekuth*, and the Christian of *unio mystica*, the Sufi of *fana*, the Taoist of *Tao* are the *result*, at least in part, of specific conceptual influences, i.e. the "starting problems" of each doctrinal, theological system' (1978, 62).

Part Five
Criteriological

17

Soteriology and Ethics

The soul of religion is the practick part.   (John Bunyan)

1 THE SOTERIOLOGICAL CRITERION

It has been self-evident, at least since the axial age, that not all religious persons, practices and beliefs are of equal value. Indeed the great founders and reformers were all acutely dissatisfied with the state of religion around them. Their criticisms have been either metaphysical (as in the case of Gautama, who rejected the prevailing *ātman* doctrine) or theological (as in the case of Muhammad, who rejected the Arabian polytheism of his day) or, much more often, moral. Thus the ancient Hebrew prophets condemned in the name of God the elevation of sacrifice and ritual above the requirements of mercy and social justice:

> I hate, I despise your feasts,
> and I take no delight in your solemn assemblies.
> Even though you offer me your burnt offerings and cereal
>   offerings,
> I will not accept them,
> and the peace offerings of your fatted beasts
> I will not look upon.
> Take away from me the noise of your songs:
> to the melody of your harps I will not listen.
> But let justice roll down like waters,
> and righteousness like an everflowing stream.
>
> (Amos 5:21–4)

In the same vein Jesus condemned some of the religious leaders of his day:

> But woe unto you, Pharisees! for ye tithe mint and rue and all
>   manner of herbs, and pass over judgment and the love of
>   God.   (Luke 11:42)

299

Later in India Guru Nanak, the founder of the Sikh tradition, criticised some of the religiousness of his own time in words reminiscent of the Semitic prophets:

> Religion lies not in the [yogi's] patched garment, nor in his staff, nor in besmearing the body with ashes. Religion lies not in suspending large rings from split ears, nor in shaving the head, nor in the blowing of horns. To live uncontaminated amid worldly temptations is to find the secret of religion. Religion lies not in empty words. He who regards all men as equal is religious.[1]

Behind all these criticisms, ethical, metaphysical and theological alike, there lies a soteriological concern. Gautama's rejection of the *ātman* doctrine was basically soteriological: for the liberation to which he pointed is liberation from all that flows from the illusion of an enduring self. The Hebrew prophets were concerned to reject the understanding of God as valuing burnt offerings more than justice and so to open their hearers to a different way of salvation. The criticisms of Jesus and later of Nanak and many others were that in devoting themselves to external rituals people were turning away from the demanding and saving presence of God. Muhammad's rejection of polytheism brought men and women to know and respond to the one and only lord of heaven and earth: *La illaha il' Allah!* For the function of post-axial religion is to create contexts within which the transformation of human existence from self-centredness to Reality-centredness can take place. Accordingly the basic criterion must be soteriological. Religious traditions and their various components – beliefs, modes of experience, scriptures, rituals, disciplines, ethics and lifestyles, social rules and organisations – have greater or less value according as they promote or hinder the salvific transformation.

2 SAINTLINESS

But how do we know when that transformation has taken or is taking place? This itself requires criteria. And on the hypothesis that the major world religions constitute varying human responses to the transcendent Reality, and are thus at least to some extent in alignment with that Reality, the available criteria will be those that have developed within them. Some of these are tradition-specific – for example, believing the distinctive doctrines of a particular movement – and cannot provide the general criterion which our hypothesis requires. But in addition to such confessional tests tradition also operates with the idea of the spiritual and moral fruits of true as distinguished from merely conventional religion. This is more promising in as much as the 'fruits of the spirit' are universally recognised and respected whereas the value of credal and communal loyalty presupposes the accident of birth at some one particular time and place.

Let us then explore the possibility that the transformation of human existence which is called salvation or liberation shows itself in its spiritual and moral fruits. 'Spiritual' is a notoriously vague term and we must resort to description. But whom shall we describe? Presumably those who have already been recognised within their own traditions as individuals in whom the signs of salvation or liberation are strikingly visible and who are accordingly known as bodhisattvas, gurus, mahatmas, masters, saints. For the sake of simplicity I shall use the concept of the 'saint' generically to cover all of these. A saint, then, is one in whom the transformation of human existence from self-centredness to Reality-centredness is so much more advanced than in the generality of us that it is readily noticed and acknowledged.[2] This is of course a stipulative definition – as is any other proposal for the use of the term. But it connects the broad hypothesis being developed in this book with the worldwide phenomenon of spiritually impressive individuals whose lives are predominantly centred in some manifestation of the Real.

The soteriological transformation normally occurs within the context of a particular tradition – indeed in the past probably almost always so –, taking a form made possible by that tradition and being identified by criteria developed within it. There are accordingly Buddhist saints, Muslim saints, Christian saints and so on, rather than simply saints. However there is an all-important common feature which we can both observe today and find reflected in the records of the past. This is a transcendence of the ego point of view and its replacement by devotion to or centred concentration upon some manifestation of the Real, response to which produces compassion/love towards other human beings or towards all life. This shift from self-centredness to Reality-centredness is capable of expression in quite diverse forms of life.

I have myself observed it in the very different lives of, for example, a Buddhist monk living in a forest hermitage in Sri Lanka and a Sikh doctor involved in a range of practical social activities in the Punjab. It can also occur in many different degrees.

William James offered a 'composite photograph of universal saintliness, the same in all religions', involving:

1. A feeling of being in a wider life than that of this world's selfish little interests; and a conviction, not merely intellectual, but as it were sensible, of the existence of an Ideal Power . . .
2. A sense of the friendly continuity of the ideal power with our own life, and a willing self-surrender to its control.
3. An immense elation and freedom, as the outlines of the confining selfhood melt down.
4. A shifting of the emotional center towards loving and harmonious affections, towards 'yes, yes,' and away from 'no,' where the claims of the non-ego are concerned.

(James [1902] 1960, 268–70)

James then listed the practical fruits of saintliness as asceticism (which, as he noted, has sometimes been carried to excess); strength of soul (expelling old fears and inhibitions); purity ('The sensitiveness to spiritual discords is enhanced, and the cleansing of existence from brutal and sensual elements becomes imperative'); and charity ('The shifting of the emotional center brings . . . increase of charity, tenderness for fellow-creatures') (James [1902] 1960, 270–1). One further characteristic, I would suggest, is the quality, a by-product of freedom from self-concern, that in its more passive form is an inner peace or serenity and in its more active form is a positive and radiant joy. (Baron von Hügel said that Pope Benedict XIV's stipulation that there should be a note of joy in the lives and influence of those put forward for canonisation was a stroke of spiritual genius (von Hügel 1927, 301).) This is indeed one of the most attractive features of saintliness and one that draws people towards religious faith in response to a quality which they find in the saints rather than in themselves. We are tempted to feel that even though we know that the saint may possibly be deluded we would rather share his or her spirit and outlook than an opposite one. But such a person at the same time makes delusion seem altogether less likely. A recent philosopher writes concerning what he calls (apologising for the phrase) a 'spiritual person':

> He has a certain serenity and inward peace which others cannot help envying and even admiring. They cannot see that he is in the least entitled to have it, in a world so full of troubles as this world is. Yet it seems a little unplausible to suppose that this serene attitude is just the product of a state of mental confusion. Indeed, the existence of such persons is in practice the most persuasive argument in favour of a religious world-outlook, and probably always has been. (Price 1969, 475)

Saintliness, or ego-transcending Reality-centredness, expresses itself, as I have already suggested, in different forms of life, some involving withdrawal from the world in prayer or meditation whilst others involve practical engagement in social or political action, and yet others in a mixture or an alternation of these. It is tempting to identify these contrasting styles of saintliness with different religious traditions, perhaps associating the world-renouncing type with Hinduism and Buddhism and the more socially active type with Judaism, Christianity and Islam. But this would be at best a considerable over-simplification. At this point however it will be useful to look more generally at the relation between inner individual and outer communal transformation and thus between religion and politics.

3 SPIRITUAL AND POLITICO-ECONOMIC LIBERATION

Within our pluralistic hypothesis salvation/liberation is defined as the transformation of human existence from self-centredness to Reality-centredness. In its traditional uses in Buddhist and Hindu discourse 'liberation' has meant the gaining of freedom from the inner suffering – of anxiety, fear, rage, jealousy, shame, remorse, resentment – caused by experiencing the world overwhelmingly as it affects the fleeting and insubstantial ego. In the second half of the twentieth century, however, the term 'liberation' has taken on a new dimension of meaning. The Christian liberation theologians, writing amidst the social and political struggles of Central and South America, have brought to consciousness in a new way the fact that God, as revealed in their scriptures, is on the side of the poor, the oppressed, the exploited. The ancient Hebrew prophets, speaking in the name of the Lord, demanded justice for the poor. Jesus belonged to the artisan class of a subject people, was (according to tradition) born in a stable, had no fixed home or income during his ministry and worked mainly with the poor. Particularly as depicted in Luke's Gospel he saw the heavenly Father as closer to the socially marginalised than to the rich and powerful.

And so the liberation theologians call for a 'preferential option for the poor' in their struggle against entrenched regimes in which a privileged few monopolise most of their country's wealth. In its social analysis this movement has drawn attention to the structural, as distinguished from purely individual, evils of the world: the capitalist system, dividing people into economic classes and countries into rich and poor, and creating vast international corporations that wield immense behind-the-scenes power over millions and are yet concerned in the end only with profits; racist structures, ranging from overt apartheid in South Africa to pervasive racial prejudice and discrimination within most white societies; and male gender domination in virtually all societies. Liberation has come to mean the freeing of whole populations from these large-scale and long-lived structural forms of oppression. How then is liberation in this sense related to the transformation of human existence from self-centredness to Reality-centredness?

We need first to note that the awareness of what we today call structural evil is a recent development in the history of human consciousness. It has been prompted by the work of Karl Marx in the nineteenth century and the subsequent writings of innumerable other economists and sociologists who have shown social structures to have identifiable material causes rather than being basic 'givens', like the terrain or the climate. Further, this new consciousness presupposes an historical situation which is itself new, namely one in which power, and hence political responsibility, have become dispersed in the democratising movements of the last two or three centuries. Until the modern period human liberation could usually only mean the inner freeing of the individual, a transformation that was expressed outwardly in works of individual charity. This kind of non-political concern for the poor and needy has in the past been common to all the great traditions. It has always been a religious duty for Hindus,

Buddhists, Jews, Christians and Muslims to give alms to the poor and to protect the weak, particularly widows and orphans; and each tradition has always been concerned to cure disease and to promote bodily health.

But it would be anachronistic to look for doctrines of universal human rights and a theology of political or economic liberation in the 'ages of faith' when political power and responsibility were beyond the horizon of all except those at the top of the social hierarchy. Indeed prior to the founding of the social sciences in the eighteenth century[3] the structures within which people lived were generally simply accepted as the divinely appointed human situation; and religion accordingly functioned, *inter alia*, as a powerful validator of the existing social order.[4] In this period liberation inevitably meant primarily a personal inner liberation. Self-transcendence was accordingly typically sought by the paths of prayer and meditation. However withdrawal from the world for the cultivation of the spiritual life, whether for the remainder of one's life (as generally in the Christian tradition) or in old age (as generally in the Hindu tradition) or for a limited period (as generally in the Buddhist tradition), should not be seen as opposed in principle to social and political activity.[5] When Christian monks pray for the world they believe that they are performing an essential work for the welfare of the community as a whole. The same is true of Buddhist monks and lay persons when in meditation they systematically radiate goodwill upon all life throughout the world. And it could indeed very well be that constructive thought and emotion, in the forms of prayer and meditation, does have real and sometimes startling positive effects.

However in the new age of sociological consciousness in which we now live the practical dispositional aspect of awareness of the Real is taking new forms. Whereas in the pre-modern era the saints within all the great traditions either lived a contemplative life in retreat from the world or engaged in charitable activities within the existing social framework, the modern world has produced a growing number of political saints whose *agape/karuṇā* is directed to changing the structures of human life. This is a new and still developing phenomenon. For modernity has arrived with different speeds and with different degrees of penetration in different parts of the world, affecting the Judeo-Christian West earlier and more deeply than the Hindu-Buddhist-Muslim East.

There have accordingly thus far been more political saints in the West than in the East. In the eighteenth and nineteenth centuries such pioneers as the Quakers opposed the institution of slavery and, with others, gradually converted enlightened opinion to see the radical evil of this age-old human institution. By the end of the nineteenth century the Christian 'social gospel' movement began to focus attention upon the structural causes of suffering, with contemporary liberation theology now carrying the analysis much further. But the powerful and indeed explosive idea of total liberation – political and economic as well as spiritual – has taken root in the East as well; and indeed its greatest exponent so far has been a Hindu, Mahatma Gandhi, whose 'experiments with Truth', both in his early days in South Africa and his later days in India, were the search for an integral inner and outer transformation. Today not only Christian priests in South America and priests and Muslim *imams* in South Africa, but also Buddhist monks in Sri Lanka[6] and Thailand, have been among its practitioners.[7]

The religious motivation for seeking structural change, now that human knowledge includes some understanding of the dynamics of social and economic life, is basically the same as for acts of individual charity in the days of pre-sociological consciousness. This motivation is two-fold. First, suffering of every kind is that from which we seek deliverance; and the awareness of the ultimate unity of the human race, which all the great traditions engender, makes it a responsibility to relieve the suffering of others whenever we can.[8] And second, the transcending of self-centredness is severely inhibited by the need anxiously to fend off starvation, disease and oppression. And so the struggle for liberation from crippling poverty, illness and exploitation is also a fight to create the conditions within which inner liberation is possible. These two motivations, which formerly typically directed *agape/karuṇā* into acts of individual charity within hierarchic social systems, today call in addition for intelligent efforts to recreate human society in a more just and equal mould. Thus from a religious point of view the basic intent of the Marxist-Leninist, Trotskyist, Maoist, and broader socialist movements, as also of 'liberation theology' and the contemporary drive for racial and gender equality, has to be interpreted as a dispositional response of the modern sociologically conditioned consciousness to the Real.

4 THE TRADITIONS AS PRODUCTIVE OF SAINTS

The production of saints, both contemplative and practical, individualistic and political, is thus one valid criterion by which to identify a religious tradition as a salvific human response to the Real.[9] In the light of this criterion we can readily see that each of the great world faiths constitutes a context for salvation/liberation: for each has produced its own harvest of saints. And what has happened to a striking extent in the saints has also been happening in lesser degrees to innumerable others within the same traditions. For the saints are not a different sort of being, travelling a different road, but are simply persons who are further ahead than the rest of us on the same road. If a religious tradition has enabled a few who are sufficiently powerfully motivated to travel fast it has also enabled many others to travel in the same direction at their own more halting pace. I believe we can see from direct observation and by attending to the reports of others that this is indeed happening within each of the great traditions. But if we now attempt comparative judgments, asking whether tradition A has produced more, or better, saints per million of population than tradition B, we quickly discover that we do not have sufficient information for an answer. All that I myself feel able to venture at present is the impressionistic judgment that no one tradition stands out as more productive of sainthood than another. I suggest that so far as we can tell they constitute to about the same extent contexts within which the transformation of human existence from self-centredness to Reality-centredness is taking place. The criterion of saintliness, then, enables us to recognise the great traditions as areas of salvation/liberation, but does not enable us to go on to grade them comparatively.

What however of the lesser traditions, and the new religious movements which have sprung up within, say, the last hundred and fifty years – including Bahai, Christian Science, Rissho Koseikai, Soka Gakkai, Tendikyo, the Church of Jesus Christ of Latter Day Saints, Spiritualism, Theosophy, the Kimbanguist movement, Johrei, the Unification Church . . .? To what extent are these also contexts of salvation/liberation? The same soteriological criterion and the same index of saintliness are valid, but are harder to apply to the much slighter data-base presented by such relatively recent phenomena. Our pluralistic hypothesis does not entail any *a priori* judgment concerning the salvific value of these new movements. It is possible in the case of each of them that it will grow to be soteriologically comparable with the present great world faiths; and also possible that it will join the many religious movements which have in the past sprung up, flourished briefly and then died out. However even ephemeral movements may be salvific within the temporary circumstances which evoked them. There is also the strong possibility that some, or even all, of these minor religious movements are salvific for some individuals at a certain stage of their personal histories, so that a number of people pass through them, perhaps thereby gaining greatly, and yet eventually finding it appropriate to move on. For whereas the great historic traditions have become internally diverse and comprehensive, so as to include within themselves most of the different types of religious outlook, the small movements tend to be more specialised and to lack this catholic appeal. However it is not part of my task, in outlining the pluralistic hypothesis, to make a detailed study of these new movements and to attempt to pronounce upon their individual soteriological efficacy.

What, again, of the great secular movements, inspired by the thought of Karl Marx, which have arisen in the twentieth century in Russia, eastern Europe, China and elsewhere? We have already noted that the communist ideology has certain features in common with the traditional religions (concepts of evil and salvation, eschatology, scriptures, a church with a priestly hierarchy and so on) as well as a major difference from them in the rejection of the idea of the transcendent. In terms of the family-resemblance analysis adopted in Chapter 1 these secular movements accordingly appear on the map of diverse overlapping phenomena covered by the umbrella term 'religion'. Are Marxist Russia and post-Maoist China, then, contexts of salvation/liberation? Once again, this is a factual question which our hypothesis does not settle *a priori*. According to that hypothesis, in pre-axial societies, before the emergence of the autonomous individual, the presence of the Real was felt in the claim of the social organism within which each person was a living cell. In the post-axial movements individuality has flourished, together with the correlative idea of individual salvation/liberation. Communism can be seen as an attempt to complete the dialectic of history by moving to a synthesis of individuality and social solidarity. Thus far however it has clearly been only very partially successful. The modern Russian empire has suffered from the same corrupting influences among its leaders as the old Christian and Muslim empires, producing the evils first of savage repression and then of immobilism and sterile conformity. However the communist experiment is very recent, indeed probably still only in its infancy. It remains to be seen to what extent it can become a form of life that makes possible a salvific self-transcendence and a recentring in the Real as manifested in the social ideals of justice, equality and the unity of the human family.

5 THE UNIVERSALITY OF THE GOLDEN RULE

The basic criterion, then, for judging religious phenomena is soteriological. The salvation/liberation which it is the function of religion to facilitate is a human transformation which we see most conspicuously in the saints of all traditions. It consists, as one of its aspects, in moral goodness, a goodness which is latent in the solitary contemplative and active in the saint who lives in society, serving his or her fellows either in works of mercy or, more characteristically in our modern sociologically-conscious age, in political activity as well, seeking to change the structures within which human life is lived. This stems in each case from a basic ethical requirement; and it is this that provides the criterion for the moral assessment of religious phenomena.

Our next task is accordingly to display this common moral requirement. In doing so we must distinguish between ethical ideals and the concrete ways in which these have been applied and misapplied at particular times and places. For such applications involve many factors other than the basic values themselves. Human reason, which is often, as David Hume said, 'the slave of the passions' (Hume [1739], II:3; 1968, 415), has regularly been used to twist moral principles in justification of individual, class and national acquisitiveness and domination. Further, a variety of empirical and metaphysical beliefs, often differing widely between different cultures and historical epochs, enter into our concrete moral judgments.

An example of this worth noting is that of the human sacrifices that were practised within many of the archaic forms of religion. In many cases these arose from conceptions of the gods as demanding and as capable of being placated by them; and in these cases our modern abhorrence echoes that of critics in the axial age:

> Shall I give my first-born for my transgression,
>   the fruit of my body for the sin of my soul?
> He has showed you, O man, what is good;
>   and what does the Lord require of you
> but to do justice, and to love kindness,
>   and to walk humbly with your God?
>
> (Micah 6:7–8)

But very often also they seem to have arisen in a quite different way, from mistaken magical or primitive scientific beliefs according to which a human death could have objective beneficial effects for the community. J. G. Frazer, in his great compendium of the phenomena of 'primitive religion', gives many examples of such beliefs. One comes from ancient Mexico:

> The ancient Mexicans conceived the sun as the source of all vital force; hence they named him Ipalnemohuani, 'He by whom men live.' But if he bestowed life on the world, he needed also to receive life from it. And as the heart is the seat and symbol of life, bleeding hearts of men and animals were presented to the sun to maintain him in vigour and enable him to run his course across the sky. Thus the Mexican sacrifices to the sun were magical rather than religious, being designed, not so much to please and propitiate him, as physically to renew his energies of heat, light, and motion. The constant demand for human victims to feed the solar fire was met by waging war every year on the neighbouring tribes and bringing back troops of captives to be sacrificed on the altar. Thus the ceaseless wars of the Mexicans and their cruel system of human sacrifices, the most monstrous on record, sprang in great measure from a mistaken theory of the solar system.[10]

Various other religio-scientific beliefs also gave point to human sacrifice. One was that the world, having originally been created as the result of a cosmic blood sacrifice, could be renewed by further such acts. 'In short, such a sacrifice – a repetition of the primordial divine act – ensures the renewal of the world, the regeneration of life, the cohesion of society' (Eliade [1978] 1982,

156). Yet another belief of this kind was that a life sacrificed at the foundation of a new building, especially a temple or palace, would ensure its durability (Eliade [1978] 1982, 91). Thus what Eliade calls 'creative murder' (134) arose from a variety of causes, some indeed reflecting conceptions of deity that have to be rejected on moral grounds, but many reflecting pre-scientific understandings of the way in which the world works. And so he warns against a too sweeping judgment upon this very widespread practice of the ancient world:

> in all traditional societies human sacrifice was fraught with a cosmological and eschatological symbolism that was singularly powerful and complex . . . This bloodstained ritual in no way indicates an intellectual inferiority or a spiritual poverty in the peoples who practice it. (152)

The main changes between the ages of ritual human sacrifice and our own day have been in our understanding of the workings of nature, and in the enlargement of moral vision from the tribal to a national and then – very tentatively and insecurely – to a global horizon. But despite these advances it remains true that our own time has seen human sacrifices on an unprecedented scale in war, holocaust and avoidable mass starvation. It is safe to say, and perhaps wise to remember, that ancient magical science allied to ancient tribal ethics sacrificed far fewer lives than modern science allied to modern nationalistic values. It is a sobering thought that, almost certainly, many more human beings have been deliberately slaughtered by their fellows in the twentieth century than in all the previous centuries of human history put together.

To select another example of cultural variation in the application of moral principles, the torture and execution of heretics in the late medieval and early modern periods of Christianity presupposed the belief that heretics who die without having recanted will suffer eternal torment in hell, together with the further assumption that a recantation made under duress can have religious value. Today virtually all Christians would agree in rejecting these beliefs. But we can distinguish them from the fundamental moral principle of promoting the good of others – both the good of the heretics who were supposedly being saved from hell, and the good of the church as a whole which was supposedly being saved from dangerous germs of spiritual corruption.

In principle, then, and to a considerable extent in practice, we can separate out basic moral values from both the magical-scientific and the metaphysical beliefs which have always entered into their application within particular cultures. From a religious point of view we must (as I have argued in Chapter 9) assume the rooting of moral norms in the structure of our human nature and the rooting of that nature in our relationship to the Real. The central moral claim upon us is accordingly to behave in accordance with our true nature, from which we have fallen into sin or into the darkness and confusion of *avidyā*. The ethical insights of the great teachers are visions of human life lived in earthly alignment with the Real, insights either heard as divine commands or intuited as the truth of the eternal Dharma or Tao or Logos. Implicit within these we can discern the utterly basic principle that it is evil to cause suffering to others and good to benefit others and to alleviate or prevent their sufferings. This is so fundamental and universally accepted a principle that it is seldom formulated. And yet if all human beings lived in accordance with it there would be no wars, no injustice, no crime, no needless suffering.

One cannot prove such a fundamental principle. It is too basic to be derived from prior premises: the whole of our moral discourse hinges upon it. When, to take an extreme case, we discover individuals who are completely amoral and who see nothing wrong in, for example, inflicting gratuitous terror and pain on a child, society can forcibly restrain them or try to control them by fear of punishment, but it cannot compel them to feel for themselves the morally evil character of such behaviour. We regard them either as insane or as lacking in an important human quality. In the end we can only say that it is human to sympathise with others in their miseries and joys and that without this fellow-feeling there would be no morality and therefore no society. The Confucian teacher Mencius (Meng Tzu, 371–289 BCE) expressed this basic insight very clearly:

> I say that every man has a heart that pities others, for the heart of every man is moved by fear and horror, tenderness and mercy, if he suddenly sees a child about to fall into a well. And this is not because he wishes to make friends with the child's

father and mother or to win praise from his countryfolk and friends, nor because the child's cries hurt him.

This shows that no man is without a merciful, tender heart, no man is without a heart for shame and hatred, no man is without a heart to give way and yield, no man is without a heart for right and wrong.   (III: 6 – Lyall 1932, 48)

The Golden Rule, in its positive or negative forms, is a widespread expression of this principle that it is good to benefit others and evil to harm them. In the Hindu scriptures we read: 'One should never do that to another which one regards as injurious to one's own self. This, in brief, is the rule of Righteousness.'[11] In the Jain *Kritānga* Sutra we read that one should go about 'treating all creatures in the world as he himself would be treated' (bk I, lect. 11: 33 – Jacoby 1968, 314).

The Buddhist scriptures do not seem to have a precise formulation of the Golden Rule, although there are several passages in which the Buddha, rebuking those who are ill-treating others, says such things as 'Life is dear to all. Comparing others with oneself, one should neither strike nor cause to strike' (*Dhammapada*, 10:2 – Narada 1972, 124; compare 10:1 and *Udāna*, V:iv). But the basic principle of universal compassion is frequently taught: for example, 'As a mother cares for her son, all her days, so towards all living things a man's mind should be all-embracing' (*Sutta Nipāta*, 149 – Hare 1945, 24). Confucius, expounding humaneness (*jen*), said, 'Do not do to others what you would not like yourself' (*Analects*, XII:2). In the Taoist *Thāi Shang* we read that the good man will 'regard [others'] gains as if they were his own, and their losses in the same way' (3 – Legge 1891, 237). The Zoroastrian *Dadistan-i-dinik* declares, 'That nature only is good when it shall not do unto another whatever is not good for its own self' (94:5 – West 1882, 271). Jesus taught, 'As ye would that men should do to you, do ye also to them likewise' (Luke 6:31). In the Jewish Talmud we read 'What is hateful to yourself do not do to your fellow man (*haver*). That is the whole of the Torah' (*Babylonian Talmud*, Shabbath 31a). And in the Hadith of Islam we read Muhammad's words, 'No man is a true believer unless he desires for his brother that which he desires for himself'.[12]

It is this principle or ideal that is spelled out and amplified in the moral precepts of the great traditions.[13] The teaching always has a particular historical location, being set in the context of the existing state of society, which was in some cases more 'primitive' and in others more 'civilised'. In terms of a given cultural-economic-political situation the teaching shows how to behave towards neighbours, parents, children, the rich, the poor, slaves, strangers, enemies . . . In each case it begins on the common ground of fair dealing and respect for others' lives and property and leads on towards the higher ground of positive generosity, forgiveness, kindness, love, compassion, where we find the ethical evidence of the transformation of human existence from self-centredness to Reality-centredness. In the next chapter the teachings of the great traditions must be traced to show rather more explicitly this common ethical criterion with which they operate.

Notes

1. Harbans Singh 1969, 212. Cf. some words of the Buddha: 'Not by matted hair, nor by family, nor by birth does one become a brahmin. But in whom there exist both truth and righteousness, pure is he, a brahmin is he' (*Dhammapada*, 26:11 – Narada 1972, 296).
2. This is not of course the same as the official sainthood conferred by the Catholic Church. In the course of history individuals have been canonised for all manner of political and ecclesiastical as well as religious reasons.
3. Don Cupitt remarks of Malthus' *Essay on the Principle of Population*, whose book-length second edition appeared in 1803, that it 'may be the first major scientific work about human society' (Cupitt 1985, 27).
4. It is true that there have also been moments when new religious movements operated to free people from a traditional domination. For example, the rise of the *bhakti* movement in India was in part a revolt against the hierarchical caste system dominated by the brahmins; and other examples could be given from each of the great traditions. But the overall picture has nevertheless been one in which religion forms part of the fabric of the socio-economic establishment.
5. There is some empirical evidence for this view. Robert Wuthnow (1978, ch. 4) found that the wave of mystical interest among western young people in the 1960s, as measured in the San Francisco area, was correlated not with withdrawal from politics but with a relatively high level of political involvement. He suggests that the relationship between mysticism and political activity depends not so much upon the nature of mysticism as upon the nature of the society within which it exists, and particularly upon the availability or otherwise of political channels and the extent to which highly differentiated social roles confine the individual's sphere of responsibility and activity.

6. Aloysius Pieris, SJ, writes that 'in Sri Lanka we have even today a small nucleus of Buddhist monks with no "power", "property", "prestige" to rely on, but only their poverty to boast of. They are radically committed to the life they share with the poor, thus voicing the systematically silenced protests of the voiceless, including the ethnic minorities. The Buddhism that appears in the columns of their explosive periodical (*Vinivida*) has made a new hermeneusis of the textual religion on the basis of the lived experience of the Poor' (Pieris 1985, sect. 5). See also Pieris 1983, 17–18, 21–25.

7. Cf. Guenter Lewy 1974.

8. It is also true, and important for a larger systematic view, that it is through the overcoming of suffering, both in the strenuous effort to remove its causes and in transmuting it when it has occurred into moral strength and compassion for others, that we grow as persons.

9. Cf. Patrick Sherry 1984.

10. Frazer [1922] 1941, 79. I do not think that it is possible to accept Wittgenstein's view that these beliefs recorded by Frazer lacked factual content: see Wittgenstein [1967] 1971. On this issue see Chapter 12.3 above. Frazer also gives numerous examples of the killing of divine kings (Frazer [1922] 1941, ch. 24). According to him these arose from the mixed religio-scientific belief that the safety of the people, and even of the world itself, was bound up with the health and strength of the sovereign regarded as an incarnation of deity. Because he must not be allowed to grow old and feeble he was executed either when he began to fail or whilst his strength was at its height and could be channelled into his successor. This particular group of examples has however been questioned (e.g. by Evans-Pritchard 1948, 20–1, 34–5) and I mention it here only as a rather famous item in the literature that has now become dubious. For a recent criticism of Frazer's general approach see Jonathan Z. Smith, 'When the Bough Breaks' (Jonathan Smith 1973).

11. *Mahabharata*, Anushana parva, 113:7 – Roy 1893, 558. Taken out of context the sentence is ambiguous and could be read as an injunction to selfishness: do not do anything to injure yourself. But the context makes it clear that the intention is the opposite.

12. This saying of Muhammad is well attested in the Hadith corpus, for example in *Muslim*, chapter on *iman*, 71–2; *Ibn Madja*, Introduction, 9; *Al-Darimi*, chapter on *riqaq*, 29; *Hambal*, 3, 1976.

13. That charity, loving kindness, forgiveness, mercy and justice are enjoined by all the great traditions is argued and illustrated by Peggy Starkey (1985). On the other hand Stewart Sutherland (1982) has questioned whether people with different religious or metaphysical beliefs can properly be said to share the same ethical principles, arguing that their different beliefs will entail their having different intentions even when they perform phenomenally similar actions. However it seems to me more correct to say that (in many cases) their different beliefs lead to their acting ethically in the same way. See also Donovan 1986.

18

The Ethical Criterion

Thou shalt love thy neighbour as thyself.
(Jesus the Christ, Matthew 22:39)

As a mother cares for her son, all her days, so towards all living things a man's mind should be all-embracing.
(Gautama the Buddha, *Sutta Nipata*, 149)

1 THE IDEAL OF GENEROUS GOODWILL, LOVE, COMPASSION

That all the great traditions teach the moral ideal of generous goodwill, love, compassion epitomised in the Golden Rule must now be confirmed by pointing to it more fully in their scriptures. It should be emphasised that I am not here trying to expound the entire ethical teachings of these traditions, nor to describe the actual behaviour of their adherents through the centuries, but to show that love, compassion, generous concern for and commitment to the welfare of others is a central ideal for each of them.

Within the many-sided and many-levelled complex of Indian traditions known to the modern West as Hinduism the basis for universal compassion lies in a belief in the hidden unity of all life. As we have already noted, there is no one universally accepted system of Hindu ideas, and the scriptures use both personal and non-personal language in speaking of the ultimate reality, Brahman. But this difference does not affect the sense of the oneness of life and hence the 'com-passion', the feeling with and for others, which it produces. Both the advaitic view that all selves are ultimately identical and the vishishtadvaitist view that they are all individually part of the one divine being point to a human unity: 'Thus one Universal Inner Self of all beings becomes one separate self for each form' (*Kaṭha* Up., II:2:10 – cf. Radhakrishnan 1969, 639). The liberated person 'sees himself in all beings, and all beings in himself' (*Bhagavad Gita*, vi:29 – Bolle

1979, 77); 'And he who sees all beings in his own self and his own self in all beings, he does not feel any revulsion' (*Īśa* Up., 6 – Radhakrishnan 1969, 572).[1] Accordingly, 'One should look upon all creatures as one's own self' (*Mahabharata*, 12:29 – Roy 1891; cf. 310, 5:33f). Or as Gandhi expressed it, 'I believe in the absolute oneness of God and therefore also of humanity. What though we have many bodies? We have but one soul' (Mahatma Gandhi 1924, 313).[2] And in the *Bhagavad Gita* (also part of the *Mahabharata*) we read this description of the good person:

> He is generous and shows self-restraint . . .
> Practices austerity
>   and honesty.
> He is gentle, truthful, not given to anger,
>   able to give up possesions.
> He has peace
>   and does not slander anyone.
> He has compassion toward all creatures
>   and no greed.
> He knows mildness and humility,
>   and is not fickle in his behavior.
> There is majesty in him.
>   He is forbearing, firm, and pure,
> Free from all treachery
>   and conceit.
>   (xvi:1–3 – Bolle 1979, 179)

Spelled out in explicitly ethical terms this requires the three '*da*'s': *damyata*, self-control; *datta*, giving; *dayadhvam*, compassion (*Bṛhadāraṇyaka* Up., V:2:2–3). Again, 'Confidence, modesty, forgiveness, liberality, purity, freedom from laziness, absence of cruelty, freedom from delusion, compassion to all creatures, absence of backbiting, joy, contentment, joviality, humility, good behaviour, purity in all action' are enjoined (*Anugītā*, xxiii – Müller [1884] 1908a, 326). The *Mahabharata*, by which so many generations of Indians have been nurtured, presents the same ideal: 'He who . . . benefits persons of all orders, who is always devoted to the good of all beings, who does not feel aversion for anybody . . . succeeds in ascending to Heaven' (Anushana parva, 145:24 – Roy 1893, 659). Again, 'Abstention from injury, truth, absence of wrath, and liberality of gifts . . . these constitute eternal

Righteousness' (Anushana parva, 142:22 – Roy 1983, 760). Or again, 'Not having done any injury to anyone, such a man lives fearlessly and with a pure heart' (Shanti parva, 259:13 – Roy 1891, 344).

Basically similar injunctions occur in the Jewish Torah, expressed here as concrete *mitzvot* for the daily life of the people:

> When you reap the harvest of your land, you shall not reap your field to its very border, neither shall you gather the gleanings after your harvest. And you shall not strip your vineyard bare, neither shall you gather the fallen grapes of your vineyard; you shall leave them for the poor and the sojourner; I am the Lord your God.
>
> You shall not oppress your neighbour or rob him. The wages of a hired servant shall not remain with you all night until the morning. You shall not curse the deaf or put a stumbling block before the blind, but you shall fear your God: I am the Lord.
>
> You shall do no injustice in judgment; you shall not be partial to the poor or defer to the great, but in righteousness shall you judge your neighbour. You shall not go up and down as a slanderer among your people, and you shall not stand forth against the life of your neighbour: I am the Lord.
>
> You shall not hate your brother in your heart, but you shall reason with your neighbour, lest you bear sin because of him. You shall not take vengeance or bear any grudge against the sons of your own people, but you shall love (*ahabta*) your neighbour (*re'a*) as yourself:[3] I am the Lord.
>
> When a stranger sojourns with you in your land, you shall not do him wrong. The stranger who sojourns with you shall be to you as the native among you, and you shall love him as yourself; for you were strangers in the land of Egypt: I am the Lord your God.   (Leviticus, 19:9–10, 11–18)

The fact that awareness of the Real, known to the Jewish people as the God of Abraham, sets human beings under a profound moral claim was likewise the powerfully reiterated message of the great Hebrew prophets:

> Woe to those who decree iniquitous decrees,
> and the writers who keep writing oppression,
> to turn aside the needy from justice

> and to rob the poor of my people of their right,
> that widows may be their spoil,
> and that they may make the fatherless their prey!
> (Isaiah 10:1–2)

For Jews, to know the Holy One, blessed be he, is to live according to God's law, which is, fundamentally, to 'do justice, to love kindness, and to walk humbly with your God' (Micah 6:8).[4]

When we turn to the Buddhist tradition we move outside the sphere of divine commands. The motivation to live rightly is neither fear of punishment nor hope of reward, except in the sense that 'All we are is the result of what we have thought: it is founded on our thoughts, and is made up of our thoughts. If a man speaks or acts with a pure thought, happiness follows him, like a shadow that never leaves him' (*Dhammapada*, 1). For the way of the Dharma is not only intrinsically connected with inner happiness but is at the same time the way to final liberation. This is the Noble Eightfold Path, some of the steps in which are directly ethical:

> Verily it is this Ariyan eightfold way, to wit: Right view (*ditthi*), right aim (*sankappa*), right speech (*vaca*), right action (*kammanta*), right living (or livelihood, *ajiva*), right effort (*vayama*), right mindfulness (*sati*), and right concentration (*samādhi*). This, monks, is that middle path which giveth vision, which giveth knowledge, which causeth calm, special knowledge, enlightenment, Nibbana.
> (*Saṃyutta Nikāya*, V:421 – Woodward 1956, 357)

Right speech, action and livelihood involve abstention from lying, backbiting, slander, abuse and idle gossip; from destroying life, stealing, dishonesty and illegitimate sexual intercourse; and from making one's living in ways that harm others, such as dealing in weapons and dangerous drugs and poisons, defrauding people or slaughtering animals.

This moral outlook, expressed in the Pali scriptures, developed in due course into the ideal of the bodhisattva: one who has attained to the verge of Nirvana and thus to the end of the process of rebirth but who out of limitless compassion (*karuṇā*) renounces final nirvanisation until the whole human race has been raised to the same level. The vow of the bodhisattva is one of self-sacrifice for the salvation of many:

> All creatures are in pain, all suffer from bad and hindering karma . . . so that they cannot see the Buddhas or hear the Law of Righteousness or know the Order . . . All that mass of pain and evil karma I take in my own body . . . I take upon myself the burden of sorrow . . . Assuredly I must bear the burdens of all beings . . . for I have resolved to save them all. I must set them all free, I must save the whole world from the forest of birth, old age, disease, and rebirth, from misfortune and sin, from the round of birth and death, from the toils of heresy . . . For all beings are caught in the net of craving, encompassed by ignorance, held by the desire for existence . . . I work to establish the kingdom of perfect wisdom for all beings . . .
>
> (*Śikṣāsamuccaya*, 278f – de Bary 1972, 84–5)

Returning to the Pali scriptures, the four cardinal virtues extolled in them are friendliness (*mettā*), compassion (*karuṇā*), sympathetic joy (*muditā*) and serenity (*samatha*). The following passage conveys the flavour of this Buddhist outlook:

> May all be happy and safe!
> May all beings gain inner joy –
> All living beings whatever . . .
> Seen or unseen,
> Dwelling afar or near,
> Born or yet unborn –
> May all beings gain inner joy.
> May no being deceive another,
> Nor in any way scorn another,
> Nor, in anger or ill-will,
> Desire another's sorrow.
> As a mother cares for her son,
> Her only son, all her days,
> So towards all things living
> A man's mind should be all-embracing.
>
> Friendliness for the whole world,
> All-embracing, he should raise in his mind,
> Above, below, and across,

Unhindered, free from hate and ill-will.
(*Sutta Nipata*, 143f – de Bary 1972, 37–8)

Essentially the same ideal of universal compassion or love
(*agape*)[5] is central to Christianity. When Jesus was asked, Which is
the greatest commandment? he answered by bringing together
two texts from the Torah: 'Thou shalt love the Lord thy God with
all thy heart, and with all thy soul, and with all thy mind. This is
the first and great commandment. And the second is like unto it.
Thou shalt love thy neighbour as thyself' (Matthew 22:36–9). The
New Testament collection of Jesus' sayings known as the Sermon
on the Mount begins with a series of beatitudes, several of which
are ethical in content:

Blessed are the meek, for they shall inherit the earth.
Blessed are those who hunger and thirst for righteousness, for
they shall be filled.
Blessed are the merciful, for they shall obtain mercy.
Blessed are the peacemakers, for they shall be called sons of
God.   (Matthew 5:5–7, 9)

The Sermon then teaches the personal love commandment and its
implication of non-violence:

Ye have heard that it hath been said, An eye for an eye, and a
tooth for a tooth: but I say unto you, That ye resist not evil: but
whosoever shall smite thee on thy right cheek, turn to him the
other also. And if any man will sue thee at law, and take away
thy coat, let him have thy cloak also. And whosoever shall
compel thee to go a mile, go with him twain. Give to him that
asketh thee, and from him that would borrow of thee turn not
thou away.

Ye have heard that it hath been said, Thou shalt love thy
neighbour, and hate thine enemy. But I say unto you, Love
your enemies, bless them that curse you, do good to them that
hate you, and pray for them that despitefully use you, and
persecute you; that ye may be the children of your Father
which is in heaven: for he maketh his sun to rise on the evil and
on the good, and sendeth rain on the just and on the unjust.
For if ye love them which love you, what reward have ye? Do
not even the publicans the same? And if ye salute your brethren

only, what do ye more than others? Do not even the publicans so? Be ye therefore perfect, even as your Father which is in heaven is perfect. (Matthew 5:38–48)

The love commandment is echoed in the letters of St John and St Paul. The former writes, 'Beloved, let us love one another: for love is of God; and every one that loveth is born of God, and knoweth God. He that loveth not knoweth not God; for God is love . . . If a man say, I love God, and hateth his brother, he is a liar: for he that loveth not his brother whom he hath seen, how can he love God whom he hath not seen?' (I John 4:7–8, 20). And St Paul writes to the Galatians that 'the fruit of the Spirit is love, joy, peace, longsuffering, gentleness, goodness, faith, meekness, temperance: against such there is no law' (Galatians 5:22–3). But the most eloquent celebration of love in the New Testament is St Paul's 'hymn':

Though I speak with the tongues of men and of angels, and have not love, I am become as sounding brass, or a tinkling cymbal. And though I have the gift of prophecy, and understand all mysteries, and all knowledge; and though I have all faith, so that I could remove mountains, and have not love, I am nothing. And though I bestow all my goods to feed the poor, and though I give my body to be burned, and have not love, it profiteth me nothing. Love suffereth long, and is kind; love envieth not: love vaunteth not itself, is not puffed up, doth not behave itself unseemly, seeketh not her own, is not easily provoked, thinketh no evil; rejoiceth not in iniquity, but rejoiceth in the truth; beareth all things, believeth all things, hopeth all things, endureth all things. Love never faileth: but whether there be prophecies, they shall fail; whether there be tongues, they shall cease; whether there be knowledge, it shall vanish away . . . And now abideth faith, hope, love, these three; but the greatest of these is love.

(I Corinthians 13:1–8, 13)

In the neighbouring Islamic tradition the moral ideal is expressed in the Qur'an and illustrated in the *hadith* reports of the sayings of Muhammad and stories of his life. The Muslim knows him or herself to be a slave of God, the Merciful, the Compassionate. This central relationship is to be lived out in a spirit of mercy and forgiveness toward others, compassion toward parents and orphans, travellers and the poor, in honesty and just dealing, faithfulness in marriage, kindness to children, cheerful courtesy and humility of bearing. For example, in Sura 17 of the Qur'an we read these injunctions, addressed to a seventh-century CE Arabian society living under harsh conditions in which the weak – widows and orphans, the poor, the old, slaves – were pitifully vulnerable, in which travel was dangerous, and in which infanticide was practised because female children were seen as an economic burden:

> Thy Lord hath decreed
> That ye worship none but Him.
> And that ye be kind
> To parents. Whether one
> Or both of them attain
> Old age in thy life,
> Say not to them a word
> Of contempt, nor repel them,
> But address them
> In terms of honour.
> And, out of kindness,
> Lower to them the wing
> Of humility, and say 'My Lord! bestow on them
> Thy Mercy even as they
> Cherished me in childhood.' (23–4)
> And render to the kindred
> Their due rights, as (also)
> To those in want,
> And to the wayfarer. (26)
> Kill not your children
> For fear of want: We shall
> Provide sustenance for them
> As well as for you.
> Verily the killing of them
> Is a great sin. (31)
> Nor come nigh to adultery:
> For it is a shameful (deed)
> And an evil, opening the road
> (To other evils). (32)
> Come not nigh

To the orphan's property
Except to improve it,
Until he attains the age
Of full strength; and fulfil
(Every) engagement,
For (every) engagement
Will be inquired into
(On the Day of Reckoning).
Give full measure when ye
Measure, and weigh
with a balance that is straight. (34–5)
Nor walk on the earth
With insolence: for thou
Canst not rend the earth
Asunder, nor reach
The mountains in height. (37)

(Trans. Yusuf Ali, 1977)

Elsewhere there is this account of true religion:

It is not righteousness
That ye turn your faces
Towards East or West;
But it is righteousness –
To believe in God
And the Last Day,
And the Angels,
And the Book,
And the Messengers;
To spend of your substance,
Out of love for Him,
For your kin,
For orphans,
For the needy,
For the wayfarer,
For those who ask,
And for the ransom of slaves;
To be steadfast in prayer,
And practise regular charity;
To fulfil the contracts
Which ye have made.
(Qur'an 2:177, trans. Yusuf Ali, 1977)

And at various places in the Qur'an we read such verses as these: 'Do thou good, as God has been good to thee' (28:77); 'Whoever submits his whole self to God and is a doer of good, he will get his reward with his Lord' (2:112).

In the *hadith* many sayings of the Prophet call for generous kindness, love, compassion for one's fellows. For example, 'It is one form of faith (*iman*) that one loves (*hub*) his brother as one loves oneself' (*Bukhari*, ch. on *iman*, 7). To take other examples from the *Al-Hadis of Miskat-ul-Masibih* (Karim 1960–4): 'Verily Allah is kind. He loves kindness; and He bestows over kindness what He bestows not over harshness' (I:253); 'He who is devoid of kindness is devoid of all good' (I:252); 'You shall not enter Paradise until you believe; and you will not believe till you love one another' (I:226); 'The main part of wisdom after religion is love for men and doing good to everyone, pious or sinner' (I:248); 'Feed the hungry, visit the sick, and free the captive' (I:220); 'The best home of Muslims is a home wherein there is an orphan who is treated well' (I:202); 'Pay trust to one who has entrusted you, and be not treacherous to one who was treacherous to you' (I:347); 'The strong man is not one who can wrestle, but the strong man is one who can control himself in the time of anger' (I:351). And concerning Muhammad himself we read that 'Forgiveness was a chief jewel in the Prophet's character. So broad was his heart that the spirit of revenge was absolutely absent from it' (IV:283); 'the Holy Prophet used always to invoke blessings on his enemies instead of taking revenge on them for the wrongs done to him' (IV:286); 'Abu Hurairah reported that it was questioned: O Messenger of Allah! curse against the polytheists. He replied: Verily I have been sent not to curse, but verily I have been raised up as mercy' (I:247).

2 AGAPE/KARUNA AS THE ETHICAL CRITERION

Love, compassion, self-sacrificing concern for the good of others, generous kindness and forgiveness – which we have seen to constitute the basic ethical principle of the great traditions – is not an alien ideal imposed by supernatural authority but one arising out of our human nature (though always in tension with other aspects of that nature), reinforced, refined and elevated to new levels within the religious traditions. This basic ideal has itself been operative in the initial acceptance of great teachers. If, for example, Gautama had preached and lived an Eightfold Path of selfishness, greed, theft, hatred, violence, slander, deceit and sensual self-indulgence, he would not have been able to set the Wheel of Dharma turning for the welfare of many. Again, if Jesus had extolled hatred instead of love, or if his own life and death had not incarnated the ideal of self-giving love that he taught, no one would have accepted him as a true son of God, revealing the heavenly Father's nature.[6] Or again, if Muhammad had not embodied in his own life the submission to God that is the central demand of the Qur'an, or had failed to live in accordance with the ethical requirements which he taught, he would not have been regarded as a true prophet of Allah. Thus the ideal of love, compassion, generosity, mercy has always been a basic factor in the recognition of someone as an authentic mediator of the Real. And having been recognised partly by their embodiment of this ideal such persons have then by their lives and teachings deepened and clarified our understanding of the ideal itself.

It is this basic norm enshrined in the great traditions that provides the broad criterion by which we can make moral judgments in the sphere of religion. In one sense its application is comparatively easy, but in another sense extremely difficult. It is easy in the sense that we can readily list actions and patterns of behaviour which are good and evil respectively under this criterion. Nazism, for example, appears somewhere within the outskirts of the spreading network of overlapping phenomena covered by the concept of religion. But whereas the other 'secular faiths' of Marxism, Maoism and Humanism contain important elements of good as well as of evil, Nazism taken as a whole appears retrospectively as unambiguously evil: for in conceiving and carrying out the Jewish holocaust it gave vent on a vast scale to the darkest and most destructive distortions of human nature. It is the common criterion of true *Menschlichkeit*, expressed in *agape* or *karuṇā*, that makes this so immediately evident to us. And as contemporary examples of evils that are identified by the same criterion we can list the continuing (although officially abolished) outcaste status within Hindu society, and the (also illegal) burning of brides because of an insufficient dowry; the cutting off of a thief's hand under the *shariah* law in the Muslim dominated Sudan and the savage persecution of the Bah'ais in Iran; the direct involvement over several generations of the dominant Christian churches in massive racial oppression in South Africa and in grossly oppressive regimes in South America; the failure to accord proper human recognition to the Palestinian people in the state of Israel. Again, one can list Hindu–Muslim and Hindu–Sikh violence in India, Catholic–Protestant violence in Northern Ireland, Christian–Muslim violence in Lebanon; and so on in a virtually endless count of religiously validated and intensified evils.

We can equally readily list religiously related activities that are admirable under this basic criterion: the provision of a basis for social cohesion for human societies, large and small; the creation of schools, universities and hospitals and the nurturing of literature, philosophy and the arts; innumerable works of mercy and charity . . . Again the list is virtually endless. But when we seek to go beyond the identification of particular phenomena as good or evil to make ethical judgments concerning the religious traditions as totalities, we encounter large complicating factors which must give pause to any project for the moral grading of the great world faiths.

The largest of these historical cross-currents has been the rise of modern science. For it is this that has made possible the rapid development of the western and northern hemisphere, lifting it out of a relatively primitive technological state and out of the generally feudal social and political conditions of the pre-modern period. This part of the world is predominantly Christian and post-Christian, so that Christianity has during the last three hundred years come to be associated with the economic affluence, the expansion of education and the intellectual ferment and political democratisation that have come in the wake of the scientific revolution. In contrast, the eastern and southern hemisphere, dominated by the Muslim, Buddhist, Hindu and African primal traditions, has been generally associated until very recently, as still today in many areas, with continuing pre-modern social, economic and political conditions.

Not only has modern science made possible the present relative affluence of the western and northern hemisphere, but it has had equally important effects on its intellectual and ethical climate. It undermined, in the seventeenth and eighteenth centuries, the generally dogmatic and superstitious mentality of medieval Europe by giving birth to the more open, critical and questioning outlook that characterises modernity. This has now become an aspect of the 'Christian West' in distinction from the still relatively medieval ethos, largely unaffected by the canons of scientific thinking, of many millions in the Islamic, Hindu, Buddhist and primal worlds. Again, as another aspect of the development of western science-based civilisation, there has been a humanisation of values producing what we may call the modern liberal ethical outlook. From this standpoint, in its ideal form, all human beings are seen as having an equal intrinsic value, and evil is accordingly discerned not only at the personal level but also in political and economic arrangements by which one group exploits another, whether the lines be drawn in terms of colour, gender, caste, class, nationality or religion. Likewise moral value is seen not only in individual acts of compassion and mutual aid within the existing social structures but also in political movements seeking to transform those structures; and the expansion of human freedom is welcomed in recognition of the equality of the sexes, in liberal education, in democratic forms of government, in life-preserving and life-enhancing applications of science, in rehabilitation as the aim of a penal system . . . And once again these liberal values have had their main development within 'Christian civilisation', though they are also now exported as secondary influences to much of Asia and Africa. Thus it seems to many that Christianity is both the source and the inspiration of a contemporary ethical outlook which matches more nearly than any other the common ideal of the great traditions.

However this comfortable assumption quickly begins to crumble under historical analysis. Modern science is not a product of Christianity as such but of the impact on Christian Europe of the Greek spirit of free enquiry during the vast cultural transformation known as the Renaissance, stimulated by a rediscovery of classical literature and thought that was rapidly spread by the new invention of printing. It is no doubt true that, as A. N. Whitehead and others have argued, the theological belief in an orderly and unitary world ordained by a rational creator provided a milieu within which this could happen (Whitehead 1926, 17–18). But that Christianity did not bring forth modern science simply from its own resources is shown by the fact that it had presided unchallenged over the life of Europe for more than a thousand years before the scientific spirit began to stir within it. And when this spirit did emerge, rapidly developing its own momentum, its most powerful foe was the church, which saw much of the new knowledge as a dangerous challenge to its established dogmas.

The Copernican revolution in astronomy, dethroning humanity from a central position in the universe; the discovery that the earth is enormously older than the biblical dating had allowed; and the Darwinian theory of evolution, entailing that the human species was not created ready-made but has gradually evolved out of lower forms of life, were felt at the time as hammer blows against the Christian revelation. The late nineteenth century saw the bitter retreat of theology before the advancing forces of science;[7] and it has only been through prolonged debates, much personal agonising and traumatic schisms between 'fundamentalists' and 'liberals' that Christianity has for the most part come to accept the new scientific picture of the world, reinterpreting many of its doctrines accordingly.

Accordingly Christianity should not be credited with the achievements and benefits of modern science – nor debited with its nuclear dangers. Modern science originated in the Christian West and could not have arisen at the same time elsewhere. But once launched it rapidly developed into an autonomous human enterprise with its own methods and outlook, owing allegiance only to the ideal of objective truth. It is not tied to the region where it first appeared and is in fact rapidly spreading throughout the world by being grafted onto the Hindu, Buddhist, Muslim, Marxist and other cultures. Christianity is the first religious tradition to have been influenced by the scientific enterprise and to be largely transformed by its new outlook and knowledge. But the same process has begun within the other great civilisations of the earth, and has been limited by material and educational resources rather than by religious backgrounds. We may surmise that the Hindu and Buddhist traditions will be able to assimilate the scientific outlook as relatively easily as post-Confucian China, whereas Islam may perhaps find the process as traumatic as Christianity has done. But to compare a West which has emerged from its medieval phase with an East which is now in the throes of emerging, attributing the wealth and productivity of the one to Christianity and the poverty and economic backwardness of the other to Hinduism, Buddhism and Islam, is to ignore the immensely important non-religious factors in history. What we see is a difference in stages of modernisation under the influence of a religiously neutral science and technology which have transformed the western and are now in the process of transforming the eastern civilisations. Thus the special relationship between Christianity and modern science, with all its good and bad effects on human life, is a contingent and temporary connection.

A second critical comment concerns the modern liberal moral outlook. This does indeed accord ideally with the basic value of generous kindness, love, compassion taught by all the great traditions and mediated to the West by Christianity. But it does not represent simply a flowering of Christian teaching. The love commandment of the Sermon on the Mount by itself, without the insistent promptings of humanist and rationalist voices, did not end slavery[8] and has not ended exploitation. Nor did it even, by itself, bring the perception that freedom and equality are ideals to be sought after. On the contrary, for more than a thousand years the application, or misapplication, of Christian ethical principles produced and validated strongly hierarchical societies in which power was narrowly concentrated in kings and emperors as God's vice-regents on earth; in which the inherited stations of 'the rich man in his castle and the poor man at his gate' were accepted as divinely established; in which women were emphatically subordinated to men;[9] and in which individual freedom of thought and action were narrowly circumscribed and punishments were brutal in the extreme. It was the fertilisation of the medieval Christian ethos by the humanistic ideals of ancient Greece, recovered in the Renaissance and consolidated in the Enlightenment of the eighteenth century, that produced the contemporary liberal moral outlook. As in the case of the rise of science, this has resulted from an interaction of cultural influences – a religious influence deriving from the Bible and another influence generated by the complex of forces creating the modern scientific worldview.

It must be added that the liberal morality pervading modern western societies has another side to it which is feared rather than envied from within the more traditional Islamic, Hindu, Buddhist, primal and also Marxist cultures. This is a combined result of the stress of dehumanising urban environments and the individualistic 'permissiveness' reflected in the divorce explosion, the resulting prevalence of one-parent families, the high rates of abortion and suicide and the widespread use of hard drugs. All this meshes with a pursuit of individual possessions and pleasure in a consumer society seeking an ever higher material standard of living through increasingly sophisticated luxuries that consume the world's resources, thereby depleting its basic non-renewable wealth. Further, as the first civilisation to have at its disposal the immense new powers of modern technology, the West has also been the first to encounter the dangers which these powers bring with them. Nuclear armaments mean that western nationalism, intensified by the capitalist–communist ideological struggle, could lead to a massive thermo-nuclear exchange creating a 'nuclear winter' in which civilisation as we know it comes to a painful end. All these factors together have created a dark shadow accompanying the bright promise of our contemporary science-oriented culture.

3 IDEALS AND APPLICATIONS: THE EXAMPLES OF CHRISTIANITY AND ISLAM

We have seen that many factors enter into the historical applications and misapplications of the common ideal of generous kindness, love, compassion. One further such factor is worth lifting up for special notice. This concerns the translation of the ideal into specific social regulations. For whilst the inner core of a religious movement usually contains highly dedicated individuals who are motivated to live out their ideals, if necessary at considerable cost to themselves, any natural human society – tribe, city, nation, empire – consists for the most part of self-concerned persons and groups, each seeking their own welfare at the expense when necessary of others. Therefore any society has to establish laws controlling social cause and effect so as to make it in the interests of the individual to respect – in act if not in desire – the rights of others. There is an important distinction between traditions in which this had to be done from the beginning and traditions in which the founder was free from any such responsibility for the maintenance of social order.

Some of the founders or initial shapers of great traditions have lived in the margins of society, without political power. Their ethical concern was accordingly limited to the relationships between individuals, it being left to later generations to adapt their teachings to guide civil societies. Chief among these have been Gautama the Buddha, who renounced his princely birth-status, and Jesus the Christ, who was born outside the power structure of the Roman world. There were however others who taught from positions of political responsibility and were obliged to give guidance for the life of their communities, consisting of ordinary selfish men and women exhibiting all the weaknesses of human nature. Such were Confucius and Plato, who were able to advise and influence rulers; Moses and the kings, priests and prophets of ancient Israel, for whom religion and politics were closely intertwined; and Muhammad who, in the conditions of the Arabia of his time, in launching a new religious movement inevitably became at the same time a political leader. The kind of moral teaching given by these great figures has been profoundly affected by their having or lacking, as the case may be, responsibility for the ordering of their societies. Broadly speaking, the more immediate and pressing this responsibility the more practical and socially oriented the teaching; whilst the more remote they were from political responsibility the more ideal and also individualistic the teaching. Thus the morally ambiguous business of legislating for human imperfection inevitably exercised the thoughts and influenced the teachings of the formative figures of ancient Judaism, and of Muhammad, but was beyond the horizon of concern of Gautama and Jesus; so that the latter were left free to challenge their contemporaries with an unqualified call to personal transformation. And because the sacred writings of a tradition reveal the Real as reflected in the mind of a human founder or founders, always embedded in a certain historical situation, the Torah and the Qur'an contain a range of detailed laws for civil society whilst the Pali scriptures and the New Testament do not.

This contrast of vocations is well illustrated by Jesus and Muhammad. Jesus was born into the artisan class of a subject people ruled by the Romans. He was thus entirely without political power or influence and was accordingly free of any need to think of ordering or reforming the society of which he was a part. Indeed any idea of social criticism or reform in the name of God – such as had been central to the work of some of the classical Hebrew prophets – was ruled out by his apocalyptic conviction of living at the end of the Age when God was about to sweep away the existing world order and bring in the divine kingdom.[10] From this standpoint Jesus could be conscious of the universal call to give oneself in a love to God that would be expressed in love to neighbour. And when he spelled this out in concrete examples it was always in relation to individual situations and never in terms of large-scale structural change.

To say this is not to deny that outstanding religious figures in the ancient world were often influential within their society. The people, and in some cases the rulers, listened to them. Thus Jesus' contemporary John the Baptist had drawn large crowds and had in his teaching publicly attacked the royal family; and the result was his arrest and execution. Jesus too drew large crowds, and his apocalyptic message, implying the imminent end of Roman rule, was potentially explosive within a situation in which there were zealot plots to overthrow that rule – such as occurred in 66 and 132 CE. He alarmed the Jewish-Roman establishment in a way that, exacerbated by his radical religious criticisms, led to Jesus' death. Thus he did have a social impact; and, further, his teaching did have hidden within it long-term social and political implications which later Christian thinkers have drawn out.

But nevertheless Jesus himself seems not to have been concerned about the reorganisation of society prior to the great Day of the Lord which was so soon to arrive, superseding all the existing social structures and superseding indeed all need for them, since it meant the divine refashioning of human nature so that men and women would live according to God's will. He was therefore not concerned with particular social and political issues – except insofar as the people pressed upon him the two questions of divorce and the payment of taxes to Rome. Thus Jesus never encountered the problems that Christianity had to face when, beginning in 310 CE, church and empire fused and it was Christianity's role to provide a framework for the lives of whole populations of people, most of whom probably had only the most rudimentary conception of Jesus' teachings. When this happened, through the adoption of Christianity by Theodosius as the official religion of the Roman world, the original gospel of love, with its pacifist implications, quickly gave way to the pragmatic law of the church-state. Bishops became chaplains and religious validators to kings and barons, or became lords themselves, ruling over large populations in a Europe that was as violent, and as heedless of the value of individual human life, as the seventh-century CE Arabia which was to be the setting for Muhammad's life.

Muhammad – in contrast to Jesus – was born into the dominant tribe of Arabia, the Quaraish, and its leading city Mecca, and was thus close to the centre of power. However his message of the unqualified oneness of God challenged the existing religious-political-commercial power structure of Mecca so that he and his companions had to flee to Medina.[11] As the new community grew there it inevitably constituted, by the very nature of Arabian society, a new political power with which the other powers had to reckon. Thus from the Hijrah onward Islam was embodied in an independent community, a political entity among the tribal groupings of the Peninsula, and its spread was co-terminous with the growth of this new political entity. In interaction with the other communities around it Islam would have been suppressed or wiped out if it had not resorted to the same methods as the neighbouring tribes, including careful political calculation and the effective use of force. Islam was thus brought after the Hijrah to the stage of morally compromised participation in the harsh dynamics of history to which Christianity arrived only with its integration into the Roman Empire.

In this respect the difference was that Christianity, coming into existence in the Mediterranean world, inherited an empire, though one already beginning to decline, whilst Islam, coming into existence in Arabia, had to forge its own empire – which also began several centuries later to decline. But in each case the religion adopted and legitimised violence as an essential means of defence, policing, thought control and the enlargement of its own borders. Thus the integration with society that took nearly three centuries in the case of Christianity, and in which the founder himself accordingly had no part, occurred in the case of Islam within the lifetime of its founder and was perforce one of his major preoccupations.

The world in fact needs to hear both the more immediate and limited and the more ultimate and unlimited claims of the Real upon our lives. Accordingly each of the great traditions, beginning with either the more earthly and social or the more ideal and individual kind of teaching, has had to generate the other to complement it.[12] Thus Christianity, beginning with the ethical ideals of the Sermon on the Mount, involving unlimited forgiveness, non-retaliation against an aggressor, renunciation of wealth and a complete trust in God without thought for tomorrow – an ideal which no Christian nation has ever seriously attempted to embody in its corporate life – , quickly developed doctrines of the ruler ordained by God, of the just war, of the proportionate punishment of sinners and the forcible suppression of heretics and social deviants, and eventually produced an elaborate casuistry covering virtually all the contingencies of life. Islam on the other hand started with the difficult but nevertheless practicable Qur'anic ethic of communal brotherhood, comprising just dealings, truth-telling, faithful performance of promises, alms-giving, and kindness to widows, orphans and slaves, and including also severe punishments for thieves and sexual offenders and an injunction to violence in certain defined circumstances. But starting with this earthly pattern, demanding but achievable, Islam later generated in its Sufi strands the love ideal that illuminates and uplifts even though it has never received a large-scale political embodiment. As an example, a poem of Jalalu'l-Din Rumi reads:

> God rebuked Moses, saying, 'O thou that has seen the rising
>   moon from thy bosom,
> Thou whom I have illumined with my Light! I am God, I fell
>   sick, thou camest not.'
> Moses said, 'O transcendent One, Thou art clear of defect.
>   What mystery is this? Explain, O Lord!'
> God said unto him again, 'Wherefore didst not thou kindly ask
>   after me when I was sick?'
> He answered, 'O Lord, Thou never ailest. My understanding is
>   lost: unfold the meaning of these words.'
> God said, 'Yea; a favourite and chosen slave of Mine fell sick. I
>   am he. Consider well:
> His infirmity is My infirmity; his sickness is My sickness.'[13]

Both groups of traditions, then, have had to apply their basic moral principles to the lives of societies, making rules to regulate the interactions and inevitable conflicts between very imperfect human beings. Such applications tend to take different forms as the moral climate changes: for example, slavery was seen as natural in the first and still in the seventh century CE, but not in the twentieth. Accordingly traditions whose scriptures eternalise laws laid down for a particular time and place are handicapped in adapting themselves to a developing moral outlook. For example, the Qur'an requires the chopping off of a thief's hand (5:41). In the harsh conditions of existence in seventh-century Arabia, when life was precarious, pain was never far away and prison systems had not yet been invented, this may have been an appropriate part of an effective system of law. But today prison sentences can provide graded punishments without the irrevocability of amputation. In this new situation, and in the changed moral climate to which it is related, the amputation of a thief's hand seems a barbarous act. But, whilst the enshrining of detailed seventh-century Arabian laws as permanent divine commands for Islamic societies has hindered the development of more humane and sophisticated penal systems, it has nevertheless fortunately not prevented many modern Islamic states from finding ways to depart in practice from the full rigour of the traditional Shariah. It has made penal advances difficult but happily not impossible.

Christianity, on the other hand, beginning with a personal ethic which included no prescriptions concerning crime and punishment or the maintenance of order in society, has been able in recent times to accept the development of penal systems more in tune with the modern moral outlook. In this particular area contemporary Christianity thus reflects the common ethical ideal better than Islam. But one can immediately think of an at least equally important area in which Islam reflects that ideal better than Christianity, namely in the matter of racial prejudice. Christian history throughout the period of European colonialism and since has been deeply disfigured by the racist assumption that black people are inherently inferior to white people and can therefore properly be exploited by them and held down in positions of servitude. This assumption was long supported by the churches, who added a further dimension to it by their denigration of Hinduism, Buddhism, Islam and African primal religions as needing to be superseded by Christianity;[14] and it continues today (though rejected and strongly criticised by many Christians) in the prevailingly racist outlook and behaviour of the peoples and governments of western Europe and North America. It is even more conspicuous in the dominant white Christian churches in South Africa, which have long validated the economic exploitation of the black majority through political and educational policies designed to keep them in a permanently inferior position. This aspect of Christian morality makes an ugly contrast with the general acceptance of black, brown and white on a basis of equality within worldwide Islam.

This then is the outcome of our discussion so far: the ethical principles of the great traditions express essentially the same ideal of love, compassion, forgiveness. But their applications of this ideal to the concrete circumstances of life in different times and places have varied greatly. Within the long shifting kaleidoscope of history we can point to both good and evil moments within each tradition, good and evil individuals, periods, structures, incidents. But it is virtually impossible to weigh up the overall moral value, in terms of the incarnation of love or compassion, of one tradition as compared with another. For we are dealing for the most part with incommensurable goods and evils. How, for example, do we weigh the integrity of family life and the support so often given to the aged in a Hindu or Muslim village against the provisions made for the often fragmented families and isolated elderly individuals in a western secular state; or weigh the endemic poverty within the largely Muslim, Hindu, Buddhist and primal Third World against the murderous persecutions of the Jews and the widespread racial oppression practised by the Christian and post-Christian civilisation of the First World? How do we weigh Third World starvation due to the devastating effects of drought and flood on subsistence economies against the miseries, producing a mounting level of crime, suicide, drug abuse and mental breakdown, in the crowded cities of the more 'advanced' countries; or weigh the caste system of India against the class system and class struggle of the industrial West; or weigh bitter communal conflicts between Muslims and Hindus in India against bitter communal conflicts between Catholics and Protestants in Northern Ireland?

Taking the great world traditions as totalities, then, we can only say that each is an unique mixture of good and evil. Each has been and is responsible for or associated with immense contributions to human welfare; each has also been and is responsible for or implicated in vast evils afflicting some part of the human race. It may be the case that, from the point of view of omniscience, one tradition stands out as morally superior to all others. But if so this is not evident from our partial human perspective. It is not possible, as an unbiased judgment with which all rational persons could be expected to agree, to assert the overall moral superiority of any one of the great religious traditions of the world. This is the rather modest conclusion to which our discussion points.

4 ETHICS AND RELIGIOUS BELIEF

We shall come in the next two chapters to the question of the status of religious belief and of the opposing doctrines of the different traditions. But before leaving the ethical criterion let us ask whether it can also be used to evaluate religious conceptions and dogmas. For it has sometimes been suggested that this might be the main basis for the comparative assessment of religious affirmations or doxastic practices.[15]

We cannot apply the common ethical ideal directly to the concept of the Real *an sich*: for, as argued in Chapter 14.2, this is the concept of that which lies beyond all (other than purely formal) human categorisation. Thus when we refer to the Real as the basis of the ultimate optimism of post-axial religion, or as the 'unity of reality and value', we are speaking from our human point of view. The Real is the ground of our values, in that it is the ground of our existence and nature; and it is good in the sense that it is to be rejoiced in as the basis of the limitlessly better possibility that is open to us. It is good, then, not in itself but in relation to the deepest concerns of human beings. On the other hand the manifestations of the Real formed in relation to culturally various modes of human consciousness are in principle open to ethical comment and criticism.

The *impersonae* – Brahman, the Tao, the Dharmakaya, Sunyata – do not have ethical qualities and cannot therefore be said to be morally good or bad. Any moral assessment must focus instead upon their effects within human behaviour. On a first view this effect has been positive. For the Real expresses itself in the lives of those who are centred in Brahman or the Dharmakaya or the Tao in a sense of human unity and in a consequent universal compassion. At the same time we have already noted (in Chapter 17.3) the criticism that Hindu and Buddhist compassion has thus far been expressed mainly in individual acts of charity, leaving untouched the structural evils of society. However we saw that this arose, not from the nature of compassion, but from a universal blindness prior to the modern sociological consciousness, a blindness that was equally evident in the expression of Christian love; and that the new awareness of structural evil is rapidly spreading within Hindu and Buddhist as well as Christian cultures, so that there is no reason to doubt that it will eventually affect the outworkings of *karuṇā* as much as of *agape*. On the more individual level, however, we must be prepared to recognise that the compassion released by negating natural self-centredness involves an objectivity and lucidity of vision which is sometimes as tough as it is tender. Thus, for example, when a woman asked the Buddha to bring her dead son back to life, he responded in a way which helped her instead to accept the universality and inevitability of death.[16] This could be seen as negative and unsympathetic, though it can also be seen as a compassionate attempt to bring her nearer to the great good of illumination.

In its *personae*, however, the Real does have ethical qualities. Adonai, Vishnu, Shiva, the heavenly Father and Allah each exist in a moral relationship with their worshippers. They accordingly come within the scope of the ethical criterion of love, compassion, generous forgiveness. In applying this criterion we need again to remember that love is inherently demanding as well as tender: to value people is to be a vehicle of the claim upon them that they become the best that they are capable of being. And generous forgiveness, whilst it may sometimes precede and evoke repentance, more often has to come after it in order to be received as genuine forgiveness. Thus the application of the common ethical ideal to concepts of God is not a matter of simple monochrome judgment. For in order to be agents of salvific transformation the divine *personae* have to be just, as well as tender, fearful and awe-inspiring as well as gracious.

However, granting these complexities, there have been conceptions of God which conflict with the common ethical ideal of the great traditions. Thus archaic images of a blood-thirsty super-power who demands human and animal sacrifices, or of a tribal or national deity who favours one section of the human community at the expense of others, are clearly morally defective. There have also been special doctrines, propounded within the particular traditions and sub-traditions, which are incompatible with the common ethical ideal. The critical purifying of doctrine in this respect has to be carried on within each tradition in its own way. I will therefore mention some possible candidates for moral scrutiny from several traditions, without attempting to reach conclusions about them, and then consider briefly one example from my own Christian tradition. The Hindu doctrine of reincarnation and the closely related Buddhist doctrine of rebirth have both been criticised as implying that those born into a disadvantaged social and economic status are not suffering an injustice, which ought to be righted, but are rather reaping an appropriate outcome of their previous lives.[17] Again, the Jewish doctrine of 'the chosen people' has been criticised as holding that God stands in a special and exclusive relationship to the Hebrew people which relegates all others to a secondary religious status.[18] And the Muslim doctrine of the *jihad* has been criticised as an incitement to religiously sanctified violence. The example that I shall draw from Christianity is the doctrine of double predestination, both in the form (taught by St Augustine[19]) that, the human race having fallen in Adam, God arbitrarily saves some and leaves others in their state of damnation, and in the form (taught by Calvin[20]) that God created some in order that they should be saved and others in order that they should be damned. Such doctrines cannot be defended by an appeal from divine love to divine justice. For in the Augustinian and Calvinist theologies all human beings are alike justly condemned by God, and the saving of some is an act of pure grace. But an act of grace which is arbitrarily extended to some and arbitrarily withheld from others cannot express the unqualified love, limitless compassion or generous forgiveness which constitutes the common ethical ideal.

These brief remarks have done no more than suggest the possibility of a systematic moral criticism, within each tradition, of its own inherited doctrines. The pluralistic hypothesis points to this possibility and suggests its appropriateness but does not prescribe its detailed conclusions; and my project here is to outline that hypothesis without attempting the impossibly large task of filling in every detail of the map which it proposes.

Notes

1. Radhakrishnan comments, 'He shrinks from nothing as he knows that the one Self is manifested in the multiple forms' (Radhakrishnan 1969, 572).
2. The Hindu philosopher Ramchandra Gandhi (a grandson of the Mahatma) has written a book entitled *I am Thou* (1984).
3. There has been considerable discussion as to who the *re'a*, neighbour, is who is to be loved. A widely held view (expressed, e.g., by Ernst Simon 1975) is that throughout most of the rabbinic period the injunction was generally understood to refer to fellow children of Israel and thus to apply only to relationships between Jews, but that it has been opened out in many modern treatments to apply universally – as by Martin Buber (1951, 69–70). It is however important to add (see Norman Solomon 1985, 6, 16) that the Jew's ethical relationship with gentiles is governed, in rabbinic thought, by certain broad principles – *'tiqqun olam* ('establishing the world aright'), *darkhe shalom* ('the ways of peace') and *'qiddush Hashem* ('sanctifying God's name') – which lead to essentially the same sort

of behaviour as to one's neighbour within the Jewish community of faith.

4. See also Nelson Glueck 1975 and the article on *hesed* in Botterweck & Ringrenn 1986, vol. 5.

5. In all the following quotations from the New Testament 'love' translates *agape* and its cognates. On the word *agape* see Victor Paul Furnish 1973, Appendix.

6. There is a striking recent example of the priority of moral judgment in the recognition of authentic religion in the statement of the Christian archbishop Desmond Tutu, opposing racial oppression in South Africa, 'If anyone were to show me that apartheid is biblical or christian . . . I would burn my Bible and cease to be a Christian' (1984, 155).

7. There is a classic account of this in A. D. White [1896] 1960.

8. In the New Testament Christian slaves are exhorted to obey their master (I Timothy 6:1–2; I Peter 2:18–20; Colossians 3:22; Ephesians 6:5).

9. In the New Testament Christian wives are exhorted to obey their husband (Ephesians 5:22; Colossians 3:18; I Peter 3:1) and to be obedient to men (I Corinthians 14:34). See also James A. Brundage 1976, 825f.

10. Mark 9:1, 13:30; Matt. 10:23, 16:28, 23:36; Luke 9:27. Some recent New Testament scholarship has been reconsidering the historicity of these sayings. But it is difficult to see why the next generation of Christians should without warrant have attributed to Jesus predictions which they knew to have been mistaken.

11. 'For the rich oligarchy of the Quraysh to renounce "paganism" was equivalent to the loss of their privileges. Moreover, to recognize Muhammad as the true Apostle of God implied the recognition of his political supremacy' (Eliade 1985, 69).

12. As Conrad Hyers has written, 'if a religion is given enough time and space, whatever its initial and prevailing orientation, it will eventually take up almost all, if not all, possible positions on any of the fundamental religious questions' (Hyers 1983, 16).

13. Nicholson 1978, 65. See also, e.g., Nasrollah Fatemi 1974.

14. Cf. Hick 1987b.

15. E.g. David E. McKenzie 1985.

16. Dhammapala's commentary on *Therīgāthā*, 213–23 – Davids 1964, 106–7. This story was used by Albert Schweitzer as showing a lack of compassion on Gautama's part (cited by Takeuchi 1983, 47).

17. This criticism was made by Max Weber ([1922] 1963, 113, 233–4). It is made even more pungently by Paul Edwards (1986/7, 42).

18. This criticism is made from a Buddhist point of view by Keiji Nishitani (1982, 203).

19. 'But the rest of mankind who are not of this number [of the saved], but who, out of the same lump of which they are, are made vessels of wrath, are brought into the world for the advantage of the elect. God does not create any of them without a purpose. He knows what good to work out of them: He works good in the very fact of creating

them human beings, and carrying on by means of them this visible system of things. But none of them does He lead to a wholesome and spiritual repentence . . . All indeed do, as far as themselves are concerned, out of the same original mass of perdition treasure up to themselves after their hardened and impenitent heart, wrath against the day of wrath; but out of that mass God leads some in mercy and repentence, and others in just judgment does not lead' (*Contra Julianum Pelagianum*, book V, ch. 14). See also *On the Soul and its Origins*, book IV, ch. 16; *On the Merits and Remission of Sins, and on the Baptism of Infants*, book II, ch. 26; *On the Predestination of the Saints*, ch. 34.

20. 'For all are not created in equal condition; rather, eternal life is foreordained for some, eternal damnation for others' (*Institutes*, book III, ch. 21, para. 5). 'Since the disposition of all things is in God's hand, since the decision of salvation or death rests in his power, he so ordains by his plan and will that among men some are born destined for certain death from the womb, who glorify his name by their destruction' (book III, ch. 23, para. 6). The Westminster Confession (1646) formulated approved Calvinist doctrine as follows: 'By the decree of God, for the manifestation of his glory, some men and angels are predestinated unto everlasting life, and others foreordained to everlasting death . . . These angels and men, thus predestinated and foreordained, are particularly and unchangeably designed; and their number is so certain and definite, that it cannot be either increased or diminished' (ch. 3, paras 3 and 4). For a theological critique of the Augustinian and Calvinist doctrines see, e.g., Hick 1985a, chs 3.10 and 6.2–3.

19

Myth, Mystery and the Unanswered Questions

Realities which 'no eye has seen, nor ear heard, nor the heart of man conceived' (I Corinthians 2:9)

1 UNANSWERED AND UNANSWERABLE QUESTIONS

We turn now from the fruits of religion in human life and history to the belief-systems of the different traditions. Here much depends upon what we regard as the epistemological status and function of these beliefs. In this connection we need, I believe, not only a doctrine of religious knowledge but also a doctrine of religious ignorance.

An important resource is to be found in the Buddha's doctrine of the *avyākata* – a term which has been variously translated as the inexpressibles, the unrevealed, the undetermined or unresolved questions. These are related to *diṭṭhi*, 'views', speculative theories and dogmas, those listed in the Pali texts being:

1 The world is eternal.
2 The world is not eternal.
3 The world is (spatially) infinite.
4 The world is not (spatially) infinite.
5 The soul (*jīva*) is identical with the body.
6 The soul is not identical with the body.
7 The Tathagata (i.e. a perfectly enlightened being) exists after death.
8 The Tathagata does not exist after death.
9 The Tathagata both exists and does not exist after death.
10 The Tathagata neither exists nor does not exist after death.

In Sutta 63 of the *Majjhima Nikāya* a monk, Malunkyaputta, complains to the Buddha that these matters are not revealed in his teaching: they 'are not explained, set aside, ignored by the Lord' (II:427 – Horner 1957, 98). He threatens to leave the

343

Buddha and revert to the secular life if he is not given the truth concerning them. 'If the Lord knows that the world is eternal, let the Lord explain to me that the world is eternal. If the Lord knows that the world is not eternal, let the Lord explain to me that the world is not eternal. If the Lord does not know whether the world is eternal or whether the world is not eternal, then, not knowing, not seeing, this would be honest, namely to say: "I do not know, I do not see"' (98). And likewise with the other questions.

In reply the Buddha first asks the monk whether he, Gautama, had ever promised to settle these questions and whether Malunkyaputta had ever made it a condition of following him that these matters should be made clear to him; and the monk grants that the answer in each case is No. The Buddha then enunciates the basic principle behind his refusal to address these questions, namely that it is not necessary for liberation to know the true answers to them. For his entire teaching has a practical and soteriological orientation: 'As the great ocean is saturated by only one taste, the taste of salt, so this teaching and system is saturated with only one taste, the taste of salvation' (*Vinaya Pitaka*, Cullavagga 9, 238 – cf. Horner 1963, 335). And so Gautama tells his parable of the man pierced by a poisoned arrow. If he insists before receiving medical treatment on knowing who shot the arrow and of what clan he is, what kind of bow he was using, what the bowstring and the shaft of the arrow were made of, from what kind of bird the feathers on the arrow came and so on, he will die before his demand for knowledge is satisfied. Likewise if we distract ourselves from the path of liberation by trying to settle these disputed cosmological and metaphysical issues we may well fail to be healed from the agonies of 'birth, ageing, dying, grief, sorrow, suffering, lamentation and despair' (*Majjhima Nikāya*, II:430 – Horner 1957, 100).

And so these matters are set aside by the Buddha because such knowledge 'is not connected with the goal, is not fundamental to the Brahma-faring, and does not conduce to turning away from, nor to dispassion, stopping, calming, super-knowledge, awakening nor to nibbana' (II:431 – Horner 1957, 101). And in Sutta 72 he says again that concern with such questions can only distract from the single-minded quest for liberation. 'To think that "the world is eternal" – this is going to a (speculative) view (*diṭṭhi*), holding a view, the wilds of views, the wriggling of views, the scuffling of views, the fetter of views; it is accompanied by anguish, distress, misery, fever; it does not conduce to turning away from, not to dispassion, stopping, calming, super-knowledge, awakening, not to nibbana' (II:485 – Horner 1957, 164).

This response to metaphysical and cosmological issues is not unique to the Buddha. A somewhat similar thought occurs within the mystical strands of a number of traditions: for example, the Christian saint, Thomas à Kempis, asks, 'What will it avail thee to be engaged in profound reasonings concerning the Trinity, if thou be void of humility, and art thereby displeasing to the Trinity?' ([15th century] I:1:3). And Julian of Norwich refers to the portion of truth that 'is hidden from us and closed, that is to say all which is additional to our salvation; for this is our Lord's privy counsel, and it is fitting to God's royal dominion to keep his privy counsel in peace, and it is fitting to his servants out of obedience and respect not to wish to know his counsel' (Julian, *Showings*, longer text, ch. 30 – 1978, 228). And again, in Judaism, the stress has always been upon right practice, both ritual and ethical, rather than right theory.

When we look carefully at the contents of the ten *avyākata* listed in the Pali texts we find that they are of two kinds. The Buddha's basic thought, that it is not necessary or conducive to liberation to know the truth of these matters, applies equally to both. But one group consists of questions which are in themselves legitimate and admit of true answers. We do not definitively know those answers, although we can develop theories and dogmas about them. The first six 'views' listed, expressing pairs of positive and negative assertions – the eternity or non-eternity and spatial infinity or finitude of the universe, and mind–body identity or non-identity – are of this kind. In these cases the translation of *avyākata* as 'the unanswered questions' seems appropriate. It is not excluded, in logic, that human beings might come to know the truth of such matters. Indeed it is possible that Gautama, after his enlightenment, did know the answers to these questions; at any rate later Buddhist writings speak of his omniscience. But it is still the case that, according to him, salvation/liberation does not depend upon such knowledge; and that for people holding different views to treat agreement about them as essential for salvation is a dangerous because soteriologically counter-productive error.

In Sutta 72 however a further idea is introduced. Here a wandering inquirer, Vacchagotta, raises the same unresolved questions and asks, 'What is the peril that the revered Gotama beholds that he thus does not approach any of these (speculative) views?' (*Majjhima Nikāya*, II:427 – Horner 1957, 164). Gautama gives essentially the same answer as in Sutta 63. But then there is a further turn to the dialogue, dealing specifically with the question of the state of a fully enlightened being, a Tathagata, beyond this life. (It should be noted that this question concerns ultimate Reality-centredness and is not the question of the more proximate condition, beyond this life, of those who are still on the way to that final state.) In response the Buddha rejects as inapplicable the entire range of possible answers in terms of which Vacchagotta had posed the question – namely by specifying where, that is in what sphere, the Tathagata arises after death:

'"Arises," Vaccha, does not apply.'
'Well then, good Gotama, does he not arise?'
'"Does not arise," Vaccha, does not apply.'
'Well then, good Gotama, does he both arise and not arise?'
'"Both arises and does not arise," Vaccha, does not apply.'
'Well then, good Gotama, does he neither arise nor not arise?'
'"Neither arises nor does not arise," Vaccha, does not apply.'
(II:486 – Horner 1957, 165)

Vaccha then expresses his bewilderment and disappointment, and the Buddha responds, 'You ought to be at a loss, Vaccha, you ought to be bewildered. For Vaccha, this *dhamma* is deep, difficult to see, difficult to understand, peaceful, excellent, beyond dialectics, subtle, intelligible to the wise . . .' (II:487 – Horner 1957, 165) – referring all the time to the mystery of Parinirvana, or Nirvana beyond this life. For it is not correct to say that after death the Tathagata exists, or does not exist, or both exists and does not exist, or neither exists nor non-exists.[1]

Gautama then illustrates the idea of a question which is so put that it has no answer by speaking of a flame that has been quenched. In which direction has the flame gone: east, west, north or south? None of the permitted answers applies. Likewise what happens after the bodily death of a Tathagata cannot be expressed in our ordinary human categories. This is not equivalent to saying, as the quenched fire image by itself might suggest, that the Tathagata ceases to exist. The proposition that he does not exist after death is among those that the Buddha refuses to accept. On the contrary, 'Freed from denotation by consciousness is the Tathagata, Vaccha, he is deep, immeasurable, unfathomable as is the great ocean' (*Majjhima Nikāya* II:487 – Horner 1957, 166). We have here the idea of realities and circumstances which transcend the categories available in our unillumined thought and language. Their total elusiveness is signalled by the Buddha's rejection not only of the straight positive and negative assertions but also of their combination and disjunction. These are matters which 'no eye has seen, nor ear heard, nor the heart of man conceived' (I Cor. 2:9). Here the translation of the *avyākata* as 'the unanswerable questions' seems more appropriate. It also seems proper to refer to their subject-matter as mysteries, realities that are beyond human comprehension and expression.

We have, then, two different kinds of question. There are those which are in principle answerable but concerning which we lack definitive information. And there are those which point to realities that cannot be expressed in human terms. In response to the first group we develop theories, which can all too easily become sanctified as dogmas. In response to the second we develop myths. But neither the theories nor the myths are necessary for salvation/liberation. To quote Thomas à Kempis once again, 'What availeth it to cavil and dispute much about dark and hidden things, for ignorance of which we shall not be reproved at the day of judgment?' ([15th century] I:3:1).

2 EXPOSITORY MYTHS

Another resource required for the discussion of religious beliefs, and their conflicts and comparative worth, has just been introduced: namely the notion of myth. We must first fix our use of the term, for there are many different definitions and it need not be assumed that one of them is right and the rest wrong. On the contrary 'myth', like 'religion', is a family-resemblance concept which has ramified out into a network of related ideas; and all that one can do is to use it consistently in the way that one has chosen. I therefore do not claim that my own definition will cover by any means all legitimate uses of the word.[2] I am concerned with it here only in the particular sense that I shall now specify.

We can approach this through a distinction between literal and mythological truth. The literal truth or falsity of a factual assertion (as distinguished from the truth or falsity of an analytic proposition) consists in its conformity or lack of conformity to fact: 'it is raining here now' is literally true if and only if it is raining here now. But in addition to literal truth there is also mythological truth. A statement or set of statements about X is mythologically true if it is not literally true but nevertheless tends to evoke an appropriate dispositional attitude to X. Thus mythological truth is practical or, in one sense of this much abused word, existential. For the conformity of myth to reality does not consist in a literal conformity of what is said to the facts but in the appropriateness to the myth's referent of the behavioural dispositions that it tends to evoke in the hearer.

As an example from ordinary life, suppose I am at a committee meeting at which what I regard as a viciously devious and unjust plan is being hatched. I might express this judgment in mythological terms by saying that what is going on here is the work of the devil. I should not, in saying this, be intending to affirm that there literally is a devil who is literally manipulating the committee. But if I am right about what is going on my statement would tend to evoke in a hearer suspicion, revulsion, condemnation which is appropriate to what is actually taking place. In so far as what is happening is indeed 'satanic' in quality my mythological statement is true – not literally true, but true in the practical sense of tending to evoke an appropriate dispositional response. And when I say that a true myth about X *tends* to evoke an appropriate dispositional attitude to X, 'tends' is meant here to suggest a natural or standard human response: as when we say that perceived danger tends to evoke fear or that perceived love tends to evoke an answering love. But what normally happens, and thus tends to happen, does not in fact occur in every instance. Thus a myth may fail to communicate successfully to a particular person at a particular time. And of course, even when it does communicate, its message may be rejected, the response which it tends to evoke being suppressed and perhaps replaced by a contrary response.

Myths now divide into two kinds. There are, first, what we can call expository myths. These say something that can also be said non-mythologically, though generally with markedly less imaginative impact. Thus, in my example, what is expressed by describing the manoeuvres at the committee meeting as the work of the devil can also be expressed literally by saying (for example) that it is a conspiracy to transfer the blame for some mistake from the person responsible to another who is innocent. Many religious myths are of this expository kind. For example, the Hebraic story of the fall of Adam and Eve in the Garden of Eden can be seen – and is today very commonly seen by Jews and Christians – as a mythic story which expresses, and thereby engraves in the imagination, the fact that ordinary human life is lived in alienation from God and hence from one's neighbours and from the natural environment. Again, the story of the Buddha's flight through the sky to Sri Lanka can be seen as a mythological way of declaring the authenticity of the ancient Buddhist tradition of that island. The belief that the suras of the Qur'an were dictated by the archangel Gabriel[3] can be seen as a mythological way of affirming that the Qur'an constitutes an authoritative divine revelation. The idea of the transsubstantiation of bread and wine into the body and blood of Christ in the eucharist can be seen as a mythological way of making the communicant's reception of them an occasion of special openness to God as known through Christ. The doctrine of reincarnation is seen by some as a mythological way of making vivid the moral truth that our actions have inevitable future consequences for good and ill, this being brought home to the imagination by the thought that the agent will personally reap those consequences in a future earthly life.

It is not however part of my present argument to claim that these, or any other specific religious stories and ideas, should in fact be regarded as mythological. I am concerned at the moment only to note that there is this expository use of mythology, from which I shall now go on to distinguish another use.

3 THE MYTHOLOGICAL CHARACTER OF LANGUAGE ABOUT THE REAL

This other use of myth has come about in response to the second kind of question identified by the Buddha, namely questions to which no answer is possible in a literal use of language; and I have suggested that such topics can appropriately be called mysteries. On the hypothesis presented in this book the Real *an sich* is the ultimate mystery. For the relationship between the Real and its *personae* and *impersonae* is, epistemologically, the relationship between a noumenal reality and the range of its appearances to a plurality of perceivers. It is within the phenomenal or experienceable realm that language has developed and it is to this that it literally applies. Indeed the system of concepts embodied in human language has contributed reciprocally to the formation of the humanly perceived world. It is as much constructed as given. But our language can have no purchase on a postulated noumenal reality which is not even partly formed by human concepts. This lies outside the scope of our cognitive capacities.

We have affirmed the noumenal Real as the necessary presupposition of the religious life. Trusting in the basically veridical character of the stream of religious experience and thought in which we participate, and extending that acceptance at least to the other major streams, we have postulated the Real as the ground of this varied realm of religious phenomena. Indeed we have already committed ourselves to such a postulate in rejecting the view of religous experience as simply human projection. For to deny that possibility is to affirm that the divine *personae* and metaphysical *impersonae* are not only shaped (as is evident) by the categories of human thought but express at the same time the presence and impact of a transcendent reality. We are thus led to affirm a noumenal ultimate reality of which the objects of religious experience are phenomenal manifestations.

This distinction between the Real as it is in itself and as it is thought and experienced through our human religious concepts entails (as we have already noted in Chapter 14.4) that we cannot apply to the Real *an sich* the characteristics encountered in its *personae* and *impersonae*. Thus it cannot be said to be one or many, person or thing, conscious or unconscious, purposive or non-purposive, substance or process, good or evil, loving or hating. None of the descriptive terms that apply within the realm of human experience can apply literally to the unexperienceable reality that underlies that realm. All that we can say is that we postulate the Real *an sich* as the ultimate ground of the intentional objects of the different forms of religious thought-and-experience. Nevertheless perhaps we can speak about the Real indirectly and mythologically. For insofar as these gods and absolutes are indeed manifestations of the ultimately Real, an appropriate human response to any one of them will also be an appropriate response to the Real. It will not be the *only* appropriate form of response because the Real is perceived in a range of ways, but it will nevertheless be *an* appropriate response.[4]

In relation to these experienced *personae* and *impersonae* language has either literal or analogical meaning. It generally has literal meaning in relation 'to divine actions on earth and analogical meaning in relation to a divine *persona* considered in him or herself or to a metaphysical *impersona* considered in itself. Thus when it is said that the Lord brought the children of Israel out of Egypt, a literal bringing is intended, even though it is a bringing such as only a very powerful deity could perform. On the other hand when it is said that God is wise or that God is good, these qualities are thought to be analogous to rather than identical with human wisdom and goodness. Again, when it is said that Brahman is *satchitānanda*, the consciousness and bliss attributed to Brahman are presumably analogous to rather than identical with the corresponding finite human qualities.

But nevertheless such literal and analogical language about the objects of religious worship or meditation always intends to be about the Real itself. And as such it functions mythologically: we speak mythologically about the noumenal Real by speaking literally or analogically about its phenomenal manifestations. We have seen (in Chapter 8) that all human awareness is in terms of meaning and that meaning always has a practical dispositional aspect: to be aware of a thing or a situation as having a particular meaning or character is to be in a dispositional state to behave in relation to it in ways that are (believed to be) appropriate to its having that character. And the function of mythology is to express the practical meaning of its referent by evoking in us an appropriate dispositional response. Thus although we cannot speak of the Real *an sich* in literal terms, nevertheless we live inescapably in relation to it, and in all that we do and undergo we are having to do with it as well as, and in terms of, our more proximate situations. Our actions are appropriate or inappropriate not only in relation to our physical and social environments but also in relation to our ultimate environment, the Real. True religious myths are accordingly those that evoke in us attitudes and modes of behaviour which are appropriate to our situation *vis-à-vis* the Real.

Discourse about the Real as it is manifested to us operates on various levels of concreteness or abstractness, the more concrete layers consisting of stories about divine beings whilst the more abstract layers consist of theologies and religious philosophies. At the level of concrete stories the Real is, as we have seen (Chapter 15), represented by implicitly finite divine figures who appear as magnified and supernaturalised humans. Yahweh walked in the Garden of Eden in the cool of the evening. The Vedic deities behaved rather like their cousins in the ancient Greek pantheon, meriting Freud's description of the gods as 'violent supermen of the beyond' – the Indian Prajapati committing incest and the Greek Chronos castrating his father Uranos. And, more attractively but no less humanly, Krishna flirted with the gopi girls of Vrindaban. At a somewhat less concrete level the gods are presented as spiritual powers working behind the scenes. Although manifesting themselves in finite contexts they are no longer themselves explicitly finite and visualisable but rather indefinitely great in their power, knowledge and wisdom. Thus in the Hebrew scriptures the Lord makes the heavens and the earth out of a primal chaos and wields historical events to punish or reward the people of Israel. In the Christian scriptures God the Father sends his son to become incarnate as Jesus the messiah. And in the Qur'an Allah gives guidance to the Muslim community in one historical situation after another, issuing the commands that have become its laws.

However, mythological thinking is not of course restricted to a narrative form. At a more abstract level there are philosophical and theological systems of ideas concerning the *personae* and *impersonae* of the Real. Examples are Hindu language concerning Brahman and the gods; Buddhist language concerning Sunyata and the Trikaya; Christian language concerning the triune nature and the metaphysical attributes of God . . . These more concrete and more abstract levels of religious language form a continuum, and actual religious discourse does not generally stay consistently on any one level but moves up and down through the different strata. But it is mythological throughout in the sense that it constitutes discourse in human terms which is ultimately about that which transcends the literal scope of human language – except, as we have already noted, when that language is purely formal and devoid of descriptive content (see Chapter 14.2). And the value of myth, whether in the form of story or of theological or philosophical schema, is practical. The truthfulness or untruthfulness of mythological stories, images and conceptions does not consist in their literal adequacy to the nature of the Real *an sich* –

in this respect it is not so much that they miss their target as that the target is totally beyond their range – but in their capacity to evoke appropriate or inappropriate dispositional responses to the Real.

But what is it for human attitudes, emotions, modes of behaviour, patterns of life to be appropriate to the Real? We can only answer within the circle of the hypothesis. It is for the god or absolute to which we relate ourselves to be an authentic manifestation of the Real and for our practical response to be appropriate to that manifestation. In so far as this is so, that *persona* or *impersona* can be said to be in soteriological alignment with the Real. For example, to love both God and one's fellow humans is a natural and appropriate response to the awareness of God as imaged in much of the Christian tradition. And to the extent that 'the God and Father of our Lord Jesus Christ' is indeed an authentic *persona* of the Real, constituting the form in which the Real is validly thought and experienced from within the Christian strand of religious history, to that extent the dispositional response appropriate to this *persona* constitutes an appropriate response to the Real. Again, an un-self-centred openness to the world and compassion for all life are the natural expressions of an awakening through meditation to the eternal Buddha nature. And to the extent that this is an authentic *impersona* of the Real, validly thought and experienced from within the Buddhist tradition, life in accordance with the Dharma is likewise an appropriate response to the Real.

4 THE MYTHOLOGICAL CHARACTER OF RELIGIOUS THOUGHT

Given the postulate of the Real *an sich*, then, and given this concept of myth, we can identify the various systems of religious thought as complex myths whose truth or untruth consists in the appropriateness or inappropriateness of the practical dispositions which they tend to evoke.[5] They are responses to the mystery of human existence. Ancient tradition has further specified this mystery in the three questions: Where do we come from?, Why are we here? and Where are we going? The last of these was the Buddha's own example of a question that cannot be answered in terms of earthly concepts; and the other two are of the same logical type. For the source and nature of human existence is as mysterious as its destiny. To each of these questions a purely naturalistic answer is possible: the physical universe has existed eternally, human life having emerged by chance within its ever changing organic forms, with each individual ceasing to exist at death. But this naturalistic answer leaves us with the original mystery, transferred now to the physical universe: *why* does it exist, with the particular basic characteristics that it has? Naturalism can urge that the question is unanswerable, but should not claim thereby to have answered it. Indeed, because we are part of the mysterious fact that we are seeking to explain it may be in principle impossible for us ever to comprehend the nature of that whole. There may be a 'Gödel's principle' in metaphysics to the effect that for any interpretive system formed from within the realm of fact being interpreted there must be at least one unanswerable question, namely the question concerning the character of that realm as a totality. And for humans this necessarily unanswerable question divides into the three-fold traditional problem of our origin, nature and destiny. At any rate let us explore the possibility that these enigmas systematically repel any solution formed in a use of language derived from the universe as encountered by an element within it.

We may begin with the Buddha's version of the third question, concerning the state of the Tathagata beyond death. This is not (as we noted in section 1) the question of the fate of ordinary unperfected human beings – the Buddha's answer to that question was the doctrine of rebirth – but of the ultimate state of perfected life in, or as, or in relation to, the Real. It is impossible to pose this question without embodying in it pre-suppositions which may, as the Buddha suggested, be inappropriate and misleading. Thus when we ask in what state humanity will be in the ultimate future, we may be using a concept of 'humanity' that will have ceased to apply. That ultimate state may not be a condition of what we now know as ourselves, nor even a state to which the notion of an individual's existing or not existing is relevant. It may entirely transcend the range of present human thought, imagination and language. It could nevertheless be that a living Tathagata is already in an earthly analogue of that state. If so, he or she will not be able to describe it directly, but only to make the kind of mysterious statement that Gautama made: 'Freed from denotation by consciousness is the Tathagata, Vaccha, he is deep, immeasurable, unfathomable as in the great ocean' (*Majjhima*

Nikāya, II:487 – Horner 1957, 166). For we cannot hope now to share the linguistically inexpressible insight or intuition of a perfected thread of the human story. Nevertheless we can understand that if the religious conviction of the reality of the Transcendent is well-founded, and there is a limitlessly greater Reality in response to which our human existence can become totally transformed, the nature of that fulfilment may at present be not only unimaginable but also conceptually ungraspable by us.

However the religious traditions have generally not been able to set this topic aside as an unresolvable issue the pursuit of which does not conduce to salvation. Instead they have developed a variety of mental pictures which seek to express the inexpressible in humanly imaginable ways. These are of two main types, found most prominently in the religions of Indian and Semitic origin respectively. The Hindu tradition, in its advaitic form, has produced images of merging into the infinite consciousness of Brahman like a drop of water into the ocean; whilst the Jewish, Christian and Muslim traditions have spoken of the vision of God, of paradise, of a divine kingdom, and of worshipping and rejoicing before the heavenly throne. These are forms of eschatological mythology, imaginative pictures of the ultimate state, produced to meet our need – a need from which the Buddha sought to free us – for something to which our minds can cling as we contemplate our own finitude.

The traditions have also created a series of pareschatological 'scenarios' picturing our more proximate state or states between death and the ultimate fulfilment; but we are concerned with these at the moment only in order to distinguish them from the properly eschatological myths. The latter can be said to be true in so far as the dispositional responses which they tend to evoke are appropriate to our actual present situation as beings on the way towards salvation/liberation. If we have been right in seeing this goal as the transformation of human existence from self-centredness to Reality-centredness, eschatological myths are valid to the extent that they promote that transformation. No doubt, as the Buddha insisted, in a single-minded pursuit of liberation one would cease to have any interest in such speculations. But for those of us who are so far from final liberation that we crave for them, it may be that mythic pictures, used in the spirit of Socrates in Plato's *Phaedo*,[6] can promote rather than hinder the soteriological process. For it would seem that in their different ways the two types of eschatological myth, cast respectively in terms of self-transcending worship of the divine Thou and absorption into the infinite life of the trans-personal Absolute, invite an overcoming of self-centredness and a re-centring in the Real.

Both demand a radical renunciation of the present grasping and self-concerned ego. The path laid out in the Indian traditions is that of a progressive deconstruction of the ego-boundaries. That developed within the Semitic traditions involves the perfecting of the individual self in relationship to God. But this latter does not in the end mean the separate perfecting of distinct atomic entities. For personality is essentially inter-personal, human perfecting consisting in a total self-giving, or *islam*, to God and a consequent transcendence of the ego boundaries. Thus the eastern and western paths constitute different forms of self-transcendence in response to the Real[7] and it may well be that their differing eschatological mythologies serve the same soteriological function.[8]

The other two of the traditional mysteries – Where do we come from and what are we here for? – are closely related, so that myths formed in response to one generally also constitute a response to the other. From the point of view of the religious conviction of the reality of the transcendent, this double question has a challenging edge. For within each of the great traditions the Real is believed to be unlimited and eternal. Why then the finite, temporal and imperfect realm of which we are part? If an ultimate One, why the fragmented many; if an eternal unchanging Reality, why the changing forms of finite existence? If God, why a world; if Brahman, why *māyā*; if the eternal Buddha nature, why *avidyā*? The answers of the religious traditions, if construed as literal factual hypotheses, are manifestly inadequate. But I want to suggest that if understood mythologically they may do something to orient us towards the Real whilst at the same time assuaging our anxiety in face of the deep mystery of our existence.

Within Christianity a traditional answer has been that God created the human species to make up the number of the citizens of heaven depleted by the defection of the fallen angels.[9] But this only directs the question back to an earlier point: why did God create the angels? Granting that they are the most perfect form of created life, why did a limitlessly perfect Being, lacking nothing, create anything at all, even angels? A more fundamental Christian answer has been that creativity is an expression of God's self-giving love. But this prompts the further question: Does God, as self-giving love, *need* a creation, so as to be lacking and incomplete without it? The dilemma is that a God who suffers from this lack is not intrinsically perfect and complete; but on the other hand if God does not need a creation, why is there one? Posed in these terms the problem is indeed insoluble.

The recent Christian movement of process theology grasps this nettle and concludes that God, instead of being limitlessly perfect, is finite, existing over against a realm of uncreated matter which God is trying, with only persuasive power, to fashion into a coherent and valuable universe. This suggestion offers a consistent picture; but at the cost of abandoning the conviction that God is that than which no more ultimate can be conceived. For on this hypothesis there is no truly ultimate reality but only a plurality of penultimates. Thus the traditional question: If God, why a world? does not arise. Instead the mystery takes the form: Why God and matter? or, in another version of process thought: Why God, matter and the power of Creativity? And this is as unanswerable as the question it sought to replace.

But although none of the Christian answers taken as literal hypotheses solves the enigma of finite existence, yet each can nevertheless be seen as painting a mythic picture that may do something to guide our human response to the Real. To believe that God created the human race to complete the heavenly household might give us a sense of the religious significance of human life. To believe that God created the world out of love might open our eyes to its goodness and enable us to receive it as a gift of grace. To believe that a loving God of limited power is trying to mould the material of the universe into something valuable and needs our co-operation might challenge us to live as God's co-workers in the cosmic task.

Within the traditions of Indian origin the mystery takes yet other forms. For Buddhism it is the question how or why the eternal Buddha nature, which is our true but presently hidden essence, has become obscured by *avidyā*, ignorance. There is no accepted answer; and if the question – which arises from later Mahayana formulations – had been put to the Buddha himself we may presume that he would have rejected it both as not conducive to liberation and as not answerable in human terms. Faced with the immediacy of *dukkha* in the shape of birth, decay, illness, sorrow and death we do not need to know how we fell into it but

only how we can get out of it. The point, we might say, echoing
Marx's dictum, is not to understand our human situation but to
change it. The Buddha taught a way of changing it, the Eightfold
Path which leads to liberation; and he would doubtless have
urged us to eschew mythological surrogates that can only distract
us from the all-important effort to attain this blessed inner
freedom.

Within the Hindu tradition the question is: Why *saṃsāra*, the
beginningless and endless process of birth, death and rebirth in
which we are enmeshed? In advaitic terms why, given the eternal
reality of Brahman, is there a realm of illusorily distinct finite
beings? Why did not the absolute Consciousness remain eternally
perfect and complete without giving rise within itself to a plurality
of selves who are only gradually and painfully discovering their
true nature as the universal *ātman* which is identical with
Brahman? Why the whole apparently unnecessary drama of
individual human existence? To this question the Upanishads
offer a mythological response. The whole complex life of the
universe, in its eternally recurring cycles of creation and
destruction, constitutes the dance of Shiva. It does not exist for
any purpose but is, like a dance, an end in itself, a dynamic
exercise of creative energy. The divine life is not static but
perpetually active, forever creating and re-creating the changing
patterns which are the life of the universe. Thus Shiva successively
creates, destroys and creates again in the endless movement of
his cosmic dance.

The mythological character of this response is evident. The
cosmic dance is not a literal dance involving the movement of
literal feet – as however it has to be depicted in the
familiar images of Shiva Nataraja. It represents a mythological
understanding of samsaric existence. And the attitude to life
which this picture tends to evoke is an acceptance of the world
and our life within it as participation in the pulsating divine life.
In all that we experience, evil as well as good, we are never
separated from Shiva but are part of his very life, swept along in
the swirling course of the cosmic dance. This acceptance of our
existence as a by-product of the exuberant divine creative energy
can help to detach us from self-regarding hopes and fears and so
may assist the salvific transition from self-centredness to Reality-
centredness.

These are examples of the mythological responses of the

different traditions to the mystery of human existence. If such mythologies were construed as literal discourse, offering factual hypotheses, they would conflict with one another. But understood mythologically the truthfulness of each consists in its aptness, as part of an unique complex of life, thought and imagination, to forward the soteriological process. They belong to different universes of discourse, or operate within different mythic spaces, and their capacity to promote the salvific human transformation can only be measured in the context of the religious totalities to which they belong. Instead then of asking which myth, taken in isolation, is true, or whether this myth is truer than that, we should look at the religious effectiveness of the vast many-sided forms of life of which they are aspects and to which they contribute.

Within the wide circumference of this basic mystery of human nature and destiny there is a further sub-issue which has challenged religious thought, evoking responses that vary not only between but also within traditions. This is the ancient problem of evil. Both the theodicies formed within the theistic religions and their non-theistic counterparts are functions of wider cosmic pictures whose mythological character they share. They are not literally true, but are nevertheless mythologically true to the extent that they tend to evoke an appropriate dispositional response to the pain and suffering of our human lot. An example, that of the Irenaean type of Christian theodicy, is outlined in the appendix which follows.

APPENDIX: THEODICY AS MYTHOLOGY

In Chapter 7.2, in response to the problem of evil considered as a challenge to theistic belief, I outlined a theodicy of the Irenaean type. How does this theodicy – or indeed any alternative Christian theodicy – fare when we think of the God of Christian faith as one among a plurality of *personae* and *impersonae* of the Real? The answer arises out of what has been said in the present chapter.

Such a theodicy is mythological in the sense that the language in which it speaks about the Real, as a personal being carrying out intentions through time, cannot apply to the ultimate transcendent Reality in itself. But such a theodicy nevertheless constitutes a true myth in so far as the practical attitudes which it tends to evoke amid the evils of human life are appropriate to our present existence in relation to the Real. The practical message of the myth is both that good can be brought out of evil and that, in Lady Julian's famous phrase, in the end 'all shall be well, and all shall be well, and all manner of thing shall be well'. This final assurance can affect our reaction to the evils that befall us. For we are to bring good out of evil by engaging in the common human struggle to avert those sufferings that can be averted and to alleviate those others which cannot; and by trying to bear without bitterness the sufferings that come upon ourselves. The myth recognises, however, that this is often an ultimate hope rather than an immediate possibility. In this present life good can often not in fact be brought out of evil. Life's pains and agonies, which sometimes help to create stronger and more compassionate men and women, at other times overwhelm and crush, leaving only despair, tragedy and disintegration. It is at this point that the myth speaks of the continuation of the creative process beyond this life and of its ultimate success in a limitless good which will justify everything that has formed the contingent series of events leading to it. Experiencing life's baffling mixture of good and evil in terms of this myth, we may be helped to live in hope, trusting in the ultimate sovereignty of God's love.

This theodicy may be – and indeed I believe it is – mythologically true. That is to say, it may be the case that seeking to bring good out of evil, both through one's own personal bearing of suffering and mutual caring in face of disasters, and by cherishing an ultimate hope beyond this life, is appropriate to the actual character of our situation in the presence of the Real.

Notes

1. Cf. *Saṃyutta Nikāya*, IV:374 – Woodward 1956, 266.
2. For a recent listing of uses of 'myth' see G. B. Caird 1980, ch. 13.
3. The Muslim tradition to this effect is based on Qur'an II:97.
4. Although the conceptual system employed by George Lindbeck in his book on the nature of doctrine differs importantly from that employed here, there is a certain overlap of conclusions. Thus, treating a religion as a vast complex proposition, he says that it 'is a true proposition to the extent that its objectives are interiorized and exercised by groups and individuals in such a way as to conform them in some measure in

the various dimensions of their existence to the ultimate reality and goodness that lies at the heart of things' (Lindbeck 1984, 51).

5. Such a view of religious concepts as human imaginative creations which may however mediate the divine reality to us has been developed by Gordon Kaufman (1981).

6. 'A man of sense ought not to say, nor will I be very confident, that the description which I have given of the soul and her mansions is exactly true. But I do say that, inasmuch as the soul is shown to be immortal, he may venture to think, not improperly or unworthily, that something of the kind is true' (*Phaedo*, 114 – Plato 1903, 268).

7. On this possibility see further Hick 1985b, part V.

8. Accordingly the pluralistic hypothesis does not have to commit itself, as D'Costa (1986, 43–5, 21–51) argues, to any one particular eschatological prediction. It can see the different pictures of the after-life as different human attempts to grasp a future whose concrete character we cannot know in advance. The 'cosmic optimism' of post-axial religion (see Chapter 4) expects a limitlessly good fulfilment of the project of human existence. But this fulfilment could take many forms, including forms that are beyond the present range of our imaginations. Our conception of the eschaton will, in that case, presumably become more adequate as we approach the reality to which it intends to refer; but it is important to insist that the basic expectation of a limitlessly good fulfilment could be correct without any of our present ways of picturing it proving adequate.

9. Augustine, *City of God*, bk XXII, ch. 1. See also Milton's *Paradise Lost*, bk ix, 135–57. Grant McColley says that 'Working from such verses as Matthew 23:30 and Luke 20:36, patristic exegetes voiced the belief that . . . God created man to fill the celestial rooms left vacant by the fallen angels' (McColley 1940, 45).

20

The Problem of Conflicting Truth-Claims

In matters of religion, whatever is different is contrary.
(David Hume)[1]

To say that God is Infinite is to say that He may be apprehended and described in an infinity of ways.   (Evelyn Underhill)[2]

1 THE PROBLEM

The 'conflicting truth-claims' of the different religious traditions pose an obvious problem for the pluralistic hypothesis. For example, Hindus believe that temporal existence is beginningless and endless, vast aeons succeeding one another in an eternal cyclical process, whereas Jews, Christians and Muslims believe that the universe began through the creative fiat of God and will end in a climactic divine judgment. Hindus and Buddhists believe that we live many times on this earth, the *liṅga śarīra* or the karmic system entering again and again into the stream of human life to form new psycho-physical persons, whereas Jews, Christians and Muslims believe that we live only once and then face an eternal heaven or hell. Hindus of the school of advaita Vedanta believe that the deepest depth of our being is the eternal and immutable *ātman*, whereas Buddhists believe that there is no such eternal *ātman* and that the human 'soul' is a transient stream of psychic events. Jews believe that the children of Israel are God's chosen people, whereas non-Jews either reject the idea of such a status or extend it to all peoples. Christians believe that Jesus was God incarnate, whereas non-Christians either deny this or extend the idea of incarnation in varying degrees to all instances of divine immanence in human life.

One could continue almost indefinitely the roll-call of such doctrinal disagreements. But even in relation to this brief list it

362

should be added that none of them constitutes an absolutely pure example of truth-claims conflict. Religious history is more complexly shaded. In the case of each pair of rival beliefs there are historical nuances and marginal exceptions. There are some Hindus and Buddhists who regard the idea of rebirth as an illuminating myth; some Christians who regard the notion of divine incarnation as a metaphorical or mythic idea; Jews who allow a sense in which all peoples are God's chosen people; and Muslims who accept a different exegesis of the Qur'anic passage about the crucifixion of Jesus. And so on. Nevertheless the basic fact of innumerable broad oppositions of religious doctrines remains; and the next step must be to distinguish their various types and levels.[3]

First, there are disagreements about what are in principle straightforward matters of historical fact. Second, there are disagreements about issues of what might be called trans-historical fact – such as whether or not human beings are involved in a process of continual reincarnation. And third, there are different stories or pictures professing to answer the ultimate questions about the nature of the Real and about the source and destiny of humanity and of the universe of which we are a part.

2 CONFLICTING HISTORICAL TRUTH-CLAIMS

There are first, then, differences of belief concerning historical events – by which is meant alleged past events of the kind that are in principle accessible to human observation. If these alleged events occurred, and if someone had been present with the appropriate equipment, it would have been possible to taperecord and/or photograph them. They belong – if they occurred – to the series of visible, audible and tangible constituents of past history. (There is of course also an at least equally important inner side, consisting of people's intentions, hopes, suspicions, fears and so on; but we are concerned at the moment only with history's publicly observable aspect.)

Here there are numerous reported happenings that are firmly believed by members of tradition A to have taken place as real historical events, but which do not figure in standard works of history written outside that tradition: for example, the Buddhist belief that the Buddha flew through the air from India to Sri

Lanka and back; the Muslim belief that Muhammad flew through the air between Mecca and Jerusalem and back;[4] the Jewish belief that the sun stood still for twenty-four hours at Joshua's command (Joshua 10:12–13); the Christian belief that Jesus came physically back to life on the third day after his death. Each of these is peculiar to the belief-system of a particular tradition. Amongst the few examples of an historical belief held within one tradition that is explicitly denied within another are the Christian belief that Jesus died on the cross, which is opposed by the Qur'anic teaching that 'they did not slay him, neither crucified him, only a likeness of that was shown to them' (4:156) and by the Ahmadiyya belief that Jesus, having survived the crucifixion, subsequently died and is buried in Kashmir; and again the Torah's statement that Abraham nearly sacrificed his son Isaac at Mount Moriah (Genesis 22) versus the Qur'anic version (Sura 37:99–111) that it was his other son Ishmael.

There are also historical disputes internal to each of the great traditions as these have developed and ramified through the centuries. Thus within Buddhism there is the disagreement between the Theravada and Mahayana as to whether it is the former that has, as it claims, preserved the original teachings of the founder. In Christianity there is the dispute between Roman Catholics and Protestants as to whether Jesus appointed St Peter to be head of his church on earth and whether the popes are his successors in this role. In Islam there is the dispute between Sunni and Shia as to whether, as the latter claim, the prophet Muhammad appointed Ali as his successor. And within each of these and other traditions there are innumerable smaller divisions, often hinging upon historically-based claims to authority.

In face of such disputes an appropriate procedure is acknowledged in principle by all who live within the intellectual world of modernity: namely that these questions can only be settled by unbiased assessment of the historical evidence. In practice, however, such rational resolutions have generally proved elusive. It remains the case that secular historians discount miracle stories whilst religious historians tend to treat as veridical some at least of those accepted within their own tradition; and that Catholic and Protestant, Sunni and Shia, Mahayana and Theravada continue to be convinced of the validity of their own traditional historical warrants. I shall not attempt to adjudicate any of these contentious issues here; my concern is rather to identify the different kinds of conflicting belief and consider to what extent they tell against the pluralistic hypothesis.

At this point much depends upon the status of these disputed historical issues within the belief systems to which they belong. For some adherents of each tradition such claims are fundamental articles of faith, not properly open to investigation and not subject to possible revision in the light of either existing or new evidence. This is indeed typically the position not only of the relatively uneducated majorities but also of many learned believers who are conservative in outlook. We therefore cannot maintain that it is psychologically possible for everyone to tolerate differences concerning the historical components of their tradition. We can only claim that some, and in the modern world a growing number, no longer regard such questions as being of the essence of their faith and accept, further, that we lack sufficient historical evidence definitively to settle most of them. But it remains true that for many other believers they *are* of the essence of their faith, so that no amount of evidence could ever change their conviction, and that for such persons the pluralist vision may well at present be inaccessible.

3 CONFLICTING TRANS-HISTORICAL TRUTH-CLAIMS

The second kind of 'conflicting truth-claims', concerning matters of trans-historical fact, are – I want to suggest – examples of the first type of *avyākata*, the 'unanswered questions', discussed in Chapter 19.1. For they have to do with questions to which there is in principle a true answer, but one which cannot be established by historical or other empirical evidence. I accordingly describe these as issues of trans-historical fact. It will be well at this point to list some examples. I shall leave aside tradition-specific issues and concentrate upon those that are concerned with universal questions to which each tradition has developed its own response.

Here the conflicts tend to be between the traditions of Indian origin and those of Semitic origin. One of the most obvious examples is that listed by the Buddha among his own unanswered questions: Is the universe eternal or did it have a beginning? This has been a matter of dispute between the theistic and non-theistic world-views; for if the universe had a beginning this may have been by an originating act of divine creation. The question –

eternal or not eternal? – is, surely in itself a valid one. For it must be the case either that the series of physical events constituting the history of the universe regresses indefinitely into the past, or that the regression terminates in a first member. Scientific cosmology may perhaps one day be able to settle the question. On the other hand, because of the unavoidable conceptual as well as observational elements in cosmological theories, it is possible that this can only be determined relatively to a current 'paradigm' which may eventually give place to another.

At the moment the evidence, hinging upon the total volume of matter, is insufficient to determine whether the universe is 'open' or 'closed'. If it is 'closed' the present expansion will eventually reverse itself and matter will return to the maximum density that produced the 'big bang' of some fifteen billion years ago. This would thus far be compatible with an oscillating model of successive expansions and contractions. Modern scientific cosmology would then be essentially in agreement with the ancient Vedic vision according to which the cosmos is repeatedly produced and destroyed in a process that has neither beginning nor end. On this view the cosmos is a pulsating drama of formation, expansion, compression and new beginning. On the other hand it may one day be established that the volume of matter is insufficient to generate a gravitational pull to counteract the impetus of the initial explosion. This would be compatible with the big bang as an absolute beginning; and the possibility then opens up that the universe was brought into existence by a power beyond itself.   '

However even if scientific cosmology should come to a definitive conclusion concerning the uniqueness or otherwise of the big bang this would not settle any religious issues. Let us take theism as our example. A universe that has existed beginninglessly into the past might still be a divine creation, depending each moment for its existence upon the creative will of God. Nor on the other hand would a singular big bang, if this were established, necessarily require a creator. For it cannot be excluded that matter might have existed eternally in some other form prior to the big bang; and even if this *could* be excluded we should still be left with a mystery that might either be resolved by postulating a maker or left unresolved as a sheer enigma. Parallel considerations apply to the question whether the universe will or will not continue endlessly into the future. Either possibility is compatible with its having been and with its not having been created *ex nihilo*. Thus the question of the eternity of the universe is only weakly and inconclusively linked with that of divine existence.

Accordingly it can hardly be necessary for salvation/liberation, even from a theistic point of view, to know whether the universe is eternal. And so when the Indian religions affirm and the Semitic religions deny its temporal infinity, this is not a dispute affecting the soteriological efficacy of either group of traditions. To believe that the universe is or is not eternal cannot significantly help or hinder the transformation of human existence from self-centredness to Reality-centredness. If it should one day become clear to all that either the traditional Indian or the traditional Semitic view on this question is mistaken, the discovery would not in any degree invalidate that family of religious traditions as contexts of salvation/liberation. Thus not only do we not know whether the universe is eternal, but this ignorance does not constitute a bar to the attainment of liberation; and further, to treat it as though it were soteriologically essential would only be likely to hinder the salvific process.

The question, then, whether the universe does or does not have a temporal beginning, and likewise whether it is created *ex nihilo*, or is a divine emanation, or a manifestation of the Real, or a product of our blindness to the Real, is not soteriologically vital. Whilst holding any or none of these theories we may still participate in the transformation of human existence from self-centredness to Reality-centredness.

A second major disagreement between what are often loosely called the eastern and western religions concerns the fate of human individuals after death. According to the wisdom of the East we are reborn again and again into this world; whereas according to the wisdom of the West we are distributed at death to an eternal heaven or hell (or perhaps to heaven via purgatory). Let us take reincarnation as our example. The debate about this is complex and many-levelled. There are a variety of significantly different reincarnation and rebirth conceptions. The popular idea is that the present conscious, remembering 'I' has lived before and will live again on earth, its memories of previous lives normally being suppressed by the traumas of birth and death. This differs from the more philosophical Vedantic conception that that which reincarnates is a deeper mental continuant which forms a new conscious self in each incarnation. And this differs again from the Buddhist conception that a stream of karmic cause and effect goes on generating new lives until total freedom from egoity is attained, thus ending the samsaric process. At different points in this spectrum empirical issues (concerning claimed memories of previous lives) and conceptual considerations (concerning the criteria of personal identity from one life to another) have to be considered.

Western writers have usually not paid sufficiently close attention to eastern thought to do more than reject reincarnation as incompatible with accepted Jewish, Christian or Muslim teaching. However the Hindu and Buddhist conceptions deserve more serious attention. There is also the possibility to be explored of speculations incorporating the basic insights of both East and West; and indeed I have tried elsewhere to outline such a speculation.[5] But there are yet other conceivable developments. One is that significant numbers within the Semitic traditions might come to accept the idea of reincarnation and proceed to build it into their own belief systems. A few Christian theologians have done this,[6] and the doctrine has also had its moments of acceptance both within Judaism[7] and on the fringes of Islam.[8] A contrary possibility is that adherents of the faiths of Indian origin might come to see reincarnation as a mythological rather than a literal truth, as has indeed happened in the case of a number of intellectuals.[9] Yet another possibility is that the view might gain ground that some people – perhaps only a minority – are reborn on earth whilst the generality of humankind are not. Or indeed more than one such development might take place at the same time.

However, apart from such possible future developments, the faiths of Indian and Semitic origin generally stand opposed on the question of reincarnation. This was not one of the Buddha's own unanswered questions. In his own time and place it was not a disputed issue: the Buddha himself and all his hearers firmly believed in Karma and rebirth. But if we ask today: Is belief, or disbelief, in reincarnation essential for salvation/liberation? the answer must surely be No. For unless one holds, as a Hindu or a Buddhist, that there is no transformation of human existence from self-centredness to Reality-centredness among the hundreds of millions who do not share the reincarnation belief or, as a Jew, a Christian or a Muslim, that there is no such transformation among the hundreds of millions who do hold that belief, one must accept that the question is not soteriologically vital. We can then agree to differ about it. We shall always hope for new evidence or new arguments which will make the truth plain to all; but in the meantime we should regard the matter as one about which it would be unwise to be unyieldingly dogmatic.

There are many other disputed trans-historical beliefs. However it is not necessary to list further examples since I want to make the same points about them all. The first is that, although there must be true answers to questions of this kind, we do not *know* the answers if 'we' here refers to humanity in general. They have not been definitively settled so as to become matters of agreed public knowledge. On the other hand if 'we' refers to some particular limited community of faith then the situation is that one such community claims to know, for example, that reincarnation is a fact whilst another claims to know the contrary. A visitor from outer space might urge them both to moderate these claims, acknowledging that each has a strong belief, backed by evidence and arguments, but nevertheless not amounting to indubitable knowledge. However many within the existing faith communities would be likely to reject such a plea. And it is at this point that my second contention becomes crucial.

This is the thought, following the insight of the Buddha, that such 'knowledge' is not necessary for salvation/liberation. Each such belief has arisen within a complex religious tradition or family of traditions to which it is integral, and each such belief contributes to one or more of the religio-cultural 'lenses' through which the Real is humanly perceived. I have argued that each of the great traditions constitutes a context and, so far as human judgment can at present discern, a more or less equally effective context, for the transformation of human existence from self-centredness to Reality-centredness. Accordingly it does not seem to make any soteriological difference whether one believes that the world is or is not eternal and its history cyclical or linear, that we do or do not reincarnate, that there are or are not angels and devils and a hierarchy of heavens and hells . . .

Such beliefs concerning matters of trans-historical fact vary in importance within the belief-system to which they belong; and at the top end of the scale they may be indispensable to a given doctrinal structure. It does not however follow that that structure is itself indispensable for salvation/liberation. On the contrary, it suggests otherwise: for it seems implausible that our final destiny should depend upon our professing beliefs about matters of trans-historical fact concerning which we have no definitive information. It seems more likely that both correct and incorrect trans-historical beliefs, like correct and incorrect historical and scientific beliefs, can form part of a religious totality that mediates the Real to human beings, constituting an effective context within which the salvific process occurs.

My far from original suggestion, then, concerning issues of trans-historical fact is (a) that they should be fully and freely recognised as matters on which directly opposed views are often held; (b) that – although by no means everyone ranged on either side of these disagreements will be able to accept this – the questions are ones to which humanity does not at present know the answers; (c) that this ignorance does not hinder the process of salvation/liberation; and (d) that we should therefore learn to live with these differences, tolerating contrary convictions even when we suspect them to be mistaken.

I have thus far been treating these trans-historical beliefs as factual in character: the Vedas are or are not eternal, the bread and wine of the eucharist do or do not become the body and blood of Christ, the words of the Qur'an were or were not recited by the angel Gabriel . . . Such beliefs can certainly be construed in this fashion, and indeed are generally so construed in the ordinary discourse and imagination of the faith-communities. But particularly in the present century, and particularly within Christianity, an awareness has developed of the mythological character of many of the beliefs that I have labelled trans-historical.

I proposed in Chapter 19 an understanding of myths as stories and systems of ideas which are not literally true of, or do not literally apply to, the divine Reality in itself but which may nevertheless be truthful in the sense that the dispositional responses which they tend to evoke are appropriate to our existence in relation to the Real. The examples that I gave there were in fact also examples of what we are now calling trans-historical beliefs. They included convictions about such matters of universal concern as the origin of the universe; the origin of our situation as sinful creatures, living in *avidyā*; and our state after death. A number of tradition-specific beliefs are also possible candidates for mythological interpretation. Within the Hindu tradition these include the Vedic stories of the gods, the doctrine of the devas and the many heavens and hells, and the idea of reincarnation. Within Judaism: Israel as God's chosen people, the numerous anthropomorphic rabbinic stories about the Lord, and the idea of the ups and downs of Jewish history as divine rewards and punishments. Within the Buddhist tradition: the idea of rebirth, the Jakata tales of the Buddha's previous lives, and discourse about the heavenly Buddhas. Within the Christian tradition: the stories of Jesus' virgin birth, bodily resurrection and ascension, and of Mary's immaculate conception and bodily assumption into heaven; the doctrine of divine incarnation, the satisfaction and penal-substitutionary conceptions of atonement, and ontological doctrines of the Holy Trinity; the image of the church as the body of Christ, and the doctrine of trans-substantiation . . .

Thus the pluralistic hypothesis suggests that a number of trans-historical beliefs, which are at present unverifiable and unfalsifiable, may well be true or false myths rather than true or false factual assertions. The hypothesis itself does not however entail that this or that specific belief *is* of this kind. The only exceptions are those that declare one particular tradition to be alone soteriologically effective: our pluralistic hypothesis holds that whilst such beliefs may in a particular phase of history be mythologically true for the particular group whose religious life they support, they do not have the literal truth that would constitute them true for everyone. Since beliefs of this kind are primarily matters for internal discussion within each faith community I shall restrict myself to an example from my own tradition. This is the belief that Jesus Christ was God (or, more precisely, the second person of the divine Trinity) incarnate as a human being. Understood literally, and taken in conjunction with the traditional conviction that this has been and will be the only occasion of divine incarnation, the doctrine entails that Christ is the sole saviour: 'there is no other name under heaven given among men by which we must be saved' than the name of Jesus Christ (Acts 4:12). This in turn entails either, as was generally believed by Christians in the past, that the other great religions of the world are non-salvific or, as is held by many theologians today, that they are salvific as realms to which the redemption won by Christ is somehow extended. The effect of this, particularly in the older and stronger version, has been to make Christians feel uniquely privileged in contrast to the non-Christian majority of the human race and accordingly free to patronise them religiously, exploit them economically and dominate them politically.

Thus the dogma of the deity of Christ – in conjunction with the aggressive and predatory aspect of human nature – has contributed historically to the evils of colonialism, the destruction of indigenous civilisations, anti-Semitism, destructive wars of religion and the burnings of heretics and witches.[10] But on the other hand it is also possible to understand the idea of divine incarnation in the life of Jesus Christ mythologically, as indicating an extraordinary openness to the divine presence in virtue of which Jesus' life and teachings have mediated the reality and love of God to millions of people in successive centuries. Thus, whereas understood literally the doctrine of an unique divine incarnation in Christ has divided humanity and has shrunk the image of God to that of the tribal deity of the West, understood mythologically it can continue to draw people to God through Christ without thereby sundering them from the rest of the human family.

4 CONCLUSIONS

In theory we can distinguish between the 'facts of faith' disclosed in the religious experience of a particular tradition and the theories subsequently developed to integrate these into a systematic world-view. Thus in an earlier book, and speaking specifically of Christian thought, I said that

> we do well to distinguish between, on the one hand, the basic convictions which directly transcribe Christian experience, providing matter for subsequent theological reflection, and on the other hand, such theological reflection itself and the formulations in which it has issued. Using the terms to express a distinction, we may call these two types of religious utterance primary affirmations of faith, and theological doctrines, respectively. The formulation of the primary affirmations of faith is a descriptive and empirical process, the aim of which is to express the basic data apprehended by faith. The theological doctrines of a religion, on the other hand, are the propositions officially accepted as interpreting its primary affirmations and relating them together in a coherent system of thought. The construction of doctrine is thus speculative in method, being

philosophical thinking undertaken within the boundaries of a particular tradition. (Hick [1957] 1987a, 218)

The 'facts of faith' are enshrined in the terms available to those who first proclaimed them. They typically contain an explicit or implicit summons to respond: for the religious fact is one which sets us under an absolute claim. Examples are the Hindu *tat tvam asi* ('This art thou'); the Buddha's Four Noble Truths; the Jewish *shemah*; the Christian recognition of Jesus as the Christ; the Islamic declaration that there is no god but God and that Muhammad is his prophet.

We have to ask concerning these primary affirmations whether they conflict with one another. They conflict in the sense that they are different and that one can only centre one's religious life wholeheartedly and unambiguously upon one of them – upon the Vedic revelation, or upon the Buddha's enlightenment, or upon the Torah, or upon the person of Christ, or upon the words of the Qur'an; but not upon more than one at once. However this is not to say that the experiences that they reflect may not constitute different ways in which the same ultimate Reality has impinged upon human life.[11] And from the point of view of a religious interpretation of the varied phenomena of religion this is how they are to be understood. For these revelatory scriptures and persons point to Brahman, or to Nirvana or Sunyata or the Dharmakaya; or to Adonai, or to the heavenly Father or the Holy Trinity; or to Allah or Vishnu or Shiva; and according to our hypothesis these are different manifestations, within different streams of human life, of the one ultimate Reality. The truth or validity or authenticity of such manifestations lies in their soteriological effectiveness. Thus to say that Adonai is an authentic *persona* of the Real in relation to the Jewish people is to say that in so far as the Jewish people respond appropriately to their Holy One, blessed be he, they are responding appropriately to the Ultimate. Or to say that the Real is authentically thought of within Mahayana Buddhism as the Dharmakaya is to say that in awakening to one's own Buddha-nature one is being effectively transformed by the Real. Thus Adonai and the Dharmakaya, although phenomenologically utterly different, may nevertheless both stand in their own soteriological alignment with the Real.

However, whilst the distinction between these primary affirmations and their interpretive theories is conceptually clear, it tends to become blurred in the actual history of the traditions. Thus in the Theravada it is hard to maintain the distinction between the experience of transience and insubstantiality and the philosophical doctrines of *pratītya samutpāda* and *anattā*. In Judaism experience and practice flow together in *midrash* and *mitzvot*; as in Islam the prophet's revelatory experience of the unity, sovereignty and compassion of Allah flows into the theological and legal elaborations of the Islamic tradition. Again, in the Vedanta and in the Mahayana the practice of meditation is inextricably linked, at any rate in the minds of the gurus, swamis and masters who transmit these traditions, with the profound and coherent systems of thought to which it has given rise. And in Christianity the original confession that 'Jesus is lord' soon began to be understood in terms either of the philosophical concept of the universal Logos which 'became flesh' in Jesus, or of the doctrine that God is three Persons in one, of whom Jesus was the second living a human life. Thus the primary affirmations of a tradition, expressing the facts of faith on which it is based, have in each case become absorbed into an interpretive context of thought; and it is this package as a whole that is taught to each new generation of believers and presented to the world as the faith by which the tradition lives.

We ought then to consider the total belief-systems of the different traditions, composed as they are of elements of diverse logical types: experiential reports, mythologies, historical and trans-historical affirmations, interpretive schemes and concepts of the ultimate. And we have to ask to what extent, or in what sense, these complex totalities conflict. We have already seen the piecemeal answer. There are, first, important ideas within the different traditions which on the surface present incompatible alternatives but which can be seen on deeper analysis to be different expressions of the same more fundamental idea: thus the Christian concept of salvation and the Hindu and Buddhist concepts of liberation are expressions of the more basic notion of the realisation of a limitlessly better possibility for human existence. Second, there are the apparently rival conceptions of the Real as personal and as non-personal. Here the pluralistic hypothesis appeals to the principle of complementarity: those whose religious practice is as prescribed by the theistic traditions experience it as a personal reality, whilst those who act in relation to it in the ways prescribed by the non-theistic traditions experience it as a non-personal reality; and the Real in itself is the noumenal ground of both of these ranges of phenomena.

Third, the concepts of Deity and of the Absolute have been schematised as the range of concrete *personae* and *impersonae* in terms of which, in the history of religions, the Real has been thought, experienced and responded to. Such varying appearances of the Real within different collective and individual consciousnesses are no more mutually incompatible than are the larger cultural complexes to which they are integral. And fourth, within the systems of thought that have been built to house these forms of religious experience, I have suggested that although conflicting historical beliefs can in principle be resolved by historical evidence they are usually not in practice settlable, and we therefore have to learn to live with them, tolerating the varying interpretations imposed by different faith-perspectives. Fifth, conflicts of trans-historical belief are even more conspicuously incapable of being resolved by presently available evidence, and I have suggested that we should recognise both the limits of our knowledge and the fact that this limitation does not hinder the all-important process of salvation/liberation.

Sixth, there are the ultimate mysteries of human existence: Where do we come from? What are we here for? Where are we going?, in response to which the religious traditions have developed their various mythologies. These mythic pictures are true in so far as the responses which they tend to elicit are in soteriological alignment with the Real. Their truthfulness is the practical truthfulness which consists in guiding us aright. They therefore do not conflict with one another as would rival factual hypotheses. Different mythologies may each be valid as ways of evoking, within the life of a particular faith community, human self-transcendence in relation to the Real. When we put all these elements together and add the other dimensions of the traditions – their cultic and liturgical activities, ethics and lifestyles, social and political embodiments – we have a number of historical totalities which, according to our hypothesis, may each mediate the Real to different groups of human beings; and which in fact do so, as far as we are able to judge, to about the same extent.

My conclusion, then, is that the differences between the root concepts and experiences of the different religions, their different and often conflicting historical and trans-historical beliefs, their incommensurable mythologies, and the diverse and ramifying belief-systems into which all these are built, are compatible with the pluralistic hypothesis that the great world traditions constitute different conceptions and perceptions of, and responses to, the Real from within the different cultural ways of being human.

Notes

1. Hume [1748] sect. X, part II – 1902, 122.
2. Underhill [1911] 1955, 238.
3. Perhaps the first significant attempt to do this was that of William A. Christian (1972).
4. Qur'an 17:1. The Hadith story is that the angel Gabriel came to the Prophet in Mecca on a horse, and that Muhammad mounted the horse and flew to the mosque in Jerusalem and back. The story has however been understood by Muslims in various ways: as a literal physical journey, as a spiritual journey, and as a dream experience. See, e.g., Al-Haj Maulana Fazlur Karim 1960–4, 378–80.
5. Hick 1985b, part IV.
6. For example, Leslie Weatherhead, 1957 and 1968, ch. XIV; Geddes MacGregor, 1978 and 1983.
7. The transmigration of souls was taught by the sixteenth-century CE Kabbalist thinker Isaac Luria and 'extended its influence with startling rapidity after 1550'. Indeed the Lurianic Kabbala 'from about 1630 onwards became something like the true *theologia mystica* of Judaism' (Gershom G. Scholem [1946] 1971a, 283–4).
8. The Druses in the Lebanon, regarding themselves as Muslims, believe in reincarnation, and a number of Ian Stevenson's collected cases of memories of previous lives come from them. He also reports cases from the Shiite sect of the Alevis. See Stevenson 1975–9.
9. See Buddhadasa 1972; Keiji Nishitani 1982, 173. See also, as western discussions, J. G. Jennings 1947, xxiv–xxv, and Eliot Deutsch [1969] 1980, ch. 5.
10. See further Hick 1987b.
11. For recent philosophical defences of this possibility see Miller 1986, Runzo 1986, and William Alston 1987.

Epilogue: The Future

What can we say, from the point of view of our pluralistic hypothesis, about the future development of the religious traditions? We cannot do more than take note of existing trends and try to plot their continuation into the future. In fact we see contrary trends at work around us. On the one hand there is a marked growth of the pluralistic outlook, particularly among educated younger people. But on the other hand there is a powerful opposite trend, a wide resurgence of the 'us against them' attitude in the forms of both religious fundamentalism and political nationalism. Thus two different trajectories are in motion, affecting different people: one moving towards a world outlook, open to the variety of human ways of thinking and feeling; and the other retrenching into intensified allegiance to one's own group, reaffirming its traditional values and modes of thought, and opposing a world-wide or species-wide loyalty.

We cannot know how the developing picture will look in a hundred years' time. But if we may take the western intellectual turmoil of the late nineteenth century as a case study, we see there at work a realistic tendency of the human mind to come to terms with new and initially disturbing knowledge. In the nineteenth century the fresh information concerned the development of life on earth. Looking back, we find that the knowledge disseminated through the debates about evolution has gradually transformed the thinking of the Christian churches. Today the new challenge comes from a flood of information about the wider religious life of humanity. And if the historical analogy provides any indication of what is likely to happen during the next hundred or so years we may expect that in due course most educated Christians will have come to take for granted a pluralistic understanding of the religious life of the world, with Christianity seen as part of that life.

Further, we may anticipate that as the communicational network grows around the globe the same need to rethink in a world perspective will progressively affect the other religious traditions. Each has within it, either latent or on the surface, the resources for a pluralist understanding of the religious situation. Thus

Judaism, with its conception of the special covenant relationship of the Jews to God, has almost of logical necessity to recognise other paths of salvation for the rest of the human race – although in practice the Jewish community has had to be so concerned about survival that questions of inter-faith theology have not been high on its agenda. Islam may be expected to go through essentially the same traumas as Christianity in its encounter both with modern science and with the emerging ecumenical outlook; only whereas the Christian trauma has been spread over a century or more Islam is having to adjust in a single generation to an already formed modern culture. It is to be hoped that the Muslim world will eventually find its own Qur'anic way of combining modern knowledge with its faith in the Transcendent and its commitment to a morality of human community. And we may further hope that this development will also include an increased recognition of the ecumenical point of view that has already been so powerfully expressed within the Sufi strand of Islam. Further east, the Hindu, Jain, Sikh and Buddhist traditions are already considerably more advanced than the faiths of Semitic origin in the development of a pluralistic outlook, and may be expected to continue to contribute to its spread.

It may seem strange to speculate even about the possibility of Marxism becoming open to those expressions of religious faith that are committed to social justice and opposed to all forms of exploitation and repression. But although Karl Marx himself was emphatically an atheist, like so many of the intellectuals of his time and circle, there is nevertheless no logical connection between atheism and Marx's account of the socio-economic dynamics of history. There is no inherent incompatibility between a basically Marxist analysis of the development of capitalist society and belief in the Transcendent. In so far as the Christian churches have normally allied themselves with the exploiting ruling classes they have been rightly condemned by the Marxists. But in this condemnation Marxism does not function in an unique role but in one that is continuous with that of the ancient Hebrew prophets and of contemporary Third World liberation theologians.

No one can profess to know whether or to what extent these various hoped-for developments will in fact take place. Those of us who want them to occur can only work for them within our own tradition whilst keeping continuously in touch, through inter-faith dialogue, with colleagues in other traditions. But if a world ecumenism does increasingly develop during the coming decades and generations this will not entail an eventual single world religion. The religious life of humanity will no doubt continue to be lived within the existing traditions, though with less and less emphasis upon their mutually exclusive claims. One will be a Christian or a Jew or a Muslim or a Buddhist or a Hindu or a Taoist or Shintoist and so on who sees one's inherited tradition as one context of salvation/liberation among others. In the meantime we have to live in the tension between the older, generally exclusivist, forms of religion and the emerging more ecumenical and pluralistic vision.

Let me now speak from within my own situation as a Christian who has already begun to see the religious situation of the human race pluralistically. Must there not be a tension, for those of us who accept a world ecumenism, between this and our continuing Christian loyalty? The answer, I think, is that there is indeed such a tension and that it is inevitable that there should be. It does not manifest itself primarily at the intellectual level. For forms of Christian belief, and in particular of Christology, Trinitarianism and atonement doctrine, have developed in our time which can claim to be true to the New Testament data and which yet do not entail the traditional Christian absolutism. I need only mention such names as the Roman Catholics Hans Küng, Edward Schillebeeckx and Karl Rahner; the Presbyterians Donald and John Baillie; and the Anglicans Maurice Wiles and Geoffrey Lampe. (For an application of Baillie's and Lampe's Christologies to our pluralistic religious situation see Hick 1988.) There are attractive forms of Christian theology available today which are compatible with the pluralistic vision. The tension comes rather at the level of the emotion and the imagination. For the idea of the absoluteness and the unique superiority of Christ, the Christian gospel and the Christian church is deeply embedded in our liturgies and cultural history as well as in the assumptions of so many of our fellow Christians. One participates in the liturgy, joins in singing the hymns, is part of the community and its history, and yet at the same time one does not share its still prevailing absolutist and exclusivist assumptions. Hence the tension; and all that we can do, I think, is to continue to live in this tension, accepting the moments of pain and turmoil that it can involve.

But on the other hand there are great gains and enrichments

available to a Christian who is able to learn from the visions, experiences and thoughts of the other great religious traditions. To see how others experience and respond to the Real can only enlarge one's own awareness of that ultimate Reality in which we all live and move and have our being. Christians already have access to the ancient Hebrew scriptures; but if we regard the Muslim and Hindu and Sikh traditions as authentic contexts of salvation/liberation we can open ourselves also to the marvellous devotional literature of Rumi and Kabir and Nanak and the Tamil poets; and if we regard the various forms of Buddhism and of non-theistic Hinduism as likewise authentic contexts of the salvific human transformation we can benefit from their long-tried methods of meditation and from their challengingly different insights. Indeed life within each tradition can be enormously enriched and expanded by openness to the accumulated experience and thought of other ways of being human in relation to the Real.

Further, within a pluralistic understanding our implicit view of other human beings must be affected. For we shall now see the transformation of human existence going on in various ways and degrees throughout the world and throughout human history, rather than only within the borders of our own tradition. This means that the entire human story, with all its light and dark, its triumphs and its tragedies, is to be affirmed as ultimately good in the sense that it is part of a universal soteriological process. What I called earlier the cosmic optimism of each of the great traditions is intensified when we see them all as pointing to the possibility of a limitlessly better existence and as affirming that the universe is such that this limitlessly better possibility is actually available to us and can begin to be realised in each present moment.

And so the kind of spirituality that is appropriate to the contemporary pluralistic vision is one that is basically trusting and hopeful and stirred by a sense of joy in celebration of the goodness, from our human point of view, of the ultimately Real. Ethically its central theme should be the love/compassion to which all the great traditions call us; and in our sociologically conscious age this is likely to be increasingly a politically conscious and active *agape/karuṇā* which seeks to change the structures of society so as to promote rather than hinder the transformation of all human life.

Reference Bibliography

NOTE: Secondary sources are cited according to the current edition. When there is an original or earlier edition its date is given in square brackets immediately following the title. Biblical quotations are from the Revised Standard Version.

Abe, Masao
    1982: 'Man and Nature in Christianity and Buddhism', in *The Buddha Eye*, ed. Frederick Franck (New York: Crossroad).
    1985a: *Zen and Western Thought* (London: Macmillan, and Honolulu: University of Hawaii Press).
    1985b: 'A Dynamic Unity in Religious Pluralism: A Proposal from a Buddhist Point of View', in *The Experience of Religious Diversity*, ed. John Hick and Hasan Askari (Aldershot, Hants, and Brookfield, VT: Gower Publishing).
Achinstein, P., and S. F. Barker (eds)
    1969: *The Legacy of Logical Positivism* (Baltimore: Johns Hopkins Press).
Adams, Robert M.
    1987: *The Virtue of Faith* (New York and London: Oxford University Press).
al 'Arabi, Ibn
    1980: *The Bezels of Wisdom* [13th century], trans. R. W. J. Austin (New York: Paulist Press, and London: SPCK).
    1990: *The Bezels of Wisdom* (New York: Paulist Press, and London: SCM Press).
Alston, William
    1956: 'Ineffability', in Philosophical Review, vol. 65, no. 4.
    1964: 'Psychological Explanations of Religious Belief', in Hick 1964.
    1967: 'Religion', *The Encyclopedia of Philosophy*, ed. Paul Edwards, vol. 7 (New York: Macmillan and Free Press, and London: Macmillan).
    1983: 'Christian Experience and Christian Belief', in Plantinga and Wolterstorff (eds) 1983.
    1987: 'Religious Experience and Religious Diversity', in *Christian Scholars Review*, vol. 16.
    1991: *Perceiving God* (Ithaca: Cornell University Press).
Anderson, Barry F.
    1975: *Cognitive Psychology: The Study of Knowing, Learning and Thinking* (New York and London: Academic Press).
Anselm, St
    1965: *St Anselm's Proslogion* [11th century], trans. M. J. Charlesworth (Oxford: Clarendon Press).
Appleby, Peter C.
    1980: 'Mysticism and Ineffability', in *International Journal for Philosophy of Religion*, vol. 11, no. 3.

Aquinas, Thomas
   1945: *Basic Writings of Saint Thomas Aquinas*, English Dominican Trans.,
      ed. Anton Pegis, vol. 2 (New York: Random House).
   1955: *On the Truth of the Catholic Faith: Summa contra Gentiles*, vol. 1,
      trans. Anton Pegis (Garden City, NY: Image Books).
Arberry, A. J.
   1979: *Sufism* (London: George Allen & Unwin [1950], and New York:
      Mandala).
Arbib, Michael A., and Mary B. Hesse
   1986: *The Construction of Reality* (London and New York: Cambridge
      University Press).
Armstrong, Karen
   1993: *A History of God* (London: Heinemann).
Aslan, Adnan
   1998: *Religious Pluralism in Christian and Islamic Philosophy: The Thought of
      John Hick and Seyyed Hossein Nasr* (Richmond: Curzon).
Augustine
   1953: *Augustine's Early Writings*, trans. J. H. S. Burleigh (London: SCM
      Press, and Philadelphia: Westminster Press).
Ayoub, Mahmoud
   1984: *The Qur'an and Its Interpreters* (Albany, NJ: State University of New
      York Press).
Baier, Kurt
   1957: *The Meaning of Life* (Canberra: Canberra University Press).
Baillie, John
   1934: *And the Life Everlasting* (London: Oxford University Press).
Ballou, Robert O.
   1948: *Pocket Bible of the World* (London: Routledge & Kegan Paul).
Banton, Michael, (ed.)
   1966: *Anthropological Approaches to the Study of Religion* (New York: F. A.
      Praeger).
Barbour, Ian
   1974: *Myths, Models and Paradigms* (New York: Harper & Row).
Barr, James
   1969: *Biblical Words for Time*, 2nd edition (London: SCM Press).
Barrow, John D., and Joseph Silk
   1984: *The Left Hand of Creation* (London: William Heinemann).
Barrow, John D., and Frank J. Tipler
   1986: *The Anthropic Cosmological Principle* (Oxford: Clarendon Press, and
      New York: Oxford University Press).
Becker, L.
   1971: 'A Note on Religious Experience Arguments', in *Religious Studies*,
      vol. 7, no. 1.
Bellah, Robert N.
   1970: *Beyond Belief: Essays on Religion in a Post-Traditional World* (New
      York and London: Harper & Row).
Bennett, James O.
   1984: 'The Meaning of Life: A Qualitative Perspective', in *Canadian
      Journal of Philosophy*, vol. 14 (December).

Berger, Peter, and Thomas Luckmann
1967: *The Social Construction of Reality* (New York: Doubleday Anchor).
Berndt, Ronald
1951: *Kunapipi* (Melbourne: Chesire).
Bertocci, Peter A., et al. (eds)
1982: *The Challenge of Religion* (New York: Seabury Press).
Betty, Stafford
1991: 'The Glitch in *An Interpretation of Religion*' in Hewett (ed.) 1991.
Bevan, Edwyn
1938: *Symbolism and Belief* (London: George Allen & Unwin, and Port Washington, NY: Kennikat Press).
Birch, Charles, and John Cobb
1981: *The Liberation of Life* (London and New York: Cambridge University Press).
Bleeker, Claas Jouco, and Geo Widengren (eds)
1969: *Historia Religionum: Handbook for the History of Religions*, vol. I (Leiden: E. J. Brill).
1971: *Historia Religionum: Handbook for the History of Religions*, vol. II (Leiden: E. J. Brill).
Boethius
1962: *Contra Eutychen et Nestorium*, III, in *Boethius: The Theological Tractates* [5th–6th century], trans. H. F. Stewart and E. K. Rand (Cambridge, MA: Harvard University Press, and London: William Heinemann).
Bolle, Kees
1979: *The Bahagavadgita: A New Translation* (Berkeley and London: University of California Press).
Botterweck, G., and H. Ringrenn (eds)
1986: *Theological Dictionary of the Old Testament*, vol. 5, trans. David Green (Grand Rapids, MI: Wm B. Eerdmans).
Bouquet, A. C.
1941: *Comparative Religion* (London: Pelican Books).
1954: *Sacred Books of the World* (ed.) (London: Penguin Books).
Bowker, John
1973: *The Sense of God: Sociological, Anthropological and Psychological Approaches to the Origin of the Sense of God* (Oxford: Clarendon Press).
1978: *The Religious Imagination and the Sense of God* (Oxford: Clarendon Press).
1987: *Licensed Insanities* (London: Darton, Longman and Todd).
Bradley, F. H.
1906: *Appearance and Reality*, 2nd edition (London: Sonnenschein, and New York: Macmillan).
Braithwaite, R. B.
1955: *An Empiricist's View of the Nature of Religious Belief* (Cambridge University Press).
Brakenhielm, Carl-Reinhold
1975: *How Philosophy Shapes Theories of Religion* (Uppsala: CWK Gleerup).
1985: *Problems of Religious Experience* (Stockholm: Almqvist & Wiksell).

Brim, Orvile G., Jr et al.
  1970: *The Dying Patient* (New York: Russell Page Foundation).
Britton, Karl
  1971: *Philosophy and the Meaning of Life* (Cambridge: Cambridge University Press).
Broad, C. D.
  1939a: 'Arguments for the Existence of God – I', in *The Journal of Theological Studies*, vol. 40 (January).
  1939b: 'Arguments for the Existence of God – II', in *The Journal of Theological Studies*, vol. 40 (April).
Brown, Stuart C. (ed.)
  1977: *Reason and Religion* (Ithaca and London: Cornell University Press).
Brundage, James A.
  1976: 'Prostitution in the Medieval Canon Law', in *Signs: Journal of Women in Culture and Society*, vol. 1, no. 4.
Brunner, Emil
  1936: *God and Man*, trans. David Cairns (London: SCM Press).
Buber, Martin
  1937: *I and Thou* [1923], trans. R. Gregor Smith (Edinburgh: T. & T. Clark).
  1951: *Two Types of Faith*, trans. Norman Goldhawk (London: Routledge & Kegan Paul).
Buddhadasa
  1972: *Toward the Truth*, ed. Donald Swearer (Philadelphia: Westminster Press).
Bultmann, Rudolf
  1984: 'The New Testament and Mythology' [1941], in *The New Testament and Mythology and Other Basic Writings*, ed. Schubert M. Ogden (Philadelphia: Fortress Press).
Burleigh, John H. S., (trans.)
  1953: *Augustine: Earlier Writings* (London: SCM Press, and Philadelphia: Westminster Press).
Butler, Cuthbert
  1967: *Western Mysticism* (London: Constable).
Butler, Bishop
  1888: *Sermons on Human Nature: Man Considered as a Moral Agent* [1726] (Edinburgh: T. & T. Clark).
Caird, G. B.
  1980: *The Language and Imagery of the Bible* (Philadelphia: Westminster Press).
Calvin, Jean
  1962: *Institutes of the Christian Religion*, 2 vols [1559], Library of Christian Classics vols 20–1, trans. Ford Lewis Battles, ed. John T. McNeill (Philadelphia: Westminster Press).
Carmody, Denise Lardner
  1981: *The Oldest God: Archaic Religion Yesterday and Today* (Nashville: Abingdon).
Carruthers, Gregory SJ
  1988: *The Uniqueness of Jesus Christ in the Theocentric Model of the Christian*

Theology of World Religions: an Elaboration and Evaluation of the Position of John Hick (Rome: Gregorian University) and 2000 (New York and London: University Press of America).

Carter, Brandon
    1974: 'Large Number Coincidences and the Anthropic Principle in Cosmology', in Longair (ed.) 1974.

Cheetham, David
    2003: *John Hick: A Critical Introduction and Reflection* (Aldershot, UK and Burlington, USA: Ashgate).

Chittick, William C., (trans.)
    1983: *The Sufi Path of Love: The Spiritual Teachings of Rumi [Mathnawi]* (Albany: State University of New York Press).

Christian, William A.
    1964: *Meaning and Truth in Religion* (Princeton: Princeton University Press).
    1972: *Oppositions of Religious Doctrines* (London: Macmillan, and New York: Herder & Herder).
    1987: *Doctrines of Religious Communities: A Philosophical Study* (New Haven and London: Yale University Press).

Clark, R. W.
    1984: 'The Evidential Value of Religious Experience', in *International Journal for Philosophy of Religion*, vol. 16, no. 3.

Cobb, John B., Jr
    1968: *The Structure of Christian Existence* (Philadelphia: Westminster Press [1967], and London: Lutterworth Press).

Cohen, John
    1966: 'Subjective Time', in J. T. Fraser (ed.) 1966.

Cohn-Sherbok, Dan
    1985: 'Don Cupitt and Judaism', in *Theology*, vol. 87, no. 726.

Collins, Steven
    1982: *Selfless Persons* (Cambridge: Cambridge University Press).

Confucius
    1938: *The Analects of Confucius*, trans. A. Waley (London: George Allen & Unwin).

Conze, Edward
    1967: *Buddhist Thought in India* (Ann Arbor: University of Michigan Press, 1967).
    1975: *Buddhism: Its Essence and Development* [1951] (New York: Harper & Row).

Cook, Robert
    1993: 'Postmodernism, pluralism and John Hick', *Themelios*, vol. 19, no. 1.

Copleston, F. C.
    1955: *Aquinas* (Harmondsworth, Middlesex: Penguin Books).
    1982: *Religion and the One* (New York: Crossroad).

Cupitt, Don
    1980: *Taking Leave of God* (London: SCM Press, and New York: Crossroad [1981]).
    1982: *The World to Come* (London: SCM Press).

1984: *The Sea of Faith* (London: BBC).

1985: *Only Human* (London: SCM Press).

1986: *Life Lines* (London: SCM Press).

Darwin, Charles

1875: *The Descent of Man*, 2nd edition (London: John Murray).

Dasgupta, Surendranath N.

1973: *Yoga as a Philosophy and Religion* [1924] (Delhi: Motilal Banarsidass).

1981: 'Sacrificial Mysticism', in *Understanding Mysticism*, ed. Richard Woods (Garden City, NY: Image Books, and London: Athlone Press).

Davids, C. A. F. Rhys. (trans.)

1950: *The Book of Kindred Sayings* (Samyutta-Nikāya), Part I (London: Luzac).

1952: *The Book of Kindred Sayings* (Samyutta-Nikāya), Part II (London: Luzac).

1964: *Psalms of the Early Buddhists* (*Therīgāthā*) (London: Luzac).

Davids, C. A. F. Rhys. and T. W. Davids (trans.)

1923: *Dialogues of the Buddha* (*Dīgha and Majjhima Nikāyas*) [1899] vol. I. (London and New York: Oxford University Press).

1938: Ibid., vol. II.

Davies, Paul

1983: *God and the New Physics* (London: J. M. Dent, and London: Pelican Books [1984]).

Davis, Stephen T.

1978: *Faith, Skepticism and Evidence* (ed.) (Lewisburg: Bucknell University Press, and London: Associated University Presses).

1983: *Logic and the Nature of God* (London: Macmillan, and Grand Rapids, MI: Wm B. Eerdmans).

1987: *Encountering Jesus* (ed.) (Atlanta: John Knox Press).

D'Costa, Gavin

1986: *Theology and Religious Pluralism* (Oxford and New York: Basil Blackwell).

1987: *John Hick's Theology of Religions* (New York and London: University Press of America).

1991: 'John Hick and Religious Pluralism' in Hewitt (ed.) 1991.

de Bary, William Theodore (ed.)

1960: *Sources of Chinese Tradition* (New York: Columbia University Press).

1972: *The Buddhist Tradition in India, China and Japan* [1969] (New York: Vintage Books).

Dember, William N.

1960: *The Psychology of Perception* (New York: Henry Holt).

de Silva, Lynn A.

1974: *Buddhism: Beliefs and Practices in Sri Lanka* (Colombo: Wesley Press).

Deutsch, Eliot

1980: *Advaita Vedanta: A Philosophical Reconstruction* [1969] (Honolulu: University of Hawaii Press).

1984: 'Art and Religion', in *Religious Pluralism*, ed. Leroy S. Rouner (Notre Dame, IN: University of Notre Dame Press).

Devine, Philip E.
  1986: 'On the Definition of Religion', in *Faith and Philosophy*, vol. 3, no. 3.
Dewey, John
  1934: *A Common Faith* (New Haven: Yale University Press, and London: H. Milford, Oxford University Press).
DeWitt, Bryce S.
  1970: 'Quantum Mechanics and Reality', in *Physics Today* (September).
DeWitt, Bryce S., and Neill Graham (eds)
  1973: *The Many-Worlds Interpretation of Quantum Mechanics* (Princeton: Princeton University Press).
Dhavamony, Mariasusai
  1971: *Love of God According to Saiva Siddhanta* (Oxford: Clarendon Press).
Diamond, Malcolm, and Thomas V. Litzenburg Jr (eds)
  1975: *The Logic of God: Theology and Verification* (Indianapolis: Bobbs-Merrill).
Dilman, Ilham
  1965: 'Life and Meaning', in *Philosophy*, vol. 40, no. 154.
Dionysius the Areopagite
  1977: *On the Divine Names and the Mystical Theology* [1920], trans. C. E. Rolt (London: SPCK).
Doniger, Simon (ed.)
  1962: *The Nature of Man in Theological and Psychological Perspective* (New York: Harper & Row).
Donovan, Peter J.
  1986: 'Do Different Religions Share Common Moral Ground?', in *Religious Studies*, vol. 22, nos 3–4.
Downing, John
  1963: 'Jesus and Martyrdom', in *Journal of Theological Studies*, vol. 14, no. 2.
Dretske, Fred I.
  1979: 'Simple Seeing', in *Body, Mind and Method*, ed. D. F. Gustafson and B. L. Tapscott (Boston: D. Reidel).
Dublin, Louis I.
  1965: *Factbook on Man – From Birth to Death*, 2nd edition (New York: Macmillan, and London: Collier-Macmillan).
Dumoulin, Heinrich
  1963: *A History of Zen Buddhism* [1959], trans. Paul Peachey (Boston: Beacon Press).
Dunfee, Susan
  1982: 'The Sin of Hiding: A Feminist Critique of Reinhold Niebuhr's Account of the Sin of Pride', in *Soundings*, vol. 65 (Fall).
Dunlop, Charles
  1984: 'Wittgenstein on Sensation and "Seeing-As"', in *Synthesis*, vol. 60, no. 3.
Duprés, Louis
  1987: 'Mysticism' in *The Encyclopedia of Religion*, vol. 10, ed. Mircea Eliade (New York: Macmillan, and London: Collier Macmillan).
Durkheim, Emile
  1963: *The Elementary Forms of the Religious Life* [1912], trans. Joseph Ward Swain (London: George Allen & Unwin [1915] and Free Press).

Eckhart, Meister
   1941: *Meister Eckhart: A Modern Translation*, trans. Raymond Blakney (New York and London: Harper Torchbooks).
Eddy, Paul Rhodes
   2002: *John Hick's Pluralist Philosophy of World Religions* (Aldershot, UK and Burlington, USA: Ashgate).
Edwardes, Denis
   1984: *Human Experience of God* (Dublin: Gill, and New York: Macmillan).
Edwards, Paul
   1986/7: 'The Case Against Reincarnation', Part II, in *Free Inquiry* (Winter).
Eisenstadt, Samuel N.
   1982: 'The Axial Age: The Emergence of Transcendental Visions and the Rise of Clerics', in *Archives Européennes de Sociologie*, vol. 33.
Eliade, Mircea
   1958: *Patterns in Comparative Religion*, trans. Rosemary Sheed (New York: New American Library).
   1971: *Cosmos and History: The Myth of the Eternal Return* [1949], trans. Willard R. Trask (Princeton: Princeton University Press).
   1978: *A History of Religious Ideas*, vol. I [1976], trans. Willard R. Trask (Chicago and London: University of Chicago Press).
   1982: *A History of Religious Ideas*, vol. II [1978].
   1985: *A History of Religious Ideas*, vol. III [1983].
Eliot, George
   1964: *Middlemarch* [1871–2] (New York: New American Library Signet Classic).
Eliot, T. S.
   1935: *Murder in the Cathedral* (New York: Harcourt, Brace & Co., and London: Faber & Faber).
   1941: *Burnt Norton* (London: Faber & Faber).
Evans, Donald
   1963: *The Logic of Self-Involvement* (London: SCM Press).
   1980: *Faith, Authenticity and Morality* (Edinburgh: Handsel Press).
Evans-Pritchard, E. E.
   1948: *The Divine Kingship of the Shilluk in the Nilotic Sudan* (Cambridge: Cambridge University Press).
Faghoury, Mostafa, and Leslie Armour
   1984: 'Wittgenstein's Philosophy and Religious Insight', in *The Southern Journal of Philosophy*, vol. 22, no. 1.
Farmer, H. H.
   1936: *The World and God* (London: Nisbet).
   1942: *Towards Belief in God* (London: SCM Press).
   1947: *God and Men* (London: Nisbet, and Nashville: Abingdon-Cokesbury).
Fatemi, Nasrollah S.
   1974: 'A Message and Method of Love, Harmony and Brotherhood', in L. F. Rushbrook (ed.) *Sufi Studies: East and West* (London: Octagon Press).

Ferré, Frederick
    1970: 'The Definition of Religion', in *Journal of the American Academy of Religion*, vol. 38, no. 1.
Feuerbach, Ludwig
    1957: *The Essence of Christianity* [1841], trans. Marion Evans [George Eliot] (New York: Harper Torchbooks).
Fiske, S. T.
    1984: *Social Cognition* (Reading, MD: Addison-Wesley).
Flew, Anthony
    1963: 'Tolstoi and the Meaning of Life', in *Ethics*, vol. 73, no. 2.
Fohrer, Georg
    1972: *History of Israelite Religion* [1968], trans. David E. Green (Nashville: Abingdon Press).
Forgie, J. William
    1985a: 'Hyper-Kantianism in Recent Discussions of Mystical Experience', in *Religious Studies*, vol. 21, no. 2.
    1985b: 'Mystical Experience and the Argument from Agreement', in *International Journal for Philosophy of Religion*, vol. 17, no. 3.
Forward, Martin (ed.)
    1995: *Ultimate Visions* (Oxford: One World).
Fox, George
    1924: *The Journal of George Fox* [1694], Everyman's Library (London: J. M. Dent, and New York: E. P. Dutton).
Fox, Marvin (ed.)
    1975: *Modern Jewish Ethics: Theory and Practice* (Columbus: Ohio State University Press).
Fraser, J. T. (ed.)
    1966: *The Voices of Time: A Cooperative Survey of Man's Views of Time as Expressed by the Sciences and by the Humanities* (New York: George Braziller, and London: Penguin Books).
Frazer, James
    1941: *The Golden Bough* [1922], abridged edition (London: Macmillan).
Freud, Sigmund
    1939: *Moses and Monotheism* [1939], in *The Standard Edition of the Complete Psychological Works of Sigmund Freud*, vol. XXIII, trans. and ed. James Strachey (London: Hogarth Press, and New York: Liveright Corp.).
    1955: *Totem and Taboo* [1913], in *The Standard Edition of the Complete Psychological Works of Sigmund Freud*, vol. XIII.
    1961: *The Future of an Illusion* [1927], in *The Standard Edition of the Complete Psychological Works of Sigmund Freud*, vol. XXI.
Furnish, Victor Paul
    1973: *The Love Command in the New Testament* (London: SCM Press).
Gade, Gerhard
    1998: *Viele Religionen – ein Wort Gottes: Einspruch gegen John Hicks pluralistichen Religionsphilosophie* (Gutersloh: Chr. Kaiser Verlag).
Galloway, George
    1914: *The Philosophy of Religion* (Edinburgh: T. & T. Clark).
Gandhi, Mahatma
    1924: *Young India* (Ahmedabad: Navajivan Publishing House).

1968: *The Selected Works of Mahatma Gandhi* (Ahmedabad: Navajivan Publishing House).

Gandhi, Ramchandra
  1984: *I am Thou* (Poona: Indian Philosophical Quarterly Publications).

Geertz, Clifford
  1979: 'Religion as a Cultural System' [1965], in Lessa and Vogt 1979.

Geivett, Douglas
  1995: *Evil and the Evidence for God: The Challenge of John Hick's Theodicy* (Philadelphia: Temple University Press).

Gillis, Chester
  1989: *A Question of Final Belief: John Hick's Pluralistic Theory of Salvation* (London: Macmillan).
  1991: 'An Interpretation of *An Interpretation of Religion*' in Hewett (ed.) 1991.

Gimello, Robert
  1978: 'Mysticism and Meditation', in *Mysticism and Philosophical Analysis*, ed. Steven Katz (New York: Oxford University Press).

Glueck, Nelson
  1975: *Hesed in the Bible*, trans. Alfred Gottschalk (New York: KTAV).

Goldstein, Valerie Saiving
  1960: 'The Human Situation: A Feminine View', in *The Journal of Religion*, vol. 40, no. 2.

Goulder, Michael
  1977: 'Jesus, the Man of Universal Destiny', in Hick (ed.) 1977.

Goulder, Michael, and John Hick
  1983: *Why Believe in God?* (London: SCM Press).

Gratton-Guinness, Ian
  1985: 'Is Psi Intrinsically Non-Linguistic?', in *Journal of the Society for Psychical Research*, vol. 53, no. 799.

Green, Ronald M.
  1978: *Religious Reason: The Rational and Moral Basis of Religious Belief* (New York: Oxford University Press).

Greenberg, Irving
  1988: *The Jewish Way* (New York: Summit Books).

Gregory of Nyssa
  1956: *Against Eunomius*, in Schaff and Wace 1956, vol. 5.
  1978: *The Life of Moses*, trans. and introduction Abraham J. Malherbe and Everett Ferguson (New York: Paulist Press).

Gregory, R. L.
  1978: *Eye and Brain*, 3rd edition [1966] (London: Weidenfeld & Nicolson, and New York: McGraw-Hill).

Gurney, Edmund (ed.)
  1886: *Phantasms of the Living*, 2 vols (London: SPR).

Hall, Lindsey
  2003: *Swinburne's Hell and Hick's Universalism: Are We Free to Reject God?* (Aldershot, UK and Burlington, USA: Ashgate).

Hanh, Thich Nhat
  1974: *Zen Keys*, trans. Albert and Jean Low (Garden City, NY: Doubleday Anchor).

Hanson, Norwood Russell
   1958: *Patterns of Discovery* (Cambridge: Cambridge University Press).
Hare, E. M.
   1945: *The Woven Cadences of Early Buddhists* (*Sutta Nipāta*) (London: Oxford University Press).
   1965: *The Book of Gradual Sayings* (*Anguttara-Nikāya*), IV (London: Luzac).
Hare, R. M.
   1973: 'The Simple Believer', in *Religion and Morality*, ed. Gene Outka and John P. Reeder (Garden City, NY: Doubleday).
Hartman, David
   1985: *A Living Covenant: The Innovative Spirit in Traditional Judaism* (New York: Free Press, and London: Collier-Macmillan).
Hartshorne, Charles
   1944: 'The Formal Validity and Real Significance of the Ontological Argument', in *The Philosophical Review*, vol. 53, no. 3.
   1961: The Logic of the Ontological Argument', in *Journal of Philosophy*, vol. 58, no. 17.
   1962: 'What Did Anselm Discover?', in *Union Seminary Quarterly Review*, vol. 17, no. 3.
   1963a: 'Necessity', in *Review of Metaphysics*, vol. 21, no. 2.
   1963b: 'Rationale of the Ontological Proof', in *Theology Today*, vol. 20, no. 2.
   196Sa: *Anselm's Discovery* (LaSalle, IL: Open Court).
   1965b: *The Logic of Perfection and Other Essays in Neoclassical Metaphysics* (LaSalle, IL: Open Court).
   1968: 'Kant's Refutation Still Not Convincing: A Reply', in *Monist*, vol. 52, no. 2.
   1969: 'Religious Aspects of Necessity and Contingency', in *And More About God*, ed. Lewis M. Rogers and Charles H. Monson Jr (Salt Lake City: University of Utah Press).
   1970: 'Six Theistic Proofs', in *Monist*, vol. 54, no. 2.
   1977: 'John Hick on Logical and Ontological Necessity', in *Religious Studies*, vol. 13, no. 2.
Harvey, O. J., David E. Hunt and Harold M. Schroder
   1961: *Conceptual Systems and Personality Organization* (New York and London: John Wiley).
Heaney, James
   1980: 'Faith and the Logic of Seeing-As', in *Sophia*, vol. 18, no. 1.
Heesterman, J. C.
   1985: *The Inner Conflict of Tradition* (Chicago and London: Chicago University Press).
Heim, Mark
   1995: *Salvations* (Maryknoll, NY: Orbis).
Heinemann, Benno
   1973: *The Maggido of Dubno and His Parables*, 3rd edition (New York: Philipp Feldheim).
Heller, Christian
   2001: *John Hicks Projekt einer religiosen Interpretation der Religionen* (Munster: Lit Verlag).

Hewett, Harold, (ed.)
  1991: *Problems in the Philosophy of Religion: Critical Studies of the Work of John Hick* (London: Macmillan).
Hick, John
  1957: *Faith and Knowledge* (2nd edition 1966) (Ithaca: Cornell University Press and London: Macmillan).
  1964: *Faith and the Philosophers* (ed.) (London: Macmillan, and New York: St. Martin's Press).
  1970: *Arguments for the Existence of God* (London: Macmillan, and New York: Herder & Herder).
  1977: *The Myth of God Incarnate* (ed.) (London: SCM Press, and Philadelphia: Westminster Press).
  1985a: *Evil and the God of Love* [1966], 2nd edition (San Francisco: Harper & Row), reissued (London: Macmillan).
  1985b: *Death and Eternal Life* [1976)], reissued (London: Macmillan).
  1987a: *Faith and Knowledge* [1957], 2nd edition reissued (London: Macmillan).
  1987b: 'The Non-Absoluteness of Christianity', in *The Myth of Christian Uniqueness*, ed. John Hick and Paul Knitter (New York: Orbis, and London: SCM Press).
  1988: 'An Inspiration Christology for a Religiously Plural World', in Stephen Davis (ed.) *Encountering Jesus* (Philadelphia: Fortress Press).
  1993: *The Metaphor of God Incarnate* (London: SCM Press, and Louisville: Westminster/John Knox Press).
  1995: *The Rainbow of Faiths* (London: SCM Press) = *A Christian Theology of Religions* (Louisville: Westminster/John Knox Press).
  1997: 'The Epistemological Challenge of Religious Pluralism' in *Faith and Philosophy*, vol. 14, no. 3.
  1999: *The Fifth Dimension*, (2nd edition 2004) (Oxford: OneWorld).
  2001: *Dialogues in the Philosophy of Religion* (London: Palgrave).
Hick, John, and Arthur C. McGill (eds)
  1967: *The Many-Faced Argument* (New York and London: Macmillan).
Hilton, Walter
  1948: *The Ladder of Perfection* [1494] (London: J. M. Watkins).
Hobbes, Thomas
  1966: *Leviathan*, English Works ed. William Molesworth, vol. III [1651], reprinted (Aalen: Scientia Verlag).
Holzner, Burkart
  1968: *Reality Construction in Society* (Cambridge, MA: Schenkman).
Hollinger, Robert
  1974: 'The Role of Aspect Seeing in Wittgenstein's Later Though', in *Cultural Hermeneutics*, ed. Robert Hollinger (Dordrecht: Reidel).
Hooke, S. H. (ed.)
  1933: *Myth and Ritual* (London: Oxford University Press).
Horner, I. B., (trans.)
  1954: *The Collection of the Middle Length Sayings* (*Majjhima Nikāya*), vol. I (London: Luzac).
  1957: *The Collection of the Middle Length Sayings*, vol. II (London: Luzac).
  1962: *The Book of the Discipline* (*Vinaya-Piṭaka*), vol. IV (London: Luzac).
  1963: *The Book of the Discipline* (*Vinaya-Piṭaka*), vol. V (London: Luzac).

Hornung, Erik
   1982: *Conceptions of God in Ancient Egypt: The One and the Many* [1971], trans. John Baines (Ithaca, NY: Cornell University Press).
Hughes, M. W.
   1968: 'Aspectual and Religious Perceptions', in *Sophia*, vol. 7, no. 1.
Hume, David
   1902: *An Enquiry Concerning Human Understanding* [1748], 2nd edition, ed. L. A. Selby-Bigge (London: Oxford University Press).
   1956: *Natural History of Religion* [1757], ed. H. E. Root (London: Adam & Charles Black).
   1968: *A Treatise of Human Nature* [1739], ed. L. A. Selby-Bigge (London: Oxford University Press).
Huxley, Julian
   1957: *Religion Without Revelation* [1927] (London: Max Parrish, and New York: Mentor Books).
Hyers, Conrad
   1983: 'The Unity and Ambiguity of Religion: Rethinking the Doctrine of Double-Truth', in *World Faiths Insight*, New Series (Summer).
Incandela, Joseph M.
   1985: 'The Appropriation of Wittgenstein's Work by Philosophers of Religion: Towards a Reevaluation and an End', in *Religious Studies*, vol. 21, no. 4.
Isherwood, Christopher
   1965: *Ramakrishna and His Disciples* (London: Methuen).
Iyer, Raghavan
   1983: *The Moral and Political Thought of Mahatma Gandhi*, 2nd edition (London and New York: Concord Grove Press).
Jacoby, Hermann
   1968: *Jaina Sutras* [1895] (Delhi: Motilal Banarsidass).
Jagadananda, Swami, (trans.)
   1970: *Upadeshasāhasrī of Sri Sankarachāria* (Madras: Sri Ramakrishna Math).
James, William
   1891: *The Principles of Psychology*, 2 vols (London: Macmillan).
   1905: *The Will to Believe and Other Essays* [1897] (New York and London: Longmans, Green & Co.).
   1920: *The Letters of William James*, vol. 2 (London: Longmans, Green & Co.).
   1960: *Varieties of Religious Experience* [1902] (London: Collins, and New York: Mentor Books).
Jaske, W. D.
   1974: 'Philosophy and the Meaning of Life', in *Australasian Journal of Philosophy*, vol. 52.
Jaspers, Karl
   1953: *The Origin and Goal of History* [1949], trans. Michael Bullock (New Haven, Conn.: Yale University Press).
Jennings, J. G.
   1947: *The Vedantic Buddhism of the Buddha* (London: Oxford University Press).

John of the Cross, St
  1958: *Ascent of Mount Carmel* [16th century], trans. E. Allison Peers (Garden City, NY: Image Books).
Julian of Norwich
  1978: *Showings* [14th century], trans. Edward Colledge and James Walsh (New York: Paulist Press).
Jung, C. G.
  1953–77: *The Collected Works of C. G. Jung*, ed. Herbert Read et al. (London: Routledge & Kegan Paul).
Kabir
  1977: *Songs of Kabir* [15th century], trans. Rabindranath Tagore [1915] (New York: Samuel Weiser).
Kalupahana, David
  1986: *Nagarjuna: The Philosophy of the Middle Way* (New York: State University of New York Press).
Kant, Immanuel
  1947: *The Moral Law* [1785], trans. M. J. Paton (London: Hutchinson).
  1956: *Critique of Practical Reason*, trans. L. W. Beck (New York: Liberal Arts Press).
  1958: *Critique of Pure Reason*, trans. Norman Kemp Smith [1929] (London: Macmillan, and New York: St. Martin's Press).
Kaplan, Stephen
  2002: *Different Paths, Different Summits: A Model of Religious Pluralism and Soteriological Diversity* (Lanham: Rowman & Littlefield).
Karim, Al-Haj Maulana Fazlur, (trans.)
  1960–4: *Al-Hadis of Miskat-ul-Masibih*, 2nd edition (Dacca).
Katz, Steven
  1978: 'Language, Epistemology, and Mysticism', in *Mysticism and Philosophical Analysis*, ed. Steven Katz (New York: Oxford University Press).
  1983: *Mysticism and Religious Traditions* (New York: Oxford University Press).
Kaufman, Gordon D.
  1972: *God the Problem* (Cambridge, MA: Harvard University Press).
  1981: *The Theological Imagination* (Philadelphia: Westminster Press).
  1985: *Theology for a Nuclear Age* (Manchester: Manchester University Press, and Philadelphia: Westminster Press).
  1993: *In Face of Mystery* (Cambridge, MA: Harvard University Press).
Keeling, Bryant, and Mario F. Morelli
  1977: 'Beyond Wittgensteinian Fideism: An Examination of John Hick's Analysis of Religious Faith', in *International Journal for Philosophy of Religion*, vol. 8, no. 4.
Kellenberger, James
  1985: *The Cognitivity of Religion* (London: Macmillan, and Los Angeles: University of California Press).
  1993: *Inter-religious Models and Criteria* (ed.) (London: Macmillan and New York: St. Martin's Press).
Kempis, Thomas à
  Of the Imitation of Christ [15th century], trans. Atkinson (London and New York: Thomas Nelson & Sons).

Kenny, Anthony
   1979: *The God of the Philosophers* (Oxford: Clarendon Press).
Klein, Kenneth H.
   1974: *Positivism and Christianity: A Study of Theism and Verifiability* (The Hague: Martinus Nijhoff).
Klemke, E. D.
   1981: *The Meaning of Life* (New York: Oxford University Press).
Klostermaier, Klaus
   1969: *In the Paradise of Krishna*, trans. Antonia Fonseca (Philadelphia: Westminster Press, and [*Hindu and Christian in Vrindaban*] London: SCM Press).
Koch, Klaus
   1982: *The Prophets*, 2 vols, trans. Margaret Kohl (Philadelphia: Fortress Press).
Kohl, Marvin
   1981: 'Meaning of Life and Happiness', in *Dialectics and Humanism*, vol. 8 (Fall).
Kroeber, A. L.
   1948: *Anthropology*, rev. edition (New York: Harcourt Brace Jovanovich).
Kümmel, Friedrich
   1966: 'Time as Succession and the Problem of Duration', in J. T. Fraser (ed.) 1966.
Kvanvig, J. L.
   1984: 'Credulism', in *International Journal for Philosophy of Religion*, vol. 16 no. 2.
Kwan, Kai-man
   2003: 'Is the Critical Trust Approach to Religious Experience Incompatible with Religious Particularism? A Reply to Michael Martin and John Hick', in *Faith and Philosophy*, vol. 20, no. 2.
Legge, James
   1891: *The Sacred Books of China: The Texts of Taoism*, Part 2 (Oxford: Clarendon Press).
Lerner, Monroe
   1970: 'When Why and Where People Die', in Brim et al. 1970.
Lessa, William A., and Evon Z. Vogt (eds)
   1979: *Reader in Comparative Religion: An Anthropological Approach*, 4th edition (New York: Harper & Row).
Leuba, James H.
   1912: *A Psychological Study of Religion: Its Origin, Function and Future* (New York: Macmillan).
Lewy, Guenter
   1974: *Religion and Revolution* (New York: Oxford University Press).
Lindbeck, George
   1984: *The Nature of Doctrine* (Philadelphia: Westminster Press, and London: SPCK).
Ling, Trevor
   1968: *A History of Religion East and West: An Introduction and Interpretation* (London: Macmillan, and New York: St. Martin's Press).
Longair, M. S. (ed.)
   1974: *Confrontation of Cosmological Theories with Observational Data,*

International Astronomical Union Symposium no. 63 (Dordrecht and Boston, MA: D. Reidel).

Losin, Peter
    1987: 'Experience of God and the Principle of Credulity: A Reply to Rowe', in *Faith and Philosophy*, vol. 4, no. 1.

Loughlin, Gerard
    1990: 'Prefacing Pluralism: John Hick and the Mastery of Religion', *Modern Theology*, vol. 7, no. 1.

Loy, David
    1985: 'Chapter One of the *Tao Te Ching*: A "New" Interpretation', in *Religious Studies*, vol. 21, no. 3.

Lyall, Leonard A., (trans.)
    1932: *Mencius* (London and New York: Longmans, Green & Co.).

MacGregor, Geddes
    1978: *Reincarnation in Christianity* (Wheaton, IL: Theosophical Publishing House).
    1983: *Reincarnation as a Christian Hope* (London: Macmillan, and New York: Barnes & Noble).

Macintyre, Alasdair, and Paul Ricoeur
    1969: *The Religious Significance of Atheism* (New York: Columbia University Press).

Macmurray, John
    1957–61: *The Form of the Personal*, 2 vols (London: Faber & Faber).

Mahadevan, T. M. P.
    1960: *Outlines of Hinduism*, 2nd edition (Bombay: Chetana Limited).

Maimonides, Moses
    1904: *Guide for the Perplexed* [12th century], trans. M. Friedlander, 2nd edition (London: Routledge & Kegan Paul).

Malcolm, Norman
    1960: 'Anselm's Ontological Arguments', in *Philosophical Review*, vol. 69, no. 1.

Malinowski, Bronislaw
    1953: *Sin and Repression in Savage Society* [1927] (London: Routledge & Kegan Paul, and New York: Humanities Press).

Malone, Michael E.
    1978: 'Is Scientific Observation "Seeing-As'?', in *Philosophical Investigations*, vol. 1.

Martin, C. B.
    1959: *Religious Belief* (Ithaca, NY: Cornell University Press).

Martin, M.
    1986: 'Swinburne's Inductive Cosmological Argument', in *Heythrop Journal*, vol. 27, no. 2.

Martineau, James
    1889: *A Study of Religion: Its Sources and Contents*, vol. 1 [1888] (Oxford: Clarendon Press).

Marx, Karl
    1963: *Manifesto of the Communist Party* [1848], ed. D. Ryazanoff (New York: Russell & Russell).

Marxsen, Willi
    1970: *The Resurrection of Jesus of Nazareth* [1968] (London: SCM Press, and Philadelphia: Fortress Press).
Mathis, Terry
    1985: *Against John Hick: An Examination of his Philosophy of Religion* (London and New York: University Press of America).
Matson, Wallace I.
    1965: *The Existence of God* (Ithaca, NY: Cornell University Press).
Matt, D. C., (trans.)
    1983: *Zohar: The Book of the Enlightenment* (New York: Paulist Press).
Mavrodes, George
    1995: 'Polytheism', in Senor 1995.
    2001: 'Responses and Discussion', in Hick 2001.
Maxwell, Robert J.
    1972: 'Anthropological Perspectives', in Henri Yaker et al. (eds) *The Future of Time* (London: Hogarth Press).
McColley, Grant
    1940: *Paradise Lost* (Chicago: Packard).
McDermott. Robert
    1970: 'The Religion Game: Some Family Resemblances', in *Journal of the American Academy of Religion*, vol. 38. no. 4.
McKenzie. David E.
    1985: 'Kant, a Moral Criterion, and Religious Pluralism', in *American Journal of Theology and Philosophy*, vol. 6, no. 1.
Meacock, Heather
    2000: *An Anthropological Approach to Theology: A Study of John Hick's Theology of Religious Pluralism* (Lanham, USA and Oxford, UK: University Press of America).
Mesle, Robert
    1991: *John Hick's Theodicy: A Process Humanist Critique* (London: Macmillan).
Miles, T. R.
    1959: *Religion and the Scientific Outlook* (London: George Allen & Unwin).
    1972: *Religious Experience* (London: Macmillan, and New York: St. Martin's Press).
Miller, Richard B.
    1986: 'The Reference of God', in *Faith and Philosophy*, vol. 3, no. 1.
Montefiore, Hugh
    1985: *The Probability of God* (London: SCM Press).
Moody, Raymond
    1975: *Life after Life* (Atlanta: Mockingbird Books).
Moore, G. F.
    1948: *History of Religions* (New York: Charles Scribner's Sons).
Müller, Max
    1908a: *The Sacred Books of the East* [1884], vol. 8 (*Anugītā*), 2nd edition (Oxford: Clarendon Press).
    1908b: *The Sacred Books of the East* [1884], vol. 21 (*Saddharma Pundarika, or Lotus of the True Law*), 2nd edition (Oxford: Clarendon Press).

Mumford, Lewis
  1957: *The Transformation of Man* (London: George Allen & Unwin).
Muntz, Peter
  1959: *Problems of Religious Knowledge* (London: SCM Press).
Murti, T. R. V.
  1955: *The Central Philosophy of Buddhism* (London: George Allen & Unwin).
Myers, F. W. H.
  1943: *Human Personality and Its Survival of Bodily Death* [1903], 2 vols (London and New York: Longmans).
Narada Mahathera (trans.)
  1972: *The Dhammapada*, 2nd edition (Colombo: Vajiranama).
Naranjo, Claudio, and Robert Ornstein
  1971: *On the Psychology of Meditation* (London and New York: Penguin Books).
Nasr, Seyyed Hossein
  1980: *Living Sufism* (London and Boston: Mandala Books).
Neville, Robert Cummings
  1991: *Behind the Masks of God* (Albany: State University of New York Press).
Nicholas of Cusa
  1990: *Nicholas of Cusa on Interreligious Harmony*, ed. James Biechler and Lawrence Bond (Lewiston, Queenston, Lampeter: Edward Mellon Press).
Nicholson, R. A.
  1963: *The Mystics of Islam* [1914] (London and Boston: Routledge & Kegan Paul).
  1978: *Rumi: Poet and Mystic* [1950] (London: George Allen & Unwin).
Niebuhr, Reinhold
  1941: *The Nature and Destiny of Man*, vol. 1 (London: Nisbet, and New York: Charles Scribner's Sons).
Nielsen, Kai
  1964: 'Linguistic Philosophy and "The Meaning of Life"', in *Cross Currents*, vol. 14, no. 3.
  1971: *Contemporary Critiques of Religion* (London: Macmillan).
  1986: 'Religion and Groundless Believing', in Runzo and Ihara (eds) 1986.
Nineham, Dennis
  1993: *Christianity Mediaeval and Modern* (London: SCM Press).
Nishitani, Keiji
  1982: *Religion and Nothingness*, trans. Jan van Bragt (Berkeley: University of California Press).
Noss, John B.
  1956: *Man's Religions* (New York: Macmillan).
Novikov, I. D.
  1984: *Evolution of the Universe* (Cambridge and New York: Cambridge University Press).
Nozick, Robert
  1981: *Philosophical Explanations* (Oxford: Clarendon Press, and Cambridge, MA: Harvard University Press).

Oakes, Robert
  1973: 'Noumena, Phenomena, and God', in *International Journal for Philosophy of Religion*, vol. 14, no. 1.
O'Connor, June
  1991: 'Sin and Salvation from a Feminist Perspective', in Hewett (ed.) 1991.
Orman, John
  1931: *The Natural and the Supernatural* (Cambridge: Cambridge University Press).
  1961: *Grace and Personality* [1917] (London: Collins Fontana, and New York: Association Press).
Otto, Rudolf
  1936: *The Idea of the Holy* [1917], trans. John H. Harvey (London and New York: Oxford University Press).
  1957: *Mysticism East and West* [1932], trans. Bertha L. Bracey and Richenda C. Payne (New York: Meridian Books).
Page, Ruth
  1985: *Ambiguity and the Presence of God* (London: SCM Press).
Paley, William
  1817: *Moral and Political Philosophy* [1786], 2nd edition (London: printed for Baldwin and Co.).
Panikkar, Raimundo
  1977: *The Vedic Experience* (Los Angeles: University of California Press).
Pannenberg, Wolfhart
  1970: *What Is Man?* [1962], trans. Duane A. Priebe (Philadelphia: Fortress Press).
  1985: *Anthropology in Theological Perspective*, trans. Matthew J. O'Connell (Philadelphia: Westminster Press, and Edinburgh: T. & T. Clark).
Parfit, Derek
  1984: *Reasons and Persons* (Oxford and New York: Oxford University Press).
Parrisikar, Vasudeva Laksmana (ed.)
  1978: *Srimad – Valmiki – Maharsi – Panitah Yogava'sistha*, 2nd edition (Bombay: Tukaram Javaji).
Parsons, Talcott
  1963: 'Introduction', in Weber 1963
Pascal, Blaise
  1932: *Pensées* [1670], ed. Leon Brunschvicg, trans. W. F. Trotter (London: J. M. Dent, and New York: E. P. Dutton).
Passmore, John
  1957: *A Hundred Years of Philosophy* (London: Duckworth).
Pegis, Anton C., (trans.)
  1945: *Basic Writings of St. Thomas Aquinas*, 2 vols (New York: Random House).
  1955: *On the Truth of the Catholic Faith: Summa contra Gentiles*, vol. 1 (Garden City, NY: Image Books).
Penelhum, Terence
  1983: *God and Skepticism* (Dordrecht: D. Reidel).
Penn, William
  1926: *Some Fruits of Solitude* (London: Constable).

Perrett, R. W.
  1984: 'John Hick on Faith: A Critique', in *International Journal for Philosophy of Religion*, vol. 15, nos 1–2.
Phillips, D. Z.
  1966: *The Concept of Prayer* (London: Routledge & Kegan Paul [1965], and New York: Schocken Books).
  1970: *Death and Immortality* (London: Macmillan, and New York: St. Martin's Press).
  1971: *Faith and Philosophical Enquiry* (London: Routledge & Kegan Paul [1970], and New York: Schocken Books).
  1977: *Religion Without Explanation* [1976] (Oxford: Basil Blackwell).
  1986: *Belief, Change and Forms of Life* (London: Macmillan).
Pieris, Aloysius, SJ
  1983: 'The Place of Non-Christian Religions and Cultures in the Evolution of Third World Theology', in *The Irruption of the Third World*, ed. Virginia Fabella and Sergio Torres (Maryknoll, NY: Orbis).
  1985: 'A Theology of Liberation in Asian Churches?' (Tokyo: 506 International Theological Symposium, Sophia University).
Plantinga, Alvin
  1967: *God and Other Minds* (Ithaca, NY: Cornell University Press).
  1974: *The Nature of Necessity* (Oxford: Clarendon Press).
  1977: *God, Freedom, and Evil* (Grand Rapids, MI: Wm B. Eerdmans).
  1980: *Does God Have a Nature?* (Milwaukee: Marquette University Press).
  1983: 'Reason and Belief in God', in Plantinga and Wolterstorff (eds) 1983.
  1986: 'On Taking Belief in God as Basic', in Runzo and Ihara (eds) 1986.
  1991: 'When Faith and Reason Clash: Evolution and the Bible', *Christian Scholar's Review*, vol. 21, no. 1, reprinted in Shatz 2002.
  1995: 'Pluralism: A Defense of Religious Exclusivism', in Senor (ed.) 1995.
  1997: 'Reformed Epistemology', in *A Companion to the Philosophy of Religion*, ed. Philip Quinn and Charles Taliaferro (Cambridge, MA and London: Blackwell).
  2000: *Warranted Christian Belief* (New York and Oxford: Oxford University Press).
Plantinga, Alvin, and Nicholas Wolterstorff (eds)
  1983: *Faith and Rationality* (Notre Dame and London: Notre Dame University Press).
Plaskow, Judith
  1980: *Sex, Sin and Grace* (Washington, DC: University Press of America).
Plato
  1903: *The Four Socratic Dialogues of Plato*, trans. Benjamin Jowett (Oxford: Clarendon Press).
Popper, Karl
  1975: *Objective Knowledge* (Oxford: Clarendon Press).
Preller, Ludwig, and Heinrich Ritter (eds)
  1913: *Historia Philosophiae Graecae: et Romanae ex Fontium Locis Contexta* [1878] (Gotha: F. A. Perthes).

Price, H. H.
   1969: *Belief* (London: George Allen and Unwin, and New York: Humanities Press).
Provost, R.
   1985: 'Swinburne, Mackie and Bayes' Theorem', in *International Journal for Philosophy of Religion*, vol. 17, no. 3.
Prozesky, Martin
   1984: *Religion and Ultimate Well-Being* (London: Macmillan).
Pseudo-Dionysius
   1987: *Pseudo-Dionysius, The Complete Works*, trans. Colm Luibheid (New York: Paulist Press).
Qur'an
   1971: trans. Zafrulla Khan (London and Dublin: Curzon Press).
   1977: trans. A. Yusuf Ali, 2nd edition (New York: American Trust Publications).
Radhakrishnan, S., (trans.)
   1968: *The Principal Upanishads* (London: George Allen & Unwin and New York: Humanities Press).
Randall, John Herman, Jr
   1954: 'Symposium: Are Religious Dogmas Cognitive and Meaningful?', in *Journal of Philosophy*, vol. 51, no. 5.
   1958: *The Role of Knowledge in Western Religion* (Boston: Starr King Press).
   1968: *The Meaning of Religion for Man* (New York: Harper Torchbooks).
Rees, Martin
   1981: 'Our Universe – and Other', in *New Scientist*, vol. 89 (January).
Reese, William L.
   1978: 'Religious Seeing-As', in *Religious Studies*, vol. 14, no. 1.
Reid, Thomas
   1785: *Essays on the Intellectual Powers of Man* (Edinburgh: John Bell; Facsimile edition, The Scholar Press).
Riser, John
   1981: 'The Meaning of Life as Social Task', in *Dialectics and Humanism*, vol. 8 (Fall).
Rizzuto, Ana-Maria
   1979: *The Birth of the Living God: A Psycho-Analytic Study* (Chicago and London: University of Chicago Press).
Robbins, J. Wesley
   1974: 'John Hick on Religious Experience and Perception', in *International Journal for Philosophy of Religion*, vol. 5, no. 2.
   1982: 'In Defence of Attitudinal Christianity', in *Religious Studies*, vol. 18, no. 1.
Romer, W. H. Ph.
   1969: 'The Religion of Ancient Mesopotamia', in Bleeker and Widengren (eds) 1969.
Rose, Kenneth
   1996: *Knowing the Real: John Hick on the Cognitivity of Religions and Religious Pluralism* (New York, Bern, Berlin: Peter Lang).

Rowe, William
  1982: 'Religious Experience and the Principle of Credulity', in *International Journal for Philosophy of Religion*, vol. 13, no. 2.
  1999: 'Religious Pluralism', *Religious Studies*, vol. 35, no. 2.
Roy, Pratapa Chandra (trans.)
  1891: *The Mahabharata*, Shanti parva (Calcutta: Bhārata Press).
  1893: *The Mahabharata*, Anushana parva (Calcutta: Bhārata Press).
Rumi, Jalalu'l-Din
  1978: *Rumi, Poet and Mystic*, trans. R A. Nicholson. (London: Unwin Mandala).
Runzo, Joseph
  1977: 'Visions, Pictures and Rules', in *Religious Studies*, vol. 13, no. 3.
  1982: 'The Radical Conceptualization of Perceptual Experience', in *American Philosophical Quarterly*, vol. 19, no. 3.
  1986: *Reason, Relativism and God* (London: Macmillan, and New York: St. Martin's Press).
Runzo, Joseph, and Craig K. Ihara (eds)
  1986: *Religious Experience and Religious Belief* (New York and London: University Press of America).
Russell, Bertrand
  1954: *Human Society in Ethics and Politics* (London: Allen & Unwin).
  1957: *Why I Am Not a Christian* (London: Allen & Unwin).
Ruusbroec, John
  1985: *John Ruusbroec: The Spiritual Espousals and Other Works*, trans. James A. Wiseman (New York: Paulist Press).
St John of the Cross
  1958: *Ascent of Mount Carmel*, trans. Allison Peers (New York: Doubleday).
Sanders, Steven, and David R. Cheney (eds)
  1980: *The Meaning of Life* (Englewood Cliffs, NJ: Prentice-Hall).
Santayana, George
  1900: *Interpretations of Poetry and Religion* (New York: Charles Scribner's Sons).
  1905: *Reason and Religion* (New York: Charles Scribner's Sons).
Sartre, Jean-Paul
  1956: *Being and Nothingness* [1943], trans. Hazel E. Barnes (New York: Philosophical Library).
Schaff, Philip and Wace
  1956: *Nicene and Post-Nicene Fathers*, Series 2 [1892] (Grand Rapids, MI: Wm B. Eerdmans).
Schechter, Solomon
  1961: *Aspects of Rabbinic Theology* [1909] (New York: Schocken Books).
Schmidt, Paul F.
  1961: *Religious Knowledge* (New York: The Free Press of Glencot).
Scholem, Gershom G.
  1971a: *Major Trends in Jewish Mysticism* [1946], rev. edition (New York: Schocken Books).
  1971b: *The Messianic Idea in Judaism* (New York. Schocken Books).
Schulweis, Harold
  1983: *Evil and the Morality of God* (New York: KTAV).

Schumann, H. Wolfgang
    1973: *Buddhism*, trans. Georg Fenerstein (London: Rider).
Schwartz, Benjamin I.
    1975a: 'Transcendence in ancient China', in *Daedalus: Wisdom, Revelation and Doubt: Perspectives on the First Millennium BC*, vol. 104, no. 2.
    1975b: 'The Age of Transcendence', in ibid.
Sellars, Roy Wood
    1938–9: 'A Statement of Critical Realism', in *Revue internationale de philosophie*, vol. I.
Senor, Thomas D. (ed.)
    1995: *The Rationality of Belief and the Plurality of Faith* (Ithaca and London: Cornell University Press).
Servadio, Emilio
    1986: 'Mysticism and Parapsychology', in *Parapsychology Review*, vol. 17, no. 3.
Shalom, Albert
    1982: 'Meaning and Life', in *Dialectics and Humanism*, vol. 9 (Winter).
Shankara
    1970: *Upadeshasahasri of Sri Sankaracharya*, trans. Swami Jagananda (Madras: Sri Ramakrishna Math).
    1978: *Crest Jewel of Discrimination* [7th–8th century], 3rd edition, trans. Swami Prabhavananda and Christopher Isherwood (Hollywood, CA: Vedanta Press).
Shatz, David (ed.)
    2002: *Philosophy and Faith: A Philosophy of Religion Reader* (New York and London: McGraw Hill).
Sherry, Patrick
    1984: *Spirit, Saints, and Immortality* (London: Macmillan).
Shinran
    1979: *Notes on 'Essentials of Faith Alone,' a Translation of Shinran's Yuishinsho-mon'i* [1250] (Kyoto: Hongwanji International Centre).
Simon, Ernst
    1975: 'The Neighbour (*Re'a*) Whom We Shall Love', in Fox (ed.) 1975.
Sinkinson, Christopher
    2001: *The Universe of Faiths: A Critical Study of John Hick's Religious Pluralism* (Carlyle, UK and Waynesboro, USA: Paternoster Press).
Singh, Harbans
    1969: *Guru Nanak and Origins of the Sikh Faith* (Bombay: Asia Publishing House).
Singh, Mohinder
    1995: 'The Sikh Vision of the Ultimate', in Forward (ed.) 1995.
Singh, Trilochan
    1969: *Sikhism* (Patiala: Punjabi University Press).
Skinner, John
    1922: *Prophecy and Religion* (Cambridge: Cambridge University Press).
Smart, Ninian
    1965: 'Interpretation and Mystical Experience', in *Religious Studies*, vol. 1, no. 1.
    1981: *Beyond Ideology: Religion and the Future of Western Civilization* (San Francisco: Harper & Row).

1984: 'Our Experience of the Ultimate', in *Religious Studies*, vol. 20, no. 1.

1986: *Concept and Empathy*, ed. Donald Wiebe (London: Macmillan, and New York: New York University Press).

Smith, John E.

1965: 'The Structure of Religion', in *Religious Studies*, vol. 1, no. 1.

Smith, Jonathan Z.

1973: 'When the Bough Breaks', in *History of Religions*, vol. 12, no. 4.

Smith, Joseph Wayne

1984: 'Philosophy and the Meaning of Life', in *Cognito*, vol. 2 (January).

Smith, Norman Kemp

1924: *Prolegomena to an Idealist Theory of Knowledge* (London: Macmillan).

1941: *The Philosophy of David Hume* (London: Macmillan).

Smith, Wilfred Cantwell

1978: *The Meaning and End of Religion* [1962] (New York: Harper & Row, and London: SPCK).

1979: *Faith and Belief* (Princeton, NJ: Princeton University Press).

1981: *Towards a World Theology* (London: Macmillan, and Philadelphia: Westminster Press).

Solomon, Norman

1985: 'Judaism and World Religions' (Birmingham: Centre for the Study of Judaism and Jewish/Christian Relations).

Stade, Robert

1970: *Ninety-Nine Names of God in Islam* (Ibadan: Daystar Press).

Stanner, W. E. H.

1979: 'The Dreaming' [1956], in Lessa and Vogt (eds) 1979.

Starkey, Peggy

1985: 'Agape: A Christian Criterion for Truth in the Other World Religions', in *International Review of Mission*, vol. 74, no. 296.

Stevenson, Ian

1975–9: *Cases of the Reincarnation Type*, 4 vols (Charlottesville: University Press of Virginia).

Streng, Frederick

1955: *Understanding Religious Life* (Belmont, CA: Wadsworth Publishing Co.).

1967: *Emptiness: A Study in Religious Meaning* (Nashville: Abingdon Press).

Strick, Kenneth A., and George F. Posner

1985: 'A Conceptual Change View of Learning and Understanding', in West and Pines (eds) 1985.

Surin, Kenneth

1989: 'Towards a "Materialist" Critique of "Religious Pluralism": A Polemical Examination of the Discourse of John Hick and Wilfred Cantwell Smith', in *The Thomist*, vol. 53, no. 4.

1990: 'A certain "Politics of Speech": "Religious Pluralism" in the Age of McDonald's Hamburger', in *Modern Theology*, vol. 7, no.1.

Sutherland, Stewart

1982: 'Religion, Ethics, and Action', in *The Philosophical Frontiers of Christian Theology*, ed. Brian Hebblethwaite and Stewart Sutherland (London and New York: Cambridge University Press).

Suzuki, D. T.
  1949: *Essays in Zen Buddhism* [1927], 1st series (London and New York: Rider).
  1950: *Essays in Zen Buddhism*, 2nd series (London and New York: Rider).
  1953: *Essays in Zen Buddhism*, 3rd series (London and New York: Rider).
  1956: *Zen Buddhism*, ed. William Barrett (Garden City, NY: Doubleday Anchor).
  1969: *An Introduction to Zen Buddhism* [1949], ed. Christmas Humphreys (London: Rider).
  1972: *The Zen Doctrine of No Mind* (York Beach, ME: Samuel Weiser).
  1982: 'The Buddhist Conception of Reality', in *The Buddha Eye*, ed. Frederick Franck (New York: Crossroad).
Swanson, G. E.
  1960: *The Birth of the Gods: The Origin of Primitive Beliefs* (Ann Arbor, MI: University of Michigan Press).
Swinburne, Richard
  1977: *The Coherence of Theism* (Oxford: Clarendon Press).
  1979: *The Existence of God* (Oxford: Clarendon Press, and New York: Oxford University Press).
  1986: *The Evolution of the Soul* (Oxford: Clarendon Press).
Taber, J. A.
  1986: 'The Philosophical Evaluation of Religious Experience', in *International Journal for Philosophy of Religion*, vol. 19, nos 1–2.
Takeuchi Yoshinori
  1983: *The Heart of Buddhism*, trans. James W. Heisig (New York: Crossroad).
Tao Te Ching
  1982: trans. Ch'u Ta-Kao (London and Boston: Mandala Books).
Temple, William
  1934: *Nature, Man and God* (London: Macmillan).
Tennant, F. R.
  1930: *Philosophical Theology I* (Cambridge: Cambridge University Press).
Teresa of Avila, St
  1960: *Autobiography* [1565], trans. E. Allison Peers (Garden City, NY: Doubleday).
Theologia Germanica [1516]
  1937: trans. Susanna Winkworth (London: Macmillan).
Tillich, Paul
  1951: *Systematic Theology*, vol. 1 (Chicago: University of Chicago Press, and London: Nisbet).
  1952: *The Courage to Be* (New Haven: Yale University Press).
  1955: 'Religious Symbols and Our Knowledge of God', in *The Christian Scholar*, vol. 38, no. 3.
  1957: *Dynamics of Faith* (New York: Harper & Brothers).
  1963: *Christianity and the Encounter of the World Religions* (New York and London: Columbia University Press).
Tutu, Desmond
  1984: *Hope and Suffering* (Johannesburg: Skotoville Publishers [1983], London: Fount Paperbacks, and Grand Rapids, MI: Wm B. Eerdmans).

Tyrell, G. N. M.
  1953: *Apparitions* (London: Gerald Duckworth).
Underhill, Evelyn
  1955: *Mysticism* [1911], 12th edition (New York: New American Library).
Urmson, J. 0.
  1956: *Philosophical Analysis: Its Development between Two World Wars* (Oxford: Clarendon Press).
van Buren, Paul
  1966: *The Secular Meaning of the Gospel* [1963] (New York: Macmillan).
van der Post, Laurens
  1958: *The Lost World of the Kalahari* (London: Hogarth Press).
Voegelin, Eric
  1954–74: *Order and History*, 4 vols (Baton Rouge and London: Louisiana University Press).
von Hügel, F.
  1927: *Selected Letters 1896–1924*, ed. Bernard Holland (London: J. M. Dent, and New York: E. P. Dutton).
von Rad, Gerhard
  1965: *Old Testament Theology*, vol. 2, trans. D. M. G. Stalker (New York and Evanston: Harper & Row).
von Stietencron, Heinrich
  1986: 'Hindu Perspectives', in *Christianity and the World Religions*, ed. Hans Küng et al. [1985], trans. Peter Heinegg (New York: Doubleday, and London: Collins).
Ward, Keith
  1974: *The Concept of God* (Oxford: Basil Blackwell).
  1987: *Images of Eternity* (London: Darton, Longman & Todd).
  1990: 'Truth and the Diversity of Religions' in *Religious Studies*, vol. 26, no. 1.
  1994: *Religion and Revelation* (Oxford: Clarendon Press).
Weatherhead, Leslie
  1957: *The Case for Reincarnation* (London: City Temple).
  1968: *The Christian Agnostic* (London: Hodder & Stoughton).
Webb, C. C. J.
  1918: *God and Personality* (London: George Allen & Unwin, and New York: Macmillan).
Webb, Mark O.
  1985: 'Religious Experience as Doubt Resolution', in *International Journal for Philosophy of Religion*, vol. 18, nos 1–2.
Weber, Max
  1963: *The Sociology of Religion* [1922], 4th edition [1956] trans. Ephraim Fischoff (Boston: Beacon Press).
Weil, Eric
  1975: 'What is a Breakthrough in History?', in *Daedalus: Wisdom, Revelation, and Doubt: Perspectives on the First Millennium BC*, vol. 104, no. 2.
Weir, Hans
  1976: *A Dictionary of Modern Written Arabic* (Ithaca, NY: Spoken Language Services).

Welbon, C. R.
    1968: *The Buddhist Nirvana and its Western Interpreters* (Chicago and London: Chicago University Press).
West, E. W.
    1882: *Pahlevi Texts* (Oxford: Clarendon Press).
West, Leo H. T., and Leon Pines (eds)
    1985: *Cognitive Structure and Conceptual Change* (New York and London: Academic Press).
White, A. D.
    1960: *A History of the Warfare of Science with Theology in Christendom* [1896], 2 vols (New York. Dover Publications).
Whitehead, Alfred N.
    1926: *Science and the Modern World* [1925] (Cambridge: Cambridge University Press).
Wicksteed, Philip
    1899: *The Religion of Time and the Religion of Eternity* (London: Philip Green).
Wiggins, David
    1967: *Identity and Spatio-Temporal Continuity* (Oxford: Basil Blackwell).
    1976: 'Truth, Invention, and the Meaning of Life', in *Proceedings of the British Academy*, vol. 62 (London).
Williams, Harry
    1972: *True Resurrection* (New York: Holt, Rinehart & Winston).
Wilson, Edward O.
    1978: *Of Human Nature* (Cambridge, MA, and London: Harvard University Press).
Winch, Peter
    1977: 'Meaning and Religious Language', in Brown (ed.) 1977.
Wisdom, John
    1965: *Paradox and Discovery* (Oxford: Basil Blackwell).
Wittgenstein, Ludwig
    1963: *Philosophical Investigations* [1953], trans. G. E. M. Anscombe (Oxford: Basil Blackwell).
    1971: 'Remarks on Frazer's "Golden Bough"' [1967], trans. A. C. Miles and Rush Rhees, in *The Human World*, no. 3.
Wolff, Hans Walter
    1977: *Joel and Amos: A Commentary on the Books of the Prophets Joel and Amos*, trans. Waldemar Janzen, S. Dean McBride Jr and Charles A. Muenchow, ed. S. Dean McBride Jr (Philadelphia: Fortress Press).
Wolfson, W. A.
    1957: 'Negative Attributes in the Church Fathers', in *Harvard Theological Review*, vol. 50.
Woodbridge, Frederick J. E.
    1926: *Realm of Mind* (New York: Columbia University Press).
    1961: *An Essay on Nature* [1940] (New York: Columbia University Press).
Woodward, Frank L. (trans.)
    1948: *The Minor Anthologies of the Pali Canon* (London: Oxford University Press).
    1951: *The Book of Gradual Sayings* (*Anguttara Nikāya*), vol. 1 (London: Luzac).

1954: *The Book of the Kindred Sayings* (*Saṃyutta Nikāya*), part 3 (London: Luzac).

1956: *The Book of the Kindred Sayings* (*Saṃyutta Nikāya*), part 4 (London: Luzac).

Wuthnow, Robert

1978: *Experimentation in American Religion* (Berkeley and London: University of California Press).

Yandell, Keith E.

1975: 'Some Varieties of Ineffability', in *International Journal for Philosophy of Religion*, vol. 6, no. 3.

1979: 'The Ineffability Theme', in *International Journal for Philosophy of Religion*, vol. 10, no. 4.

Zaehner, R. C.

1961: *Mysticism Sacred and Profane* (London: Oxford University Press).

1966: *Hinduism*, 2nd edition (London: Oxford University Press).

1969: *The Bhagavad Gita* (Oxford: The Clarendon Press).

Index of Names

Index of Subjects